Organizational Behavior: Tools for Success

2E

Phillips | Gully

 CENGAGE
Learning®

Australia • Brazil • Japan • Korea • Mexico • Singapore • Spain • United Kingdom • United States

CENGAGE
Learning

**Organizational Behavior:
Tools for Success, 2E**

Organizational Behavior: Tools for Success
Phillips | Gully

For product information and technology assistance, contact us at
Cengage Learning Customer & Sales Support, 1-800-354-9706

For permission to use material from this text or product,
submit all requests online at **cengage.com/permissions**
Further permissions questions can be emailed to
permissionrequest@cengage.com

This book contains select works from existing Cengage Learning resources and was produced by Cengage Learning Custom Solutions for collegiate use. As such, those adopting and/or contributing to this work are responsible for editorial content accuracy, continuity and completeness.

Compilation © 2015 Cengage Learning

ISBN: 9781305759701

WCN: 01-100-101

Cengage Learning
20 Channel Center Street
Boston, MA 02210
USA

Cengage Learning is a leading provider of customized learning solutions with office locations around the globe, including Singapore, the United Kingdom, Australia, Mexico, Brazil, and Japan. Locate your local office at:
www.international.cengage.com/region.

Cengage Learning products are represented in Canada by Nelson Education, Ltd.

For your lifelong learning solutions, visit **www.cengage.com/custom.**

Visit our corporate website at **www.cengage.com.**

Jean Phillips

Jean Phillips is a professor in the Human Resource Management department in the School of Management and Labor Relations at Rutgers University. She earned her Ph.D. from Michigan State University in organizational behavior and human resource management. She has taught classroom and hybrid classroom/online courses in topics including organizational behavior, strategic human resource management, staffing, and teams and leadership in the United States, Iceland, and Singapore at the undergraduate, master's, Ph.D., and executive master's levels.

Jean has authored or presented more than eighty papers, research articles, books, and book chapters and has coauthored or edited more than eighteen books. She was among the top 5 percent of published authors in *Journal of Applied Psychology* and *Personnel Psychology* during the 1990s and received the 2004 Cummings Scholar Award from the Organizational Behavior Division of the Academy of Management. Her research interests focus on recruitment and staffing, leadership and team effectiveness, and issues related to learning organizations. Her research has appeared in *Academy of Management Journal*, *Journal of Applied Psychology*, *Organizational Behavior and Human Decision Processes*, *Personnel Psychology*, *Small Group Research*, *Journal of Business and Psychology*, and *International Journal of Human Resource Management*. She has served on the editorial boards of *Journal of Applied Psychology*, *Journal of Management*, *Personnel Psychology*, and the *Journal of Business and Psychology*.

Her consulting work includes the creation and evaluation of strategic recruitment and staffing programs, evaluating recruiting source effectiveness, coaching on enhancing leadership performance and work team effectiveness, and the development and evaluation of employee survey programs.

Stan Gully

Stan Gully is a professor in the Human Resource Management department in the School of Management and Labor Relations at Rutgers University. He earned his Ph.D. from Michigan State University in Industrial and Organizational Psychology. He has taught courses at the undergraduate, master's, Ph.D., and executive master's level covering content such as organizational learning and innovation, recruiting and staffing, human resource management, performance management, training and development, data analysis, and leadership. He has taught using traditional and hybrid technologies in the United States, Iceland, Singapore, and Indonesia.

Stan has authored or presented more than eighty papers, research articles, and book chapters on a variety of topics and was recognized in 2012 as one of the most highly cited management scholars in the past thirty years. Stan has coauthored or edited more than eighteen books. His work has appeared in *Research in Personnel and Human Resources Management, Journal of Applied Psychology, Organizational Behavior and Human Decision Processes, Journal of Organizational Behavior, Organizational Research Methods,* and *Advances in Interdisciplinary Studies of Work Teams,* among other outlets. Stan has served on the editorial boards of *Academy of Management Journal, Journal of Management, Journal of Organizational Behavior,* and *Journal of Applied Psychology.* He has won several awards for his research, teaching, and service, including Rutgers' 2010 Jim Chelius Best Teacher Award. He is a former coeditor of the Academy of Management Research Methods Division Newsletter.

Stan once worked in management at UPS (brown uniform and all!). His consulting work includes evaluating predictors of pharmaceutical salesperson effectiveness, assessing the effectiveness of an employer branding initiative, and implementing a multisource feedback system. He has also designed various training programs on topics including leadership and the evaluation of recruiting source effectiveness. His research interests include employee wellness, strategic recruiting, leadership and team effectiveness, training, and organizational learning.

Jean and Stan married after meeting in graduate school and have two sons, Tyler and Ryan.

We dedicate this book to our sons, Ryan and Tyler, who make our lives complete.

PREFACE

No matter what your field of study, organizational behavior is one of the most important classes you will take when it comes to launching and advancing your career. Organizational behavior (OB) explains how organizations work, why people behave the way they do, and how you can be more effective when working alone or with others. Other classes will help you to develop the technical skills required for success in your chosen career. We wrote this book to help you to acquire the "soft skills" that make the difference between being an average and an excellent performer in any job. In other words, this book won't teach you accounting, nursing, or other technical information, but it will help you to have a more successful career as an accountant, nurse, or whatever profession you choose.

Why Learn About OB?

If you want to find and excel at a job you love, understanding how your unique characteristics fit with different organizations and jobs and understanding how to manage yourself and others will help you do it. If you are interested in getting promoted, then understanding communication, politics, influence, and decision making, and learning how to motivate and lead individuals and teams will be critical to your advancement. Understanding what people think and feel, knowing how to persuade and motivate them, and being able to resolve conflicts and forge cooperation are among the most important skills of successful leaders. Even in today's increasingly "flat" organizations, which give employees more responsibilities as management layers are removed, OB skills are essential to success. Effective managers distinguish themselves by understanding people, motivation, and team dynamics, in addition to having strong technical knowledge or expertise.

We also feel strongly that organizational behavior should be one of the most interesting and fun classes you will take. People are fascinating! Understanding what makes different people productive and happy will help you to manage your career in a fulfilling way. Better understanding yourself and your strengths will enable you to identify the opportunities you will be happiest pursuing and most successful in. Learning about yourself as well as others is both important and enjoyable. We provide a variety of self-assessments, skill-building activities, Internet resources, and company examples to make the material engaging and interesting to read.

Another great thing about learning organizational behavior is the fact that it also applies to your daily life. Moods and emotions, goals, communication, diversity, career management, and decision making are just some of the many OB topics that are relevant to both your personal and professional experiences every day. Mastering the topics in this book will make you more effective in the non-work areas of your life as well.

Our Goals

The focus of this textbook is on developing your personal and managerial skills by:

- Helping you *understand yourself*, *understand organizations*, and understand the role of OB in *your personal career success*
- Cultivating an understanding of and ability to apply knowledge about *individual and group behavior in organizations* as well as appreciating how *the entire organizational system* operates
- Enhancing your understanding of how to *flexibly apply the OB concepts* that are appropriate for different problems or situations
- Creating an understanding of the modern OB context, including *ethics, diversity, competitive advantage, technology,* and *the global context*

The field of organizational behavior is constantly changing as old theories are modified (or even disproven) and new ones are proposed. This book is grounded in state-of-the-art research knowledge and will help you to understand how to best utilize what we know about OB. Our intent is to give you the information you need to understand what is going on in organizations today.

Second Edition Updates

In this edition we updated many of the chapter opening real world challenges and case studies to keep the examples current. We also updated the supporting citations in all chapters, and updated research findings where appropriate. Statistics and examples in the text were also updated. We also created a chapter indexed list of Ivey, Harvard Business School, and other case studies and activities available from Harvard Business School Press, available in the instructor's manual.

Features

This textbook contains several features designed to reinforce the themes of the book and further develop your OB skills.

Real World Challenge. To help you recognize OB-relevant issues in organizations, each chapter begins with a *Real World Challenge* that describes a real challenge or problem faced by a person or organization that relates to that chapter's content. The chapter then concludes with a description of how the company or individual addressed the challenge.

Global Issues. A *Global Issues* feature in each chapter highlights the global implications of some of the chapter's content.

Case Study. A *Case Study* in each chapter reinforces some of each chapter's material and gives you the opportunity to apply what you learn in the chapter to a real organizational situation.

Understand Yourself. To help you better understand your own characteristics, an *Understand Yourself* feature in each chapter gives you the chance to assess yourself on a variety of topics relevant to OB. This feature will help you better understand what motivates you, how you view money, your leadership style, your emotional intelligence, and your diversity awareness, among other things.

Improve Your Skills. Each chapter also contains an *Improve Your Skills* box to help you become more effective in different areas including dealing with challenging managerial behaviors, interviewing, managing stress, negotiating, and assessing an organization's culture and political environment.

So What? To help you understand the usefulness of OB topics in your life now and in the future, we've identified *So What?* moments throughout each chapter. These will show you how OB can make an immediate impact on your personal success and influence your managerial future.

Now What? Videos. Captivating *Now What?* decision-making videos put you in the manager's chair. Four videos are included for each chapter, with the first video presenting a business challenge, and three shorter videos providing "correct" and "incorrect" responses to the challenge. A short synopsis and discussion questions to accompany each video are included at the end of the chapter.

Workplace Videos. Also included with each chapter are *Workplace* videos featuring real-world companies to show managerial challenges. Video cases and discussion questions appear at the end of each chapter.

Technology Coverage. Technology has become an integral part of doing business. In addition to showing how technology can make learning fun, throughout the book we've included coverage of technology's influences and impacts on today's workplace. For example, in the motivation chapter, we discuss how technology can help to empower employees, monitor employee productivity, provide real-time feedback on performance, and enhance positive reinforcement.

Personal and Organizational Competitive Advantage Exercises. Each chapter also contains an activity designed to develop your personal skills and an activity designed to enrich your understanding of how the chapter topic can create a competitive advantage for an organization. The personal competitive advantage exercise at the end of each chapter is intended to help you develop your personal skills in an area covered by the chapter. Topics include active listening, making a great first impression, motivating others, negotiating a job offer, and understanding your leadership potential.

The organizational competitive advantage exercise at the end of each chapter helps you apply chapter material to the creation of a competitive advantage for organizations. Because organizational behavior affects the entire organization, these exercises are intended to focus your attention on the broader impact of organizational behavior. Topics include creating a competitive advantage through multiculturalism, influencing ethical decisions, motivating a sales staff, and short case studies.

Summary and Discussion Questions. We also provide chapter summaries and discussion questions at the end of each chapter. Each chapter concludes with a variety of exercises that will help to further develop your OB skills and to enable a better understanding of how OB can enhance both your personal success and the organization's competitive advantage.

For All Career Stages

We wrote this book to help you find and excel at a job you like, no matter what career stage you're in. We want to help you get a better job and a better career, and to be a better manager. The concepts discussed and skills developed throughout this book apply to people at all job levels. We've even included a special chapter called "Managing Your Career" that we hope will help you develop your own career path.

We'd love to hear your feedback and ideas for further improving the book and associated materials. E-mail us any time at phillipsgully@gmail.com. We hope you enjoy the book!

Student Learning Tools

CourseMate. Now you can make the most of your study time by accessing everything you need to succeed in one, convenient online site. Read your text online with a complete e-book, take notes, review flashcards, watch videos, and take practice quizzes—all conveniently online with CourseMate. This wealth of study resources will enhance the learning experience, providing the tools you need to master OB concepts and succeed in your OB course.

CengageNOW. CengageNOW is an easy-to-use online resource that helps you study in LESS TIME to get the grade you want NOW. A Personalized Study diagnostic tool assists you in accessing areas where you need to focus study. Built-in technology tools help you master concepts as well as prepare for exams and daily class.

Instructor Teaching Tools

We offer the tools you need to successfully teach your OB course—in person or online. All ancillary material is brand new to fit this text, and everything has been checked and rechecked for quality and accuracy. In addition, text authors Jean Phillips and Stan Gully have been instrumental in designing the ancillary package and vetting content to ensure the highest quality.

Video DVD Package. The engaging DVD package includes three sets of videos.

Now What? decision-making videos are a captivating four-video set that accompanies each text chapter. The first video presents a business challenge, while three shorter videos provide "correct" and "incorrect" responses to the OB challenge. These videos were written and designed by the text authors.

Workplace videos profile real-world companies to show challenges managers face in the workplace. Featured companies include Evo, Numi Organic Tea, and Flight 001, among others.

Chapter Indexed Case Studies. The instructor's manual now includes a chapter indexed list of case studies and additional activities from Harvard Business School, Ivey, and others available on the Harvard Business School website.

Write Experience. Cengage Learning's Write Experience allows you to assess written communication skills without adding to your workload! Write Experience utilizes artificial intelligence to score student writing instantly and accurately, while also providing students with detailed revision goals and feedback on their writing to help them improve written communication and critical thinking skills. Write Experience is the first product designed and created specifically for the higher education market through an exclusive agreement with McCann Associates, and powered by e-Write IntelliMetric Within™. IntelliMetric is the gold standard for automated scoring of writing and is used to score the Graduate Management Admissions Test® (GMAT®) analytical writing assignment.

The Phillips/Gully YouTube Channel. The authors have painstakingly collected a large number of engaging informational videos that can be used to supplement and reinforce student knowledge. Several activities for each chapter that are linked to these YouTube videos are also available on the instructors' companion website for use in both online and face-to-face courses. You can access these videos at http://www.youtube.com/user/phillipsgullyob/videos.

Instructor's Resource CD-ROM. Find all of the helpful, time-saving teaching resources you need to create a dynamic, interactive OB course in this all-in-one Instructor's Resource CD. Everything you need to plan, teach, grade, and effectively assess student understanding and progress is at your fingertips. The Instructor's Resource CD includes a robust *Instructor's Manual* with Media Guide, verified Test Bank, easy-to-use ExamView® software, and two sets of PowerPoint® presentation slides—basic and premium.

CourseMate. Interested in a simple way to complement *Organizational Behavior* and your course content with study and practice materials? Cengage's Management CourseMate brings concepts to life with interactive learning, study, and exam preparation tools that support the printed text. Watch student comprehension soar with flashcards and engaging games, audio summaries, self-assessments, streaming videos, and more in this textbook-specific website. A complete e-book provides you with the choice of an entire online learning experience. Management CourseMate goes beyond the book to deliver what you need!

CengageNOW. This robust, online course management system gives you more control in less time and delivers better student outcomes—NOW. CengageNOW includes teaching and learning resources organized around lecturing, creating assignments, grading, quizzing, and tracking student progress and performance. Flexible assignments, automatic grading, and a gradebook option provide more control while saving you valuable time. A Personalized Study diagnostic tool empowers students to master concepts, prepare for exams, and become more involved in class.

***Instructor's Manual* with Media Guide.** The robust *Instructor's Manual* to accompany the text includes these resources:

- Chapter Overview
- Learning Objectives
- Key Terms
- Opening Real World Challenge
- Chapter Outline with:
  - In-depth explanation of chapter concepts
  - So What? moments
  - Expanded coverage of *Global Issues, Improve Your Skills, Understand Yourself,* and *Case Study* features

- PowerPoint references that tie the *Instructor's Manual* to the premium and basic PowerPoint presentations
- Blank lines for instructor notes
- Answers to end-of-chapter Discussion Questions and Exercises
- Extra Exercises

Also included in the *Instructor's Manual* is a complete guide covering how to incorporate media and technology into your classroom, including *Now What?* and *Workplace* videos.

Text authors Jean Phillips and Stan Gully reviewed all *Instructor's Manual* chapters, and chapters have also been proofread to ensure accuracy and completeness. The *Instructor's Manual* with Media Guide is available on the Instructor's Resource CD-ROM and on the text support website.

PowerPoint Presentation Files. Two PowerPoint presentation files have been prepared for each text chapter. The Premium PowerPoint presentation includes all learning objectives, text figures and tables, photos, *So What?* features, end-of-chapter discussion questions and exercises, and robust coverage of key chapter topics. The Basic PowerPoint presentation is a simpler version, with a bit less included, for instructors who like to develop their own PowerPoint programs.

Both Premium and Basic PowerPoint presentations include lecture notes in the Notes section of each slide to provide extra tips for the instructor. All slides have been reviewed by text authors Jean Phillips and Stan Gully, and all have been proofread for accuracy. The PowerPoint presentations are available on the Instructor's Resource CD-ROM and on the text support website.

Test Bank. The Test Bank contains more than 2,500 questions, including multiple-choice, true/false, short answer, and essay. Each question is brand-new for this brand-new textbook, and each has been carefully verified for accuracy by Hoyt Hayes, Columbia College. Questions are tagged to AACSB guidelines, as well as Bloom's Taxonomy. Level of difficulty, text page reference, and chapter topic information is included for each question. Text authors Jean Phillips and Stan Gully have reviewed each Test Bank chapter. The Test Bank is available on the Instructor's Resource CD-ROM and on the text support website.

ExamView. This supplement contains all of the questions in the Test Bank. The program is easy-to-use test creation software compatible with Microsoft Windows and Macintosh. Instructors can add or edit questions, instructions, and answers and select questions (randomly or numerically) by previewing them on the screen. Instructors can also create and administer quizzes online, whether over the Internet, a local area network (LAN), or a wide area network (WAN). ExamView is available on the Instructor's Resource CD-ROM in Windows format. Macintosh files are available upon request. Please contact your Cengage sales representative to request a Macintosh ExamView CD.

Instructor's Companion Website. Access important teaching resources on this companion website. For your convenience, you can download electronic versions of the instructor supplements at the password-protected section of the site, including the *Instructor's Manual* with Media Guide, Test Bank, and PowerPoint presentations.

To access these additional course materials and companion resources, please visit www.cengagebrain.com. At the CengageBrain.com home page, search for the ISBN of your title (from the back cover of your book) using the search box at the top of the page. This will take you to the product page where free companion resources can be found.

ACKNOWLEDGMENTS

Although only our names appear on the cover of this book, we are a small part of a team of many talented people responsible for making it happen. We greatly appreciate the many coordinative, organizational, and motivational talents of developmental editor Erin Guendelsberger. She did an excellent job managing the process of making this book and was a true pleasure to work with. Developmental editor Joanne Dauksewicz also kept the project moving and was terrific at managing the many details of the project. Executive editor Scott Person and marketing managers Clint Kernen and Jon Monahan were also instrumental in helping to develop the book. They really helped us to set the "vision" for this project. We appreciate senior acquisitions editor Michele Rhoades for being willing to take on this project. She was also terrific in helping us develop our ideas. We are also grateful for the continuing support of editor-in-chief Melissa Acuna who kept the project on track.

Senior art director Tippy McIntosh did a wonderful job developing an engaging layout and design for the book. Media editor Rob Ellington was great at identifying and incorporating the most cutting-edge technology. The entire presentation of the text and other materials is a result of their talents in creating an engaging experience from beginning to end.

Senior editorial assistant Ruth Belanger did a great job keeping us organized and meeting deadlines. We also appreciate the talents and efforts of content project manager Jana Lewis, director of development John Abner, marketing coordinator Julia Tucker, and senior marketing communications manager Jim Overly. We could not have completed this project without their help.

We would also like to thank Linda Ireland for doing a great job copyediting the book and Raquel Sousa and Josh Brown for tracking down an amazing number of interesting photos for the book. Print buyer Arethea Thomas did a terrific job coordinating the manufacturing process. We want to recognize Martha Hall for securing relevant text permissions and John Hill for securing relevant photo permissions that allow you to see these materials.

We also want to thank the Rutgers' iTV studio team for helping to develop and make the videos. We thank the cast and crew for helping us to create engaging and interesting videos that bring the book concepts to life:

Cast

Aaron McDaniel as Alex

Kyla V. Garcia as Amy

Sarah Sirota as Allison

Rowan Meyer as Ryan

Amanda Brooke Lerner as Billie

Joanna Hartshorne as Mary

Arielle Uppaluri as Karen

Aidan Kinney as Joe

John Keller as John

Crew

Producer - Hébert Peck, Jr.

Director – J. Allen Suddeth

Assistant Director - John Keller

Lighting Director - Pete Troost

Audio - Mark Andersen

Chief Engineer - Alex Fahan

Technical Director - Tom Sanitate

Camera Operator - Greg Bryant

Camera Operator - Tim Stollery

Camera Operator - Steve Barcy

Grip - Jon Celiberti

Production Coordinator - Deb Andriano

Make Up - Maddy Schlesinger

Floor Manager - Mindy Hoffman

Administrative Assistant - Diane Thorn

Production Assistant - Natalie Flynn

Production Assistant-Patricia Montero

Editor - Pete Troost

We had a lot of fun working on this book, and appreciate the opportunity to have been a part of such a high performing team.

We also want to acknowledge the high quality feedback provided from the following people. Their comments and suggestions were invaluable in improving and developing this book.

H. Lon Addams
Weber State University

Jackie Anderson
Davenport University

Joe S. Anderson
Northern Arizona University

Roxanne Beard
Ohio Dominican University

Joy E. Beatty
University of Michigan–Dearborn

H. Michael Boyd
Bentley University

Michael S. Duchon
Cleveland State University

Megan W. Gerhardt
Miami University

Banu Goktan
University of North Texas at Dallas

Jim Gort
Davenport University

Jonathon Halbesleben
University of Wisconsin–Eau Claire

Nancy Hanson-Rasmussen
University of Wisconsin–Eau Claire

Paul Harvey
University of New Hampshire

Hoyt Hayes
Columbia College

Kathie K. Holland
University of Central Florida

Monika L. Hudson
University of San Francisco

Eli Kass
University of San Francisco and U.C. Berkeley

Kevin B. Lowe
University of North Carolina–Greensboro

Karen S. Markel
Oakland University

Lauryn A. Migenes
University of Central Florida

Regina M. O'Neill
Suffolk University

Rhonda S. Palladi
Georgia State University

Ray Read
Baylor University

Gary Renz
Webster University

Robert W. Robertson
Saint Leo University

Anita Satterlee
Liberty University

Donald R. Schreiber
Baylor University

Holly A. Schroth
University of California, Berkeley

Jenna P. Stites
Penn State University

Paige P. Wolf
George Mason University

Carolyn M. Youssef
Bellevue University

Personal Acknowledgment

Along with this book, we are co-authors of *Human Resource Management*, 1st edition, *Strategic Staffing*, 2nd edition, and a five-book series entitled *Staffing Strategically*. We spend most of our free time having fun with our boys Ryan and Tyler, cooking, gardening, exploring, and spoiling our dog (Murphy) and cat (Mooch). We wish to thank our family for their patience and support while we were writing this book. They kept us grounded, happy, and sane throughout the entire project.

BRIEF CONTENTS

CONTENTS

PART 1

The Organizational Behavior Context

CHAPTER 1

What Is Organizational Behavior?

Becton, Dickinson, and Co. pursues its corporate purpose of "helping all people lead healthy lives" through its research and its attention to corporate social responsibility.

LEARNING OBJECTIVES

1. What is "organizational behavior"?

2. How can OB make you a more effective employee and manager?

3. How can OB improve a firm's performance?

4. Why do OB concepts need to be applied flexibly to match a company's diverse employee needs?

5. What role does OB play in organizational ethics?

6. From where does our knowledge about OB come?

7. Why is the "scientific process" relevant to OB?

REAL WORLD CHALLENGE

CORPORATE SOCIAL RESPONSIBILITY AT BECTON, DICKINSON, AND Co.

As a large global healthcare company, Becton, Dickinson, and Co. has the potential to influence the health and life of many people around the world. BD is focused on improving drug delivery, enhancing the quality and speed of diagnosing infectious diseases and cancers, and advancing research, discovery and production of new drugs and vaccines. [1]

BD CEO Edward Ludwig believes that corporations have a fundamental and long-term obligation to be socially responsible. BD is committed to its corporate purpose of "helping all people live healthy lives." BD wants to become "the organization best known for eliminating unnecessary suffering and death from disease and, in so doing, become one of the best performing companies in the world." [2]

Imagine that Ludwig learns that you are taking a course on organizational behavior and asks for your advice on how Becton Dickinson can increase its corporate social responsibility. After studying this chapter, you should have some good ideas.

© JERRY MCCREA/STAR LEDGER/CORBIS

SO WHAT?
Because it explains how organizations work, knowing about OB is essential to being effective at all organizational levels.

organizational behavior

Explains and predicts how people and groups interpret events, react, and behave in organizations; describes the role of organizational systems, structures, and processes in shaping behavior

organization

Consists of people with formally assigned roles working together to achieve common goals

managers

Organizational members who are responsible for the attainment of organizational goals by planning, organizing, leading, and controlling the efforts of others in the organization

Our goal in writing this book is to help you get a better job and enjoy a better career, and to be a better manager. As the title suggests, we want to help you better understand yourself, understand organizations, and understand the role of organizational behavior in your personal career success. Organizational behavior (OB) is the cornerstone of success for everyone in organizations. Even the most skilled accountant, researcher, marketer, engineer, or anything else will be ineffective as an employee and as a manager without good interpersonal and communication skills and a solid understanding of managing and motivating individuals and teams.

The field of *organizational behavior* is about understanding how people and groups in organizations behave, react, and interpret events. It also describes the role of organizational systems, structures, and processes in shaping behavior, and explains how organizations *really work*. Drawing from fields including management, anthropology, sociology, information technology, ethics, economics, and psychology, OB provides a foundation for understanding the "soft skills" that enable the effective management of people in organizations. Because it explains how organizations work from individual motivation to team dynamics to organizational structure, knowing about OB is essential to being effective at all organizational levels.

Learning about yourself and constantly developing your skills is important to succeeding in any career. An *organization* is a group of people with formally assigned roles working together to achieve common goals. *Managers* are organizational members who are responsible for the attainment of organizational goals by planning, organizing, leading, and controlling the efforts of others in the organization.[3] Breaking these four managerial functions down further:

- *Planning.* Planning involves setting goals, establishing a strategy to pursue those goals, and forecasting future threats and opportunities that might influence the company's needs and strategies.
- *Organizing.* Organizing involves designing the organization's or workgroup's structure, identifying what tasks need to be done, hiring the right people, delegating and assigning each task, establishing a chain of command, and creating rules for communication and decision making.
- *Leading.* Leading involves directing and coordinating the work of others, influencing and motivating others, maintaining morale, and resolving individual and group conflicts.
- *Controlling.* Controlling involves monitoring performance to ensure that it is consistent with quality and quantity standards, and taking appropriate actions to get back on track if necessary.

Imagine this scenario. You decide to start a company to create a new series of iPhone applications. What do you need to do? The first thing you need to do is *plan*. What is the market like for different types of applications? What niche do you want to pursue? After making decisions and setting goals for your new company, you establish an overall strategy to achieve these goals. Then, you *organize*. You identify the tasks that need to be done and hire people with the skills your company needs to be successful. You assign tasks to the people best able to execute them, and develop and communicate work rules and procedures to get the work done. You also create a culture and compensation system to motivate employees to meet organizational goals and standards.

You then need to *lead* your team by communicating and keeping them focused on their goals. You might also need to coordinate the work of different employees if one employee cannot do her part of a project until another employee finishes his part. If two employees are not getting along, you may need to influence them to reduce the conflict and keep them productive and engaged. You also need to *control* the project to ensure that deadlines are being met, and that the work is up to your quality and quantity standards. If the team falls behind schedule, you will need to find a way to get it back on track by hiring more help, dividing the work differently, or some other means.

From this example, you can see the importance of many different OB concepts in the practice of management. Decision making, communicating, leading, conflict management, influencing, motivating, and designing an effective organizational structure are all important to even a small organization like the one in our example. The effects of good management are amazing. Dun & Bradstreet claims that about 90 percent of new businesses fail, usually because of poor management. Think of an organization with which you are familiar, perhaps your own school or current employer, and imagine how it might be different with a skilled versus an unskilled leader. Understanding OB and how and when to apply different concepts will give you the tools you need to be effective in any managerial role.

In addition to helping you better understand yourself, organizational behavior can help you understand why people and groups behave the way they do in organizations. Using your knowledge about OB can help you to perform better and to be a more effective manager. Think about it this way: When you shop at a store, eat at a restaurant, or call for customer service, do all employees with whom you interact behave the same way? If you have worked, were there some bosses or coworkers with whom you preferred to work? Have you ever seen or heard about employees doing things to undermine each other or that would compromise the performance of the business? OB helps to explain and understand why these things happen, and gives you the tools you need to change them.

There is no one best way to manage—effective employees and managers understand that they need to be flexible in adapting to work challenges. This book will give you a variety of skills and tools to use in almost any work situation. After studying this book, you should have good answers to the questions in Table 1-1, and many others.

Having a toolkit of OB skills and flexibly applying them to match the current situation is essential to managing the variety of situations employees and managers face. No matter what the challenge, there are OB tools that will

Table 1-1

Some Questions Organizational Behavior Can Help Answer

- How can diversity both help and hurt team performance?
- Why are emotions important at work?
- Are some personality characteristics related to higher job performance?
- Is there more than one way to "fit" in an organization?
- Is there one best way to lead?
- Is saying, "Do your best!" the best way to motivate high performance?
- What are some common decision-making errors, and how can I avoid them?
- What is the role of politics at work?
- What steps can I take to effectively manage my career?
- What are the positive and negative effects of stress at work?
- What is globalization, and how does it affect me?
- What is "organizational culture" and why is it important?
- How can technology leverage what we know about organizational behavior to improve work performance?
- Why do some people behave unethically in organizations?
- Why are some teams more effective than others?

help you to succeed. The *Understand Yourself* feature in each chapter will help you to learn more about some of the aspects of your personality, perceptions, values, needs, and goals that are relevant to management by providing a variety of self-assessment tools. The feedback provided with some of the tools will help you to interpret your score and learn how to develop yourself in each area. The *Improve Your Skills* feature in each chapter will help you to improve some aspect of your OB skills. Investing now in developing your OB skills will prepare you to be a more effective employee and manager, and help you move up faster in any organization. It takes time to understand yourself and to develop your OB skills. The sooner you start, the faster you will prepare yourself for succeeding in your career.

In this chapter, we first briefly discuss the importance of OB to your career as well as to a firm's competitive advantage and strategic execution. We then briefly discuss the history of OB. We also explain and provide an overview of some current issues in organizational behavior, and discuss how we know what we know about OB. We conclude by describing the organization of the rest of this book.

SO WHAT

Investing now in developing your OB skills will prepare you to be a more effective employee and manager, and help you move up faster in any organization.

WHY IS OB IMPORTANT?

You may still be wondering about the relevance of OB to your current major or career path. You might be thinking, "I don't know any organizational behaviorists. Why is this topic important?" We field this question all the time from people unfamiliar with OB. The core of OB is being effective at work. Understanding how people behave in organizations and why they do what they do is critical to working effectively with and managing others. OB gives everyone the knowledge and tools they need to be effective at any organizational level. OB is an important topic for anyone who works or who will eventually work in an organization, which is the case for most people.

Whenever managers are surveyed ten to fifteen years out of school and asked to identify the most important classes they ever took, OB is usually one of them. This is not because it made them technically better in their area of specialty, but because it made them more effective employees and better managers. As one expert has put it, "It is puzzling that we seek expert advice on our golf game but avoid professional advice on how we can deal with other people."[4] Using your knowledge of OB can help you to succeed faster in any organization or career.

Organizations as a whole also benefit from OB. Imagine the difference between a company with motivated, engaged employees with clear goals aligned with the business strategy and one with unhappy employees, a lot of conflict, weak leadership, and a lack of direction. Effectively implementing OB principles is what creates effective and successful companies. OB is clearly important to organizations. By appropriately applying OB knowledge about individuals, groups, and the effect of organizational structure on worker behavior, the conditions can be created that make organizations most effective.

SO WHAT

Effectively implementing OB concepts increases organizational performance.

OB also helps companies perform well. A mounting body of evidence shows that an emphasis on the softer side of business positively influences bottom line results. By listening to employees, recognizing their work, building trust, and behaving ethically, managers have boosted such performance measures as operating earnings, return on investment, and stock price.[5] In addition to financial performance and job satisfaction, OB also influences absenteeism and turnover. Reducing absenteeism and turnover can be worth millions of dollars to organizations through increased productivity and customer service and decreased staffing costs.

Successful business strategies are grounded in creating and maintaining a sustainable *competitive advantage*, which exists any time an organization has an edge over rivals in attracting customers and defending itself against competition. The effective management of people is key to the creation of a competitive advantage and business strategy execution. As former General Electric CEO Jack Welch said, "We now know where productivity—real and limitless productivity—comes from. It comes from challenged, empowered, excited, rewarded teams of people."[6] We next discuss how firms can gain a competitive advantage through OB.

competitive advantage
Anything that gives a firm an edge over rivals in attracting customers and defending itself against competition

GAINING A COMPETITIVE ADVANTAGE THROUGH OB

Not all organizations are able to create a competitive advantage. Michael Treacy and Fred Wiersma have identified many sources of competitive advantage including having the best-made or cheapest product, providing the best customer service, being more convenient to buy from, having shorter product development times, and having a well-known brand name.[7] Because it is an organization's *people* who are responsible for gaining and keeping any competitive advantage, effective management is critical to business success.[8]

Warehouse retailer Costco's strong and loyal customer base, access to a broad range of high-quality products for a low price, and committed employees give it a competitive advantage over smaller and lesser-known retailers. Although Costco pays its employees substantially more than its closest competitor, Sam's Club, it has similar financial returns on its labor costs due to lower turnover and higher levels of employee productivity.[9] This, in turn, results in a higher-quality customer experience.

"We now know where productivity—real and limitless productivity—comes from. It comes from challenged, empowered, excited, rewarded teams of people." —*Jack Welch, Former General Electric CEO*

According to Michael Porter, to have a competitive advantage a company must ultimately be able to give customers *superior value for their money* (a combination of quality, service, and acceptable price)—either a better product that is worth a premium price or a good product at a lower price can be a source of competitive advantage.[10] Table 1-2 lists some possible sources of

Table 1-2

Sources of Competitive Advantage

- *Innovation:* developing new products, services, and markets and improving current ones
- *Distribution:* dominating distribution channels to block competition
- *Speed:* excelling at getting your product or service to consumers quickly
- *Convenience:* being the easiest for customers to do business with
- *First to market:* introducing products and services before competitors
- *Cost:* being the lowest-cost provider
- *Service:* providing the best customer support before, during, or after the sale
- *Quality:* providing the highest-quality product or service
- *Branding:* developing the most positive image

© CENGAGE LEARNING 2012

competitive advantage. You should note that an organization's talent is the key to securing each of these.

One of the most important things managers do is execute a firm's business strategy. We next discuss business strategy in more detail, as well as how OB can reinforce the organization's overall business strategy and support its execution.

Types of Business Strategies

A company may create value based on price, technological leadership, customer service, or some combination of these and other factors. Business strategy involves the issue of how to compete, but also encompasses:

- The strategies of different functional areas in the firm
- How changing industry conditions such as deregulation, product market maturity, and changing customer demographics will be addressed
- How the firm as a whole will address the range of strategic issues and choices it faces

Business strategies are partially planned, and partially reactive to changing circumstances.

A large number of possible strategies exist for any organization, and an organization may pursue different strategies in different business units. Companies may also pursue more than one strategy at a particular time. According to Michael Porter, businesses can compete successfully by being the cheapest producer, by making unique products valued by consumers, or by applying their expertise in a narrow market segment to meet that segment's particular product or service needs.[11] These three primary business strategies are:

1. Cost leadership
2. Differentiation
3. Specialization

Another strategic choice is whether to grow the business, and if so how to do it. We next discuss each of these strategies and their implications for OB.

cost leadership strategy
Striving to be the lowest-cost producer for a particular level of product quality

Cost Leadership Strategy. Firms pursuing a *cost leadership strategy* strive to be the lowest-cost producer in an industry for a particular level of product quality. These businesses are typically good at designing products that can be efficiently manufactured (e.g., designing products with a minimum number of parts needing assembly) and engineering efficient manufacturing processes to keep production costs and customer prices low. Walmart is a good example of a firm pursuing a cost leadership strategy.

operational excellence
Maximizing the efficiency of the manufacturing or product development process to minimize costs

Organizations pursuing a strategy of keeping costs and prices low try to develop a competitive advantage in *operational excellence*. Employees in these firms need to identify and follow efficient processes and engage in continuous improvement. Manufacturing and transportation companies frequently adopt this approach. These organizations continually look for ways to modify their operational systems in order to reduce costs and lower prices while offering a desirable product that competes successfully with competitors' products. Dell Computers, Federal Express, and Walmart are good examples of companies whose competitive advantage is based on operational excellence.

Most operationally excellent firms require managers to hire and train flexible employees who are able to focus on shorter-term production objectives, who avoid waste, and who are concerned about minimizing production costs.[12]

Operationally excellent organizations function with tight margins and rely more on teamwork than individual performance.

Differentiation Strategy. A *differentiation strategy* calls for the development of a product or service with unique characteristics valued by customers. The value added by the product's uniqueness may enable the business to charge a premium price for it. The dimensions along which a firm can differentiate include image (Coca-Cola), product durability (Wrangler clothing), quality (Lexus), safety (Volvo), and usability (Apple Computer). Some companies, such as Southwest Airlines and ING Direct bank, differentiate themselves from their competitors by pursuing a strategy based on only providing no-frills, basic products and services at a low cost. Companies can pursue more than one strategy at a time. In this case, Southwest Airlines and ING Direct are both cost leaders and differentiators.

differentiation strategy
Developing a product or service that has unique characteristics valued by customers

Organizations pursuing a differentiation strategy often try to develop a competitive advantage based on *product innovation*. This requires employees to continually develop new products and services to create an advantage in the market. These companies create and maintain a culture that encourages employees to bring new ideas into the company. These companies then listen to and consider these ideas, however unconventional they might be. For these companies, the frequent introduction of new products is key to staying competitive. This strategy is common in technology and pharmaceutical companies. Johnson & Johnson, Nike, and 3M are good examples of organizations whose competitive advantage is based on product innovation.

product innovation
Developing new products or services

Product innovators must protect their entrepreneurial environment. To that end, managers develop and reinforce an innovative culture. Instead of selecting job candidates based only on their related experience, they also assess whether a candidate can work cooperatively in teams and

ADVERTISING ARCHIVES

Companies including 3M that pursue a product innovation strategy require employees to continually develop new products and services.

whether the candidate is open-minded and creative.[13] An organization with a product innovation competitive advantage would likely seek a core workforce of research and development employees who have an entrepreneurial mindset, longer-term focus, high tolerance for ambiguity, and an interest in learning and discovery. Employees who need stability and predictability would not fit as well. Managers in innovative companies also need to motivate and empower employees.[14]

specialization strategy

Focusing on a narrow market segment or niche and pursuing either a differentiation or cost leadership strategy within that market segment

Specialization Strategy. Businesses pursuing a *specialization strategy* focus on a narrow market segment or niche—a single product, a particular end use, or buyers with special needs—and pursue either a differentiation or cost leadership strategy within that market segment. Successful businesses following a specialist strategy know their market segment very well, and often enjoy a high degree of customer loyalty. This strategy can be successful if it results in either lower costs than competitors serving the same niche, or in an ability to offer customers something other competitors do not (e.g., manufacturing nonstandard parts). Red Lobster, Dunkin' Donuts, and Starbucks are examples of companies pursuing a specialization strategy.

customer intimacy

Delivering unique and customizable products or services to meet customers' needs and increase customer loyalty

Organizations pursuing a specialization strategy often try to develop a competitive advantage based on *customer intimacy* and try to deliver unique and customizable products or services to meet their customers' needs and increase customer loyalty. This approach involves dividing markets into segments or niches and then tailoring the company's offerings to meet the demands of those niches. Creating customer loyalty requires employees to combine detailed knowledge about their customers with operational flexibility so they can respond quickly to almost any customer need, from customizing a product to fulfilling special requests. Consulting, retail, and banking organizations often adopt this approach.

Most service-quality experts say that talent is the most critical element in building a customer-oriented company.[15] Hiring active learners with good customer relations skills and emotional resilience under pressure would complement a customer intimacy competitive advantage, and help ensure that the organization continually enhances its ability to deliver on promises to customers.[16] Because employee cooperation and collaboration are important to developing customer intimacy, managers should also focus on building effective teams and creating effective communication channels.

Companies such as Starbucks are able to get a high price for their products because of their focus on customer relationships. Imagine if Starbucks began to hire cheaper labor, including people with weak communication skills, and cut back on its investments in employee training and satisfaction. Starbucks' competitive advantage would quickly erode, and the company would have to reduce the price of its coffee to keep customers coming back. This could eventually result in Starbucks pursuing a cost leadership strategy rather than a specialization strategy because they failed to attract, motivate, and retain the right types of employees.

growth strategy

Company expansion organically or through acquisitions

Growth Strategy. Another strategic choice is whether to expand the company and seek to increase business. Companies often pursue a *growth strategy* in response to investor preferences for rising earnings per share, and the required business expansion generally requires the acquisition of additional talent. For example, growth-oriented chains such as Chipotle Mexican Grill regularly open new stores that require additional management, employees, and even product distribution staff.

The success of a growth strategy depends on the firm's ability to find and retain the right number and types of employees to sustain its intended growth. Growth can be *organic*, happening as the organization expands from within by opening new factories or stores. If it is, it requires an investment in recruiting, selecting, and training the right people to expand the company's operations. Firms can also pursue growth strategies through *mergers* and *acquisitions*. Mergers and acquisitions have been a common way for organizations to achieve growth, expand internationally, and respond to industry deregulation. In addition to expanding the organization's business, mergers and acquisitions can also be a way for an organization to acquire the quality and amount of talent it needs to execute its business strategy.

When using mergers and acquisitions as a way to implement a growth strategy, it is important to consider the match between the organizations' cultures, values, and organizational structures. Mismatches between merged or acquired organizations can result in underperformance and the loss of talented employees. Mergers and acquisitions often fail because of culture issues rather than technical or financial issues.[17] The failed DaimlerChrysler, HP and Compaq, and AOL-Time Warner mergers are just a few prominent examples.

Changing Business Strategy

Strategy implementation and strategic change require large-scale organizational changes; two of the largest may be the new organizational culture and new behaviors required of employees. Depending on the nature of a strategic change, some employees are likely to lack the willingness or even the ability to support the new strategy. Targeting management efforts to coach, motivate, and influence the people who are critical to implementing a new strategy may help it to take hold and ultimately influence the strategy's effectiveness.

Imagine an organization currently manufacturing semiconductor chips. The competitive environment is such that the organization must compete on cost. The organization is focused on operational efficiencies to control expenses. Its focus is on keeping costs contained, and the culture reinforces strict adherence to operating rules to help achieve these goals. Now consider what would change if the organization were to identify a better competitive position by specializing in designing new and innovative computer chips and outsourcing their production. The organization's focus would now be on innovation, problem solving, and teamwork. Managers would need to do less rule enforcement and more leading, motivating, and communicating. Employee involvement in decision making might also increase. Intel went through this type of transformation in the early 1970s when it moved from being a producer of semiconductor memory chips to programmable microprocessor chips.

The previous discussion should help you to understand the role of OB in executing a variety of business strategies. Effective managers understand what needs to be done to execute a company's business strategy, then they plan, organize, direct, and control the activities of employees to get it done. Managers do not accomplish organizational objectives by themselves—they get work done through others. Flexibly applying OB principles will help you to do that most effectively.

WHERE DOES OB COME FROM?

OB could date back to caveman times, when people first started trying to understand, motivate, and lead others. The Greek philosopher Plato contemplated the essence of leadership, and Aristotle discussed persuasive communication. The foundation of organizational power and politics can be found in the more than 2,300-year-old writings of Sun-Tzu and 16th-century Italian philosopher Machiavelli. Charismatic leadership was later discussed by German sociologist Max Weber. OB topics have clearly been of interest to many people for a long time. Let's briefly review some history to better understand the origins of the scientific study of OB.

Formal study of OB began in the 1890s, following the industrial relations movement spawned by Adam Smith's introduction of the division of labor. In the 1890s, Frank and Lillian Gilbreth and Frederick Winslow Taylor identified the positive effects of precise instructions, goal setting, and rewards on motivation. Their ideas became known as *scientific management*, and are often considered the beginning of the formal study of OB.

scientific management
Based on the belief that productivity is maximized when organizations are rationalized with precise sets of instructions based on time-and-motion studies

Scientific management is based on the belief that productivity is maximized when organizations are rationalized with precise sets of instructions based on time-and-motion studies. The four principles of Taylor's scientific management are:[18]

1. Replace rule-of-thumb work methods with methods based on scientifically studying the tasks using time-and-motion studies.
2. Scientifically select, train, and develop all workers rather than leaving them to passively train themselves.
3. Managers provide detailed instructions and supervision to workers to ensure that they are following the scientifically developed methods.
4. Divide work nearly equally between workers and managers. Managers should apply scientific management principles to planning the work, and workers should actually perform the tasks.

SO WHAT
Don't focus only on productivity—you must also meet workers needs to be an effective leader.

Although scientific management improved productivity, it also increased the monotony of work. Scientific management left no room for individual preferences or initiative, and was not always accepted by workers. At one point, complaints that it was dehumanizing led to a congressional investigation.[19]

After World War I, attention shifted to understanding the role of human factors and psychology in organizations. This interest was spawned by the discovery of the *Hawthorne effect* in the 1920s and 1930s. The Hawthorne effect occurs when people improve some aspect of their behavior or performance simply because they know they are being assessed. This effect was first identified when a series of experiments that came to be known as the Hawthorne studies were conducted on Western Electric plant workers in Hawthorne, just outside of Chicago, to see the effects of a variety of factors, including individual versus group pay, incentive pay, breaks, and snacks, on productivity.

Hawthorne effect
When people improve some aspect of their behavior or performance simply because they are being assessed

One of the working conditions tested at the Hawthorne plant was lighting. When they tested brighter lights, production increased. When they tested dimmer lights, production also increased! Researchers observed that productivity almost always improved after a lighting change—any change—but eventually returned to normal levels. Workers appeared to try harder when the lights were dimmed just because they knew they were being evaluated. George Elton Mayo, founder of the human relations movement initiated by the Hawthorne studies, explained this finding by saying that the workers tried harder because of the sympathy and interest of the observers. Mayo stated that the reason workers are more strongly motivated by informal things is that individuals have a deep psychological need to believe that their organization cares about them.[20] Essentially, workers are more motivated when they believe their organization is open, concerned, and willing to listen.

The Hawthorne studies prompted further investigation into the effects of social relations, motivation, communication, and employee satisfaction on factory productivity. Rather than viewing workers as interchangeable parts in mechanical organizations as the scientific management movement had done, the *human relations movement* viewed organizations as cooperative systems and treats workers' orientations, values, and feelings as important parts of organizational dynamics and performance. The human relations movement stressed that the human dimensions of work, including group relations, can supersede organizational norms and even an individual's self-interests.

human relations movement
Views organizations as cooperative systems and treats workers' orientations, values, and feelings as important parts of organizational dynamics and performance

Unsophisticated research methods did render some of the conclusions of human relations researchers incorrect.[21] For example, the relationship between employee satisfaction and performance is more complex than researchers initially thought. Nonetheless, the movement ushered in a new era of more humane, employee-centered management by recognizing employees' social needs, and highlighted the importance of people to organizational success.

During the human relations movement, Chester I. Barnard's classic 1938 book, *Functions of the Executive*,[22] described organizations as systems of cooperative human activity. Barnard supported using natural groups, in which social aspects supersede functional organizational structures. He also advocated for the use of *two-way communication*, by which communication is from worker to chief executive, as well as vice versa. In convincing subordinates to cooperate, Barnard proposed that persuasion was preferable to economic incentives.[23] Barnard also believed in the importance of good leadership in communicating goals and ensuring effective decision making. Barnard identified three core executive functions:[24]

two-way communication
Communication is from worker to chief executive, as well as vice versa

1. Establishing and maintaining a system of communication
2. Securing essential services from other members
3. Formulating organizational purposes and objectives

Harvard social work professor and management consultant Mary Parker Follett was known as a "prophet of management" because her ideas were ahead of her time. Follett discovered a variety of phenomena, including creativity exercises such as brainstorming, the "groupthink" effect in meetings (in which faulty decisions are made because group members try to minimize conflict and reach consensus by neglecting to critically analyze and test ideas), and what later became known as "management by objectives" and "total quality management." Follett also advocated for power-sharing arrangements in organizations. In the 1950s, Japanese managers discovered her writings and credit her ideas, along with those of W. Edwards Deming, in revitalizing their industrial base.

W. Edwards Deming is known as the "guru of quality management." In postwar Japan, Deming taught Japanese industrialists statistical process control and quality concepts. His classic 1986 book[25] describes how to do high-quality, productive, and satisfying work. Deming's plan-do-check-act cycle of continuous improvement promoted the adoption of fourteen principles to make any organization efficient and capable of solving almost any problem. Deming believed that removing fear from the workplace gives employees pride in their workmanship, which increases production. Deming also felt that when things go wrong, there is a 94 percent chance that the system (elements under managerial control including machinery and rules) rather than the worker is the cause.[26] He believed that making changes in response to normal variations was unwise, and that a proper understanding of variation includes the mathematical certainty that variation will normally occur within a certain range. Deming's fourteen principles of transformation for improving the practice of management are:[27]

1. Create constancy of purpose toward improvement of product and service.
2. Adopt a new philosophy for a new economic age.
3. Cease dependence on inspection to achieve quality.
4. Minimize total cost.
5. Improve constantly and forever.
6. Institute training on the job.
7. Institute leadership.
8. Drive out fear.
9. Break down barriers between departments.
10. Eliminate slogans.
11. Eliminate quotas.
12. Remove barriers to pride of workmanship.
13. Institute a vigorous program of education and self-improvement.
14. Involve everyone in the organization to work toward transformation.

Source: Deming, W. Edwards, Out of the Crisis, pp. 23–24, Deming's 14 Points of Management, © 2000 Massachusetts Institute of Technology, by permission of The MIT Press.

The total quality management movement initiated by Deming again highlights the importance of people, teamwork, and communication in an organization's success.

You will read much more about the evolution of OB throughout this book, but this brief history helps to set the stage for how we got this far. We now turn our attention to some modern OB issues and discuss why they are important to understand.

CURRENT OB ISSUES

OB helps us to understand organizations by helping us to understand the effects of the various systems and contexts in which they are embedded. Some modern managerial and organizational challenges relevant to OB are globalization and diversity, technology, ethics, and social responsibility. We introduce these topics next and will continue to discuss them throughout the book, as they are essential to effectively managing modern organizations.

Globalization

The internationalization of business has become the norm for many organizations. For example, when a Penske truck is leased for an interstate trip, Genpact's staff in India checks the customer's credit and acquire permits. If the truck is stopped at a weigh station because it lacks a required fuel permit, Indian workers transmit the necessary document to the weigh station to get the vehicle back on the road within a half-hour. After a trip, the driver's log is shipped to a Genpact facility in Juarez, Mexico, where mileage, tax, toll, and fuel data are entered into Penske computers and processed in India. When Penske sells the truck, staff in Mexico records the transaction.[28]

In addition to the globalization of business processes, the globalization of the U.S. workforce has also increased the importance of diversity awareness on the part of managers and employees. ***Parochialism*** occurs when the world is

parochialism

Viewing the world solely through one's own eyes and perspective viewed solely through one's own eyes and perspective. To some extent everyone is parochial, as all of us interpret things in the way we have come to understand the world. Nonetheless, Americans are often accused of having a more parochial perspective than people from other cultures. This may be due to the large domestic market, and the fact that English has been adopted as the international language of business.[29] Nonetheless, the fact that the international economy no longer revolves around the United States means that global thinking is increasingly necessary. As Lester Thurow, former dean of MIT's Sloan School of Management, has stated, managers "must have an understanding of how to manage in an international environment. . . . To be trained as an *American* manager is to be trained for a world that is no longer there."[30]

Much of the research on organizational behavior has been done in the United States; however, what is true for Americans working in the United States may not be true for anyone else, including non-Americans working in the United States. Assuming that everyone in the world shares the same values, norms, and expectations about work is incorrect. National boundaries no longer limit many organizations, and many U.S. companies employ people from around the world.

In this book, the *Global Issues* feature in each chapter will highlight global issues that are relevant to the concepts we discuss. In the *Global Issues* feature in this chapter, you will learn more about how effective motivation and leadership vary in different cultures.

We will discuss diversity and the importance of flexibly applying OB concepts to different people throughout the book. This chapter's *Improve Your Skills* feature gives you the opportunity to better understand your **global mindset**, or set of individual attributes that enable you to influence individuals, groups, and organizations from diverse socio/cultural/institutional systems.[35] Global mindset combines cultural intelligence and a global business orientation.[36] Most chief executives of large multinational organizations believe that having a strong cadre of globally minded leaders would strengthen their organization's competitiveness.[37]

SO WHAT

Being able to recognize, manage, and leverage cultural differences in an organization can enhance both personal and organizational success.

global mindset

Set of individual attributes that enable you to influence individuals, groups, and organizations from diverse socio/cultural/institutional systems

GLOBAL ISSUES

MANAGING ACROSS CULTURES

Effective management requires flexibility and an appreciation that people's expectations and values differ. The U.S. workforce is already very diverse, and is expected to become even more diverse in coming years. The more comfortable you are in tailoring your motivation and leadership efforts to the people you want to lead, the more effective you will be as an employee and as a manager.

Although good pay and interesting work appear to be universally motivating,[31] people from different cultures have different traditions, are often motivated by different things, and communicate in different ways.[32] For example, some cultures communicate directly while others are more reserved. Some cultures put a high value on family life whereas others stress the importance of work. As one expert puts it, "to understand why people do what they do, we have to understand the cultural constructs by which they interpret the

world."[33] Clearly, motivating employees in a multinational organization is challenging, particularly if managers adopt a "one-size-fits-all" motivation strategy.

Cultural differences also influence the effectiveness of different leadership behaviors.[34] Effective leadership behaviors are determined by the roles of expectations, norms, and traditions in the particular society. Managers supervising employees from different cultures must recognize these differences and adapt their behaviors and relationships accordingly. For example, societies such as the United States, Sweden, and Germany have small variation in the distribution of power across supervisors and employees, but others such as Japan and Mexico have a large power difference. If employees feel that large power differences are legitimate and appropriate, they may be uncomfortable if their supervisor tries to reduce the expected power difference by acting more friendly and accessible.

IMPROVE YOUR SKILLS

GLOBAL MINDSET

A global mindset reflects your ability to influence people, groups, and organizations from a variety of backgrounds and cultures. Multinational companies' ability to create globally integrated systems depends on their ability to get employees, managers, and executives to understand and adapt to the realities of a globalized economy. The ability to integrate talent from many parts of the world faster and more effectively than other companies is a source of a firm's competitive advantage[38] as well as your own personal competitive advantage.

Please use the following scale in responding to the ten questions below. When you are finished, follow the scoring instructions at the bottom to calculate your score. Then read more about what your score means, and how you can improve your global mindset.

strongly disagree	disagree	neutral	agree	strongly agree
1	2	3	4	5

___ 1. In interacting with others, I assign equal status to people regardless of their national origin.

___ 2. I consider myself as equally open to ideas from other countries and cultures as I am to ideas from my own country and culture of origin.

___ 3. Finding myself in a new cultural setting is exciting.

___ 4. I see the world as one big marketplace.

___ 5. When I interact with people from other cultures, it is important to me to understand them as individuals.

___ 6. I regard my values to be a hybrid of values acquired from multiple cultures as opposed to just one culture.

___ 7. I get very curious when I meet someone from another country.

___ 8. I enjoy trying food from other countries.

___ 9. In this interlinked world of ours, national boundaries are meaningless.

___ 10. I believe I can live a fulfilling life in another culture.

Scoring: Add up your responses to identify your global mindset score.

Interpretation: Because experiences influence global mindset in a positive or negative manner,[39] you can take steps to improve your global mindset. Based on your score, you might consider some of the personal development activities identified below, or you might come up with others.

If your score is *between 10 and 20*, you have a relatively low global mindset. Formal training/educational programs, self-study courses, university courses, or in-company seminars or management development programs can help you to increase your global mindset.

If your score is *between 21 and 35*, you have a moderate global mindset. You do not exhibit extremely high parochialism, but at the same time you are not as open to people from other cultures as you could be. In addition to the self-development activities listed above, you might consider joining some culturally diverse student organizations and making a point of befriending some people from other cultures to gain more experience and become more comfortable with people from other cultures.

If your score is *between 36 and 50*, you have a high global mindset. This means that you are open to meeting people from a variety of cultures, and are comfortable with global diversity. This does not mean you cannot improve further! Joining international student organizations, working with international volunteer organizations, and befriending people from a variety of cultures will further develop your global mindset.

Source: Adapted from Gupta, A.K., & Govindarajan, V. 2002. Cultivating a global mindset. Academy of Management Executive. 16, 1, 116–126; Kefalas, A.G., Neuland, E.W., 1997. Global mindsets: an exploratory study. Paper presented at the Annual Conference of the Academy of International Business, Moneterrey, Mexico, 4–7 October; Nummela, Niina – Saarenketo, Sami – Puumalainen, Kaisu (2004) Global mindset – a prerequisite for successful internationalisation? Canadian Journal of Administrative Sciences, Vol. 21 No.1, 51–64.

Because global mind-set is learned, experiences can influence it in a positive or negative manner.[40] Every year, the financial services giant HSBC sends promising new hires and managers into long-term business experiences abroad to build a cohort of international officers. Locations include western countries as well as Saudi Arabia, Indonesia, and Mexico. To make a career at HSBC, managers must perform these international missions. This enables HSBC to develop a continuous supply of globally minded managers capable of cross-border learning. Similar approaches are pursued by other multinationals to enable them to transfer expertise and know-how across geographical, cultural, and political divides.[41]

Technology

From automated telephone systems to global positioning systems to electronic inventory controls, technology has forever changed the way firms conduct business. Technology has also changed the practice of management. Production technology can increase work group autonomy, decision making, and responsibility. Technology can also be a training and organizational change aid, a communication media like instant messaging or email, or a tool for managing the interrelatedness of organizational subunits. Automated performance feedback, teleconferencing, and virtual teams whose members are located around the globe are just a few modern management tools and challenges made possible by technology.

People differ in their enthusiasm and attitudes toward technology. Some older workers, although definitely not all, resist learning new technologies, which can inhibit managers' success in implementing technological solutions. Effective management can help give these workers the confidence and motivation to learn new skills. Throughout this book, we highlight ways technology is being used by organizations to apply OB concepts, and give you tips on how to use it most effectively.

SO WHAT

Technology can help organizations implement OB concepts more effectively.

Ethics

Ethics refers to standards of behavior about how people ought to act in different situations. As author Aldo Leopold put it, "Ethical behavior is doing the right thing when no one else is watching—even when doing the wrong thing is legal."[42] But the right thing with regard to the effects of different choices and in relationships with employees, customers, and other stakeholders is often not obvious. Most ethical dilemmas in the workplace are not as simple as "Should I take credit for Laura's idea?" or "Should I claim pay for hours I never worked?" Often there is no clear moral compass to guide employees and managers through complex dilemmas.

ethics

Standards of behavior about how people ought to act in different situations

Managing this challenge is further complicated by the diverse values that exist in today's global workplace. Because some people feel that business ethics, with its message of "do the right thing," only states the obvious, they do not take business ethics seriously. For many others, ethical principles go right out the door during times of stress.[43] Putnam Investments promotes ethical behavior by reducing employee stress and creating a work environment that encourages its employees, rather than dictating to them.

MONTY RAKUSEN / CULTURA / JUPITER IMAGES

Technology has made it easier to communicate and conduct business more efficiently with employees and customers located around the world.

Although it might seem intuitive that firms should behave ethically, a glance at the news headlines suggests that employees' and companies' unethical behavior is more common than you might think. The Chief Operating Officer at the fertilizer producer Intrepid Potash, Patrick L. Avery, resigned after confirming that he did not receive previously claimed degrees from the University of Colorado and Loyola Marymount University.[44] Corporate espionage by Formula One racing team McLaren on rival Ferrari[45] and civil fraud charges against Goldman Sachs[46] are additional high-profile ethical lapses. And U.S. Secret Service agents received two days of ethics training after a prostitution scandal in Colombia.[47]

> "Ethics, values, and strong organizational cultures are the very fabric of business." —*Wayne Cascio and Peter Cappelli, management experts*

Some unethical behaviors occur because people are simply less ethical than others, but many issues occur because of the broader organizational context and systems. Company leaders often give too little thought and time to developing and reinforcing an organizational culture in which people can and do act ethically. There are three types of systemic errors organizations often make that undermine their ethics efforts:[48]

1. *Omission errors*—a lack of written rules
2. *Remission errors*—pressure by a manager or others to make unethical choices
3. *Commission errors*—a failure to follow sound, established operational and ethical practices

All three of these errors can have obvious negative consequences.

OB can give you tools to use both in creating an ethical organization and in making more ethical choices yourself.[49] Table 1-3 describes why employees sometimes act unethically.

Table 1-3

Why Employees Act Unethically

A survey of 1,121 managers and human resources experts from around the world investigated the top reasons why employees break the rules. Each participant was asked, "What are the top three factors that are most likely to cause people to compromise an organization's ethical standards?" Here are the results:

Pressure to meet unrealistic business objectives/deadlines	69.7%
Desire to further one's career	38.5%
Desire to protect one's livelihood	33.8%
Working in environment with cynicism or diminished morale	31.1%
Improper training/ignorance that the act was unethical	27.7%
Lack of consequence if caught	24.3%
Need to follow boss's orders	23.5%
Peer pressure/desire to be a team player	14.9%
Desire to steal from or harm the organization	9.5%
Wanting to help the organization survive	8.7%
Desire to save job	7.9%
A sense of loyalty	6.9%

Source: Marquez, J. (2006). Rebalancing Putnam, Workforce Management, May 22, 2006, pp. 1, 18–22, available online at: http://www.workforce.com/archive/feature/24/38/83/index.php.

You are probably already familiar with the moral benefits of paying attention to business ethics. However, there are other types of benefits from managing ethics in the workplace:[50]

- Attention to business ethics can substantially improve society.
- Ethics programs help maintain a moral course in times of change.
- Ethics programs cultivate teamwork and productivity.
- Ethics programs support employee growth.
- Ethics programs help ensure that policies are legal.
- Ethics programs help avoid criminal acts of omission and can result in lower fines.
- Ethics programs help manage values associated with quality management, strategic planning, and diversity management.
- Ethics programs promote a strong public image

Ethical employee behavior determines short-term organizational performance and long-term organizational success. If employees do not consistently behave ethically, long-term sustainability is unlikely for any organization. As noted, management experts Wayne Cascio and Peter Cappelli state, "Ethics, values, and strong organizational cultures are the very fabric of business."[51] Despite the obvious problems that can result from unethical employee behavior, many organizations do not have a comprehensive ethics and compliance program.

Organizational culture—a system of shared values, expectations, and behaviors that guide members' attitudes and behaviors—establishes the context for everything people in an organization do. Strong ethical cultures are created when leaders live ethically every day and clearly communicate the firm's expectations to prospective and new employees.

Organizations frequently adopt a code of ethics to clarify what is and what is not acceptable. According to the Federal Sentencing Guidelines for Organizations, several elements are important to a complete ethics and compliance program:[52]

1. Written standards for ethical conduct
2. Ethics training
3. Providing a way for seeking ethics-related advice or information
4. Providing a mechanism for reporting misconduct anonymously
5. Disciplining employees who violate the standards of the organization or the law
6. Evaluating ethical behavior as part of an employee's regular performance appraisals

Codes of conduct specify expected and prohibited actions in the workplace, and give examples of appropriate behavior. A *code of ethics* is a decision-making guide that describes the highest values to which an organization aspires. It specifies the ethical rules of operation in terms of what employees should and should not do. Relying solely on codes of conduct and ethics to manage ethical behavior in the workplace is insufficient, however. Treating employees fairly, aligning formal and informal organizational systems to promote ethical behavior, and having ethical leaders at all levels of the company who regularly communicate and reinforce the values behind the code are critical.

Having policies promoting ethical behavior is not enough to establish an ethical culture. Having a clear system of reward and punishment is also important. Effective managers both reward ethical behavior and respond to ethical

SO WHAT
Although ethical dilemmas are not always easy to manage, ethics is essential to long-term organizational performance.

organizational culture
A system of shared values, norms, and assumptions that guide members' attitudes and behaviors

code of conduct
Specifies expected and prohibited actions in the workplace, and gives examples of appropriate behavior

code of ethics
A decision-making guide that describes the highest values to which an organization aspires

Figure 1-1

A Formula for Ethical Behavior

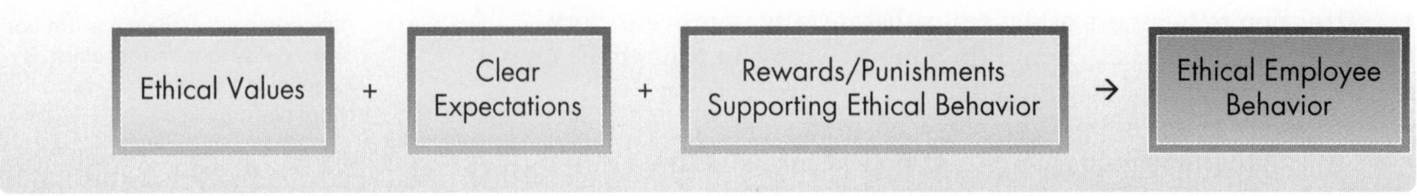

breaches. As shown in Figure 1-1, ethical employee behavior results from ethical values, clear expectations, and rewards and punishments supporting ethical behavior. Five managerial practices that promote ethical behavior are:[53]

1. Close any gaps between knowledge about what to do and actual behaviors. Employees know what is right; now they need to do it.
2. Be selective about who you hire—hiring the right people is critical to long-term success. Because values drive behavior, values can be as important as skills.
3. Socialize new hires to promote ethical values.
4. Implement systems and procedures to promote accountability for ethical behavior.
5. Fairly allocate organizational resources. All managerial leaders manage the five key resources of time, people, money, information, and capital assets. The distribution of these resources should create perceptions of equity and fairness.

In this book we will regularly discuss the role of ethics in organizational behavior. This chapter's case study describes how food manufacturer Smucker has created a strong ethical culture, and how this has helped the company prosper.

Social Responsibility

An important business challenge relevant to OB is adopting a broader stakeholder perspective and looking beyond shareholder value or the short-term stock price. Ethical behavior and social responsibility are increasingly seen as appropriate ways of managing and conducting business. The negative impact of the unethical behaviors of Bernie Madoff, Enron, and others on their communities, workforces, and other stakeholders has been devastating, and has refocused many organizations on doing the right thing by their stakeholders.[54]

corporate social responsibility
Businesses living and working together for the common good and valuing human dignity

Definitions of *corporate social responsibility* often include businesses living and working together for the common good and valuing human dignity. An important part of this is how employers treat their employees. Organizations are increasingly interested in balancing their financial performance with their employees' quality of life, and improving the local community and broader society. One expert defined corporate social responsibility this way: "Regardless of how many people with whom you come in contact, every one of them should be better off for having known you and your company."[55]

But is it really the responsibility of businesses to be good citizens? Doing so can help a firm attract the best talent, and customers are increasingly favoring companies that do the right thing. As Walter J. Cleaver, President and CEO of the Human Resource Planning Society, has put it, "Sustainability is not just looking at the short term; it's building for the long haul. A lot of companies are looking at the financial, social, and environmental impact of what they do. Starbucks pays more for coffee beans because it donates a certain

CASE STUDY

The J.M. Smucker Company

From its founding in 1897, when Jerome Monroe Smucker sold apple butter from the back of a horse-drawn wagon, the J.M. Smucker Company has recognized that acting ethically is a key element of its success. The Orrville, Ohio, manufacturer wants to ensure that its signature comfort foods—fruit spreads, frostings, juices, and beverages—remain American staples, and that its daily operations are guided by honesty, respect, trust, responsibility, and fairness.

Ensuring that the company meets the highest ethical standards starts with hiring people who already have a strong personal value system. To do this, Smucker steeps job candidates in its ethical standards and refers frequently to how company values relate to the particular position a job candidate is seeking. The company also engages in rigorous reference checks. Once hired, the ethics emphasis intensifies. Each new hire attends a daylong training seminar that includes presentations by company officials, videos, and breakout sessions on moral awareness, moral courage, and values.

The discussions go much deeper than a superficial review of how to be a good person. One session concentrates on three ways to make a decision when faced with a dilemma. One option is seeking to do the greatest good for the greatest number of people. The second is a rules-based approach in which the decision will set a standard that everyone else follows. The final alternative is to use the Golden Rule: "Treat others as you would like to be treated."

The sessions also explore the complexity of ethics. Employees are rarely in a clear-cut situation where right and wrong are obvious. Ethical decisions often involve a nuanced balance between right and right. For example, the choice an employee has to make may involve questions related to the pulls between truth and loyalty, the individual versus the community, and short-term versus long-term approaches to business decisions. Smucker communicates that it wants its employees to act with truth over loyalty, community over the individual, and long-term over short-term company interests.

All employees go through the ethics program again every three to five years, and sign a detailed nine-page ethics statement annually to ensure that they truly understand the level of performance Smucker expects from them.

Smucker also strongly believes in environmental sustainability, including utilizing renewable energy, improving wastewater management, using sustainable raw materials, and reusing resources rather than consuming new ones. Smucker promotes social sustainability in the communities in which it operates, promoting initiatives and programs that support and enhance the quality of life. The J.M. Smucker Company has consistently appeared on *Fortune* magazine's "100 Best Places to Work For" list, which it attributes in part to its strong culture.

Questions:

1. Why would ethics be important to a company like Smucker? How can its focus on ethics improve its business performance?
2. Appearing on "best places to work" lists can increase an employer's popularity, even among lower-qualified applicants. The increased volume of applicants can be costly and time-consuming. What do you feel are the benefits and drawbacks to being on this type of list? Do you think that it is generally beneficial to be publicly recognized as a good employer? Why or why not?
3. Does Smucker's culture appeal to you as a potential employee? Why or why not?

Source: Smucker Gift Will Establish Business Leadership Institute (2012). The University of Akron, April 23. Available online: http://www.uakron.edu/im/online-newsroom/news_details.dot?newsId=d24e5be1-b6fc-431b-871c-164ada224a69&crumbTitle=Smucker%20gift%20will%20establish%20business%20leadership%20institute; Harrington, A. (2005). Institute for Global Ethics Expands Focus on Business Practices with Center for Corporate Ethics, CSRWire, January 27. Available online at: http://www.csrwire.com/News/3473.html; Schoeff, M. (2006). Workforce Management, March 13, p. 19; "Award-Winning Company," smuckers.com. Available online at: http://www.smuckers.com/family_company/join_our_company/award_winning_company.aspx; "Sustainability," smuckers.com. Available online at: http://www.smuckers.com/family_company/join_our_company/sustainability.aspx.

"Sustainability is not just looking at the short term; it's building for the long haul." *—Walter J. Cleaver, President and CEO of the Human Resource Planning Society*

amount to the farmers and schools (of a foreign country) so they can keep a good supply source. A company's long-term existence is in many ways connected to how the public perceives it in terms of values."[56]

Ethical behavior and socially responsible business practices have been extensively discussed and have been accepted as significant aspects of management practice. Although most agree with their importance in principle, some people still believe that managers should focus solely on stockholders' interests. Others argue that because business is an influential element of society, it has an obligation to solve problems of public concern, that it is in the enlightened self-interest of organizations to be socially responsible. In other words, social responsibility supporters believe that ethical behavior is more profitable and more rational than unethical behavior, and crucial for the effectiveness of business organizations.

This chapter's *Understand Yourself* feature gives you the opportunity to evaluate how important ethics and social responsibility are to you.

UNDERSTAND YOURSELF

HOW IMPORTANT ARE ETHICS AND SOCIAL RESPONSIBILITY TO YOU?

There is some controversy about the importance of ethics and social responsibility in organizations and their relevance to organizational effectiveness. This series of statements will help you to better understand your beliefs about the role ethics and social responsibility should play in companies. Please use the following scale in responding to the ten statements below. When you are finished, follow the scoring instructions at the bottom to calculate your score. Then read more about what your score means.

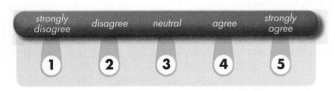

strongly disagree (1)   disagree (2)   neutral (3)   agree (4)   strongly agree (5)

___ 1. It is more important for a company to be ethical and socially responsible than anything else.

___ 2. Businesses have a responsibility to do more than just make a profit.

___ 3. Organizations must be ethical and socially responsible if they are to survive.

___ 4. A company will be more profitable in the long term if it is ethical and socially responsible.

___ 5. Being ethical improves the overall effectiveness of a business

___ 6. Being socially responsible improves the overall effectiveness of a business.

___ 7. Being ethical improves a company's global competitiveness.

___ 8. Being socially responsible improves a company's global competitiveness.

___ 9. In a crisis, survival should more important to a company than ethics or social responsibility.

___ 10. Stockholders are a company's most important stakeholders.

Scoring: Add up your responses to identify your perceived importance of ethics and social responsibility score.

Interpretation: If your score is *between 10 and 20*, you tend to place a higher value on financial performance than on social responsibility and business ethics. This could present challenges for you in balancing what is right with what you feel you need to do to succeed. Following a company's code of conduct and code of ethics will be important to your future success.

If your score is *between 21 and 35*, you tend to strike a balance between performance and social responsibility and business ethics. This is not inherently good or bad, but it is important for you to think about your ethical principles and fully evaluate the impacts of your decisions.

If your score is *between 36 and 50*, you tend to put ethics and social responsibility before making a profit. This is clearly the moral "high road" and the one least likely to get you into legal trouble, but do not forget that profits and shareholders matter too.

To have lasting effects, social responsibility efforts should be integrated into the culture of the organization.[57] Corporate social responsibility has the biggest impact when it is integrated with business priorities, relevant to achieving business objectives, inclusive of both internal and external stakeholder needs, and consistent with the firm's cultural values and brand identity.[58] Serving stockholders as well as the larger population of stakeholders, which includes workers, customers, the community, and even the planet, are not mutually exclusive.

Supermarket Trader Joe's has long urged shoppers to bring their own bags to promote recycling. Two Costco warehouses in Palm Springs, California, send their waste produce to a worm farm, where it is composted into mulch.[59] Starbucks Shared Planet initiative has a goal of obtaining LEED third-party green certification for all new company-operated stores worldwide. Starbucks states, "Starbucks™ Shared Planet™ is our commitment to do business in ways that are good for people and the planet."[60]

Corporate sustainability initiatives can be top-down, with someone in a position of authority dictating to managers and employees what to do. Corporate sustainability efforts can also be grassroots, with employees identifying projects and taking the initiative to organize their own activities. For example, Google's employee shuttle system was created by an employee, and employees in two of its offices decided to eliminate water bottles.[61] Whereas the support of top management is critical to the success of any initiative, the involvement of employees creates a lasting culture change.

Socially responsible programs and policies being implemented by U.S. corporations include:

- Workplace diversity
- Favorable working conditions
- Nonexploitation of workers, including discrimination and harassment
- Work-life balance initiatives
- Community volunteerism and charitable giving programs
- Environmental "green" programs including recycling and resource conservation
- Reducing carbon emissions
- Partnering with environmentally friendly suppliers and companies

Employee participation in social responsibility initiatives not only can motivate employees, but also can generate some good ideas. When a major printing company set a goal to reduce its waste by 20 percent over five years, its executive team naturally focused on finding ways to streamline its printing operations to reduce paper waste. After a series of brainstorms, a receptionist pointed out that the number of individual lunches delivered to the office every day created a significant amount of food packaging waste. By investing in a small café and encouraging employees to eat a buffet-style lunch, the printer reduced twice as much waste as it did by streamlining its printing operations.[62] Google calculates that it takes over 2,000 cars off the road every day through its free electric car charging stations, its electric car-sharing program for employees, and its employee shuttle.[63] Nearly 50 percent of Walmart employees signed up for the company's personal sustainability project, which encourages employees to live more sustainable lives by educating them on ways to conserve resources and reduce energy consumption at home.[64]

The International Organization for Standardization (ISO) has created a variety of standards that help organizations gain international acceptance of their practices and outcomes.[65] In addition to environmentally related standards such as sustainability and carbon emissions, the ISO publishes management standards including those for leadership, customer focus, involvement of

SO WHAT
Social responsibility initiatives can motivate employees and improve organizational performance.

people, and continual improvement. These standards can help managers meet their environmental and social responsibility objectives.

Managers have a great deal of influence over the execution of corporate responsibility programs, and need to be aware of any likely challenges to successful implementation. A Grant Thorton Corporate Responsibility Survey reported the four greatest obstacles to successful execution of corporate responsibility programs are:[66]

1. A focus on quarterly earnings or other short-term targets
2. The cost of implementation
3. Difficulty in measuring and quantifying return on investment
4. An unsupportive corporate culture

Each of these obstacles can be reduced through the application of OB concepts including goal setting, feedback, decision making, influence, and organizational culture.

HOW DO WE KNOW WHAT WE KNOW?

An important part of being an effective manager is understanding the quality of the information you use to make decisions. Not all information is accurate! Accordingly, it is important for you to understand the processes that have been used to establish our knowledge about OB, and why we know what we know.

Intuition

Many people feel that they have a good understanding of other people from observing them all of their lives. When you want to persuade or motivate a friend or colleague to do something, for example, you likely use various techniques and tricks that have worked for you in the past. So why should you study OB?

Although we can certainly develop a good understanding of many of the norms, expectations, and behaviors of others by living and working with them, there are many things that are not well understood without more systematic study. Decades of research have both reinforced some of the things many people intuitively believe and identified common misunderstandings or misperceptions about OB. For example, when are different leadership approaches most effective? What are the advantages and disadvantages of different influence approaches? What goal level will best motivate someone? How important is employee satisfaction to job performance? Is stress always bad? The answers to some of these questions may surprise you, and will help make you a more successful manager.

We encourage you to read this book with an open mind, and to not assume that you know all there is to know about a topic before you have studied it. Our goal is to help you be as effective as possible in organizations, and to help you create successful organizations. Help us help you succeed by being open to challenging and replacing popular but incorrect notions you may have about OB.

scientific method

Method of knowledge generation that relies on systematic studies that identify and replicate a result using a variety of methods, samples, and settings

The Scientific Method

Rather than relying on experience or intuition, or just assuming that ideas are correct because they seem to make sense, the *scientific method* relies on systematic studies that identify and replicate a result using a variety of methods, samples, and settings. Although he himself was not a distinguished scientist, Sir Francis Bacon developed the scientific method, shown in Figure 1-2, in the 1600s.[67]

The scientific method begins with *theory*, which is a collection of verbal and symbolic assertions that specify how and why two or more variables are related, and the conditions under which they should and should not relate.[68] Theories describe the relationships that are proposed to exist among certain variables, when, and under what conditions. Until they are proven to be correct, theories are no guarantee of fact. It is important to systematically test any theory to verify that its predictions are accurate.

The second step in the scientific method is the development of *hypotheses*, or written predictions specifying expected relationships between certain variables. "Setting a goal will be positively related to the number of products assembled" is an example of a hypothesis (and, in fact, it's true!). So how can you test this hypothesis?

Hypothesis testing can be done using a variety of research methods and statistical analyses. For our purposes, assume we collect data on our predictor, or *independent variable*, and our criterion, or *dependent variable*. In this hypothetical case, setting a specific, difficult, achievable goal is the independent variable, and the number of products assembled is our dependent variable. We identify a representative group of assemblers, and record their goals and their performance during a one-hour work period. We can then analyze the *correlation*, abbreviated *r*, between the two variables to test our hypothesis. The correlation reflects the strength of the statistical relationship between two variables. Rather than answering a question with a "yes" or "no," the correlation answers with "how strong the relationship is."

The correlation ranges from -1 to +1, and can be positive or negative. A correlation of 0 means that there is no statistical relationship. We can also imagine a correlation as a graph. As you can see from Figure 1-3, in the context of our example, a correlation of 0 would mean that setting a goal has no effect on the number of products assembled, while a correlation of +1 means

theory
A collection of verbal and symbolic assertions that specify how and why variables are related, and the conditions under which they should and should not relate

hypotheses
Written predictions specifying expected relationships between certain variables

independent variable
The variable that is predicted to affect something else

dependent variable
The variable predicted to be affected by something else

correlation
Reflects the size and strength of the statistical relationship between two variables; ranges from −1 to +1

Figure 1-2

The Scientific Method

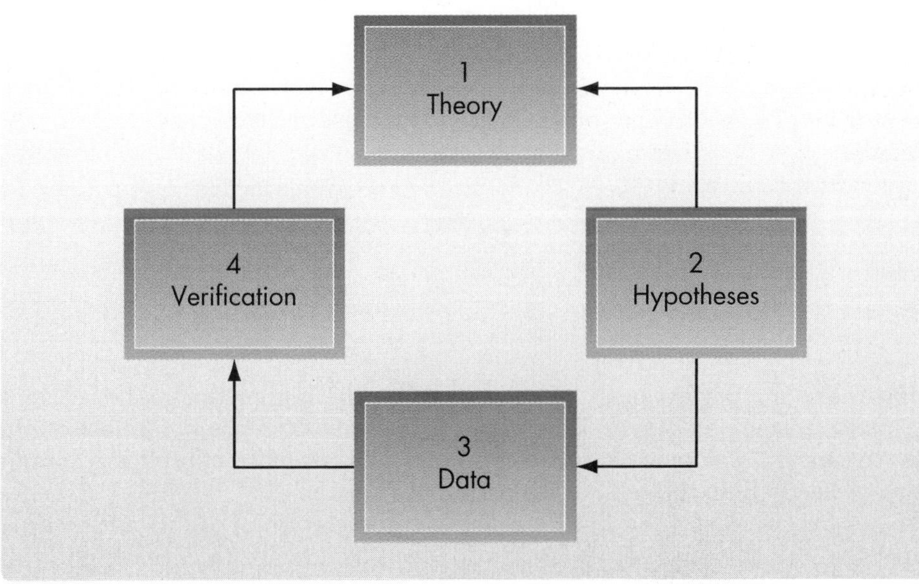

© CENGAGE LEARNING 2012

Figure 1-3
Interpreting Correlations

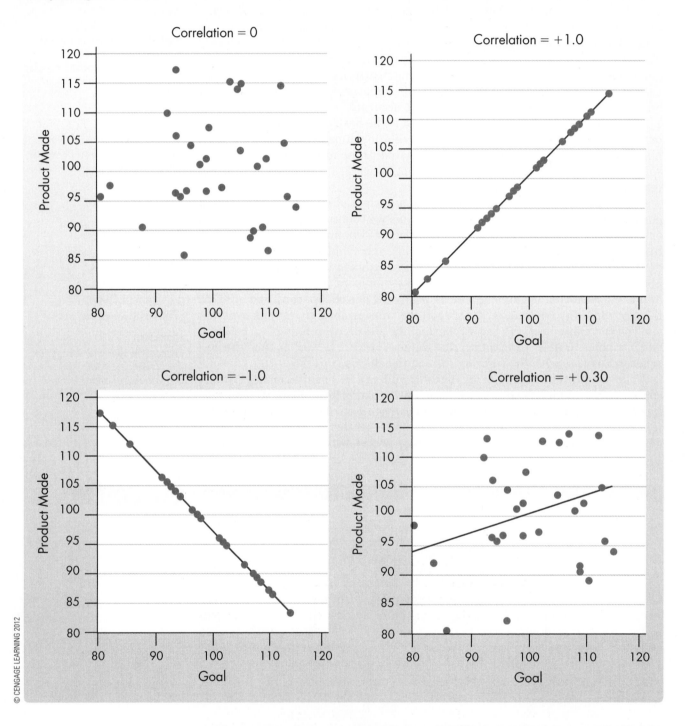

that there is a perfect positive relationship—the higher the goal, the more products assembled. A correlation of +1.0 is as strong a positive relationship as we can get, and shows that we can predict the number of products assembled perfectly from the level of the assembler's goals.

As you can also see from Figure 1-3, a correlation of -1.0 is as strong a negative relationship as we can get. It would indicate that the higher an assembler's goal, the lower her performance. A negative correlation is not necessarily bad. In this case, it would simply mean that to maximize assemblers' performance, the manager should set *lower* goals (perhaps goals for lower error rates or faster assembly times). In reality, we never see perfect +1.0 or -1.0 correlations when it comes to people's behavior—people are just too complicated. Nonetheless, being able to visualize what these relationships look like can help you to understand the relationships. In Figure 1-3, we also include a correlation of +0.30, which is more common in OB research.

The evaluation of relationships between organizational actions and outcomes can help organizations execute strategy more effectively and improve performance. Texas-based Sysco, a marketer and distributor of food-service products, is a good example. Reducing customer churn can improve performance for companies in low-margin industries like Sysco's. Sysco maintains low fixed costs and periodically conducts customer and associate work-climate surveys to assess and correlate employee satisfaction with customer satisfaction. The company has found that customer loyalty and operational excellence are affected by a satisfied, productive, and committed workforce.[69]

High employee retention also cuts the cost of operations. Because of the important relationship it identified between associate satisfaction and commitment, and the satisfaction of all other constituents (customers, communities, suppliers, and shareholders), Sysco has implemented a rigorous set of programs to enhance the retention and satisfaction of its employees.[70]

Meta-Analysis. A statistical technique called *meta-analysis* is used to combine the results of many different research studies done in a variety of organizations and for a variety of jobs. The goal of meta-analysis is to estimate the true relationship between various constructs and to determine whether the results can be generalized to all situations or if the relationship works differently in different situations.

meta-analysis

A statistical technique used to combine the results of many different research studies done in a variety of organizations and for a variety of jobs

Although meta-analysis can often give useful insights into the strength of the relationships between the variables in the studies included in the analysis, there is no guarantee that any one organization would find the same relationship. This is because many situational factors exist in every organization that may drastically impact the strength of the relationship, including differences in the job context and differences in the definition of job success. It is important to always test hypotheses and validate theories in your own organization before making decisions based on them.

Uncommon Sense. People sometimes believe that OB is simply a collection of common sense ideas because the theories can seem obvious. For example, everyone knows that having higher goals and confidence leads to better performance, more job satisfaction leads to greater productivity, greater group cohesion will lead to higher group performance, and valuing rewards leads to greater motivation, right? So if it is all common sense, why do we need OB research? And why do we need to study these theories?

The answer is that common sense isn't so common. People don't always agree. If ten different people see the same leadership interaction you may find ten different "common sense" perspectives on what leadership is and how it works. Even if you don't find ten different perspectives, you will certainly not find perfect agreement on the same phenomenon. Take two common sense statements: "Absence makes the heart grow fonder" and "When the cat is away the mice will play." Which one is correct? Why?

Another answer is that common sense is not always right. Findings may seem common sense after the research is done, but beforehand we don't really know what is going on. For example, in this book you will learn that each of the common sense statements made earlier is either false or conditional. Goals and confidence do not always work, satisfaction does not always lead to productivity, cohesion does not always enhance group performance, and having valued rewards sometimes doesn't motivate people. So it isn't just common sense. We need science and research because it is built on careful and systematic testing of assumptions and conclusions. This process allows us to evolve our understanding of how things work and it allows us to learn when goals, confidence, satisfaction, cohesion, and rewards affect outcomes and why it happens. That is why you need to learn the theories and why you can't just operate on common sense.

ORGANIZATION OF THE BOOK

Organizational behavior takes a systems approach to how individuals and groups act in organizations. Employees relate to organizations in several ways. Individual employees relate to each other as individuals. Individual employees also relate to workgroups and to the organization as a whole. Organizations are social systems, and managing the resulting social dynamics is a critical part of effective job performance and effective management.

The model shown in Figure 1-4 reflects the organization of this book. The first two chapters describe the OB context, and the importance of national and organizational cultures in OB. We then move from managing individual behavior to managing groups and teams to understanding and managing organizations, organizational change, and your own career.

Figure 1-4

Model of This Book

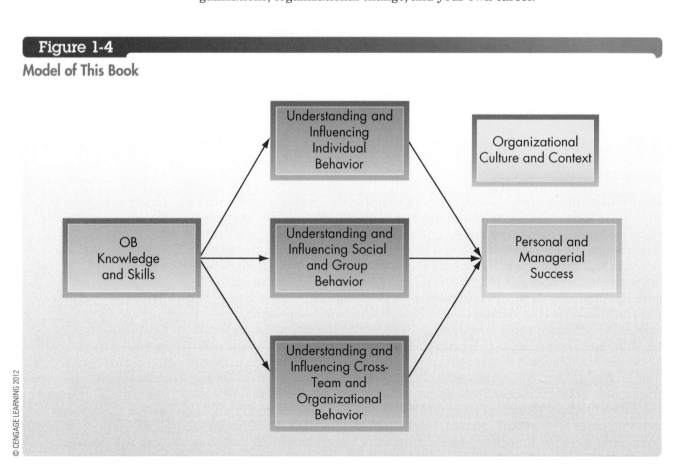

REAL WORLD RESPONSE

CORPORATE SOCIAL RESPONSIBILITY AT BECTON, DICKINSON, AND Co.

In addition to regularly donating cash and products to global nonprofits, BD partnered with Direct Relief International to provide free diabetes insulin-injection products to Americans needing financial help during the financial downturn. It also partnered with the Foundation for Innovative New Diagnostics to promote access to early and accurate diagnosis of tuberculosis in India.

Recognizing that human health and a healthy environment are inseparable, BD also recognizes the importance of environmental responsibility. BD has a strategy to reduce its environmental footprint and help its customers reduce theirs through renewable energy use and other environmental performance programs including minimizing material use and reducing the impacts of product disposal.

BD's employee Volunteer Service Trip gives associates the opportunity to participate in company-sponsored volunteer trips that address global health issues. The company also recognizes creativity and excellence in its associates and retirees community involvement by making contributions in the awardees' names to the organizations in which they volunteer. Eligible employees are also given up to two full days of paid time off every year to volunteer for community service.

BD focuses its social responsibility efforts on areas where it can have the greatest impact including providing resources for disaster relief and recovery, supporting immunization campaigns, and promoting healthcare worker safety. The company also sets goals for its social and environmental responsibility performance, and tracks its progress in meeting them. Reflecting its success in the area of social responsibility, BD has been awarded numerous awards for good citizenship, ethics, the environment, and being an employer of choice.

Source: Ludwig, E. (2012). CEO Forum: Corporate Responsibility During a Downturn, NYSE Magazine. http://www.nysemagazine.com/ceoforum; Sustainabil-ity at BD (2012). Available online: http://www.bd.com/sustainability/; New Collaboration Aims to Improve Access to TB Diagnostics (2012). Available online at: http://www.bd.com/contentmanager/b_article.asp?Item_ID=26649&ContentType_ID=1&BusinessCode=20001&d=BD+Worldwide&s=&dTitle=&dc=&dcTitle=; 2010 Sustainability Report (2010). Becton Dickinson. Available online at: http://www.bd.com/sustainability/2010/environment/sustainable_operations.aspx; Legacy of Caring (2012). Becton Dickinson. Available online at: http://www.bd.com/responsibility/legacy_of_caring/awards_recognitions.asp.

SUMMARY AND APPLICATION

Why is it that some people rise in organizations despite being only average accountants, marketers, researchers, and so on? Often the answer is that those people know how to interact effectively with other people. Effective interaction with people is critical for advancement in organizations, and often for effective job performance. Being able to understand what people think and feel, knowing how to persuade and motivate others, and knowing how to resolve conflicts and forge cooperation are among the most important skills of successful leaders.[71] "People skills" are often what make the difference between an average and an excellent performer in almost any job.

As we said at the beginning of this chapter, we want to help you get a better job and a better career, and to be a better manager. This book can help you better understand yourself, understand organizations, understand the role of organizational behavior in your personal career success, and improve your OB skills. All we can do, however, is make these things possible: You need to make them happen. We encourage you to stay open-minded and receptive to new ideas and to information that disconfirms some of your current assumptions about people, organizations, and management. By studying the chapters and putting some thought into how you can use various the concepts in different situations, you will be taking an important step in advancing your career.

✓ TAKEAWAY POINTS

1. Organizational behavior describes how people and groups in organizations behave, react, and interpret events. It also describes the role of organizational systems, structures, and processes in shaping behavior. Drawing from fields including management, anthropology, sociology, information technology, ethics, economics, and psychology, OB provides a foundation for the effective management of people in organizations.

2. OB can make you a more effective employee and manager by making you more effective at performing the four managerial functions of planning, organizing, directing, and controlling. No matter what managerial challenge is being faced, there are OB tools that will help you to succeed.

3. OB can improve a firm's performance by positively influencing bottom line results. Listening to employees, recognizing their work, and behaving ethically can improve such performance measures as operating earnings, return on investment, and stock price.

4. OB concepts need to be applied flexibly to match a company's business strategy and its diverse employee needs. The U.S. workforce is already very diverse, and is expected to become even more diverse in coming years. Recognizing, managing, and leveraging cultural differences can lead to enhanced personal and organizational success.

5. Ethical organizational cultures are created or undermined by managers. Because OB helps to understand and influence individual behavior, it is an important managerial tool for promoting ethical employee behaviors.

6. Scientific management, the human relations movement, and the quality management movement provide some of the foundations of our knowledge about OB.

7. The "scientific process" is how we have learned what we know about OB. Correlation coefficients are one of the methods used to establish the relationships between two or more variables.

DISCUSSION QUESTIONS

1. In the opening real world challenge, how can social responsibility help BD pursue its business strategy?
2. What do you think are the most important things a manager does? Is how a manager does these things also important? Why or why not?
3. Why do you think some employees behave unethically? What can you, as a manager, do to promote ethical employee behavior?
4. Why do you think the Hawthorne effect exists?
5. Why will learning about OB help you to get a better job and a better career, and be a better manager?
6. Why do you want to learn more about OB?
7. Think of something that you believe leads to employee productivity based on intuition that may not prove to be true if tested systematically. Now apply the scientific method and describe how you might test your theory.

EXERCISES

Your Motivation to Lead

Being motivated to lead is insufficient to guarantee that someone will become a leader—you must also have the ability to lead and the opportunity to do so. Nonetheless, some personal characteristics have been found to be correlated with leadership and managerial motivation. This measure is a shortened version of the "motivation to lead" instrument developed by Kim-Yin Chan and Fritz Drasgow.[72] Although your results do not perfectly predict whether or not you will eventually become a manager, the motivation to lead self-assessment can give you some insight into your leadership potential and your interest in pursuing a career in management.

Using the 1–5 scale below, indicate your agreement with each of the following nine statements. When you are finished, follow the scoring instructions to calculate your motivation to manage and interpret your score using the information below. There are no right or wrong answers—please answer honestly to give yourself the best feedback! When you have scored your responses, answer the questions below.

strongly disagree	disagree	neutral	agree	strongly agree
1	2	3	4	5

___1. Most of the time, I prefer being a leader rather than a follower when working in a group.
___2. I am the type of person who likes to be in charge of others.
___3. I have a tendency to take charge in most groups or teams that I work in.
___4. I would agree to lead others even if there are no special rewards or benefits with that role.

___5. I never expect to get more privileges if I agree to lead a group.
___6. I feel that I have a duty to lead others if I am asked.
___7. I have been taught that I should always volunteer to lead others if I can.
___8. It is an honor and a privilege to be asked to lead.
___9. People should volunteer to lead rather than wait for others to ask or vote for them.

Scoring: Add up your scores to the nine statements. The total is your motivation to lead score.

Interpretation: Motivation to lead is a dynamic construct. It is not only affected by personality, but also is changeable through experience. Career advancement generally requires you to take on leadership responsibilities with projects, work groups, teams, or departments. It is a good idea to reflect on why you might not have a stronger desire to lead, and think about what you might do to increase your motivation in this area.

If your score is *between 9 and 18,* you have a relatively low motivation to lead. This suggests that you don't seek out or respond favorably to leadership opportunities and may not be as likely to advance very far in organizations.

If your score is *between 19 and 32,* you have a moderate motivation to lead. You do not shy away from leadership opportunities, but you often do not seek them out and do not always welcome them.

If your score is *between 33 and 45,* you have a relatively high motivation to lead. This suggests that you like to lead, and often find ways to lead others.

Questions

1. Do you think that your score accurately reflects your motivation to lead? Why or why not? What is missing from the assessment, if anything?
2. What might you do in the next year to improve your motivation to lead?
3. What are the implications for an organization if most of its employees have a low motivation to lead? What can a firm do to increase its employees' leadership motivation?

The People Make the Place

Form small groups of four to five students. Working individually, take a few minutes to make a list of characteristics that describe someone you would most like to have as a coworker (or think of someone who you have enjoyed working with in the past). Then make a list of characteristics that describe someone you would least like to work with (or someone you have disliked working with in the past). Now have each group member share ideas as you go around the group, taking turns and presenting one good and one undesirable characteristic at a time. Once all group members' ideas have been shared, discuss the following three questions. Be prepared to share your answers with the class.

Questions

1. Why do you think some people might act like you described a desirable coworker acting?
2. As a manager, what could you do to create a workgroup in which all employees behaved like you described your most preferred coworker and not like your least preferred coworker?
3. If all of a company's managers behaved like your good example, what would the effect be on the organization?

NetApp

After reading this chapter, you understand how important employees are to organizational performance. In 2009, NetApp, a $3 billion data storage and management solutions company with 8,000 worldwide employees, was rated number one on *Fortune* magazine's list of the "100 Best Companies to Work For." Point your browser to NetApp's Careers page at http://www.netapp.com /us/careers/ and read about how the company presents itself to potential employees. Explore the website and learn more about working at NetApp, and then answer the following questions.

Questions

1. Which topics from this chapter relate to NetApp?
2. How are ethics and diversity valued by NetApp?
3. Based on what you learned from its website, does NetApp seem like a company you would enjoy working for? Why or why not?

VIDEO CASES

Now What?

Imagine being a new manager at Happy Time Toys, a company that designs and manufactures novelty toys. While attending a group meeting with your boss and two coworkers, your boss asks for ways of better using the organization's talent to create a competitive advantage. *What do you say or do?* Go to this chapter's "Now What?" video, watch the challenge video, and choose the best response. Be sure to also view the outcomes of the two responses you didn't choose.

(Continued)

Discussion Questions

1. Which aspects of management and organizational behavior discussed in this chapter are illustrated in these videos? Explain your answer.
2. How could a company's talent strategy undermine its ability to create a competitive advantage?
3. How else might you answer the question of how Happy Time Toys can create a competitive advantage through its talent?

Workplace | City of Greensburg, Kansas: Ethics and Social Responsibility

May 4, 2007, started out like any day for the 1,500 residents of Greensburg, Kansas. Weather forecasters predicted afternoon storms, but few residents paid much attention. By 6 p.m., the National Weather Service issued a tornado warning for Kiowa County. Around 9:20 p.m., storm sirens sounded, and residents took cover in bathrooms and basements. When they emerged from their shelters, their town was gone.

With 700 homes to rebuild, the residents were prepared to start with a clean slate. City Administrator Steve Hewitt and Mayor Lonnie McCollum rallied the people and vowed to rebuild a green town. Although both Hewitt and McCollum believed Greensburg should be rebuilt in a socially responsible way, using sustainable practices, designs, and materials; they faced some ethical dilemmas. Hewitt frequently explained his broad view of the stakeholders affected by their choices, "We're making 100-year decisions that will affect our children and our children's children."

Greensburg upped the cost of rebuilding when city council approved an ordinance declaring all municipal buildings would be built to the highest green building rating for sustainability: "LEED-Platinum." Leadership in Energy and Environmental Design (LEED) promotes a whole-building approach to sustainability by recognizing performance in five key areas of human and environmental health: materials selection, sustainable site development, energy efficiency, water savings, and indoor environmental quality. In Hewitt's mind, Greensburg had an economic responsibility to construct buildings that achieved maximum energy efficiency. So even if it cost more initially to build LEED-Platinum facilities, the town's energy costs as well as its operating costs would be significantly lower in the future.

Today, the initiative to rebuild Greensburg is a group effort. John Deere, BTI Greensburg, and Honda are but a few of the businesses aiding the cause. Greensburg GreenTown, a 501(c)(3) not-for-profit organization, is the town's central organizer, providing Greensburg with the information, support, and resources necessary to rebuild as a green community. Although many challenges lie ahead, leaders of the town will not be deterred. As they say in Greensburg: "Rebuilding green is the right thing to do."

Discussion Questions

1. In what ways do the activities of Greensburg exemplify good ethics and social responsibility? Explain.
2. What are the potential consequences of rebuilding Greensburg without concern for green practices?
3. What risks are involved in rebuilding Greensburg as a green town?

CENGAGENOW™ includes **teaching and learning resources** to supplement the text, and is designed specifically to **help students "think like managers"** by engaging and challenging them to think critically about managerial situations. **CengageNOW uses today's technology to improve the skills** of tomorrow's managers.

END NOTES

[1]Becton Dickinson (2012). News Release, August 2. Available on-line: http://www.bd.com/resource.aspx?IDX=27604.

[2]Sustainability at BD (2012). Becton Dickinson. Available online: http://www.bd.com/sustainability/.

[3]Fayol, H. (1949). *General and Industrial Management,* trans. Constance Storrs. London: Sir Isaac Pittman.

[4]Lubit, R. (2004, March/April). The Tyranny of Toxic Managers: Applying Emotional Intelligence to Deal with Difficult Personalities. *Ivey Business Journal.* Available online: http://wwwold.iveybusinessjournal.com/article.asp?intArticle_ID=475.

[5]Pfeffer, J. (2003). *Business and the Spirit: Management Practices That Sustain Values, Handbook of Workplace Spirituality and Organizational Performance,* eds. R. A. Giacolone and C. L. Jurkiewicz (pp. 29–45). New York: M. E. Sharpe Press; Ulrich, D., & Smallwood, N. (2003). *Why the Bottom Line Isn't! How to Build Value Through People and Organization.* New Jersey: John Wiley & Sons, Inc.

[6]Jack Welch speech to the Economic Club of New York, Detroit, May 16, 1994.

[7]Treacy, M., & Wiersema, F. (1997). *The Discipline of Market Leaders.* New York: Perseus Books.

[8]Lado, A. A., Boyd, N. G., & Wright, P. (1992). A Competency-Based Model of Sustainable Competitive Advantage: Toward a Conceptual Integration. *Journal of Management, 18,* 77–91.

[9]Worrell, D. (2011). Higher Salaries: Costco's Secret Weapon, Allbusiness.com. Available online: http://www.allbusiness.com/staffing-hr/16745820-1.html.

[10]Porter, M. E. (1985). *Competitive Advantage.* New York: Free Press.

[11]Porter, M. E. (1985). *Competitive Advantage.* New York: Free Press; Porter, M. E. (1998). *Competitive Strategy: Techniques for Analyzing Industries and Competitors.* New York: Free Press.

[12]Beatty, R. W., & Schneier, C. E. (1997). New HR Roles to Impact Organizational Performance: From "Partners" to "Players." *Human Resource Management, 36,* 29–37; Deloitte & Touche, LLP. (2002). *Creating Shareholder Value Through People: The Human Capital ROI Study.* New York: Author; Treacy, M., & Wiersema, F. (1993). Customer Intimacy and Other Value Disciplines. *Harvard Business Review, 71,* 84–94.

[13]Beatty, R. W., & Schneier, C. E. (1997). New HR Roles to Impact Organizational Performance: From "Partners" to "Players." *Human Resource Management, 36,* 29–37; Deloitte & Touche, LLP. (2002). *Creating Shareholder Value Through People: The Human Capital ROI Study.* New York: Author; Treacy, M., & Wiersema, F. (1993). Customer Intimacy and Other Value Disciplines. *Harvard Business Review, 71,* 84–94.

[14]Pieterse, A.N., van Knippenberg, D., Schippers, M., & Stam, D. (2010). Transformational and Transactional Leadership and Innovative Behavior: The Moderating Role of Psychological Empowerment, *Journal of Organizational Behavior, 31,* 609–623.

[15]Groth, M. & Goodwin, R.E. (2011). Customer Service. In S. Zedeck (ed.), *APA Handbook of Industrial and Organizational Psychology: Maintaining, Expanding, and Contracting the Organization* (vol. 3, pp. 329–357) Washington, DC: American Psychological Association.

[16]Beatty, R. W., & Schneier, C. E. (1997). New HR Roles to Impact Organizational Performance: From "Partners" to "Players." *Human Resource Management, 36,* 29–37; Deloitte & Touche, LLP. (2002). *Creating Shareholder Value Through People: The Human Capital ROI Study.* New York: Author; Treacy, M., & Wiersema, F. (1993). Customer Intimacy and Other Value Disciplines. *Harvard Business Review, 71,* 84–94.

[17]Weber, Y. & Fried, Y. (2011), Guest Editors' Note: The Role of HR Practices in Managing Culture Clash During the Postmerger Integration Process, *Human Resource Management, 50,* 565–570.

[18]Taylor, F. W. (1911). *The Principles of Scientific Management.* New York: Harper & Brothers.

[19]Spender, J. C., & Kijne, H. (1996). *Scientific Management: Frederick Winslow Taylor's Gift to the World?* Boston: Kluwer.

[20]Mayo, E. (1945). *The Social Problems of an Industrial Civilization.* Boston: Harvard Univ. Press.

[21]Organ, D. W. (2002, March–April). Elusive Phenomena. *Business Horizons,* 1–2.

[22]Barnard, C. I. (1938/1968). *The Functions of the Executive.* Cambridge, MA: Harvard University Press.

[23]Barnard, C. I. (1938/1968). *The Function of the Executive.* Cambridge, MA: Harvard University Press.

[24]Barnard, C. I. (1938/1968). *The Functions of the Executive.* Cambridge, MA: Harvard University Press.

[25]Deming, W. E. (1986). *Out of the Crisis.* Boston: Massachusetts Institute of Technology.

[26]Deming, W. E. (1986). *Out of the Crisis.* Boston: Massachusetts Institute of Technology, p. 315.

[27]Deming, W. Edwards, *Out of the Crisis,* pp. 23–24, Deming's 14 Points of Management, © 2000 Massachusetts Institute of Technology, by permission of The MIT Press.

[28]Engardio, P. (2006, January 30). Penske's Offshore Partner in India. *BusinessWeek.* Available online: http://www.businessweek.com/magazine/content/06_05/b3969414.htm.

[29]Adler, N. N. (2008). *International Dimensions of Organizational Behavior* (5th ed.). Mason, OH: Thompson Higher Education.

[30]Global Strategist. (1988, March 7). *U.S. News & World Report,* 50.

[31]Festing, M., Engle, A. D. Sr., Dowling, P. J. & Sahakiants, I. (2012). Human Resource Management Activities: Pay and Rewards. In C. Brewster & W. Mayrhofer (Eds.), *Handbook of Research on Comparative Human Resource Management* (pp. 139–163). Northampton, MA: Edward Elgar Publishing.

[32]Forstenlechner, I., & Lettice, F. (2007). Cultural Differences in Motivating Global Knowledge Workers. *Equal Opportunities International, 26*(8), 823–833.

[33]D'Andrade, R. G., & Strauss, C. (1992). *Human Motives and Cultural Models* (p. 4). Cambridge, UK: Cambridge University Press.

[34]Ayman, R. & Korabik, K. (2010). Leadership: Why Gender and Culture Matter. *American Psychologist, 65,* 157–170.

[35]Javidan, M., Steers, R. M., & Hitt, M. A. (2007). *The Global Mindset, Advances in International Management* (vol. 19). New York: Elsevier.

[36]Story, J.S.P. & Barbuto, J.E. (2011). Global Mindset: A Construct Clarification and Framework, *Journal of Leadership & Organizational Studies, 18*(3), 377–384.

[37] Dumaine, B. (1995, August). Don't Be an Ugly American Manager. *Fortune,* 225.

[38]Javidan, M., Steers, R. M., & Hitt, M. A. (2007). *The Global Mindset, Advances in International Management* (vol. 19). New York: Elsevier.

[39]Arora, A., Jaju, A., Kefalas, A. G., & Perenich, T. (2004). An Exploratory Analysis of Global Managerial Mindsets: A Case of U.S. Textile and Apparel Industry. *Journal of International Management, 10,* 393–411.

[40]Lane, H.W., Maznevski, M., Dietz, J. (2009). *International Management Behavior: Leading with a Global Mindset* (6th ed.). Sussex, UK: Wiley.

[41]Warren, K. (2009). *Developing Employee Talent to Perform,* eds. J. M. Phillips and S. M. Gully. New York: Business Expert Press.

[42]Leopold, A. Available online: http://www.goodreads.com/quotes/show/355449.

[43]Knutson, J. (2001). *Project Management for Business Professionals.* New York: John Wiley & Sons.

[44]Bloomberg. (2009, February 11). Intrepid Potash's Avery Quits After Misrepresentation (Update 1). Available online: http://www.bloomberg.com/apps/news?pid=newsarchive&sid=avvKZdohHtWY.

[45]Lemkin, R. (2008, February 1). Dirty Little Secrets: Corporate Espionage. BBC News. Available online: http://news.bbc.co.uk/2/hi/business/7220063.stm.

[46] Jacobs, S. (2010, April 18). Fraud Charge Deals Big Blow to Goldman's Image. The Seattle Times. Available online: http://seattletimes.nwsource.com/html/businesstechnology/2011639548_apusgoldmansachsreputation.html.

[47]Secret Service to Undergo Ethics Training (May 1, 2012). Boston Globe. Available online: http://www.boston.com/news/nation/articles/2012/05/01/secret_service_to_undergo_ethics_training/.

[48]Knutson, J. (2001). *Project Management for Business Professionals.* New York: John Wiley & Sons.

[49]Moore, C., Detert, J.R., Treviño, L.K., Baker, V.L. & Mayer, D.M. (2012). Why Employees Do Bad Things: Moral Disengagement and Unethical Organizational Behavior, *Personnel Psychology, 65*(1), 1–48.

[50]Knutson, J. (2001). *Project Management for Business Professionals.* New York: John Wiley & Sons.

[51]Cascio, W. F. & Cappelli, P. (2009, January). Mesh Values, Incentives, and Behavior. *HR Magazine,* 47–50.

[52] United States Sentencing Commission (2011). 2011 Federal Sentencing Guidelines Manual. Available online: http://www.ussc.gov/Guidelines/2011_guidelines/Manual_HTML/8b2_1.htm.

[53]Kerns, C. D. (2003). Creating and Sustaining an Ethical Workplace Culture. *Graziadio Business Report, 6*(3). Available online: http://gbr.pepperdine.edu/033/ethics.html.

[54]Carroll, A. B. & Buchholtz, A. K. (2012). *Business & Society: Ethics, Sustainability, and Stakeholder Management* (8th ed.). Mason, OH: Cengage Learning.

[55]Sanders, T. (2008). *Saving the World at Work.* New York: Doubleday Business.

[56]5 Questions for Walter J. Cleaver, President and CEO of the Human Resource Planning Society. (2006, July 31). *Workforce Management,* 7.

[57]Maon, F., Lindgreen, A., & Swaen, V. (2010). Organizational Stages and Cultural Phases: A Critical Review and a Consolidative Model of Corporate Social Responsibility Development, *International Journal of Management Reviews, 12,* 20–38.

[58]Rupp, D. E., Williams, C. & Aguilera, R. (2011). Increasing Corporate Social Responsibility through Stakeholder Value Internalization (and the Catalyzing Effect of New Governance): An Application of Organizational Justice, Self-Determination, and Social Influence Theories, In M. Schminke (ed.) *Managerial Ethics: Managing the Psychology of Morality.* Routledge/Psychology Press.

59Talevich, T. (2008, July). Green Makes Sense at Costco. *The Costco Connection,* 22.

60Starbucks. (2012). Starbucks Shared Planet. Available online: http://www.starbucks.com/responsibility/learn-more/starbucks-shared-planet.

61Woodward, N. H. (2008, June). New Breed of Human Resource Leader. *HR Magazine,* 52–56.

62McClellan, J. (2008, June 27). Get Your Employees Excited About Sustainability. Society for Human Resource Management. Available online: http://www.shrm.org/hrdisciplines/ethics/articles/pages/employeesandsustainability.aspx.

63Wasserman, T. (2011). Google Offers Employees 30 More Electric Cars to Share, Mashable.com, June 9. Available online: http://mashable.com/2011/06/09/google-electric-vehicles/.

64McClellan, J. (2008, June 27). Get Your Employees Excited About Sustainability. Society for Human Resource Management. Available online: http://www.shrm.org/hrdisciplines/ethics/articles/pages/employeesandsustainability.aspx.

65For additional information, see http://www.iso.org/iso/iso_catalogue/management_standards/iso_9000_iso_14000/qmp.htm.

66Thornton, G. (2007). Executives Say Corporate Responsibility Can Be Profitable. Available online: http://www.csrwire.com/press_releases/15302-Executives-Say-Corporate-Responsibility-Can-Be-Profitable.

67Bacon, F., Silverthorne, M., & Jardine, L. (2000). *The New Organon.* Cambridge, UK: Cambridge University Press.

68Campbell, J. P. (1990). The Role of Theory in Industrial and Organizational Psychology. In *Handbook of Industrial and Organizational Psychology,* eds. M. D. Dunnette and L. M. Hough (vol. 1, pp. 39–74). Palo Alto, CA: Consulting Psychologists Press.

69Carrig, K., & Wright, P. M. (2007, January). Building Profit Through Building People. *Workforce Management.* Available online: http://www.workforce.com/section/09/feature/24/65/90/index.html.

70Carrig, K., & Wright, P. M. (2007, January). Building Profit Through Building People. *Workforce Management.* Available online: http://www.workforce.com/section/09/feature/24/65/90/index.html.

71Lubit, R. (2004, March/April). The Tyranny of Toxic Managers: Applying Emotional Intelligence to Deal with Difficult Personalities. *Ivey Business Journal.* Available online: http://wwwold.iveybusinessjournal.com/article.asp?intArticle_ID=475.

72Chan, K.Y. & Drasgow, F. (2001). Toward a Theory of Individual Differences and Leadership: Understanding the Motivation to Lead, *Journal of Applied Psychology,* 86(3), 481–498. Reprinted with permission of APA.

CHAPTER 2

Diversity

ConAgra values the ideas and contributions of all of its employees, and believes that its diversity helps it better serve its communities, customers, and stakeholders.

© ANDREW HOLBROOKE/CORBIS NEWS/CORBIS

REAL WORLD CHALLENGE

CREATING A CLIMATE FOR DIVERSITY AT CONAGRA FOODS

ConAgra Foods is a leading food company in North America with brands including Healthy Choice, Hunt's, Orville Redenbacher's, and Reddi-wip. The company serves a broad base of customers and consumers, and seeks the full contribution of all employees.[1] ConAgra believes that its diverse employees help it to forge stronger relationships in its communities, in the marketplace, and with its stakeholders. ConAgra also wants to leverage its diverse talent for future leadership positions[2] and build a culture in which all employees can be authentic and know that their diverse ideas and capabilities are valued.[3]

ConAgra considers diversity to include a broad range of characteristics including race, age, gender, cultural background, sexual orientation, personal experiences, and style.[4] Imagine that ConAgra asks you for advice about how it can become an even more inclusive organization. What would you tell them? After reading this chapter, you should have some good ideas.

LEARNING OBJECTIVES

1. Describe the difference between surface-level and deep-level diversity.

2. Describe how diversity can benefit organizations.

3. Describe how diversity can have negative effects in organizations.

4. Explain various barriers to creating inclusive organizations.

5. Give examples of several diversity assessment methods.

6. Explain how societal culture affects how people interpret others and how others interpret them.

7. Describe the role of cultural competence in organizations.

People are obviously different, but what are the differences that matter to organizations? Some people look different from others. Does that matter? Men and women communicate humor differently.[5] Is that important? What about differences in how people think and make decisions?

Organizations care about diversity for legal reasons,[6] but also because it has the potential to improve organizational performance.[7] In this chapter you will learn about why diversity can be both good and bad for business, different types of diversity, and barriers to diversity. You will also learn about some tools to use in managing diversity, and why societal culture is an important diversity issue for organizations today.

WHAT IS DIVERSITY?

diversity
The variety of observable and unobservable similarities and differences among people

What does it mean to be diverse? ***Diversity*** refers to the variety of observable and unobservable similarities and differences among people. Some differences, such as gender, race, and age, are often the first diversity characteristics to come to mind. ITT Corporation also considers diversity to include life experience, educational background, and the part of the world the individual is from.[8] When Rob Keeling, Vice President of Diversity at banking giant Capital One, is asked how diverse his diversity team is, he responds: "Capital One's diversity team represents various groups, including White males, African Americans, Asian Americans, women, LGBT (lesbian, gay, bisexual, and transsexual), persons under and over forty, native born Americans, those born outside the United States, people from HR and people from the business sector."[9] And these categories are only a partial list of all the ways people can be considered to be similar or different. Clearly, there are many ways to be diverse!

Diversity is much more than demographics and can reflect combinations of characteristics rather than a single attribute. Each individual also has a variety of characteristics, and combinations of them can result in diversity. For example, a person named Rosa could identify herself as an experienced Hispanic female attorney. However, different situations may increase or decrease the salience of each characteristic.[10] In some situations Rosa might identify the most with being an attorney and in other situations she might identify herself as an Hispanic female.

We next discuss some of the many types of diversity relevant to organizations, and how understanding diversity can help you to be a more effective employee and manager.

TYPES OF DIVERSITY

surface-level diversity
Observable differences in people, including race, age, ethnicity, physical abilities, physical characteristics, and gender

deep-level diversity
Individual differences that cannot be seen directly, including goals, values, personalities, decision-making styles, knowledge, skills, abilities, and attitudes

Have you ever met someone, thought he or she was different from you, and then learned that the two of you actually had a lot in common? This reflects two types of diversity: surface-level diversity and deep-level diversity. ***Surface-level diversity*** refers to observable differences in people, including race, age, ethnicity, physical abilities, physical characteristics, and gender. Surface-level diversity reflects characteristics that are observable and known about people as soon as you see them.

Deep-level diversity refers to individual differences that cannot be seen directly, including goals, values, personalities, decision-making styles, knowledge, skills, abilities, and attitudes. These "invisible" characteristics in others take more time to learn about, but can have stronger effects on group and organizational performance than surface-level characteristics. Even pay differences[11] in a group and differences based on rank or power can affect group processes and performance.[12]

SO WHAT
What people look like is much less important to individual and group performance than their deeper characteristics like knowledge, abilities, and attitudes.

We can think of diversity as a characteristic of a workgroup, such as when we describe a group as being diverse with respect to one or more member characteristics—the age, organizational rank, or gender diversity of a group, for example. Diversity can also be thought of from an individual's perspective in terms of that person's differences from and similarities to other group members—such as being the lowest-paid member of the group, or the only person in a group who does not have a lot of work experience. The latter diversity perspective is called *relational demography*.[13] The more different you perceive yourself to be from the other group members, the more aware you are of these differences. Being the only new hire in a meeting feels different from being in a meeting in which half of the attendees are also new hires.

Have you ever been in a group and felt different for some reason? Perhaps you were the only female, the only person of your race, or the youngest group member by several years. Being a *token*, or in the numerical minority in a group based on some unique characteristic, can affect majority members' perceptions of token minority members.

Tokens are mistakenly assumed to fully represent all members of their subgroup, and are often included in the group only to look good to the public. Motivation can obviously be reduced if the token member feels that he or she is there only because of the differentiating characteristic (e.g., we need a black female staff member to avoid looking bad publicly). Supporting this, research has found that racial minorities perceive lower fairness and experience lower job satisfaction.[14] This places greater performance pressures on minority group members, increases the tendency to conform with others, increases stereotyping, and creates more boundaries between majority and minority group members.[15] With that said, being a token is not the same experience for everyone. Being the sole male in a workgroup is often a different experience from that of being the sole female.

Two prominent diversity researchers, David Harrison and Katherine Klein, identified three other types of within-group diversity that reflect different types of deep-level diversity:[16]

1. *Separation*: differences in position or opinion among group members reflecting disagreement or opposition—dissimilarity in an attitude or value, for example, especially with regard to group goals or processes
2. *Variety*: differences in a certain type or category, including group members' expertise, knowledge, or functional background
3. *Disparity*: differences in the concentration of valuable social assets or resources—dissimilarity in rank, pay, decision-making authority, or status, for example

As an example of these three types of diversity, consider three six-member teams, each of which is responsible for generating a new product idea. Team Separation's diversity is in their attitudes toward the best approach to use. Half of the team prefers creative brainstorming while the other half prefers basing the product on objective, data-based customer analysis. Members of Team Variety vary in their functional areas of expertise. One is a marketing professional, one a materials specialist, and the others represent manufacturing, product safety, advertising, and law. Lastly, members of Team Disparity vary in their rank in the organization. One member of the team is a vice president, two are mid-level managers, and three are lower-level employees. The diversity in each team is obvious, yet you can imagine how the effects of the diversity will likely differ across each team. Table 2-1 summarizes the five types of diversity we have just discussed.

relational demography
A single group member's similarities to and differences from other group members.

token
Being in the numerical minority in a group based on some unique characteristic and being assumed to fully represent that minority group

separation
Differences in position or opinion among group members reflecting disagreement or opposition—dissimilarity in an attitude or value, for example, especially with regard to group goals or processes

variety
Differences in a certain type or category, including group members' expertise, knowledge, or functional background

disparity
Differences in the concentration of valuable social assets or resources—dissimilarity in rank, pay, decision-making authority, or status, for example

SO WHAT
When building a workgroup or team, it is important to attend to many different types of diversity to ensure the team has what it needs to succeed.

Table 2-1	

Five Types of Diversity

1. *Surface-level diversity:* observable differences in people, including gender, race, age, ethnicity, and physical abilities

2. *Deep-level diversity:* individual differences that cannot be seen directly, including goals, values, personalities, decision-making styles, knowledge, and attitudes

3. *Separation:* differences in position or opinion among group members reflecting disagreement or opposition, especially with regard to group goals or processes—dissimilarity in an attitude or value, for example (a type of deep-level diversity)

4. *Variety:* differences in a certain type or category, including group members' expertise, knowledge, or functional background (a type of deep-level diversity)

5. *Disparity:* differences in the concentration of valuable social assets or resources—including dissimilarity in rank, pay, decision-making authority, or status (a type of deep-level diversity)

© CENGAGE LEARNING 2012

BUSINESS CASE FOR DIVERSITY

Why should we care about diversity? Because as employees, the better we are able to work with all types of people, the more effective we will be in our jobs. As managers, diversity awareness will enable us to hire, retain, and engage the best talent, which will help to maximize the organization's performance. Diversity also fosters greater creativity and innovation.[17] As one Xerox vice president put it, "When you try to be more open, as opposed to using the ideas of one group limited by their experiences, you get a chance to tap into the total spectrum of creativity."[18] Additionally, the business context is becoming increasingly globalized. Employees are more and more likely to work with diverse groups of people or deal with customers from many different countries and backgrounds. In addition, acquiring and managing diversity is both an ethical and legal necessity. We next elaborate on the business case for diversity.

Performance Benefits

Realizing the potential positive effects of diversity depends on employees' attitudes toward diversity. Recent research has found that firm performance increases when employees have more positive attitudes toward diversity.[19]

As Beth Axelrod, Senior VP of HR for the online auction site eBay once said, "It's . . . important for companies to define how diversity links to their business results. Otherwise, there will be no compelling reason for leaders to focus on diversity."[20] Diversity contributes to a firm's competitive advantage when it enables all employees to contribute their full talents and motivation to the company. The primary motivation for effectively managing diversity is the fact that doing so brings out the best in all employees, allowing each of them to contribute maximally to the firm's performance in an increasingly competitive business environment. As the Coast Guard's official diversity statement notes, "Diversity is not a program or a policy; it is a state of being. It provides well-rounded perspectives in problem-solving that let us identify better ways of performing the duties entrusted to us by our government and fellow citizens."[21]

> "It's . . . important for companies to define how diversity links to their business results. Otherwise, there will be no compelling reason for leaders to focus on diversity." —*Beth Axelrod, Senior VP of HR for eBay*

Purdue University's police department believes that an important element in community policing is having police officers who look like part of the community in which they work.[22] At cereal giant Kellogg Company, headquartered in Battle Creek, Michigan, diversity and inclusion are critical to competing successfully in the global marketplace. The company's strategy includes building accountability for diversity and inclusion throughout the organization. To execute this strategy, Kellogg created an Executive Diversity and Inclusion Council, a cross-functional team led by CEO David Mackay, to embed diversity and inclusion within the organization.[23]

Diversity as a Source of Competitive Advantage

Although many managers view diversity as a benefit to their companies,[24] researchers are more divided on the effects diversity has on workgroup performance.[25] Some people consider diversity to be a source of competitive advantage for organizations.[26] For example, some studies have found that culturally diverse work teams make better decisions over time than do homogeneous teams.[27] Diverse groups can use their diverse backgrounds to develop a more comprehensive view of a problem and a broader list of possible solutions. The broader social network of diverse employees also can give workgroups and organizations access to a wider variety of information and expertise.

Diversity can be a source of creativity and innovation that can create a competitive advantage.[28] A review of decades of research found that diversity can enhance creativity and improve a team's decision making.[29] Research by noted management expert Rosabeth Moss-Kanter found that innovative companies intentionally use heterogeneous teams to solve problems and do a better job of eliminating racism, sexism, and classism.[30] Having more women in top management positively affects the performance of firms pursuing an innovation strategy.[31]

Furniture manufacturer Steelcase understands the importance of diversity to its business success. "To grow and prosper in today's global marketplace, our company depends increasingly on employees who know how to live and work with a great variety of people," says Steelcase President and CEO James P. Hackett. "That's especially true at this time when many of the barriers that once separated the world's people—time, distance, politics and language, for example—are falling. Not only will our customers, colleagues and fellow citizens come from a variety of places, cultures, religions and racial backgrounds, our lives will be richer for it."[32]

> "To grow and prosper in today's global marketplace, our company depends increasingly on employees who know how to live and work with a great variety of people." —*James P. Hackett*, *CEO and President of Steelcase*

ANDRE JENNY STOCK CONNECTION WORLDWIDE/NEWSCOM

Kellogg feels so strongly that diversity and inclusion are critical to its success that its strategy includes building accountability for diversity and inclusion throughout the company.

Legal Issues

Although many other antidiscrimination laws exist, one of the most important is Title VII of the Civil Rights Act of 1964, amended in 1991. It prohibits employment discrimination based on race, color, religion, sex, or national origin. Title VII prohibits not only intentional discrimination but also practices that have the effect of discriminating against individuals because of their race, color, national origin, religion, or sex. Other laws offer protections to additional groups, including employees with disabilities[33] and workers over the age of forty.[34] Under Title VII, it is an unlawful employment practice for an employer:[35]

1. "to fail or refuse to hire or to discharge any individual, or otherwise to discriminate against any individual with respect to his compensation, terms, conditions, or privileges of employment, because of such individual's race, color, religion, sex, or national origin;"
2. "to limit, segregate, or classify his employees or applicants for employment in any way which would deprive or tend to deprive any individual of employment opportunities or otherwise adversely affect his status as an employee, because of such individual's race, color, religion, sex, or national origin."

Congress established that intentional discrimination occurred "when a complaining party demonstrates that race, color, religion, sex, or national origin was a motivating factor for any employment practice, even though other factors also motivated the practice."[36] The Civil Rights Act of 1991 allows monetary damages in cases of intentional employment discrimination.

One of the largest employment discrimination lawsuits was settled for more than $11.7 million against Walmart and Sam's Club.[37] Thousands of female employees filed a class-action suit over alleged denial of advancement, equal pay, promotions, and raises based on the fact that they were women.[38] Fortunately, obeying the law and promoting diversity is consistent with hiring the people best suited for the job and organization.

DIVERSITY TRENDS

As the great U.S. baseball manager Yogi Berra once observed, "It's tough to make predictions, especially about the future." Nonetheless, some short-term demographic trends are strong enough to suggest that the changing demographic mix in the workforce will continue to increase the importance of understanding and leveraging diversity. For example, the ethnic and cultural mix of the U.S. workforce is changing. The Census Bureau projects that by 2020 the U.S. workforce will consist of 62.3 percent White non-Hispanics, 18.6 percent Hispanics, 12 percent Blacks, and 5.7 percent Asians. Longer-term U.S. demographic projections further highlight the increasingly diverse character of the United States:[39]

- The population is projected to become older. By 2030, about one in five people will be sixty-five or over.
- By 2050, the total population is forecasted to grow from 282.1 million in 2000 to 419.9 million, a 49 percent increase. (This is in sharp contrast to most European countries, whose populations are expected to decline by 2050.)
- Non-Hispanic Whites are expected to decrease from the current 69.4 percent of the total population to 50.1 percent by 2050.
- People of Hispanic origin (of any race) are projected to increase from 35.6 million in 2002 to 102.6 million in 2050, an increase of 188 percent.

Table 2-2

Projected Change in the U.S. Working Population by Race between 2008 and 2050[40]

Year	Hispanic (any race)	Black	Asian
2008	15%	15%	5.1%
2050	30%	15%	9.2%

This would nearly double the Hispanic share of the nation's population, from 12.6 percent to 24.4 percent.

- The Black population is projected to rise from 35.8 million in 2000 to 61.4 million in 2050, an increase of about 26 million or 71 percent. This would increase the Black share of the population to 14.6 percent from 12.7 percent.
- The Asian population is forecasted to grow 213 percent, from 10.7 million in 2000 to 33.4 million in 2050. This would double the Asian share of the population from 3.8 percent to 8 percent.

Non-Whites are expected to make up half of the working-age population in 2039 and more than 55 percent in 2050—up from 34 percent today. Table 2-2 shows the U.S. Census Bureau's projected change in the working population by race between 2008 and 2050.

As shown in Figure 2-1, the U.S. Bureau of Labor Statistics projects a dramatic increase in workers age sixty-five and older during the next decade,

Figure 2-1

Projected Percentage Change in the U.S. Labor Force by Age from 2006 to 2016[43]

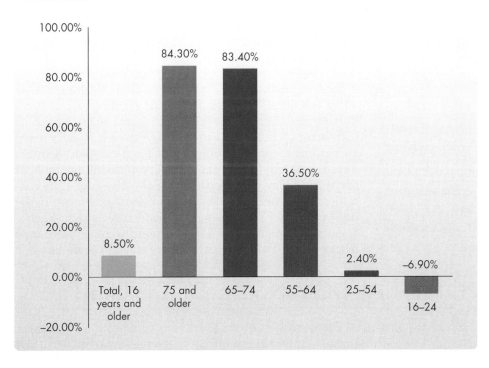

while the percentage of younger workers is expected to decrease. This obviously increases the need for succession planning at many organizations to ensure the continuity of leadership. Due to the aging of the U.S. workforce, and to the clearly differentiated characteristics of the generations that comprise it (including veterans, baby boomers, gen-Xers, and millennials), firms are also paying more attention to how workers of different ages work together.

Work teams are often age diverse, and it is increasingly likely that an older employee will report to a younger supervisor. A survey conducted by the Society for Human Resource Management found that in organizations with 500 or more employees, 58 percent of HR professionals reported conflict between younger and older workers, largely due to their different perceptions of work ethics and work-life balance.[41] As Ed Reilly, President of the American Management Association, says, younger workers "are going to be the eventual managers. They will be as interested in keeping older workers as older workers today are interested in figuring out how to work with the younger generations."[42]

Although the Bureau of Labor Statistics reported in 1996 that almost half of all management positions in the United States were held by White men, diversity remains elusive in the top jobs. Ninety-six percent of the CEOs of companies in the 2007 Fortune 1,000 were White males (the list also included twenty-one White women, ten African American men, six Hispanic men, and three Asian women).[44]

Many countries and regions face talent shortages at all levels, and those gaps are expected to worsen. By 2040, Europe is forecast to have a shortfall of 24 million workers aged fifteen to sixty-five; raising the proportion of women in the workplace to that of men would cut the gap to 3 million. In the United States, the retirement of the baby boomer generation will probably mean the loss of large numbers of senior-level employees in a short period of time—nearly one-fifth of the working-age population (sixteen and older) of the United States will be at least sixty-five by 2016.[45]

Talent shortages are forecast to rise globally. In the United Kingdom, male-dominated sectors with a shortage of workers include engineering, IT, and skilled trades—yet 70 percent of women with science, engineering, or technology qualifications are not working in these fields.[46] Pursuing diversity can allow firms to attract and retain scarce talent as well as reach other business goals. One European Commission study showed that 58 percent of companies with diversity programs reported higher productivity, improved employee motivation, and greater efficiency; and 62 percent said that the programs helped to attract and retain top talent.[47]

Today's war for talent is global, making recruiting and retaining a diverse workforce a more competitive business issue than ever. Beth Axelrod, Senior VP of HR for eBay noted, "Increasingly, diverse talent reflecting this competitive landscape is one of the most critical factors a business can leverage to consistently drive successful results. It's important for a company's workforce to not only reflect the diversity of talent available in the world today but also to mirror the diversity of its customer base." Because eBay recognizes that women make most consumer purchasing decisions, it feels that placing talented women in key decision-making roles helps it to better understand its customers' needs and preferences.[48]

SO WHAT

Increasing diversity can improve organizational performance and manage talent shortages, but only if it is properly managed.

"Increasingly, diverse talent reflecting this competitive landscape is one of the most critical factors a business can leverage to consistently drive successful results."
—*Beth Axelrod, Senior VP of HR for eBay*

POTENTIAL DOWNSIDE OF DIVERSITY

Despite the potential for positive outcomes, diversity can be a two-edged sword.[49] Diversity can cause misunderstanding, suspicion, and conflict in the workplace that can result in absenteeism, poor quality, low morale, and loss of competitiveness[50] as well as lowered workgroup cohesiveness.[51] Diverse groups are less able to provide for all of their members' needs and tend to have less integration and communication and more conflict than do homogeneous groups.[52]

Importantly, the effects of diversity seem to depend on the type of diversity. While age diversity in top management teams and workgroups is related to increased turnover and absenteeism,[53] there is little evidence that it influences group performance. Additionally, there is mixed evidence that a group's age diversity positively affects group processes such as communication, conflict, and cohesion.[54] There is also little evidence that age similarity between supervisors and subordinates positively influences interpersonal liking and performance.[55] However, there is some evidence that age differences that violate social status norms associated with age have negative implications for subordinates. For example, research found that supervisors rated subordinates who were older than them lower on task performance and extra role behaviors (going beyond job requirements) than subordinates who were younger or similar in age.[56]

Research findings on the effects of other types of diversity are frequently inconclusive. A review of twenty-four different studies of diversity's effects on team performance found that neither job-related diversity (including functional background, industry, and occupation) nor demographic diversity (age, gender, race, and ethnicity) was related to team cohesion or performance. The authors concluded that rather than having positive or negative effects, diversity may have no direct effect on team cohesion or performance.[57] Rather than having no effect at all, however, it is likely that diversity affects individual and organizational outcomes through its effects on other things, like conflict, which we will discuss later in this chapter.

Because the effects of diversity depend on the type of diversity, it is impossible to state that diversity in itself is good or bad for all workgroups. With that said, it is important to note that although the possible benefits of diversity are not guaranteed, the costs associated with mismanaging diversity are quite clear, including reduced motivation, increased turnover and absenteeism among disenfranchised groups, and costly lawsuits.[58] Companies that develop a poor reputation in the area of diversity also lose their edge in recruiting the best talent, and can have difficulty marketing their products to an increasingly diverse customer base[59] and competing in the international marketplace.[60]

The effects of relational demography also depend on which characteristic makes the individual as similar or different from the group. Being of the same race as other workgroup members is associated with higher workgroup productivity, higher commitment to the workgroup, and better perceptions of advancement opportunities.[61] Although not true for all men, men in groups made up mostly of women have been found to be less attached to the group, absent more often, and report a lower intention to stay with the company.[62] Whereas non-Whites tend to be unaffected by being different from others, this difference can negatively affect White team members.[63] Gender differences have been found to negatively affect superior-subordinate relationships. One study found that subordinates with a supervisor of the other gender experienced greater role ambiguity and role conflict, and their supervisors reported liking them less and gave them lower performance ratings than subordinates of the same gender.[64]

The number and strength of subgroups in a workgroup also can influence the group's performance. ***Faultlines*** determine the existence and strength of subgroups, and depend on the composition and alignments of different group member demographic characteristics.[65] Faultlines in the earth have the potential to fracture a particular geographic region into multiple pieces. Similarly, faultlines in groups can break them into multiple subgroups. Faultlines can result in rifts that may form in different ways, depending on the patterns and characteristics of the subgroups. For example, a workgroup may have a faultline creating

faultlines

Separation based on the existence and strength of subgroups due to the composition and alignments of different group member characteristics

a subgroup of young White females who are all new to the group. It might have another subgroup of older Hispanic males who have similar education and expertise. Because of weak faultlines and the absence of strong subgroups, homogeneous teams and highly heterogeneous teams with many subgroups have better long-term performance than moderately heterogeneous teams.[66]

Interestingly, people sometimes discriminate against people similar to them. Research on tokenism has found a greater perception of competition among women in male-dominated than in gender-integrated organizations.[67] In firms with few women at the top, women also tend to perceive greater differences between men and women, and gender perceptions are more strongly aligned with gender role stereotypes.[68]

HOW DOES DIVERSITY INFLUENCE INDIVIDUAL AND ORGANIZATIONAL OUTCOMES?

Does just being different make a difference to group or organizational outcomes? In fact, differences among group members do not in themselves create positive or negative outcomes.[69] Any relationships found between workgroup diversity and individual, group, or organizational outcomes are likely due to a variety of processes underlying demographic group memberships rather than to the demographic differences themselves.[70] Organizational outcomes can thus be more affected by how the firm leverages its diversity than by the diversity itself.[71] One study found that although racial diversity in firms did not influence firm performance, it interacted with business strategy to have a positive impact on firm outcomes.[72]

So what are some of the processes through which diversity has its effects? *Social integration* is one important process. When we feel like we are part of a group socially as well as in a task performance capacity, we feel more committed to the group. Greater diversity is related to less social integration in workgroups, which increases turnover.[73]

Status and power effects that are often related to demographic group membership can also lead to reduced group cohesiveness and other negative diversity effects.[74] Lower-status organization members are often more self-conscious in the presence of higher-ranking members, and are less likely to share their ideas or challenge the ideas of the higher-status members.

Team conflict is another way diversity affects workgroup outcomes. Different types of diversity have been found to be related to two types of conflict. *Task conflict* is conflict over task issues, such as goals, deadlines, or work processes. *Relationship conflict* is interpersonal conflict, including personality clashes. Different types of diversity tend to lead to different types of conflict. Gender diversity can lead to greater relationship conflict, whereas educational diversity is associated with greater task conflict.[75] Group members' value similarity is related to lower task and relationship conflict.[76]

Surface-level diversity has been found to affect relationship conflict, while diversity in job-related characteristics such as education or tenure affect task conflict.[77] Relationship conflict is strongly related to lower team performance and lower member satisfaction, particularly when the task is highly complex (i.e., decision making or project teams rather than production teams).[78] In contrast, team interactions that include opposing views about tasks and strategic decision-making processes increase the tendency for diversity to enhance top management team performance.[79] It is important for people to be willing to challenge each other's ideas and positions in order to obtain the best possible

social integration
When members feel they are a core part of the group

SO WHAT
Conflict is not always bad, and can enhance performance if it helps groups generate better ideas or find better ways of doing things

task conflict
Conflict over task issues, such as goals, deadlines, or work processes

relationship conflict
Interpersonal conflict including personality clashes

outcomes, so appropriate levels of task conflict can improve performance. Task conflict likely has a curvilinear relationship with team performance in that work teams do best under moderate levels of task conflict—too much or too little can hurt performance.[80] Figure 2-2 illustrates this relationship.

Collaborative problem solving can reduce the negative effects of task conflict and help teams better translate their diversity into greater innovation.[81] Also, surface-level diversity becomes less important over time, and deep-level diversity becomes more important to group cohesiveness.[82] This suggests that conflict is dynamic and evolves over time.

Having diverse employees does not guarantee that a firm treats all of its employees equally or that the potential benefits of the diversity are realized. *Inclusion* is the sense of being safe, valued, and engaged in a group regardless of similarities to or differences from other group members. Inclusion in a workgroup meets employees' needs for both belonging and uniqueness.[83] Inclusion focuses on bringing out the excellence in each individual employee through increased employee involvement and integration.[84] An inclusive workplace values the many differences within its workforce and utilizes the full potential of all of its employees.[85] If diverse employees are not included in organizational decision making, or if they are marginalized at work, not only are their potential contributions not being realized, but they also are more likely to leave the organization entirely.

Perceptions of discrimination lead to negative organizational and personal outcomes. Perceptions of age discrimination, regardless of one's age, is related to lower employee self-esteem and perceived control, and ultimately to stress, burnout, and job dissatisfaction.[86]

Leveraging diversity is about developing an organization that includes the contributions of all of its members. Later in the chapter we discuss ways firms can create a culture of inclusion that supports diversity. Diverse team members who feel included and respected are more likely to share ideas, be committed to group goals, and feel engaged. Cooperative group norms tend to increase in diverse groups over time, particularly when members communicate with and see each other more often.[87] This suggests that time and group member contact can increase the positive effects of diversity.

SO WHAT

Don't rush to judge other people—over time, surface-level characteristics become less important and deep-level diversity becomes more important in terms of conflict, cooperation, and performance.

inclusion
The sense of being safe, valued, and engaged in a group

SO WHAT

To capitalize on the potential advantages of diversity, take the time to enhance the inclusion of all group members.

Figure 2-2

Curvilinear Relationship Between Task Conflict and Team Performance

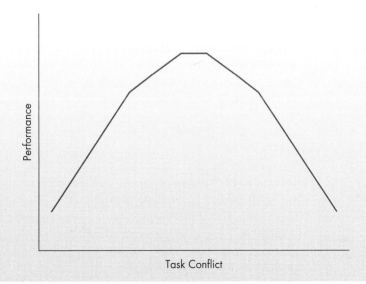

© CENGAGE LEARNING 2012

information processing

A change in the way groups integrate information and reconcile different perspectives

Information processing is a change in the way groups integrate information and reconcile different perspectives to make decisions or take action. Diverse teams have members with a broader range of experiences, knowledge, and backgrounds that give them a larger pool of resources, which may be helpful in dealing with unusual problems or situations. The need to integrate diverse information and reconcile different perspectives may stimulate more creative thinking and prevent premature agreement on courses of action, which can lead to better solutions and innovative performance.[88]

Table 2-3 summarizes the ways diversity can affect individual and organizational outcomes.

BARRIERS TO INCLUSION

What prevents companies from becoming inclusive and making the most of their diversity? A report of the U.S. Equal Employment Opportunity Commission identified several common diversity barriers that exist in many organizations.[89] These barriers stem from a variety of decision-making and psychological factors as well as from employee unawareness. Understanding and proactively addressing these barriers can minimize their impact and enhance inclusion.

The "Like Me" Bias

"like me" bias

A bias resulting from people's preference to associate with other people who they perceive to be like themselves

Consciously or unconsciously, we tend to associate with others who we perceive to be like ourselves. This bias is part of human nature. Although it can create a higher comfort level in working relationships, the *"like me" bias* can also lead to a tendency to employ and work with people like ourselves in terms of protected characteristics such as race, color, sex, disability, and age; and it can result in an unwillingness to employ people unlike ourselves. Perceived cultural and religious differences and ethnocentrism can feed on the "like me" bias and restrict inclusion. Because the "like me" bias can influence the assessment of performance norms, there may be a perception that someone "different" is less able to do a job and that someone "like me" is better able to do a job.

Table 2-3

Mechanisms through Which Diversity Affects Outcomes

Social integration	Feeling like part of a group socially as well as in a task performance capacity increases commitment to the group.
Differences in status and power	Lower-status group members are less likely to share their ideas or challenge the ideas of the higher-status members.
Task conflict	Conflict over task issues, such as goals, deadlines, or work processes, has the potential to improve group performance if it is not too low or too high.
Relationship conflict	Interpersonal conflict, including personality clashes, detracts from group performance and group member satisfaction.
Inclusion	The sense of being safe, valued, and engaged in a group results in more information sharing and commitment.
Information processing	A change in the way groups integrate information and reconcile different perspectives results in more creative thinking and prevention of premature consensus.

© CENGAGE LEARNING 2012

The "like me" bias is consistent with *social categorization theory,* which proposes that we categorize others into in-groups of people like ourselves and out-groups of dissimilar people. Because we tend to trust, cooperate with, and like in-group members more than out-group members, we are attracted to and favor in-group members and groups comprised of group members similar to us.[90] This suggests that more homogeneous workgroups should experience lower relationship conflict and higher member commitment and cohesion. Consistent with this idea, research that has found that group homogeneity is better than heterogeneity in terms of affecting positive work-related behavior and attitudes.[91]

social categorization theory
Similarities and differences among people form the basis for sorting self and others into similar in-group members and dissimilar out-groups

Stereotypes

A *stereotype* is a belief about an individual or a group based on the idea that everyone in that particular group will behave the same way. For example, "all men are strong," "all women are nurturing," and "people who look a certain way are dangerous" are all examples of stereotypes. A male research scientist who tends to believe that women make poor scientists is unlikely to hire, mentor, or seek the opinion of a female scientist. Stereotypes can reduce inclusion opportunities for minorities, women, persons with disabilities, and older workers. Stereotypes are harmful because they result in judgments about an individual based solely on his or her being part of a particular group, regardless of his or her unique identity.

stereotype
A belief about an individual or a group based on the idea that everyone in that particular group will behave the same way

People may have stereotypes of other individuals based on their race, color, religion, national origin, sex, disability, or age, among other things. Stereotypes are often negative and erroneous, and thus adversely affect the targeted individuals.[92] Because stereotypes can breed subtle racism, sexism, prejudice, and discomfort, they must be addressed in the diversity context. Recruiters and hiring managers may have stereotypes of what makes good or poor employees that can adversely affect equal employment opportunities and undermine diversity efforts.

Prejudice

It is also possible that outright bigotry still occurs on the part of an employer or its management for or against a targeted group, despite Title VII now having been in existence for more than forty years.[93] Even if an organization has a strong commitment to inclusion, it is possible that the beliefs and actions of individual employees or managers are inconsistent with the organization's policies and values. Organizations can help to reduce the occurrence of prejudice by carefully selecting and training managers and employees, evaluating their inclusion behaviors, and tracking the promotion rates of members of different groups who work for different supervisors to identify possible discriminatory trends that warrant further attention.

Perceived Threat of Loss

As voluntary efforts are made by companies to promote inclusion, members of groups who traditionally have been the predominant employees of a particular workforce or occupation may grow anxious or angry. If they perceive a direct threat to their own career opportunities, they may feel that they need to protect their own prospects by impeding the prospects of others.[94] This can influence employees' willingness to help minority employees, recruit diverse candidates for a position, and support diversity initiatives.

Steve Larson, Senior Diversity Consultant for Wachovia, firmly believes that you cannot have a successful diversity program without engaging White males. According to Larson, "If White men are not included, they can feel threatened and are likely to fear they will be negatively impacted by, and at worst targeted by, diversity initiatives." Excluding White men can contribute to their skepticism and resistance to ongoing diversity efforts. This can lead to any number of unintended consequences, including actively undermining diversity initiatives.[95]

Ethnocentrism

ethnocentrism
The belief that one's own language, native country, and cultural rules and norms are superior to all others

Ethnocentrism reflects the belief that one's own language, native country, and cultural rules and norms are superior to all others. Ethnocentrism often has less to do with prejudice and more to do with inexperience or ignorance about other people and environments. Because people know more about the cultural and behavioral norms of their home country, they have a better understanding of people from that country. Education and experiences that promote greater cross-cultural awareness can foster a conscious effort to value and promote cultural diversity.

Unequal Access to Organizational Networks

organizational networks
Patterns of task and personal relationships among employees

All organizations have formal and informal networks. These *organizational networks* influence knowledge sharing, resource accessibility, and work opportunities. Women and minorities are often excluded from informal organizational networks, which can be important to job performance, mentoring opportunities, and being seen as a candidate for promotion.[96] Research has associated male domination at the upper ranks of a firm with female executives' reports of barriers to advancement and exclusion from informal networks.[97] Companies including ConAgra Foods, featured in this chapter's Real World Challenge, proactively use employee networks to promote diversity and inclusion.

Table 2-4 summarizes these six barriers to inclusion.

Table 2-4

Barriers to Inclusion

The "like me" bias	People prefer to associate with others they perceive to be like themselves.
Stereotypes	A belief about an individual or a group based on the idea that everyone in a particular group will behave the same way or have the same characteristics.
Prejudice	Outright bigotry or intolerance for other groups.
Perceived threat of loss	If some employees perceive a direct threat to their own career opportunities, they may feel that they need to protect their own prospects by impeding diversity efforts.
Ethnocentrism	The belief that one's own language, native country, and cultural rules and norms are superior to all others.
Unequal access to organizational networks	Women and minorities are often excluded from organizational networks, which can be important to job performance, mentoring opportunities, and being seen as a candidate for promotion.

© CENGAGE LEARNING 2012

MANAGING DIVERSITY

It is clear that diversity alone does not guarantee positive organizational outcomes—how effectively diversity is managed is what makes the difference. The most important element in effectively leveraging the positive potential of diversity is top management support for diversity and for diversity initiatives. If top managers do not promote inclusion and respect diversity, lower-level managers and employees are not likely to do so either. In addition, an inclusive environment is created when all employees' cultural awareness and empathy are enhanced through diversity training and all employees are given equal access to mentors and other influential company employees. Creating fair company policies and practices that give all employees equal access to performance feedback, training and development, and advancement opportunities is also critical.

Diversity is more likely to positively affect companies that support diverse employees in higher-level positions and help all employees effectively interact with people who are different from them. Diversity initiatives are more successful when the company is able to keep employees thinking about diversity issues, even when they do not feel a direct, negative impact.[98] We next discuss some tools and techniques that companies use to promote diversity.

Tools

The foundation for effective diversity management is top management support and hiring people likely to succeed in an inclusive organization. Training and mentoring can also help. ***Reciprocal mentoring,*** which matches senior employees with diverse junior employees to allow both individuals to learn more about a different group, is one technique used to promote diversity awareness and inclusion. Human resource outsourcing firm Hewitt Associates' Cross-Cultural Learning Partners Program paired the CEO and each of his direct reports with diverse associates. Each partner was e-mailed different "lessons" on an aspect of diversity each month, and the partners met to discuss, reflect on, and apply what they learned. Dale Gifford, former Chairman and CEO of Hewitt, said of the experience, "I learned how other people might view me based on my being a White male, as opposed to just thinking about diversity in terms of how I viewed others."[99]

Diversity initiatives at PNC Financial Services include a career development program, networking opportunities, and mentoring programs for all employees.[100] Top executives within aerospace giant Boeing are asked to mentor at least one person each, and many of its businesses require that each senior executive mentor three people, including at least one woman and one minority person.[101]

To more effectively hire and retain diverse employees, it is

reciprocal mentoring
Matches senior employees with diverse junior employees to allow both people to learn more about a different group

DMITRIY SHIRONOSOV/SHUTTERSTOCK

Reciprocal mentoring between senior and junior employees increases the diversity awareness of all employees and promotes inclusion.

important to be vigilant about first making sure that highly qualified job candidates are diverse. Companies must focus on being a meritocracy, promote awareness of how different groups communicate differently, and ensure that the assessment and promotion process does not inadvertently misinterpret those styles. Ensuring that the promotion process proactively identifies diverse candidates in the pipeline helps to prevent inadvertently overlooking them. When senior female women at eBay communicated their commitment to the success of other women in the company, it reinforced female employees' emotional attachment to the firm and strengthened their belief that eBay is a great place to work.[102]

Diversity training and diversity education need to communicate that bias is a part of being human. It is not realistic to claim or to pursue an "I'm totally unbiased" stance with regard to diversity. Everyone has biases whether or not they are aware of them—diversity training should enable employees to become aware of them and learn to control them to prevent both explicit and implicit displays of bias.

To promote awareness and empathy, MetLife began a series of "diversity live" programs in which professional actors present a variety of scenarios, leading to a lively audience discussion of what was done and how it could have been done better. One scenario involves an American-born IT pro in the United States interacting with an Indian teammate in Delhi; others touch on work-life, cross-cultural and gay/lesbian themes. MetLife believes that these programs have contributed to its success in promoting diversity. In its 1998 biannual survey, a little more than half of the respondents agreed that MetLife values diversity. The number surged to 79 percent in 2006, but the firm will not consider its program a complete success until the surveys indicate 100 percent agreement.[103]

Diversity at global giant Siemens is driven from the corporate level. Mike Panigel, SVP for Siemens corporate HR in the United States and the Americas, states, "We value the important role that managers play in ensuring inclusion. This is why we've made diversity leadership training an integral component of our 'managing at Siemens' leadership development program."[104]

Although White men make up the majority of the U.S. workforce, in some companies they are the least engaged in diversity efforts. Diversity and inclusion efforts have historically had a strong focus on minorities and women, and as such, many companies may be leaving out the majority of their workforce—often White men. In doing so, companies might be inadvertently creating a culture of *exclusion*, which goes against the core of what it means to be an inclusive organization that values its people.[105] In many companies, the terms *diversity* and *White men* are seen as an oxymoron. When the subject is race, the experiences of people of color are discussed; when the issue of gender arises, the experiences of women are examined. As a result, White men may feel alienated and can become angry, confused, or indifferent to diversity efforts, feeling that their companies are offering something for everyone but them.[106]

Shell Oil is one example of a company that has held several White Men's Caucus workshops to enable White males to come together and discuss "White male privilege" and other issues. Michael Andries, a Shell management consultant, said, "This caucus was the first opportunity I have had to explore how I really felt about diversity and other groups, in the company of others like myself . . . . As a result I believe I am beginning to 'get it.'"[107]

To manage diversity effectively as both an employee and a manager, it is important to be aware of your biases and attitudes toward diversity. This chapter's *Understand Yourself* feature will help you to understand your own level of diversity awareness.

SO WHAT

Involve everyone in diversity initiatives, not just minorities, to maximize participation and commitment.

Assessment

Diversity metrics allow companies to monitor their progress and to define their priorities for future action. Frequently used indicators include:

- The diversity of job applicants and new hires
- The proportion of people with different demographics in a company's business units at each level of employment

UNDERSTAND YOURSELF

DIVERSITY AWARENESS SELF-ASSESSMENT

In this chapter, you learned about the effects of diversity in organizations. Diversity awareness helps managers to lead more effectively, and to more accurately interpret and understand the behaviors of others.

To get some insight into your own diversity awareness, which is the first step in improving yourself in this area, please indicate how often you do the behaviors described in the following twelve statements using the scale below. Record your response to the left of each statement. Then score your responses using the instructions at the end of this assessment.

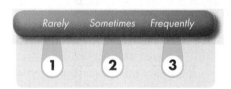

Rarely — 1   Sometimes — 2   Frequently — 3

___ 1. I am comfortable in groups that are diverse in age, gender, ethnicity, and culture.
___ 2. I regularly assess my own tendencies to show bias and prejudice and continually try to improve my attitudes and perspectives on diversity.
___ 3. When speaking with someone for whom English is not his or her primary language, I do not consider that person's English proficiency to reflect their intelligence.
___ 4. I try to be aware of the main characteristics, values, and habits of my culture and ethnic group.
___ 5. When I see someone else exhibiting cultural insensitivity or racial or gender bias, I voice my disapproval.
___ 6. I understand and accept that people with diverse cultural backgrounds living in my country may desire different degrees of acculturation into my culture.
___ 7. I apologize when I have offended someone.
___ 8. Even though my values and opinions may differ from theirs, I accept and respect the rights of others to make decisions that affect their lives.
___ 9. I am comfortable discussing diversity.
___ 10. Some of my friends are different from me in age, race, background, etc.
___ 11. I take advantage of opportunities to learn more about different cultures and ethnicities.
___ 12. I treat people the way they prefer to be treated.

Add up the numbers to the left of each statement. If your score is:

Between 12 and 20: Your diversity awareness is low. This does not mean that you are prejudiced. Your score could reflect a lack of information or an unwillingness to take risks and experience new or unfamiliar situations. You might consider working on your self-awareness and self-knowledge in the area of diversity, perhaps actively improving your diversity awareness through workshops and self-assessment instruments, reading diversity publications, and actively getting to know people who are different from you.

Between 21 and 28: You have a moderate degree of diversity awareness. You might benefit from reading diversity publications, practicing "putting yourself in others' shoes" to reflect on how their experiences and perceptions might differ from yours, and actively getting to know people who are different from you.

Between 29 and 36: You have high diversity awareness and are comfortable with many different types of people and in many different situations. You might continue to learn about diversity through reading diversity publications, befriending people who are different from you, and continuing working on your communication and leadership skills with a variety of people.

- The pay levels and attrition rates of people with different demographics in comparable positions
- The ratio of people with different demographics promoted to those eligible for promotion

At the bank Lloyds TSB, the CEO reviews the progress of women with the managing directors of the business units, and the company regularly profiles its workforce at all levels to measure its progress in improving the gender diversity of its workforce.[108] Linking part of each business unit's bonus pool specifically to diversity goals helped financial firm ING raise the proportion of its top-management positions around the world held by women by 25 percent over four years.[109]

When health system Trinity Health began its diversity and inclusion program, it recognized the importance of accountability and structure. It developed a three-year plan with clearly defined outcomes and measures. The health care provider then applied a leadership team incentive-pay clause called a "circuit breaker" to meet its diversity and inclusion objectives. The entire group forfeits the year's incentive pay if a single member of the 200-person leadership team fails to meet the objectives.[110]

Every quarter MetLife publishes a diversity progress report divided by lines of business. The reports go to the chair and top seventy-five company executives. The reports look at recruiting, retention, and development, among other metrics, and reflect how MetLife and each of its lines of business are performing in the area of diversity.[111]

This chapter's *Case Study* feature describes the many diversity activities and programs at Johnson & Johnson.

THE ROLE OF SOCIETAL CULTURE

Another important source of diversity is societal culture. A society's culture is comprised of assumptions that become taken for granted by its members. Culture is passed from generation to generation through stories, activities, and by observing family, friends, teachers, and others with whom we interact.

National boundaries do not always coincide with cultural boundaries. Because societal culture reflects language, politics, religion, and values, among other things, it is not unusual for a single country, such as China or Russia, to have multiple cultures. Do you think that Texas, California, Mississippi, Alaska, and Vermont have at least somewhat different cultures despite all being part of the United States? Similarly, societal culture can vary across nearby countries, as is the case with many of the former Soviet republics. It is helpful to remember that just because two countries are located near each other, such as Britain and Ireland, their societal cultures can be very different due to differences in religion, language, politics, and other factors.

Why is understanding societal culture important? Because it influences the diverse values, customs, language, and expectations we bring with us to work, which affect our reactions, preferences, and feelings.[114] For example, societies differ in the degree to which they are comfortable challenging supervisors' ideas, taking risks, and seeing rewards distributed unequally. Being five minutes late to a meeting in Switzerland would be met with stern disapproval, but meetings often begin late in the Philippines (although foreigners should always arrive on time).

CASE STUDY

Diversity at Johnson & Johnson

Johnson & Johnson, a global manufacturer of health care products headquartered in New Brunswick, New Jersey, takes diversity very seriously. In 2009, J&J's Chairman and CEO William C. Weldon received a perfect score from *Diversity Inc.* magazine for his diversity commitment. In addition to meeting regularly with employee groups, Weldon has J&J's chief diversity officer report directly to him and holds a senior position on a nonprofit organization tied to a multicultural group. He ties more than 6 percent of his direct reports' bonuses to diversity results.

J&J's online Diversity University provides diversity-related resources, cultural awareness training tools featuring country-specific content, and classes that introduce the concepts, personal benefits, and business advantages of diversity. J&J's workforce and managerial ranks also reflect the demographics of the communities the company serves. The company is even committed to diversity among its suppliers and participates in the National Minority Manufacturing Institute.

Diversity drives J&J's innovation and performance. As one vice president stated, "We recognize that diversity leads to innovation and innovation leads to business success, which in turn, leads to fulfilling opportunities for our employees."[112]

J&J's commitment to diversity has paid off. Women comprise 31 percent of its most senior-level executives, and 47 percent of the company's highest-paid employees. As Weldon states, "Diversity and inclusion are part of the fabric of our businesses and are vital to our future success worldwide. The principles of diversity and inclusion are rooted in Our Credo and enhance our ability to deliver products and services to advance the health and well-being of people throughout the world. We cannot afford to reduce our focus on these critical areas in any business climate."[113]

Questions:

1. How do J&J's diversity programs help it to better compete?
2. Which of the programs described in this case study do you think would be most effective at promoting and leveraging diversity at J&J?
3. Do you think diversity can lead to negative outcomes at J&J? If so, which outcomes and why?

Source: Based on No. 1 Johnson & Johnson (2009). Diversity Inc. Available online at: http://www.diversityincbest-practices.com/bp/5449.php; Diversity is the Byword at J&J. (2008). The Metropolitan Corporate Counsel, March 1. http://www.metrocorpcounsel.com/current.php?artType=view&artMonth=March&artYear=2008&EntryNo=8030; Johnson & Johnson (2007). Diversity University Meets Education Needs. Available online at: http://careers.jnj.com/careers/global/workforce_diversity/diversity_resources/diversity_university/index.htm;jsessionid=NKTKP4KAZUEHE CQPCB3WU3QKB2IIWTT1.

Hofstede's Cultural Values

Based on thousands of interviews and more than a decade of research on over forty countries, culture scholar Geert Hofstede[115] identified five dimensions that tend to distinguish cultures across countries:

1. *Power distance*: the degree of inequality that exists and that is accepted among people with and without power. Higher power distance (e.g., Philippines, Guatemala, and Malaysia) is associated with hierarchical, centralized companies that have large gaps in authority, respect, and compensation; while lower power distance (e.g., Austria, Israel, and Denmark) is reflected in flatter organizations in which employees and supervisors are considered almost as equals.

power distance

The degree of inequality that exists and that is accepted among people with and without power

individualism
Reflects the strength of the ties people tend to have with others in their community

masculinity
How much a society values and exhibits traditional male and female roles and expects them to be distinct

uncertainty avoidance
The degree of anxiety members feel in uncertain or unfamiliar situations

long-term orientation
Reflects a focus on long-term planning, delivering on social obligations, and avoiding "losing face"

2. *Individualism*: refers to the strength of the ties people tend to have with others in their community. Higher individualism (e.g., United States, Australia, and New Zealand) indicates loose ties with others and is reflected in greater valuation of people's time and need for freedom, whereas lower individualism (e.g. Guatemala, Equador, and Bangladesh) is reflected in placing a high value on harmony rather than honesty, and an emphasis on intrinsic rewards.

3. *Masculinity*: refers to how much a society values and exhibits traditional male and female roles and expects them to be distinct. In highly masculine cultures, men are expected to be assertive and strong and to be the sole provider for the family. Higher masculinity (e.g., Japan, Hungary, Slovakia) is reflected in a distinction between men's work and women's work, while lower masculinity (e.g., Denmark, Sweden, Norway) is reflected in equal employment opportunity and respect for successful and powerful women.

4. *Uncertainty avoidance*: is the degree of anxiety members feel in uncertain or unfamiliar situations. Higher uncertainty avoidance (e.g., Greece, Portugal, and Uruguay) is associated with a need for structure, avoiding differences, and very formal business conduct governed by many rules, whereas lower uncertainty avoidance (e.g., Singapore, Jamaica, and Hong Kong) is characterized by an informal business culture, acceptance of risk, and more concern with long-term strategy and performance than with daily events.

5. *Long-term orientation*: reflects a focus on long-term planning, delivering on social obligations, and avoiding "losing face." A longer-term orientation (e.g., China and Taiwan) is reflected in a strong work ethic and placing high value on education and training, whereas a shorter-term orientation (e.g., West Africa, Czech Republic, and Canada) is characterized by higher individualism, creativity, and equality.

Understanding a society's culture in these ways can help you to be more effective as an employee and as a manager. For example, if you are in a higher power distance culture, acknowledge and respect the leader's power. In a lower power distance culture, try to involve as many people as possible in decision making and use teamwork where possible. In a highly individualistic culture, encourage others to express their ideas and be sure to acknowledge their accomplishments and contributions. In lower individualistic cultures, focus on working harmoniously with others, and show respect for traditions.

In cultures higher in masculinity, be aware of possible bias concerning appropriate male and female roles. In cultures lower in masculinity, treat men and women equally. In higher uncertainty avoidance cultures, set clear goals and expectations and provide detailed plans and instructions. In lower uncertainty avoidance cultures, minimize structure and provide capable subordinates more latitude in making decisions. In cultures with a longer-term orientation, reward loyalty, commitment, and perseverance and avoid doing anything that would cause someone to "lose face." In cultures with a shorter-term orientation, you can introduce changes more quickly and expect employees to be more innovative.

An additional cultural dimension is the influence of *context*, or the degree to which tradition and protocol dictate how communication should proceed. High-context cultures, including China and Japan, place greater emphasis on protocol, subtlety, and indirectness. Low-context cultures, including the United States and most western cultures, communicate more directly and place the purpose and outcome of the communication over the interpersonal relationships involved. The directness of low-context cultures often appears pushy and insensitive to members of a high-context culture, and the lengthy and indirect communications of high-context cultures often seems evasive and time wasting to members of low-context cultures.[116]

It is important to remember that belonging to a particular culture or being from a particular country does not ensure that the culture describes a particular individual. Individuals from the same area or culture are not all the same, and cultural values can change over time.

The GLOBE Project

A large-scale, eleven-year study of global leadership effectiveness extended Geert Hofstede's work by investigating the leadership beliefs of people in sixty-one different societal cultures.[117] A primary goal of the Global Leadership and Organizational Behavior Effectiveness (GLOBE) Research Program, which sponsored the study, is to develop societal and organizational measures of culture and leader attributes that are appropriate to use across all cultures. The team of 170 scholars from around the world wants to ultimately describe, understand, and predict the impact of cultural variables on leadership and organizational processes and the effectiveness of these processes. The nine cultural dimensions being studied by the GLOBE project are:[118]

1. *Assertiveness*: How confrontational and aggressive should people be in social relationships?
2. *Uncertainty avoidance*: How much should social norms, rituals, rules, and bureaucratic practices be relied on to limit unpredictability?
3. *In-group collectivism*: How much pride and loyalty should individuals have for their family or organization?
4. *Institutional collectivism*: How much should leaders reward and encourage collective distribution of resources and collective action rather than the pursuit of individual goals?
5. *Performance orientation*: How much should people be rewarded for improvement and excellence?
6. *Future orientation*: How much should people delay gratification through planning for the future and saving?
7. *Power distance*: How unequally should power be distributed in organizations and in society?
8. *Humane orientation*: How much should society encourage and reward kindness, fairness, generosity, and friendliness?
9. *Gender egalitarianism*: How much should gender role differences be minimized?

One of the goals of the research is to identify the ways in which middle managers worldwide distinguish between effective and ineffective leadership. These attributes are not statements about how different cultures define outstanding leadership—they are the ways in which people across the world distinguish between effective and ineffective leaders. The GLOBE study defines leadership as the ability of an individual to influence, motivate, and enable others to contribute toward the effectiveness and success of the organizations of which they are members. People who engage in this process are called leaders.[119]

The GLOBE team identified many leader attributes *universally* seen as being at least somewhat responsible for a leader's effectiveness or ineffectiveness, including self-protection, team integration, modesty, autocracy, integrity, decisiveness, and performance orientation. They also identified a large number of *culturally contingent* attributes, whose effects on leadership effectiveness differed across different cultures. These attributes include compassion, ambition, caution, class consciousness, and cunning. A summary of the effects of culture on perceptions of leaders' attributes is in Table 2-5.

Table 2-5		
Cultural Effects on Perceptions of Leaders' Attributes[120]		
Universal *Positive* Leader Attributes	**Universal *Negative* Leader Attributes**	***Culturally Contingent* Leader Attributes**
Intelligent	Asocial	Cunning
Dependable	Dictatorial	Orderly
Excellence oriented	Noncooperative	Subdued
Honest	Irritable	Individualistic
Encouraging	Egocentric	Ruler

As Table 2-5 illustrates, effective leadership behaviors differ depending on the culture the leader is in. Given the important role of the followers in determining whether a leader will be effective, it is important to adjust your leadership style to the preferences and expectations of your subordinates, particularly if you are working in another country as an *expatriate*. We now turn our attention to understanding and improving your cultural competence, which will allow you to be a more flexible and therefore more effective performer and leader.

expatriate

Person temporarily or permanently living in a country other than that of legal residence.

Cultural Competence

Italians often perceive people from the United States as people who are always working, talking about business over lunch and drinking their coffee while running in the street instead of enjoying those activities with others. Does this mean that Italians are lazy and Americans are hyperactive? No, it means that people from different cultures give different meanings to some activities. In Italy, where relationships are highly valued, lunch, dinner, and pauses for coffee have a social purpose—people get together to relax and to get to know each other better. In the United States, where time is money, business can be part of lunch, deals are discussed during dinner, and contracts are signed over coffee.[121]

One of the worst, yet easiest, mistakes people can make is to assume that other people are just like them. People from different cultures see and do things in different ways. *Cultural competence* is the ability to interact effectively with people of different cultures. A culturally competent person has a respectful awareness and understanding of cultural differences. There are four components of cultural competence:[122]

SO WHAT

People from different cultures often have different interpretations of the same event—don't assume that everyone shares your views.

cultural competence

The ability to interact effectively with people of different cultures

1. *Awareness of our own cultural worldview, and of our reactions to people who are different*: A security guard who knows that she profiles teenagers as "troublemakers" is culturally aware of her reactions to this group.
2. *Our attitude toward cultural differences*: This reflects a willingness to honestly understand our beliefs and values about cultural differences.
3. *Knowledge of different worldviews and cultural practices*: Research has found that our values and beliefs about equality may be inconsistent with our behaviors. Many people who scored low on a prejudice test did things in cross-cultural situations that reflected prejudice.[123]
4. *Cross-cultural skills*: This component addresses the importance of practicing cultural competence, including nonverbal communication, to become effective cross-culturally.

IMPROVE YOUR SKILLS

UNDERSTANDING YOUR CULTURE

As you have learned in this chapter, cultural competence requires an awareness of your own cultural practices and worldview. This worksheet will help you to analyze some of the features of your own societal culture. For each cultural feature, identify an example that represents most of the people in your primary culture. Then take a minute to reflect on how other cultures might differ, and how these differences might lead to misunderstanding.

Cultural Feature	Example of Feature Representing Your Primary Culture	How Feature Might Differ and Cause Misunderstanding in Other Cultures
1. Social greetings		
2. Attitudes toward privacy		
3. Appropriate decision making speed		
4. Openness of communication		
5. Gestures that reflect that you understand what you have just been told		
6. Personal grooming		
7. Deference to authority figures		
8. Acceptable personal space		
9. Timeliness		
10. Work ethic		

Although some people are naturally culturally competent, most of us have to put effort into developing this skill. This requires honestly examining our prejudices and biases, actively developing cross-cultural skills, learning from role models, and having a positive attitude about cultural issues. The key to cross-cultural success is awareness—being aware of how culture influences your interpretations of others, your own behavior, and how people from other cultures may see you. Understanding why we do things in certain ways, how we see the world, and why we react as we do is an important part of being culturally aware.

Cultural awareness can improve performance in culturally diverse organizations, or when a firm's customers are diverse. This chapter's *Improve Your Skills* feature will help you understand some of the characteristics of your own culture that are likely to differ in other areas of the world.

BRANKOKOSTESKI/ISTOCKPHOTO.COM

What does this mean? In the United Kingdom and the United States, it means "okay." But in Japan, it means money; in Turkey and Brazil, it is an insult; in Portugal and Greece, it means, "no good"; and in Russia, it indicates the number zero.

GLOBAL ISSUES

CULTURAL ETIQUETTE QUIZ

Successfully managing or conducting business across cultures involves knowing what to say, when to arrive for meetings, what to wear, what gifts are acceptable, and what greeting to give, among many other things. It takes a continued effort to recognize and appreciate the other party's expectations and business practices. This quiz will give you an idea of how aware you are of the business cultures of other areas of the world. Answers are at the bottom of the quiz.[124]

_____ 1. Which culture often views professional titles as arrogant?

_____ 2. Where should you not use red ink on your business card because the color red has a negative connotation?

_____ 3. In this culture, it may be considered an insult to leave immediately following a meeting, as this may suggest that you are not interested in getting to know the other party.

_____ 4. If you compliment someone in this country on one of their personal items, he or she may insist that you accept it as a gift.

_____ 5. In this country, tapping your nose signals that something is to be kept secret or confidential.

_____ 6. In this country, beckoning someone with your palm up while wagging one finger can be taken as an insult.

_____ 7. In what country do people who have worked together for years still shake hands every morning as if they were meeting for the first time?

_____ 8. In this country, negotiations usually take a long time and are chaotic, with numerous people often speaking simultaneously.

_____ 9. The "thumbs up" gesture is offensive in this country.

_____ 10. Be sensitive to the volume of your voice in this country. Americans' loud voices are known to be offensive in meetings as well as in restaurants and on the street.

_____ 11. Negotiations and meetings with people from this country often involve flared tempers, and temper tantrums and walkouts often occur. Standing with your hands in your pockets is also considered rude in this culture.

_____ 12. Because saving face is so important in this culture, you will often hear "It's inconvenient" or "I'll look into it" instead of being told "no."

Answers: (1) Ireland; (2) Madascar; (3) Columbia; (4) Bahrain; (5) England; (6) India (and China); (7) Germany; (8) Spain; (9) Saudi Arabia; (10) France; (11) Russia; (12) China

Just for fun, take the Cultural Etiquette Quiz in this chapter's _Global Issues_ feature (above) and see how much you know about working and doing business in other cultures.

SUMMARY AND APPLICATION

Diversity is much more than demographics and can reflect combinations of characteristics in addition to a single attribute. Each individual also has a variety of characteristics that can be considered diverse. There are many types of diversity, including surface-level and deep-level diversity. Diversity can be examined as a group characteristic, as in "this group is diverse with regard to gender, race, and experience," or as an individual characteristic in terms of a person's similarity to

REAL WORLD RESPONSE

CREATING A CLIMATE FOR DIVERSITY AT CONAGRA FOODS

ConAgra Foods sees diversity as the foundation of its future success. Having a diverse culture brings to the company a wide variety of perspectives and talents that strengthen its ability to better serve both customers and consumers. By creating an inclusive culture that leverages the diversity of its employees, ConAgra empowers its talent to grow to their fullest potential.

ConAgra has built a strong business case for diversity and inclusion, enabling the company to create a culture that attracts, retains and engages people from all walks of life. Believing that workforce diversity enables stronger relationships in the community, the marketplace, and with stakeholders, ConAgra operates and sponsors the Diversity and Inclusion Leadership Council, a group of senior executives who provide guidance, support, and sponsorship of diversity initiatives.[125]

Fundamental to building a diverse and inclusive culture are the ConAgra Employee Resource Networks (ERNs), which give hundreds of employees of similar and differing cultures, backgrounds, and lifestyles the opportunity to promote inclusion across the company, advance business objectives, and enhance their personal and professional growth through networking and mentoring. The ERNS include the ConAgra Black Employee Network, Women's Leadership Council, ConAgra Asian Network, ConAgra Latino Network, ConAgra Young Professional Network and Illuminations (Lesbian, Gay, Bisexual, Transgender and Allies). A mentoring program allows each network access to mentoring circles where senior leaders provide coaching and share insights.[126] ConAgra received an International Innovation in Diversity Award for its use of ERNs to advance diversity.[127]

ConAgra is also sensitive and responsive to diversity among its suppliers, customers, consumers, and the communities in which it works. It also expects its employees to act at all times in a manner that values diversity among customers and employees.[128]

or difference from the other group members. Having a token minority member in a group affects the majority members' perceptions of that minority group, placing greater performance pressures on minority group members, increasing stereotyping, and creating more boundaries between majority and minority group members.

Diversity affects individual and organizational outcomes through processes including social integration, differences in status and power, task conflict, relationship conflict, inclusion, and information processing. Barriers to inclusion include the "like me" bias, stereotypes, prejudice, perceptions of loss by persons who feel threatened by diversity initiatives, ethnocentrism, and unequal access to organizational networks. Organizations promote diversity through top management commitment, staffing, training, and mentoring. Diversity metrics allow companies to monitor their progress and to define their priorities for future action.

Societal culture reflects language, politics, religion, and values among other things, and societal culture can vary within a single country or across nearby countries. Because societal culture influences the diverse values, customs, language, and expectations we bring with us to work, it is important to understand its effects on our own as well as on other people's behaviors. Societal cultures can differ on a variety of characteristics, including collectivism, power distance, future orientation, and gender egalitarianism as well as determine what employees consider desirable leadership characteristics. You will be a more effective performer and leader if you are culturally aware.

It is important to be aware of and continually develop your cultural awareness and understanding of how culture influences your interpretations of others, your own behavior, and how people from other cultures may see you. Diversity has the potential to enhance organizational performance, particularly for firms serving a diverse customer base or as an innovation strategy, but it must be effectively managed. Creating a culture of inclusion and hiring, training, and rewarding employees for inclusive behaviors will help in taking advantage of the positive potential of diversity and will minimize the potential for negative individual and organizational outcomes.

 TAKEAWAY POINTS

1. *Surface-level diversity* refers to the observable differences in people that are known about people as soon as you see them. Examples include race, age, ethnicity, physical abilities, physical characteristics, and gender. *Deep-level diversity* refers to the individual differences that cannot be seen directly, including goals, values, personalities, decision-making styles, knowledge, skills, abilities, and attitudes.

2. Diversity can enhance a firm's competitive advantage when it enables all employees to contribute their full talents and motivation to the company. Effectively managing diversity brings out the best in all employees, allowing each of them to contribute maximally to the firm's performance. Diversity can improve decision making, enhance creativity, and enable a company to better relate and respond to its customers.

3. If poorly managed, diversity can have negative effects in organizations. Poorly managed diversity can cause misunderstanding, suspicion, and conflict that can result in absenteeism, poor quality, low morale, loss of competitiveness, and lowered workgroup cohesiveness. Diverse groups tend to have less integration and communication and more conflict than do homogeneous groups.

4. Barriers to creating inclusive organizations include the *"like me" bias*, when people prefer to associate with others they perceive to be like themselves; *stereotypes*, or beliefs about an individual or a group based on the idea that everyone in a particular group will behave the same way or have the same characteristics; *prejudice*, or outright bigotry or intolerance for other groups; *perceived threat of loss,* when some employees perceive a direct threat to their own career opportunities and feel that they need to protect their own prospects by impeding diversity efforts; *ethnocentrism*, or the belief that one's own language, native country, and cultural rules and norms are superior to all others; and *unequal access to organizational networks,* which occurs when women and minorities are excluded from organizational networks that are important to job performance, mentoring opportunities, and being candidates for promotion.

5. Diversity assessment methods include the diversity of job applicants and new hires, the proportion of people with different demographics in a company's business units at each level of employment, the pay levels and attrition rates of people with different demographics in comparable positions, and the ratio of people with different demographics promoted to those eligible for promotion.

6. Societal culture affects how people interpret others and how others interpret them by influencing the diverse values, customs, language, and expectations people bring to work.

7. Cultural competence is the ability to interact effectively with people of different cultures. A culturally competent person has a respectful awareness and understanding of cultural differences. In multicultural organizations, or when a company's customers are diverse, this skill can enhance your effectiveness.

DISCUSSION QUESTIONS

1. Which do you think is more important to team performance, surface-level or deep-level diversity? Why?
2. How can diversity create a competitive advantage for a firm?
3. How can managers help teams to overcome the potential negative effects of diversity?
4. If a subordinate came to you and said that they felt the company's new diversity hiring initiative was unfair and would compromise their well-deserved opportunities for advancement, how would you respond?
5. How can White males be effectively included in diversity initiatives?
6. What can leaders do to be effective when team members are from different cultures and have different expectations about how the leader should behave?

EXERCISES

What Does Culture Mean to You?

This exercise is done as a class, and the instructor plays the role of class secretary. First working alone, think about what "societal culture" means. For five minutes, think about your own culture. Write down how you think a dictionary would define the word, then write down all of the cultural dimensions you can think of that you would use to describe it.

After five minutes, the instructor will call on students to share some of their ideas and record them on a chalkboard, flip chart, or something else. Try to identify categories into which the ideas can be placed. Then answer the following questions as a class.

Questions

1. How might multiculturalism create a competitive advantage for an organization?
2. What categories are the most important to teams working in organizations?
3. What categories are the least important to teams working in organizations?
4. What does your list suggest that managers wanting to promote a multicultural workplace might do?

Diversity at Microsoft

As you learned in this chapter, diversity is not only a legal and ethical necessity, but it also can improve business results. Microsoft believes that diversity enriches its products, and the company engages in many activities to promote inclusion. Explore the information about diversity at Microsoft by pointing your browser to http://www.microsoft.com/about/diversity/en/us/default.aspx. Then answer the questions that follow.

Questions

1. In what ways does Microsoft seem to define diversity?
2. Which of Microsoft's diversity programs and initiatives do you think are most important to the company's future success? Why?
3. After exploring Microsoft's website, how do you evaluate the company as a potential employer? Why?

VIDEO CASES

Now What?

Imagine trying to write a project status report for Happy Time Toys with three other team members when an older team member tries to take the project over, believing that you're too inexperienced to do a good job. *What do you say or do?* Go to this chapter's "Now What?" video, watch the challenge video, and choose a response. Be sure to also view the outcomes of the two responses you didn't choose.

Discussion Questions

1. What type(s) of conflict is (are) this group experiencing?
2. How can diversity be a source of competitive advantage for this group?
3. If you were the CEO of Happy Time Toys, how would you create a culture of inclusion to help your company realize the benefits of diversity?

Workplace | Evo: Managing in a Global Environment

Fast-growing online retailer Evo has an exciting new problem: It has more international customers than ever before. In 2001, the Seattle-based company began selling brand name ski-and-skate gear to U.S. consumers, and today Evo delivers products to places as far away as Bahrain, Turkey, Japan, and Bali.

Selling to global markets is loaded with difficulties, however, and Evo's customer service representatives have stories to tell about their challenging interactions with international consumers. For starters, overseas callers are often disappointed to learn that they cannot order items due to international licensing and distribution agreements. In addition, language barriers between Evo's employees and international customers make certain orders impossible to transact.

Daily operations have unusual twists as well, especially in the area of supply chain management. "Manufacturers overseas can impact us," said Evo marketer Molly Hawkins. "There was a lock at all the ports in China and we couldn't import any of their products. Therefore, a lot of soft goods like jackets and pants couldn't be shipped."

Globalization is affecting products as well. In addition to selling skis, snowboards, and related gear, Evo now offers an international travel package for sport adventurers. Known as evoTRIP, the travel service provides guided ski, snowboarding, and surf expeditions to exotic destinations in South America, Japan, Indonesia, and Switzerland. "This concept is near and dear to what all of us value," said Bryce Phillips, Evo's founder. "It's getting out there, learning more about different cultures, doing the activities in different parts of the world, and seeing beautiful locations you've never seen before."

To offer the richest, most authentic cultural experience, evoTRIP relies on local guides. Professional athletes selected from each country travel with groups so that evoTrippers can experience rich cultural nuances from place to place.

Although Evo's largest customer base continues to reside in the United States, Phillips is excited about expanding his company's global reach. As licensing practices change to reflect the boundary-free world of e-commerce, and as Evo becomes a global brand, ski-and-board enthusiasts all over the world may soon identify themselves as loyal Evo customers.

Discussion Questions

1. How might globalization affect Evo's commitment to diversity?
2. What are the advantages and disadvantages of diversity for Evo's business?
3. What cultural differences should Evo and evoTRIP managers pay attention to when traveling abroad?

DO WHAT

CENGAGENOW™ includes **teaching and learning resources** to supplement the text, and is designed specifically to **help students "think like managers"** by engaging and challenging them to think critically about managerial situations. **CengageNOW uses today's technology to improve the skills** of tomorrow's managers.

END NOTES

[1]Leadership Statement on Diversity and Inclusion (2012). ConAgra Foods. Available online: http://phx.corporate-ir.net /phoenix.zhtml?c=202310&p=comm_leadership.

[2]ConAgra Foods Recognized for Innovation in Diversity (2010). Diversity Best Practices. Available online: http://www .diversitybestpractices.com/news-articles/conagra-foods- recognized-innovation-diversity.

[3]Diversity and Inclusion (2012). ConAgra. Available online: http://company.conagrafoods.com/phoenix.zhtml?c= 202310&p=comm_main.

[4]CPGjobs Featured Employer: ConAgra (2012). Available online: http://www.cpgjobs.com/559/.

[5]Cox, J. A., Read, J. L., & van Auken, P. M. (1990). Male-Female Differences in Communicating Job-Related Humor: An Ex- ploratory Study. *Humor: The International Journal of Humor Research, 3,* 287–295.

[6]See http://www.eeoc.gov/employers/index.cfm for more informa- tion on Federal laws prohibiting employment discrimination.

[7]McKay, P., Avery, D. R., & Morris, M. A. (2008). Mean Racial- Ethnic Differences in Employee Sales Performance: The Moderat- ing Role of Diversity Climate. *Personnel Psychology, 61,* 349–374.

[8]ITT Corp Promotes Technical Diversity Around the World, Di- versity/Careers in Engineering and Information Technology, August/September 2008. Available online: http://www.diversity- careers.com/articles/pro/08-augsep/dia_ITT_corp.html.

[9]Diversity Best Practices, White Male Engagement: Inclusion is Key. CDO Insights, April 2007. Available online: http://www .diversitybestpractices.com/content/cdo-insights-white-male- engagement.

[10]Nkomo, S. N., & Cox, T. H., Jr. (1996). Diverse Identities in Or- ganizations. In S. R. Clegg, C. Hardy, & W. R. Nord (eds.), *Hand- book of Organization Studies* (pp. 338–356). London: Sage.

[11]Bloom, M., & Michel, J. G. (2002). The Relationships Among Or- ganizational Context, Pay Dispersion, and Managerial Turnover. *Academy of Management Journal, 45,* 33–42.

[12]Linnehan, F., & Konrad, A. M. (1999). Diluting Diversity: Impli- cations for Inter-Group Inequality in Organizations. *Journal of Management Inquiry, 8,* 399–414.

[13]See Tsui, A. S., & O'Reilly, C. A. (1989). Beyond Simple Demo- graphic Effects: The Importance of Relational Demography in Superior-Subordinate Dyads. *Academy of Management Journal, 32,* 402–423.

[14]Wesolowski, M. A., & Mossholder, K. W. (1997). Relational Demography in Supervisor-Subordinate Dyads: Impact on Subor- dinate Job Satisfaction, Burnout, and Perceived Procedural Jus- tice. *Journal of Organizational Behavior, 18,* 351–362.

[15]Kanter, R. M. (1977). *Men and Women of the Corporation.* New York: Basic Books.

[16]Harrison, D. A., & Klein, K. J. (2007). What's the Difference? Diversity Constructs as Separation, Variety, or Disparity in Orga- nizations. *Academy of Management Review, 32,* 1199–1228.

[17] Yang, Y. & Konrad, A.M. (2010). Diversity and Organizational Innovation: The Role of Employee Involvement, *Journal of Organizational Behavior, 32,* 1062–1083; Harrison, D. A., & Klein, K. J. (2007). What's the Difference? Diversity Constructs as Separation, Variety, or Disparity in Organizations. *Academy of Management Review, 32,* 1199–1228.

[18]Diversity Programs: A Strategic Business Initiative That Helps U.S. Corporations Compete Globally. (1996, July). Black Enterprise. Available online: http://www.questia.com/read/1G1-18407141 /diversity-programs-a-strategic-business-initiative

[19]McKay, P. F., Avery, D. R., & Morris, M. A. (2008). Mean Racial- Ethnic Differences in Employee Sales Performance: The Moderat- ing Role of Diversity Climate. *Personnel Psychology, 61,* 349–374.

[20]McPherson, J. R., & Mendonca, L. T. (2008, September 30). The Challenge of Hiring and Retaining Women: An Interview with the Head of HR at eBay. *The McKinsey Quarterly.* Available on- line: http://www.mckinseyquarterly.com/Organization/Talent /The_challenge_of_hiring_and_retaining_women_An_interview _with_the_head_of_HR_at_eBay_2184.

[21]Allen, T. W. (2007). Diversity Policy Statement. U.S. Coast Guard. Available online: http://www.uscg.mil/RESERVE/msg07 /alcoast/coast059_07.htm.

[22]Schenke, J. (2008). Purdue University Honors, Rewards Diver- sity Efforts. (September 12). Available online: http://news.uns .purdue.edu/x/2008b/080912OlsenCatalyst.html.

[23]Diversity Is the Key Ingredient to Kellogg's Global Success. (2008, March). Diversityinc.com. Available online: http://www .diversityinc-digital.com/diversityincmedia/200803?pg=64#pg64.

[24]Robinson, G., & Dechant, K. (1997). Building a Business Case for Diversity. *Academy of Management Executive, 11,* 21–30.

[25]See reviews by Webber, S. S., & Donahue, L. M. (2001). Impact of Highly and Less Job-Related Diversity on Work Group Cohe- sion and Performance: A Meta-Analysis. *Journal of Management,* 141–162; Williams, K. Y., & O'Reilly III, C. A. (1998). Demography and Diversity in Organizations: A Review of 40 Years of Research. *Research in Organizational Behavior, 20,* 77–140.

[26]Ragins, B. R., & Gonzalez, J. A. (2003). Understanding Diver- sity in Organizations: Getting a Grip on a Slippery Construct. In *Organizational Behavior: The State of the Science,* ed. J. Greenberg (pp. 125–163). Mahwah, NJ: Lawrence Erlbaum Associates.

[27]Triandis, H. C., Kurowski, L. L., & Gelfand, M. J. (1993). Work- place Diversity. In *Handbook of Industrial and Organizational Psychology,* eds. H. C. Triandis, M. Dunnette, & L. Hough (4th ed., pp. 769–827). Palo Alto, CA: Consulting Psychologists Press; McLeod, P. L., Lobel, S., & Cox, T. H. (1996). Ethnic Diversity and Creativity in Small Groups. *Small Group Research, 27,* 248–264.

[28]Bassett-Jones, N. (2005). The Paradox of Diversity Manage- ment, Creativity and Innovation. *Creativity and Innovation Management, 14,* 169–175.

[29]Williams, K. Y. (1998). Demography and Diversity in Organiza- tions: A Review of 100 Years of Research. In *Research in Organi- zational Behavior,* eds. B. M. Staw and L. L. Cummings (Vol. 20, pp. 77–140). Greenwich, CT: JAI Press.

[30]Moss-Kanter, R. (1983). *The Change Masters.* New York: Simon & Schuster.

[31]Deszõ, C. L., & Gaddis Ross, D. (2008, July 17). "Girl Power": Female Participation in Top Management and Firm Quality. Working paper series.

[32]Steelcase's Legacy of Diversity. (2008, March). Diversityinc .com. Available online: http://www.diversityinc-digital.com/ diversityincmedia/200803?pg=66#pg66.

[33]For more information, see http://www.ada.gov.

[34]U.S. Equal Employment Opportunity Commission. The Age Discrimination in Employment Act of 1967. Available online: http://www.eeoc.gov/policy/adea.html.

[35]See SEC. 2000e-2. [Section 703] of the Civil Rights Act of 1964. Available online: http://www.eeoc.gov/policy/vii.html.

[36]Sec. 703 (m) of Title VII.

[37]EEOC. (2010, March 1). Walmart to Pay More Than $11.7 Million to Settle EEOC Sex Discrimination Suit. U.S. Equal Employment Opportunity Commission. Available online: http://www .eeoc.gov/eeoc/newsroom/release/3-1-10.cfm.

[38]Glater, J. D. (2004, June 27). Attention Wal-Mart Plaintiffs: Hurdles Ahead. *The New York Times.* Available online: http:// select.nytimes.com/gst/abstract.html?res=F00B13FD3D5C0C748 EDDAF0894DC404482&n=Top%2fNews%2fBusiness%2fCompa nies%2fWal%2dMart%20Stores%20Inc%2e.

[39]Toossi, M. (2012). Labor Force Projections to 2020: A More Slowly Growing Workforce, *Monthly Labor Review*, January, 43–64.

[40]U.S. Census Bureau, 2008.

[41]Schramm, J. (2006, June). *SHRM Workplace Forecast*. Alexandria, VA: Society for Human Resource Management.

[42]Frauenheim, E. (2007, March 12). Aging Boomers Require Workplace Flexibility, Says American Management Association. *Workforce Management, 6.*

[43]U.S. Bureau of Labor Statistics, July 2008.

[44]Fortune 1000. (2007). Available online: http://www.money.cnn .com.

[45]Desvaux, G., Devillard-Hoellinger, S., & Meany, M. C. (September 2008). A Business Case for Women. *The McKinsey Quarterly*. Available online: http://www.mckinseyquarterly.com /Organization/Talent/A_business_case_for_women_2192.

[46]See Wittenberg-Cox, A., & Maitland, A. (2008). *Why Women Mean Business: Understanding the Emergence of Our Next Economic Revolution.* Chichester, England: John Wiley & Sons.

[47]Desvaux, G., Devillard-Hoellinger, S., & Meaney, M. C. (2008, September). A Business Case for Women. *The McKinsey Quarterly*. Available online: http://www.mckinseyquarterly.com /Organization/Talent/A_business_case_for_women_2192.

[48]McPherson, J. R., & Mendonca, L. T. (2008, September 30). The Challenge of Hiring and Retaining Women: An Interview with the Head of HR at eBay. *The McKinsey Quarterly*. Available online: http://www.mckinseyquarterly.com/Organization/Talent /The_challenge_of_hiring_and_retaining_women_An_interview _with_the_head_of_HR_at_eBay_2184.

[49]Millikin, F. J., & Martins, L. L. (1996). Searching for Common Threads: Understanding the Multiple Effects of Diversity in Organizational Groups. *Academy of Management Review, 21*, 402–433.

[50]See Bassett-Jones, N. (2005). The Paradox of Diversity Management, Creativity and Innovation. *Creativity and Innovation Management, 14*, 169–175.

[51]See Jackson, S. E., Stone, V. K., & Alvarez, E. B. (1992). Socialization Amidst Diversity: The Impact of Demographics on Work Team Old-Timers and Newcomers. In *Research in Organizational Behavior*, eds. L. L. Cummings and B. M. Staw (Vol. 15, pp. 45–109). Greenwich, CT: JAI.

[52]Williams, K. Y., & O'Reilly III, C. A. (1998). Demography and Diversity in Organizations: A Review of 40 Years of Research. *Research in Organizational Behavior, 20*, 77–140.

[53]See, e.g., Jackson, S. E., Brett, J. F., Sessa, V. I., Cooper, D. M., Julin, J. A., & Peyronnin, K. (1991). Some Differences Make a Difference: Individual Dissimilarity and Group Heterogeneity as Correlates of Recruitment, Promotions, and Turnover. *Journal of Applied Psychology, 76*, 675–689; O'Reilly, C. A., Caldwell, D. F., & Barnett, W. P. (1989). Work Group Demography, Social Integration, and Turnover. *Administrative Science Quarterly, 34*, 21–37; Riordan, C. M. (2000). Relational Demography Within Groups: Past Developments, Contradictions, and New Directions. *Research in Personnel and Human Resources Management, 19*, 131–173; Tsui, A. S., Egan, T. D., & O'Reilly, C. A. (1992). Being Different: Relational Demography and Organizational Attachment. *Administrative Science Quarterly, 37*, 547–579.

[54]See, e.g., O'Reilly, C. A., Caldwell, D. F., & Barnett, W. P. (1989). Work Group Demography, Social Integration, and Turnover. *Administrative Science Quarterly, 34*, 21–37; Pelled, L. H., Eisenhardt, K. M., & Xin, K. R. (1999). Exploring the Black Box: An Analysis of Work Group Diversity, Conflict, and Performance. *Administrative Science Quarterly, 44*, 1–28; Webber, S. S., & Donahue, L. M. (2001). Impact of Highly and Less Job-Related Diversity on Work Group Cohesion and Performance: A Meta-Analysis. *Journal of Management, 27*, 141–162.

[55]Liden, R. C., Stilwell, D., & Ferris, G. R. (1996). The Effects of Supervisor and Subordinate Age on Objective Performance and Subjective Performance Ratings. *Human Relations, 49*, 327–347; Shore, L. M., Cleveland, J. N., & Goldberg, C. B. (2003). Work Attitudes and Decisions as a Function of Manager Age and Employee Age. *Journal of Applied Psychology, 88*, 529–537; Tsui, A. S., & O'Reilly, C. A. (1989). Beyond Simple Demographic Effects: The Importance of Relational Demography in Superior-Subordinate Dyads. *Academy of Management Journal, 32*, 402–423; Vecchio, R. P. (1993). The Impact of Differences in Subordinate and Supervisor Age on Attitudes and Performance. *Psychology and Aging, 8*, 112–119.

[56]Tsui, A. S., Porter, L. W., & Egan, T. D. (2002). When Both Similarities and Dissimilarities Matter: Extending the Concept of Relational Demography. *Human Relations, 55*, 899–929.

[57]Webber, S. S., & Donahue, L. M. (2001). Impact of Highly and Less Job-Related Diversity on Work Group Cohesion and Performance: A Meta-Analysis. *Journal of Management, 27*, 141–162.

[58]Robinson, G., & Dechant, K. (1997). Building a Business Case for Diversity. *Academy of Management Executive, 11*, 21–30.

[59]Cox, T. H., Jr., & Blake, S. (1991). Managing Cultural Diversity: Implications for Organizational Competitiveness. *Academy of Management Executive, 5*, 45–67; Robinson, G., & Dechant, K. (1997). Building a Business Case for Diversity. *Academy of Management Executive, 11*, 21–30.

[60]Fernandez, J. P. (1991). *Managing a Diverse Workforce*. Lexington, MA: Lexington Books.

[61]Riordan, C. M., & Shore, L. M. (1997). Demographic Diversity and Employee Attitudes: An Empirical Examination of Relational Demography Within Work Units. *Journal of Applied Psychology, 82*, 342–358.

[62]Tsui, A. S., Egan, T. D., & O'Reilly III, C. A. (1992). Being Different: Relational Demography and Organizational Attachment. *Administrative Science Quarterly, 37*, 549–579.

[63]Tsui, A. S., Egan, T. D., & O'Reilly III, C. A. (1992). Being Different: Relational Demography and Organizational Attachment. *Administrative Science Quarterly, 37*, 549–579.

[64]Tsui, A. S., & O'Reilly, C. A. (1989). Beyond Simple Demographic Effects: The Importance of Relational Demography in

Superior-Subordinate Dyads. *Academy of Management Journal, 32,* 402–423.

[65]Lau, D. C., & Murnighan, J. K. (1998). Demographic Diversity and Fault Lines: The Compositional Dynamics of Organizational Groups. *Academy of Management Review, 23,* 325–340.

[66]Earley, P. C., & Mosakowski, E. (2000). Creating Hybrid Team Cultures: An Empirical Test of Transnational Team Functioniong. *Academy of Management Journal, 43,* 26–49.

[67]Ely, R. J. (1994). The Effects of Organizational Demographics and Social Identity on Relationships Among Professional Women. *Administrative Science Quarterly, 39,* 203–238.

[68]Ely, R. J. (1995). The Power in Demography: Women's Social Constructions of Gender Identity at Work. *Academy of Management Journal, 38,* 589–634.

[69]See Smith, K. G., Smit, K. A., Olian, J. D., Sims, H. P., O'Bannon, D. P., & Scully, J. A. (1994). Top Management Team Demography and Process: The Role of Social Integration and Communication. *Administrative Science Quarterly, 39,* 412–438.

[70]Ragins, B. R., & Gonzalez, J. A. (2003). Understanding Diversity in Organizations: Getting a Grip on a Slippery Construct. In *Organizational Behavior: The State of the Science,* ed. J. Greenberg (pp. 125–163). Mahwah, NJ: Lawrence Erlbaum Associates.

[71]Schneider, S. K., & Northcraft, G. B. (1999). Three Social Dilemmas of Workforce Diversity in Organizations: A Social Identity Perspective. *Human Relations, 52,* 1445–1467.

[72]Richard, O. C. (2000). Racial Diversity, Business Strategy, and Firm Performance: A Resource-Based View. *Academy of Management Journal, 43,* 164–177.

[73]O'Reilly, C. A., Caldwell, D. F., & Barnett, W. P. (1989). Work Group Demography, Social Integration, and Turnover. *Administrative Science Quarterly, 34,* 21–37.

[74]Konrad, A. M. (2003). Defining the Domain of Workplace Diversity Scholarship. *Group and Organization Management, 28,* 4–17.

[75]Jehn, K. A., Chadwick, C., & Thatcher, S. M. B. (1997). To Agree or Not to Agree: The Effects of Value Congruence, Individual Demographic Dissimilarity, and Conflict on Workgroup Outcomes. *International Journal of Conflict Management, 8,* 287–305.

[76]Jehn, K. A., Chadwick, C., & Thatcher, S. M. B. (1997). To Agree or Not to Agree: The Effects of Value Congruence, Individual Demographic Dissimilarity, and Conflict on Workgroup Outcomes. *International Journal of Conflict Management, 8,* 287–305.

[77]Pelled, L. H. (1996). Demographic Diversity, Conflict, and Work Group Outcomes: An Intervening Process Theory. *Organization Science, 7,* 615–631; Pelled, L. H., Eisenhardt, K. M., & Xin, K. R. (1999). Exploring the Black Box: An Analysis of Work Group Diversity, Conflict, and Performance. *Administrative Science Quarterly, 44,* 1–28.

[78]De Dreu, C. K. W., & Weingart, L. R. (2003). Task Versus Relationship Conflict, Team Performance, and Team Member Satisfaction: A Meta-Analysis. *Journal of Applied Psychology, 88,* 741–749.

[79]Fredrickson, J. W. (1984). The Comprehensiveness of Strategic Decision Processes: Extension, Observations, Future Directions. *Academy of Management Journal, 27,* 445–466.

[80]De Dreu, C. K. W. (2006). When Too Little or Too Much Hurts: Evidence for a Curvilinear Relationship Between Task Conflict and Innovation in Teams. *Journal of Management, 32,* 83–107.

[81]De Dreu, C. K. W. (2006). When Too Little or Too Much Hurts: Evidence for a Curvilinear Relationship Between Task Conflict and Innovation in Teams. *Journal of Management, 32,* 83–107.

[82]Harrison, D. A., Price, K. H., & Bell, M. P. (1998). Beyond Relational Demography: Time and the Effects of Surface- and Deep-Level Diversity on Work Group Cohesion. *Academy of Management Journal, 41,* 96–107.

[83]Shore, L.M., Randel, A.E., Chung, B.G., Dean, M.A., Ehrhart, K.H., & Singh, G. (2011). Inclusion and Diversity in Work Groups: A Review and Model for Future Research, *Journal of Management, 37,* 1262–1289.

[84]Roberson, Q. (2006). Disentangling the Meanings of Diversity and Inclusion in Organizations. *Group and Organization Management, 31,* 212–236.

[85]Mor Barak, M. E. (2005). *Managing Diversity: Toward a Globally Inclusive Workplace.* Thousand Oaks, CA: Sage.

[86]Perrewé, P. L., Brymer, R. A., Stepina, L. P., & Hassell, B. L. (1991). A Causal Model Examining the Effects of Age Discrimination on Employee Psychological Reactions and Subsequent Turnover Intentions. *International Journal of Hospitality Management, 10,* 245–260.

[87]Harrison, D. A., Price, K. H., & Bell, M. P. (1998). Beyond Relational Demography: Time and the Effects of Surface- and Deep-Level Diversity on Work Group Cohesion. *Academy of Management Journal, 41,* 96–107.

[88]van Knippenberg, D., DeDreu, C. K. W., & Homan, A. C. (2004). Work Group Diversity and Group Performance: An Integrative Model and Research Agenda. *Journal of Applied Psychology, 89,* 1008–1022; van Knippenberg, D., & Schippers, C. (2007). Work Group Diversity. *Annual Review of Psychology, 58,* 515–541.

[89]U.S. Equal Employment Opportunity Commission. (2012). *Best Practices of Private Sector Employers.* Available online: http://www.eeoc.gov/eeoc/task_reports/best_practices.cfm.

[90]van Knippenberg, D., DeDreu, C. K. W., & Homan, A. C. (2004). Work Group Diversity and Group Performance: An Integrative Model and Research Agenda. *Journal of Applied Psychology, 89,* 1008–1022; van Knippenberg, D., & Schippers, C. (2007). Work Group Diversity. *Annual Review of Psychology, 58,* 515–541.

[91]Jackson, S. E., & Joshi, A. (2004, September). Diversity in Social Context: A Multi-Attribute, Multi-Level Analysis of Team Diversity and Sales Performance. *Journal of Organizational Behavior,* 675–702.

[92]Federal Glass Ceiling Commission. (1995, March). *Good for Business: Making Full Use of the Nation's Human Capital.* Fact-Finding Report of the Federal Glass Ceiling Commission.

[93]Federal Glass Ceiling Commission. (1995, March). *Good for Business: Making Full Use of the Nation's Human Capital* (pp. 28–29). Fact-Finding Report of the Federal Glass Ceiling Commission.

[94]Federal Glass Ceiling Commission. (1995, March). *Good for Business: Making Full Use of the Nation's Human Capital* (pp. 31–32). Fact-Finding Report of the Federal Glass Ceiling Commission.

[95]Diversity Best Practices. (2007, April). White Male Engagement: Inclusion Is Key. CDO Insights. Available online:http://www.diversitybestpractices.com/content/cdo-insights-white-male-engagement.

[96]Perrewé, P. L., & Nelson, D. L. (2004, December). Gender and Career Success: The Facilitative Role of Political Skill. *Organizational Dynamics, 366–378.*

[97]Lyness, K. S., & Thompson, D. E. (2000). Climbing the Corporate Ladder: Do Female and Male Executives Follow the Same Route? *Journal of Applied Psychology, 85,* 86–101.

[98]Spelman, D., Addison-Reid, B., Avery, E., & Crary, M. (2006). Sustaining a Long-Term Diversity Change Initiative: Lessons from a Business University. *The Diversity Factor, 14*(4), 19–25.

[99]Winters, M. F. (2006). *CEOs Who Get It.* Washington, DC: Diversity Best Practices.

[100]Diversity at PNC. (2010). Available online: https://www.pnc.com/webapp/unsec/Blank.do?siteArea=/PNC/Careers/Why+PNC/Diversity+at+PNC.

[101]Diversity Efforts Are Big at Boeing. (2008, February/March). Diversity/Careers in Engineering and Information Technology. Available online: http://www.diversitycareers.com/articles/pro/08-febmar/dia_boeing.htm.

[102]McPherson, J. R., & Mendonca, L. T. (2008, September 30). The Challenge of Hiring and Retaining Women: An Interview with the Head of HR at eBay. *The McKinsey Quarterly.* Available online: http://www.mckinseyquarterly.com/Organization/Talent/The_challenge_of_hiring_and_retaining_women_An_interview_with_the_head_of_HR_at_eBay_2184.

[103]At MetLife, Diversity Is About "The Way We Do Business." (2008, June/July). Diversity/Careers in Engineering and Information Technology. Available online: http://www.diversitycareers.com/articles/pro/08-junjul/dia_MetLife.html.

[104]Siemens IT Solutions & Services Looks for Top IT Talent. (2008, June/July). Diversity/Careers in Engineering and Information Technology. Available online: http://www.diversitycareers.com/articles/pro/08-junjul/dia_siemens.html.

[105]Diversity Best Practices. (2007, April). White Male Engagement: Inclusion Is Key. CDO Insights. Available online: http://www.diversitybestpractices.com/content/cdo-insights-white-male-engagement.

[106]Diversity Best Practices. (2007, April). White Male Engagement: Inclusion Is Key. CDO Insights. Available online: http://www.diversitybestpractices.com/content/cdo-insights-white-male-engagement.

[107]Atkinson, W. (2001, September). Bringing Diversity to White Men. *HR Magazine, 46*(9), 76–83.

[108]Desvaux, G., Devillard-Hoellinger, S., & Meaney, M. C. (2008, September). A Business Case for Women. *The McKinsey Quarterly.* Available online: http://www.mckinseyquarterly.com/Organization/Talent/A_business_case_for_women_2192.

[109]Desvaux, G., Devillard-Hoellinger, S., & Meaney, M. C. (2008, September). A Business Case for Women. *The McKinsey Quarterly.* Available online: http://www.mckinseyquarterly.com/Organization/Talent/A_business_case_for_women_2192.

[110]Metrics Tied to Pay Usher in Diversity at Trinity Health. (2008, March). Diversityinc.com. Available online: http://www.diversityinc-digital.com/diversityincmedia/200803?pg=70#pg70.

[111]At MetLife, Diversity Is About "The Way We Do Business." (2008, June/July). Diversity/Careers in Engineering and Information Technology. Available online: http://www.diversitycareers.com/articles/pro/08-junjul/dia_MetLife.html.

[112]Diversity Is the Byword at J&J. (2008, March 1). The Metropolitan Corporate Counsel. Available online: http://www.metrocorpcounsel.com/current.php?artType=view&artMonth=March&artYear=2008&EntryNo=8030.

[113]No. 1 Johnson & Johnson. (2009). Diversity Inc. Available online: http://www.diversityinc-digital.com/diversityincmedia/200905/?pg=42#pg42.

[114]Peretz, H. & Fried, Y. (2012). National Cultures, Performance Appraisal Practices, and Organizational Absenteeism and Turnover: A Study Across 21 Countries, *Journal of Applied Psychology, 97*(2), 448–459.

[115]Hofstede, G. (2001). *Culture's Consequences: Comparing Values, Beliefs, Behaviors, Institutions, and Organizations Across Nations.* Thousand Oaks, CA: Sage; Hofstede, G., & Hofstede, G. J. (2004). *Cultures and Organizations: Software of the Mind.* New York: McGraw-Hill; Hofstede, G. (1980). *Culture's Consequences: International Differences in Work-Related Values.* Newbury Park, CA: Sage.

[116]Hunt, J. M. & Weintraub, J. R. (2007). *The coaching organization: A Strategy for Developing Leaders.* Thousand Oaks, CA, US: Sage Publications, Inc.

[117]Dorfman, P., Javidan, M., Hanges, P., Dastmalchian, A., & House, R. (2012). GLOBE: A Twenty Year Journey Into the intriguing World of Culture and Leadership, Journal of World Business. Proof available online: http://dx.doi.org/10.1016/j.jwb.2012.01.004.

[118]House, R., Javidian, M., Hanges, P., & Dorfman, P. (2002, Spring). Understanding Cultures and Implicit Leadership Theories across the Globe: An Introduction to Project GLOBE. *Journal of World Business, 37,* 3–10; Javidan, M., Stahl, G. K., Brodbeck, F., & Wilderom, C. P. M. (2005, May). Cross-Border Transfer of Knowledge: Cultural Lessons from Project GLOBE. *Academy of Management Executive,* 59–76.

[119]House, R. J., & Javidan, M. (2004). Overview of GLOBE. In R. J. House, P. J. Hanges, M. Javidan, P. W. Dorfman, & V. Gupta, *Culture, Leadership, and Organizations: The GLOBE Study of 62 Societies* (pp. 9–28). Thousand Oaks, CA: SAGE, 15.

[120] Based on House, R. J., Hanges, P. J., Javidan, M., Dorfman, P. W., & Gupta, V. (2004). *Culture, Leadership, and Organizations: The GLOBE Study of 62 Societies.* London: Sage.

[121]Quappe, S., & Cantatore, G. (2007, November). What Is Cultural Awareness, Anyway? How Do I Build It? Culturosity.com. Available online: http://www.culturosity.com/articles/whatisculturalawareness.htm.

[122]Adapted from Martin, M., & Vaughn, B. (2007, Spring). Cultural Competence: The Nuts and Bolts of Diversity and Inclusion. *Strategic Diversity & Inclusion Management Magazine,* 31–38.

[123]Kassof, A. (1958). The Prejudiced Personality: A Cross-Cultural Test. *Social Problems, 6,* 59–67.

[124]Based on "Cultural Business Etiquette," U.S. Commercial Service, United States of America Department of Commerce. Available online at: http://www.buyusa.gov/iowa/etiquette.html . Accessed September 20, 2008; "United Kingdom," International Business Etiquette and Manners. Available online at: http://www.cyborlink.com/besite/united_kingdom.htm. Accessed September 30, 2008; "India," International Business Etiquette and Manners. Available online at: http://www.cyborlink.com/besite/india.htm. Accessed September 30, 2008; "Germany," International Business Etiquette and Manners. Available online at: http://

www.cyborlink.com/besite/germany.htm. Accessed September 30, 2008; "Spain," International Business Etiquette and Manners. Available online at: http://www.cyborlink.com/besite/spain.htm. Accessed September 30, 2008; "Saudia Arabia," International Business Etiquette and Manners. Available online at: http://www.cyborlink.com/besite/saudi-arabia.htm. Accessed September 30, 2008; "France," Interna.

[125]CPGjobs Featured Employer: ConAgra (2012). Available online: http://www.cpgjobs.com/559/.

[126]ConAgra Foods Recognized for Innovation in Diversity (2010). Diversity Best Practices. Available online: http://www.diversitybestpractices.com/news-articles/conagra-foods-recognized-innovation-diversity.

[127]ConAgra Foods Recognized for Innovation in Diversity (2010). Diversity Best Practices. Available online: http://www.diversitybestpractices.com/news-articles/conagra-foods-recognized-innovation-diversity.

[128]Leadership Statement on Diversity and Inclusion (2012). ConAgra Foods. Available online: http://phx.corporate-ir.net/phoenix.zhtml?c=202310&p=comm_leadership

PART 2

Individual Effectiveness

CHAPTER **3**

Individual Differences I: Demographics, Personality, and Intelligence

Southwest Airlines' business strategy execution depends on its employees providing outstanding customer service. To support its strategy, it hires empathetic, creative, fun-loving people with a positive attitude.

REAL WORLD CHALLENGE

INDIVIDUAL DIFFERENCES THAT MAKE A DIFFERENCE AT SOUTHWEST AIRLINES

Fun and friendly customer service is essential to the success of Southwest Airlines' business strategy.[1] Southwest's Vice President of People feels that fun balances the stress of hard work. Because Southwest believes that fun is about attitude, it hires for personality and attitude. CEO Herb Kelleher believes that with the exception of a few technically oriented positions, such as pilots, Southwest can train new hires on whatever they need to do, but it cannot change employees' inherent nature.[2]

Southwest Airlines' mission statement includes, "Creativity and innovation are encouraged for improving the effectiveness of Southwest Airlines."[3] To support its goals of hiring fun, creative, innovative employees, Southwest Airlines looks for leadership and a sense of humor in the people it hires. The company looks for empathetic people with other-oriented, outgoing personalities who work hard and have fun at the same time. Southwest's learning-oriented, fun culture gives employees the freedom to be themselves and become passionate about their jobs.[4]

Southwest asks for your advice about how to better hire empathetic employees with creativity and fun-loving characteristics who fit with the company's unique culture. After reading this chapter, you should have some good ideas.

© IVAN CHOLAKOV/SHUTTERSTOCK.COM

LEARNING OBJECTIVES

1 Explain why demographic characteristics should not be used to make organizational decisions.

2 Describe two different personality traits and discuss how they influence work behaviors.

3 List the "Big Five" personality traits and discuss how they are important to organizations.

4 Describe how personality can help us better understand bullying at work.

5 List and describe Gardner's seven different types of intelligence.

6 Describe emotional intelligence and discuss how it can help managers be more effective.

Are your family and friends all the same in what they do well and what they like to do? Probably not. Employees are not the same either. Effective managers appreciate the ways their employees differ, and do their best to bring out the excellence in each individual. Good managers help their employees succeed in their current role; great managers understand each of their employees' talents and create the perfect role for each person.[5] Doing this requires an understanding of the ways people differ, which is the focus of the next several chapters.

Individual differences are important to organizations because they influence outcomes ranging from job performance to turnover.[6] Just imagine how introverted, formal, soft-spoken people would feel as employees of Southwest Airlines, given the description of their culture you read about in the chapter opening *Real World Challenge*. Because it would not be a good fit for them, they would be unlikely to be successful employees.

Your personality, abilities, and work style define who you are, how you think, how you lead, and how comfortable you feel in different settings. Understanding your own constellation of talents and traits will help you to select the job and organization in which you will be happiest and most successful. It will also give you insights about which of your behaviors or reactions you need to adjust to be most effective in different situations and with different people.

Individual differences could be the topic of an entire book. We will focus our attention on some that are most important in work organizations. Specifically, in this chapter we will discuss demographic characteristics, personality, and mental abilities.

DEMOGRAPHIC CHARACTERISTICS

demographic characteristics
Physical and observable characteristics of individuals, including gender, ethnicity, and age

Demographic characteristics refer to individuals' physical and observable characteristics, including gender, ethnicity, and age. We next discuss a variety of demographic characteristics and the role they play in organizations.

Race, Nationality, and Ethnicity

The United States is diverse and its diversity is increasing.[7] Understanding the implications of racial, national origin, and ethnic diversity is important in organizations because of our tendency to favor colleagues of our own race in hiring, performance evaluations, pay raises, and promotions.[8]

In the United States, people from minority backgrounds are more likely to feel stress, threatened by stereotypes,[9] and perceive discrimination.[10] In the realm of skills assessment (like hiring assessments), they are less likely to perceive tests as being relevant, less likely to feel the situation is fair, and more likely to be concerned about performance. Although this can cause Blacks to underperform Whites on the mental ability tests commonly used in training, hiring, promotion, and other organizational outcomes, well-developed tests can predict job or training success equally well for members of both groups.

stereotype threat
Awareness of subgroup differences on standardized tests creates frustration among minority test takers and ultimately lowers test scores

Due to subgroup members' awareness of subgroup differences on standardized tests, the administration of such tests can produce a *stereotype threat* that creates frustration among minority test takers and ultimately lowers test scores.[11] Additionally, this threat lowers expectations and effort, thus producing lower scores among individuals affected by the stereotype threat. Together, these factors can lead to differences in test performance.[12] Individual differences in perceptions of stereotype threat are related to lower test-taking motivation and higher anxiety.[13] One study found that greater anxiety and lower motivation predicted African Americans' increased likelihood of withdrawing from a job selection process.[14]

Age

Four generations are currently represented in the workforce. According to date of birth, they are: seniors (1922–1943); baby boomers (1943–1963); Generation X (1964–1980); and Generation Y or the Millennial Generation (1980–2000). As each generation brings their unique experiences, values, and worldview, each also brings changes to workplace policies and procedures. For example, many seniors are staying in the workforce longer than previous generations, leading many firms to revamp their retirement policies and offer these experienced workers part-time jobs. Baby boomers' interest in wellness is changing the fitness programs and wellness benefits many employers provide. Many Generation Xers are concerned about maintaining balance in their lives, increasing many companies' interest in work-life balance programs. Generation Y members are technologically savvy, the most diverse of any generation, and are considered to be the biggest workplace influence since the baby boomers.

The U.S. workforce is aging at the same time Generation Y, the largest generation since the baby boomers, is entering the workforce. This increases the importance of understanding the role of age in organizations, and how to manage generational differences at work. Danielle Robinson, Director of Diversity, Talent, and Organizational Design for global premium drinks company Diageo, believes that Generation Y's entrance into the workplace "has added a layer of complexity to an already complex work environment."[15]

Age tends to be positively related to job performance,[16] although not all research has supported this relationship.[17] The influence of age in training environments has been extensively studied. Age was negatively associated with learning scores in an open learning program for managerial skills.[18] Older trainees demonstrated lower motivation, reduced learning, and less post-training confidence in comparison to younger trainees.[19] This suggests that age has a negative relationship with learning, and that part of its influence may be due to motivation. This could be because speed of processing slows as age increases.[20] Such speed is likely to be most important in jobs requiring high levels of intense, rapid processing of information (e.g., air-traffic controllers). It is important to note that this relationship does not hold for everyone—some older employees are likely to be good learners, and some younger employees are likely to perform poorly in training.

Increasing conscientiousness and knowledge counteract some of the negative effects of aging that result from reductions in information processing speed and motivation to learn.[21] It is likely that age is related to anxiety and other emotional variables, particularly in a complex or technologically oriented setting. Older trainees also may have concerns about their ability to rapidly process new complex information and as a result, suffer from a variation of the stereotype threat that ethnic minorities sometimes experience. Consistent with this view, older workers may not participate in learning and development activities as much as younger workers, in part due to a decline in confidence in their skills.[22] Beliefs in one's skill adequacy influence decisions to exert and maintain effort, particularly in the face of challenges. Older adults may benefit from self-paced learning environments, which may allow additional time. Additionally, confidence-boosting interventions can help to address the negative effects of anxiety and reduced confidence.

SO WHAT

You will need to work effectively with coworkers from several different generations who have different values, skills, and expectations

Some organizations are using reverse mentoring to bridge generational differences and transfer the technology skills younger workers bring to the workplace to more senior employees. *Reverse mentoring* pairs a senior employee with a junior employee, but unlike the top-down focus of traditional mentoring, the focus is on transferring the skills of the junior employee to the senior employee.[23]

Reverse mentoring was made popular by GE CEO Jack Welch, who realized that the web was going to transform business and knew that GE's younger, "webified" employees had better Internet skills and e-business knowledge than did GE's older and higher-ranking executives. He decided to pair an Internet savvy employee with one of GE's 600 worldwide executives to share their expertise about the new technology. In addition to building the e-business capabilities of his managers, this unique "mentoring up" program made managers at all levels more comfortable with each other, and transferred a lot of technology knowledge throughout GE.[24]

reverse mentoring

Pairs a senior employee with a junior employee to transfer the skills of the junior employee to the senior employee

Gender

Few, if any, differences between women and men are known that are relevant to managerial performance. No consistent differences in analytical skills, problem-solving ability, motivation, competitiveness, learning ability, or sociability have been found.[25] Given the lack of research evidence and the legal risks of gender discrimination, it is best to assume that there is no meaningful difference in managerial performance between women and men.[26]

Underlying Factors

In many cases, demographic characteristics are indicators of other underlying characteristics that are the real drivers of behavior, attitude, and other differences. For example, the effects of ethnicity and race may be due to exposure to prejudice, previous job opportunities, and cultural values. Similarly, gender effects may be due to different interests, self-beliefs when performing traditional gender-role jobs (e.g., nursing, plumbing), or differences in leadership style. Age can be an indicator of generational differences as well as differences in knowledge, work experience, and fluid or crystallized intelligence. In contrast to demographic characteristics, personality, value, attitude, interest, and lifestyle attributes are called *psychographic characteristics*.

For every demographic variable, there are many possible underlying explanatory variables.[27] Rather than using a demographic characteristic to make organizational decisions, it is best to focus on the underlying characteristic that drives any differences in behavior. Generalizing to everyone based on a demographic characteristic is often misguided, and can get a manager in legal trouble through a violation of employment discrimination laws.

SO WHAT

Instead of relying on demographic characteristics when making hiring decisions, focus on the psychographic characteristics that are the real cause of performance differences.

psychographic characteristic

Any personality, value, attitude, interest, or lifestyle attribute

PERSONALITY

Personality refers to the dynamic mental attributes and processes that determine individuals' emotional and behavioral adjustments to their environments.[28] Although personality continues to evolve throughout our lifetimes, it is also fairly consistent over time and is generally stable in the context of work. An ambitious new hire is likely to remain ambitious throughout her

personality

The dynamic mental attributes and processes that determine individuals' emotional and behavioral adjustments to their environments

career. The less flexible someone is in different situations and in interactions with a variety of people, the more permanent and stable the individual's personality. Personality can influence our choice of career and employer, as well as job satisfaction, leadership, stress, job performance, and even how long we stay with an employer.

Gordon W. Allport was the first psychologist to examine the concept of personality traits.[29] A *trait* refers to a tendency to behave consistently over time and in a variety of situations. Personality traits are associated with differences in motivational states, self-set goals, assessments and interpretations of situations, and reactions to these interpretations, including anxiety.[30] We next discuss several personality traits important to organizations.

trait

A tendency to behave consistently over time and in a variety of situations

Achievement Motivation

Two of the most important traits for work organizations are high achievement orientation and low fear of failure. Alex Haley, author of the book *Roots*, endured rejection for seven years while trying to publish his first book. During this time he regularly submitted manuscripts, viewed rejection as a learning opportunity, and persisted in his belief that through his hard work and tenacity he would succeed as an author. This illustrates the personality trait of *achievement motivation*.

Achievement motivation reflects strong desires to accomplish something meaningful, and take pleasure in succeeding at something important and demanding.[31] People high in achievement motivation are willing to dedicate significant effort to achieve ambitious goals and tasks, often for long periods. People lower in achievement motivation are more focused on the consequences of failure and fixate on the disappointment, shame, and embarrassment that may follow if they attempt something and fail.

achievement motivation

Strong desires to accomplish something important, and take pleasure in succeeding at something important and demanding

Fear of Failure

Fear of failure is an anticipatory feeling of anxiety about attempting a challenging task, failing, and appearing incompetent.[32] Wanting to reduce this anxiety lowers our interest in pursuing achievement-related goals or increases our intent to quit challenging tasks quickly if success is not immediate. This anxiety can actually become a self-fulfilling prophecy—being afraid of failing can increase the chances that we will fail by interfering with our performance. Obviously this trait can be devastating to organizations. Employees with a fear of failure may try to disperse responsibility to others or choose to pursue lower goals or easier tasks.

The strength of our achievement motivation relative to the strength of our fear of failure determines how we react to achievement-oriented situations. Managers whose achievement motivation is greater than their need to avoid failure tend to be promoted more rapidly. Most people have a clearly dominant need or tendency to favor one of the two attributes.[33] For approximately 10 percent of people, neither achievement motivation nor fear of failure is dominant because both traits are strong, both are weak, or both are of moderate strength.[34] If both traits are strong or moderate, intense approach-avoidance conflicts are likely to result. If both traits are weak, the person is likely to simply be indifferent to achievement-oriented situations.[35]

Traits describe *what* people do, but not *why* they do it.[36] We behave in ways consistent with our traits because of our needs and motives. For example, people with the trait of high achievement motivation may have a strong need (or motive) to improve how things are done, while those with a fear of failure

fear of failure

An anticipatory feeling of anxiety about attempting a challenging task, failing, and appearing incompetent

SO WHAT

Fearing failure can reduce job performance.

may have a need to protect themselves from the disappointment of failure. Effective managers focus on the underlying reasons for behavior when trying to coach subordinates. By giving feedback about employees' strengths and giving them the resources and training necessary for success, managers can increase their perception that they can succeed. When people believe they have what it takes to succeed, they tend to exert more effort and avoid focusing on their doubts and the challenges that arise.

Tolerance for Ambiguity

tolerance for ambiguity
Propensity to view ambiguous situations as either threatening or desirable

Tolerance for ambiguity reflects the tendency to view ambiguous situations as either threatening or desirable.[37] Intolerance for ambiguity reflects a tendency to perceive or interpret information marked by vague, incomplete, fragmented, multiple, inconsistent, or contradictory meanings as an actual or potential source of psychological discomfort or threat.[38] Being tolerant of ambiguity is related to creativity, positive attitudes toward risk, and orientation to diversity.[39] Managers with a low tolerance for ambiguity tend to be more directive with their staff and do not empower them to make their own decisions at work. The best managerial strategy is to place individuals with a low tolerance for ambiguity in well-defined and regulated tasks.

Although some ambiguity is unavoidable at work, Table 3-1 gives you some tips for reducing ambiguity for your own subordinates.

Table 3-1

Reducing Ambiguity for Your Employees[40]

Although some ambiguity at work cannot be avoided, ambiguity due to indecisive leaders or unclear managerial instructions can be frustrating for employees and can compromise an organization's performance. Although micromanaging is not the answer, one of the important roles of a manager is to provide clear direction to employees and ensure that their work stays on task. This table highlights some strategies you can use to reduce unnecessary ambiguity among your own staff.

- Take the time to plan projects and give employees clear goals and objectives. All employees should understand their short- and long-term goals, even if you leave the details of their execution up to them. Feeling as though they are on a team working toward a shared goal can also decrease feelings of ambiguity.

- Recognize that there is usually more than one way to accomplish a task and be open to employees' suggestions and ideas. It is more difficult for employees to try to guess what you want and try to do a task your way than it is to give a task their best effort and do the work you hired them to do.

- Be available and encourage follow-up questions if employees need clarification on goals or instructions.

- Be willing to make decisions and take action. As a manager, this is your job and sometimes it is necessary to take action without being absolutely certain of the accuracy of your choice.

- Coach employees with a lower tolerance for ambiguity to be more confident and comfortable making decisions. Give employees the opportunity to practice analyzing problems and making decisions on smaller tasks to build their confidence and skills.

- Train employees to deal quickly with ambiguity in ways consistent with company policy and the organization's values. Take time at meetings to pose scenarios to your staff and ask them how they would handle them. This will help them to act decisively and correctly when similar situations happen on the job.

- Establish metrics around key goals to help employees get the feedback they need to know how they are doing and where adjustments may be needed. People with a lower tolerance for ambiguity often require more frequent and more detailed feedback to feel comfortable.

- Recognize that people from different cultures can have different tolerances for ambiguity. Some people will need more detailed instructions than will others to feel comfortable completing assignments.

- Identify the importance for ambiguity tolerance in different jobs and include this as an evaluation criterion when staffing. If a job requires a high tolerance for ambiguity, someone with a low ambiguity tolerance is not likely to be a high performer even if they are good at the technical requirements of the job.

It might seem like personality traits, including tolerance for ambiguity, would be difficult for employers to assess in job applicants. In fact, assessment methods such as interviews can be quite effective at assessing many personality traits. Table 3-2 provides some sample interview questions that assess tolerance for ambiguity.

Locus of Control

Locus of control reflects the degree to which a person generally perceives events to be under his or her control (internal locus) or under the control of others (external locus).[41] An external locus of control is related to passivity and learned helplessness,[42] while an internal locus is related to confidence in one's ability to successfully perform tasks.[43] An internal locus of control is positively related to both job satisfaction and job performance.[44] Locus of control is also an important determinant of training and coaching outcomes. Trainees with a greater internal locus of control have more positive attitudes toward learning because they believe that it is more likely to be useful and beneficial.[45]

locus of control

The degree to which a person generally perceives events to be under his or her control (internal locus) or under the control of others (external locus)

Table 3-2

Assessing Ambiguity Tolerance in an Interview

The following are examples of questions that could be used in an interview to assess a job candidate's tolerance for ambiguity.

1. Tell me about a time at work when the line of control was confusing. What did you do?
2. Describe a time when the expectations for a project were unclear. What did you do?
3. Tell me about a time when you had conflicting goals given to you at work. How did you stay effective?
4. Describe a time when you were in a workgroup and it wasn't clear what you were supposed to do. How did you handle the situation?

Table 3-3

Effects of Locus of Control on Organizational Outcomes

Organizational Outcome	Internal versus External Locus of Control
Job satisfaction	Internals are generally more satisfied with their job, pay, supervisor, and coworkers.
Commitment	Internals are more committed and have lower absenteeism.
Job motivation	Internals have greater task motivation, job involvement, and self-confidence than do externals.
Job performance	Internals tend to have higher job performance than externals.
Career success	Internals tend to earn a higher salary than do externals.
Conflict and stress	Internals report lower role conflict, work-family conflict, burnout, and stress than do externals.
Social integration	Internals tend to be more socially integrated at work and report more favorable relationships with their supervisors.

Source: See Ng, T.W.H., Sorensen, K.L., & Eby, L.T. (2006). Locus of Control at Work: A Meta-Analysis, *Journal of Organizational Behavior*, 27, 1057–1087.

Locus of control is also related to ethical behavior.[46] People with an internal locus of control are more likely to see the connection between their own behavior and its outcomes. They are thus more likely to take responsibility for their ethical behavior and act according to their own judgment of what is right.[47] An internal locus of control has been found to reduce the effects of work conflict on psychological strain due to the use of a problem-solving conflict management strategy.[48] An internal locus of control is also related to stronger feelings of being embedded in the organization as a result of more proactive networking.[49] Table 3-3 summarizes current research findings on the different reactions internals and externals have to various organizational factors.

This chapter's *Understand Yourself* feature gives you the opportunity to evaluate your locus of control when it comes to work.

Type A personality

Impatient, competitive, ambitious, and uptight; experiences a frustrated sense of wasting time when not actively engaged in productive activity

Type B personality

Relaxed and easygoing; less overly competitive than Type A

Personality Type A and Personality Type B

In 1973, two cardiologists identified two different personality profiles they called Type A and Type B. The *Type A personality* is impatient, competitive, ambitious, and uptight. The *Type B personality* is more relaxed and easygoing and less overly competitive than Type A. Type Bs are not without stress, but they confront challenges and external threats less frantically. Unlike Type As, Type Bs rarely experience a frustrated sense of wasting time when not actively engaged in productive activity.[51] Although Type As often have higher job performance than Type Bs,[52] Type As are also more prone to stress and coronary heart disease.

Although the idea that a cause-and-effect relationship exists between Type A behavior and coronary artery disease is controversial, some effects of Type A stress are definitely known. Stress causes

© STOCKLITE/SHUTTERSTOCK.COM

People with Type B personalities are more relaxed and easygoing than are people with more competitive Type A personalities. Which personality type do you think this person is likely to possess?

UNDERSTAND YOURSELF

WORK LOCUS OF CONTROL

Using the scale below, write a number from 1 to 7 that reflects your agreement or disagreement with the statements below. When you are finished, follow the scoring instructions at the bottom to interpret your score.

strongly disagree	disagree	slightly disagree	neutral	slightly agree	agree	
1	2	3	4	5	6	7

___ 1. A job is what you make of it.

___ 2. On most jobs, people can pretty much accomplish whatever they set out to accomplish.

___ 3. If you know what you want out of a job, you can find a job that gives it to you.

___ 4. If employees are unhappy with a decision made by their boss, they should do something about it.

___5. Getting the job you want is mostly a matter of luck.

___6. Making money is primarily a matter of good fortune.

___7. Most people are capable of doing their jobs well if they make the effort.

___8. In order to get a really good job, you need to have family members or friends in high places.

___9. Promotions are usually a matter of good fortune.

___10. When it comes to landing a really good job, who you know is more important than what you know.

___11. Promotions are given to employees who perform well on the job.

___12. To make a lot of money you have to know the right people.

___13. It takes a lot of luck to be an outstanding employee on most jobs.

___14. People who perform their jobs well generally get rewarded for it.

___15. Most employees have more influence on their supervisors than they think they do.

___16. The main difference between people who make a lot of money and people who make a little money is luck.

Scoring: First recalculate your responses to items 1, 2, 3, 4, 7, 11, 14, and 15 by subtracting the number you wrote from 7 (6 = 1; 5 = 2; 4 = 3; 3 = 4; 2 = 5; 1 = 6). Cross out the number you initially wrote and replace it with the recoded value—only the new values will be used in scoring. Now add up your scores to all sixteen items to get your work locus of control score.

Interpretation: Higher scores reflect a more external locus of control. Managers tend to have a more internal locus of control.[50]

Source: Copyright Paul E. Spector, All rights reserved, 1988.

an increase in blood pressure; if the stress is constant, the heart and arteries begin to show signs of damage. It has been estimated that 14 to 18 percent of sudden heart attacks occur immediately after an emotional stress and are more likely to occur when a person is angry.[53]

Understanding the personality type of your coworkers and boss can help you to better understand and manage this potential source of work conflicts. Recognizing your personality type can help you to identify work situations that are good fits for you. High Type As need greater stimulation than Type Bs and are more likely to overschedule themselves. In managers, having a high Type A personality and an external locus of control is associated with greater levels of perceived stress, lower job satisfaction, and poorer physical and mental health compared to those with a Type B personality and an internal locus of control. Some researchers have even suggested that negative health consequences may outweigh the superficial attractiveness of the Type A personality in a managerial position.[54]

Researchers also have identified a lack of time as the prevalent attitude that reduces pro-social behavior, or acts of kindness that benefit others, including sharing, cooperating, and helping.[55] Because people in a hurry (like high Type As) will not help others, high Type A personalities may show less ethical and helpful behavior even in an ethical organizational culture than do Type Bs.

SO WHAT

Although having a Type A personality can be good for job performance, if it is not managed properly, the Type A personality can contribute to poor health.

The "Big Five"

Over the years, as many as 1,700 adjectives have been used to describe various aspects of personality.[56] Accordingly, efforts have been made to create more simplified groupings of traits that capture most of these characteristics. The *Big Five* is one of the more established personality frameworks. The five personality dimensions are:[57]

Big Five

A personality framework consisting of extroversion, emotional stability, agreeableness, conscientiousness, and openness to experience

1. *Extraversion*: being sociable, assertive, talkative, and energetic. The opposite trait is *introversion*.
2. *Emotional stability*: associated with not being anxious, depressed, angry, and insecure. The opposite trait is *neuroticism*.
3. *Agreeableness*: being polite, flexible, trusting, cooperative, forgiving, and tolerant. The opposite trait is *disagreeableness*.
4. *Conscientiousness*: associated with being careful, thorough, responsible, organized, and prone to planning as well as being hardworking, achievement-oriented, and persistent. The opposite trait is *lazy*.
5. *Openness to experience*: being imaginative, cultured, curious, broad-minded, and artistically sensitive. The opposite trait is *closed-mindedness*.

So what do these Big Five traits mean to organizations? Of the five, emotional stability and conscientiousness tend to have the strongest and most consistently positive relationship with performance motivation.[58] Conscientiousness is known to be positively associated with a variety of work outcomes, including training performance. Highly conscientious individuals also have greater confidence in their abilities.[59] However, some aspects of conscientiousness, including dependability, order, and dutifulness, can reduce performance when adaptability to changing task conditions is important.[60] Lower emotional stability may result in reductions in attention and reduced motivation, in part through reductions in self-confidence.

More open individuals are, by definition, more receptive to experiencing and learning new things. As a result, they are more likely to maintain their focus on learning and on sustaining motivation when learning becomes challenging.[61] Evidence suggests that openness to experience is a good predictor of training success, while the evidence for conscientiousness appears to be mixed.[62] Openness is also related to success in expatriate assignments.[63]

Extraversion is positively related to training outcomes,[64] possibly because extroverted individuals are more energetic, assertive, and sociable. Extroverted individuals may also be better able to maintain an outward focus, enabling learning. Other than web-based or computer programs, many training programs include some component of interpersonal interaction. To the degree that training and learning require social interaction, extraversion is likely to facilitate and enhance such interactions, reducing anxiety and increasing motivation to learn.[65]

Murray Barrick and Mick Mount reviewed 117 studies with 23,994 participants and found that conscientiousness was consistently positively related to all performance criteria for all occupational groups. Extraversion was a good predictor of performance for occupations involving social interaction (e.g. management and sales). Extraversion and openness to experience were good predictors of training proficiency criteria.[66] Agreeableness has also been found to predict job[67] and training performance.[68] Emotional stability, extraversion, conscientiousness, and agreeableness are all positively related to job satisfaction.[69] Emotionally stable, agreeable, and conscientious people tend to set higher goals, and emotionally stable extroverts tend to have higher self-confidence.[70]

Theories of personality generally assume stability in traits such as conscientiousness, but emerging evidence suggests that age is related to changes in personality. In particular, agreeableness and conscientiousness seem to show increases with age whereas extraversion, neuroticism, and openness show declines.[71]

It is important to remember that the Big Five traits do not explain all of human personality. Traits including honesty, conservativeness, sense of humor, and manipulativeness are not captured by these five traits. The factors are also not completely independent. For example, emotional stability is often positively related to extraversion—people who are not anxious or insecure tend to be more outgoing. The most significant contribution of the Big Five model is the establishment of a taxonomy that helps to organize a previously scattered and disorganized group of personality traits.

Machiavellianism

Machiavellianism is defined as an individual's general strategy for dealing with other people and the degree to which they feel they can manipulate others in interpersonal situations.[72] With its roots in Machiavelli's publication of *The Prince* in 1532, a Machiavellian personality has been defined as someone who "employs aggressive, manipulative, exploiting, and devious moves to achieve personal or organizational objectives."[73]

The Machiavellian individual manipulates others for his or her own purpose—the needs, feelings, or rights of others are secondary.[74] The characteristics of a Machiavellian include deceit, manipulation (although not obvious), suspicion of others, and emotional detachment. Machiavellians also tend to be impersonal, opportunistic, ambitious, impatient, and appear unresponsive to personal or ethical concerns of others.[75] No difference in intelligence has been found between high and low Machiavellian individuals.[76]

Since Machiavellian characteristics exist in most individuals in differing degrees, managers need to learn about this characteristic. Two important reasons for understanding Machiavellianism are the issues of loyalty and ethics. Loyalty refers to a person's commitment to another person, task, or organization. Self-interest is the most powerful force affecting loyalty and ethics. Machiavellian employees are less likely to be loyal to their job or organization. Highly Machiavellian people are also less ethically sensitive than are lower Machiavellian people, and they agree less with ethical policies and rules of behavior. Highly Machiavellian managers tend to perceive ethical problems as less serious and are less likely to take action in the face of ethical breaches.[77] The positive effects of ethical leader behavior on employee engagement are also reduced when the leader is more highly Machiavellian.[78]

Because Machiavellian managers are reluctant to punish unethical behavior, enforcing an ethical code of conduct is essential. Organizations must make it in the best interest of Machiavellians to behave ethically—severe punishments for unethical behavior and significant rewards for ethical behavior are what Machiavellians respond to the most.[79] Machiavellian employees have also been found to prefer transactional relationships with their employers that increase the likelihood of deviant behaviors.[80] An opportunity to assess your own Machiavellianism is presented in Table 3-4.

The results of research on Machiavellianism have found that:

1. Men are generally more Machiavellian than women.
2. Older adults tend to have lower Mach scores than younger adults.
3. There is no significant difference between high Machiavellians and low Machiavellians on measures of intelligence or ability.

Machiavellianism

An individual's general strategy for dealing with other people and the degree to which they feel they can manipulate others in interpersonal situations

Table 3-4

How Machiavellian Are You?

To assess your Machiavellianism, please respond honestly to the nine statements using the scale below.

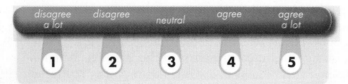

disagree a lot	disagree	neutral	agree	agree a lot
1	2	3	4	5

___1. The best way to handle people is to tell them what they want to hear.

___2. When you ask someone to do something for you, it is best to give the real reason for wanting it rather than giving reasons that might give more weight.

___3. Anyone who completely trusts anyone else is asking for trouble.

___4. It is hard to get ahead without cutting corners here and there.

___5. It is safest to assume that all people have a vicious streak, and it will come out when they are given a chance.

___6. One should take action only when it is morally right.

___7. Most people are basically good and kind.

___8. There is no excuse for lying to someone else.

___9. Generally speaking, people won't work hard unless they're forced to do so.

Scoring: For questions 2, 6, 7, and 8, subtract your score from 6 and replace your original score with this new score. Then add these scores to your scores for the other five questions to calculate your Machiavellianism score.

Interpretation: The higher your score, the more Machiavellian you tend to be. The average adult score is 23.[81]

If your score is *below 18,* you rarely use manipulation as a tool.

If your score is *between 19 and 28,* you sometimes use manipulation as a tool.

If your score is *between 29 and 35,* you often use manipulation as a tool.

If your score is *over 36,* you almost always use manipulation as a tool.

Machiavellian principles are manipulative, deceiving, dishonest, and favor political usefulness over morality. These are undesirable and unethical tactics that are not recommended for managers or anyone else. People often recognize and resent manipulative tactics, which can derail your career.

Source: This article was published in Studies in Machiavellianism, Christie, Richard, Geis, Florence L., page 17. Academic Press. © Elsevier, 1970.

4. Machiavellianism is not significantly related to demographic characteristics such as educational level or marital status.

5. High Machiavellians tend to be in professions that emphasize the control and manipulation of individuals—for example, lawyers, psychiatrists, and behavioral scientists.[82]

An understanding of this type of aggressive personality and leadership style can help you to be more effective in your job. If you can recognize high Machiavellian characteristics in coworkers or supervisors, you can take action to prevent damage to yourself or to your organization.

SO WHAT

Highly Machiavellian personalities should be identified during the hiring process and selected out.

The Bullying Personality

workplace bullying

A repeated mistreatment of another employee through verbal abuse; conduct that is threatening, humiliating, or intimidating; or sabotage that interferes with the other person's work

Workplace bullying is a repeated mistreatment of another employee through verbal abuse; conduct that is threatening, humiliating, or intimidating; or sabotage that interferes with the other person's work.[83] Popular media such as *Time, Management Today,* and *Psychology Today* have all featured stories on the pervasiveness of bullying. Bullying costs employers through higher turnover, greater absenteeism, higher workers' compensation costs, and higher disability insurance rates, not to mention a diminished reputation as a desirable place to work.[84]

Fifty percent of the U.S. workforce reports either being bullied at work (35 percent) or witnessing bullying (15 percent). It is four times more common than harassment. Eighty-one percent of bullying behavior is done by supervisors.[85] Forty-five percent of targets report stress-related health problems, and targeted individuals suffer debilitating anxiety, panic attacks, clinical depression, and even post-traumatic stress. Once targeted, employees have a 64 percent chance of losing their job for no reason. Despite this, 40 percent of targets never report it. Only 3 percent sue and 4 percent complain to state or federal agencies.[86]

Who tends to become a bully? Bullying is complex and comes in a variety of forms, but common to all types is the abuse of authority and power, stemming from the bully's need to control another person. Machiavellianism may lead to bullying. High Machiavellians exhibit a resistance to social influence, an orientation to cognitions (rational thoughts) rather than emotions, and initiating and controlling structure (components of bossiness). High Machiavellians manipulate and exploit others to advance their personal agendas, which is the foundation of bullying.[87]

If personality helps to explain why some people are bullies, can it also help us understand why some people are more likely to be targets of bullying? Although there is no clear personality profile that predicts who will be targeted, people who are more introverted, less agreeable, less conscientious, less open to experience, and more emotionally unstable seem to be more likely to be bullied.[88] This chapter's *Improve Your Skills* feature describes ways managers can be bullies (or just toxic), and describes various survival tactics (that we hope you'll never have to use!).

SO WHAT
Although costly to many organizations, bullying is often ineffectively managed.

Where Does Personality Come From?

Personality is shaped by both genetic and environmental factors.[89] To some extent we are born who we are—people have different temperaments from birth. But our life experiences, culture, and environment also shape our personalities. In fact, one of the most important environmental influences on personality is culture.[90] Culture provides the context in which personality develops and acquires meaning.

"Over the past decade I have come to expect that all basic features of trait psychology are universal, and that personality traits are a characteristic of the human species." —*Robert R. McCrae, Noted Personality Scholar*

© PRODAKSZYN/SHUTTERSTOCK.COM

Workplace bullying may be more common than you think. Fifty percent of the U.S. workforce reports either being bullied at work or witnessing bullying. Most, but not all, workplace bullying is done by supervisors.

Because personality is a product of both heredity and environment, and because we know that culture can influence personality, an important question is whether personality traits are the same worldwide or unique to each culture. Much of what we know about personality is the result of research done in the United States. Does this knowledge generalize globally, or does personality vary by culture as dramatically as language and food do? Research in this area has focused on the Big Five personality traits, and has supported the universality of the Big Five worldwide.[91] After initially expecting to find personality differences across cultures, noted personality scholar Robert R. McCrae found no evidence of cultural differences in the Big Five. He states, "Over the past decade I have come to expect that all basic features of trait psychology are universal, and that personality traits are a characteristic of the human species."[92]

Myers-Briggs Type Indicator

Myers-Briggs Type Indicator
A personality inventory based on Carl Jung's work on psychological types

The 126-item *Myers-Briggs Type Indicator*[93] (MBTI) is an extremely popular personality inventory. More than 2 million people worldwide take the self-assessment inventory every year.[94] It is based upon Carl Jung's work on

IMPROVE YOUR SKILLS

CHALLENGING MANAGERIAL BEHAVIORS AND HOW TO RESPOND

Varieties	Primary Traits	Objective	Subordinate Survival Tactics	Superior's Actions
Grandiose: Psychodynamic	Outward grandiose self-image; exploits others; devalues others; enraged if self-esteem threatened; limited conscience and capacity for empathy; desperately protects underlying fragile self-esteem	Be admired	Show admiration; avoid criticizing them; consult with mentor or executive coach	Close oversight of managers is needed to continually assess their treatment of others
Grandiose: Learned	Grandiose self-image; exploits others out of carelessness; is inconsiderate in treatment of others due to not receiving negative feedback for behavior	Be admired	Show admiration; avoid criticizing them; consult with mentor or executive coach	Do not automatically believe superiors over subordinates
Control Freak	Micromanages; seeks absolute control of everything; inflated self-image and devaluation of others' abilities; fears chaos	Control others	Avoid direct suggestions; let them think new ideas are their own; don't criticize them; show admiration and respect; don't outshine them; play down your accomplishments and ambition; document your work; build relationship with a mentor; look for other positions	360-degree feedback; place them where they cannot do serious harm; consider getting rid of them; don't ignore signs of trouble
Antisocial	Takes what he or she wants; lies to get ahead and hurts others if they are in his or her way; lacks both a conscience and capacity for empathy	Excitement of violating rules and abusing others	Avoid provoking them; transfer out before they destroy you; do not get dragged into their unethical or illegal activities; seek allies in coworkers and mentors; seek executive coach to help you cope	Consider possible presence of depression, anxiety, alcohol

Source: From Lubit, R. (2004). The Tyranny of Toxic Managers: Applying Emotional Intelligence to Deal with Difficult Personalities. *Ivey Business Journal*, March/April, p. 4.

psychological types. Psychologist Carl Jung was a contemporary of Sigmund Freud and a leading exponent of Gestalt personality theory. The MBTI was first developed by Isabel Briggs Myers (1897–1979) and her mother, Katharine Cook Briggs, to help people understand themselves and each other so that they could find work that matches their personality. They put Jung's concepts into everyday language. Isabel Myers's 1980 book *Gifts Differing*, and her philosophy of celebrating individual differences, encouraged the workplace diversity movement.

The MBTI uses four scales with opposite poles to assess four sets of preferences. The four scales are:[95]

1. *Extroversion (E)/Introversion (I)*: Extroverts are energized by things and people. They are interactors and "on the fly" thinkers whose motto is, "ready, fire, aim." Introverts find energy in ideas, concepts, and abstractions. They can be social, but also need quiet time to recharge their batteries. They are reflective thinkers whose motto is, "ready, aim, aim." Do you like to focus on the outer world (extroversion) or on your own inner world (introversion)?

2. *Sensing (S)/Intuition (N)*: Sensing people are detail oriented. They want and trust facts. Intuitive people seek out patterns and relationships among the facts they have learned. They trust their intuition and look for the "big picture." Do you prefer to focus on the information you take in (sensing) or do you like to interpret and add meaning (intuition)?

3. *Thinking (T)/Feeling (F)*: Thinkers value fairness, and decide things impersonally based on objective criteria and logic. Feelers value harmony, and focus on human values and needs as they make decisions or judgments. When you make decisions, do you like to first look at logic and consistency (thinking) or at the people and special circumstances involved (feeling)?

4. *Judging (J)/Perceiving (P)*: Judging people are decisive and tend to plan. They focus on completing tasks, take action quickly, and want to know the essentials. They develop plans and follow them, adhering to deadlines. Perceptive people are adaptable, spontaneous, and curious. They start many tasks, and often find it difficult to complete them. Deadlines are meant to be stretched. In dealing with the world, do you like to get things decided quickly (judging) or do you prefer to stay open to new information and options (perceiving)?

The possible combinations of these preferences result in sixteen personality types, which are identified by the four letters that represent one's tendencies on the four scales. For example, ENTJ reflects extraversion, intuition, thinking, and judging. You can complete a brief Myers-Briggs type self-assessment online at http://www.humanmetrics.com/cgi-win/JTypes2.asp.

Although the Myers-Briggs instrument was not developed or intended to be used to identify personality profiles and label people, too often this is what is done with the results. This is problematic as it can lead to discrimination and poor career counseling. Employers should not hire, fire, or assign employees by personality type, because the MBTI is not even reliable at identifying a person's type. When retested, even after intervals as short as five weeks, as many as 50 percent of people are classified into a different type. There is little support for the claim that the MBTI can justify job discrimination or be a reliable aid to someone seeking career guidance.[96]

Jung never intended for his work to be applied to a personality inventory. He noted, "My scheme of typology is only a scheme of orientation. There is such a factor as introversion, there is such a factor as extraversion. The classification of individuals means nothing, nothing at all. It is only the instrumentarium for the practical psychologist to explain, for instance, the husband to a wife or vice versa."[97] Nonetheless, the MBTI has become so popular that it is likely that you will encounter it during your career.[98] It can be a fun team-building tool for illustrating some of the ways that people differ, but it should not be used in making organizational decisions including hiring and promotions.

SO WHAT

The Myers-Briggs instrument can be useful for teambuilding, but should not be used in making organizational decisions

Role of the Situation

The relationship between personality and behavior changes, depending on the strength of the situation we are in. We might be extroverted in nature but, in a situation like a lecture or an important meeting, suppress our tendencies and behave in a more quiet and reserved way. When situational pressures are weak, we are better able to be ourselves and let our personalities guide our behaviors. Strong organizational cultures might decrease the influence of personality on employee behaviors by creating clear guidelines for employee behavior. Weaker organizational cultures might allow greater individual employee expression, resulting in a wider variety of employee behaviors.

GLOBAL ISSUES

HOW OTHERS SEE AMERICANS

Characteristics Most Commonly Associated with Americans

France	Japan	Western Germany	Great Britain	Brazil	Mexico
Industrious	Nationalistic	Energetic	Friendly	Intelligent	Industrious
Energetic	Friendly	Inventive	Self-indulgent	Inventive	Intelligent
Inventive	Decisive	Friendly	Energetic	Energetic	Inventive
Decisive	Rude	Sophisticated	Industrious	Industrious	Decisive
Friendly	Self-indulgent	Intelligent	Nationalistic	Nationalistic	Greedy

Characteristics Least Commonly Associated with Americans

France	Japan	Western Germany	Great Britain	Brazil	Mexico
Lazy	Industrious	Lazy	Lazy	Lazy	Lazy
Rude	Lazy	Sexy	Sophisticated	Self-indulgent	Honest
Honest	Honest	Greedy	Sexy	Sexy	Rude
Sophisticated	Sexy	Rude	Decisive	Sophisticated	Sexy

Source: Adler, N.J. (2008). International Dimensions of Organizational Behavior. Mason, OH: Thompson/South-Western, p. 82, Table 3-1.

You now have a good understanding of some of the ways we all differ. It is also interesting to think about how frequently there are differences in how people from other cultures perceive us. Asking foreigners to describe people from your country is a powerful way to understand how others perceive you. This chapter's *Global Issues* feature is from a *Newsweek* survey reporting the characteristics foreigners most and least often associate with Americans. It may give you some insight into how an American might be perceived differently in different parts of the world.

INTELLIGENCE

There are many types of intelligence, or mental abilities, including general mental ability, information processing capacity, verbal ability, and emotional intelligence. We next discuss some of the types of intelligence most relevant to organizations.

General Mental Ability

General mental ability is the capacity to rapidly and fluidly acquire, process, and apply information. It involves reasoning, remembering, understanding, and problem solving. It is associated with the increased ability to acquire, process, and synthesize information and has been defined simply as the ability to learn.[99] The strong association between measures of general mental ability and performance in a wide variety of task domains is one of the most consistent findings in the field of organizational behavior.[100] Research has supported the idea that mental ability is most important in complex jobs, when individuals are new to the job, and when there are changes in the workplace that require workers to learn new ways of performing their jobs.[101] Some companies, including the Internet search firm Google, prefer to hire for general mental ability rather than experience.[102]

general mental ability
The capacity to rapidly and fluidly acquire, process, and apply information

Information processing capacity involves the manner in which individuals process and organize information. Information processing capacity also helps explain differences between experts and novices on task learning and performance, as experts process and organize information more efficiently and accurately than novices.[103] General mental ability influences information processing capacity.[104] Age also explains differences in information processing capacity. Relative to younger adults, older adults tend to have access to a wider amount and variety of information, although they are less able to process novel information quickly.[105]

information processing capacity
The manner in which individuals process and organize information

Mental ability tests typically use computerized or paper-and-pencil test formats to assess general mental abilities, including verbal or mathematical reasoning, logic, and perceptual abilities. Because scores on these tests can predict a person's ability to learn in training or on the job,[106] be adaptable and solve problems, and tolerate routine, their predictive value may increase given the trend toward jobs requiring innovation, continual training, and nonroutine problem solving. There are many different types of mental ability tests, including the Wonderlic Personnel Test, Raven's Progressive Matrices, the Kaufman Brief Intelligence Test, and the Wechsler Abbreviated Scale of Intelligence. Table 3-5 contains some questions like those found on the Wonderlic Personnel Test.

mental ability tests
Assess general mental abilities including verbal and mathematical reasoning, logic, and perceptual abilities

Despite being easy to use and one of the most valid selection methods for all jobs, mental ability tests produce racial differences that are three to five times larger than other methods, such as structured interviews, that are also valid predictors of job performance.[108] Although the reasons for the different results are not fully understood, it is thought that factors including culture, differential access to test coaching and test preparation programs, and different

Table 3-5

Mental Ability Test Items[107]

The following questions are similar to those found on the Wonderlic Personnel Test measuring mental ability. The answers are at the bottom of the table.

1. Assume the first two statements are true. Is the final one (1) true (2) false or (3) not certain?
   - The girl plays soccer.
   - All soccer players wear cleats.
   - The girl wears cleats.
2. Paper sells for $0.36 per pad. What will three pads cost?
3. How many of the five pairs of items listed below are exact duplicates?

Pullman, K. M.	Puilman, K. M.
Jeffrey, C. K.	Jeffrey, C. K.
Schoeft, J. P.	Shoeft, J. P.
Lima, L. R.	Lima, L. R.
Woerner, K. E.	Woerner, K. C.

4. PRESENT PRESERVE—Do these words
   1. Have similar meanings?
   2. Have contradictory meanings?
   3. Mean neither the same nor the opposite?

Answers: (1) true; (2) $1.08; (3) 1; (4) 2.

test motivation levels could be important factors.[109] Job applicants also often dislike mental ability tests because they do not seem to be job related.[110]

Because hiring discrimination can be legally problematic when using mental ability tests,[111] it is best to evaluate the effect of mental ability tests on protected groups before using them on job candidates. Because mental ability tests can be combined with other predictors to reduce adverse impact and increase prediction accuracy, and because alternative predictors with less adverse impact can be used to predict job success comparably to mental ability tests used alone, generally mental ability tests should not be used alone.[112] Many organizations use mental ability tests, including the National Football League.[113]

Multiple Intelligences

Intelligence tests often involve a range of abstract questions designed to assess your language, spatial awareness, and numerical ability. However, to think that your score on a single test reflects your actual intelligence ignores your many other mental abilities. A lower score on a particular intelligence test result simply means you are less skilled at whatever type of intelligence that particular test measures—while reflecting nothing about your level of any other type of intelligence.

Increasingly, researchers and scholars are realizing that there is more than one way to be smart.[114] Gardner's ***theory of multiple intelligences*** suggests that there are a number of distinct forms of intelligence that each individual possesses in varying degrees:[115]

theory of multiple intelligences
There are a number of distinct forms of intelligence that each individual possesses in varying degrees

1. *Linguistic:* words and language
2. *Logical-mathematical:* logic and numbers
3. *Musical:* music, rhythm, and sound
4. *Bodily-kinesthetic:* body movement and control

5. *Spatial-visual:* images and space
6. *Interpersonal:* other people's feelings
7. *Intrapersonal:* self-awareness

The different intelligences represent not only different content domains but also learning preferences. The theory suggests that assessment of abilities should measure all forms of intelligence, not just linguistic and logical-mathematical, as is commonly done (e.g., in college admissions tests like the ACT, SAT, GMAT, and GRE).[116]

According to Gardner, learning and teaching should focus on the particular intelligences of each person. For example, if you have strong spatial or linguistic intelligences, you should be encouraged to develop these abilities.[117] This relates to the strengths-based development described in this chapter's *Case Study* feature.

Gardner also emphasizes the cultural context of multiple intelligences. He observed that the needs of different cultures lead them to emphasize different types of intelligence. For example, the high spatial abilities of the Puluwat people of the Caroline Islands enable them to navigate their ocean canoes, and a balance of personal intelligences is required in Japanese society.[119]

SO WHAT

Few people are good at everything. Try to maximize the fit between employees' strengths and the requirements of their jobs.

CASE STUDY

Strengths-Based Development

When drought threatened the survival of Ohio farming co-op Auglaize Provico, CEO Larry Hammond realized that he would have to change the business model. Grain elevators were sold, headcount was carefully reduced 25 percent, and the co-op took on work outside of its previous core business. Hammond even cut his own pay.

Hammond then implemented strengths-based development to leverage the unique strengths and talents of each employee. The strengths approach recognizes that everyone has different talents and natural patterns of thought, feeling, and behavior. Recognizing and building on those talents with pertinent skills and knowledge creates strengths. People who are applying a true strength tend to perform well. Hammond hoped that encouraging employees to leverage their innate talents would enable them to drive the business forward.

Auglaize's management had previously used a "deficit" development approach, spending a lot of time identifying employees' weaknesses and trying to correct them. This meant that a lot of Auglaize's management was relatively negative. Hammond wanted to change that approach. He says, "If you really want to [excel], you have to know yourself—you have to know what you're good at, and you have to know what you're not so good at, and a lot of people don't. Most of us know what we're not good at because people tell us. And we also tend to want to fix it." The idea that workers should "fix" their weaknesses is common, but it can be problematic because attempts to fix weaknesses take time, attention, and energy away from maximizing naturally powerful talents. Employees also enjoy using their talents and doing something well instead of struggling against their weaknesses to produce mediocre work.

Every employee in the co-op took an assessment to measure and identify his or her top five talents, and received at least two consultations on their individual strengths. This enabled Auglaize to build on what its employees naturally do best. Employees became more engaged, productive, and energized, and the organization became more successful. As one expert says, "One issue is that the people who are really valued often don't know who they are, especially in times of change. If managers regularly give positive feedback to key performers, it increases their confidence to undertake greater challenges and reinforces their commitment."[118]

(Continued)

Questions:

1. Do you think it is better to focus on assessing and developing employees' weaknesses, or to focus on their strengths? Why?
2. Why would strengths-based development increase employee engagement?
3. If you were a manager, how might you interact with employees differently if you were using strengths-based development rather than deficit-based development?

Source: Robison, J. (2007). *Great Leadership Under Fire. Gallup Management Journal.* http://gmj .gallup.com/content/26569/Great-Leadership-Under-Fire.aspx; Local Ag Companies Merge to Form New Cooperative.February 20, 2008. Sidney Daily News, p. 8; Hodges, T. D., & Clifton, D. O. (2004). Strengths-based development in practice. In P. A. Linley & S. Joseph (Eds.), *International handbook of positive psychology in practice: From research to application* (pp. 256–268). New York: Wiley.

SO WHAT

Understanding that there are multiple ways to be intelligent helps you to achieve your potential and helps you to bring out the excellence in each of your subordinates as well.

Knowing your strongest areas of intelligence can guide you to the most appropriate job and learning environments to enable you to achieve your potential. Compare your intelligence strengths to the job types in Table 3-6.

As a manager, it is possible to develop the same skills in different ways for different subordinates. For example in diversity training, bodily-kinesthetic learners could engage in role-plays while spatial-visual subordinates could create posters conveying the material being taught. Using a person's preferred learning style helps to make learning easy and enjoyable.

Table 3-6

Matching Intelligence Types with Career Choices

Type of Intelligence	Related Careers	Preferred Learning Style
Bodily-Kinesthetic: physical agility and balance; body control; hand-eye coordination	Athletes, firefighters, chefs, actors, gardeners	Touch and feel, physical experience
Interpersonal: ability to relate to others and perceive their feelings; interprets behaviors of others; relates to emotional intelligence	Psychologists, doctors, educators, salespeople, politicians	Human contact, teamwork
Intrapersonal: self-awareness; understands oneself and one's relationship to others and to the world; relates to emotional intelligence	Related to success in almost all careers	Self-reflection, self-discovery
Linguistic: verbal and written language; explaining and interpreting ideas and information	Authors, speakers, lawyers, TV and radio hosts, translators	Verbal and written words and language
Logical-Mathematical: logic and pattern detection; analytical; problem solving; excels at math	Engineers, directors, scientists, researchers, accountants, statisticians	Logic and numbers
Musical: recognition of rhythm and tonal patterns; musical ability; high awareness and use of sound	Musicians, DJs, music teachers, acoustic engineers, music producers, composers	Music, sounds, rhythm
Spatial-Visual: creation and interpretation of visual images; visual and special perception	Artists, engineers, photographers, inventors, beauty consultants	Pictures, shapes, visually

Source: Based on Gardner, H. (1983). *Frames of Mind.* New York: Basic Books; Gardner, H. (1993a). *Multiple Intelligences: The Theory in Practice.* NY: Basic Books; Gardner, H. (1993b). *Creating Minds.* NY: Basic Books; Marks-Tarlow, T. (1995). *Creativity Inside Out: Learning Through Multiple Intelligences.* Reading, MA: Addison-Wesley.

Emotional Intelligence

Emotional intelligence (EI) is an interpersonal capability that includes the ability to perceive and express emotions, to understand and use them, and to manage emotions in oneself and other people.[120] Expert Daniel Goleman defines emotional intelligence as "the capacity for recognizing our own feelings and those of others, for motivating ourselves, and for managing emotions well in ourselves and in our relationships."[121] He describes five dimensions of EI that include three personal competencies (self-awareness, self-regulation, and motivation) and two social competencies (empathy and social skills). Emotional capabilities may operate at multiple levels to influence change in organizations.[122] EI may also influence employee emotional reactions to job insecurity and their coping with associated stresses.[123]

One expert says, "If we liken the mind to a high-performance engine, then emotional intelligence would be the oil that enables us to maintain and manage ourselves to perform to our full potential."[124] Emotional intelligence involves using emotional regulatory processes to control anxiety and other negative emotional reactions and to generate positive emotional reactions.[125] Negative emotions, such as anxiety or frustration, are distracting and result in diminished learning and performance.[126] Emotional regulation and control may also be important in managing distracting positive emotions at work. Emotional intelligence is composed of five dimensions:

1. *Self-awareness*: being aware of what you are feeling
2. *Self-motivation*: persisting in the face of obstacles, setbacks, and failures
3. *Self-management*: managing your own emotions and impulses
4. *Empathy*: sensing how others are feeling
5. *Social skills*: effectively handling the emotions of others

People differ in the degree to which they are able to recognize the emotional meaning of others' facial expressions, although seven universal emotions are expressed in the face in exactly the same way regardless of race, culture, ethnicity, age, gender, or religion:[127]

1. Joy
2. Sadness
3. Fear
4. Surprise
5. Anger
6. Contempt
7. Disgust

Recognizing and understanding these emotions is important in communicating, establishing relationships, building rapport, negotiation, and many other managerial tasks. More effective communicators better recognize the emotions being conveyed by peoples' facial expressions.[128]

There is some evidence that components of EI are malleable skills that can be developed,

emotional intelligence
An interpersonal capability that includes the ability to perceive and express emotions, to understand and use them, and to manage emotions in oneself and other people

© YURI ARCURS/SHUTTERSTOCK.COM

Seven universal emotions are expressed in the face in exactly the same way regardless of age, race, culture, ethnicity, or gender. What emotion is this woman expressing?

including facial expression recognition.[129] The ability to understand what others think and feel, knowing how to appropriately persuade and motivate them, and knowing how to resolve conflicts and forge cooperation are some of the most important skills of successful managers. You can get a rough estimate of your EI by taking the EI self-assessment from About.com at http://psychology.about.com/library/quiz/bl_eq_quiz.htm.

Much controversy surrounds the notion of EI.[130] Some have argued that its theoretical conceptualization is unclear because it is overly inclusive, lacks specificity, and encompasses both static trait components and malleable state components. It is not clear if it is simply a learned skill or an innate capability. Several researchers have also argued that EI is simply a surrogate for general intelligence and well-established personality traits.[131] However, a number of studies have supported the usefulness of EI.[132] EI has been found to be related to, and yet distinct from, personality dimensions; and various measures of EI provided incremental predictive power regarding life satisfaction and job performance, even after controlling for Big Five personality dimensions.[133]

It appears that, although controversies still exist, EI is distinct from other ability and personality trait measures. There is some ambiguity about the degree to which EI is considered a malleable and trainable set of competencies versus a stable set of personality traits or emotional abilities; however, EI does relate to job performance, adjustments to stressful situations, and pro-social behaviors.

SUMMARY AND APPLICATION

Everyone is different. We each have different personalities, demographics, and intelligences. By understanding the characteristics of your coworkers and subordinates, you will be best able to choose the OB tool or management style that will be most effective. Remember, flexibility is the key to effective management.

 **TAKEAWAY POINTS**

1. In many cases, demographic characteristics are indicators of other underlying characteristics that are the real drivers of behavior and other differences. For every demographic variable, there are many possible underlying explanatory variables. Rather than using a demographic characteristic to make organizational decisions, it is best to focus on the underlying characteristic that drives any differences in behavior. Generalizing to everyone based on a demographic characteristic is often misguided, and can get a manager in legal trouble through a violation of employment discrimination laws.

2. People high in achievement motivation are willing to dedicate significant effort to achieve ambitious goals and tasks, often for long periods. Employees coping with a fear of failure may try to disperse responsibility to others or choose to pursue lower goals and easier tasks. Being tolerant of ambiguity is related to creativity, positive attitudes toward risk, and orientation to diversity. Trainees with a greater internal locus of control have more positive attitudes toward learning because they believe that it is more likely to be useful and beneficial. Locus of control is also related to ethical behavior. Having a Type A personality and an external locus of control is associated with greater levels of perceived stress, lower job satisfaction, and poorer physical and mental health than that of managers with a Type B personality and an internal locus of control.

REAL WORLD RESPONSE

INDIVIDUAL DIFFERENCES THAT MAKE A DIFFERENCE AT SOUTHWEST AIRLINES

Southwest Airlines looks for employees with positive attitudes and leadership skills, who fit well with the company's fun and unique culture. Their investment of time and resources in finding the right talent has paid off in lower turnover, increased internal promotion rates, and higher productivity.[134]

Instead of evaluating flight attendant candidates on a fixed set of skills, Southwest looks for their attitude toward others, work ethic, and their ability to work effectively on a team.[135] Flight attendant candidates do more than interview for a job, they audition—and the audition begins the moment they request an application. Managers jot down anything memorable about the initial conversation, both good and bad. When flying candidates out for interviews, their special tickets alert gate agents, flight attendants, and others to pay special attention to them. Employees observe whether recruits are consistently friendly to the crew and to other passengers or if they are complaining and drinking cocktails at 9 a.m. they pass these observations on to the People Department.[136]

Flight attendant recruits are evaluated even when they think that they are not being assessed. During the five-minute speeches flight attendant job candidates give about themselves (in front of as many as fifty other recruits), managers watch the audience as closely as the speaker. Unselfish people who enthusiastically support their potential coworkers are the ones who catch Southwest's eye, not the applicants who seem bored or use the time to improve their own presentations. [137]

Prospective employees are often asked during an interview how they recently used their sense of humor in a work environment and how they have used humor to defuse a difficult situation. Southwest also looks for humor in the interactions people have with each other during group interviews.[138] To assess leadership, Southwest Airlines uses a group assessment exercise called Fallout Shelter, in which candidates imagine they are a committee charged with rebuilding civilization after a nuclear war. Groups are given a list of fifteen people from different occupations, including nurse, teacher, all-sport athlete, biochemist, and pop singer, and have ten minutes to make a unanimous decision about which seven people can remain in the only available fallout shelter. Each candidate is graded on a scale ranging from "passive" to "active" to "leader" as they propose, discuss, and debate the decision.[139]

Southwest consistently has the highest productivity numbers in the industry.[140] Southwest's hiring methods not only ensure that it hires people whose personalities fit the company's culture, but also help the company execute its customer service strategy.

3. The "Big Five" personality traits are:
   1. *Extroversion*: being sociable, assertive, talkative, and energetic
   2. *Emotional stability*: associated with not being anxious, depressed, angry, and insecure
   3. *Agreeableness*: being polite, flexible, trusting, cooperative, forgiving, and tolerant
   4. *Conscientiousness*: associated with being careful, thorough, responsible, organized, and prone to plan as well as being hardworking, achievement-oriented, and persistent
   5. *Openness to experience*: being imaginative, cultured, curious, broad-minded, and artistically sensitive

   Of the five, emotional stability and conscientiousness tend to be the strongest and most consistently related to motivation. Conscientiousness is positively associated with a variety of work outcomes, including training performance. Highly conscientious individuals also have greater confidence in their abilities. However, some aspects of conscientiousness, including dependability, order, and dutifulness, can reduce performance when adaptability to changing task conditions is important. Lower emotional stability may result in reductions in attention and reduced motivation, in part through reductions in self-confidence.

4. The foundation of bullying is the abuse of authority and power, stemming from the bully's need to control another person. High Machiavellians manipulate and exploit others to advance their personal agendas, which is the foundation of bullying.

5. Gardner's seven different types of intelligence are:
   1. *Linguistic:* words and language
   2. *Logical-mathematical:* logic and numbers
   3. *Musical:* music, rhythm, and sound
   4. *Bodily-kinesthetic:* body movement and control
   5. *Spatial-visual:* images and space
   6. *Interpersonal:* other people's feelings
   7. *Intrapersonal:* self-awareness

6. Emotional intelligence is an interpersonal capability that includes the ability to perceive and express emotions, to understand and use them, and to manage emotions in oneself and other people. It is important in communicating, establishing relationships, building rapport, negotiation, and many other managerial tasks.

DISCUSSION QUESTIONS

1. What individual differences do you feel are most important to organizations? Why?
2. If you were denied a job because of your score on a personality test, what would be your reaction?
3. If your supervisor exhibited bullying behaviors, what would you do?
4. Which of Gardner's multiple intelligences do you feel are most important for managers?
5. Do you think emotional intelligence is important to managers? How would you assess emotional intelligence in deciding who to promote to a managerial position?
6. If you were a manager, what individual differences would be important to you in hiring an assistant? Why?

EXERCISES

Individual Differences in Teams

In this exercise you will be asked to role-play a particular personality in a work team. After dividing into teams of four people, count off one to four to identify your role in the team by reading the description below. If your team has more than four people, restart the numbering at one when you get to the fifth person. If you need to be reminded of what each characteristic is and how a person with it might behave, review that section of the chapter.

Role 1: Low tolerance for ambiguity

Role 2: High fear of failure

Role 3: High conscientiousness

Role 4: High self-confidence

For the next five to ten minutes (until the instructor tells you to stop), your team's task is to discuss possible uses for an empty soda can and identify your team's favorite three ideas. When your instructor tells you, your role will change to be the opposite of what you just were.

Role 1: High tolerance for ambiguity

Role 2: Low fear of failure

Role 3: Low conscientiousness

Role 4: Low self-confidence

You will spend the next five to ten minutes (until the instructor tells you to stop) discussing possible uses for an old shirt and deciding on your group's favorite three ideas. When your instructor ends the task, address the following questions as a group and be prepared to share your answers with the class.

Questions

1. Which characteristics were most helpful to your group's performance? Why?
2. Which characteristics were least helpful to your group's performance? Why?
3. What could a leader do to effectively manage a group with these characteristics?
4. How easy was it to play both the high and low levels of your assigned characteristic?

Leveraging Individual Differences at Southwest Airlines

Southwest Airlines believes that it needs employees with creativity, humor, and the ability to work well with others to successfully execute its business strategy. This chapter's opening *Real World Challenge* provided some information about how the company currently assesses job candidates on these dimensions. Reread the opening *Real World Challenge* and its conclusion, and answer the following questions in a group of three to five people. Be prepared to share your answers with the class.

Questions

1. Do you think that it is appropriate for Southwest Airlines to assess creativity and humor during its assessment process?
2. How would you react if you went through Southwest's assessment process? Identify some things that you would both like and dislike, and explain why.
3. What other individual differences might be important for flight attendants? Why?

Generational Diversity

As you learned in this chapter, four generations are currently represented in the U.S. workforce. Many companies are taking steps to reach out to different generations to appeal to them as an employer.

Use the Internet to research why companies including Walmart and The Home Depot are actively recruiting "mature" workers (age fifty and older). Then answer the following questions.

Questions

1. Why are companies like Walmart and The Home Depot recruiting mature workers?
2. How can companies better recruit mature workers?
3. What job-seeking advice would you give to a mature worker who has not looked for a job for twenty years?

Emotional Intelligence

Point your favorite browser to http://www.queendom.com/tests/access_page/index.htm?idRegTest=1121 and complete the emotional intelligence assessment. After finishing the assessment, review your free feedback and answer the following questions.

Questions

1. Do you agree with the description of your emotional intelligence?
2. What can you do to further improve your emotional intelligence?
3. How can your answers to questions like these help to predict how effective you would be as a manager?

*We thank Professor Lauryn Migenes at the University of Central Florida for suggesting this exercise.

VIDEO CASES

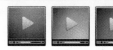

Now What?

While waiting for a phone call with two subordinates, imagine that another subordinate walks into the room and has a loud, frustrated outburst after being unable to find something. The other employees in the room clearly feel uncomfortable as a result of this behavior. *What do you say or do?* Go to this chapter's "Now What?" video, watch the challenge video, and choose a response. Be sure to also view the outcomes of the two responses you didn't choose.

Discussion Questions

1. Which aspects of management and organizational behavior discussed in this chapter are illustrated in these videos? Explain your answer.
2. Which do you feel is more important at work, an employee's behavior or performance? Why?
3. As a manager, what else might you do to effectively handle this situation?

Workplace | Scholfield Honda: Change and Innovation

Not long ago, the phrase "hybrid SUV" would have been considered an oxymoron. But almost overnight, hybrid cars of all shapes and sizes became mainstream. As gas prices soared and concerns about the environment deepened, many people were looking for innovative solutions to energy problems and wondering about the cars of the future.

Enter Lee Lindquist, alternative fuels specialist at Scholfield Honda in Wichita, Kansas. Lindquist loves technology, is a passionate environmentalist, and has found the perfect way to make a difference at work. While researching alternative fuel vehicles for a presentation at the local Sierra Club, he learned Honda had been selling a natural gas vehicle in New York and California since 1998, where it was marketed as a way for municipalities and fleet customers to address air quality issues. He also discovered that the Honda Civic GX was the greenest model currently available for sale in the United States.

Lindquist couldn't believe Honda's most innovative car had been on the market for ten years and yet hadn't been embraced by Honda dealerships or consumers. One challenge of offering the Civic GX to the public was the lack of natural gas fueling stations and the high cost of purchasing and installing individual fueling stations for home use. With any new technology, a critical mass of early adopters helped lay groundwork for others. In the case of the Civic GX, Honda dealerships weren't adopting or promoting the new technology, and Lindquist viewed this lack of entrepreneurship as unacceptable.

(Continued)

Rising fuel prices provided the perfect opportunity to introduce the Civic GX to cost-conscious green-minded customers. When Lindquist first brought the Civic GX idea to dealership owner Roger Scholfield, his boss was skeptical. Scholfield had long been promoting Honda vehicles as fuel-efficient and didn't want to confuse customers with the "new" vehicle. Nevertheless, Scholfield warmed to the idea and, with Lindquist's help, began marketing the car to corporate and government customers.

Since that time, Scholfield Honda has seen many big changes. The dealership has stocked up on recycling bins and compostable cups, launched tree giveaway promotions, donated a Civic GX to a nearby tornado-stricken town, and formed a "Green Team" that meets regularly to identify what's next for Scholfield's ever-changing workplace.

Discussion Questions

1. How might the demographic characteristic of age affect the willingness of Scholfield Honda managers to embrace new high-tech green vehicles?
2. What can organizations do to address potential negative effects of age on employee performance?
3. Explain how the personality traits of achievement motivation, fear of failure, and tolerance for ambiguity play a role in Roger Scholfield's decision to go green with alternative fuel vehicles.

DO WHAT

CENGAGENOW™

CENGAGENOW™ includes **teaching and learning resources** to supplement the text, and is designed specifically to **help students "think like managers"** by engaging and challenging them to think critically about managerial situations. **CengageNOW uses today's technology to improve the skills** of tomorrow's managers.

END NOTES

[1]Pfeffer, J. (1998). *The Human Equation: Building Profits by Putting People First.* Boston, MA: Harvard Business School Press.

[2]Rutherford, L. (2012). How Does Southwest Airlines Screen Candidates for Culture? Workforce.com, April 3. Available online: http://www.workforce.com/article/2012040/DEAR_WORKFORCE/120409976.

[3]The Mission of Southwest Airlines. Available online: http://www.southwest.com/html/about-southwest/index.html.

[4]Maxon, T. (2010). Southwest Airlines Ranks No. 2 on List of "Best Companies for Leadership." Dallas News, February 17. Available online: http://aviationblog.dallasnews.com/archives/2010/02/southwest-airlines-ranks-no-2.html.

[5]Bregman, P. (2009). Susan Boyle: A Lesson in Talent Management. Available online: http://blogs.harvardbusiness.org/bregman/2009/04/susan-boyle-a-lesson-in-talent.html.

[6]Hunter, J. E., & Hunter, R. F. (1984). Validity and Utility of Alternative Predictors of Job Performance. *Psychological Bulletin, 96,* 72–98; Gully, S. M., & Chen, G. (2010). Individual Differences, Attribute-Treatment Interactions, and Training Outcomes. In S. W. J. Kozlowski & E. Salas (eds.), *Learning, Training, and Development in Organizations* (pp. 3–64). SIOP Organizational Frontiers Series. San Francisco, CA: Jossey-Bass.

[7]U.S. Census Bureau Reports, March 2004; Camarota, S. A., & McCardle, N. (2003, September). Where Immigrants Live: An

Examination of State Residency of the Foreign Born by Country of Origin in 1990 and 2000. Washington, DC: Center for Immigration Studies.

[8]Powell, G. N., & Butterfield, D. A. (2002). Exploring the Influence of Decision Makers' Race and Gender on Actual Promotions to Top Management. *Personnel Psychology, 55,* 397–428; Butterfield, D. A., & Grinnell, J. P. (1999). "Re-viewing" Gender, Leadership, and Managerial Behavior: Do Three Decades of Research Tell Us Anything? In *Handbook of Gender and Work* (pp. 223–238). London: Sage.

[9]Steele, C. M., & Aronson, J. (1995). Stereotype Threat and the Intellectual Test Performance of African Americans. *Journal of Personality and Social Psychology, 69,* 797–811.

[10]Contrada, R. J., Ashmore, R. D., Gary, M. L., Coups, E., Egeth, J. D., Sewell, A., Ewell, K., Goyal, T. M., & Chasse, V. (2001). Measures of Ethnicity-Related Stress: Psychometric Properties, Ethnic Group Differences, and Associations with Well-Being. *Journal of Applied Social Psychology, 31*(9), 1775–1820.

[11]Steele, C. M., & Aronson, J. (1995). Stereotype Threat and the Intellectual Test Performance of African Americans. *Journal of Personality and Social Psychology, 69,* 797–811.

[12]Grand, J.A., Ryan, A.M., Schmitt, N., & Hmurovic, J. (2010). How Far Does Stereotype Threat Reach? The Potential Detriment of Face Validity in Cognitive Ability Testing, *Human Performance, 24,* 1–28; Chan, D., Schmitt, N., DeShon, R. P., Clause, C. S., & Delbridge, K. (1997). Reactions to Cognitive Ability Tests: The Relationships Between Race, Test Performance, Face Validity Perceptions, and Test-Taking Motivation. *Journal of Applied Psychology, 82,* 300–310; Ployhart, R. E., Ziegert, J. C., & McFarland, L. A. (2003). Understanding Racial Differences on Cognitive Ability Tests in Selection Contexts: An Integration of Stereotype Threat and Applicant Reactions Research. *Human Performance, 16*(3), 231–259.

[13]Ployhart, R. E., Ziegert, J. C., & McFarland, L. A. (2003). Understanding Racial Differences on Cognitive Ability Tests in Selection Contexts: An Integration of Stereotype Threat and Applicant Reactions Research. *Human Performance, 16*(3), 231–259.

[14]Schmit, M. J., & Ryan, A. M. (1997). Applicant Withdrawal: The Role of Test-Taking Attitudes and Racial Differences. *Personnel Psychology, 50*(4), 855–876.

[15]Grillo, J. (2009, May/June). Gen Y: How Millennials Are Changing the Workplace. *Diversity Executive, 20.*

[16]Waldman, D. A., & Avolio, B. J. (1986). A Meta-Analysis of Age Differences in Job Performance. *Journal of Applied Psychology, 71,* 33–38.

[17]McEvoy, G. M., & Cascio, W. F. (1989). Cumulative Evidence of the Relationship Between Employee Age and Job Performance. *Journal of Applied Psychology, 74,* 11–17.

[18]Warr, P., & Bunce, D. (1995). Trainee Characteristics and the Outcomes of Open Learning. *Personnel Psychology, 48*(2), 347–375.

[19]Colquitt, J. A., LePine, J. A., & Noe, R. A. (2000). Toward an Integrative Theory of Training Motivation: A Meta-Analytic Path Analysis of 20 Years of Research. *Journal of Applied Psychology, 85*(5), 678–707.

[20]Hertzog, C. (1989). Influences of Cognitive Slowing on Age Differences in Intelligence. *Developmental Psychology 25,* 636–651.

[21]Gully, S. M., & Chen, G. (2010). Individual Differences, Attribute-Treatment Interactions, and Training Outcomes. In S. W. J. Kozlowski & E. Salas (eds.), *Learning, Training, and Development in Organizations* (pp. 3–64). SIOP Organizational Frontiers Series. San Francisco, CA: Jossey-Bass.

[22]Maurer, T. J. (2001). Career-Relevant Learning and Development, Worker Age, and Beliefs About Self-Efficacy for Development. *Journal of Management, 27*(2), 123–140; Maurer, T. J., Weiss, E. M., & Barbeite, F. G. (2003). A Model of Involvement in Work-Related Learning and Development Activity: The Effects of Individual, Situational, Motivational, and Age Variables. *Journal of Applied Psychology, 88*(4), 707–724.

[23] Chaudhuri, S. & Ghosh, R. (2012). Reverse Mentoring: A Social Exchange Tool for Keeping the Boomers Engaged and Millennials Committed. *Human Resource Development, 11,* 55–76.

[24]Breen, B. (2001, November). Trickle-Up Leadership. *Fast Company, 52,* 70.

[25]See, e.g., Hyde, J. S. (1981, October). How Large Are Cognitive Gender Differences? *American Psychologist,* 892–901; Black, M.M., & Holden, E. W. (1998). The Impact of Gender on Productivity and Satisfaction Among Medical School Psychologists. *Journal of Clinical Psychology in Medical Settings, 5*(1), 117–131; Powell, G. N., & Graves, L. M. (2003). *Women and Men in Management* (3rd ed.). New York: Sage; Re-viewing Gender, Leadership and Managerial Behavior: Do Three Decades of Research Tell Us Anything? In *Gender and Work,* ed. Powell, G.N. Newbury Park: Sage.

[26]Black, M. M., & Holden, E. W. (1998). The Impact of Gender on Productivity and Satisfaction Among Medical School Psychologists. *Journal of Clinical Psychology in Medical Settings, 5*(1), 117–131; Powell, G. N., & Graves, L. M. (2003). *Women and Men in Management* (3rd ed.). New York: Sage.

[27] Gully, S. M., & Chen, G. (2010). Individual differences, attribute-treatment interactions, and training outcomes. In S. W. J. Kozlowski & E. Salas (eds.), *Learning, Training, and Development in Organizations* (pp. 3–64). SIOP Organizational Frontiers Series. San Francisco, CA: Jossey-Bass.

[28]Allport, G. W. (1937). *Personality-A Psychological Interpretation.* New York: Henry Holt; James, L. R., & Mazerolle, M. D. (2002). *Personality in Work Organizations.* Thousand Oaks, CA: Sage.

[29]Allport, G. W. (1937). *Personality-A Psychological Interpretation.* New York: Henry Holt; James, L. R., & Mazerolle, M. D. (2002). *Personality in Work Organizations.* Thousand Oaks, CA: Sage.

[30]Chen, G., Gully, S. M., Whiteman, J. A., & Kilcullen, B. N. (2000). Examination of Relationships Among Trait-Like Individual Differences, State-Like Individual Differences, and Learning Performance. *Journal of Applied Psychology, 85,* 835–847; Kanfer, R., & Heggestad, E. D. (1997). Motivational Traits and Skills: A Person-Centered Approach to Work Motivation. In *Research in Organizational Behavior,* eds. L. L. Cummings and B. M. Staw (Vol. 19, pp. 1–56). Greenwich, CT: JAI Press; Herold, D. M., Davis, W., Fedor, D. B., & Parsons, C. K. (2002). Dispositional Influences on Transfer of Learning in Multistage Training Programs. *Personnel Psychology, 55*(4), 851–869.

[31]McClelland, D. C. (1985). *Human Motivation.* New York: Cambridge University Press.

[32]Atkinson, J. W. (1957). Motivational Determinants of Risk-Taking Behavior. *Psychological Review, 64,* 359–372.

[33]James, L. R. (1998). Measurement of Personality via Conditional Reasoning. *Organizational Research Methods, 1,* 131–163.

[34]James, L.R. (1998). Measurement of Personality via Conditional Reasoning. *Organizational Research Methods, 1,* 131–163.

[35]James, L. R., & Mazerolle, M. D. (2002). *Personality in Work Organizations.* Thousand Oaks, CA: Sage.

[36]James, L. R., & Mazerolle, M. D. (2002). *Personality in Work Organizations.* Thousand Oaks, CA: Sage.

[37]Budner, S. (1962). Intolerance of Ambiguity as a Personality Variable. *Journal of Personality, 30,* 29–50; MacDonald, A. P., Jr. (1970). Revised Scale for Ambiguity Tolerance: Reliability and Validity. *Psychological Reports, 26,* 791–798.

[38]Furnham, A. (1995). Tolerance of Ambiguity: A Review of the Concept, Its Measurement and Applications. *Current Psychology, 14,* 179.

[39]See Kirton, M. J. (2004). *Adaption-Innovation in the Context of Diversity and Change.* Oxford: Routledge; Wilkinson, D. (2006). *The Ambiguity Advantage: What Great Leaders Are Great At.* London: Palgrave Macmillan; Lauriola, M., & Levin, I. P. (2001). Relating Individual Differences in Attitude Toward Ambiguity to Risky Choices. *Journal of Behavioral Decision Making, 14,* 107–122.

[40]McFarlin, K. (2012). Howt o Deal With Ambiguity in the Workplace, The Houston Chronicle. Available online: http://smallbusiness.chron.com/deal-ambiguity-workplace-10051.html. Accessed December 27, 2012; Ambiguity—How Do You Deal With It? Assessment Business Center, January 12, 2012. Available online: http://assessmentbusinesscenter.wordpress.com/2012/01/12/ambiguity-how-do-you-deal-with-it/; Davis, R. (2011). Dealing With Ambiguity in the Workplace, TroyMedia, October 19. Available online: http://www.troymedia.com/2011/10/19/dealing-with-ambiguity-in-the-workplace/.

[41]Rotter, J. B. (1990). Internal Versus External Control of Reinforcement: A Case History of a Variable. *American Psychologist, 45,* 489–493.

[42]Rotter, J. B. (1992). Cognates of Personal Control: Locus of Control, Self-Efficacy, and Explanatory Style. Comment. *Applied and Preventive Psychology, 1,* 127–129.

[43]Phillips, J. M., & Gully, S. M. (1997). The Role of Goal Orientation, Ability, Need for Achievement, and Locus of Control in the Self-Efficacy and Goal Setting Process. *Journal of Applied Psychology, 82,* 792–802.

[44]Judge, T. A., & Bono, J. E. (2001). Relationship of Core Self-Evaluations Traits—Self-Esteem, Generalized Self-Efficacy, Locus of Control, and Emotional Stability—With Job Satisfaction and Job Performance: A Meta-Analysis. *Journal of Applied Psychology, 86,* 80–92.

[45]Noe, R. A., & Schmitt, N. (1986). The Influence of Trainee Attitudes on Training Effectiveness: Test of a Model. *Personnel Psychology, 39,* 497–523.

[46]Forte, A. (2005). Locus of Control and the Moral Reasoning of Managers. *Journal of Business Ethics, 58,* 65–77.

[47]Treviño, L. K., & Youngblood, S. A. (1990). Bad Apples in Bad Barrels: A Causal Analysis of Ethical Decision Making Behavior. *Journal of Applied Psychology, 75*(4), 447–476.

[48]Dijkstra, T.M., Beersma, B., & Evers, A. (2011). Reducing Conflict-Related Employee Strain: The Benefits of an Internal Locus of Control and a Problem-Solving Conflict Management Strategy. *Work & Stress: An International Journal of Work, Health & Organisations, 25*(2), 167–184.

[49]Ng, T.W.H., & Feldman, D.C. (2011). Locus of Control and Organizational Embeddedness, *Journal of Occupational and Organizational Psychology, 84*(1), 173–190.

[50]Spector, P. E. (1988). Development of the Work Locus of Control Scale. *Journal of Occupational Psychology, 61,* 335–340.

[51]Applebaum, S. H. (1981). *Stress Management for Health Care Professionals.* Rockville, MD: Aspen Publications.

[52]Kunnanatt, J. T. (2003). Type A Behavior Pattern and Managerial Performance: A Study Among Bank Executives in India. *International Journal of Manpower, 24,* 720–734.

[53]Ferroli, C. (1996, January/February). Anger Could Be a Fatal Fault. *The Saturday Evening Post,* pp. 18–19.

[54]Kirkcaldy, B. D., Shephard, R. J., & Furnham, A. F. (2002). The Influence of Type A Behaviour and Locus of Control upon Job Satisfaction and Occupational Health. *Personality and Individual Differences, 33*(8), 1361–1371.

[55]Darley, J. M., & Batson, C. D. (1973). "From Jerusalem to Jericho": A Study of Situational and Dispositional Variables in Helping Behavior. *Journal of Personality and Social Psychology, 27,* 100–108.

[56]Ashton, M. C., Lee, K., & Goldberg, L. R. (2004). A Historical Analysis of 1,710 English Personality-Descriptive Adjectives. *Journal of Personality and Social Psychology, 87,* 707–721.

[57]Barrick, M. R., & Mount, M. K. (1991). The Big Five Personality Dimensions and Job Performance: A Meta-Analysis. *Personnel Psychology, 44,* 1–26.

[58]Judge, T. A., & Ilies, R. (2002). Relationship of Personality to Performance Motivation: A Meta-Analytic Review. *Journal of Applied Psychology, 87,* 797–807.

[59]Cheramie, R.A., & Simmering, M.J. (2010). Improving Individual Learning for Trainees with Low Conscientiousness, *Journal of Managerial Psychology, 25,* 44–57; Martocchio, J. J., & Judge, T. A. (1997). Relationship Between Conscientiousness and Learning in Employee Training: Mediating Influences of Self-Deception and Self-Efficacy. *Journal of Applied Psychology, 82,* 764–773; Colquitt, J. A., & Simmering, M. J. (1998). Conscientiousness, Goal Orientation, and Motivation to Learn During the Learning Process: A Longitudinal Study. *Journal of Applied Psychology, 83,* 654–665.

[60]LePine, J. A., Colquitt, J. A., & Erez, M. (2000). Adaptability to Changing Task Contexts: Effects of General Cognitive Ability, Conscientiousness, and Openness to Experience. *Personnel Psychology, 53,* 563–593.

[61] Gully, S. M., & Chen, G. (2010). Individual Differences, Attribute-Treatment Interactions, and Training Outcomes. In S. W. J. Kozlowski & E. Salas (eds.), *Learning, Training, and Development in Organizations* (pp. 3–64). SIOP Organizational Frontiers Series. San Francisco, CA: Jossey-Bass.

[62]Bell, B. S., & Kozlowski, S. W. J. (2009). Toward a Theory of Learner-Centered Training Design: An Integrative Framework of Active Learning. In S. W. J. Kozlowski & E. Salas (eds.), *Learning, Training, and Development in Organizations* (pp. 263–300). New York: Routledge; Colquitt, J. A., LePine, J. A., & Noe, R. A. (2000). Toward an Integrative Theory of Training Motivation: A Meta-Analytic Path Analysis of 20 Years of Research. *Journal of Applied Psychology, 85*(5), 678–707.

[63]Caligiuri, P. M. (2000). The Big Five Personality Characteristics as Predictors of Expatriate Success. *Personnel Psychology, 53,* 67–88.

[64]Barrick, M. R., & Mount, M. K. (1991). The Big Five Personality Dimensions and Job Performance: A Meta-Analysis. *Personnel Psychology, 44,* 1–26; Major, D. A., Turner, J. E., & Fletcher, T. D. (2006). Linking Proactive Personality and the Big Five to Motivation to Learn and Development Activity. *Journal of Applied Psychology, 91*(4), 927–935.

[65] Gully, S. M., & Chen, G. (2010). Individual differences, attribute-treatment interactions, and training outcomes. In S. W. J. Kozlowski & E. Salas (eds.), *Learning, Training, and Development in Organizations* (pp. 3–64). SIOP Organizational Frontiers Series. San Francisco, CA: Jossey-Bass.

[66]Barrick, M. R., & Mount M. K. (1991). The Big Five Personality Dimensions and Job Performance: A Meta-Analysis. *Personnel Psychology, 44,* 1–26; Mount, M. K., & Barrick, M. R. (1998). Five

Reasons Why the "Big Five" Article Has Been Frequently Cited. *Personnel Psychology, 51,* 849–857.

[67]Tett, R. P., Jackson, D. N., & Rothstein, M. (1994). Meta-Analysis of Personality-Job Performance Relations: A Reply of Ones, Mount, Barrick, and Hunter. *Personnel Psychology, 47,* 157–172.

[68]Salgado, J. E. (1997). The Five Factor Model of Personality and Job Performance in the European Community. *Journal of Applied Psychology, 82*(1), 30–43.

[69]Judge, T. A., Heller, D., & Mount, M. K. (2002). Five-Factor Model of Personality and Job Satisfaction: A Meta-Analysis. *Journal of Applied Psychology, 87,* 530–541.

[70]Judge, T. A., & Ilies, R. (2002). Relationship of Personality to Performance Motivation: A Meta-Analytic Review. *Journal of Applied Psychology, 87*(4), 797–807.

[71]Noftle, E.E., & Fleeson, W. (2010). Age Differences in Big Five Behavior Averages and Variabilities Across the Adult Life Span: Moving Beyond Retrospective, Global Summary Accounts of Personality, *Psychology and Aging, 25,* 95–107; Warr, P., Miles, A., & Platts, C. (2001). Age and Personality in the British Population Between 16 and 64 Years. *Journal of Occupational and Organizational Psychology, 74,* 165–199.

[72]Robinson, J. P., & P. R. Shaver. (1973). *Measures of Social Psychological Attitudes.* Ann Arbor, MI: Institute for Social Research.

[73]Calhoon, R. P. (1969). Niccolo Machiavelli and the Twentieth Century Administrator. *Academy of Management Journal, 2*(12), 211.

[74]Christie, R., & Geis, F. L. (1970). *Studies in Machiavellianism.* New York: Academic Press.

[75]Christie, R., & Geis, F. L. (1970). *Studies in Machiavellianism.* New York: Academic Press.

[76]Calhoon, R. P. (1969). Niccolo Machiavelli and the Twentieth Century Administrator. *Academy of Management Journal, 2*(12), 205–212.

[77]Singhapakdi, A., & Vitell, S. J. (1990). Marketing Ethics: Factors Influencing Perceptions of Ethical Problems and Alternatives. *Journal of Macromarketing, 10,* 4–19.

[78]Hartog, N.D., & Belschak, F.D., (2012). Work Engagement and Machiavellianism in the Ethical Leadership Process. *Journal of Business Ethics, 107,* 35–47.

[79]Rayburn, J. M., Overby, J., & Hammond, K. (2003). Differences in Charisma, Ethics, Personality, and Machiavellian Characteristics of Male and Female Marketing Students. *Academy of Marketing Studies Journal,* 107–125.

[80]Zagenczyk, T.J., Restubog, S.L.D., Kiewitz, C., Kiazad, K., & Tang, R.L. (in press). Psychological Contracts as a Mediator between Machiavellianism and Employee Citizenship and Deviant Behaviors, *Journal of Management.*

[81]Adapted from Christie, R., & Geis, F. L. (1970). *Studies in Machiavellianism* (p. 17). New York: Academic Press.

[82]Adapted from Christie, R., & Geis, F. L. (1970). *Studies in Machiavellianism* (pp. 82–83). New York: Academic Press.

[83]Fitzpatrick, M.E., Cotter, E.W., Bernfeld, S.J., Carter, L.M., Kies, A., & Fouad, N.A. (2011). The Importance of Workplace Bullying to Vocational Psychology: Implications for Research and Practice. *Journal of Career Development, 38,* 479–499; Workplace Bullying Institute (2010). Results of the 2010 and 2007 WBI U.S. Workplace Bullying Survey. Workplace Bullying Institute. Available online: http://www.workplacebullying.org/wbiresearch/2010-wbi-national-survey/.; Namie, G. (2007). The Challenge of Workplace Bullying. *Employment Relations Today, 34*(2), 43–51.

[84]Namie, G. (2008). U.S. Workplace Bullying Survey. Workplace Bullying Institute. Available online: http://www.workplacebullying.org/docs/zogbyflyer.pdf.

[85]Namie, G., & Namie, R. (2000, Autumn). Workplace Bullying: Silent Epidemic. *Employee Rights Quarterly.*

[86]Workplace Bullying Institute (2010). Results of the 2010 and 2007 WBI U.S. Workplace Bullying Survey. Workplace Bullying Institute. Available online: http://www.workplacebullying.org/wbiresearch/2010-wbi-national-survey/.

[87]Namie, G., & Namie, R. (2009). *The Bully at Work* (2nd ed.). Naperville, IL: Sourcebooks.

[88]Glaso, L., Matthiesen, S. B., Nielsen, M. B., & Einarsen, S. (2007). Do Targets of Workplace Bullying Portray a General Victim Pesonality Profile? *Scandinavian Journal of Psychology, 48*(4), 313–319; Coyne, I., Seigne, E., & Randall, P. (2000). Predicting Workplace Victim Status from Personality. *European Journal of Work and Organizational Psychology, 9,* 335–349.

[89]Joseph, J. (2010). Genetic Research in Psychiatry and Psychology: A Critical Overview. In K. Hood, C. Tucker Halpern, G. Greenberg, & R. Lerner (eds.), *Handbook of Developmental Science, Behavior, and Genetics* (pp. 557–625). Malden, MA: Wiley-Blackwell.

[90]Benet-Martínez, V., & Oishi, S. (2008). Culture and Personality. In *Handbook of Personality: Theory and Research,* eds. O. P. John, R. W. Robins, and L. A. Pervin (3rd ed.). New York: Guilford Press.

[91]Allik, J., & McCrae, R. R. (2004). Escapable Conclusions: Toomela (2003) and the Universality of Trait Structure. *Journal of Personality and Social Psychology, 87,* 261–265; McCrae, R. R., Terracciano, A., and 78 members of the Personality Profiles of Cultures Project. (2005). Universal Features of Personality Traits from the Observer's Perspective: Data from 50 Cultures. *Journal of Personality and Social Psychology, 3,* 547–561.

[92]McCrae, R. R. (2002). Cross-Cultural Research on the Five-Factor Model of Personality. In *Online Readings in Psychology and Culture,* eds. W. J. Lonner, D. L. Dinnel, S. A. Hayes, and D. N. Sattler (Unit 6, Chapter 1). Bellingham, WA: Center for Cross-Cultural Research, Western Washington University. Available online: http://www.wwu.edu/culture/mccrae.htm.

[93]The MBTI instrument is available from Consulting Psychological Press in Palo Alto, California.

[94]*MBTI Basics.* (2009). The Myers & Briggs Foundation. Available online: http://www.myersbriggs.org/my-mbti-personality-type/mbti-basics/.

[95]Based on Briggs Myers, I. (1995). *Gifts Differing: Understanding Personality Type.* Palo Alto, CA: Davies-Black; Brightman, H. J. (2009). *GMU Master Teacher Program: On Learning Styles.* Available online: http://www2.gsu.edu/~dschjb/wwwmbti.html; *MBTI Basics.* (2009). The Myers & Briggs Foundation. Available online: http://www.myersbriggs.org/my-mbti-personality-type/mbti-basics/.

[96]Pittenger, D. J. (1993, Fall). Measuring the MBTI and Coming Up Short. *Journal of Career Planning and Placement.* Available online: http://www.indiana.edu/~jobtalk/HRMWebsite/hrm/articles/develop/mbti.pdf.

[97]McGuire, W., & Hull, R. F. C. (eds.). (1977). *C. G. Jung Speaking.* Princeton, NJ: Princeton University Press, p. 305.

[98]Lloyd, J.B. (2012). The Myers-Briggs Type Indicator and Mainstream Psychology: Analysis and Evaluation of an Unresolved Hostility. *Journal of Beliefs & Values: Studies in Religion & Education, 33,* 23–34; Waters, R.J. (2012). Learning Style Instruments: Reasons Why Research Evidence Might Have a Weak Influence on Practitioner Choice. *Human Resource Development International, 15*(1), 119–129.

[99]Hunter, J. E. (1986). Cognitive Ability, Cognitive Aptitudes, Job Knowledge, and Job Performance. *Journal of Vocational Behavior, 29,* 340–362.

[100]Hunter, J. E., & Hunter, R. F. (1984). Validity and Utility of Alternative Predictors of Job Performance. *Psychological Bulletin, 96,* 72–98; Ree, M. J., Carretta, T. R., & Teachout, M. S. (1995). Role of Ability and Prior Knowledge in Complex Training Performance. *Journal of Applied Psychology, 80*(6), 721–730.

[101]Hunter, J. E. (1986). Cognitive Ability, Cognitive Aptitudes, Job Knowledge, and Job Performance. *Journal of Vocational Behavior, 29*(3), 340–362; Murphy, K. (1989). Is the Relationship Between Cognitive Ability and Job Performance Stable Over Time? *Human Performance, 2,* 183–200; Ree, M. J., & Earles, J. A. (1992). Intelligence Is the Best Predictor of Job Performance. *Current Directions in Psychological Science, 1,* 86–89.

[102]Conlin, M. (2006, June). Champions of Innovation. *IN,* 18–26.

[103]Chase, W. G., & Simon, H. A. (1973). The Mind's Eye in Chess. In *Visual Information Processing,* ed. W. G. Chase (pp. 215–281). New York: Academic Press; Chi, M. T. H., Glaser, R., & Rees, E. (1982). Expertise in Problem Solving. In *Advances of the Psychology of Human Intelligence,* ed. R. J. Sternberg (Vol. 1, pp. 7–75). Hillsdale, NJ: Erlbaum.

[104]Ree, M. J., Carretta, T. R., & Teachout, M. S. (1995). Role of Ability and Prior Knowledge in Complex Training Performance. *Journal of Applied Psychology, 80*(6), 721–730; Schmidt, F. L., & Hunter, J. E. (1981). Employment Testing: Old Theories and New Research Findings. *American Psychologist, 36,* 1128–1137; Schmidt, F. L., & Hunter, J. E. (1998). The Validity and Utility of Selection Methods in Personnel Psychology: Practical and Theoretical Implications of 85 Years of Research Findings. *Psychological Bulletin, 124,* 262–274.

[105]Kanfer, R., & Ackerman, P. L. (2004). Aging, Adult Development and Work Motivation. *Academy of Management Review, 29,* 1–19.

[106]Gully, S. M., Payne, S. C., & Koles, K. L. K. (2002). The Impact of Error Training and Individual Differences on Training Outcomes: An Attribute-Treatment Interaction Perspective. *Journal of Applied Psychology, 87,* 143–155.

[107]Cognitive Ability Tests (2012). U.S. Office of Personnel Management. Available online: http://apps.opm.gov/adt/content.aspx?page=3-04&AspxAutoDetectCookieSupport=1&JScript=1; Schmidt, F. L., & Hunter, J. (2004). General Mental Ability in the World of Work: Occupational Attainment and Job Performance. *Journal of Personality & Social Psychology, 86*(1), 162–173.

[108]Outtz, J. L. (2002). The Role of Cognitive Ability Tests in Employment Selection. *Human Performance, 15,* 161–171.

[109]Hough, L., Oswald, F. L., & Ployhart, R. E. (2001). Determinants, Detection and Amelioration of Adverse Impact in Personnel Selection Procedures: Issues, Evidence and Lessons Learnt. *International Journal of Selection and Assessment, 9*(1/2), 152–194.

[110]Smither, J. W., Reilly, R. R., Millsap, R. E., Pearlman, K., & Stoffey, R. W. (1993). Applicant Reactions to Selection Procedures. *Personnel Psychology, 46,* 49–76.

[111]Roth, P. L., Bevier, C. A., Bobko, P., Switzer, F. S., & Tyler, P. (2001). Ethnic Group Differences I Cognitive Ability in Employment and Educational Settings: A Meta-Analysis. *Personnel Psychology, 54*(2), 297–330; Murphy, K. R. (2002). Can Conflicting Perspectives on the Role of g in Personnel Selection Be Resolved? *Human Performance, 15,* 173–186; Murphy, K. R., Cronin, B. E., & Tam, A. P. (2003). Controversy and Consensus Regarding Use of Cognitive Ability Testing in Organizations. *Journal of Applied Psychology, 88,* 660–671.

[112]Outtz, J. L. (2002). The Role of Cognitive Ability Tests in Employment Selection. *Human Performance, 15,* 161–171.

[113]Walker, S. (2005, September 30). The NFL's Smartest Team. *Wall Street Journal Online.* Available online: http://online.wsj.com/article_email/SB112804210724556355 -IRjf4NjlaZ4n56rZ H2JaqWHm4.html.

[114]For more information, see Sternberg, R. J. (1997). *Thinking Styles.* New York: Cambridge University Press; Guilford, J. P. (1967). *The Nature of Human Intelligence.* New York: McGraw-Hill.

[115]Gardner, H. (1983). *Frames of Mind.* New York: Basic Books; Gardner, H. (1993a). *Multiple Intelligences: The Theory in Practice.* New York: Basic Books; Gardner, H. (1993b). *Creating Minds.* New York: Basic Books; Marks-Tarlow, T. (1995). *Creativity Inside Out: Learning Through Multiple Intelligences.* Reading, MA: Addison-Wesley.

[116]Gardner, H. (1983). *Frames of Mind.* New York: Basic Books; Gardner, H. (1993a). *Multiple Intelligences: The Theory in Practice.* New York: Basic Books; Gardner, H. (1993b). *Creating Minds.* New York: Basic Books; Marks-Tarlow, T. (1995). *Creativity Inside Out: Learning Through Multiple Intelligences.* Reading, MA: Addison-Wesley.

[117]Gardner, H. (2011). Frames of Mind: The Theory of Multiple Intelligences. Philadelphia, PA: Basic Books.

[118]Sommerville, H. (2007, January 23). Staff Engagement: A Question of Motive. *Personnel Today.* Available online: http://www.personneltoday.com/articles/2007/01/23/38955/staff -engagement-a-question-of-motive.html.

[119]Gardner, H. (1983). *Frames of Mind.* New York: Basic Books; Gardner, H. (1993a). *Multiple Intelligences: The Theory in Practice.* New York: Basic Books.

[120]Mayer, J. D., & Salovey, P. (1993). The Intelligence of Emotional Intelligence. *Intelligence, 17,* 433–442; Mayer, J. D., & Salovey, P. (1997). What Is Emotional Intelligence? In *Emotional Development and Emotional Intelligence,* eds. P. Salovey & D. J. Sluyter. New York: Basic Books.

[121]Goleman, D. (1998). *Working with Emotional Intelligence* (p. 317). New York: Bantam.

[122]Huy, Q. N. (1999). Emotional Capability, Emotional Intelligence, and Radical Change. *Academy of Management Review, 24*(2), 325–345.

[123]Jordan, P. J., Ashkanasy, N. M., & Hartel, C. E. J. (2002). Emotional Intelligence as a Moderator of Emotional and Behavioral Reactions to Job Insecurity. *Academy of Management Review, 27*(3), 361–372.

[124]Maddocks, J. (2011). A Decade of Emotional Intelligence, JCA. Available online: http://www.jca.eu.com/pdf/DecadeofEIReport .pdf.

[125]Kanfer, R., Ackerman, P. L., & Heggestad, E. D. (1996). Motivational Skills and Self-Regulation for Learning: A Trait Perspective. *Learning and Individual Differences, 8,* 185–209; Kanfer, R., & Heggestad, E. D. (1997). Motivational Traits and Skills: A Person-Centered Approach to Work Motivation. In *Research in Organizational Behavior,* eds. L. L. Cummings and B. M. Staw (Vol. 19, pp. 1–56). Greenwich, CT: JAI Press.

[126]Chen, G., Gully, S. M., Whiteman, J. A., & Kilcullen, B. N. (2000). Examination of Relationships Among Trait-Like Individual Differences, State-Like Individual Differences, and Learning Performance. *Journal of Applied Psychology, 85,* 835–847; Colquitt, J. A., LePine, J. A., & Noe, R. A. (2000). Toward an Integrative Theory of Training Motivation: A Meta-Analytic Path Analysis of 20 Years of Research. *Journal of Applied Psychology, 85*(5), 678–707.

[127]Ekman, P., & Friesen, W. V (1969). The Repertoire of Nonverbal Behavior: Categories, Origins, Usage, and Coding. *Semiotica*, 1, 49–98.

[128]Goleman, D. (2006). *Social Intelligence: The New Science of Human Relationships*. New York: Bantam.

[129]Dulewicz, V., & Higgs, M. (2004). Can Emotional Intelligence Be Developed? *International Journal of Human Resource Management, 15*(1), 95–111.

[130]Locke, E. A. (2005). Why Emotional Intelligence Is an Invalid Concept. *Journal of Organizational Behavior, 26*(4), 425–431.

[131]Schulte, M. J., Ree, M. J., & Carretta, T. R. (2004). Emotional Intelligence: Not Much More than g and Personality. *Personality and Individual Differences, 37*(5), 1059–1068.

[132]O'Boyle, E.H., Humphrey, R.H., Pollack, J.M., Hawver, T.H., & Story, P.A. (2011). The Relation Between Emotional Intelligence and Job Performance: A Meta-Analysis, *Journal of Organizational Behavior, 32*(5), 788–818; Cote, S., & Miners, C. T. H. (2006). Emotional Intelligence, Cognitive Intelligence, and Job Performance. *Administrative Science Quarterly, 51*(1), 1–28; Fox, S., & Spector, P. E. (2000). Relations of Emotional Intelligence, Practical Intelligence, General Intelligence, and Trait Affectivity with Interview Outcomes: It's Not All Just "G." *Journal of Organizational Behavior, 21,* 203–220; Law, K. S., Wong, C. S., & Song, L. J. (2004). The Construct and Criterion Validity of Emotional Intelligence and Its Potential Utility for Management Studies. *Journal of Applied Psychology, 89*(3), 483–496; Tett, R. P., & Fox, K. E. (2006). Confirmatory Factor Structure of Trait Emotional Intelligence in Student and Worker Samples. *Personality and Individual Differences, 41*(6), 1155–1168; Van Rooy, D. L., & Viswesvaran, C. (2004). Emotional Intelligence: A Meta-Analytic Investigation of Predictive Validity and Nomological Net. *Journal of Vocational Behavior, 65*(1), 71–95; Van Rooy, D. L., Viswesvaran, C., & Pluta, P. (2005). An Evaluation of Construct Validity: What Is This Thing Called Emotional Intelligence? *Human Performance, 18*(4), 445–462.

[133]Law, K. S., Wong, C. S., & Song, L. J. (2004). The Construct and Criterion Validity of Emotional Intelligence and Its Potential Utility for Management Studies. *Journal of Applied Psychology, 89*(3), 483–496.

[134] Rutherford, L. (2012). How Does Southwest Airlines Screen Candidates for Culture? Workforce.com, April 3. Available online: http://www.workforce.com/article/20120403/DEAR _WORKFORCE/120409976.

[135] Rutherford, L. (2012). How Does Southwest Airlines Screen Candidates for Culture? Workforce.com, April 3. Available online: http://www.workforce.com/article/20120403 /DEAR_WORKFORCE/120409976.

[136]Kaihla, P. (2006, March 23). Best-Kept Secrets of the World's Best Companies. *Business 2.0*. Available online: http://money.cnn .com/2006/03/23/magazines/business2/business2_bestkeptsecrets /index.htm.

[137]Kaihla, P. (2006, March 23). Best-Kept Secrets of the World's Best Companies. *Business 2.0*. Available online: http://money.cnn. com/2006/03/23/magazines/business2/business2_bestkeptsecrets /index.htm; Freiberg, K., & Freiberg, J. (1996). *Nuts! Southwest Airlines' Crazy Recipe for Business and Personal Success*. Austin: Bard Press.

[138]Freiberg, K., & Freiberg, J. (1996). *Nuts! Southwest Airlines' Crazy Recipe for Business and Personal Success*. Austin: Bard Press.

[139]Carbonara, P. (1996, August). Hire for Attitude, Train for Skill. *Fast Company, 4,* 73.

[140]Lichtenwalner, B. (2011). Southwest Airlines 2011 Results Reflect Benefits of Servant Leadership, Modern Servant Leader. Available online: http://modernservantleader.com/servant-leadership/southwest-airlines-2011-results-reflect-benefits-of-servant-leadership/.

CHAPTER

4

Individual Differences II: Self-Concept, Learning Styles, and Types of Fit

This Apple Computer billboard reflects the company's strong disruptive innovation culture. Hiring people who fit its culture and who are enthusiastic about making people's lives better is critical to the company's success.

REAL WORLD CHALLENGE

APPLE'S EMPLOYER BRAND

Apple has created one of the strongest and most valuable brands in the world.[1] It has also created a strong culture around disruptive innovation and creating products that make people's lives better. Apple knows that hiring people who fit its culture and who are enthusiastic about making people's lives better through technology and creating innovative new products are key to its success and the execution of its business strategy.[2]

Imagine that Apple asks for your advice on how to use its employer brand to hire more people who fit the company and who can help it execute its business strategy. After reading this chapter, you should have some good ideas.

LEARNING OBJECTIVES

1. Define self-concept and describe what managers can do to enhance its effects in the workplace.

2. Explain the difference between a learning orientation and a performance orientation.

3. Explain how learning styles differ.

4. Describe the four different types of fit.

5. Describe psychological contracts and the role they play in organizations.

6. Explain how realistic job previews can be used to support psychological contracts.

What we think of ourselves and our abilities often becomes a self-fulfilling prophecy. As Mary Kay Ash, founder of the Mary Kay cosmetics company said, "If you think you can, you can. If you think you can't, you're right." Our self-concept influences many important organizational outcomes including job performance and learning. If we believe we are unable to achieve a goal or learn something new, it is unlikely that we will be able to. Effective managers appropriately influence the self-concept of their staff to maximize their performance.

> "If you think you can, you can. If you think you can't, you're right." —*Mary Kay Ash, Founder of Mary Kay Cosmetics*

Understanding how people learn is also important for managers. Because people learn differently, effective leaders match their teaching and coaching style to fit the needs of the person being developed.

In this chapter we turn our attention to self-concept and learning styles. At the end of the chapter we will discuss different ways people can "fit" with an organization. Selecting employees for the individual differences that best fit the job, organization, and business strategy can increase firm performance.[3] We also discuss the role psychological contracts and realistic job previews play in shaping employees' expectations.

SELF-CONCEPT

self-concept

A person's perceptions of him- or herself as a physical, spiritual, or moral being

Self-concept refers to a person's perceptions of him- or herself as a physical, spiritual, or moral being.[4] It is formed through our experiences and interactions with others and is especially influenced by evaluations by significant others, reinforcements, and attributions for our behavior. Self-concept traits are related to other personality measures but contain distinct components including self-evaluation, self-worth, and self-determination that only partially overlap with personality.[5] The three primary self-concept traits are self-esteem, core self-evaluations, and self-efficacy, which we discuss next.

Self-Esteem

self-esteem

Our feelings of self-worth and our liking or disliking of ourselves

Self-esteem refers to our feelings of self-worth and our liking or disliking of ourselves.[6] Research suggests that self-esteem is strongly related to motivational processes such as specific self-efficacy, self-set goals, and effort as well as emotional processes, such as anxiety and regulating emotion.[7] Self-esteem is positively related to job performance[8] and learning.[9]

Core Self-Evaluations

core self-evaluations

Fundamental premises people hold about themselves and their functioning in the world

Core self-evaluations are fundamental premises people hold about themselves and their functioning in the world.[10] Core self-evaluations comprise four more specific personality traits:

1. *Self-esteem*: the basic appraisal and overall value placed on oneself as a person
2. *General self-efficacy*: a judgment of how well we can perform successfully in a variety of situations
3. *Locus of control*: the perceived degree of control we have over what happens to us; people with an *internal locus of control* view themselves as in

control of what happens to them whereas people with an *external locus of control* see factors external to themselves (such as luck or powerful others) as responsible for what happens to them

4. *Neuroticism* (or its converse, *emotional stability*): the tendency to experience poor emotional adjustment and negative affective states including hostility, fear, and depression

More positive and internal core self-evaluations are related to higher job performance,[11] job satisfaction,[12] life satisfaction,[13] and motivation.[14]

Self-Efficacy

Self-efficacy is our confidence in our ability to cope, perform, and be successful on a specific task. It is possible to have high self-esteem (I generally like myself and feel that I am a competent person) but low self-efficacy for certain tasks (I am poor at learning foreign languages). Self-efficacy is a key factor influencing motivation and engagement in an activity. It has also been found to reduce the negative effect of low job autonomy on psychological and physical stress.[15]

General self-efficacy reflects a generalized belief that we will be successful at whatever challenges or tasks we might face.[16] Because self-efficacy and general self-efficacy are related to setting higher goals, persisting in the face of obstacles, and performing better, it is important for you to maintain a positive sense of self-efficacy. Self-efficacy is even related to developing your skills, setting more challenging goals, seeking social support, and persisting longer in the face of challenges can help to build self-efficacy.

This chapter's *Understand Yourself* feature gives you the opportunity to evaluate your own general self-efficacy.

Goal Orientation

Individuals with a high *learning goal orientation* believe they can improve their skills and abilities. Learning goal oriented individuals are interested in developing new competencies, understanding and improving their work, improving their skills, and achieving task mastery based on self-referenced standards. The focus of LGO is on task mastery, including learning through experimentation and failure.[17]

Individuals with a high *performance goal orientation* believe that their ability is fixed.[18] People with a high PGO want to demonstrate their ability by outperforming others, exceeding normative standards, and achieving success with limited effort. They may also have an increased fear of failure and of negative evaluations by others.[19]

High LGO has been positively related to feedback seeking,[20] complex learning strategies,[21] and adaptability.[22] Higher LGO individuals have greater motivation to learn[23] and set higher goals, including those for development.[24] In general, LGO is associated with positive learning and training outcomes because higher LGO individuals better focus their attention, sustain their motivation, have higher self-efficacy, and have less anxiety than those lower in LGO.[25] Learning oriented individuals like high-effort experiences, which characterizes most novel situations. Learning oriented individuals welcome opportunities to develop new skills, understand and improve their work, and improve their level of competence.[26]

SO WHAT

Because believing that we are not good at something makes it less likely that we will perform well at it, effective managers try to boost employees' self-efficacy on tasks subordinates should be able to do well.

self-efficacy
A person's confidence in his or her ability to organize and execute the courses of action necessary to accomplish a specific task

general self-efficacy
Your generalized belief that you will be successful at whatever challenges or tasks you might face

learning goal orientation
Characterized by a belief that abilities are changeable and a desire to increase task mastery or competence

performance goal orientation
A belief that abilities are fixed and a desire to demonstrate high ability and to be positively evaluated by others

UNDERSTAND YOURSELF

WHAT IS YOUR GENERAL SELF-EFFICACY?

Below are several statements about you with which you may agree or disagree. Before answering the questions, think about your everyday life and all of your activities. This set of questions asks you to describe how you personally feel about your life in general. Answer honestly—there are no right or wrong answers. Using the response scale below, indicate your agreement or disagreement with each item by placing the appropriate number on the line preceding that item. You must answer all eight questions to interpret your score.

strongly disagree	disagree	neutral	agree	strongly agree
1	2	3	4	5

___ 1.   I will be able to achieve most of the goals that I have set for myself.

___ 2.   When facing difficult tasks, I am certain that I will accomplish them.

___ 3.   In general, I think that I can obtain outcomes that are important to me.

___ 4.   I believe I can succeed at most any endeavor to which I set my mind.

___ 5.   I will be able to successfully overcome many challenges.

___ 6.   I am confident that I can perform effectively on many different tasks.

___ 7.   Compared to other people, I can do most tasks very well.

___ 8.   Even when things are tough, I can perform quite well.

Scoring: Add up your total points. This is your general self-efficacy score. You can determine where you fall along the following scale. The interpretation of your score is based on research using samples of working professionals in the United States. Most people in the United States generally feel efficacious and would tend to rate each item above the neutral point (3) on the scale. As a result, the average score is approximately 33. It is possible that different results would be obtained in different countries and cultures.

Interpretation: If your score is *8 to 29*, you are comparatively low in general self-efficacy, as compared to working professionals in the United States. In confidence, you are probably in the bottom 10 to 15 percent of the U.S. working population. You do not feel you can effectively perform tasks or achieve goals you have set. You feel that in general you cannot perform better than others and cannot overcome challenges. You are likely to set lower goals than others, feel more anxiety when facing difficult situations, and more likely

to give up when you face obstacles. Slowly and systematically building your competence in core areas of your life will be important if you are low in general self-efficacy. Finding sources of personal support that will encourage your efforts may be important.

If your score is *30 to 33*, as compared to working professionals in the United States, you have somewhat low general self-efficacy. You may feel you cannot perform tasks effectively or you may be concerned about achieving goals you have set. It is possible that you feel you cannot perform better than others and you may feel concerned about overcoming challenges. You may set lower goals or feel more anxiety when facing difficult situations. You are more likely to give up when you face obstacles than people who feel more efficacious. Slowly and systematically building your competence in core areas of your life will help build general self-efficacy. Finding sources of personal support that will encourage your efforts may be important.

If your score is *34 to 37*, you are somewhat high in general self-efficacy, as compared to working professionals in the United States. You probably feel you can perform most tasks effectively and you have confidence you can achieve goals you have set. Most likely you feel you can perform better than others and you believe you can overcome challenges. You probably set challenging goals or feel excitement when facing difficult situations. You are not likely to give up when you face obstacles. Continuing to build your competence in core areas of your life will maintain your general self-efficacy. It may be important not to become overly efficacious, lest you find yourself becoming arrogant or discounting the input of others. Research is building in this area, but it appears that people can have too much confidence and that such confidence may reduce willingness to alter courses of action when required or may lead to the discounting of suggestions by others.

If your score is *38 to 40*, as compared to working professionals in the United States, you have very high general self-efficacy. You are probably in the top 10 or 15 percent of the population in your confidence. You are sure you can perform tasks effectively and you have strong confidence that you can achieve goals you have set. You feel you can perform better than others and you believe you can overcome almost any challenge you face. You probably set challenging goals or feel excitement when facing difficult situations. You are very unlikely to give up when you face obstacles. Your confidence will serve you as a great source of strength and motivation. However, you will have to avoid being arrogant and overly sure of yourself. Research is building in this area, but it appears that people can have too much confidence and that such confidence may reduce willingness to alter courses of action when required or may lead to the discounting of suggestions by others.

Source: G. Chen, S. M. Gully, & D. Eden, "Validation of a New General Self-efficacy Scale," Organizational Research Methods, 2001, 4, 62–83. © 2001 by SAGE Publications. Reprinted by Permission of SAGE Publications.

People high in PGO have been found to choose less subjectively difficult and challenging tasks, which might threaten their perceived level of competence, whereas people high in LGO are more likely to choose difficult tasks and to persist in the tasks they choose.[27] High PGO individuals, particularly those with a fear of failure, are less likely to seek feedback[28] and have lower motivation to learn.[29] PGO may reduce motivation because high PGO can be negatively related to self-efficacy, especially when fear of failure is high.[30] It increases anxiety, which also reduces self-efficacy.[31] However, having high PGO is not necessarily dysfunctional.[32] PGO is positively related to performance, but it is also positively related to task-related cognitive interference, which is negatively related to performance. Thus, PGO has counteracting effects on performance.

Although people tend to have a predisposition to a certain level of PGO and LGO, they can also be influenced by others. Telling people that they can improve their skills in an area and giving them the opportunity to succeed early in the training can increase their LGO, decrease their anxiety, and improve their ability to learn the material.[33]

LEARNING STYLES

Learning style refers to individual differences and preferences in how we process information when problem solving, learning, or engaging in similar activities.[34] There are numerous typologies, measures, and models that capture these differences and preferences. Most of these approaches have focused on child learning, but there is evidence that these differences are important for adults as well.[35] Next we'll discuss several of the most popular approaches to learning styles.

Sensory Modalities

One approach addresses our preference for sensory modality. A **sensory modality** is a system that interacts with the environment through one of the basic senses.[36] The most important sensory modalities are:

- *Visual*: learning by seeing
- *Auditory*: learning by hearing
- *Tactile*: learning by touching
- *Kinesthetic*: (learning by doing)

According to researchers, about 20 to 30 percent of American students are auditory; about 40 percent are visual; and the remaining 30 to 40 percent are either tactile/kinesthetic, visual/tactile, or some combinations of the above major senses.[37]

SO WHAT

If you increase people's belief that they are able to learn something or improve their abilities, they are more likely to succeed.

SO WHAT

Accommodating our own and subordinates' preferred sensory modalities can increase learning and performance.

sensory modality
A system that interacts with the environment through one of the basic senses

© Ian Shaw/Alamy

People learn best in different ways and using different sensory modalities. Understanding how you learn best can make it easier to identify the instructional methods that work best for you. What sensory modalities being used by this child to learn?

Learning Style Inventory

A second approach to understanding learning styles, the Kolb Learning Style Inventory, is one of the more dominant approaches to categorizing cognitive styles.[38] According to David Kolb, the four basic learning modes are active experimentation, reflective observation, concrete experience, and abstract conceptualization. In addition, the learning process is considered from the two dimensions of active/passive and concrete/abstract.[39] According to Kolb, there are four basic learning styles:[40]

1. *Convergers*: depend primarily on active experimentation and abstract conceptualization to learn. People with this style are superior in technical tasks and problems and inferior in interpersonal learning settings.

2. *Divergers*: depend primarily on concrete experience and reflective observation. People with this style tend to organize concrete situations from different perspectives and structure their relationships into a meaningful whole. They are superior in generating alternative hypotheses and ideas, and tend to be imaginative and people- or feeling-oriented.

3. *Assimilators*: depend on abstract conceptualization and reflective observation. These individuals tend to be more concerned about abstract concepts and ideas than about people. They also tend to focus on the logical soundness and preciseness of ideas, rather than the ideas' practical values; they tend to work in research and planning units.

4. *Accommodators*: rely mainly on active experimentation and concrete experience, and focus on risk taking, opportunity seeking, and action. Accommodators tend to deal with people easily and specialize in action-oriented jobs, such as marketing and sales.

Learning style predicted preference for training delivery mode at a large U.S. financial institution, although there was an overall preference for classroom-based delivery regardless of learning style.[41]

Although much has been written about cognitive styles, there are wide gaps in our current understanding. There are many differences in how styles are conceptualized,[42] and there have been numerous criticisms of Kolb's measures and the underlying theory.[43] These measures are subject to a variety of statistical and inferential problems, and many show low reliability.[44] Most of the research has also focused on children—less work has focused on how the styles influence adult learning. Despite these limitations, evidence suggests that cognitive and learning styles may be important for understanding human behavior and performance in a variety of contexts.

Learning Style Orientations

Annette Towler and Robert Dipboye[45] developed a learning style orientation measure to address some of the limitations of the Kolb inventory and identify key styles and preferences for learning. They demonstrated that learning style orientations predict preferences for instructional methods beyond the Big Five personality traits. They identified five key factors:

1. *Discovery learning*: an inclination for exploration during learning. Discovery learners prefer subjective assessments, interactional activities, informational methods, and active-reflective activities.

2. *Experiential learning*: a desire for hands-on approaches to instruction. Experiential learning is positively related to a preference for action activities.

3. *Observational learning*: a preference for external stimuli such as demonstrations and diagrams to help facilitate learning. Observational learning is positively related to preference for informational methods and active-reflective methods.
4. *Structured learning*: a preference for processing strategies such as taking notes, writing down task steps, and so forth. Structured learning is related to preferences for subjective assessments.
5. *Group learning*: a preference to work with others while learning. Group learning is related to preferences for action and interactional learning.

This chapter's *Improve Your Skills* feature (page 116) gives you the opportunity to evaluate your own preferred learning styles using the Towler and Dipboye measure to better understand the learning environments that are best for you.

TYPES OF FIT

Why are some very talented people undesirable coworkers or employees despite being very talented at what they do? The answer lies in the many ways in which people need to fit with an employment opportunity to be a successful match. Being good at our job is important, but is not enough—we need to fit with our organization and workgroup as well. We next describe each of these dimensions of fit in greater detail.[46]

Person-Job Fit

Person-job fit is the fit between a person's abilities and the demands of the job, and the fit between a person's desires and motivations and the attributes and rewards of a job.[47] An employee's talents need to meet a job's requirements, and the job needs to meet the employee's needs and motivations.[48] Because job performance is usually the most important determinant of an employee's success, person-job fit is usually the primary focus of most staffing efforts.

person-job fit
The fit between a person's abilities and the demands of the job and the fit between a person's desires and motivations and the attributes and rewards of a job

From the employee's perspective, if the job does not meet his or her financial, career, lifestyle, and other needs, then the match is not ideal. An individual motivated by commissions and merit pay is not likely to be a good fit with a job based on teamwork and group rewards. Similarly, an individual who does not enjoy working with people is not likely to succeed in a sales position. It is important to consider not only the fit between an individual's talents and the job requirements, but also the fit between an individual's motivations and the rewards offered by the job.

Research suggests that person-job fit leads to higher job performance, satisfaction, organizational commitment, and intent to stay with the company.[49] Because people differ in their personality and motivations as well as their skills, consider individual differences beyond skills when making hiring decisions.

To maximize your own career success, start by setting specific career goals that align with your personal talents, desires, and values. Then create short-term and long-term plans to acquire the talents you will need to succeed in the job or series of jobs you identify.

IMPROVE YOUR SKILLS

WHAT IS YOUR LEARNING STYLE?

Annette Towler and Robert Dipboye's[50] learning style orientation measure identifies your preferred learning and instructional methods. This feature gives you the opportunity to use a condensed version of their scale to better understand your preferred learning style. Understanding your learning style will help you to choose development and learning opportunities that you can most enjoy and perform best in.

Using the scale below, record your response to each item on the line in front of it. Then follow the scoring instructions below and interpret your scores.

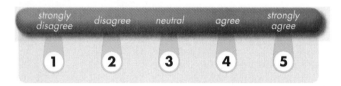

strongly disagree	disagree	neutral	agree	strongly agree
1	2	3	4	5

___ 1. I like instructors who make me think about abstract ideas.

___ 2. I enjoy learning subjects that deal with abstract ideas.

___ 3. I enjoy abstract ideas when learning.

___ 4. I like to learn subjects that allow me to ponder.

___ 5. I like problems that do not have a definitive solution.

___ 6. I like classes where there is no one correct answer but a matter of opinion.

___ 7. I am a reflective person when learning.

___ 8. I like to theorize abstract ideas.

___ 9. I like instructors who allow me to explore my own ideas.

___10. I enjoy classes when the instructor deviates from the text.

___11. I like instructors who are spontaneous.

___12. I learn a lot from instructors who stray from the main topic.

___13. I enjoy studying in a group.

___14. I prefer to study in a group.

___15. When learning, I like to go through the process with others.

___16. When learning, I do not enjoy working through problems alone.

___17. I like discussion groups.

___18. I like to put my ideas straight into practice when learning.

___19. I enjoy jumping into a task when learning.

___20. I learn best when I am given the opportunity to obtain practical experience.

___21. I like to put new knowledge to immediate use.

___22. I like to dive in and practice.

___23. For me, the best way to learn something is to put an idea straight into practice.

___24. I like to turn ideas into practical applications when learning.

___25. I enjoy being given hands-on experience.

___26. I enjoy learning practical topics.

___27. Learning material that requires action appeals to me.

___28. I enjoy work schedules.

___29. I enjoy making outlines of text and lecture material.

___30. I like to make a plan before I set out to learn something new.

___31. Devising a work schedule is something I enjoy.

___32. When learning, I like to make an outline of the ideas.

___33. When learning a new task, I like to first write down the steps I need to perform.

___34. I like to take notes while reading or listening to a lecture.

___35. I have good study habits.

___36. I like to break a task into simpler terms.

___37. I like the instructor to give me many practical examples.

___38. I like to see actual demonstrations of what I am learning.

___39. I learn best when I am given specific examples.

___40. I learn best when pictures or diagrams are provided.

___41. I prefer that the instructor provides handouts or slides covering each part of the lecture.

___42. When learning a new task, I need the instructor to give me specific guidance.

___43. To understand an abstract subject, I need to relate it to practical situations.

___44. I need the instructor to give me guidance.

___45. I prefer things that I can actually see or touch.

Scoring: Add up your responses to items 1 to 12 to get your score for discovery learning. Add up your responses to items 13 to 17 to get your score for group learning. Add up your responses to items 18 to 27 to get your score for experiential learning. Add up your responses to items 28 to 36 to get your score for structured learning. Add up your responses to items 37 to 45 to get your score for observational learning.

Interpretation: Identify your highest two scores—these are your preferred learning styles. Now read the descriptions below to learn about how you can maximize the fit of your learning environment with your preferred learning styles.

Discovery learners enjoy a broad range of learning situations, such as interactional lectures and active-reflective activities that allow them to contemplate complex issues. In particular, they enjoy subjective assessments without a right or wrong answer. Discovery learners perform well on creative tasks in unstructured learning situations. You probably perform less well in situations that require attention to detail.

Group learners enjoy learning with others and enjoy learning through group and one-on-one discussions through interpersonal contact. Group learners perform worse when they have to sit and watch. A lack of face-to-face interaction might impede your learning.

Experiential learners enjoy jumping straight into a task and putting newly acquired knowledge to immediate use. Experiential learners enjoy exercises such as role plays and simulations rather than lectures, where they must be passive. Accordingly, you might perform better in training courses that emphasize experiences.

Structured learners rely on their own information-processing strategies to learn, and prefer to impose their own structure on learning. Through their attention to detail, structured learners might be more insecure, nervous, and apprehensive in their effort to achieve perfection.[51] You perform best in learning situations where you are given autonomy and choices in training.

Observational learners tend to be passive learners who need external cues to help them learn. Observational learners do not enjoy activities that require the use of logical and abstract thinking, preferring concrete experiences organized by others, such as films or field trips that are realistic and concrete. Observational learners perform best in structured training that provides immediate and practical experiences. You will probably do less well in learning situations that are student-centered and require a high level of autonomy.

Source: Towler, A., & Dipboye, R. L., Development of a Learning Style Orientation Measure. Organizational Research Methods, 6, 216–235. © 2003 by SAGE Publications. Reprinted by Permission of SAGE Publications.

Person-Group Fit

In addition to fit with the job, the fit between the employee and his or her workgroup and supervisor is also important. Good *person-group fit* (or person-team fit) means that an individual fits with the workgroup's work styles, skills, and goals. Person-group fit recognizes that employees often must work effectively with their workgroup or teammates to be successful. Person-group fit leads to improved job satisfaction, organizational commitment, and intent to stay with the company.[52v]

Teamwork, communication, and interpersonal competencies can be as critical to team performance as team members' ability to perform core job duties. Person-group fit is thus particularly important in team-oriented work environments.[53] Men's Wearhouse CEO George Zimmer rewards team selling because the company's customers want to have a positive store experience. Team selling is taken so seriously that the company once terminated one of its most successful salespeople because he focused only on maximizing his own sales. After firing the salesperson, the store's total sales volume increased significantly.[54]

person-group fit
Match between an individual and his or her supervisor and workgroup

SO WHAT

Selecting members whose individual characteristics and personal goals are consistent with the needs of the workgroup is particularly important in team-based environments.

Person-Organization Fit

Person-organization fit is the fit between an individual's values, beliefs, and personality and the values, norms, and culture of the organization.[55] The strength of this fit influences important organizational outcomes including job performance, retention, job satisfaction, and organizational commitment.[56] As one expert states, "If you're in the right environment, it's like you're hooked up to a generator with positive power continuously surging into you. If you're not culturally aligned, it's like you're draining power from a NiCad battery that eventually will run dry."[57] Organizational values and norms that are important for person-organization fit include integrity, fairness, work ethic, competitiveness, cooperativeness, and compassion for fellow employees and customers.

Person-organization fit has a strong positive relationship with job satisfaction, organizational commitment, and intent to stay with the company, and can influence employee attitudes and citizenship behaviors beyond the job requirements, such as helping others or talking positively about the firm.[58] It also has a modest impact on turnover and tenure, but little to no impact on meeting job requirements.[59] Despite the potential overlap between person-job and person-organization fit, research suggests that people may experience differing degrees of fit with the job and with the organization.[60] Essentially, it is

person-organization fit
Fit between an individual's values, beliefs, attitudes, and personality and the values, norms, and culture of the organization

Zappos understands the importance of hiring employees who are a good fit with its strong culture of providing excellent customer service. One way it pursues this goal is to offer new customer service agents $2,000 to leave the company after the initial training period if the employee feels that he or she is not a good fit with Zappos.

© Ronda Churchill/Bloomberg /Getty Images

possible to like what you do but not where you do it, or to like where you work but not what you do there.

So how can you maximize person-organization fit? A good place to start is to identify those qualifications, competencies, and traits that relate to the organization's strategy, values, and processes and hire people with those characteristics. For example, even if Maria is technically well qualified as a researcher, if she avoids risk, is indecisive, and tends to ruminate over a decision, she may be unsuccessful in an innovative, fast-paced company.

Online shoe retailer Zappos.com attributes its success to its culture of great customer service, high energy, and employee autonomy. Because it does not monitor its customer service agents' call times or give them scripts, it is critical to make sure they are a good fit with the Zappos culture. One of the ways the company does that is to offer new customer service agents $2,000 to leave the company after the initial training period if they feel that they are a poor fit.[61] To find the best matches for their culture and business, The Container Store's online application includes questions asking job candidates to reveal their favorite Container Store product. Additional questions explore communications skills and other characteristics. Using the website also helps the candidate learn more about the company and be better prepared for an interview. This process helps to persuade strong candidates that The Container Store is a good fit for their interests and needs.

Employees must be able and willing to adapt to a company by learning, negotiating, enacting, and maintaining the behaviors appropriate to the company's environment.[62] To successfully adapt, employees must be open-minded and have sufficient information about organizational expectations and standards, and their own performance in light of those standards. Employees also must be able and willing to learn new behaviors and habits (e.g., low anxiety, high self-esteem, good time management skills, etc.).

Hiring for any type of fit does not mean simply hiring those with whom we are most comfortable, which can lead to dysfunctional stereotyping and discrimination against people who may actually contribute a great deal to the company's success. One company that assesses and selects employees based on their fit with the organization's core values is Johnson & Johnson (J&J). J&J's credo[63] clearly spells out J&J's values: customer well-being, employee well-being, community well-being, and shareholder well-being, in that order. Johnson & Johnson recruits, hires, and evaluates employees against their credo, which is central to J&J's organizational culture. Ralph Larsen, J&J Chairman and CEO, attributes the majority of J&J's success to the company's core values.[64]

Table 4-1 summarizes some common characteristics of organizational culture and identifies some personality traits that fit each one. Think about your own personality, and use this table to reflect on what type of organization might be the best fit for you.

Person-Vocation Fit

Person-vocation fit is the fit between a person's interests, abilities, values, and personality and a profession.[66] Our adjustment and satisfaction are greater when our occupation meets our needs. For example, a social individual who is low in conscientiousness and dislikes working with numbers would be a poor fit with the engineering vocation.

person-vocation fit
The fit between a person's interests, abilities, values, and personality and a profession

John Holland proposed a six-dimensional vocational model that represents characteristics of the work environment, personality traits, and interests of working people.[67] These dimensions are:

1. *Realistic*: building, practical, hands-on, tool-oriented, physical
2. *Investigative*: analyzing, intellectual, scientific
3. *Artistic*: creating, original, independent, chaotic
4. *Social*: supporting, helping, cooperative, healing
5. *Enterprising*: persuading, leadership, competitive
6. *Conventional*: detail-oriented, organizing, clerical

Table 4-1

Personality Traits and Workplace Culture[65]

Organizational Culture Characteristic	Matching Personality Trait
High ability to influence	Challenges authority; likes being empowered
Low ability to influence	Respects hierarchical structure; needs direction
High comfort with ambiguity	Adventurous, risk taking
Low comfort with ambiguity	Cautious, rigorous
High achievement	Achievement striving, assertive, high activity level
Low achievement	A follower, contemplative, less concerned with high performance
Collectivist	Cooperative, trusting, altruistic
Individualist	Independent, low in trust, low in altruism
Public	Friendly, seeks company of people, extroverted
Private	Reserved, needs privacy, self-conscious

Holland viewed vocational interests as an expression of personality. There is some overlap between his six dimensions and other personality frameworks such as the Big Five.[68] The pattern of personality variables associated with occupational success is consistent with Holland's framework.[69] Success in artistic occupations depends on high scores for openness along with low scores for conscientiousness, for example, and success in conventional occupations depends on low scores for openness and high scores for conscientiousness.

Although individuals usually choose a vocation long before applying to an organization, understanding person-vocation fit can still be useful to organizations and managers. Companies wanting to develop their own future leaders, or smaller organizations that need employees to fill multiple roles, may be able to use vocational interests in determining whether job applicants would be a good fit with the organization's future needs.

Some people pursue two or more different vocations over the course of their careers because they have diverse interests or because they become bored working a long time in the same career. Organizations may better retain valued career changers by understanding their vocational preferences and designing career tracks for them that place them in new roles in the organization over time that are consistent with their vocational interests and aptitudes. This allows valued employees who would otherwise be likely to leave the organization to pursue a different type of vocation to pursue multiple vocations within the company.

Table 4-2 summarizes these four different types of fit.

complementary fit

The degree to which an employee adds something that is missing in the organization or workgroup by being different from the others

Complementary and Supplementary Fit

People can fit into an organization or workgroup in two ways.[70] *Complementary fit* is the degree to which an employee adds something that is missing

Table 4-2

Dimensions of Fit

Type of Fit	Possible Dimensions of Fit
Person-Job Fit: Does the person meet the needs of the job and does the job meet the needs of the person?	Intelligence Job-related skills Job knowledge Previous work experience Personality related to performing job tasks
Person-Group Fit: Does the employee fit the workgroup, including the supervisor?	Teamwork skills Knowledge and ability relative to other team members Conflict management style Preference for teamwork Communication skills Personality related to working well with others
Person-Organization Fit: Does the individual's values, beliefs, and personality fit the values, norms, and culture of the organization?	Alignment between personal motivations and the organization's culture, mission, and purpose Values Goals
Person-Vocation Fit: Does the person's interests, abilities, values, and personality fit his or her occupation?	Aptitudes Interests Personal values Long-term goals

© CENGAGE LEARNING 2012

in the organization or workgroup by being different from the others, often by having different abilities or expertise.[71] A consumer products company seeks complementary fit, for example, when it seeks product development specialists with new backgrounds and skills to work with existing employees to develop a new line of products.

As J. J. Allaire, Founder, Chairman, and Executive VP of Products at Allaire Corporation, said, "It's tempting not to hire people who compensate for your weaknesses—because you don't want to admit that you have any. But . . . you've got to understand the strengths and weaknesses of your entire group and hire accordingly."[72] Although culture alignment increases employees' comfort levels, too much comfort can lead to complacency and groupthink.

Supplementary fit is the degree to which a person's characteristics are similar to those that already exist in the organization.[73] Supplementary fit can be important when a firm needs to replace a departing reservations agent with someone who can perform the job similarly to the other agents. In this case, the company would try to hire a reservations agent with characteristics similar to its current employees.

Both complementary and supplementary fit are important. Together they help to ensure that new hires will fit in with the workgroup and organization but also bring new skills and perspectives that will enhance the workgroup's and organization's performance. When SCA Tissue North America realized that it had such a high level of respect in its culture that it became demotivating, the company responded by adding new employees who understood the value of challenging others' ideas.[74]

Ben Schneider's Attraction-Selection-Attrition[75] (ASA) framework proposes that over time, the processes of attraction to organizations, selection into organizations, and attrition from organizations creates a restriction of range on a wide variety of individual differences. Consequently, the people who remain in an organization end up working with colleagues much like themselves because the "fit" is better.

> "It's tempting not to hire people who compensate for your weaknesses—because you don't want to admit that you have any. But . . . you've got to understand the strengths and weaknesses of your entire group and hire accordingly." —*J. J. Allaire, Founder, Chairman, and Executive VP of Products at Allaire Corporation*

supplementary fit
The degree to which a person's characteristics are similar to those that already exist in the organization

SO WHAT
Sometimes workgroups need members to have similar skills; other times they need members who have different skills.

Psychological Contracts

A *psychological contract* refers to employer and employee expectations of the employment relationship, including mutual obligations, values, expectations, and aspirations that operate over and above the formal contract of employment.[76] If the employer and employee do not agree about what the contract involves, employees may feel that promises have been broken, or that the psychological contract has been violated.

Employees hold many different types of employee expectations both consciously (e.g., expectations about job performance, security, and financial rewards) and unconsciously (e.g, being looked after by the employer).[77] For example, an employer may expect a worker not to harm the company's public image, and an employee may expect to not be terminated after many years' service. The psychological contract is dynamic and evolves over time as a result of both the employees' and employer's changing needs and relationships. These expectations may not be written into any formal agreement, but they are powerful determinants of behavior. Because psychological contract violations have negative implications for employee trust,[78] performance,[79] and behavior,[80] they are important in understanding and managing behavior in organizations.[81]

psychological contract
Employer and employee expectations of the employment relationship, including mutual obligations, values, expectations, and aspirations that operate over and above the formal contract of employment

Esteemed management scholar Denise Rousseau differentiates "relational contracts," which depend on trust and loyalty, from "transactional contracts" in which employees do not expect a long-lasting relationship with their organization. In a transactional contract, employees view their employment as a transaction in which, for example, long hours and extra work are provided in exchange for good pay and benefits.[82]

Both individual and organizational factors are involved in the development of the psychological contract. Individual determinants include experiences and expectations that may have been formed about employment relationships prior to employment, during recruitment, during early organizational socialization, or from experiences in the course of employment.[83] These experiences and expectations may vary according to individual differences including age, gender, level of education, and union membership.[84] Organizational factors, including human resource policies and practices, can indicate certain promises or obligations on the part of the employer and influence employees' expectations.[85] Many organizations are operating with a cultural lag from the old psychological contract.[86] They want the flexibility of "new" contracts but retain the artifacts of a traditional contract (e.g. career paths, benefits, etc.). This indicates a need for employers to be clearer and more explicit about mutual obligations and to communicate them unambiguously.

There is evidence that older members of the workforce feel that the psychological contract, as they understand it, has been violated, and that they have lost trust in their organizations.[87] Younger workers may have different expectations for their contracts[88] that reflect the changing realities of the labor market and the employment relationship.[89] A sense of violation is related to different expectations or perceived promises. Among younger workers, for example, there may be less sense of violation if job descriptions change, and a higher sense of violation for a denial of quick advancement or challenging work[90] or for lack of work-life support.[91]

One expert states, "The best contract you can have is where the individual does not ask the organization to do the impossible and the individual does not expect the impossible of the organization."[92] Some companies like the pharmaceutical firm AstraZeneca are careful to manage the psychological contract with their employees. An AstraZeneca representative states, "We articulate the psychological contract—what our commitment is to the employee, and what we expect of them. They have this the minute they come into the organization. For some, the motivation is simply to come to work and get paid, for others it's about nourishing their soul. The important thing is that they are honest about their aspirations."[93]

This chapter's *Global Issues* feature describes some global differences in psychological contracts.

Realistic Job Previews

When communicating the nature of the work and the organization to job candidates, companies can choose how objective to be. Many firms choose to disclose as little potentially undesirable information as possible to reduce the chance that it will make the position unappealing. Essentially, some firms believe that if they tell recruits what it is really like to work there, the recruits will not want the job. However, this focus on hiring people without giving them a thorough understanding of what they are getting themselves into can backfire.

SO WHAT
Clear psychological contracts promote trust and increase employee motivation.

GLOBAL ISSUES

GLOBAL DIFFERENCES IN PSYCHOLOGICAL CONTRACTS

Psychological contracts create implied promises and obligations between employees and the employer. Because what the exchange means to workers or employers is subjective and affected by personal values, upbringing, the broader society, and the history of the relationship, psychological contracts can be influenced by national culture. For example:[94]

- In French employment relationships, psychological contracts are based more on conflict than on agreement.
- The Japanese experience of organizational membership places a sense of belonging at the center of the employment relationship.

- Workers' perceptions of whom their employment relationship is with differs across countries: Workers in the United States view the relationship as being with the employer; Australians view it as being with coworkers; and French workers view it as being with the state itself.
- Being singled out for high performance is seen as undesirable by workers in some societies including Australia, Japan, and The Netherlands.

Your effectiveness as a manager will increase if you recognize and attend to the different expectations of employees from different cultures.

Different people prefer different types of jobs and organizations. If the fit is not good once people are hired, they tend to leave. Companies are increasingly putting interactive features and questionnaires on their websites to communicate their culture and give applicants insights into what it is like to work there. This increases the accuracy of new employees' expectations, and decreases psychological contract violations.

Realistic job previews (RJPs) involve the presentation of both positive and potentially negative information to job candidates. Rather than trying to sell candidates on the job and company by presenting the job opportunity in the most positive light, the company strives to present an accurate picture through an RJP. The goal is not to deter candidates, but rather to provide accurate information about the job and organization and build trust.[95] Hiring customers and using employee referrals are among the methods many companies, including Apple featured in this chapter's opening real world challenge, use to give job candidates realistic information about what it would be like to work at that company.

Walt Disney World in Lake Buena Vista, Florida, employing more than 55,000 people and hiring an average of 200 people a day, uses realistic job previews. Before completing an application or being interviewed, candidates view a film illustrating what working at Disney is like. After viewing it, about 10 percent of candidates drop out of the hiring process. Disney sees this as a good thing, as those self-selecting themselves out probably would not have been a good fit with the organization.[96] Cisco Systems' Make Friends @ Cisco program uses employee volunteers to answer phone or e-mail queries from job seekers who would like more information about working at Cisco.

If a common reason for employees leaving an organization is that the job is not what they expected, this is a good sign that the recruiting message can be improved. Giving applicants the opportunity to self-select out of the hiring process if they do not perceive themselves to be good fits with the position or organization increases the likelihood that the applicants ultimately hired will be good fits and will be better employees as a result. Given the relatively low cost associated with their development, RJPs may be useful for organizations trying to reduce turnover rates for jobs that departing employees say were not what they expected when they accepted job offers.

This chapter's *Case Study* feature describes how Hilton has used RJPs to hire employees who are less likely to quit in the first 90 days.

realistic job previews
Provide both positive and potentially negative information to job candidates

SO WHAT
Giving prospective employees realistic information about what the job will be like helps poor fits self-select themselves out of consideration.

CASE STUDY

....

Improving Retention through RJPs at Hilton

Hilton Hotels appreciates the important role its employees play in customer satisfaction and retention.[97] The company also recognizes that turnover costs Hilton in terms of lost training investment, increased hiring costs, and lower job performance.

Hilton was experiencing annual turnover among its housekeeping staff that approached 100 percent. Hilton realized that the reason turnover was highest during the first 60 days is because housekeeping job applicants do not have a good understanding of what commercial cleaning consists of. Because of these inaccurate perceptions about the job, the company thought that realistic job previews might help to improve the accuracy of new hires' job expectations and improve retention.[98]

Housekeeping job candidates now first sign a waiver freeing Hilton of liability and acknowledging that the voluntary job tryout is one of several factors that will be used to evaluate the candidate for employment. Candidates then participate in a four-hour job trial exercise, which includes making six beds. The effort has reduced housekeeping turnover by 30 percent.[99]

Hilton also created a demanding twenty-four-hour assessment involving a series of simulations to provide a realistic preview of the demands and pace of managerial jobs. Candidates appreciated the realistic indication of the job demands and the quality of new hires increased.[100]

Questions:

1. What types of fit was Hilton interested in improving?
2. How can recruitment messages improve different types of fit?
3. How did the job trial provide a realistic job preview? How else could Hilton improve the fit of its housekeepers with their jobs and with the company?

Some companies have used realistic job previews to counter inaccurate employer images. The fast-food giant McDonald's has responded to critics in the United Kingdom who claimed it was a poor employer by launching a poster campaign using the slogan "Not bad for a McJob," detailing the company's benefits and flexible hours. This is the first time McDonald's has tried to combat the negative misconceptions that have been associated with the title "McJob" since the term was first used by Douglas Copeland in his bestselling novel *Generation X: Tales for an Accelerated Culture*. A McDonald's executive who believes that a huge gap exists between the external perception and the internal reality of working at McDonald's states, "Our employer reputation isn't justified; we have to accept that this association exists and correct it."[101]

SUMMARY AND APPLICATION

Front line managers are essential to attracting and retaining talented employees—any company lacking great front-line managers will suffer. The best managers recognize and appreciate the differences in their employees and build on each person's unique strengths rather than trying to fix his or her weaknesses. They also focus on finding the right job fit for each person, even if that is not the next typical promotion from the employee's current job.[102] Understanding how people differ in their self-concepts and learning styles can help you match your management style and OB tools to each employee. By identifying your own characteristics, you also can best select the jobs and companies in which you are most likely to enjoy working and succeed.

REAL WORLD RESPONSE

APPLE'S EMPLOYER BRAND

Hiring employees who view their role as attacking the status quo helps to spur the continuous and disruptive innovation that is central to Apple's business strategy.[103] The management team at Apple Computer understands the importance of a strong brand image in appealing to both customers and recruits. Apple closely integrates its product brand with its employer brand to persuasively communicate its employer brand to targeted recruits. Videos and images in the main career areas of Apple's website contain messages including, "Amaze yourself. Amaze the world," "Part career, part revolution," and "Whatever your job is here, you'll be part of something big."[104]

Apple's emotionally compelling "Think Different" commercial highlighting famous risk takers including Albert Einstein, Amelia Earhart, and Martin Luther King also helped to clearly identify Apple's employment brand. Creative people who take risks and who do things against the grain, and who think differently are good fits with Apple's culture.

To staff its retail stores, Apple does not look for technical mastery or exceptional intelligence. Apple wants enthusiastic, friendly, appealing employees who enjoy helping others discover tools they can use to enhance their lives. Apple recruiters look for people who smile warmly throughout the rigorous interview process, and are nice to everyone they meet. In group interviews hiring managers look for humble, outgoing, team-oriented people who are willing to help others and ask for assistance when needed.[105]

Although Apple pays its employees on par with other retailers, by hiring employees with the individual differences that fit its culture and who are enthusiastic about their job of helping improve people's lives it enjoys low employee turnover, high customer satisfaction, and high profit per employee.[106]

✓ TAKEAWAY POINTS

1. Self-concept is a person's perceptions of him- or herself. It is formed through our experiences and interactions with others. The three primary self-concept traits are self-esteem, core self-evaluations, and self-efficacy. Because believing that we are not good at something makes it less likely that we will perform well at it, effective managers try to boost employees' self-efficacy on tasks that the employees should be able to do well.

2. A *learning goal orientation* reflects a belief that abilities are changeable, and a desire to increase task mastery or competence. Learning goal oriented individuals are interested in developing new skills, understanding

and improving their work, improving their competence, and achieving task mastery based on self-referenced standards. Individuals with a high *performance goal orientation* believe that their ability is fixed and want to demonstrate their ability by outperforming others, exceeding normative standards, and achieving success with limited effort. They also may have an increased fear of failure and of negative evaluations by others.

3. *Experiential learners,* who enjoy exercises such as role plays and simulations rather than lectures where they must be passive, might perform better in training courses that emphasize experiences. *Group learners,* who enjoy learning with others and through group and one-on-one discussions with interpersonal contact, perform worse when they have to sit and watch. *Discovery learners* enjoy a broad range of learning situations, such as interactional lectures, active-reflective activities that allow them to contemplate complex issues, and, in particular, subjective assessments without a right or wrong answer. They perform well on creative tasks in unstructured learning situations. *Observational learners* tend to be passive learners who need external cues to help them learn, and do not enjoy activities that require the use of logical and abstract thinking. They prefer concrete experiences organized by others, such as films or field trips that are realistic and concrete, and perform best in structured training that provides immediate and practical experiences. *Structured learners,* who rely on their own information-processing strategies to learn and prefer to impose their own structure on learning, perform best in learning situations where they are given autonomy and choices in training.

4. *Person-job fit* reflects the fit between a person's abilities and the demands of the job and the fit between a person's desires and motivations and the attributes and rewards of a job. *Person-group fit* reflects the fit between the person and his or her workgroup and supervisor. *Person-organization fit* reflects the fit between the person and the organization's values, norms, and culture. *Person-vocation fit* reflects the fit between a person's interests, abilities, values, and personality and his or her chosen occupation, regardless of the person's employer.

5. A psychological contract refers to employer and employee expectations of the employment relationship, including mutual obligations, values, and expectations that operate over and above the formal contract of employment. Realistic job previews involve the presentation of both positive and potentially negative information to job candidates so that they can self-assess their fit with the organization and the psychological contract it offers.

6. Realistic job previews can support psychological contracts by increasing the accuracy of employees' expectations of the employer.

DISCUSSION QUESTIONS

1. If an employee of yours had low self-efficacy toward a work task that you felt she or he should be able to do, what would you do?
2. Which do you feel is more important to career success, self-efficacy or general self-efficacy?
3. When would a learning goal orientation be preferred to a performance goal orientation? When would a performance goal orientation be preferred to a learning goal orientation?
4. Think of a time when the learning environment did not match your preferred learning style. What happened and how did you cope with the misfit?

5. As a manager, how can you effectively use knowledge of your subordinates' learning styles to improve your coaching of them?
6. Which type of fit do you feel is most important to organizations? Why?
7. Would learning realistic information about a job or organization make you more or less likely to pursue the job opportunity? What types of information would discourage you from pursuing the job? Why?

EXERCISES

What Is Your Goal Orientation?[107]

This exercise gives you the opportunity to better understand your learning and performance goal orientations.

Instructions: Below are several statements about you with which you may agree or disagree. There are no right or wrong answers. Using the response scale below, indicate your agreement or disagreement with each item by placing the appropriate number on the line preceding that item.

strongly disagree	disagree	neutral	agree	strongly agree
1	2	3	4	5

___ 1. The opportunity to do challenging work is important to me.
___ 2. I do my best when I'm working on a fairly difficult task.
___ 3. I try hard to improve on my past performance.
___ 4. When I have difficulty solving a problem, I enjoy trying different approaches to see which one will work.
___ 5. The opportunity to learn new things is important to me.
___ 6. The opportunity to extend the range of my abilities is important to me.
___ 7. I prefer to work on tasks that force me to learn new things.
___ 8. When I fail to complete a difficult task, I plan to try harder the next time I work on it.
___ 9. The things I enjoy the most are the things I do the best.
___10. I feel smart when I can do something better than most other people.
___11. I like to be fairly confident that I can successfully perform a task before I attempt it.
___12. I am happiest at work when I perform tasks on which I know that I won't make any errors.
___13. I feel smart when I do something without making any mistakes.
___14. I prefer to do things that I can do well rather than things that I do poorly.
___15. The opinions others have about how well I can do certain things are important to me.
___16. I like to work on tasks that I have done well on in the past.

Scoring: Add up your scores for questions 1 to 8. This is your learning goal orientation score. Now add up your scores for questions 9 to 16. This is your performance goal orientation score.

Source: Reprinted from Organizational Behavior and Human Decision Processes, 67, Button, S. B., Mathieu, J. E., & Zajac, D. M., "Goal Orientation in Organizational Research: A Conceptual and Empirical Foundation", 26–48, 1996, with permission from Elsevier.

Interpretation:[108]

Learning goal orientation:

If your score is *below 25,* you have a relatively low learning goal orientation.

If your score is *between 25 and 35,* you have an average learning goal orientation.

If your score is *above 35,* you have a relatively high learning goal orientation

Performance goal orientation:

If your score is *below 25,* you have a relatively low performance goal orientation.

If your score is *between 25 and 35,* you have an average performance goal orientation.

If your score is *above 35,* you have a relatively high performance goal orientation.

Now reread the part of the chapter that discusses learning and performance goal orientations to interpret your scores and answer the following questions.

Questions

1. Do you agree or disagree with your scores for your learning and performance goal orientations? Do the scores match your self-perceptions? What aspects of the descriptions of these orientations best describe you?
2. When do you think it would be best to adopt a learning goal orientation? Why? Given that a learning goal orientation is malleable, what might you do to increase your learning goal orientation in these situations?
3. When do you think it would be best to adopt a performance goal orientation? Why? Given that a performance goal orientation is malleable, what might you do to increase your performance goal orientation in these situations?

Fitting In at Johnson & Johnson

In a group of four to five people, read J&J's credo (http://www.jnj.com/connect/about-jnj/jnj-credo/) and answer the questions below. Be prepared to share your answers with the class.

Questions

1. Given the information in the Credo, what types of people (i.e., what individual differences) would be a good fit with Johnson & Johnson?
2. How could selecting people who fit with its Credo create a competitive advantage for J&J?
3. What types of fit do you think J&J would be most interested in maximizing in new hires? Why? How could it maximize this fit?

VIDEO CASES

Now What?

Imagine meeting with a subordinate who has been working at Happy Time Toys for a month and can't yet meet the company's goals. The subordinate tried hard to perform well during the training session to look good compared to the other new hires, but the others are doing a lot better on the job. The subordinate communicates frustration about being unable to learn the new job. *What do you say or do?* Go to this chapter's "Now What?" video, watch the challenge video, and choose a response. Be sure to also view the outcomes of the two responses you didn't choose.

Discussion Questions

1. Why do you think the employee was unable to perform better at first?
2. Which aspects of organizational behavior discussed in this chapter are illustrated in these videos? Explain your answer.
3. How else would you handle this situation? Explain your answer.

Workplace | Numi Organic Tea: Dynamics of Behavior in Organizations

Getting a job offer from Numi Organic Tea is kind of like getting accepted into a big mafia family, minus the illegal activities and violence. Fierce loyalty is critical for survival. A willingness to work long, odd hours is non-negotiable.

When asked about Numi's hiring practices, co-founder Ahmed Rahim responded, "People are everything for a company. You can have a great product and great mission, but without the right people, you don't have the right formula."

Numi hasn't had much trouble finding and retaining talent. Approximately fifty people work for the progressive Oakland-based company, and Rahim has reduced the potential for turnover by making sure every candidate has the right skills and experience and fits well with the organization's culture.

In particular, Numi executives seek individuals who are passionate about Numi tea and share the organization's commitment to organics, sustainability, and fair trade. Employees who share Numi's cultural values can effectively represent the organization in any situation.

Although many companies have employees who are ambitious and hardworking, Numi is fully staffed with high-achieving, high-performance types that will do whatever it takes to make Numi the most successful tea brand in the world.

(Continued)

Discussion Questions

1. What question does Numi owner Ahmed Rahim ask job candidates to help evaluate person-organization fit? Why is this important?

2. What individual qualities are difficult to assess through a typical interviewing process, and how might realistic job previews help Numi increase the effectiveness of its recruitment efforts?

3 Do you think an individual motivated by traditional pay and bonuses would be a good fit with Numi? Why or why not?

DO WHAT CENGAGENOW

CENGAGENOW™ includes **teaching and learning resources** to supplement the text, and is designed specifically to **help students "think like managers"** by engaging and challenging them to think critically about managerial situations. **CengageNOW uses today's technology to improve the skills** of tomorrow's managers.

END NOTES

[1]Prodhan, G. & Sharp, A. (2011, May 9) Apple Usurps Google as World's Most Valuable Brand, *Reuters*. Available online: http://www.reuters.com/article/2011/05/09/us-apple-brand-idUSTRE74800D20110509.

[2] Sullivan, J. (2011, September 26). Talent Management Lessons from Apple...A Case Study of the World's Most Valuable Firm, ERE.net. Available online: http://www.ere.net/2011/09/26/talent-management-lessons-from-apple%E2%80%A6-a-case-study-of-the-worlds-most-valuable-firm-part-3-of-4/.

[3]Collins, C., Ericksen, J., & Allen, M. (2005). Human Resource Management Practices, Workforce Alignment, and Firm Performance. CAHRS Working Paper Series. Cornell University ILR School, Working Paper 05-05.

[4]Shavelson, R. J., Hubner, J. J., & Stanton, G. C. (1976). Self-Concept: Validation of Construct Interpretations. *Review of Educational Research, 46*, 407–441.

[5]Shavelson, R. J., Hubner, J. J., & Stanton, G. C. (1976). Self-Concept: Validation of Construct Interpretations. *Review of Educational Research, 46*, 407–441, p. 411.

[6]Brockner, J. (1988). *Self-Esteem at Work: Research, Theory, and Practice.* Lexington, MA: Lexington Books; Chen, G., Gully, S. M., & Eden, D. (2004). General Self-Efficacy and Self-Esteem: Toward Theoretical and Empirical Distinction Between Correlated Self-Evaluations. *Journal of Organizational Behavior, 25*, 375–395.

[7]Chen, G., Gully, S. M., & Eden, D. (2004). General Self-Efficacy and Self-Esteem: Toward Theoretical and Empirical Distinction Between Correlated Self-Evaluations. *Journal of Organizational Behavior, 25*, 375–395.

[8]Judge, T. A., & Bono, J. E. (2001). Relationship of Core Self-Evaluations Traits—Self-Esteem, Generalized Self-Efficacy, Locus of Control, and Emotional Stability—With Job Satisfaction and Job Performance: A Meta-Analysis. *Journal of Applied Psychology, 86*(1), 80–92.

[9]Chen, G., Gully, S. M., & Eden, D. (2004). General Self-Efficacy and Self-Esteem: Toward Theoretical and Empirical Distinction Between Correlated Self-Evaluations. *Journal of Organizational Behavior, 25*, 375–395.

[10]Chen, G. (2012). Evaluating the Core: Critical Assessment of Core Self-Evaluations Theory, *Journal of Organizational Behavior, 33*(2), 153–160; Judge, T. A., & Larsen, R. J. (2001). Dispositional Source of Job Satisfaction: A Review and Theoretical Extension. *Organizational Behavior and Human Decision Processes, 86*, 67–98.

[11]Judge, T. A., & Bono, J. E. (2001). Relationship of Core Self-Evaluations Traits—Self-Esteem, Generalized Self-Efficacy, Locus of Control, and Emotional Stability—With Job Satisfaction and Job Performance: A Meta-Analysis. *Journal of Applied Psychology, 86*, 80–92.

[12]Judge, T. A., Locke, E. A., Durham, C. C., & Kluger, A. N. (1998). Dispositional Effects on Job and Life Satisfaction: The Role of Core Evaluations. *Journal of Applied Psychology, 83*, 17–34.

[13]Heller, D., Judge, T. A., & Watson, D. (2002). The Confounding Role of Personality and Trait Affectivity in the Relationship Between Job and Life Satisfaction. *Journal of Organizational Behavior, 23*, 815–835.

[14]Erez, A., & Judge, T. A. (2001). Relationship of Core Self-Evaluations to Goal Setting, Motivation, and Performance. *Journal of Applied Psychology, 86,* 1270–1279.

[15]Nauta, M.M., Liu, C. & Li, C. (2010). A Cross-National Examination of Self-Efficacy as a Moderator of Autonomy/Job Strain Relationships, *Applied Psychology, 59*(1), 159–179.

[16]Chen, G., Gully, S. M., & Eden, D. (2001). Validation of a New General Self-Efficacy Scale. *Organizational Research Methods, 4,* 62–83.

[17]Dweck, C. S. (1986). Motivational Processes Affecting Learning. *American Psychologist, 41,* 1040–1048.

[18]Dweck, C. S. (1986). Motivational Processes Affecting Learning. *American Psychologist, 41,* 1040–1048; Farr, J. L., Hofmann, D. A., & Ringenbach, K. L. (1993). Goal Orientation and Action Control Theory: Implications for Industrial and Organizational Psychology. In *International Review of Industrial and Organizational Psychology,* eds. C. L. Cooper and I. T. Robertson (pp. 193–232). New York: Wiley; Phillips, J. M., & Gully, S. M. (1997). The Role of Goal Orientation, Ability, Need for Achievement, and Locus of Control in the Self-Efficacy and Goal Setting Process. *Journal of Applied Psychology, 82,* 792–802; VandeWalle, D. (1997). Development and Validation of a Work Domain Goal Orientation Instrument. *Educational and Psychological Measurement, 57,* 995–1015.

[19]VandeWalle, D. (1997). Development and Validation of a Work Domain Goal Orientation Instrument. *Educational and Psychological Measurement, 57,* 995–1015.

[20]Payne, S. C., Youngcourt, S. S., & Beaubien, J. M. (2007). Meta-Analytic Examination of the Goal Orientation Nomological Net. *Journal of Applied Psychology, 92,* 128–150; chughati, A. A. & Buckley, F. (2010). Assessing the Effects of Organizational Identification on In-Role Job Performance and Learning Behaviour: The Mediating Role of Learning Goal Orientation, *Personnel Review, 39*(2), 242–258.

[21]Payne, S. C., Youngcourt, S. S., & Beaubien, J. M. (2007). Meta-Analytic Examination of the Goal Orientation Nomological Net. *Journal of Applied Psychology, 92,* 128–150.

[22]Kozlowski, S. W. J., Gully, S. M., Brown, K. G., Salas, E., Smith, E. M., & Nason, E. R. (2001). Effects of Training Goals and Goal Orientation Traits on Multi-Dimensional Training Outcomes and Performance Adaptability. *Organizational Behavior and Human Decision Processes, 85,* 1–31.

[23]Colquitt, J. A., & Simmering, M. J. (1998). Conscientiousness, Goal Orientation, and Motivation to Learn During the Learning Process: A Longitudinal Study. *Journal of Applied Psychology, 83,* 654–665.

[24]Brett, J. F., & VandeWalle, D. (1999). Goal Orientation and Goal Content as Predictors of Performance in a Training Program. *Journal of Applied Psychology, 84*(6), 863–873; Phillips, J. M., & Gully, S. M. (1997). The Role of Goal Orientation, Ability, Need for Achievement, and Locus of Control in the Self-Efficacy and Goal Setting Process. *Journal of Applied Psychology, 82,* 792–802.

[25]Gully, S. M., & Chen, G. (in press). Individual Differences, Attribute-Treatment Interactions, and Training Outcomes. To appear in: *Learning, Training, and Development in Organizations,* eds. S. W. J. Kozlowski and E. Salas. SIOP Organizational Frontiers Series. San Francisco, CA: Jossey-Bass.

[26]Farr, J. L., Hofmann, D. A., & Ringenbach, K. L. (1993). Goal Orientation and Action Control Theory: Implications for Industrial and Organizational Psychology. In *International Review of Industrial and Organizational Psychology,* eds. C. L. Cooper and I. T. Robertson (pp. 193–232). New York: Wiley; DeGeest, D & Brown, K.G. (2011). The Role of Goal Orientation in Leadership Development, *Human Resource Development Quarterly, 22*(2), 157–175.

[27]Farr, J. L., Hofmann, D. A., & Ringenbach, K. L. (1993). Goal Orientation and Action Control Theory: Implications for Industrial and Organizational Psychology. In *International Review of Industrial and Organizational Psychology,* eds. C. L. Cooper and I. T. Robertson (pp. 193–232). New York: Wiley; Gully, S. M., & Phillips, J. M. (2005). A Multilevel Application of Learning and Performance Orientations to Individual, Group, and Organizational Outcomes. In *Research in Personnel and Human Resources Management,* ed. J. Martocchio (Vol. 24, pp. 1–51). Greenwich, CT: JAI Press/Elsevier Science.

[28]Payne, S. C., Youngcourt, S. S., & Beaubien, J. M. (2007). Meta-Analytic Examination of the Goal Orientation Nomological Net. *Journal of Applied Psychology, 92,* 128–150.

[29]Colquitt, J. A., & Simmering, M. J. (1998). Conscientiousness, Goal Orientation, and Motivation to Learn During the Learning Process: A Longitudinal Study. *Journal of Applied Psychology, 83,* 654–665.

[30]Payne, S. C., Youngcourt, S. S., & Beaubien, J. M. (2007). Meta-Analytic Examination of the Goal Orientation Nomological Net. *Journal of Applied Psychology, 92,* 128–150.

[31]Chen, G., Gully, S. M., Whiteman, J. A., & Kilcullen, B. N. (2000). Examination of Relationships Among Trait-Like Individual Differences, State-Like Individual Differences, and Learning Performance. *Journal of Applied Psychology, 85,* 835–847.

[32]Hofmann, D. A. (1993). The Influence of Goal Orientation on Task Performance: A Substantively Meaningful Suppressor Variable. *Journal of Applied Social Psychology, 23,* 1827–1846.

[33]Weissbein, D.A., Huang, J.L., Ford, J.K., & Schmidt, A.M. (2011). Influencing Learning States to Enhance Trainee Motivation and Improve Training Transfer, *Journal of Business and Psychology, 26*(4), 423–435; Martocchio, J. J. (1994). The Effects of Conceptions of Ability on Self-Efficacy Beliefs and Learning in Training. *Journal of Applied Psychology, 79,* 819–825.

[34]Liu, Y., & Ginther, D. (1999). Cognitive Styles and Distance Education. *Online Journal of Distance Learning Administration, 2*(3). State University of West Georgia, Distance Education. Available online: http://www.westga.edu/~distance/ojdla/fall23/liu23.html/; Robertson, I. T. (1985). Human Information-Processing Strategies and Style. *Behavior and Information Technology, 4*(1), 19–29; Sadler-Smith, E. (1997). "Learning Style": Frameworks and Instruments. *Educational Psychology, 17*(1–2), 51–63; Sternberg, R. J., & Zhang, L. (eds.). (2001). *Perspectives on Thinking, Learning, and Cognitive Styles.* Mahwah, NJ: LEA; Zhang, L., & Sternberg, R. J. (2006). *The Nature of Intellectual Styles.* Mahwah, NJ: LEA.

[35]Sternberg, R. J., & Zhang, L. (eds.). (2001). *Perspectives on Thinking, Learning, and Cognitive Styles.* Mahwah, NJ: LEA.

[36]Bissell, J., White, S., & Zivin, G. (1971). Sensory Modalities in Children's Learning. In *Psychology and Educational Practice,* ed. G. S. Lesser (pp. 130–155). Glenview, IL: Scott, Foresman, & Company.

[37]Dunn, R. S., & Dunn, K. J. (1979). Learning Styles/Teaching Styles: Should They . . . Can They . . . Be Matched? *Educational Leadership, 36,* 238–244.

[38]Tennant, M. (1988). *Psychology and Adult Learning.* London: Routledge.

[39]Kolb, D. A. (1984). *Experiential Learning: Experience as the Source of Learning and Development.* Englewood Cliffs, NJ: Prentice-Hall.

[40]Kolb, D. A. (1984). *Experiential Learning: Experience as the Source of Learning and Development.* Englewood Cliffs, NJ: Prentice-Hall.

[41]Buch, K., & Bartley, S. (2002). Learning Style and Training Delivery Mode Preference. *Journal of Workplace Learning, 14*(1), 5–10.

[42]Cassidy, S. (2004). Learning Styles: An Overview of Theories, Models, and Measures. *Educational Psychology, 24*(4), 419–444.

[43]Towler, A., & Dipboye, R. L. (2003). Development of a Learning Style Orientation Measure. *Organizational Research Methods, 6,* 216–235.

[44]Duff, A., & Duffy, T. (2002). Psychometric Properties of Honey and Mumford's Learning Styles Questionnaire. *Personality and Individual Differences, 33,* 147–163; Newstead, S. E. (1992). A Study of Two "Quick-and-Easy" Methods of Assessing Individual Differences in Student Learning. *British Journal of Educational Psychology, 62*(3), 299–312; Wilson, D. K. (1986). An Investigation of the Properties of Kolb's Learning Style Inventory. *Leadership & Organization Development Journal, 7*(3), 3–15.

[45]Towler, A., & Dipboye, R. L. (2003). Development of a Learning Style Orientation Measure. *Organizational Research Methods, 6,* 216–235.

[46]Towler, A., & Dipboye, R. L., Development of a Learning Style Orientation Measure. *Organizational Research Methods, 6,* 216–235. © 2003 by SAGE Publications. Reprinted by permission of SAGE Publications.

[47]Mount, M. K., & Barrick, M. R. (1995). The Big Five Personality Dimensions. *Research in Personnel and Human Resource Management, 13,* 153–200.

[48]For a more extensive discussion, see Kristof-Brown, A. L., Zimmerman, R. D., & Johnson, E. C. (2005). Consequences of Individuals' Fit at Work: A Meta-Analysis of Person-Job, Person-Organization, Person-Group, and Person-Supervisor Fit. *Personnel Psychology, 58,* 281–342.

[49]Adapted from Edwards, J. R. (1991). Person-Job Fit: A Conceptual Integration, Literature Review, and Methodological Critique. In *International Review of Industrial and Organizational Psychology*, eds. C. L. Cooper and I. T. Robertson (Vol. 6, pp. 283–357). New York: Wiley.

[50]Caldwell, D. F., & O'Reilly, C. A. (1990). Measuring Person-Job Fit Within a Profile Comparison Process. *Journal of Applied Psychology, 75,* 648–657; Edwards, J. R. (1991). Person-Job Fit: A Conceptual Integration, Literature Review, and Methodological Critique. In *International Review of Industrial and Organizational Psychology*, eds. C. L. Cooper and I. T. Robertson (Vol. 6, pp. 283–357). New York: Wiley.

[51]Kristof-Brown, A. L., Zimmerman, R. D., & Johnson, E. C. (2005). Consequences of Individuals' Fit at Work: A Meta-Analysis of Person-Job, Person-Organization, Person-Group, and Person-Supervisor Fit. *Personnel Psychology, 58,* 281–342.

[52]Kristof-Brown, A. L., Zimmerman, R. D., & Johnson, E. C. (2005). Consequences of Individuals' Fit at Work: A Meta-Analysis of Person-Job, Person-Organization, Person-Group, and Person-Supervisor Fit. *Personnel Psychology, 58,* 281–342.

[53]Werbel, J. D., & Gilliland, S. W. (1999). Person-Environment Fit in the Selection Process. In *Research in Personnel and Human Resource Management*, ed. G.R. Ferris (Vol. 17, pp. 209–243). Stamford, CT: JAI Press.

[54]Sinton, P. (2000, February 23). Teamwork the Name of the Game for Ideo. *San Francisco Chronicle*. Available online: http://www.sfgate.com/business/article/Teamwork-the-Name-of-the-Game-for-Ideo-3304722.php.

[55]Kristof, A. L. (1996). Person-Organization Fit: An Integrative Review of Its Conceptualizations, Measurement, and Implications. *Personnel Psychology, 49,* 1–50; Kristof, A. L. (2000). Perceived Applicant Fit: Distinguishing Between Recruiters' Perceptions of Person-Job and Person-Organization Fit. *Personnel Psychology, 53,* 643–671.

[56]E.g., Chatman, J. (1989). Improving Interactional Organizational Research: A Model of Person-Organization Fit. *Academy of Management Review, 14,* 333–349; Chatman, J. (1991). Matching People and Organizations: Selection and Socialization in Public Accounting Firms. *Administrative Science Quarterly, 36,* 459–484; Vancouver, J. B., & Schmitt. N. W. (1991). An Exploratory Examination of Person-Organization Fit: Organizational Goal Congruence. *Personnel Psychology, 44,* 333–352.

[57]Grossman, R. J. (2009, February). Hiring to Fit the Culture. *HR Magazine,* 44.

[58]Kristof-Brown, A. L., Zimmerman, R. D., & Johnson, E. C. (2005). Consequences of Individuals' Fit at Work: A Meta-Analysis of Person-Job, Person-Organization, Person-Group, and Person-Supervisor Fit. *Personnel Psychology, 58,* 281–342.

[59]Kristof-Brown, A. L., Zimmerman, R. D., & Johnson, E. C. (2005). Consequences of Individuals' Fit at Work: A Meta-Analysis of Person-Job, Person-Organization, Person-Group, and Person-Supervisor Fit. *Personnel Psychology, 58,* 281–342.

[60]Sekiguchi, T. & Huber, V.L. (2011). The Use of Person-Organization Fit and Person-Job Fit Information in Making Selection Decisions, *Organizational Behavior and Human Decision Processes, 116*(2), 203–216; O'Reilly, III, C. A., Chatman, J., & Caldwell, D. V. (1991). People and Organizational Culture: A Profile Comparison Approach to Assessing Person-Organization Fit. *Academy of Management Journal, 34,* 487–516.

[61]McGregor, J. (2009, March 23 & 30). Zappos' Secret: It's an Open Book. *BusinessWeek,* 62.

[62]Ashford, S. J., & Taylor, M. S. (1990). Adaptations to Work Transitions: An Integrative Approach. In *Research in Personnel and Human Resources Management,* eds. G. Ferris & K. Rowland. (Vol.8, pp. 1–39).

[63]Johnson & Johnson. (2009). Our Credo. http://careers.jnj.com/careers/global/shared_values/our_credo/index.htm;jsessionid=C2T1QOMNC5LY4CQPCB3WU3QKB2IIWTT1.

[64]Michaels, L. (2002). The HR Side of Competitive Advantage. *Thunderbird Magazine, 55*(1).

[65]Adapted from Mallinger, M., & Rizescu, I. (2001). Personality Traits and Workplace Culture. *Graziadio Business Report.*

[66]Holland, J. L. (1985). *Making Vocational Choices: A Theory of Vocation Personalities and Work Environments.* Englewood Cliffs, NJ: Prentice-Hall.

[67]Holland, J. L. (1997). *Making Vocational Choices.* Odessa, FL: Psychological Assessment Resources, Inc.

[68]Hogan, R., & Blake, R. (1999). John Holland's Vocational Typology and Personality Theory. *Journal of Vocational Behavior, 55,* 41–56.

[69]Hogan, R., & Hogan, J. (1991). Personality and Status. In *Personality, Social Skills, and Psychopathology,* eds. D. G. Gilbert and J. J. Conley (pp. 137–154). New York: Plenum.

[70]Muchinsky, P. M., & Monahan, C. J. (1987). What Is Person-Environment Congruence? Supplementary Versus Complementary Models of Fit. *Journal of Vocational Behavior, 31,* 268–277.

[71]Muchinsky, P. M., & Monahan, C. J. (1987). What Is Person-Environment Congruence? Supplementary Versus Complementary Models of Fit. *Journal of Vocational Behavior, 31,* 269.

[72]Anders, G. (2000, June). Talent Bank. *Fast Company,* 94.

[73]Muchinsky, P. M., & Monahan, C. J. (1987). What Is Person-Environment Congruence? Supplementary Versus Complementary Models of Fit. *Journal of Vocational Behavior, 31,* 269.

[74]Grossman, R. J. (2009, February). Hiring to Fit the Culture. *HR Magazine,* 44.

[75]Schneider, B. (1987). The People Make the Place. *Personnel Psychology, 40,* 437–453; Schneider, B., Goldstein, H. W., & Smith, D. B. (1995). The ASA Framework: An Update. *Personnel Psychology, 48,* 747–773; Schneider, B., Smith, D. B., Taylor, S., & Fleenor, J. (1998). Personality and Organizations: A Test of the Homogeneity of Personality Hypothesis. *Journal of Applied Psychology, 83,* 462–470.

[76]Argyris, C. (1960). *Understanding Organizational Behavior.* Homewood, IL: Dorsey Press.

[77]Argyris, C. (1960). *Understanding Organizational Behavior.* Homewood, IL: Dorsey Press; Levinson, H., Price, C., Munden, K., Mandl, H., & Solley, C. (1962). *Men, Management, and Mental Health.* Cambridge, MA: Harvard University Press.

[78]Robinson, S., & Rousseau, D. (1994). Violating the Psychological Contract: Not the Exception but the Norm. *Journal of Organizational Behavior, 16,* 289–298.

[79]Robinson, S., & Wolfe-Morrison, E. (1995). Psychological Contracts and Organizational Citizenship Behaviour: The Effect of Unfulfilled Obligations on Civic Virtue Behaviour. *Journal of Organizational Behavior, 16,* 289–298.

[80]Nicholson, N., & Johns, G. (1985). The Absence Culture and the Psychological Contract. *Academy of Management Review, 10,* 397–407.

[81]Nadin, S.J. & Williams, C.C. (2011). Psychological Contract Violation Beyond an Employees' Perspective: The Perspective of Employers, *Employee Relations, 34*(2), 110–125; Schein, E. H. (1965). *Organizational Psychology.* Englewood Cliffs, NJ: Prentice-Hall.

[82]Rousseau, D. M., & Wade-Benzoni, K. A. (1995). Changing Individual-Organizational Attachments: A Two-Way Street. In *The Changing Nature of Work,* ed. A. Howard. San Francisco, CA: Jossey-Bass.

[83]Rousseau, D. M. (2001). Schema, Promise and Mutuality: The Building Blocks of the Psychological Contract. *Journal of Occupational and Organizational Psychology, 74*(4), 511–542.

[84]Guest, D., & Conaway, N. (1998). *Fairness at Work and the Psychological Contract.* London: Institute of Personnel and Development.

[85]Guest, D., & Conaway, N. (1998). *Fairness at Work and the Psychological Contract.* London: Institute of Personnel and Development.

[86]Noer, D. (2000). Leading Organizations Through Survivor Sickness: A Framework for the New Millennium. In *The Organisation in Crisis,* eds. R. Burke and C. L. Cooper. Oxford: Blackwell.

[87]Herriot, P., Manning, W. E. G., & Kidd, J. M. (1997). The Content of the Psychological Contract. *British Journal of Management, 8,* 151–162.

[88]Turnley, W. H., & Feldman, D. C. (1999). A Discrepancy Model of Psychological Contract Violations. *Human Resource Management Review, 9*(3), 367–386; Smithson, J., & Lewis, S. (2000). Is Job Insecurity Changing the Psychological Contract? Young People's Expectations of Work. *Personnel Review, 29*(6), 680–702.

[89]Brannen, J., Lewis, S., Nilsen, A., & Smithson, J. (eds.). (2002). *Young Europeans, Work and Family: Futures in Transition.* London: Routledge.

[90]Turnley, W. H., & Feldman, D. C. (1999). The Impact of Psychological Contract Violations on Exit, Voice, Loyalty and Neglect. *Human Relations, 52*(7), 895–922.

[91]Brannen, J., Lewis, S., Nilsen, A., & Smithson, J. (eds.). (2002). *Young Europeans, Work and Family: Futures in Transition.* London: Routledge.

[92]Sommerville, H. (2007, January 23). Staff Engagement: A Question of Motive. *Personnel Today.* Available online: http://www .personneltoday.com/articles/2007/01/23/38955/staff-engagement -a-question-of-motive.html.

[93]Sommerville, H. (2007, January 23). Staff Engagement: A Question of Motive. *Personnel Today.* Available online: http://www .personneltoday.com/articles/2007/01/23/38955/staff-engagement -a-question-of-motive.html.

[94]Chao, J.M.C., Cheung, F.Y.L. & Wu, A.M.S. (2011). Psychological Contract Breach and Counterproductive Workplace Behaviors: Testing Moderating Effect of Attribution Style ad Power Distance, *The International Journal of Human Resource Management, 22*(4), 763–777; Rousseau, D. M., & Schalk, R. (2000). *Psychological Contracts in Employment: Cross-National Perspectives.* Thousand Oaks, CA: Sage.

[95]See Earnest, D.R., Allen, D.G. & Landis, R.S. (2011). Mechanisms Linking Realistic Job Previews with Turnover: A Meta-Analytic Path Analysis, *Personnel Psychology, 64*(4), 865–897; Phillips, J. M. (1998). Effects of Realistic Job Previews on Multiple Organizational Outcomes: A Meta-Analysis. *Academy of Management Journal, 41,* 673–690.

[96]Lynch, L. (2001, June/July). Recruiting, Retaining the Best. Accessed on the *MRO Today* website at http://mrotoday.com.

[97]Grow With Us (2012). Hilton Worldwide. Available online: http://www.hiltonworldwide.com/careers/why-work-at-hilton/.

[98]Tucker, M.A. (2012). Show and Tell, *HR Magazine, 57(1).* Available online: http://www.shrm.org/Publications/hrmagazine /EditorialContent/2012/0112/Pages/0112tucker.aspx.

[99]Tucker, M.A. (2012). Show and Tell, *HR Magazine, 57(1).* Available online: http://www.shrm.org/Publications/hrmagazine /EditorialContent/2012/0112/Pages/0112tucker.aspx.

[100] Hilton Gains Edge in Race for Management Talent (2012). SHL. Available online: http://www.shl.com/images/uploads/cs _Hilton.pdf.

[101]McDonald's Recruitment Drive Hits Back at Critics. (2006, April 21). Personneltoday.com. Available online: http://www .personneltoday.com/Articles/21/04/2006/34977/McDonald39s -recruitment-drive-hits-back-at-critics.htm.

[102]Buckingham, M., & Coffman, C. (1999). *First, Break All the Rules.* New York: Simon & Schuster.

[103] Sullivan, J. (2011, September 26). Talent Management Lessons from Apple...A Case Study of the World's Most Valuable Firm, ERE.net. Available online: http://www.ere.net/2011/09/26 /talent-management-lessons-from-apple%E2%80%A6-a-case -study-of-the-worlds-most-valuable-firm-part-3-of-4/.

[104] Kolflat, L. (2012). Mission: Brand Alignment, *HRO Today, 11*(3). Available online: http://www.hrotoday.com/content/5111 /mission-brand-alignment.

[105] Adams, S. (2012, April 3). How to Get Hired at an Apple Store, *Forbes.* Available online at: http://www.forbes.com/sites /susanadams/2012/04/03/how-to-get-hired-at-an-apple-store/.

[106] Poeter, D. (2011, December 8). How Much Money Do Apple Store Employees Make for Apple? *PC Mag.* Available online: http://www.pcmag.com/article2/0,2817,2397421,00.asp.

[107]Reprinted from Organizational Behavior and Human Decision Processes, 67, Button, S. B., Mathieu, J. E., & Zajac, D. M., "Goal Orientation in Organizational Research: A Conceptual and Empirical Foundation", 26–48, 1996, with permission from Elsevier.

[108]Normative information is from Phillips, J. M., & Gully, S. M. (1997). The Role of Goal Orientation, Ability, Need for Achievement and Locus of Control in the Self-Efficacy and Goal Setting Process. *Journal of Applied Psychology, 82,* 792–802.

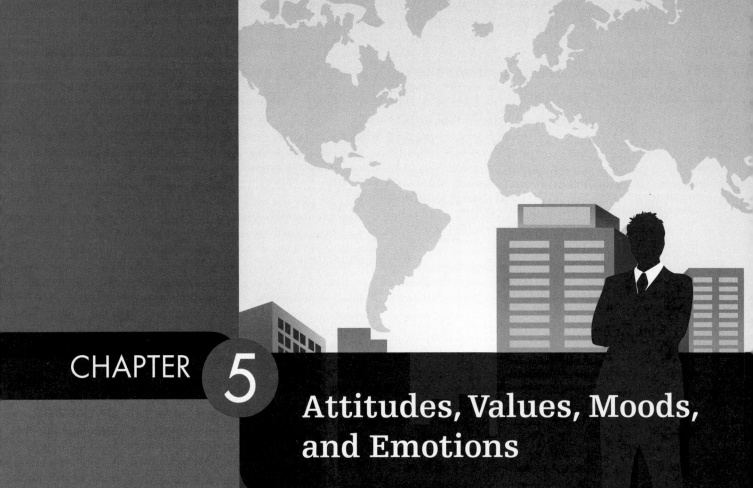

CHAPTER **5**

Attitudes, Values, Moods, and Emotions

John Yokoyama of Seattle's Pike Place Fish Market focused on improving employees' attitudes and better involving them in the business to turn his company around.

AP PHOTO/ELAINE THOMPSON

REAL WORLD CHALLENGE

ATTITUDE IS A CHOICE AT PIKE PLACE FISH MARKET[1]

John Yokoyama did not plan on owning Seattle's Pike Place Fish Market. Selling fish is a tough job. The days are long—most employees at Seattle's Pike Place Fish work from 6:30 A.M. to 6:30 P.M.—and the work can be boring and tiring. But when the owner of the business decided to get out, Yokoyama decided to buy the business instead of losing his job.

As a manager, Yokoyama demanded results from his employees and came down hard on their mistakes. He never went on vacation, and insisted on managing all of his company's activities himself. He emulated the previous owner's negative attitudes, anger, and fear-based management style. No one working there was having fun, including Yokoyama.

As his business struggled, employee turnover was high and morale was low. Yokoyama knew he was not getting the best from his employees and recognized that he needed to change his managerial values and style to save his business. He realized that if he could better involve his employees and improve their attitudes, his business would be likely to improve. Yokoyama asks you for advice on improving his employees' attitudes. After reading this chapter, you should have some good ideas for him.

LEARNING OBJECTIVES

1. Describe three types of value conflicts.

2. Explain how attitudes affect behavior and describe the three attitudes that are most important for organizational outcomes.

3. Discuss the three types of organizational commitment.

4. Explain why emotions are important to organizations.

5. Discuss the difference between positive and negative affect.

6. Describe emotional labor and discuss its possible positive and negative outcomes.

7. Describe how emotions are related to stress and how some stress can be beneficial.

If your boss asked you to work harder, could you? Most of us could probably give our employer at least an additional 10 to 20 percent effort if we chose to do so. Because values, attitudes, moods, and emotions all influence our behavior and job satisfaction, effectively managing them is one way to increase employees' discretionary effort and improve performance. Employees work harder and are less likely to quit their jobs when their personal values are consistent with the organization's values, when they are satisfied with their jobs, and when they have positive attitudes about the company and the work environment.[2]

This chapter will further your understanding of how values, attitudes, moods, and emotions influence work behavior. As a manager, this information will help you to better hire, motivate, and retain talented employees. Because emotions are closely linked to stress, we also discuss the positive and negative sides of stress, and how to manage your own and others' stress. This chapter should also help you to improve your skills in understanding and managing your own attitudes and emotions so you can become even more effective at work.

VALUES

values

Ways of behaving or end-states desirable to a person or to a group

Values are ways of behaving or end-states that are desirable to a person or to a group. Values can be conscious or unconscious.[3] Although our values tend to be fairly well established by the time we are teenagers, our values can be reshaped by major life events including the birth of a child, going to war, the death of a loved one, illness, or even business failure. Work values influence important individual and organizational outcomes including performance and retention, and are often considered to be important work outcomes in themselves.[4]

A company leader's personal values affect the firm's business strategy[5] and all aspects of organizational behavior including staffing, reward systems, manager-subordinate relationships, communication, conflict management styles, and negotiation approaches.[6] Personal values also influence ethical choices. When there are no clear rules for dealing with specific ethical problems, we tend to respond to each situation on an individual basis depending on our values at that time.[7] Our personal values combine with organizational influences like company culture to generate decisions that can be significantly different from those made based solely on our personal values.[8] Strong company cultures help to guide us when making these ambiguous choices. However, if personal values conflict with the organization's cultural values, it is difficult to maintain ethical norms.[9]

Types of Values

Values can be described as terminal or instrumental, and as intrinsic or extrinsic. Let's explore each of these distinctions.

Terminal and Instrumental Values. Noted values researcher Milton Rokeach[10] identified two types of values: terminal and instrumental. *Terminal values* reflect our long-term life goals, and may include prosperity, happiness, a secure family, and a sense of accomplishment. People who value family more than career success will work fewer hours and spend more time with their kids than people whose values put career success first. Of course, this does not mean that having strong family values will prevent one from having a successful career.

terminal values

Long-term personal life goals

David Neeleman, CEO of JetBlue, keeps weekends as free as possible and tries to make it home every night to spend quality time with his family. He feels that following these rules has had a positive effect on JetBlue's performance.

RICK MAIMAN/BLOOMBERG/GETTY IMAGES

David Neeleman, CEO of JetBlue, established personal rules to allow him to spend time with his family. He keeps weekends as free as possible, tries to make it home every night to spend quality time with his family, and schedules vacations when his kids are out of school. He feels that following these rules has also had a positive effect on JetBlue's performance.[11]

Terminal values can change over time depending on our experiences and accomplishments. When a career-oriented person sells her business for a lot of money, her prosperity goals may be reached and family may then become most important. One way to rank your most important terminal values is to ask yourself, "If I can't have everything I want, in twenty years, what would I be most disappointed about *not* having?" The answer can often clarify tough choices about how to prioritize terminal values and how to divide time among pursuing different outcomes including work, family, and personal interests.

Instrumental values are our preferred means of achieving our terminal values or our preferred ways of behaving. Terminal values influence what we want to accomplish; instrumental values influence how we get there. Honesty, ambition, and independence are examples of instrumental values that guide our behavior in pursuit of our terminal goals. The stronger an instrumental value is, the more we act on it. People who value honesty behave more ethically in pursuing the terminal value of prosperity and a sense of accomplishment than do people with a lower honesty instrumental value.

A CEO's instrumental values have a strong influence on his or her organization's culture and processes. Six primary values tend to influence managers' behaviors and choices and thus are important to understanding managerial behavior:[12]

1. *Collectivism*: concern for a family or social group as opposed to oneself
2. *Rationality*: valuing fact-based and emotion-free decisions and actions
3. *Novelty*: valuing change
4. *Duty*: valuing obligation, loyalty, and the integrity of reciprocal relationships

instrumental values

Our preferred means of achieving our terminal values or our preferred ways of behaving

5. *Materialism*: valuing wealth and tangible possessions
6. *Power*: valuing control of situations and other people

Managers with different levels of these six values behave differently in setting and pursuing organizational strategies and goals. Hiring people whose values are consistent with the organizational values and culture can improve their fit with their jobs and with the company and improve their job performance.

Leaders of Oregon's Full Sail Brewing have strong values around environmental responsibility. The brewery has used reclaimed and recycled building materials in building a cannery, uses energy-efficient lighting and air compressors, and has adopted a four-day workweek to reduce water and energy consumption by 20 percent. It also operates an on-site wastewater treatment facility.[13]

SO WHAT

Understanding what you want to achieve as well as how you want to achieve it helps you to make effective career and life decisions.

intrinsic work values
Values related to the work itself

Intrinsic and Extrinsic Work Values. *Intrinsic work values* relate to the work itself.[14] For example, some employees want challenging jobs with a lot of variety that require them to continually learn new things, whereas others prefer simpler jobs they can perform in the same way every day. Most people need to find some personal intrinsic value in their work to feel truly satisfied with it.[15] As philosopher Albert Schweitzer once said, "Success is not the key to happiness. Happiness is the key to success. If you love what you are doing, you will be successful."[16]

> "Success is not the key to happiness. Happiness is the key to success. If you love what you are doing, you will be successful."
> —*Albert Schweitzer, Philosopher*

Valuing challenging work and learning new skills can help advance your career. Anne Sweeney, President of Disney/ABC Cable Networks and President of the Disney Channel, worked her way up from an assistant position by always being willing to try new things and take on new responsibilities. As she states, "It is important to always find the unknown exciting."[17]

extrinsic work values
Values related to the outcomes of the work

Extrinsic work values are related to the outcomes of doing work.[18] Employees who work to earn money or to have health benefits are satisfying extrinsic work values. Having high status in the company, getting recognized for quality work, and having job security are extrinsic work values.

Table 5-1 lists some common intrinsic and extrinsic work values.

Table 5-1

Intrinsic and Extrinsic Work Values

Intrinsic Work Values	Extrinsic Work Values
Challenging work	Financial gain
Adventurous work	Benefits
Having autonomy	Social contact
Having a lot of responsibility	Time with family
Being creative	Time for volunteering
Helping others	Time for hobbies
Working with others	Job security
Competition	Public recognition
Becoming an expert	Free time

© CENGAGE LEARNING 2012

When Values Conflict

Intrapersonal, interpersonal, and individual-organization value conflicts all influence employee attitudes, retention, job satisfaction, and job performance. Let's explore each of these in greater detail.

Intrapersonal Value Conflict. When highly ranked instrumental and terminal values conflict and both cannot be met, we experience inner conflict and stress. At some point in their career, many managers experience an *intrapersonal value conflict* between the instrumental value of ambition and the terminal value of happiness. If being happy pulls us to spend quality time with our family or pursuing a hobby we love, but personal ambition pulls us to work longer hours and pursue promotions, we feel conflicted.

intrapersonal value conflict
When highly ranked instrumental and terminal values conflict

As South African leader Nelson Mandela said, "I really wanted to retire and rest and spend more time with my children, my grandchildren, and of course with my wife. But the problems are such that for anybody with a conscience who can use whatever influence he may have to try to bring about peace, it's difficult to say no."[19] People are generally happier and less stressed when their instrumental and terminal values are aligned.

Interpersonal Value Conflict. Unlike intrapersonal value conflicts, which are internal to an individual, *interpersonal value conflicts* occur when two different people hold conflicting values. Interpersonal value conflicts are often the cause of personality clashes and other disagreements. Consider this conversation:

interpersonal value conflicts
When two different people hold conflicting values

> Maria: "I can't believe you quit your job. The pay was the best around."
>
> Steve: "My old job certainly paid better, but I didn't like the way they treated customers. My new job may not pay as well, but the management is much more ethical, and I am enjoying myself a lot more."

Maria's materialistic values clearly differ from Steve's ethical focus. As a manager, it is important to remember that people's constellations of instrumental and terminal values differ. These differences can lead to differences in work styles, work preferences, and reactions to announcements or events.

SO WHAT
Understanding people's values can help you to best match incentives, feedback, and job assignments to each employee.

Individual-Organization Value Conflict. Just as two different employees' values can conflict, an employee's values can conflict with the values of the organization, creating *individual-organization value conflict*. Lower individual-organization value conflict leads to greater job satisfaction, higher performance, lower stress, and greater job commitment.[20]

individual-organization value conflict
When an employee's values conflict with the values of the organization

Many firms are using technology during the recruiting process to communicate the values they seek in employees. Southwest Airlines' blog, "Nuts about Southwest," reflects the company's playful spirit. In addition to employee posts, a video blog, news section, and links to Flickr, LinkedIn, YouTube, Facebook, and Twitter, official video and photo galleries and the airline's podcast further help socialize employees and reinforce the values it expects employees to display.[21]

The Home Depot offers four "realistic job preview" videos that use footage of real employees to describe and demonstrate various positions. This honest but upbeat format provides a conduit for organizational values, and helps reduce individual-organization value conflict by allowing people whose values are not a good fit to drop out of the hiring process.[22]

Onboarding and socialization practices introduce new hires to the organization, its culture, and its values. Onboarding is critical in communicating a company's culture, aligning new hires' values with those of the company, and increasing employees' connection with the firm.

When window treatment manufacturer Hunter Douglas researched why its turnover rate six months post-hire was 70 percent, it found that new hires did not feel connected to the company or its values. The company realized that this was probably due to the ten-minute orientation new hires received before starting their jobs. After revamping its onboarding process, turnover fell to 6 percent.[23] As one expert says, "A successful onboarding program is one that inspires new employees; that makes them passionate about the company."[24]

How Values Differ around the World

Global differences in values can lead to different managerial behaviors. For example, Latin Americans tend to highly value family loyalty, which leads them to hire competent family members whenever possible.[25] Managers in the United States tend to strongly value individual achievement, which leads them to emphasize a candidate's previous performance and skill assessments rather than family ties.

Values are influenced by culture. Research has found that a large number of basic values can be condensed into two major dimensions that vary across cultures: (1) traditional/secular-rational values and (2) survival/self-expression values.[26] Traditional/secular-rational values reflect the contrast between societies in which religion is very important and those in which it is not. More traditional societies emphasize the importance of parent-child ties and deference to authority, which is reflected in high levels of national pride and a nationalistic outlook. Societies with secular-rational values have the opposite characteristics.

Survival values emphasize economic and physical security. Self-expression values emphasize subjective well-being, self-expression, and quality of life, giving high priority to environmental protection, diversity tolerance, and participation in decision making. Societies that rank high on self-expression values also tend have higher interpersonal trust and tolerance and value individual freedom and self-expression.[27]

Figure 5-1 illustrates how these two major dimensions of values differ in a variety of countries.

ATTITUDES

attitude

Expresses our values, beliefs, and feelings toward something, and inclines us to act or react in a certain way toward it

An ***attitude*** expresses our values, beliefs, and feelings toward something, and inclines us to act or react in a certain way toward it. We all have attitudes about many aspects of our jobs, organizations, bosses, and careers. Having a "negative attitude toward hard work" reflects a person's work values and bias against working hard. A negative attitude toward something reflects a belief that something undesirable is going to happen, whereas a positive attitude reflects an optimistic belief that good things are coming. As Irving Berlin said, "Our attitudes control our lives. Attitudes are a secret power working twenty-four hours a day, for good or bad. It is of paramount importance that we know how to harness and control this great force."[29] Like values, attitudes influence important individual and organizational outcomes including performance and retention, and are often considered to be important work outcomes in themselves.[30]

Liz Fetter, President and CEO of NorthPoint Communications, recites inspirational quotes to herself to keep her attitude on track when things are getting tough. Her favorite is, "If you know how to swim, it doesn't matter

> "Our attitudes control our lives. Attitudes are a secret power working twenty-four hours a day, for good or bad. It is of paramount importance that we know how to harness and control this great force."
>
> —*Irving Berlin, Songwriter*

Figure 5-1

How Values Differ around the World[28]

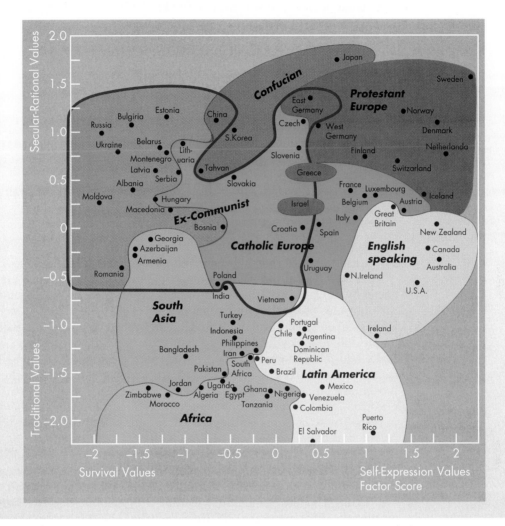

Source: Inglehart, R., & Welzel, C. (2005). Modernization, Cultural Change and Democracy (p. 64). New York: Cambridge University Press. Based on the World Values Surveys, see http://www.worldvaluessurvey. Org. Copyright © 2005 Ronald Inglehart and Christian Welzel. Reprinted with the permission of Cambridge University Press.

how deep the water is."[31] She has reached a high level of career success by staying in control of her attitude and mindset.

Where Do Attitudes Come From?

Attitudes are formed over the course of a person's lifetime through experiences, family, culture, religion, and socioeconomic factors. Our values also influence our attitudes. Despite these influences, ultimately our attitudes are chosen by us. If the attitude we have at a moment is not generating the outcomes or reactions we want, we can change our attitude and try again.

As a manager, it is important to remember that changing employee attitudes toward work, as well as corresponding behaviors, can take time. Some attitudes are more difficult to change than others. Peter Nelson, Southwest Airline's manager of creative development, says that because a customer-friendly attitude is "excruciatingly hard to instill in people," Southwest hires people who already possess that trait. Southwest has always emphasized that

SO WHAT

Maintaining a positive attitude enhances performance and persistence.

people are "hired and fired for attitude." Herb Kelleher, the company's co-founder and former CEO, gives this example: "One of our pilot applicants was very nasty to one of our receptionists, and we immediately rejected him. You can't treat people that way and be the kind of leader we want."[32]

Attitudes are composed of three components:

1. *Beliefs* are your judgments about the object of the attitude that result from your values, past experiences, and reasoning. For example, your beliefs about doing a difficult job reflect your values and perceptions about doing hard work. Some people might believe that doing hard work is healthy, while others might believe it is stressful.
2. *Feelings* reflect your evaluations and overall liking of the object of the attitude, and can be positive or negative. For example, some people feel that doing hard work is good and enjoy it, whereas others feel that it is bad and dislike it.
3. *Behavioral intentions* reflect your motivation to do something with respect to the object of the attitude. You might intend to either avoid or volunteer for a project requiring hard work.

Our beliefs tend to drive our feelings; our beliefs and feelings in turn influence our attitudes, which then affect our behavior through intentions (see Figure 5-2).

Our behavioral intentions stem from our feelings, but they also are influenced by our personalities, values, past experiences, and expectations about the outcomes of the different behaviors we could choose. People with the same feelings about something may develop different behavioral intentions. For example, one person who dislikes physical work might turn down a physical job while another person who dislikes physical work might take the job anyway because alternative job opportunities are scarce. People choose the behavioral intention that they feel will best meet their needs or that will make them the most comfortable. As a manager, understanding that people behave differently in response to the same feelings will help you to best match your actions to the person and situation you are dealing with.

Our intentions do not always lead to the execution of intended behaviors. We might fully intend to give a staff member feedback on the great job he did managing a challenging customer issue, but not get around to it due to conflicting schedules and a busy workload. Nonetheless, intentions are better predictors of behavior than feelings or beliefs because they address specific behavior choices rather than more generalized beliefs and feelings.

Cognitive Dissonance

Assume that you strongly believe that all companies need to be environmentally responsible, and that you are the new CEO of a company that is a terrible polluter. You learn that reducing your company's carbon emissions would be so expensive that the company would no longer be profitable. What would

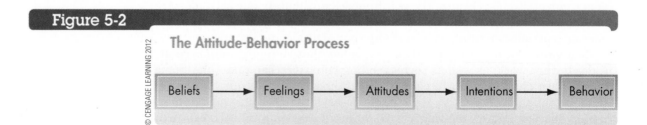

Figure 5-2

© CENGAGE LEARNING 2012

The Attitude-Behavior Process

Beliefs → Feelings → Attitudes → Intentions → Behavior

you do? The gap between your environmentally responsible attitude and your attitude that your responsibility is to run a profitable company creates what is called cognitive dissonance. ***Cognitive dissonance*** is an incompatibility between behavior and an attitude or between two different attitudes.[33] Several options exist for dealing with cognitive dissonance:

cognitive dissonance
An incompatibility between behavior and an attitude or between two different attitudes

1. You can *change your behavior* and reduce the company's carbon emissions.
2. You can *reduce the felt dissonance* by reasoning that the pollution is not so important when compared to the goal of running a profitable company.
3. You can *change your attitude* toward pollution to decrease your belief that pollution is bad.
4. You can *seek additional information* to better reason that the benefits to society of manufacturing the products outweigh the societal costs of polluting.

Your choice of whether or not to try to reduce feelings of cognitive dissonance is affected by:

1. *Your perception of the importance of the elements that are creating the dissonance*: Given your strong belief about the importance of environmental responsibility, it will be more difficult for you to ignore the dissonance. If the elements involved in the dissonance are less important to you, it is easier to ignore it.
2. *The amount of influence you feel you have over these elements*: If you are being prevented by the Board of Directors from investing in pollution reducing technology, it would be easier to rationalize the dissonance and not take action. If you are making the decision alone, however, then you are more likely to address the dissonance in a more active way.
3. *The rewards involved in the dissonance*: Rewards for dissonance tend to decrease our reactions to it. If your sizeable annual bonus is based on the firm's financial performance, for example, and not its environmental record, then you would likely be less inclined to take action to address the dissonance.

What Attitudes Are the Most Important for Organizations?

Of the many attitudes people can hold, three are most often studied in organizational behavior because of the effects they have on important organizational outcomes such as job performance and turnover. They are: job satisfaction, organizational commitment, and job engagement. Let's learn more about each of these attitudes.

Job Satisfaction. Job satisfaction is one of the most commonly studied organizational outcomes in the field of organizational behavior. Our *job satisfaction* reflects our attitudes and feelings about our job. The factors that have the greatest influence on job satisfaction are: the work itself, attitudes, values, and personality (see Figure 5-3).

job satisfaction
Reflects our attitudes and feelings about our job

Satisfaction with the nature of the work itself is the largest influence on job satisfaction. If you do not like the work you are doing, it is hard to be satisfied with your job. Challenging work, autonomy, variety, and job scope also increase job satisfaction.[34] As a manager, if you want to increase your subordinates' job satisfaction, focus first on improving the nature of the work they do.[35] Coworkers, bosses, and subordinates are part of the work experience and can also influence job satisfaction. Their attitudes and perceptions can

Figure 5-3

Influences on Job Satisfaction

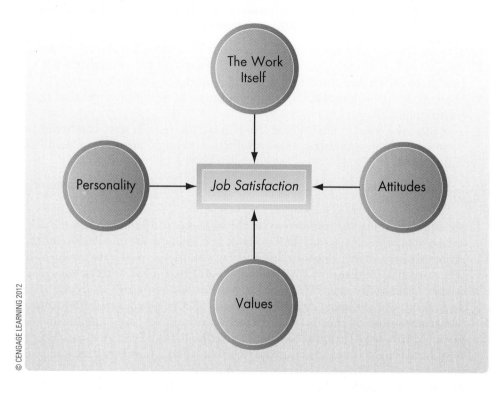

© CENGAGE LEARNING 2012

organizational citizenship behaviors

Discretionary behaviors (e.g., helping others) that benefit the organization but that are not formally rewarded or required

be contagious, especially for new hires forming impressions about the job and company. If coworkers are unhappy and dissatisfied with their jobs, new hires are more likely to be dissatisfied than if they regularly interact with happy and satisfied coworkers.

Our attitudes and values about work also influence our job satisfaction. Someone with a negative attitude toward work is less likely to be satisfied with any job than someone with a positive attitude toward work. Employees who find intrinsic value in their work are doing what is important to them. If someone values challenge and variety in work, that person will be more satisfied with jobs with these characteristics than with monotonous work.

Interestingly, our job satisfaction is somewhat stable over time, even when we change jobs or employers.[36] Some people are rarely satisfied with their jobs, and others tend to be satisfied no matter what job they have. Research evidence suggests that differences in job satisfaction are due in part to differences in employees' genetics and personality.[37] In particular, core self-evaluation,[38] extroversion, and conscientiousness[39] influence job satisfaction. Accordingly, selecting extroverted, conscientious people who are a good fit with the job and who have high core self-evaluations (a broad, general, positive self-regard[40]) can enhance employees' job satisfaction.

But are happy employees really more productive employees? The answer is yes. And the positive relationship between job satisfaction and job performance is even stronger for complex, professional jobs.[41] Satisfied employees also benefit organizations because job satisfaction positively influences employees' attitudes and *organizational citizenship behaviors*, or discretionary behaviors (e.g., helping others) that benefit the organization but that are not formally rewarded or required.[42]

Job dissatisfaction is related to higher absenteeism and turnover, as well as to other withdrawal behaviors such as lateness, drug abuse, grievances, and retirement decisions.[43] It isn't just the level of job satisfaction that matters, however. If job satisfaction is declining, turnover intentions and actual turnover are particularly likely to increase.[44] Because of the potentially high cost of these employee behaviors, the financial impact of improving employees' job satisfaction can make it worthwhile for managers to invest in improving employee attitudes toward their jobs and the company.

Organizational Commitment. *Organizational commitment* reflects the degree to which an employee identifies with the organization and its goals and wants to stay with the organization. There are three ways we can feel committed to an employer:

1. *Affective commitment*: positive emotional attachment to the organization and strong identification with its values and goals. Employees of a children's hospital may be affectively committed to the organization because of its goal of providing top-quality health care to kids. Affective commitment leads employees to stay with an organization *because they want to*, and is related to higher performance.
2. *Normative commitment*: feeling obliged to stay with an organization for moral or ethical reasons. An employee who has just finished an MBA paid for by a firm's tuition reimbursement program might feel a moral obligation to stay with the employer for at least a few years to repay the debt. Normative commitment is related to higher performance and leads employees to stay with an organization *because they feel they should*.
3. *Continuance commitment*: staying with an organization because of perceived high economic (taking another job would mean losing valuable stock options) and/or social costs (friendships with coworkers) involved with leaving. Continuance commitment leads employees to stay with an organization *because they feel that they have to*.

These three types of organizational commitment are not mutually exclusive. It is possible to be committed to an organization in affective, normative, and continuance ways at the same time, at varying levels of intensity. At any point in time, an employee has a "commitment profile" that reflects high or low levels of all three types of organizational commitment.[45] Different profiles have different effects on workplace behavior such as job performance, absenteeism, and the chance that the organization member will quit.[46]

Employee Engagement. If you did not like your coworkers, your boss was mean, and you did not have the resources you needed to get your job done, how would you feel about your job? Would you put 100 percent into your work? When we feel respected and see how our work matters to the company and to others, we feel more enthusiastic and engaged. *Employee engagement* is "a heightened emotional and intellectual connection that an employee has for his/her job, organization, manager, or coworkers that, in turn, influences him/her to apply additional discretionary effort to his/her work."[47]

Engaged employees give their full effort to their jobs, often going beyond what is required because they are passionate about the firm and about doing their jobs well. Disengaged workers do not perform close to their potential capability, lacking the emotional and motivational connections to their employer that drive discretionary effort. Rather than *wanting* to do the work and wanting to do their best, disengaged workers feel they *have* to do the work, and generally do only what they have to do as a result.

organizational commitment
The degree to which an employee identifies with the organization and its goals and wants to stay with the organization

affective commitment
Positive emotional attachment to the organization and strong identification with its values and goals

normative commitment
Feeling obliged to stay with an organization for moral or ethical reasons

continuance commitment
Staying with an organization because of perceived high economic and/or social costs involved with leaving

SO WHAT
Employees who stay with a job because they want to, not because they feel that they should or that they have to, identify more strongly with the organization and its goals.

employee engagement
A heightened emotional and intellectual connection that an employee has for his/her job, organization, manager, or coworkers that, in turn, influences him/her to apply additional discretionary effort to his/her work

One study found that more than 50 percent of senior executives have "less than ideal emotional connection and alignment" to their organization.[48] This is particularly troubling given the financial consequences of low engagement. High employee engagement is related to superior business performance. Towers Perrin found that high-engagement organizations have a 28 percent earnings-per-share (EPS) growth rate compared to low-engagement organizations' 11 percent EPS decline.[49] A report from the Society for Human Resource Management found that strengthening employee engagement saved one company $1.7 million in just one year.[50]

As a manager, remember that the drivers of employee engagement can differ from the drivers of employee attraction and retention—what gets employees into an organization is not the same as what keeps them engaged and keeps them from leaving.[51] Engagement is enhanced when employees:

- Have clear goals and roles
- Have the resources needed to do a good job
- Get meaningful feedback on their performance
- Are able to use their talents
- Are recognized for doing a good job
- Have positive relationships with coworkers
- Have opportunities to learn and grow
- Have supportive leadership

Table 5-2 summarizes the results of a recent global Towers Perrin survey on the different worldwide drivers of employee attraction, retention, and engagement by generation.

Table 5-2

Top Three Worldwide Drivers of Employee Attraction, Retention, and Engagement for Different Age Groups

Top Drivers of Attraction for 18- to 24-Year-Olds	Top Drivers of Retention for 18- to 24-Year-Olds	Top Drivers of Engagement for 18- to 24-Year-Olds
Career advancement opportunities	Have excellent career advancement opportunities	Organization develops leaders at all levels
Competitive base pay	Work in an environment where new ideas are encouraged	Organization quickly resolves customer concerns
Learning and development opportunities	Satisfaction with the organization's business decisions	Senior management is sincerely interested in employee well-being
Top Drivers of Attraction for 45- to 54-Year-Olds	**Top Drivers of Retention for 45- to 54-Year-Olds**	**Top Drivers of Engagement for 45- to 54-Year-Olds**
Competitive base pay	Organization's reputation as a great place to work	Senior management is sincerely interested in employee well-being
Challenging work	Satisfaction with the organization's people decisions	Improved my skills and capabilities over the last year
Convenient work location	Understand potential career track within the organization	The organization's reputation for social responsibility

Source: Based on information provided in Exhibits 14, 15, and 16 of *Towers Perrin Global Workforce Study — Global Report* at http://www.towersperrin.com/tp/getwebcachedoc?webc=HRS/USA/2008/200803/GWS_Global_Report20072008_31208.pdf.

EMOTIONS AND MOODS

Do you behave the same way or perform as well when you are excited as you do when you are unhappy or afraid? Of course not—which is the reason why emotions play an important role in the workplace. It is easy to imagine the performance difference of unhappy salespeople compared to a happy sales staff. Employees who effectively manage their emotions and moods can create a competitive advantage for a company. Would Starbucks or Nordstrom be as successful with moody employees? It is not likely.

We all experience emotions at work. Our behaviors are not guided solely by conscious, rational thought. In fact, emotion often plays a larger role in our behaviors than does conscious reasoning. *Emotions* are intense, short-term physiological, behavioral, and psychological reactions to a specific object, person, or event that prepare us to respond to it. Let's break this definition down into its four important elements:

emotions
Transient physiological, behavioral, and psychological episodes experienced toward an object, person, or event that prepare us to respond to it

1. *Emotions are short events or episodes*. Emotions are relatively short-lived. Excitement about making a big sale or anxiety over a looming deadline subsides after a little while.
2. *Emotions are directed at something or someone*. This differentiates emotions from *moods*, which are short-term emotional states that are not directed toward anything in particular.[56] Moods are less intense than emotions and can change quickly. The cause of emotions can be readily identified—making a big sale or facing a deadline, for example.
3. *Emotions are experienced*. They involve involuntary changes in heart rate, blood pressure, facial expressions, animation, and vocal tone. We *feel* emotion.
4. *Emotions create a state of physical readiness through physiological reactions*. Increased heart rate, adrenaline, and eye movements prepare our bodies to take action. Particularly strong emotions including fear, anger, and surprise can demand our attention, interrupt our thoughts, and motivate us to respond by focusing our attention on whatever is generating the emotion.

moods
Short-term emotional states not directed toward anything in particular

Whereas an attitude can be thought of as a judgment about something, an emotion is experienced or felt. Emotions do not last as long as attitudes. As two experts put it, "The major aspect of emotion is the aspect of passions that urges people to do things."[57] Emotions influence how we perceive the world, help us interpret our experiences, and prime us to respond.

Why is understanding the role of emotions important to organizations? First, because they are malleable, effective employees and managers know how to positively influence their own emotions and the emotions of others.[58] Second,

SATCHAN/ZEFA/CORBIS

Positive and happy sales staff can help to create positive emotions and moods in customers, creating a competitive advantage for the company.

CASE STUDY

Rules of Engagement at SuccessFactors

The California-based software company SuccessFactors does not tolerate nasty or demeaning employees. One of the company's founding principles is: "No jerks! Our organization will consist only of people that absolutely love what we do, with a white hot passion. We will have utmost respect for the individual in a collaborative, egalitarian, and meritocratic environment—no blind copying, no politics, no parochialism, no silos, no games, no cynicism, no arrogance—just being good!"[52] CEO Lars Dalgaard feels that there is a strong business case against tolerating nasty and demeaning people. Not only do firms that tolerate jerks have more difficulty recruiting and retaining the best talent, but they also are prone to higher customer churn and weakened investor confidence.[53]

SuccessFactors does not expect perfect employees, but when errors are made, employees are expected to repent. Dalgaard himself is not above the rule and admits to occasionally blowing it at meetings. He once apologized to all 400-plus people in his company, not just to the people at the meeting, because he knew that word about his behavior would get out and could hurt the company's strong culture of trust and respect.[54]

The company asks all new hires to sign its Rules of Engagement, which are essentially a contract for how employees agree to behave. SuccessFactors' Rules of Engagement are:[55]

1. I will be passionate about SuccessFactors' mission, about my work. I will love what we do for companies and employees everywhere.
2. I will demonstrate respect for the individual. I will be nice and listen to others, and respect myself. I will act with integrity and professionalism.
3. I will do what it takes to get the job done, no matter what it takes, but within legal and ethical boundaries.
4. I know that this is a company, not a charity. I will not waste money. I will question every cost.
5. I will present an exhaustive list of solutions to problems and suggest actionable recommendations.
6. I will help my colleagues and recognize the team when we win. I will never leave them behind when we lose.
7. I will constantly improve—Kaizen! I will approach every day as an opportunity to do a better job, admitting to and learning from my mistakes.
8. I will selflessly pursue customer success.
9. I will support the culture of meritocracy and pay for performance.
10. I will focus on results and winning-scoring points, not just gaining yardage.
11. I will be transparent. I will communicate clearly and be brutally honest, even when it's difficult, because I trust my colleagues.
12. I will always be in sales and drive customer satisfaction.
13. I will have fun at work and approach my work with enthusiasm.
14. I will be a good person to work with—I will not be a jerk.
15. I will not BCC (blind copy) anyone and never talk negatively and destructively behind someone's back (character assassination); rather, I will confront them with the issue I am facing or wanted to comment to others about, to allow us a trusting and hyper-productive collaborative environment.
16. I recognize that I am personally a steward of this "Olympic flame," and I know that if I lose my edge, it will trigger a wildfire, and we together have both the power to keep this open honest culture, or break it. DON'T DO IT. BE GOOD.
17. I agree to live these values. If my colleagues fail to live up to any of these rules, I will speak up and will help them correct; in turn, I will be open to constructive criticism from my colleagues should I fail to live by these values. I understand that my performance will be judged in part by how well I demonstrate these values in my daily work.

Questions:

1. What effect would SuccessFactors' Rules of Engagement have on employee attitudes?
2. Do you think that the company's strong values and Rules of Engagement help or hurt its performance? Why?
3. How can SuccessFactors screen job applicants to find those who best fit its values?
4. What else can the company do to reinforce its values with its employees?

Source: SuccessFactors (2009), Rules of Engagement. © 2010 SuccessFactors, Inc. All rights reserved. Available online at: http://www.successfactors.com/company/rules/.

emotions influence both the creation and maintenance of our motivation to engage or to not engage in certain behaviors. Third, research has found that emotion can influence turnover, decision making, leadership, helping behaviors, and teamwork behaviors.[59] The quality of subordinates' emotional exchanges with their leader also influences the affective tone of the workgroup.[60] Effective leaders use emotion to generate positive follower behaviors.

Effective managers establish appropriate emotional expression norms for their workgroups. Norms for excessive politeness may result in anger suppression and the withholding of vital emotional information that ultimately hurts the organization.[61] Similarly, norms allowing for frequent display of anger, particularly by company leaders, can create climates of fear and defensiveness. Managers should clarify when and where anger expressions are appropriate, so that employees know when and how to safely express their justified anger. Expressing anger often leads to positive consequences when patience is used in judging whether the expression is warranted. Even an uncomfortable exchange can result in employees' needs and perceptions receiving appropriate attention. By not stigmatizing appropriate anger expressions, managers may be able to address problems earlier, rather than creating an environment where chronically suppressed anger is released in harmful ways.[62]

Emotional displays are not acceptable in all cultures, as we discuss further in this chapter's Global Issues feature.

GLOBAL ISSUES

EMOTIONAL DISPLAYS IN DIFFERENT CULTURES

People from different cultures have different expectations about displaying or hiding their emotions. Cultural display rules are learned in childhood to help us manage and modify our emotional expressions based on the social circumstance we are in.[63] Some cultures have strong norms about regulating emotions to satisfy organizational roles and norms, whereas other cultures are more impulsive and value expressing unregulated emotions.[64] The United States tends to expect employees to act positively and hide negative emotions—thus the popular "service with a smile" slogan. France, on the other hand, has a more impulsive orientation toward emotional displays at work.[65] Some cultures, including Austria, Korea, and Japan, expect people to display a neutral emotional state. In these cultures, subdued emotional expressions and monotonic vocal intonation are expected.

People in cultures with a more impulsive orientation to emotional expression are likely to feel more personal control over their expressions than people who must behave as the organization requires. This control can result in more of a buffer against experienced strain and emotional exhaustion.[66] In one study of employees who work on jobs involving client interaction and emotional labor, employees in a more impulsive-oriented culture (France) showed lower degrees of emotional exhaustion than did U.S. employees.[67]

As a manager and employee in a multicultural workplace, it is helpful to remember that some emotional displays may not be considered appropriate by all employees. For example, in the Japanese culture, anger between colleagues is considered highly inappropriate,[68] yet in the United States anger and open disagreements between colleagues who know and like each other are relatively common and accepted. Understanding how displaying different emotions is perceived by people from different cultures will help you to be more effective as both an employee and a manager in a multicultural workplace.

Where Do Moods Come From?

Although the cause of emotions tends be obvious, the cause of mood tends to be more unfocused and diffused. Unlike instant reactions that produce emotion, and that change with expectations of future pleasure or pain, moods are harder to cope with, can last for days, weeks, months, or even years.[69] Our mood at the start of a workday influences how we see and react to work events, which influences our performance.[70] Because moods reflect an individual's emotional state, researchers typically infer the existence of moods from a variety of behavioral cues.

Our moods can be influenced by others. Nasty interactions with coworkers can impact our mood five times more strongly than positive interactions.[71] Workgroups tend to experience shared group moods when they can display mood information to each other through facial, vocal, and behavioral cues.[72] Subordinates' attributions of their leader's sincere versus manipulative intentions also influence their emotional responses to the leader.[73] Altering characteristics of the group's work, changing elements of the work context, or changing group membership in a way that changes the manner in which coworkers interact can change the amount and type of mood information members get from each other and influence employees' moods.

Affectivity

affectivity

A general tendency of an individual to experience a particular mood or to react to things in a particular way or with certain emotions

positive affect

Reflects a combination of high energy and positive evaluation characterized in such emotions as elation

negative affect

Comprises feelings of being upset, fearful, and distressed

Affectivity represents our tendency to experience a particular mood or to react to things with certain emotions.[74] Researchers have identified two types of affectivity: positive and negative. Individuals with a high positive affectivity experience tend to experience more positive emotions including cheerfulness or enthusiasm. Individuals higher in negative affectivity tend to experience more negative emotions, such as irritation or nervousness.

The two dominant dimensions of mood are, *positive affect,* which reflects a combination of high energy and positive evaluation characterized by emotions like elation, and *negative affect,* which comprises feelings of being upset, fearful, and distressed.[75] As shown in Figure 5-4, positive and negative affect are not opposites, but are two distinct dimensions.[76] Not being elated does not mean that I am upset, and not being sad does not mean that I am elated. Affect tends to be somewhat dispositional and fairly stable over time. Some people just tend to be more positive and optimistic than others.[77]

Negative affect is related to lower organizational citizenship behaviors, greater withdrawal and counterproductive work behaviors, lower job satisfaction, and greater injuries.[78] Affectivity can also be important to training outcomes. Employees with greater positive affect or lower negative affect experience a greater increase in self-efficacy after training. This suggests that affectivity may be an important thing to consider when choosing people to participate in development programs.[79]

Figure 5-4
Positive and Negative Affect

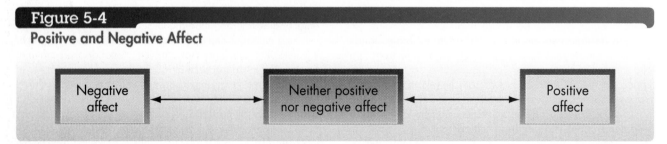

Source: Thompson, E. R., Development and Validation of an Internationally Reliable Short-Form of the Positive and Negative Affect Schedule (PANAS), Journal of Cross-Cultural Psychology, 38(2), 227–242. © 2007 by SAGE Publications. Reprinted by Permission of SAGE Publications.

Moods and emotions can influence our satisfaction with our jobs and employers. Higher positive affect is related to increased creativity, openness to new information, and efficient decision making.[80] Positive affectivity also increases the likelihood of cooperation strategies in negotiations, improving the results.[81] Numerous studies show that happy individuals are successful in many areas of their lives, including marriage, health, friendship, income, and work performance.[82]

SO WHAT

Positive affect promotes success, and success makes people happy.

Why Do Emotions Matter?

Creating an environment that elicits and sustains positive emotional states in employees can positively impact a company's bottom line.[83] Emotions affect productivity, creativity, and career success. As one expert explains:

> If service workers are angry, demoralized, or just plain disinterested, no amount of training will offset the service climate their emotional state creates. The economic consequence of not addressing front line employee emotions is disastrous. Customer service research shows that 68 percent of customers defect from a company because they were treated with an attitude of indifference. Thus, 68 percent of what leads to customer defection is related to emotion—or in this case, the lack of emotion.[84]

Emotions are also related to stress. Emotional distress compromises intellectual functioning in a variety of ways. As we become more stressed, our thinking becomes increasingly more simplistic, unimaginative, and even

UNDERSTAND YOURSELF

POSITIVE AND NEGATIVE AFFECTIVITY

strongly disagree	disagree	neutral	agree	strongly agree
1	2	3	4	5

___9. Afraid
___10. Active

Scoring: Add up your scores for items 3, 5, 7, 8, and 10. This is your positive affectivity score. Now add up your scores for items 1, 2, 4, 6, and 9. This is your negative affectivity score.

Using the scale above, and thinking about yourself and how you usually feel, indicate before each item below to what extent you generally feel:

___1. Upset
___2. Hostile
___3. Alert
___4. Ashamed
___5. Inspired
___6. Nervous
___7. Determined
___8. Attentive

Interpretation: If your *positive affectivity score is greater than 19.7*, it is above average compared to a sample of 411 U.S. undergraduates. If your *negative affectivity score is greater than 11.3*, it is above average compared to the same sample of 411 U.S. undergraduates. To reduce your negative affectivity, try to think more positively and focus on those things for which you can be grateful. Keeping a gratitude journal can help you reflect positively on the things that happen in your life.

Source: Thompson, E. R., Development and validation of an internationally reliable short-form of the positive and negative affect schedule (PANAS), Journal of Cross-Cultural Psychology, 38(2), 227–242. © 2007 by SAGE Publications. Reprinted by Permission of SAGE Publications.

primitive—we literally become "dumbed down." Creating a flexible, focused, and responsive workforce requires a workplace that elicits and sustains positive emotional states.[85]

Emotions also matter because they influence moods and behavior, including ethical behavior. According to a former derivatives trader, the dominant emotion of the finance-led boom in the early 2000s was "infectious greed." Economists, bankers, politicians, and regulators shared the mindset of infectious greed and optimism, generating behavior that no regulatory mechanism could have controlled.[86]

Recent research suggests that emotions can both motivate and interfere with ethical behavior.[87] A number of researchers have demonstrated a modest relationship between empathy and helping behaviors.[88] Emotions also can change the extent to which we use advice in making decisions. Gratitude leads to greater weighing of advice, whereas anger results in people weighing advice less heavily than people do when in a neutral emotional state. Angry people also show the least trust, while people experiencing gratitude show the most.[89]

Emotions can interrupt our concentration and ability to get work done. Imagine being a relatively new hire working for a company that just announced the necessity for layoffs. Would you be able to concentrate on your work, or would your fear of losing your job interfere with your performance?

Emotional Contagion

emotional contagion

One person's expressed emotion causes others to express the same emotion

Have you ever noticed that being around angry people makes you feel at least a little angrier, too? *Emotional contagion* reflects the phenomenon where one person's expressed emotion causes others to express the same emotion. Research has found that emotional contagion can enhance leadership effectiveness[90] as well as satisfaction, productivity, performance, and workgroup cohesion.[91] Aggressive and mean leaders tend to create aggressive and mean workgroups.[92] Once ignited, mistrust and disrespect can spread fast among employees through emotional contagion.[93]

Because of the strong effects the emotions and dispositions of your boss and coworkers can have on you, when you are looking for a job it is worth investigating these dimensions in your future workgroup. One expert suggests taking a close look at the people you will be working with when you are evaluating a job offer. If your potential colleagues are self-centered, nasty, narrow-minded, or unethical, you have little chance of turning them into better human beings or of transforming the workplace into a healthy one, even in a small company. In fact, the odds are that you will turn into a jerk as well.[94]

SO WHAT

Managing your own emotions can increase others' positive emotions.

Understanding emotional contagion gives you an additional tool to use in managing employees' moods and emotions. If you consistently display a positive attitude, pride, and confidence in the organization, this can increase these feelings in your subordinates and coworkers.

Emotional Labor

emotional labor

Displaying the appropriate emotion regardless of the emotion actually felt

If you have ever experienced the difference between a grouchy and a cheerful salesperson, then you understand the importance of emotions in many jobs. Even when they are not feeling cheery, employees in some jobs—especially service jobs—need to display positive emotions. At Walt Disney World, employees are trained to display specific emotions, particularly when they are "onstage" with Disney guests, no matter how unpleasant the guests happen to be and how angry the employees feel.[95] *Emotional labor* is the act of displaying the appropriate emotion regardless of the emotion we actually feel.[96] It occurs whenever employees have to regulate their emotions in a manner consistent with the company's rules. Because almost all jobs require some sort of emotional labor to conform to organizational norms and expectations in meetings and in interacting with coworkers and customers, it is helpful to understand more about it.

Service businesses and customers share a set of expectations about the emotions that should be displayed during a service encounter.[97] These expectations are a function of societal, occupational, and organizational norms.[98] Emotional labor can be thought of as the "acting" that employees perform on the job to meet these expectations. If we think of eating lunch in a restaurant, for example, the service is a "show" where the server is an "actor," the customer is the "audience," and the restaurant is the stage. The restaurant provides the setting and context that allows actors (employees) to perform for an audience (customers).

The interaction between the actors and the audience is based on their mutual expectations about which emotions ought to be expressed and which ought to be disguised,[99] which create *display rules*. For example, employees in the United States are often expected to maintain "professionalism" by suppressing both positive and negative emotions.[100] Emotional display rules apply to leaders as well. Research has found that when a product has failed, a leader expressing sadness has been evaluated more favorably than a leader expressing anger.[101]

There is no universal conclusion about whether emotional labor is helpful or harmful to employees—research has often found contradictory results.[102] As a result, emotional labor is often described as a double-edged sword. There is a clear relationship between our emotional state and our physical state. Efforts to display unfelt positive emotions or suppress felt negative emotions often lead to patterns of physiological responses that precede illnesses ranging from lower immune levels[103] to cancer.[104] Job burnout,[105] emotional exhaustion,[106] and job dissatisfaction[107] also can result. For example, prison officers report that suppressing emotion in the workplace is positively associated with overall stress and negatively associated with job satisfaction.[108] Other consequences of emotional labor include poor self-esteem, depression, and cynicism.[109]

However, people do not all respond to emotional labor in the same way.[110] The negative effects of emotional labor are greater for some individuals than for others. Some service employees are unique in the way that they enjoy working with people, helping people, and making the world a better place. This likely reflects differences in employees' instrumental values and personality. Research has also found that when workers are able to correctly identify others' emotions the negative impact of emotional labor is reduced.[111]

Some research has identified positive consequences of emotional labor for both organizations and employees. For the company, regulating employees' emotional displays in a highly scripted manner can ensure task effectiveness and service quality,[112] and increase sales and repeat business.[113] For employees, the positive aspects of emotional labor can include financial rewards (higher tips or salaries);[114] increased satisfaction, security, and self-esteem;[115] increased self-efficacy and psychological wellbeing;[116] and decreased stress.[117] When expressed feelings are congruent with experienced emotions, employees experience "emotional harmony," which is an indicator of a good fit between the person and the job requirements.[118] When there is a lack of congruence between our characteristics and job requirements, job satisfaction drops and stress increases.[119] We then usually seek opportunities to leave the situation.[120]

display rules

Shared expectations about which emotions ought to be expressed and which ought to be disguised

Interacting with a variety of people, being at the center of attention, and experiencing a sense of joy when genuinely helping others can all provide intrinsic rewards when performing emotional labor.[121] Effective leaders also use emotional labor to regulate their own emotions and to manage the job attitudes, moods, and performance of their followers.[122]

Managing Emotions and Moods

Emotional intelligence is an interpersonal skill that includes the ability to perceive and express emotions, to understand and use them, and to manage emotions in oneself and other people.[123] An emotionally intelligent employee knows the best time to talk to a coworker, and knows when not to make a suggestion to the boss. Higher emotional intelligence is related to higher individual problem-solving skills, negotiation skills, and performance. Emotionally intelligent people are good at recognizing their own and others' emotions and tailoring their own behaviors and emotions accordingly. Emotional intelligence can be learned and improves with practice.

Our emotions and moods change over the course of a day in response to what happens to us, but we can do several things to stay in control of them. The most important thing is to recognize the moods and emotions we are feeling and to try to understand their source. We can also try to avoid spending time with negative coworkers, and make a point of not being bothered by negative coworkers, in order to decrease the possibility of emotional contagion. Doing small things to create feelings of gratitude and happiness in coworkers can improve their emotions and moods, which might further improve ours. As a manager, remember the positive influence you can have on your subordinates' emotions and moods by not micromanaging, by listening to their suggestions, and by respecting and trusting them.

SO WHAT

You can increase other people's positive moods and emotions by trusting, respecting, and listening to them.

STRESS

The American Institute of Stress estimates that stress costs American businesses $300 billion annually.[124] Health care expenditures alone are nearly 50 percent higher for workers reporting high levels of stress.[125] In an extreme example, in one five-month period, three engineers at one firm committed suicide due to their anxiety about unreasonable workloads, high-pressure management tactics, exhaustion, and even humiliating criticism in front of colleagues during performance reviews. In response, the company committed $10 million to combat workplace stress, added employees, and trained 2,100 managers on how to avoid negative stress and how to teach their subordinates to do the same. Psychologists were even brought in to teach 150 senior executives methods of identifying warning signs that people may be at risk, and how to communicate with them.[126]

Although individual differences exist in what people find stressful, excessive workload demands, job insecurity, and conflicting expectations are stressful to most people. Incivility in the workplace is also a common source of stress.[127] Table 5-3 identifies some job conditions that can lead to stress.

Experiencing stress in response to a potentially stressful event is not inevitable—it depends greatly on how we interpret or appraise the event. Noted psychologist Richard Lazarus[128] was the first to recognize that

Table 5-3

Job Conditions That May Lead to Stress

Lack of Autonomy	Employees around the world prefer to have some control over their work
Job Design	Long work hours, a heavy workload, repetitive tasks, and jobs that do not utilize workers' skills
Management Style	Bullying and incivility, lack of worker participation in decisions, poor communication, lack of feedback
Conflicting Roles	Conflicting work roles or goals or too many roles
Coworker Relationships	Lack of coworker support and help
Career Issues	Lack of advancement opportunity; job insecurity
Work Conditions	Dangerous or unpleasant working conditions including noise, smells, pollution, and overcrowding

Source: Stress . . . At Work (1999). NIOSH Publication No. 99–101. Available online at: http://www.cdc.gov/niosh/docs/99-101/. Accessed February 4, 2010.

challenging events are stressful only when also accompanied by negative emotions.[129] This knowledge gives us great power to manage stress in ourselves and in others. Often the easiest way to reduce stress is to change our interpretation or appraisal of an event, replacing negative emotions with positive or neutral emotions.

Functional and Dysfunctional Stress

Stress is not always a bad thing—probably nothing worthwhile is accomplished without at least some degree of stress. Mild stress generates a small amount of adrenaline that makes action more likely and even increases the brain's ability to form new memories.[130] Good stress is called *functional stress*,[131] which is the experience of manageable levels of stress for a reasonable period of time that generates positive emotions including satisfaction, excitement, and enjoyment. An example of functional stress might be a challenging assignment given by your boss.

> **functional stress**
> *Manageable levels of stress for reasonable periods of time that generate positive emotions including satisfaction, excitement, and enjoyment*

Dysfunctional stress refers to an overload of stress from a situation of either under- or over-arousal stemming from too few or too many demands that continues for too long. Factors including bureaucracy and role ambiguity interfere with our performance and lead to dysfunctional stress.

> **dysfunctional stress**
> *An overload of stress from a situation of either under- or over-arousal that continues for too long*

Although both functional and dysfunctional stress can lead to negative outcomes like emotional exhaustion, dysfunctional stress is also related to withdrawal behaviors and turnover. Functional stress can lead to positive outcomes including job satisfaction, but if the resulting anxiety is unmanaged, it can lead to counterproductive behaviors.[132]

Figure 5-5 illustrates the desirability of having some stress in our lives while guarding against having too much. As you can see in the figure, at lower levels of arousal, we experience an increased risk of feeling bored and experiencing dysfunctional stress that can hurt our performance, satisfaction, and well-being. At higher levels of arousal, we are also more likely to experience dysfunctional stress due to work overload. At moderate levels of stress, we are the most likely to experience functional stress, enjoying what we do and performing well at it.

Figure 5-5

The Stress Continuum

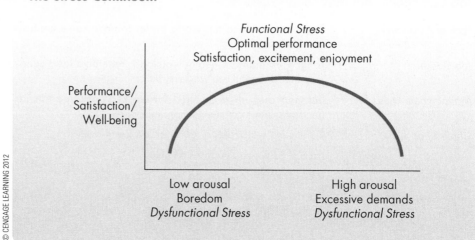

© CENGAGE LEARNING 2012

Different people thrive under different levels of stress. Some people need low levels, and others thrive on challenges. Only unpleasant stressors produce harmful stress reactions—essentially, challenges are not harmful as long as we enjoy the challenge. This is relevant to the setting of stretch goals, or asking employees to aim for targets slightly higher than their current ability or performance levels. Stretch goals are often used to increase motivation and improve performance. They can work, but only if they are attainable—no one is motivated by unachievable goals. Setting a subordinate up for failure is more likely to trigger distress and anxiety than higher performance. Supporting employees and removing obstacles to their performance are important in maximizing the benefits of challenging goals.[133]

Stress Stages

Our response to stress happens in three stages: alarm, resistance, and exhaustion.[134] The *alarm stage* is triggered whenever we face any danger. Our energy is increased, our breathing quickens, our pulse races, and our body quickly readies itself to either fight or flee the danger. If the alarm stage is triggered by a specific event, like your boss entering the room angry and yelling, it is called *primary stress*. If it is triggered by anxiety over something that is about to happen, like a performance review at a time the company is about to lay off some employees, it is called *secondary stress*. Warning signs that we are beginning to experience stress include headaches, sleep problems, difficulty concentrating, upset stomach, short temper, and job dissatisfaction.

When the first stage of stress is not relieved, our energy starts to fall and we enter the *resistance stage*. But because our bodies want to continue fighting off the danger, we become impatient. As our bodies release stored sugars and fats into our system, our physical and mental behavior patterns change as we become exhausted, forgetful, and anxious. Because our immune system is weakened, we are also more likely to get sick.

If we are unable to resolve the stress in the second stage, the third stage of *exhaustion* develops and we are tired and listless. Because our system is broken down at this stage, it can lead to complications like heart disease and ulcers. If not properly managed, stress can lead to increased risk of musculoskeletal disorders, psychological disorders including depression, and burnout, injury, and illness.

Bullying

Bullying can increase stress and decrease performance as well as decrease the organization's productivity, reputation, legal issues, and culture.[135] Between 30 and 53[136] percent of employees report having felt bullied at some point in their working lives.[137] Bullying is a repeated mistreatment of another employee through verbal abuse; conduct that is threatening, humiliating, or intimidating; or sabotage that interferes with the other person's work. Targets of bullying and observers report psychological problems such as distress, humiliation, anger, anxiety, embarrassment, discouragement, feelings of inadequacy, hopelessness, depression, burnout, lower job satisfaction, a perceived lack of support from colleagues and workgroup cohesiveness, eroded attachment to the job and organization, and greater intention to leave.[138] Twenty percent of victims leave their jobs.[139]

Research also suggests that psychological well-being is impaired more through psychologically abusive behavior than physically abusive behavior.[140] Damage to the organization occurs through absenteeism, high turnover, and time and money lost due to stress, reduced productivity during work distractions, and vengeful activities. Research suggests that as many as 71 percent of bullies are in management positions and 29 percent are peers and subordinates.[141]

SO WHAT

Effective managers are not bullies and do not tolerate bullying behavior by their employees.

Managing Stress

We put more energy into activities we enjoy. Having fun doing things that we enjoy and are good at while accomplishing important organizational goals improves attitudes, moods, emotions, and organizational performance. Problem-focused coping strategies that deal directly with stressors are more effective than emotion-focused coping strategies that focus on the emotions brought on by the stressors.[142] Actively promoting positive employee attitudes, moods, and emotions fights stress and burnout, and improves employees' performance and job satisfaction.

Stress can be managed through various coping strategies that focus on:

1. Changing the situation through *direct action* (e.g., quitting the job or hiring an assistant)
2. Changing the way we think about the situation through *cognitive reappraisal* (e.g., focusing on the developmental aspects of a challenging assignment)
3. Focusing on *managing the stress reaction symptoms* (e.g., working out or meditating)

Positive stress symptom management strategies include social support, meditation, time management, exercise, a positive and relaxed outlook, and getting enough rest. Other symptom-focused coping strategies can be harmful, including drinking, drug use, and overeating. Removing the source of the stress is more effective than managing its symptoms.[143]

Positive management, giving positive feedback, and assigning employees to tasks and projects that utilize their strengths energize employees to have positive attitudes and emotions and put their full effort into their jobs. Giving negative feedback leads workers to focus disproportionately on their weaknesses rather than their strengths. As management expert Peter Cappelli says, "Cranking up negative consequences, which seems to be the dominant view of motivation, is not really good for people's mental health."[144] Unfortunately, negative feedback, like "You really messed up that project," seems to increase during challenging times that are already stressful enough.

Too often, job stress is treated with medication or counseling rather than by making appropriate changes in the workplace and to workloads. When leaders at Merck, the pharmaceutical company based in Whitehouse Station, New Jersey, listened to employee complaints about problems including overwork, inadequate training, and lack of communication, they created employee teams to address them. Work was analyzed and reorganized to give workers more control over their workloads and schedules. In payroll, for example, the company learned that most employees' work was most critical earlier in the week. To reduce the amount of overtime payroll employees had to put in, they were allowed to telecommute more often and to work compressed workweeks. These changes reduced overtime costs, absenteeism, and turnover.[145]

Some companies are realizing that helping employees balance work and life demands can reduce employees' stress. Management consultant Booz Allen Hamilton Inc. creates a sort of social contract where employees identify their life responsibilities and then work is arranged around those commitments. Some companies, like research and development firm Draper Laboratory in Cambridge, Massachusetts, even refuse to buy cell phones and other communication devices for employees to prevent them from being "on call" twenty-four hours a day.[146]

Table 5-4 gives you some tips on how to prevent stress in your own life and for those you manage.

For most people, occasional stress is a part of work life. Successful managers handle stress well.[147] Stress management tools like time management, exercise, meditation, and time away from the television and cell phone can help you better manage pressure. This chapter's *Improve Your Skills* feature gives you some additional tips for managing stress.

Table 5-4

How to Change the Organization to Prevent Job Stress

- Ensure that workloads match employees' capabilities and resources.
- Design jobs to provide meaning, stimulation, and opportunities for employees to use their skills.
- Clearly define employee roles and responsibilities.
- Give employees the opportunity to participate in decisions and actions affecting their jobs.
- Improve communication and reduce uncertainty about career development and future employment prospects.
- Provide opportunities for social interaction among employees.
- Establish work schedules that are compatible with demands and responsibilities outside the job.

Source: How to Change the Organization to Prevent Job Stress (1999). NIOSH Publication No. 99–101. http://www.cdc.gov/niosh/docs/99-101/.

IMPROVE YOUR SKILLS

STRESS MANAGEMENT TIPS

We all feel stress from time to time. Knowing how to manage your stress will help to keep you healthy and productive. Two main strategies for managing stress are: (1) generate calm or relaxed feelings to counteract the biological state of exhaustion or over-arousal, and (2) change your appraisal of the stress-inducing situation to reduce negative emotions. Below are some tips for using each strategy.

Generating Calm or Relaxed Feelings

1. Eat healthy and avoid too much caffeine.
2. Get enough high-quality sleep; take a nap if necessary.
3. Exercise.
4. Practice relaxation techniques including meditation. These are known to relax muscles and reduce adrenaline levels.
5. Develop affectionate relationships. Giving and getting hugs, petting a dog or cat, or having conversations with friends can all reduce feelings of stress.
6. Prioritize your to-do list. As Scarlett O'Hara says in the movie *Gone with the Wind*, "I can't think about that right now. If I do, I'll go crazy. I'll think about that tomorrow."
7. Learn to say "No," "Not now," and "I really can't"—no one can do everything!

Changing Your Appraisal of the Situation

1. Try to view crises or stressful events as opportunities. The Chinese character for crisis, *wei ji,* is made up of two component characters. One is the character for danger, and the other is the character for opportunity. Framing a crisis as an opportunity decreases negative emotions and increases positive emotions, reducing stress.
2. Reframe the stressor. Casting the situation in a less stressful or threatening way can decrease negative emotions and stress. For example, the boss is not really trying to make your job difficult; she is just very busy and has deadlines to meet.
3. Try to find the silver lining. Your boss's moving up the deadline for that big report is challenging, but it gives you a chance to show your talent, and it will soon be done!

Job Burnout

Burnout refers to "exhaustion of physical or emotional strength or motivation usually as a result of prolonged stress or frustration."[148] Boston Consulting Group proactively looks for employees who are working too hard and putting in so many hours that they are at risk of burning out. When issues are identified, managers help team members balance workload, prioritize goals, and keep employees focused on delivering to the client rather than working the most hours.[149]

The Professional Renewal Center in Lawrence, Kansas, is a career rehabilitation program for executives with substance abuse, sexual harassment, and emotional issues at work. One thing their burned-out patients usually have in common is that they never took vacation.[150] PricewaterhouseCoopers tracks employees who have not taken enough vacation, sending them and their supervisor reminders that they should do so.[151]

To best help yourself and your employees, it is a good idea to learn to recognize the symptoms of burnout. Table 5-5 describes some of the physical and behavioral signs of burnout as well as some of the effects burnout has on work performance.

burnout
Exhaustion of physical or emotional strength or motivation usually as a result of prolonged stress or frustration

YURI ARCURS/SHUTTERSTOCK

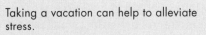
Taking a vacation can help to alleviate stress.

Table 5-5

Signs of Burnout and Effects on Work Performance

The signs of burnout tend to fall into the three categories of physical symptoms, behavioral changes, and work performance.

Physical Symptoms	Behavioral Changes	Work Performance
Weight loss	Increase in risky behavior	Decreased performance
Sleeplessness	Irritability	Lowered initiative
Frequent illness	Moodiness	Less interest in working
Headaches	Increased suspicion of others	Less efficiency at work

© CENGAGE LEARNING 2012

SUMMARY AND APPLICATION

Values, attitudes, emotions, and moods are important aspects of organizational behavior because of the effects they have on what we choose to do and how we choose to do it. When our personal values are consistent with the organization's values, when we are satisfied with our jobs, and when we have positive attitudes about the company and the work environment, we work harder, perform better, and are less likely to quit our jobs. That makes the effective management of attitudes, values, and emotions an important personal and managerial tool.

As a manager, it is important to recognize that you are always "on stage" and that your employees constantly look to you for signs that communicate how things are going in the organization. If you often have a worried expression on your face, this can impact employees' moods, emotions, and stress. Managers with greater positivity make better decisions, have more effective relationships with subordinates, and create better coordination among their workgroups by transferring positive affect to their subordinates.[152]

 TAKEAWAY POINTS

1. Intrapersonal value conflict occurs when highly ranked instrumental and terminal values conflict. Interpersonal value conflict occurs when two different people hold conflicting values. Individual-organization value conflict happens when an employee's values conflict with the values of the organization.

2. Our beliefs and feelings about something influence our attitudes about it. Our attitudes then affect our behavior through our intentions. The three most important job-related attitudes are job satisfaction, organizational commitment, and employee engagement. Job satisfaction reflects our attitudes and feelings about our job. Organizational commitment is the degree to which an employee identifies with the organization and its goals and wants to stay with the organization. Employee engagement reflects a heightened emotional and intellectual connection that an employee has for his or her job, organization, manager, or coworkers that, in turn, influences the employee to apply additional discretionary effort to his or her work.

3. The three types of organizational commitment are affective (I want to stay), normative (I should stay), and continuance (I have to stay).

REAL WORLD RESPONSE

ATTITUDE IS A CHOICE AT PIKE PLACE FISH MARKET

John Yokoyama had recently purchased Seattle's Pike Place Fish Market. Continuing the previous owner's fear-based management style led to low morale, high turnover, and bad employee attitudes. To revive his flagging business, he decided to share his vision of being world famous with his employees, and empowered them to pursue this vision. He gave his employees permission to have fun with their jobs and to perform their best by bringing their whole selves to work every day. Together, Yokoyama and his employees developed four guiding principles:

1. *Choose your attitude*: We may have no control over what job we have, but we do control how we approach our job.

2. *Make their day*: Engage and delight customers and coworkers; don't grudgingly do the bare minimum.

3. *Be present*: Don't dwell on where you aren't; instead, make the most of where you are. When talking to customers and coworkers, look them in the eye and give them your full attention.

4. *Play*: Have as much fun as you can at whatever you're doing to cultivate a spirit of innovation and creativity.

As one fishmonger explains, "My buddies and I realized that each day when we come to the fish market we bring an attitude. We can bring a moody attitude and have a depressing day. We can bring a grouchy attitude and irritate our coworkers and customers. Or we can bring a sunny, playful, cheerful attitude and have a great day. We can choose the kind of day we will have. We spent a lot of time talking about this choice, and we realized that as long as we are going to be at work, we might as well have the best day we can have." [153]

Yokoyama's goal of being world famous has also been realized. The market is known worldwide for its fun atmosphere and positive employee attitudes. The fishmongers enjoy letting customers know they are important whether they buy anything or not, and constantly entertain them. Employees sing, throw fish, and play jokes on each other and on customers.

Throwing fish and playing jokes on customers obviously would not work as well for every business as it did for Seattle's Pike Place Fish Market. But by developing healthy work relationships and creating positive attitudes and emotions in employees and customers, the business is now worth 1,000 times more than Yokoyama paid for it more than thirty-five years ago. The market has been featured on numerous television shows, and was even named one of the most fun places to work in America by CNN.

Sources: Christensen, J. (2003). First Person: Gone Fishin', Sales and Marketing Management, 155(4), 53; Hein, K. (2002). Hooked on Employee Morale, Incentive, 176(8), 56–57; Lundin, S.C., Paul, H., & Christensen, J. (2000). Fish! A remarkable Way to Boost Morale and Improve Results. New York: Hyperion; Yerkes, L. (2007). Fun Works: Creating Places Where People Love to Work. San Francisco: Berrett-Koehler.

4. Emotions influence both the creation and maintenance of our motivation to engage and to not engage in certain behaviors. Emotions also influence turnover, decision making, leadership, helping behaviors, and teamwork behaviors. Effective leaders use emotion to generate positive follower behaviors.

5. Positive affect reflects a combination of high energy and positive evaluation characterized by emotions like elation. Negative affect involves feelings of fearfulness and distress, which comprises feelings of being upset. Positive and negative affect are not opposites, but rather are two distinct dimensions.

6. Emotional labor is the act of displaying the appropriate emotion regardless of the emotion we actually feel. It occurs whenever employees have to regulate their emotions in a manner consistent with the company's rules. When expressed feelings are congruent with experienced emotions, employees experience "emotional harmony," which is an indicator of a good fit between the person and the job requirements. When there is a lack of congruence between our characteristics and job requirements, job satisfaction drops and stress increases. For the company, regulating employees' emotional displays in a highly scripted manner can increase sales and repeat business. For employees, the positive aspects of emotional labor can include higher tips or salaries; increased satisfaction, security, and self-esteem; increased psychological well-being; and decreased stress.

7. Our emotions influence whether we feel stress. Challenging events are stressful only when also accompanied by negative emotions. Some stress is actually beneficial. Functional stress is the experience of a manageable level of stress for a reasonable period of time that generates positive emotions including satisfaction, excitement, and enjoyment. Dysfunctional stress is an overload of stress from a situation of either under- or over-arousal that continues for too long.

DISCUSSION QUESTIONS

1. Do terminal or instrumental values have a larger influence on your behavior at work? Explain.

2. If your boss was not sure if it would be worth the investment to change the company's hiring practices to include an evaluation of applicants' attitudes, what would you tell him or her?

3. Do you think that it would be easier to influence a subordinate's attitudes, values, or emotions? Why? Which would have the largest influence on the employee's behavior? Why?

4. Have you ever had to engage in emotional labor and display an emotion that you did not actually feel? What did you do? How well did it work? How did it make you feel?

5. If you wanted to use your knowledge of emotional contagion to improve the mood of your workgroup, what would you do?

6. As a manager, how could you ensure that your employees were experiencing functional rather than dysfunctional stress?

7. Describe a time when you were highly engaged at work. Why did you feel this way? What could you do as a manager to promote engagement among your employees?

8. Do you know anyone who has been bullied at work? What happened and what did they do about it? What can you do as a manager to prevent bullying among your employees?

EXERCISES

The Effect of Emotion on Team Performance

In this exercise you will be asked to role-play a particular emotion as a member of a work team. After dividing into teams of four people, count off one to four to identify your role in the team by reading the description below. If your team has more than four people, restart the numbering at 1 when you get to the fifth person.

Role 1: Grouchy, negative affect

Role 2: Calm

Role 3: Happy, positive affect

Role 4: Calm

For the next five to ten minutes (until the instructor tells you to stop), your team's task is to discuss possible slogans for the field of organizational behavior and identify your team's favorite idea. When your instructor tells you, your role will change to the following:

Role 1: Calm

Role 2: Happy, positive affect

Role 3: Calm

Role 4: Grouchy, negative affect

You will spend the next five to ten minutes (until the instructor tells you to stop) discussing the best ways for the manager of a local McDonald's restaurant to improve the employees' job engagement and deciding on your group's favorite three ideas. When your instructor ends the task, address the following questions as a group and be prepared to share your answers with the class.

Questions

1. Did your emotion influence your own performance or behavior in your team?
2. Did any emotional contagion occur in your team? If so, was the positive (happy) or negative (grouchy) emotion more contagious? Why do you think this was so?
3. What could a leader do to effectively manage a team's emotion? Is it worth trying?

Who Stays and Who Goes?

Form groups of three to five students. Imagine yourselves as managers asked to downsize the employees in your departments by 25 percent. Ignoring issues such as performance and seniority, what factors would you use to help the managers decide who stays and who goes? Be ready to share your ideas and your reasons for them with the class.

*We thank Professor Kathie K. Holland at the University of Central Florida for suggesting this exercise.

Managing Stress

Form groups of three to five students. Each student then independently generates a list of what he or she does to relieve stress in his or her life. For fifteen minutes, each team shares and discusses each idea and creates a list of the team's top five ideas. These ideas are then shared with the class to generate fresh ideas to help the class better combat stress.

*We thank Professor H. Lon Addams at Weber State University for suggesting this exercise.

Positive and Negative Affectivity

Complete and score the positive and negative affectivity self-assessment in this chapter. The instructor will pair you with another student with whom you will have two minutes to discuss anything you like. After the two minutes are up, each student tries to guess the other's emotional disposition (you do not have to reveal your actual score if you do not want to).

*We thank Professor Paul Harvey at the University of New Hampshire for suggesting this exercise.

VIDEO CASES

Now What?

Imagine listening to a coworker complain that Happy Time Toys' production goals for a product that is tricky to assemble are unrealistic. The coworker believes that the company is too concerned about quality at the expense of productivity. The coworker feels that the company could make a lot more money if they let some of the team's borderline products go through. The coworker is going to continue to tell the team to pass borderline products to help the team meet its production goals to earn the bonus. This would reduce the employee's stress and, after all, the products are not *that* bad. *What do you say or do?* Go to this chapter's "Now What?" video, watch the challenge video, and choose a response. Be sure to also view the outcomes of the two responses you didn't choose.

Discussion Questions

1. What do you think is more important, quality or quantity? Why?
2. What are some other examples of common individual-organization values conflicts?
3. How is cognitive dissonance illustrated in these videos?

Workplace | Flight 001: Planning and Goal Setting

Until the late 1990s, Brad John and John Sencion worked in different areas of New York's fashion industry. Both traveled often between the United States, Europe, and Japan for work. No matter how many times they began a trip, they spent the days and hours racing all over town picking up last-minute essentials. By the time they got to the airport, they were sweaty, stressed, and miserable—not exactly the glamorous existence they envisioned when they got into the fashion industry.

Then during a flight from New York to Paris in 1998, the weary travelers came up with an idea for a one-stop travel shop targeted at fashion-forward globetrotters like themselves. They called it Flight 001 and began selling guidebooks, cosmetics, laptop bags, luggage, electronic gadgets, passport covers, and other consumer products.

Today, as the company enters its second decade, Flight 001 is hailed as one of the most exciting businesses in the industry. In addition to selling useful travel merchandise, the New York-based retailer offers a unique shopping experience: Flight 001 stores are shaped like airplane fuselages tricked out with retro airport décor and accessories. The company has multiple stores in the United States and a boutique in Harvey Nichols—an upscale department store in the United Arab Emirates. In the years to come, the founders expect to be in every major city in the United States, Europe, and Asia.

But as the company embarks on a new five-year plan, the stretch goal of opening as many as thirty new stores in the United States and overseas is beginning to hit turbulence. Co-founder Brad John is determined to make Flight 001 the international authority on travel, but ambitious plans will require changes to the company's staffing, merchandising, and financial planning.

With all the talk about expansion and new product lines, it will be increasingly important that Flight 001 not become distracted from what makes it special in the first place: location, design, and an impeccable product line.

Discussion Questions

1. What are Flight 001's goals, and what intrinsic work values motivate the company's founders to think big for the future?
2. What plans at Flight 001 are creating stress for Crew Development Manager Emily Griffin?
3. Identify whether the stress placed upon Emily Griffin is functional or dysfunctional, and list ways in which Griffin can manage the stress.

CENGAGENOW™ includes **teaching and learning resources** to supplement the text, and is designed specifically to **help students "think like managers"** by engaging and challenging them to think critically about managerial situations. **CengageNOW uses today's technology to improve the skills** of tomorrow's managers.

END NOTES

[1] Powell, D.J. (2011). Learning From Fish, Counselor, February 8. Available online: http://www.counselormagazine.com/component/content/article/44-clinical-supervision/1160-learning-from-fish; Chittim, G. (2011). Monkfish Scares Last Tourist at Pike Place Market, King5.com, November 11. Available online: http://www.king5.com/news/environment/Fish-Market-Releases-Fan-Favorite-133722773.html; Christensen, J. (2003). First Person: Gone Fishin'. *Sales and Marketing Management, 155*(4), 53; Lundin, S.C., Paul, H., & Christensen, J. (2000). *Fish! A Remarkable Way to Boost Morale and Improve Results.* New York: Hyperion.

[2] Hom, P. W., & Griffeth, R. W. (1995). *Employee Turnover.* Cincinnati, OH: Southwestern.

[3] Kluckhohn, F., & Strodtbeck, F. L. (1961). *Variations in Value Orientations.* Evanston, IL: Row, Peterson.

[4] Schleicher, D.J., Hansen, S., Fox, D., & Kevin, E. (2011). Job Attitudes and Work Values. In S. Zedeck (ed.), *APA Handbook of Industrial and Organizational Psychology: Maintaining, Expanding, and Contracting the Organization,* Vol. 3 (137–189). Washington, DC: American Psychological Association.

[5] Boyacigiller, N., Kleinberg, J. M., Phillips, M. E., & Sackman, S. (1996). Conceptualizing Culture. In *Handbook for International Management Research,* eds. B. J. Punnett and O. Shenkar (pp. 157–208). Cambridge: Blackwell; Erez, M., & Earley, C. P. (1993). *Culture, Self-Identity, & Work.* New York: Oxford University Press; Hampden-Turner, C., & Trompenaars, F. (1993). *The Seven Cultures of Capitalism: Value Systems for Creating Wealth in the United States, Britain, Japan, Germany, France, Sweden, and the Netherlands.* New York: Doubleday.

[6] Bartlett, C.A., & Sumantra, G. (1998). *Managing Across Borders: The Transnational Solution* (2nd ed.). Boston: Harvard Business School Press; Porter, M. E. (1990). *The Competitive Advantage of Nations.* New York: Free Press; Posner, B. Z., & Munson, J. M. (1979). The Importance of Values in Understanding Organizational Behavior. *Human Resource Management, 18,* 9–14.

[7] Fritzsche, D. J., & Becker, H. (1982). Business Ethics of Future Marketing Managers. *Journal of Marketing Education, 4,* 2–7.

[8] Fritzsche, D. J. (1991). A Model of Decision-Making Incorporating Ethical Values. *Journal of Business Ethics, 10,* 841–852.

[9] Paine, L. S. (1994). Managing for Organizational Integrity. *Harvard Business Review, 72*(2), 106–117.

[10] Rokeach, M. (1973). *The Nature of Values.* New York: Free Press.

[11] The Best Advice I Ever Got. (2005, March 21). *Fortune,* 112.

[12] Hambrick, D. C., & D. L. Brandon. (1988). Executive Values. In *The Executive Effect: Concepts and Methods for Studying Top Managers,* ed. D. C. Hambrick (pp. 3–34). Greenwich, CT: JAI Press.

[13] Full Sail, New Belgium Breweries Push Sustainability. (2009, June 9). *Environmental Leader.* Available online: http://www.environmentalleader.com/2009/06/09/full-sail-new-belgium-breweries-push-sustainability/.

[14] Nord, W. R., Brief, A. P., Atieh, J. M., & Doherty, E. M. (1988). Work Values and the Conduct of Organizational Behavior. In *Research in Organizational Behavior,* eds. B. M. Staw and L. L. Cummings (pp. 1–42). Greenwich, CT: JAI Press.

[15] Malka, A., & Chatman, J. A. (2003). Intrinsic and Extrinsic Work Orientations as Moderators of the Effect of Annual Income on Subjective Well-Being: A Longitudinal Study. *Society for Personality and Social Psychology, Inc., 29,* 737–746.

[16] Available online: http://www.brainyquote.com/quotes/quotes/a/albertschw155988.html.

[17] Pestrak, D. (2008). If You Want to Succeed, a Positive Attitude Is Everything. Women's Media. Available online: http://www.womensmedia.com/new/Pestrak-Attitude.shtml.

[18] Nord, W. R., Brief, A. P., Atieh, J. M., & Doherty, E. M. (1988). Work Values and the Conduct of Organizational Behavior. In *Research in Organizational Behavior,* eds. B. M. Staw and L. L. Cummings (pp. 1–42). Greenwich, CT: JAI Press.

[19] Nelson Mandela: The U.S.A. Is a Threat to World Peace. (2002, September 10). *Newsweek.* Available online: http://www.newsweek.com/2002/09/09/nelson-mandela-the-u-s-a-is-a-threat-to-world-peace.html.

[20] Edwards, J. R. (2004). Complementary and Supplementary Fit: A Theoretical and Empirical Integration. *Journal of Applied Psychology, 89,* 822–834; Amos, E. A., & Weathington, B. L. (2008). An Analysis of the Relation Between Employee-Organization Value Congruence and Employee Attitudes. *Journal of Psychology: Interdisciplinary and Applied, 142*(6), 615–632.

[21] Impastato, J. (2009, January). Integrate Web 2.0 into the On-Boarding Experience. *Talent Management,* 18–20.

[22] Impastato, J. (2009, January). Integrate Web 2.0 into the On-Boarding Experience. *Talent Management,* 18–20.

[23] Impastato, J. (2009, January). Integrate Web 2.0 into the On-Boarding Experience. *Talent Management,* 18–20.

[24] Impastato, J. (2009, January). Integrate Web 2.0 into the On-Boarding Experience. *Talent Management,* 19.

[25] Adler, N. J. (2008). *International Dimensions of Organizational Behavior.* Mason, OH: Thompson/South-Western.

[26] Inglehart R., & Welzel, C. (2005). *Modernization, Cultural Change and Democracy.* New York: Cambridge University Press.

[27] Inglehart R., & Welzel, C. (2005). *Modernization, Cultural Change and Democracy.* New York: Cambridge University Press.

[28]Inglehart, R., & Welzel, C. (2005). *Modernization, Cultural Change and Democracy* (p. 64). New York: Cambridge University Press. Based on the World Values Surveys, see http://www.worldvaluessurvey. Org. Copyright © 2005 Ronald Inglehart and Christian Welzel. Reprinted with the permission of Cambridge University Press.

[29]Available online: http://www.career-success-for-newbies.com/attitude-quotes.html.

[30] Robertson, I.T., Birch, A.J. & Cooper, C.L. (2012). Job and Work Attitudes, Engagement and Employee Performance: Where Does Psychological Well-Being Fit In?, *Leadership & Organization Development Journal, 33*(3), 224–232.

[31] Pestrak, D. (2008). If You Want to Succeed, a Positive Attitude Is Everything. Women's Media. Available online: http://www.womensmedia.com/new/Pestrak-Attitude.shtml.

[32]Cohen, A., Watkinson, J., & Boone, J. (2005, March 28). Southwest Airlines CEO Grounded in Real World. SearchCIO.com. Available online: http://searchcio.techtarget.com/news/article/0,289142,sid182_gci1071837,00.html.

[33]Festinger, L. (1957). *A Theory of Cognitive Dissonance*. Stanford, CA: Stanford University Press.

[34]Gagné, M. & Bhave, D. (2011). Autonomy in the Workplace: An Essential Ingredient to Employee Engagement and Well-Being in Every Culture. In V.I. Chirkov et al. (eds.), *Human Autonomy in Cross-Cultural Context, Cross-Cultural Advancements in Positive Psychology, 1*(2), 163–187; Fried, Y., & Ferris, G. R. (1987). The Validity of the Job Characteristics Model: A Review and Metaanalysis. *Personnel Psychology, 40*(2), 287–322; Parisi, A. G., & Weiner, S. P. (1999, May). Retention of Employees: Country-Specific Analyses in a Multinational Organization. Poster at the Fourteenth Annual Conference of the Society for Industrial and Organizational Psychology, Atlanta, GA.

[35]Saari, L., & Judge, T. A. (2004). Employee Attitudes and Job Satisfaction. *Human Resource Management, 43*(4), 395–407.

[36]Staw, B. M., & Ross, J. (1985). Stability in the Midst of Change: A Dispositional Approach to Job Attitudes. *Journal of Applied Psychology, 70,* 469–480.

[37]Judge, T.A., Ilies, R., & Zhang, Z. (2012). Genetic Influences on Core Self-Evaluations, Job Satisfaction, and Work Stress: A Behavioral Genetics Mediated Model, Organizational Behavior and Human Decision Processes, 117(1), 208–220; House, R. J., Shane, S. A., & Herold, D. M. (1996). Rumors of the Death of Dispositional Research Are Vastly Exaggerated. *Academy of Management Review, 21,* 203–224.

[38]Judge, T. A., & Bono, J. E. (2001). Relationship of Core Self-Evaluations Traits—Self-Esteem, Generalized Self-Efficacy, Locus of Control, and Emotional Stability—With Job Satisfaction and Job Performance: A Meta-Analysis. *Journal of Applied Psychology, 86,* 80–92.

[39]Judge, T. A., Heller, D., & Mount, M. K. (2002). Five-Factor Model of Personality and Job Satisfaction: A Meta-Analysis. *Journal of Applied Psychology, 87,* 530–541.

[40]Judge, T. A., Erez, A., Bono, J. E., & Thoresen, C. J. (2003). The Core Self-Evaluations Scale: Development of a Measure. *Personnel Psychology, 56,* 304.

[41]Judge, T. A., Thoresen, C. J., Bono, J. E., & Patton, G. K. (2001). The Job Satisfaction–Job Performance Relationship: A Qualitative and Quantitative Review. *Psychological Bulletin, 127,* 376–407.

[42]Organ, D. W. (1988). *Organizational Citizenship Behavior—The Good Soldier Syndrome* (1st ed.). Lexington, MA/Toronto: D.C. Heath & Company; Smith, C. A., Organ, D. W., & Near, J. P. (1983). Organizational Citizenship Behavior: Its Nature and Antecedents. *Journal of Applied Psychology, 68,* 653–663; Williams, L. J., & Anderson, S. E. (1991). Job Satisfaction and Organizational Commitment as Predictors of Organizational Citizenship and In-Role Behaviors. *Journal of Management, 17,* 601–617; LePine, J. A., Erez, A., & Johnson, D. E. (2002). The Nature and Dimensionality of Organizational Citizenship Behavior: A Critical Review and Meta-Analysis. *Journal of Applied Psychology, 87,* 52–65.

[43]Hulin, C. L., Roznowski, M., & Hachiya, D. (1985). Alternative Opportunities and Withdrawal Decisions: Empirical and Theoretical Discrepancies and an Integration. *Psychological Bulletin, 97,* 233–250; Kohler, S. S., & Mathieu, J. E. (1993). An Examination of the Relationship Between Affective Reactions, Work Perceptions, Individual Resource Characteristics, and Multiple Absence Criteria. *Journal of Organizational Behavior, 14,* 515–530.

[44]Chen, G., Ployhart, R.E., Thomas, H.C., Anderson, N. & Bliese, P.D. (2011). The Power of Momentum: A New Model of Dynamic Relationships between Job Satisfaction Change and Turnover Intentions. *Academy of Management Journal, 54*(1), 159–181.

[45]Meyer, J. P., & Allen, N. J. (1997). *Commitment in the Workplace: Theory, Research, and Application*. Thousand Oaks, CA: Sage.

[46]Meyer, J.P., Stanley, L.J. & Parfyonova, N.M. (2012). Employee Commitment in Context: The Nature and Implication of Commitment Profiles. *Journal of Vocational Behavior, 80*(1), 1–16; Taylor, S.G., Bedeian, A.G. & Kluemper, D.H. (in press). Linking Workplace Incivility to Citizenship Performance: The Combined Effects of Affective Commitment and Conscientiousness, *Journal of Organizational Behavior*; Meyer, J., Stanley, D., Herscovich, L., & Topolnytsky, L. (2002). Affective, Continuance, and Normative Commitment to the Organization: A Meta-Analysis of Antecedents, Correlates, and Consequences. *Journal of Vocational Behavior, 61,* 20–52; Klein, H., Becker, T., & Meyer, J. (2009). *Commitment in Organizations: Accumulated Wisdom and New Directions*. New York: Taylor & Francis.

[47]Gibbons, J. (2006). *Employee Engagement: A Review of Current Research and Its Implications* (p. 5). New York: The Conference Board.

[48]In Gurchiek, K. (2008, April 23). Many Senior Executives Not Engaged with Their Organizations. Society for Human Resource Management. Available online: http://www.shrm.org/hrnews_published/articles/CMS_025415.asp.

[49]Towers Perrin (2008). Closing the Engagement Gap: A Road Map for Driving Superior Business Performance. Towers Perrin Global Workforce Study 2007–2008. Available online: http://www.towersperrin.com/tp/getwebcachedoc?webc=HRS/USA/2008/200803/GWS_Global_Report20072008_31208.pdf.

[50]Gurchiek, K. (2008, April 23). Many Senior Executives Not Engaged with Their Organizations. Society for Human Resource Management. Available online: http://www.shrm.org/Publications/HRNews/Pages/SeniorExecutivesNotEngaged.aspx.

[51]Macey, W.H,, Schneider, B. Barbera, K. and Young, S.A (2009). *Employee Engagement: Tools for Analysis, Practice and Competitive Advantage*. Boston: Wiley-Blackwell.

[52]Dalgaard, L. (2001, May 23). Founding Principles. Available online: http://www.successfactors.com/company/founding-principles/.

[53]Sutton, R. (2007, May). Building the Civilized Workplace. *The McKinzey Quarterly*. Available online: http://www.mckinseyquarterly.com/Organization/Talent/Building_the_civilized_workplace_1963#foot3.

[54]Sutton, R. (2007, May). Building the Civilized Workplace. *The McKinzey Quarterly*. Available online: http://www.mckinseyquarterly.com/Organization/Talent/Building_the_civilized_workplace_1963#foot3.

[55]SuccessFactors. (2009). Rules of Engagement. Available online: http://www.successfactors.com/company/rules/.

[56]Kanfer, R., & Klimoski, R. J. (2002). Affect and Work: Looking Back to the Future. In *Emotions in the Workplace,* eds. R. G. Lord, R. J. Klimoski, and R. Kanfer (pp. 473–490). San Francisco, CA: Jossey-Bass.

[57]Dingfelder, S., & Frijda, N. H. (2008, May 20). *Monitor on Psychology.*

[58]Elfenbein, H. A. (2007). Emotion in Organizations: A Review of Theoretical Integration. In *The Academy of Management Annals,* eds. J. P. Walsh and A. P. Brief (Vol. 1, pp. 315–386). New York: Taylor & Francis.

[59]Amabile, T., Barsade, S., Mueller, J., & Staw, B. (2005). Affect and Creativity at Work. *Administrative Science Quarterly, 50*(3), 367–403.

[60]Tse, H. M., & Dasborough, M. T. (2008). A Study of Exchange and Emotions in Team Member Relationships. *Group & Organization Management: An International Journal, 33,* 194–215.

[61]Pinder, C. C., & Harlos, K. (2001). Employee Silence: Quiescence and Acquiescence as Response to Perceived Injustice. *Research in Personnel and Human Resources Management, 20,* 331–369.

[62]Gibson, D. E., & Callister, R. R. (2010). Anger in Organizations: Review and Integration. *Journal of Management, 36,* 66–93.

[63]Ekman, P., & Friesen, W. (1969). The Repertoire of Nonverbal Behavior: Categories, Origins, Usage, and Coding. *Semiotica, 1,* 49–98.

[64]Gordon, S. L. (1989). Institutional and Impulsive Orientations in Selective Appropriating Emotions to Self. In *The Sociology of Emotions: Original Essays and Research Papers,* eds. D. D. Franks and D. McCarthy (pp. 115–136). Greenwich, CT: JAI Press.

[65]Hallowell, R., Bowen, D. E., & Knoop, C. I. (2002). Four Seasons Goes to Paris. *Academy of Management Executive, 16*(4), 7–24.

[66]Gordon, S. L. (1989). Institutional and Impulsive Orientations in Selective Appropriating Emotions to Self. In *The Sociology of Emotions: Original Essays and Research Papers,* eds. D. D. Franks and D. McCarthy (pp. 115–136). Greenwich, CT: JAI Press.

[67]Grandey, A. A., Fisk, G. M., & Steiner, D. D. (2005). Must "Service with a Smile" Be Stressful? The Moderate Role of Personal Control for American and French Employees. *Journal of Applied Psychology, 90*(5), 893–904.

[68]Markus, H., & Kitayama, S. (1991). Culture and the Self: Implications for Cognition, Emotion, and Motivation. *Psychological Review, 98,* 224–253.

[69]Schucman, H., & Thetford, C. (1975). *A Course in Miracles.* New York: Viking Penguin.

[70]Rothbard, N.P. & Wilk, S.L. (2011). Waking Up on the Right or Wrong Side of the Bed: Start-of-Workday Mood, Work Events, Employee Affect, and Performance, *Academy of Management Journal, 54*(5), 959–980.

[71]Miner, A. G., Glomb, T. M., & Hulin, C. (2005, June). Experience Sampling Mood and Its Correlates at Work: Diary Studies in Work Psychology. *Journal of Occupational and Organizational Psychology, 78*(2), 171–193.

[72]Bartel, C. A., & Saavedra, R. (2000). The Collective Construction of Work Group Moods. *Administrative Science Quarterly, 45,* 197–231.

[73]Dasborough, M. T., & Ashkanasy, N. M. (2002). Emotion and Attribution of Intentionality in Leader-Member Relationships. *The Leadership Quarterly, 13,* 615–634.

[74]Smith, C. A., & Lazarus, R. S. (1993). Appraisal Components, Core Relational Themes, and the Emotions. *Cognition and Emotion, 7,* 233–269.

[75]Watson, D., & Tellegen, A. (1985). Toward a Consensual Structure of Mood. *Psychological Bulletin, 98,* 219–235.

[76]Watson, D., & Tellegen, A. (1985). Toward a Consensual Structure of Mood. *Psychological Bulletin, 98,* 219–235.

[77]Watson, D., Clark, L. A., & Tellegen, A. (1988). Development and Validation of Brief Measures of Positive and Negative Affect: The PANAS Scales. *Journal of Personality and Social Psychology, 54,* 1063–1070.

[78]Dimotakis, N., Scott, B.A. & Koopman, J. (2011). An Experience Sampling Investigation of Workplace Interactions, Affective States, and Employee Well-Being. *Journal of Organizational Behavior, 32*(4), 572–588; Kaplan, S., Bradley, J. C., Luchman, J. N., & Haynes, D. (2009). On the Role of Positive and Negative Affectivity in Job Performance: A Meta-Analytic Investigation. *Journal of Applied Psychology,* 94, 162–176.

[79]Gerhardt, M. W., & Brown, K. G. (2006). Individual Differences in Self-Efficacy Development: The Effects of Goal Orientation and Affectivity. *Learning and Individual Differences, 16,* 43–59.

[80]Isen, A. M. (2004). An Influence of Positive Affect on Decision Making in Complex Situations: Theoretical Issues with Practical Implications. *Journal of Consumer Psychology, 11*(2), 75–85.

[81]Forgas, J. P. (1998). On Feeling Good and Getting Your Way: Mood Effects on Negotiator Cognition and Behavior. *Journal of Personality and Social Psychology, 74,* 565–577; Van Kleef, G. A., De Dreu, C. K. W., & Manstead, A. S. R. (2004). The Interpersonal Effects of Anger and Happiness in Negotiations. *Journal of Personality and Social Psychology, 86,* 57–76.

[82]Lyubomirsky, S., King, L., & Diener, E. (2005). The Benefits of Frequent Positive Affect: Does Happiness Lead to Success? *Psychological Bulletin, 131*(6), 803–855.

[83]Donaldson, S.I., Csikszentmihalyi, M., & Nakamura, J. (Eds.). (2011). *Applied Positive Psychology: Improving Everyday Life, Health, Schools, Work, and Society.* London: Routledge Academic.

[84]Lee, D. (2008). How Employee Emotions Affect Your Organization's Ability to Compete. HumanNature@Work. Available online: http://www.humannatureatwork.com/articles/employee_morale/Employee_Emotions-2.htm.

[85]Lee, D. (2008). The Emotional Side of Intellectual Capital. HumanNature@Work. Available online: http://www.humannatureatwork.com/articles/IntellectualCapital/Intellectual-Capital-Articles-1.htm.

[86]Whimster, S. (2009, February 20). To Understand Economics, We Have to Consider Emotions, Too. *The Guardian.* Available online: http://www.guardian.co.uk/commentisfree/2009/feb/20/economics-emotions-human-values.

[87]Eisenberg, N. (2000). Emotion, Regulation, and Moral Development. *Annual Review of Psychology, 51,* 665–697, p. 665.

[88]For a review, see Eisenberg, N. (2000). Emotion, Regulation, and Moral Development. *Annual Review of Psychology, 51,* 665–697.

[89]Gino, F., & Schweitzer, M. (2008). Blinded by Anger or Feeling the Love: How Emotions Influence Advice Taking. *Journal of Applied Psychology, 93*(5), 1165–1173.

[90]Bono, J., & Ilies, R. (2006). Charisma, Positive Emotions and Mood Contagion. *Leadership Quarterly, 17*(4), 317–334.

[91]Sy, T., Côté, S., & Saavedra, R. (2005). The Contagious Leader: Impact of the Leader's Mood on the Mood of Group Members, Group Affective Tone, and Group Processes. *Journal of Applied Psychology, 90*(2), 295–305.

[92]Anderson, C., & Thompson, L. (2004). Affect from the Top Down: How Powerful Individuals' Positive Affect Shapes Negotiations. *Organizational Behavior & Human Decision Processes, 95*(2), 125–139.

[93]Hatfield, E., Cacioppo, J. T., & Rapson, R. L. (1994). *Emotional Contagion.* Cambridge, England: Cambridge University Press.

[94]Sutton, R. (2007, May). Building the Civilized Workplace. *The McKinsey Quarterly.* Available online: http://www.mckinseyquarterly.com/Organization/Talent/Building_the_civilized_workplace_1963.

[95]Rafaeli, A., & Sutton, R. (1989). The Expression of Emotion in Organizational Life. In *Research in Organizational Behavior,* eds. B. M. Staw and L. L. Cummings (pp. 1–42). Greenwich, CT: JAI Press.

[96]Based on Ashforth, B. E., & Humphrey, R. H. (1993). Emotional Labor in Service Roles: The Influence of Identity. *Academy of Management Review, 18,* 88–115.

[97]Hochschild, A. (1983). *The Managed Heart: Commercialization of Human Feeling.* Berkeley: University of California Press.

[98]Rafaeli, A., & Sutton, R. (1989). The Expression of Emotion in Organizational Life. In *Research in Organizational Behavior,* eds. B. M. Staw and L. L. Cummings (pp. 1–42). Greenwich, CT: JAI Press.

[99]Ekman, P. (1973). Cross Culture Studies of Facial Expression. In *Darwin and Facial Expression: A Century of Research in Review,* ed. P. Ekman (pp. 169–222). New York: Academic Press.

[100]Kramer, M. W., & Hess, J. A. (2002). Communication Rules for the Display of Emotions in Organizational Settings. *Management Communication Quarterly, 16*(1), 66–80.

[101]Madera, J. M., & Smith, D. B. (2009). The Effects of Leader Negative Emotions on Evaluations of Leadership in a Crisis Situation: The Role of Anger and Sadness. *The Leadership Quarterly, 20*(2), 103–114.

[102]Hülsheger, U. R. & Schewe, A.F. (2011). On the Costs and Benefits of Emotional Labor: A Meta-Analysis of Three Decades of Research, *Journal of Occupational Psychology, 16*(3), 361–389.

[103]Cohen, S., & Herbert, T. B. (1996). Health Psychology: Psychological Factors and Physical Disease from the Perspective of Human Psychoneuroimmunology. *Annual Review of Psychology, 47,* 113–142.

[104]Watson, M., Pettingale, K. W., & Greer, S. (1984). Emotional Control and Autonomic Arousal in Breast Cancer Patients. *Journal of Psychosomatic Research, 28,* 467–474.

[105]Hochschild, A. (1983). *The Managed Heart: Commercialization of Human Feeling.* Berkeley: University of California Press.

[106]Morris, J., & Feldman, D. (1997). Managing Emotions in the Workplace. *Journal of Managerial Issues, 9,* 257–274.

[107]Morris, J., & Feldman, D. (1996). The Dimensions, Antecedents, and Consequences of Emotional Labor. *Academy of Management Review, 21,* 986–1010.

[108]Rutter, D. R., & Fielding, P. J. (1988). Sources of Occupational Stress: An Examination of British Prison Officers. *Work and Stress, 2,* 292–299.

[109]Ashforth, B. E., & Humphrey, R. H. (1993). Emotional Labor in Service Roles: The Influence of Identity. *Academy of Management Review, 18,* 88–115.

[110]See, e.g., Kiffin-Petersen, S.A., Jordan, C.L. & Soutar, G.N. (2011). The Big Five, Emotional Exhaustion and Citizenship Behaviors in Service Settings: The Mediating Role of Emotional Labor, *Personality and Individual Differences, 50*(1), 43–48; Rafaeli, A., & Sutton, R. (1989). The Expression of Emotion in Organizational Life. In *Research in Organizational Behavior,* eds. B. M. Staw and L. L. Cummings (pp. 1–42). Greenwich, CT: JAI Press; Wharton, A. (1999). The Psychosocial Consequences of Emotional Labor. In R. J. Steinberg and D. M. Figart (Eds.), *Emotional Labor in Service Economy 561,* 38–45. *The Annals of the American Academy of Political and Social Science.*

[111]Bechtoldt, M.N., Rohrmann, S., DePater, I.E. & Beersma, B. (2011). The Primacy of Perceiving: Emotion Recognition Buffers Negative Effects of Emotional Labor, *Journal of Applied Psychology, 96*(5), 1087–1094.

[112]Ashforth, B. E., & Humphrey, R. H. (1993). Emotional Labor in Service Roles: The Influence of Identity. *Academy of Management Review, 18,* 88–115.

[113]Rafaeli, A., & Sutton, R. (1987). Expression of Emotion as Part of the Work Role. *Academy of Management Review, 12,* 23–37.

[114]Rafaeli, A., & Sutton, R. (1987). Expression of Emotion as Part of the Work Role. *Academy of Management Review, 12,* 23–37.

[115]Strickland, W. (1992). Institutional Emotional Norms and Role Satisfaction: Examination of a Career Wife Population. *Sex Roles, 25,* 423–439; Tolich, M. B. (1993). Alienation and Liberating Emotions at Work. *Journal of Contemporary Ethnography, 22,* 361–381.

[116]Ashforth, B. E., & Humphrey, R. H. (1993). Emotional Labor in Service Roles: The Influence of Identity. *Academy of Management Review, 18,* 88–115.

[117]Conrad, C., & Witte, K. (1994). Is Emotional Expression Repression Oppression? Myths of Organizational Affective Regulation. In *Communication Yearbook,* ed. S. Deetz (Vol. 17, pp. 417–428).

[118]Rafaeli, A., & Sutton, R. (1987). Expression of Emotion as Part of the Work Role. *Academy of Management Review, 12,* 23–37.

[119]Dawis, R. V., & Lofquist, L. H. (1984). *A Psychological Theory of Work Adjustment.* Minneapolis: University of Minnesota Press.

[120]Chau, S. L., Dahling, J. J., Levy, P. E., & Diefendorff, J. M. (2009). A Predictive Study of Emotional Labor and Turnover. *Journal of Organizational Behavior, 30,* 1151–1163.

[121]Shuler, S., & Sypher, B. D. (2000). Seeking Emotional Labor: When Managing the Heart Enhances the Work Experience. *Management Communication Quarterly, 14,* 50–89, p. 83.

[122]Humphrey, R.H. (in press). How do Leaders Use Emotional Labor? *Journal of Organizational Behavior.*

[123]Mayer, J. D., & Salovey, P. (1993). The Intelligence of Emotional Intelligence. *Intelligence, 17,* 433–442; Mayer, J. D., & Salovey, P. (1997). What Is Emotional Intelligence? In *Emotional Development and Emotional Intelligence,* eds. P. Salovey and D. J. Sluyter. New York: Basic Books.

[124]Sturgeon, J. (2009, April). Stress Management. *Talent Management Magazine.*

[125]Goetzel, R.Z., Anderson, D.R., Shitmer, R.W., Ozminkowski, R.J., Dunn, R. L., & Wasserman, J. (1998). The Relationship Between Modifiable Health Risks and Health Care Expenditures: An Analysis of the Multi-Employer HERO Health Risk and Cost Database. *Journal of Occupational & Environmental Medicine, 40,* 843–854.

[126]Goudreau, J. (2007, August 6). Dispatches from the War on Stress. *BusinessWeek,* 74–75.

[127]Sliter, M., Sliter, K. & Jex, S. (2012). The Employee as a Punching Bag: The Effect of Multiple Sources of Incivility on Employee Withdrawal Behavior and Sales Performance, *Journal of Organizational Behavior, 33*(1), 121–139.

[128]Lazarus, R.S. (1993). Coping Theory and Research: Past, Present, and Future. *Psychosomatic Medicine, 55,* 234–247.

[129]Lazarus, R. S. (1993). Why We Should Think of Stress as a Subset of Emotion. In *Handbook of Stress: Theoretical and Clinical Aspects,* eds. L. Goldberger and S. Breznitz (2nd ed.). New York: Free Press.

[130]McGaugh, J. L. (2000). Memory: A Century of Consolidation. *Science, 287,* 248–251.

[131]Selye, H. (1956). *The Stress of Life.* New York: McGraw-Hill.

[132]Rodell, J. B., & Judge, T. A. (2009). Can "Good" Stressors Spark "Bad" Behaviors? The Mediating Role of Emotions in Links of Challenge and Hindrance Stressors with Citizenship and Counterproductive Behaviors. *Journal of Applied Psychology, 94,* 1438–1451.

[133]Wallace, C. J., Edwards, B. D., Arnold, T., Frazier, L. M., & Finch, D. M. (2009). Work Stressors, Role-Based Performance, and the Moderating Influence of Organizational Support. *Journal of Applied Psychology, 94,* 254–262.

[134]Girdano, D., Everly, G. S., & Dusek, D. E. (2009). *Controlling Stress and Tension* (8th ed.). San Francisco, CA: Benjamin Cummings.

[135]Bartlett, J.E. & Bartlett, M.E. (2011). Workplace Bullying: An Integrative Literature Review. *Advances in Developing Human Resources, 13*(1), 69–84.

[136]Porhola, M., Karhunen, S., & Rainivaara, S. (2006). Bullying at School and in the Workplace: A Challenge for Communication Research. In *Communication Yearbook,* ed. C. Beck (Vol. 30, pp. 249–301). Hillsdale, NJ: Erlbaum; Rayner, C. (1997). The Incidence of Workplace Bullying. *Journal of Community & Applied Social Psychology, 7,* 199–208; Jennifer, D., Cowie, H., & Ananiadou, K. (2003). Perceptions and Experience of Workplace Bullying in Five Different Working Populations. *Aggressive Behavior, 29,* 489–496.

[137]Mattice, C., & Spitzberg, B. (2008). Bullies in Business: Self-Reports of Tactics and Motives. Poster session presented at the 6th International Conference on Workplace Bullying, Montreal, Canada.

[138]Ashforth, B. E. (1994). Petty Tyranny in Organizations. *Human Relations, 47,* 755–778; Ashforth, B. E. (1997). Petty Tyranny in Organizations: A Preliminary Examination of Antecedents and Consequences. *Canadian Journal of Administrative Sciences, 14,* 126–140; Infante, D. A., & Gordon, W. I. (1986). Superiors' Argumentativeness and Verbal Aggressiveness as Predictors of Subordinates' Satisfaction. *Human Communication Research, 12,* 117–125; Rayner, C., Hoel, H., & Cooper, C. L. (2002). *Workplace Bullying: What We Know, Who Is to Blame, and What Can We Do?* New York: Taylor & Francis; Rayner, C., & Keashly, L. (2005). Bullying at Work: A Perspective from Britain and North America. In *Counterproductive Work Behavior: Investigations of Actors and Targets,* eds. S. Fox and P. E. Spector (pp. 271–296). Washington, DC: American Psychological Association; Tepper, B. J. (2000). Consequences of Abusive Supervision. *Academy of Management Journal, 43,* 178–190.

[139]Rayner, C. (1997). The Incidence of Workplace Bullying. *Journal of Community & Applied Social Psychology, 7,* 199–208.

[140]Dailey, R., Lee, C., & Spitzberg, B. H. (2007). Psychological Abuse and Communicative Aggression. In *The Dark Side of Interpersonal Communication,* eds. B. H. Spitzberg & W. R. Cupach (2nd ed., pp. 297–326). Mahwah, NJ: Lawrence Erlbaum Associates.

[141]Rayner, C. (1997). The Incidence of Workplace Bullying. *Journal of Community & Applied Social Psychology, 7,* 199–208.

[142]Callan, V. J. (1993). Individual and Organizational Strategies for Coping with Organizational Change. *Work and Stress, 7,* 63–75; Folkman, S., Lazarus, R. S., Gruen, R. J., & DeLongis, A. (1986). Appraisal, Coping, Health Status, and Psychological Symptoms. *Journal of Personality and Social Psychology, 50,* 571–579.

[143]Cooper, C. L., & Cartwright, S. (1994). Healthy Mind; Healthy Organization—A Proactive Approach to Occupational Stress. *Human Relations, 47,* 455–472.

[144]Goudreau, J. (2007, August 6). Dispatches from the War on Stress. *BusinessWeek,* 74–75.

[145]Laabs, J. (1999). Workforce Overload. *Work Force,* 30–37.

[146]Goudreau, J. (2007, August 6). Dispatches from the War on Stress. *BusinessWeek,* 74–75.

[147]Kawada, T. & Otsuka, T. (2011). Relationship Between Job Stress, Occupational Position and Job Satisfaction Using a Brief Job Stress Questonniare (BJSQ), *Work: A Journal of Prevention, Assessment, and Rehabilitation, 40*(4), 393–399.

[148]*Merriam-Webster's Collegiate Dictionary.* (2009). Available online: http://careerplanning.about.com/gi/dynamic/offsite.htm?zi=1/XJ &sdn=careerplanning&cdn=careers&tm=83&gps=390_280_829_ 502&f=20&su=p554.12.336.ip_&tt=2&bt=0&bts=0&zu=http%3A// www.m-w.com/.

[149]Goudreau, J. (2007, August 6). Dispatches from the War on Stress. *BusinessWeek,* 74–75.

[150]Conlin, M. (2007, May 21). Do Us a Favor, Take a Vacation. *BusinessWeek,* 88–89.

[151]Conlin, M. (2007, May 21). Do Us a Favor, Take a Vacation. *BusinessWeek,* 88–89.

[152]Fredrickson, B. (2009). *Positivity.* New York: Crown.

[153]Lundin, S.C., Paul, H., Christensen, J. & Blanchard, K. (2000). *Fish! A Proven Way to Boost Morale and Improve Results.* New York: Hyperion, 38.

CHAPTER 6

Social Perception, Attributions, and Perceived Fairness

The President and CEO of Beth Israel Deaconess Medical Center understands the important role all hospital employees play in providing quality health care. This led to a focus on being fair to lower-wage employees while making changes to improve the hospital's financial condition.

REAL WORLD CHALLENGE

AVOIDING LAYOFFS AT BETH ISRAEL HOSPITAL[1]

Paul Levy, President and CEO of Beth Israel Deaconess Medical Center in Brookline, Massachusetts, is worried. With the economy in free-fall, the hospital faces a revenue shortfall of $20 million. Beth Israel hired about a quarter of its 8,000 staff over the last six years, and Levy knows that it will be difficult for all of them to keep their jobs and benefits much longer.

As Levy walks around the hospital, he watches a variety of lower-wage employees doing their jobs. He sees the transporters who push patients around in wheelchairs talk to patients and put them at ease. He also sees the people who deliver food, change sheets, and wash floors chat with patients and their families, and is reminded of the important role they play in health care. As he watches his lowest-paid employees work, he thinks about how many of them have second jobs and are just scraping by in the tough economy.

As Levy considers what to do to improve the hospital's finances, he wants to be fair to the lower-wage earners and not put an additional burden on them. Their salaries are so low already, and laying them off would certainly create hardships for their families. Levy asks you for ideas about how he can be fair to all of his employees and still improve the hospital's financial condition. After reading this chapter, you should have some good ideas.

JUPITERIMAGES/PHOTOS.COM

If you tried a new task and failed, would you try again if you felt that you failed because of your lack of skill? Would your answer change if you thought you failed because of bad luck? Our reality is what we perceive. Our perceptions and attributions about what happens to us and around us influence our behavior. This is as true in organizations as it is in the rest of our lives.

Fairness perceptions also influence our behavior. If a subordinate feels that a manager is unfair despite the manager's best intentions to be fair, the subordinate will base his or her reactions on the perceived unfairness. If a hiring manager mistakenly perceives a job candidate to be a poor fit with the job based on a stereotype of a good hire, the candidate will not get the job. Understanding how our innate information processing biases work can help us to stay objective and make the best decisions possible. In this chapter, you will learn about how social perception, attributions, and fairness perceptions shape our behavior, and how you can use this information to be a more effective manager.

SOCIAL PERCEPTION

social perception

The process through which we use available information to form impressions of others

We see the world and other people not as they are, but as we construct them.[2] *Social perception* is the process through which we use available information to form impressions of others. The way we view someone may be very different from the way the other person views him- or herself. We base our impressions on the information we obtain from the environment, our previous attitudes, and our current mood.

Perception Shortcuts

We constantly receive so much information that we cannot process it all. To process the maximum amount of information using minimal cognitive effort, we often use both functional and dysfunctional perception "shortcuts." Let's explore some of them.

schema

Organized patterns of thoughts or behaviors to help us quickly interpret and process information

Schema and Stereotypes. We all create organized patterns of thoughts or behaviors to help us quickly interpret and process information.[3] These *schemas* are helpful because they allow us to make sense of a person, place, situation, or event quickly based on limited information. A schema guides our actions and responses: immediately calling your supervisor when you see an upset customer enter the store is an example of an activated schema. An activated schema "fills in" missing details. We use schema every day to organize our knowledge and provide a framework for our future understanding. Examples of schema include social roles and scripts about how to behave in certain situations like business meetings.

Schemas are usually very helpful. We are constantly bombarded with so much information that it would be impossible to process it all without their help. Schemas help us to identify what information to ignore and what to pay attention to, and help us quickly make sense of ambiguous information and situations.

Schemas are normally developed through experience, but they can be formed with limited or no experience (as is often true of stereotypes). Schemas guide our attention to certain information in our environments, which ultimately influences the way we understand our world and what we remember later. Table 6-1 summarizes the four main benefits of using schemas.

Table 6-1

Benefits of Schemas

1   *They allow us to focus on some information and ignore other information.* For example, if we perceive our coworkers to be friendly and supportive, we can interact with them without being defensive or guarded.

2   *They allow us to infer facts beyond the information immediately available to us.* For example, when negotiating a job offer, we might recognize that the other person represents the company's interests and infer that the person's refusal of some of our requests is not personal but simply reflects company policies.

3.   *They help us properly relate to our surroundings.* If we recognize some coworkers as gossips, we might remain guarded with them but confide in other coworkers who we perceive as trustworthy.

4.   *They allow us to predict behavior.* For example, when frustrated, our supervisor will close the office door.

© CENGAGE LEARNING 2012

When schemas lead us to form inaccurate perceptions or jump to the wrong conclusion, they can be dysfunctional. A *stereotype* is a dysfunctional schema that is essentially an oversimplified schema for a group of people. Stereotypes can contain both positive and negative assumptions—"dumb blonde," for example, or "smart librarian." Obviously, there are many smart blonde-haired people and not all librarians are smart.

Stereotyping is a negative perceptual shortcut that involves forming oversimplified beliefs about an individual or a group based on the idea that everyone in that particular group will behave the same way. For example, if someone shows up in class wearing athletic clothes and carrying a basketball, you might stereotype that person as an athlete.

Stereotypes assign people to a schema based on as little as one distinguishing characteristic, often in appearance or behavior. The stereotype we assign to someone then fills in missing information about that person's beliefs, behaviors, motivations, interests, and so on, based on our assumptions about a similar group of individuals. After stereotyping the student as an athlete, you would make assumptions about him or her based on your stereotype for athletes.

Attributing a fixed set of characteristics to all group members enables us to make quick judgments, but often we are wrong because stereotypes rarely match what the targeted person is really like. Stereotypes based on age, race, and gender are the cause of discrimination both in the workplace and in society. This has been a particular problem for Arab Americans and Muslims since the terrorist attacks of September 11, 2001.[4] Because people tend to welcome evidence that confirms their stereotypes and to ignore or explain away any disconfirming evidence, stereotypes are difficult to change.

Perception Errors. One perception shortcut is *categorization*, which reflects our tendency to put things into groups or categories (e.g., Southerner, energetic, athlete, etc.). We then exaggerate the similarities within and the differences between the groups. This explains our tendency to see members of a particular group to which we do not belong as being more alike than they actually are. Have you ever seen someone work quickly and thought to yourself how good he or she is at that job? If so, you may have put that person into a "high performer" category.

Once we put people into categories, *selective perception* leads to selectively interpreting what we see based on our interests, expectations, experience, and attitudes. Once we categorize someone (a cashier named Sue, for

stereotype
A dysfunctional schema that is essentially an oversimplified schema for a group of people

stereotyping
Forming oversimplified beliefs about an individual or a group based on the idea that everyone in that particular group will behave the same way

SO WHAT
Stereotypes may help us to make quick judgments, but often they are wrong.

categorization
Our tendency to put things into groups or categories

selective perception
Selectively interpreting what we see based on our interests, expectations, experience, and attitudes

our running example) as a high performer, we focus more on (and will better remember) information related to her high performance, and we tend to disregard information reflecting her low performance. If we saw Sue make an error on the cash register, we might discount it by attributing it to a fluke or to a problem with the machine, and focus only on her superior item-scanning speed.

Selective perception reinforces stereotypes as the perceiver focuses on information and behaviors that confirm rather than negate the assigned stereotype. A supervisor who believes that a subordinate has high potential will interpret what is observed through that positively biased lens, while a supervisor who believes a subordinate has low ability will interpret the same information negatively to reinforce expectations of low performance. Managers need to be aware of this bias in order to evaluate subordinates more objectively and accurately.

The ***halo effect*** is when we form a general impression about something or someone based on a single (typically good) characteristic. For example, people tend to associate beauty with other positive characteristics. We often assume that physically attractive people possess more socially desirable personalities than less beautiful people do, and that they lead happier and more successful lives.[5] Similarly, because you perceive Sue to be a high performer, you might assume that she is also intelligent, energetic, or whatever else you associate with high performers.

As an example of the halo effect in organizations, when Cisco Systems was growing rapidly in the 1990s, it was widely praised for its great strategy, management of acquisitions, and customer focus. But after the technology bubble burst, the same observers often made opposite attributions: Now Cisco had a flawed strategy, poor acquisition management, and bad customer relations. In reality, Cisco really had not changed very much—a performance change simply led people to see the company differently.[6]

The ***contrast effect*** occurs when we evaluate our own or another person's characteristics through comparisons with other people we have recently encountered who rank higher or lower on the same characteristics. After encountering Sue, if we see an average cashier, we might evaluate him as below average because we thought so highly of Sue's performance. The contrast effect is common among college students who—because they are used to being around people who have relatively high intelligence and ambition compared to the general public, and because they compare themselves to other smart, motivated people—conclude that they are only average when, in fact, they are above average.

Projection occurs when we project our own characteristics onto other people. If a hiring manager is interviewing someone who reminds him of himself when he was just starting out, he may assume that the candidate also shares his values, work ethic, and abilities.

The common perception shortcuts we just discussed are summarized in Table 6-2.

First Impressions

Perceptions are difficult to change once they are formed. Remember what your mother told you about the importance of first impressions? It's true! Research has found that not only do we tend to avoid people after we have had a negative reaction to them,[7] but also negative impressions are harder to change than positive ones.[8] First impressions are formed quickly. If you find yourself making negative assumptions about someone you have just met, it can be a

halo effect

Forming a general impression about something or someone based on a single (typically good) characteristic

contrast effect

Evaluating a person's characteristics through comparisons with other people we have recently encountered who rank higher or lower on the same characteristics

projection

Attributing our own characteristics to other people

SO WHAT

Perception shortcuts decrease the accuracy of our evaluation of others, even during job interviews and performance appraisals.

Table 6-2

Social Perception Shortcuts

Schema	Abstract mental structures used for organizing information; can be functional in helping us process a high volume of information or dysfunctional (stereotypes)
Categorization	Our tendency to put things into groups or categories
Selective perception	Selectively interpreting what we see on the basis of our interests, background, experience, and attitudes
Halo effect	Drawing a general impression about an individual on the basis of a single (typically good) characteristic
Contrast effect	Evaluating a person's characteristics through comparisons with other people we have recently encountered who rank higher or lower on the same characteristics
Projection	Attributing our own characteristics to other people

© CENGAGE LEARNING 2012

good idea to quickly look for positive information that disconfirms your negative assumptions before they become too strongly held.

This chapter's *Improve Your Skills* feature will help you to make great first impressions in job interviews.

Our social perceptions can obviously be flawed—even the most skilled observers can misperceive and misjudge others. Once we form wrong impressions, they are likely to persist. When we have the motivation and the resources to think carefully about something, we usually will, but even then the various cognitive biases can influence our perceptions.

IMPROVE YOUR SKILLS

MAKING A GREAT FIRST IMPRESSION IN A JOB INTERVIEW

The old saying "You don't get a second chance to make a good first impression" highlights the importance of making first interactions count. People look at how you dress, how you talk, and how you act to infer additional characteristics about you and form a positive or negative attitude toward you. Speed dating is a great example of this process. Research has found that impressions are formed in the first thirty seconds of meeting someone,[9] so it is worth concentrating on making that first interaction count!

Practice can make you more comfortable engaging in the behaviors that are likely to lead to a good first impression. Introduce yourself to new classmates and other people you have not formally met and develop a style you are comfortable with. Here are some tips you can use to help you make your best first impression in a job interview:

- *Dress appropriately—nothing sloppy.* When in doubt, dress conservatively. Be neat, and have well-groomed hair and nails.

- *Give a firm, dry, confident one-handed handshake.* If you are nervous, keep a handkerchief in your pocket to wipe off your hand first.

- *Use an appropriate speaking style.* In business situations, this typically involves clear enunciation, a

varied pitch, and no mumbling.[10] Avoid using slang expressions, including words like *dude,* and do not pepper sentences with words such as *like* and *you know.*

- *Use positive emotion words* (e.g., happy, good, glad) and try to avoid negative emotion words (e.g., sad, wrong, bad).[11]

- *Try to use nonverbal communication to express yourself.* Using animated facial expressions tends to be interpreted as being friendly, confident, and popular.[12] Use good posture and natural gestures, and avoid fidgeting, clenching your fists, and playing with a pen. Try not to appear stiff or uncomfortable.[13]

- *Don't focus on yourself.* Show interest in the interviewer as well. Good listening skills make good first impressions.[14]

- *Convey appropriate enthusiasm, warmth, and sincerity.* Remember to give a genuine smile!

- *Subtly mirroring the interviewer's body language, tone, and posture* can generate a positive impression.

- *Be polite, and avoid making any jokes that could be misinterpreted.*[15]

How Do We Decide How to Classify People?

Now that you understand more about how we use a variety of shortcuts to form impressions of others, you are probably curious about how we decide which shortcuts to use. We next discuss the three primary factors that influence how we classify others.

Goals of the Perceiver. We try to identify how the other person will affect our pursuit of our goals. The goal of customs inspectors, for example, is to determine if each traveler getting off a plane is safe or threatening, and whether and how much of a search is needed. The inspector quickly scans each traveler for traits that fit the inspector's schema of a businessperson, smuggler, vacationer, or terrorist. The same group of travelers, however, evaluates each other for cues of possibly rewarding interactions. They screen each other for a different set of traits that fit their schema of a potential friend, conversation partner, and so on.

Social Context. The setting and context around us plays a large part in how we classify people and interpret their behavior. We expect people to display certain activities in certain settings, and we look for consistencies between our schema for the particular setting and the behaviors of the people present. For example, if someone enters a restaurant at lunchtime wearing a Hawaiian shirt and Bermuda shorts and orders a tropical drink, we might categorize him as a vacationer. If the same thing happened at a business lunch, we might think that the person is nuts.

Accessibility in Memory. When a person's behavior is ambiguous or when we encounter unfamiliar or conflicting characteristics, it can be unclear which schema or category to apply. The more easily we can remember a category, the more accessible it is and the more likely we are to use it. Repeated or recent use may make some classifications more accessible than others. For example, imagine that you just learned that your roommate broke an arm mountain biking. If you recently discussed with friends how reckless some students are, you might be more likely to perceive your roommate's behavior as irresponsible rather than adventurous.

implicit personality theories
Assumptions about how personality traits are related

In one study that illustrates accessibility effects,[16] students read two different descriptions of a guest lecturer. The two descriptions were identical, except that half the students were told the speaker was cold and the rest were told he was warm. Those who had read that the guest lecturer was cold rated him as less considerate, sociable, popular, good-natured, humorous, and humane than those who had read he was warm. Why did this happen? Because we each have *implicit personality theories*, which are assumptions about how personality traits are related and which ones tend to go together. If you learn that a new classmate is shy, you may also assume that she is humorless and unpopular.

People's implicit personality theories differ based on past experiences that focus attention on certain traits when forming impressions. For example, when meeting someone for the first time, some people attend most to

TOM MERTON/JUPITER IMAGES

Because you don't get a second chance to make a good first impression, it is helpful to practice how you will behave when meeting someone. Appropriate dress, politeness, and positive non-verbal behaviors can help others form a positive impression of you.

extroversion, others to intelligence, and still others to physical appearance. Imagine Juan, a person who is intelligent and outgoing. Someone who attends strongly to intelligence is likely to perceive Juan as competent, hardworking, and creative, as these traits tend to go with intelligence for most people. Someone else who focuses on extroversion may form an impression of Juan as warm and friendly, as these traits tend to accompany extroversion. Both impressions are true, but they reflect very different perceptions and impressions. If asked to describe Juan to someone else, each person would likely describe him in very different ways.

It is important to remember that the impressions we form of others reflect as much about our own ways of perceiving as they do about the characteristics of the person being perceived. What does this mean to managers? Think about what happens when a supervisor is asked to evaluate subordinates' performance. Perceptual errors may lead a supervisor to selectively remember only the performance information that is consistent with his or her overall impressions of each subordinate, which can be influenced by the halo effect, stereotypes, implicit personality theories, and other perceptual processes that can be wrong. Hiring managers can similarly focus on information that confirms their initial perceptions of a job candidate and discount objective information about the person's qualifications and actual fit with the job and organization.

Self-Fulfilling Prophecies

Professor Richard Wiseman's book *The Luck Factor* describes how people's habits create both good and bad luck. When we expect good luck we might try harder and persist longer, which leads to greater success.[17] Because lucky people expect good luck, their subsequent openness, persistence, and other behaviors reinforce this expectation and create more good luck, becoming *self-fulfilling prophecies*.

self-fulfilling prophecies
When expectations create behaviors that cause the expectations to come true

Our impressions and expectations of others also can become self-fulfilling prophecies. If we categorize Gianna as untrustworthy, we are likely to treat her with suspicion and distrust. These actions then evoke appropriate guarded reactions from Gianna, and her reactions in turn serve to confirm our initial impressions. One of the first experiments on the self-fulfilling prophecy effect in work settings was conducted in a job training program for disadvantaged employees.[18] Trainees labeled "high aptitude" (though randomly selected) achieved more on objective tests, were rated higher by their supervisors and peers, and had lower dropout rates than the trainees who were not labeled in that way.

Researchers working with the Israel Defense Forces found that:

- Self-fulfilling prophecies work in different cultures.[19]
- The effect can work for groups, not just individuals (e.g., expecting high performance of a workgroup can also become self-fulfilling).[20]
- Self-fulfilling prophecies work negatively as well as positively—in fact, pessimistic expectations can have an even more powerful effect on behavior than optimistic expectations.[21] Unless counteracted through verbal persuasion, compliments, expressing confidence in the person, or in some other way, lower expectancies tend to lower performance.[22]

Expectations can even have physiological effects. One study split naval cadets preparing to embark on their first cruise into two groups. One group was told that their responses to an earlier questionnaire suggested that they were unlikely to experience seasickness and that, even if they did, it would not affect their performance. The other group of cadets received noncommittal information. After the cruise, cadets in the first group reported less seasickness than those in the second group and received higher performance evaluations from training officers unaware of the manipulation.[23]

Self-fulfilling prophecies are widespread in organizations. High expectations have a stronger effect on disadvantaged groups or those stereotyped as low achievers, and on people who are unsure of their abilities in a particular situation.[24] Self-fulfilling prophecies also seem to work best in newly established relationships.

Managers use four factors in conveying their expectations to subordinates:[25]

1. *Climate*: A climate is the social and emotional atmosphere leaders create. Managers often create a warmer and more supportive social and emotional climate for subordinates of whom they expect a lot. Supervisors signal positive expectations by nodding and smiling, making frequent eye contact, and using a warm tone of voice.[26]

2. *Input*: People labeled high performers receive more opportunities to develop their skills and to perform well. The number and type of assignments high-expectation employees are given can spark a positive performance spiral. As employees successfully complete projects, they gain confidence in themselves and the confidence of their superiors, as well as higher visibility in the organization. They are then given more challenging assignments, which they are then more likely to complete successfully.

3. *Output*: High-expectation employees often receive more opportunities to express their opinions, speak at meetings, and contribute to solving problems. Managers pay closer attention to their contributions, and give them more assistance in overcoming obstacles.

Figure 6-1

The Self-Fulfilling Expectation Process

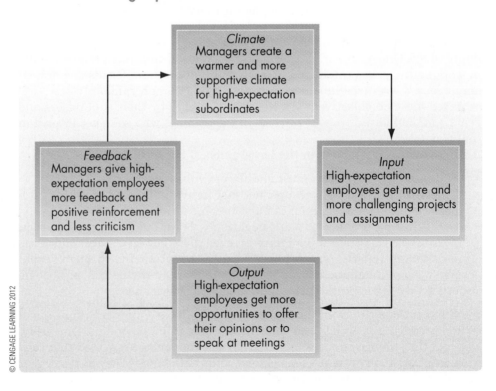

© CENGAGE LEARNING 2012

4. *Feedback*: High expectations tend to generate more positive feedback and reinforcement and less criticism for failure.[27] Managers also tend to give more detailed performance feedback to employees of whom they have high expectations.[28] Managers praise employees perceived as poor performers less often, which reinforces the impression that less is expected from them and weakens their confidence.

SO WHAT
Communicating only positive expectations about people can increase their performance.

These four factors are summarized in Figure 6-1.

Managers' perceptions of subordinates affect an organization's performance. Because company leaders often have a huge impact on employee behavior, self-fulfilling prophecies are a powerful management tool. Although you cannot turn a truly bad employee into a superstar, communicating positive expectations rather than negative ones can help employees reach their full potential. Ethically speaking, it is also important to monitor your own behavior to reduce inequities in how you treat others, even if the differences seem small. Using self-fulfilling prophecies to your own advantage by maintaining high self-expectations and standards even if others expect less of you can help to insulate you from any negative expectations of your own supervisors.

ATTRIBUTIONS

Have you ever noticed that when classmates do well on a test, they often attribute it to their own effort and ability, but when they learn that you did well, they seem to attribute it more to luck or to easy grading by the instructor? This tendency is a perfectly normal outcome of attributions. *Attribution* refers to the way we explain the causes of our own as well as other people's behaviors and achievements, and understand why people do what they do.[29] Our job performance and even our ultimate survival in an organization often depend on the accuracy of our attributions for our own and supervisor, coworker, and customer behaviors and outcomes.

attribution
How people explain the causes of their own as well as other people's behaviors and achievements

The strongest attribution people tend to make is whether their own or others' behaviors or outcomes are due to the individual (internal factors) because of things like effort or ability or to the environment (external factors) because of things like luck, a lack of resources, or other people. We rely on three rules to evaluate whether to assign an internal or an external attribution to someone's behavior or outcome:[30]

1. *Consistency*: Has the person regularly behaved this way or experienced this outcome in the past? If your roommate consistently earns good grades in a subject, you are more likely to attribute a recent high test grade to an internal cause like ability or effort. If his or her grades earlier in the semester have been lower, you are more likely to attribute the grade to an external cause like luck. Consistency leads to internal attributions.
2. *Distinctiveness*: Does the person act the same way or receive similar outcomes in different types of situations? Low distinctiveness occurs when the person frequently acts in a certain way or receives certain outcomes and leads to internal attributions. If your roommate is a straight-A student, the distinctiveness of his or her recent high grade would be low, and you would make internal attributions for it. If your roommate is a C student, the distinctiveness of the recent high grade would be high and you would attribute it to external causes.
3. *Consensus*: Would others behave similarly in the same situation, or receive the same outcome? If almost everyone earns an A in the course in which your roommate just did well, consensus would be high and you would

make external attributions for your roommate's grade. If consensus is low and few students do well in the class, you would make internal attributions for the grade.

As a manager, understanding that a subordinate's own perceptions or attributions for success or failure determine the amount of effort he or she will expend on that activity in the future is a powerful motivational tool. Employees' perceptions and attributions determine the amount of effort they will exert on that activity in the future, and those attributions may differ across people. An employee may believe that she expended a great deal of effort when in fact she did not, or perceive an objectively easy task to be difficult. Attributing success to internal causes builds self-efficacy and increases the motivation to try hard and persist in the face of failure.

Attribution Errors

A core assumption of attribution theory is that people strive to maintain a positive self-image through *self-serving attributions*, or attributing our successes to ourselves and our failures to external factors. Self-serving attributions enable us to feel good about ourselves. In general, this means that we make self-serving attributions that credit successes to our own efforts or abilities, but blame failures on factors beyond our control, such as bad leadership or bad luck. Even professional athletes make self-serving attributions.[31]

Why do we make self-serving attributions? There are three reasons. One is to maintain or enhance our sense of self-worth. Achievement is strongly related to self-esteem. As attribution pioneer Bernard Weiner states,

> Causal attributions determine affective reactions to success and failure. For example, one is not likely to experience pride in success, or feelings of competence, when receiving an "A" from a teacher who gives only that grade, or when defeating a tennis player who always loses. . . . On the other hand, an "A" from a teacher who gives few high grades or a victory over a highly rated tennis player following a great deal of practice generates great positive affect.[32]

The second reason is to maintain others' positive perceptions of us. We enjoy having others think of us as competent and successful. The third reason is that the information we have about our past performance in similar situations can prompt us to attribute unexpected negative outcomes to the situation. In other words, if you know that you successfully performed a similar assignment last year, you are likely to blame external factors for your failure this time.

Self-serving attributions are not necessarily dysfunctional. They can increase our expectations for success, which help us to deal with challenges and setbacks and stay motivated. If we do not expect to succeed at a task, we are not motivated to try and will probably fail as a result.

The *fundamental attribution error* refers to our tendency to underestimate the impact of external factors and overestimate the impact of internal factors in explaining other people's behavior. In explaining our own behaviors, we tend to overemphasize the role of external factors and underestimate the role of internal factors, including our own personalities. Attribution is a two-step process in which we first spontaneously make an internal attribution of others' behavior, and then more consciously adjust the attribution to account for situational factors. Because this second step requires greater time and effort, we may not get to it if we are distracted or preoccupied, causing us to underweight its influence.[33]

SO WHAT

Managing your own and subordinates' attributions can improve effort, persistence, and ultimate success.

self-serving attributions

Attributing our successes to ourselves and our failures to external factors

fundamental attribution error

Our tendency to underestimate the impact of external factors and overestimate the impact of internal factors in explaining other people's behavior

Defensive attributions are explanations for negative outcomes, such as tragic events like job loss or serious injury, which help us to avoid feelings of vulnerability and mortality. One defensive attribution is unrealistic optimism about the future. We tend to think that good things are more likely and that bad things are less likely to happen to us than to others. Another way we deal with tragic information about others is to believe that a similar thing could never happen to us. A belief in a just world[34] is a defensive attribution in which we assume that bad things happen to bad people and good things happen to good people. Because most of us see ourselves as good, this reassures us that bad things will not happen to us.

This chapter's *Understand Yourself* feature may help you to better understand some of the attributions you make in your own life.

defensive attributions
Explanations for negative outcomes, such as tragic events, that help us to avoid feelings of vulnerability and mortality

Managerial Implications

Research has found that lower-level employees tend to attribute failure to external factors and attribute success to themselves. Executives, on the other hand, tend to take a more balanced perspective and attribute success to external factors and only partially to themselves. Executives also tend to assume greater personal responsibility for failure.[35]

We persist at tasks the most when we attribute our successes to internal factors. If you want your staff to persist at tasks, help them to establish a sincere belief that they are competent and can succeed if they work hard, and that occasional setbacks or failures are due to some other factor (such as bad luck) that is unlikely to influence future performance.

UNDERSTAND YOURSELF

SELF-HANDICAPPING ATTRIBUTIONS

Self-handicapping occurs when people create obstacles for themselves that make success less likely. Examples include drug and alcohol use, refusing to practice, and reducing effort. Creating these impediments obviously decreases motivation and performance. These behaviors may sound silly, but they are very real and serve to protect the person's sense of self-competence. If a self-handicapping person does poorly, the obstacle creates an easy explanation for the failure. If the person succeeds in spite of the obstacle, the success seems even greater.

Students sometimes use self-handicapping attributions, perhaps by not studying for a test. They might feel that:

- If they study hard and give it their best shot but fail, they will look and feel incompetent.

- If they study hard and pass, the hard work will reduce the meaning of the success. If they were really smart, they would not have had to work so hard.

- If they do not study and fail, the failure can be easily explained by the lack of effort. They can still believe that

they could have succeeded if they had really tried. Even if they fail the test, no one will have evidence that they are stupid.

- If they do not study but still manage to succeed, then the only explanation for the success is that they have really high ability.

This kind of reasoning is obviously counterproductive, because someone who expends less effort is obviously less likely to succeed. Self-handicapping tends to emerge during adolescence among persons with a high concern about looking competent. Focusing on effort attributions and developing feelings of self-efficacy help overcome this behavior.

Have you ever engaged in this type of behavior? Be honest with yourself and try to identify areas in your academic or work life in which you might be holding back effort through self-handicapping attributions. Then make an action plan to put greater effort into these tasks and see what happens to your performance.

SO WHAT

The ideal attribution for success is, "I was successful because I am competent at this task and I worked hard."

Although ability attributions for success are generally beneficial, it is not beneficial to attribute successes *entirely* to ability. If Tony thinks he already has all the ability he needs, he may feel that additional effort is unnecessary. The ideal attribution for success is, "I was successful because I am competent at this task and I worked hard." In the face of failure, persistence and eventual success are more likely if failure is attributed to a lack of appropriate effort. If a new employee who could be successful begins to perceive herself as a failure at the new job, it is important to help her develop the belief that she can still succeed if she gives it her best effort. Obviously it is also important to be realistic. If an employee really is not likely to succeed at a task, telling her that it is only a matter of effort when no amount of effort is likely to raise performance to an acceptable level is unethical and only postpones the inevitable removal of the person from the position.

It is motivationally deadly to fail repeatedly after making a serious effort at a task. When this happens, we either stop believing we are competent, or stop attributing our failure to lack of effort. Both of these outcomes reduce our persistence and effort. It is very important, therefore, for managers to ensure that talented subordinates who work hard are able to perceive themselves as successful.

Managers also need to ensure that subordinates internalize a correct understanding of effort. Just trying harder or spending more time doing ineffective activities does not represent effort. What you want to promote are not simply effort attributions, but *strategic effort attributions*. People need to believe that working hard *in an effective way* is what leads to success.[36] Consistently helping employees make strategic effort attributions encourages them to view failures as problem-solving situations in which the search for an improved strategy becomes the main focus.[37] If you can show subordinates ways to improve their efforts and channel their energies more effectively, this can give them an accurate perception that increased strategic effort is likely to pay off.

When a subordinate believes that she or he has low ability, it is necessary to intervene. Such a person is likely to attribute any success to luck or other external causes, and is unlikely to be very motivated to exert maximum effort. It is very difficult to change this belief because it requires changing the person's self-concept, which takes time. Some strategies to address this challenge include:[38]

- Focusing heavily on the person's effort as a cause of success
- Identifying areas in which the subordinate perceives him- or herself as competent
- Showing connections between that competence and the task being addressed
- Promoting short-term motivation to increase successes, which over time can alter the person's self-concept and attributions
- Reinforcing effort attributions[39]
- Training that shows the person that he or she can do the task and that promotes attributions that lead to greater motivation and performance[40]

Managing attributions is also important in external communications. One study found that organizations that made "self-disserving" internal and controllable attributions for negative events had higher stock prices one year later.[41] Organizations taking personal responsibility for negative events appear more in control, leading to more positive investor impressions.

Wise managers know to be wary of their own attributions. They ask themselves, "If I didn't know how this employee was performing, what would I think about his or her effort, skills, or fit with our culture?" Always look for independent evidence rather than quickly accepting the idea that a successful employee has great skills or motivation or that a struggling employee must have poor skills and motivation.[42] Wise managers resist the natural tendency to make attributions based solely on outcomes and look for the real causes of performance.[43]

Understanding social perception and attributions is important to promoting and managing organizational diversity. The meaning of a particular behavior or experience may differ across cultures due to differences in norms, values, experiences, and role perceptions. Employees from different backgrounds and cultures use different implicit and explicit frameworks in interpreting their experiences.[44] This can lead culturally diverse people to interpret the same behavior or experience very differently.

Although it is important to remember that not everyone in a particular subgroup will interpret things the same way, between-group differences can lead to conflict and misunderstandings because of the differential attributions likely to occur.[45] For example, the silence of an individual from an Asian culture may be attributed by a coworker from the United States to indifference or laziness even though it is intended only as respect. Similarly, a compliment may be misinterpreted as a manipulation attempt, offers of help can be seen as demeaning, and a gift can be seen as a bribe. Discrepant attributions result in misunderstandings, rejection, and even conflict.[46] These types of discrepancies are more likely to occur in cross-cultural interactions because of differences in the norms, roles, values, and expectations each culture has developed in its adaptation to the rigors of life in its particular geographic, economic, and historical circumstances.[47] This chapter's *Global Issues* feature describes additional cultural issues in attributions.

SO WHAT

Employees from different cultures can interpret the same behavior or experience very differently.

GLOBAL ISSUES

HOW CULTURE CAN INFLUENCE ATTRIBUTIONS

In intercultural interactions, the interpretations of behaviors are often more important than the actual behaviors themselves.[48] Because Western cultures emphasize individual freedom and autonomy, people in these cultures prefer dispositional explanations, while people from collectivist cultures that emphasize group membership and conformity to group norms tend to prefer situational explanations.[49]

One study showed American and Chinese participants a picture of an individual fish swimming in front of a group of fish. More American than Chinese participants attributed the individual fish's behavior as internally

GEORGETTE DOUWMA/PHOTOGRAPHER'S CHOICE/GETTY IMAGES

Why do you think the fish is swimming outside of the school of fish?

rather than externally caused.[50] This attributional difference may be due to the way people with different cultural orientations perceive themselves in their environment. Westerners, who tend to be more individualistic, often see themselves as independent entities and therefore tend to notice individual objects more than contextual details.[51]

Understanding a coworker's behavior requires understanding his or her subjective culture. Attributional training can help us understand the appropriate attributions for the behaviors of diverse coworkers.

PERCEIVED FAIRNESS

Think of a time when you felt unfairly treated at work or school. Why did you feel that way? What did you do about it? When we perceive unfairness, we are often motivated to do something about it. In organizations, perceptions of unfairness (also referred to as injustice) can exist in numerous situations. Layoffs and downsizings are often seen as unfair by those dismissed as well as by the employees who remain. Hiring and promotion decisions are often seen as unfair by those not chosen. In unionized settings, both managers and union representatives often perceive the other to be unfair. Even organizational change can be viewed as unfair by those asked to learn new systems or do new things.

Jerald Greenberg coined the term *organizational fairness* to refer to employees' perceptions of organizational events, policies, and practices as being fair or not fair.[52] Fairness is a primary concern in relationships where subordinates must rely on others in higher positions.[53]

organizational fairness
Employees' perceptions of organizational events, policies, and practices as being fair or not fair

Researchers view individuals' reactions to unfairness as an evolutionary-based response that is automatic, emotional (anger, for example), retributive, and sometimes irrational (at least in the short term).[54] Research has found that we will often punish others' unfair behavior even if we make personal sacrifices to do so.[55] We tend to label actions as unfair if we think the person could and should have behaved differently and the outcome could have been more favorable.[56]

Outcomes of Perceived Fairness

Why should you care about fairness? You should care because perceptions of fairness affect a wide variety of employee attitudes and behaviors including satisfaction, commitment, trust, and turnover. A number of negative behaviors can result from perceptions of unfairness, including theft, sabotage, and other unethical behaviors.[57] Perceived unfairness also increases the chances that employees will file lawsuits against their employers.[58] Most of these outcomes of fairness perceptions can have an obvious economic impact on organizations.

As a manager, it is critical to remember that it is insufficient to just *be* fair; you must also be *perceived* as fair by your subordinates. Perceptions are what drive responses, and subordinates' attributions and interpretations of your behaviors and decisions may not reflect your intentions or your own beliefs. The demographic diversity of the U.S. workforce requires many managers to handle differences among employees regarding characteristics ranging from ethnicity to religion to political ideology—all of which can be a source of conflict and misunderstanding.[59] Effectively managing organizational fairness perceptions and attributions can help managers prevent or effectively manage any conflict or misunderstandings that occur.

Understanding fairness is important for ethical reasons as well.[60] There has been no shortage of high-profile ethical lapses in recent years, ranging from Enron to Bernie Madoff to mortgage fraud. Training all employees, including company leaders, in organizational fairness principles helps guide them in making ethical decisions. When employees perceive general organizational fairness and an organizational desire to follow through on formal ethics programs, unethical behavior is reduced and employees are more willing to report problems to management.[61] Also, individuals' expectations for fairness produce expectations that those who violate ethical expectations will be disciplined.[62] Failure to meet employees' fairness expectations can lead them to engage in unethical behavior.[63]

Types of Fairness Perceptions

We think of fairness in three main ways:

1. *Distributive fairness*: Did we get what we wanted?
2. *Procedural fairness*: Were the procedures used in making the decision fair?
3. *Interactional fairness*: Were we treated with respect (interpersonal fairness) and given adequate and timely information (informational fairness) during the decision-making process?[64]

We next elaborate on each of these fairness types.

Distributive Fairness. *Distributive fairness* refers to the perceived fairness of the outcome received, including resource distributions, promotions, hiring and layoff decisions, and raises.[65] Imagine that you and a friend both apply for a job with a local company at the same time. Although you believe that you are more qualified, your friend is offered a job and you are not. Would this feel fair? Your belief about the fairness of you not getting the job reflects your perception of distributive fairness. Distributive fairness relates only to the outcome received, not to the fairness of the process that generated the decision.

In 1965, John Stacey Adams[66] developed equity theory to describe how people decide whether or not a decision is fair. Essentially, employees expect a fair return for what they contribute—this is often referred to as the *equity norm*.[67] A key component of equity theory is social comparison—employees compare their own input/outcome ratios with the input/outcome ratios of other employees,[68] and seek to maintain an equitable ratio.[69] Inputs include time, effort, ability, training, personal sacrifice, and enthusiasm. Outcomes include pay, appreciation, bonuses, benefits, recognition, and flexible work arrangements. This comparison process is reflected in the formula shown in Figure 6-2.

As shown in Figure 6-2, according to equity theory, your ratio of inputs compared to outcomes in comparison to the other person's ratio is what matters, not just the relative level of the outcomes you receive. If your comparison person has more favorable outcomes than you do, you may perceive this to be fair if you acknowledge that she also contributes more to the organization (by performing better, working longer, etc.). Research has supported this theory and it has become one of the most useful frameworks for understanding work motivation.

Perceiving that another employee has a more favorable ratio than you do (e.g., you are underpaid) often leads to emotional reactions (such as anger) and attempts to restore equity. Adams proposed a number of ways that people act to resolve perceived inequities and to balance the ratio. For example, imagine a situation where someone feels underpaid compared to a coworker. To restore feelings of equity, the worker could react by:[70]

- *Decreasing his or her inputs* (maybe work slower or less carefully)
- *Increasing his or her outcomes* (ask for a raise or steal)
- *Trying to get the coworker to increase his or her inputs* (work harder)

distributive fairness
The perceived fairness of the outcome received

equity norm
People are rewarded based on their relative level of contributions

SO WHAT

If employees perceive that an inequity exists, they are likely to withhold some of their contributions, either consciously or unconsciously, to bring the situation into better balance.

Figure 6-2

Equity Theory

You		Comparison Person	Perceived Equity
Input/Outcome	<	Input/Outcome	You feel overpaid.
Input/Outcome	=	Input/Outcome	You feel pay is fair.
Input/Outcome	>	Input/Outcome	You feel underpaid.

© CENGAGE LEARNING 2012

- *Trying to reduce the coworker's outcomes* (e.g., by spreading rumors, sabotage)
- *Choosing a different comparison person who provides a better ratio comparison* (this could be a different coworker or someone outside the company, such as a friend working in a similar job)
- *Cognitively distorting the comparison* and convincing him- or herself that the situation is equitable
- *Leaving the organization*

Imagine, for example, that you work hard at your job for forty hours a week and earn a salary of $50,000, but a colleague with the same job and same hours earns $60,000 in salary. In assessing the equity of the situation, you realize that your colleague has advanced training, has worked for ten years longer than you have, and is more productive. You decide that given your colleague's greater job inputs, the greater outcome (salary) is fair. You might know of another colleague, however, who has the same effort level, work experience, productivity, and education that you do, but who makes $55,000. In this instance, you may feel that the situation is unfair because you perceive the inputs as being roughly equal, and yet your colleague makes $5,000 more a year than you do.

So what happens if the inequity is in your favor? If your boss pays you $150 for a day's work and pays a coworker $140 for the same work, how would you react? Would you return the extra $10 or keep it as a "bonus"? As you might expect, we are more likely to notice, and to be upset with, being underpaid than being overpaid.[71] Some people temporarily increase their productivity to make the situation more equitable, but this effect gradually wears off.[72] This probably happens because we reevaluate our inputs (we worked hard, we did a good job, etc.) to justify the difference in pay. Research has found that employees who feel that they were hired for jobs that exceed their qualifications (and who thus feel over-rewarded) engage in more helping behaviors and have higher organizational commitment.[73]

Equity theory has wide-reaching implications for employee productivity, motivation, and turnover. Managers need to be aware of these important implications, including:

- People consider the balance of their inputs and outcomes—a working parent may accept lower pay in return for more flexible working hours.
- Employees place different personal values on various inputs and outcomes. Two employees with similar experience and qualifications may have different perceptions of the fairness of doing the same work for the same pay.
- People use a variety of cognitive shortcuts in evaluating equity and often do not have complete information when making fairness judgments.
- Because employees' perceptions of their and their coworkers' inputs and outcomes may be incorrect, their perceptions must be effectively managed.
- As a manager, some of the ways you can use equity theory to motivate subordinates are:
- Have regular one-on-one meetings with employees to discuss their goals and career development.
- Give employees regular feedback so they know how they are doing.
- Ensure that you recognize and reward good performance.
- Try to influence employees' choice of comparison person to improve equity perceptions.

Although equity theory was originally concerned with differences in pay, it is also applicable to other forms of tangible and intangible rewards in the workplace.[74] That is, if any employee input is not balanced with a fair outcome, motivation will be more difficult.

In addition to equity, rewards or outcomes can be based on either equality or need. Equality and equity are not the same. *Equality* means that everyone's outcomes are identical. Southwest Airlines, for example, tends to reward employees collectively through stock options and profit sharing rather than paying employees based on their individual performance. Executives also do not receive large raises if lower-level employees are under a wage freeze.[75]

Equity means that everyone's outcomes are fair based on their relative level of contributions—some people may get more (or less) than others if they contributed more (or less). Equity theory does *not* propose that outcomes (e.g., pay) need to be equal across employees. Employees will not think it is unfair if a comparison employee is receiving more from the organization (e.g., getting paid more) if the person also contributes more to the organization (by being a better performer, working longer hours, etc.).

When outcomes are distributed based on *need*, the people most in need of rewards benefit first. For example, a parent with an out-of-work spouse might be protected in this round of layoffs. Needs can be based on just about anything—financial, personal, or other factors. In collectivist cultures, compensation decisions are highly influenced by "need."

Most research on distributive fairness has explored equity. Although research has not yet clarified how employees tend to choose a response to perceived inequity, one of the factors may be the employee's culture. For instance, someone from a more collectivist culture may be more likely to use an equality norm, especially with immediate coworkers. Table 6-3 summarizes the three possible fairness norms of equity, equality, and need.

The reality of managing is that not everyone can get what they want. But how do people react when they do not get what they want? Most people feel that positive outcomes are fair and that undesirable outcomes are not fair. But how they react to undesirable outcomes depends on their perceptions of two other types of fairness: procedural fairness and interactional fairness.

Procedural Fairness. A fair process is as important as a fair outcome. *Procedural fairness* addresses the fairness of the procedures used to generate the outcome (e.g., what rules were followed, whether people had the opportunity to express opinions and influence the outcome, etc.).[76] For example, let's continue the example of your applying for a job at the same time as your friend but your friend getting the position. What if you learned that the hiring manager is your friend's cousin, so your friend was offered the job even though you were more qualified? Bending the rules for a relative would probably violate your standards for what constitutes a fair hiring procedure.

Low procedural fairness increases negative outcomes, such as lower job performance and withdrawal behaviors like coming to work late or putting in

SO WHAT

People do not always have to be rewarded identically for them to perceive the rewards to be fair.

procedural fairness
Perceptions of the fairness of the policies and procedures used to make decisions

---

Table 6-3

Examples of Rewards Distributed Based on Equity, Equality, and Need

Equity	Promotions should be given to the person who is most qualified (i.e., has the strongest skills or is capable of contributing the most to the organization in the new role).
Equality	Health benefits should be given equally to all employees, not just to those people who have higher-level positions.
Need	When an employee has a family emergency, the supervisor should approve time off to deal with it.

© CENGAGE LEARNING 2012

less effort. But if procedural fairness is high, negative reactions are much less likely. Six rules apply to procedural fairness:[77]

1. *Representativeness*: Representativeness means "that all phases of [the] allocation process must reflect the basic concerns, values, and outlook of important subgroups in the population of individuals affected by the allocation process."[78] This often involves giving individuals a chance to speak on their own behalf. *Instrumental voice* occurs when the comments a person makes can influence the decision. *Noninstrumental voice*, on the other hand, occurs when the comments will have no bearing on the outcome (e.g., the comments were allowed only after the decision had been made). Both types of voice can be effective in different situations.

2. *Consistency*: A procedure should be used consistently across time and across employees.

3. *Bias suppression*: The decision maker's personal biases should not influence the decision and the decision maker should not be so influenced by prior beliefs that he or she does not give all points of view adequate and reasonable consideration.

4. *Accuracy*: The information being used in the decision should be perceived as accurate.

5. *Correctability*: A grievance or appeals process should exist in case mistakes are made.

6. *Ethicality*: Ethical standards should guide the decision.

So why does procedural fairness matter? There are two reasons.[79] First, employees use perceptions of the current decision-making procedures to predict how they will likely fare in the organization in the future. Second, fair procedures signal that employees are valued and accepted by the organization.

Procedural fairness increases in importance when the outcome of a decision is unfavorable. If we get what we want, we are not as bothered by questionable policies or procedures. But if an outcome is unfavorable, the means justify the ends—we tend to react less negatively if we think the procedure used in making the decision was fair. If procedures are seen as unfair, the favorability of the outcome matters more. Because employees will sometimes go against their own self-interest if a situation violates their rules about fairness and justice, managers should pay careful attention to achieving a fair process and fair outcomes when making changes to company structures, processes, systems, and incentives.[80]

Interactional Fairness. *Interactional fairness* is whether the amount of information about the decision and the process was adequate, and the perceived fairness of the interpersonal treatment and explanations received during the decision-making process. Does an employee who did not receive a performance bonus feel that the supervisor adequately explained the reason? When we assess undesirable outcomes, how we are treated can be just as important as the outcomes we receive. It is difficult to give our best effort to someone who treats us rudely or disrespects us. Deception or abusive words or actions can be seen as having low interactional fairness.[81]

Although providing adequate information and treating people respectfully may not sound like powerful tools in work motivation, interactional fairness reduces negative reactions to undesirable work outcomes. In one company,[82] two plants announced 15 percent pay cuts for their workers. At one plant, the CEO gave employees extensive explanations about why the pay cuts were necessary, and regretfully and explicitly explained that they would allow the company to avoid layoffs. Employees at the second plant were given only a short explanation that a pay cut was going to take place to avoid layoffs, and received no apology. Interactional fairness was therefore high in the first plant and low in the second plant. After the announcement, theft increased in both plants but was significantly higher in the plant that received an inadequate explanation for the pay cuts. Voluntary turnover was also higher in the plant that perceived low interactional fairness.

Interactional fairness describes two specific types of interpersonal treatment.[83] The first type is ***interpersonal fairness***, which reflects the degree to which people are treated with politeness, dignity, and respect by authorities or third parties involved in executing procedures or determining outcomes. The second type is ***informational fairness***, which focuses on the extent to which employees receive adequate information and explanations about decisions affecting their working lives.[84]

It is important that a high degree of interactional fairness exist in the relationship between a supervisor and a subordinate. Low interactional fairness can lead to feelings of resentment toward either the supervisor or the organization.[85] A victim of interactional unfairness often has increased expressions of hostility toward the supervisor or company, which can lead to negative work behaviors and decrease the effectiveness of organizational communication.[86] Explanations increase job applicants' fairness perceptions, perceptions of the hiring organization, test-taking motivation, and performance on cognitive ability tests.[87]

Table 6-4 summarizes the effects of the different types of fairness perceptions on a variety of important organizational outcomes.

Fairness perceptions are important to customers as well as employees.[88] Would you shop at a store again if the employees treated you rudely? In a study of retail customers, interactional fairness had a larger impact on continued patronage and negative word-of-mouth intentions than did distributive or procedural fairness.[89] Employees' fairness perceptions can also spill over and influence their interactions with customers.[90]

interpersonal fairness
The degree to which people are treated with politeness, dignity, and respect by authorities or third parties involved in executing procedures or determining outcomes

informational fairness
The extent to which employees receive adequate information and explanations about decisions affecting their working lives

SO WHAT
Undesired outcomes increase the importance of fair procedures and fair interpersonal treatment.

Table 6-4

Effects of Fairness Perceptions on Organizational Outcomes

Outcome	Correlation with Procedural Fairness	Correlation with Distributive Fairness	Correlation with Interpersonal Fairness	Correlation with Informational Fairness
Job satisfaction	.62	.56	.35	.43
Organizational commitment	.57	.51	.19	.29
Trust	.61	.57	n/a	.51
Withdrawal	−.46	−.50	−.02	−.24
Performance	.36	.15	.03	.13
Negative employee reactions	−.31	−.30	−.35	−.33

Note: Correlations range from −1 to +1; 0 represents no relationship, −1 represents a perfect inverse relationship, and +1 represents a perfect positive relationship (as the fairness perception rises, the outcome increases); numbers closer to 1 or −1 reflect stronger relationships, positive numbers reflect positive relationships, and negative numbers reflect inverse relationships.

Source: Based on Colquitt, J.A., Conlon, D.E., Wesson, M.J., Porter, C.O., Ng, K.Y. (2001), "Justice at the millennium: A meta-analytic review of 25 years of organizational justice research", Journal of Applied Psychology, Vol. 86(3): 425–45. Reprinted by permission of APA.

At this point you might be wondering how fairness perceptions can be measured. Table 6-5 shows one popular questionnaire for assessing the different types of fairness perceptions.

Table 6-5

Measuring Fairness Perceptions

Think about a past outcome you received, and think of it as you answer all the questions below. You might think about a course grade you got, a raise you received, or some other situation. Use the following scale and record your response to the left of each question.

To a small extent		To a moderate extent		To a large extent
1	2	3	4	5

Procedural Fairness
The following questions refer to the procedures used to arrive at your outcome. To what extent:
___1. Were you able to express your views and feelings during those procedures?
___2. Did you have influence over your outcome arrived at by those procedures?
___3. Were those procedures applied consistently?
___4. Were those procedures free of bias?
___5. Were those procedures based on accurate information?
___6. Were you able to appeal your outcome arrived at by those procedures?
___7. Did those procedures uphold ethical and moral standards?

Distributive Fairness
The following questions refer to your outcome. To what extent:
___1. Did your outcome reflect the effort you put into your work?
___2. Was your outcome appropriate for the work you completed?
___3. Did your outcome reflect what you contributed to the organization?
___4. Was your outcome justified, given your performance?

Interpersonal Fairness
The following questions refer to the authority figure who enacted the procedure. To what extent:
___1. Did he/she treat you in a polite manner?
___2. Did he/she treat you with dignity?
___3. Did he/she treat you with respect?
___4. Did he/she refrain from improper remarks or comments?

Informational Fairness
The following questions refer to the procedures used to arrive at the outcome. To what extent:
___1. Was the authority figure candid in his/her communications with you?
___2. Did he/she explain the procedures thoroughly?

___3. Were his/her explanations regarding the procedures reasonable?

___4. Did he/she communicate details in a timely manner?

___5. Did he/she seem to tailor his/her communications to individuals' specific needs?

Scoring and Interpretation:
Add up your scores to each of the subscales and record the totals below. Then divide each total by the number of items in that subscale, as shown below, to identify your average rating for each type of fairness. Higher scores reflect greater fairness perceptions.
Procedural fairness: _____ / 7 = _____ average procedural fairness rating
Distributive fairness: _____ / 4 = _____ average distributive fairness rating
Interpersonal fairness: _____ / 4 = _____ average interpersonal fairness rating
Informational fairness: _____ / 5 = _____ average informational fairness rating

Source: Copyright © 2001 by the American Psychological Association. Adapted with permission. Table 1 (adapted), page 389, from Colquitt, J. A. (2001). On the dimensionality of organizational justice: A construct validation of a measure. *Journal of Applied Psychology,* 86(3), 386–400. No further reproduction or distribution is permitted without written permission from the American Psychological Association.

Trust

One of the most important outcomes of consistently treating others fairly is trust. *Trust* is the expectation that another person will not act to take advantage of us regardless of our ability to monitor or control them.[91] Trust has been called "the social glue that holds things together"[92] and is critical to long-term relationships.[93] Trust is positively related to job performance.[94] Trusting work relationships enable employees to focus on their work and not waste time and energy "watching their backs." As Berkshire Hathaway Chairman Warren Buffet said, "Trust is like the air we breathe. When it's present, nobody really notices. But when it's absent, everybody notices."[95]

> "Trust is like the air we breathe. When it's present, nobody really notices. But when it's absent, everybody notices." —*Warren Buffet, Berkshire Hathaway Chairman*

trust
The expectation that another person will not take advantage of us regardless of our ability to monitor or control them

Trust is particularly important to the developmental stages of relationships,[96] and is positively related to a company's financial performance.[97] One survey of 500 business professionals found that having a trusting relationship with one's manager was the main factor in deciding to stay.[98]

If another person is not perceived as ethical or fair, it is unlikely that they will be seen as trustworthy. Trust is at the discretion of the other person and must be earned. As American Airlines CEO Gerard Arpey says, "The only way to build trust professionally or personally is by being trustworthy."[99] After surveying up to twenty employees in fifty-seven different companies, Development Dimensions International found that the top two trust-building behaviors for leaders were making sure their words are consistent with their actions and showing confidence in direct reports.[100] The same survey found that the top two trust-reducing behaviors for leaders were being concerned about their own welfare above anything else and sending mixed messages.

SO WHAT
Earning others' trust is essential to developing good relationships.

California training and consulting organization HeartMath LLC promotes employee trust by ensuring an open communication flow. Information about the financial health of the company is shared with employees, and the staff is involved in decisions that affect them.[101]

This chapter's *Case Study* feature gives you the opportunity to think about the implications of trust during a merger.

CASE STUDY

Regaining Trust After a Merger

When US Airways and America West joined forces to become US Airways Group,[102] integrating the companies' very different cultures and regaining employees' trust were critical to the new company's survival. The merger was intended to make both carriers more efficient. "This is a teamwork business," the CEO says. "You have to have people work together in some sort of team." As he greets employees just off the tarmac at the frozen Philadelphia airport, the CEO says he wants US Airways employees to know that the company is changing in a positive direction. "As much as I would like them to see that this [company] will be different, I know trust is earned," he adds. "I'm going to earn it."[103]

The cultures of the two companies are quite different—US Airways is more mature and formal while America West is seen as more of an enthusiastic youngster. To help merge the two different cultures, Larry LeSueur, a longtime America West employee, was appointed as vice president of culture to impart CEO Doug Parker's message that every employee is valued and that we "expect you to treat customers well, and we, as a leadership team, will do the same for you."[104]

Because of several previous bankruptcies, along with wage and benefit givebacks, the US Airways workforce had lost trust with management. To rebuild trust, LeSueur spent time listening to their pent-up frustration and anger.[105] Because of the challenging economy and competitive industry, earning employees' trust and focusing them on performing their jobs well cannot happen quickly enough.

Questions:

1. If you were an employee at US Airways Group, what would your main concerns be?
2. How could your trust be earned by the company following the merger?
3. What might happen if employees continued to distrust management? Explain why, using what you have learned in this chapter.

Psychological Contract Violations

There are two primary types of employment contracts: (1) the formal contract and (2) the equally important, informal, and unwritten psychological contract that establishes how people think they should be treated. The informal psychological contract refers to employer and employee expectations of the employment relationship, including mutual obligations, values, and expectations that operate over and above the formal contract of employment.[106] Both types of contracts involve rights, obligations, and expectations on the part of the employer and the employee, and a breach in one can have important effects on the other. For example, how people feel they are being treated by the organization can affect their perception of their pay.[107] Psychological contracts can include expectations of financial rewards, performance-based pay, career advancement, and job stability.

Businesses are increasingly using psychological contracts to clarify understandings between themselves and their employees. As shown in Figure 6-3, sandwich company Prêt à Manger's website frames its psychological contract with store employees as what employees can expect from the company and what the company expects from its employees.

Although they can change over time, psychological contracts are promise-based and become a schema that is relatively stable and durable.[109] They also establish a foundation for employee expectations of procedural, distributive, and interactional fairness. The employer and employee may not agree about

Figure 6-3

The Psychological Contract at Prêt à Manger[108]

United Kingdom–based sandwich company Prêt à Manger tries to clarify its psychological contract before employees are even hired. Here are some excerpts from its website that explain what it expects from employees and what employees can expect from Prêt à Manger.

What Prêt à Manger expects from employees:

- Good communication
- Teamwork
- Enthusiasm
- Going the extra mile

What employees can expect from Prêt à Manger:

- Get paid as much as we can afford rather than as little as we can get away with
- Cosmopolitan atmosphere due to diverse employee backgrounds
- Training & development
- Promotion opportunities

Sources: Prêt à Manger (2010). Working as a Team Member, Pret.com. http://www.pret.com/jobs/working_shop/. Prêt à Manger (2010). Working at Pret, Pret.com. Available online at: http://www.pret.com/jobs/. Accessed March 9, 2010.

what the contract actually involves, which can lead to feelings that the psychological contract has been violated.

Psychological contract violations have important implications for employee trust,[110] performance,[111] and behavior.[112] Perceiving that the employer has breached the psychological contract can create feelings of injustice, deception, or betrayal.[113] Downsizings and layoffs are often seen by employees as violations of the psychological contract. Specific circumstances, such as layoff timing and labor market factors (e.g., whether there is a perceived need for cutbacks), are particularly associated with employees feeling that their psychological contract has been violated.[114]

Employees with different understandings of their psychological contracts respond differently to contract violation and to planned organizational change.[115] For example, employees in Singapore, with an unstructured labor market and many short-term contracts, and "transactional" psychological contracts, show a lower sense of obligation to employers than U.S. employees, and less perceived violation when changes are introduced.[116] The negative impact of breaking psychological contracts can be offset if employees' trust in their employer remains high.[117]

SO WHAT

Maintaining trust helps reduce the negative effects of breaking a psychological contract.

SUMMARY AND APPLICATION

Understanding how our innate information processing biases work can help us to stay objective and make the best decisions possible for ourselves and our organizations. The attributions we make explain a great deal of our choices to persist in or to quit various tasks. If we attribute success to ourselves, we are likely to persist at the task. If we attribute failure to internal causes like low ability, we are less likely to persist. One of the most powerful managerial tools is the ability to understand and influence the attributions others make and guide them to more productive explanations for their outcomes.

REAL WORLD RESPONSE

AVOIDING LAYOFFS AT BETH ISRAEL HOSPITAL

Beth Israel Deaconess Medical Center was in a tough position. With the falling economy, the hospital's finances were in dire straits. Rather than making closed-door decisions, President and CEO Paul Levy openly blogged about the hospital's finances in great detail, and explained what they could mean to the hospital in terms of layoffs. He thought of ways to protect his lowest-paid but critical employees, and assembled his employees to update them on the situation. He said:

> I want to run an idea by you that I think is important, and I'd like to get your reaction to it. I'd like to do what we can to protect the lower-wage earners—the transporters, the housekeepers, the food service people. A lot of these people work really hard, and I don't want to put an additional burden on them. Now, if we protect these workers, it means the rest of us will have to make a bigger sacrifice. It means that others will have to give up more of their salary or benefits.[118]

He had barely gotten the words out of his mouth when employees erupted in thunderous, sincere applause.

Levy then asked his employees to send him ideas about saving money. Employees responded quickly—at one point Levy was receiving 100 messages an hour. Hospital employees did not want anyone to get laid off and were willing to forego pay raises and benefits to make that possible. Higher-paid staff members gave up bonuses and benefits to help protect the jobs of the lowest-paid employees. Other employee suggestions included eliminating the employee barbecue, saving $50,000, and ending reimbursement for cell phones and BlackBerrys.

Beth Israel employees realized that employees are all in the same boat in the tough economy, and wanted to be fair to everyone. Nurse Linda Trainor said she was pleased with how the challenges were handled. "Most people are willing to make a sacrifice so that our colleagues won't have to lose their jobs, or not as many. When I see people at AIG getting raises after a bailout and I see our CEO taking a pay cut, it makes me glad I work here. Sacrifice is the name of the game and not greed."[119]

Handling the challenge with fairness and equity also helped to maintain employee morale. Lissa Kapust, a hospital employee for thirty years, added, "Walking through the hallways here, there's a feeling of anxiety, but also a sense we are going to pull together to get through this together."[120]

Sources: Based on Cullen, K. (2009). A Head with a Heart. *The Boston Globe*, March 12. Available online at: http://www.boston.com/news/local/massachusetts/articles/2009/03/12/a_head_with_a_heart/. Accessed July 10, 2009; Cooney, E. (2009). Sparing 450 Jobs at Beth Israel. *The Boston Globe*. Available online at: http://www.boston.com/news/local/massachusetts/articles/2009/03/19/sparing_450_jobs_at_beth_israel/. Accessed July 10, 2009; Ribbler, J. (2009). Paul Levy of Beth Israel Deaconess Medical Center Inspires Execs, Employees to Share Sacrifice and Wins Ribby Award. Available online at: http://media-proinc.com/ribblog/http://media-proinc.com/ribblog/04/2009/paul-levy-of-beth-israel-deaconess-medical-center-inspires-execs-employees-to-share-sacrifice-and-wins-ribby-award, accessed July 10, 2009.

Although the various cognitive shortcuts can help us to quickly process information and determine appropriate reactions, they can be wrong. The "facts" we hold about groups of people can be incorrect. Categorization and stereotypes distort what we perceive about other people, and subsequent selective perception can lead us to ignore important facts that disconfirm our initial perceptions.

Fairness perceptions stem in part from our attributions, and have a strong impact on a variety of organizational outcomes. Our perceptions of the fairness of the outcomes, processes, interpersonal treatment, and information received during the decision-making process are all important determinants of our reactions. Perceiving fairness is important to establishing trust. Establishing trusting relationships with supervisors and subordinates will help you to focus on your job performance, and improve the performance of the people around you.

✓ TAKEAWAY POINTS

1. We tend to categorize people into groups and then use selective perception to quickly process additional information about them. The halo effect occurs when we form an overall impression about someone on the basis of a single (typically good) characteristic. The contrast effect happens when we evaluate someone by comparing that person to other people we have recently encountered who rank higher or lower on the same characteristics. We also project our own characteristics onto others who we perceive to be similar to us in some ways.

2. We decide how to classify others based on our personal goals, the social context, and how easily we can remember a category.

3. Self-fulfilling prophecies occur when our impressions and expectations of ourselves or others cause us to do things that make those prophecies more likely to come true. Managers who communicate positive expectations and not negative ones can help their employees reach their full potential.

4. Internal attributions include ability and effort. External attributions include luck, not having sufficient resources, and the interference or help of other people.

5. Helping employees establish a sincere belief that they are competent and can succeed if they work hard, and that occasional setbacks or failures are due to some other factor (such as bad luck) that is unlikely to influence future performance, encourages task persistence.

6. Distributive fairness is the perception of fairness of the outcome received. If employees do not earn a performance bonus, do they think this is fair? Procedural fairness is the fairness of the policies and procedures used to make the decision and determine the outcomes. Interpersonal fairness refers to the politeness, dignity, and respect with which people were treated during the decision-making process. Informational fairness focuses on the adequacy of the information and explanations received during the decision-making process. Imagine a situation in which you are competing with three other employees for a desired promotion. The organization has decided to make a choice based on a combination of two factors: an interview with the hiring manager (30 percent) and the candidates' previous performance appraisal scores (70 percent). Your belief that the right person got promoted is your perception of distributive fairness. Your belief that it is fair to make the decision based 70 percent on the performance appraisal scores and 30 percent on the interview is your perception of procedural

fairness. Your perception of interpersonal fairness would reflect whether you feel you were treated respectfully, and your perception of informational fairness would reflect whether you felt that the information you received throughout the decision-making process was accurate.

7. Trust is an outcome of fairness. If another person is not perceived as fair, it is unlikely that the person will be seen as trustworthy. To improve subordinates' fairness perceptions, managers can try to ensure that outcomes are perceived as equitable and make sure that none of the six procedural fairness rules are violated. To improve interactional fairness perceptions, managers can give adequate explanations for decisions, and treat subordinates with sincerity and respect.

DISCUSSION QUESTIONS

1. Describe a time when you were unfairly treated at work. Why did you perceive unfairness?
2. How would you allocate pay raises across a group of employees in a way that would be fair to everyone? How would you allocate grades to students in this class in a way that would be fair to everyone? If your preferences differ in each situation, why?
3. What are the implications for projection and for the contrast effect in job interviews? What can the interviewer do to reduce the effects of projection and the contrast effect?
4. Describe a time when a self-fulfilling prophecy negatively influenced you. What could you have done differently to obtain a more positive outcome?
5. Think about the attributions you tend to make for your academic performance. Is there anything you can do differently to leverage what you now know to improve your performance?
6. Which type of fairness do you think is most important to organizations? Why?
7. Imagine that you are a company manager and have three great subordinates who are all competing for a single open promotion. What could you do during the promotion process to ensure that all three feel fairly treated even though only one will get promoted?
8. How do you think trust influences organizations? Do you believe that trust can create a competitive advantage for a company? Why or why not?

EXERCISES

Making a Great First Impression

The purpose of this exercise is to give you practice making a great first impression. Refer to this chapter's *Improve Your Skills* feature and read over the tips. Take a few minutes to think about how you can comfortably display the behaviors discussed in the feature. You want to be yourself—don't try to overact or treat the tips like a checklist. Think through a couple of different versions of how the first couple minutes of a job interview meeting might go.

Now find two classmates to work with for this exercise. One of you will role-play the interviewer, one will be him- or herself as the interviewee, and the third will observe and give feedback to the interviewee. Take turns role-playing the initial introductions and small talk that might occur during the first two or three minutes of a job interview. When each person is finished, give the interviewee feedback on how to make a great first impression. Do the exercise with both partners to improve your skills in this important area.

Beth Israel Hospital

Form a group of four to five people and reread this chapter's opening *Real World Challenge* (both the introduction and the conclusion) about how Beth Israel Hospital dealt with its financial challenges. Decide who will record the group's ideas, and discuss the four questions below. Be prepared to share your insights with the class.

Questions

1. In what ways were equity, equality, and need norms illustrated in this story?
2. What types of fairness perceptions are relevant to the story? How so?
3. Would the actions taken by Beth Israel Hospital build or undermine trust? With whom?
4. How could the actions taken by Beth Israel Hospital create a competitive advantage for the organization?

VIDEO CASES

Now What?

Imagine that a coworker is complaining to you about being upset after learning that another coworker is being paid more despite the complaining coworker being at the company a year longer. *What do you say or do?* Go to this chapter's "Now What?" video, watch the challenge video, and choose a response. Be sure to also view the outcomes of the two responses you didn't choose.

Discussion Questions

1. Which aspects of organizational behavior discussed in this chapter are illustrated in these videos? Explain your answer.
2. How is ethics illustrated in these videos? Explain your answer.
3. As a manager, how else might you handle this situation?

(Continued)

Workplace | Recycline Preserve: Strategy and the Partnership Advantage

When Recycline set out to differentiate itself from conventional consumer goods manufacturers, the company had no idea how the public would perceive its green marketing efforts. The company began in 1996 when founder Eric Hudson designed an innovative toothbrush out of all-recycled material. Today, Recycline's eco-friendly product line, Preserve, includes a range of personal care items, tableware, and kitchen goods.

Recycline's materials may be recycled, but its strategy is completely new. By offering products that makes consumers feel good about their purchases, Recycline not only delivers higher value products but also introduces fresh ideas in the industry. The company's partnership with Stonyfield Farm is a good example. During one Earth Day in Boston, an employee from Stonyfield approached Recycline to ask if the company had a use for scrap plastic from its yogurt containers. Recycline immediately saw the benefit of working with Stonyfield Farm, and now the scrap plastic is used to create Preserve brand products including toothbrushes and razors.

Although the partnership with Stonyfield Farm has yielded amazing results, Recycline wouldn't be where it is today without Whole Foods. "Our company was born in the natural channel," noted C. A. Webb, Recycline's director of marketing. "Whole Foods has been our number one customer. Not only have they done an amazing job of telling our story in their stores, they are the ultimate retail partner for us because they are so trusted. Customers have a sense that when they enter a Whole Foods market, every product has been carefully hand selected in accordance with Whole Food's mission."

In 2007, Whole Foods and Recycline launched a line of kitchenware products that included colanders, cutting boards, mixing bowls, and storage containers. "Together we did the competitive research, we speced out the products, and we developed the pricing strategy and designs," Webb said. "It created less risk on both sides."

Through its various partnerships, Recycline was able to take an untested product and sell it at the nation's largest and most respected natural foods store. Whole Foods in turn used its experience and resources to ensure the product sold well. "We gave Whole Foods a twelve-month exclusive on the line," Webb said, "which in turn gave them a great story to tell."

Discussion Questions

1. What is your perception of CEO Eric Hudson? On what do you base your perception?
2. What is the public's perception of green products according to Marketing Director C. A. Webb? Why do some people have that perception, and what can Recycline do to change it?
3. To what do you attribute Recycline's success?

DO WHAT

CENGAGENOW™ includes **teaching and learning resources** to supplement the text, and is designed specifically to **help students "think like managers"** by engaging and challenging them to think critically about managerial situations. **CengageNOW uses today's technology to improve the skills** of tomorrow's managers.

END NOTES

[1]Based on Cullen, K. (2009, March 12). A Head with a Heart. *The Boston Globe.* Available online: http://www.boston.com/news/local/massachusetts/articles/2009/03/12/a_head_with_a_heart/; Cooney, E. (2009). Sparing 450 Jobs at Beth Israel. *The Boston Globe.* Available online: http://www.boston.com/news/local/massachusetts/articles/2009/03/19/sparing_450_jobs_at_beth _israel/; Ribbler, J. (2009). Paul Levy of Beth Israel Deaconess Medical Center Inspires Execs, Employees to Share Sacrifice and Wins Ribby Award. Available online: http://media-proinc.com/paul-levy-of-beth-israel-deaconess-medical-center-inspires-execs-employees-to-share-sacrifice-and-wins-ribby-award/.

[2]Ross, L., & Nisbett, R. E. (1991). *The Person and the Situation: Perspectives of Social Psychology.* New York: McGraw-Hill.

[3]Bartlett, F. C. (1932). *Remembering: A Study in Experimental and Social Psychology.* Cambridge, England: Cambridge University Press.

[4]Babcock, P. (2006, September 3). Backlash Discrimination Lasts Five Years After 9/11. *HR Magazine.*

[5]Dion, K. K., Berscheid, E., & Walster, E. (1972).What Is Beautiful Is Good. *Journal of Personality and Social Psychology, 24,* 285–290.

[6]Mendonca, L., & Miller, M. (2007, November). Crafting a Message That Sticks: An Interview with Chip Heath. *The McKinsey Quarterly.* Available online: http://www.mckinseyquarterly.com/Governance/Leadership/Crafting_a_message_that_sticks_An_interview_with_Chip_Heath_2062.

[7]Denrell, J. (2005). Why Most People Disapprove of Me: Experience Sampling in Impression Formation. *Psychological Review, 112*(4), 951–978.

[8]Kammrath, L. K., Ames, D. R., & Scholer, A. A. (2007). Keeping Up Impressions: Inferential Rules for Impression Change Across the Big Five. *Journal of Experimental Social Psychology, 43*(3), 450–457.

[9]See Ambady, N., & Rosenthal, R. (1993). Half a Minute: Predicting Teacher Evaluations from Thin Slices of Nonverbal Behavior and Physical Attractiveness. *Journal of Personality and Social Psychology, 64,* 431–441.

[10]Lampton, W. (1999). *The Complete Communicator.* Franklin, TN: Hillsboro Press.

[11]Berry, D. S., Pennebaker, J. W., Mueller, J. S., & Hiller, W. S. (1997). Linguistic Bases of Social Perception. *Personality and Social Psychology Bulletin, 23*(5), 526–537.

[12]DePaulo, B. M. (1992). Nonverbal Behavior and Self-Presentation. *Psychological Bulletin, 111,* 203–243; Riggio,

R. E., & Friedman, H. S. (1986). Impression Formation: The Role of Expressive Behavior. *Journal of Personality and Social Psychology, 50,* 421–427.

[13]Moosad, G. (2009, April 21). 16 Tips to Make a Great First Impression. Available online: http://ezinearticles.com/?16-Tips-to-Make-a-Great-First-Impression&id=2250755.

[14]Lampton, W. (1999). *The Complete Communicator.* Franklin, TN: Hillsboro Press.

[15]Moosad, G. (2009, April 21). 16 Tips to Make a Great First Impression. Available online: http://ezinearticles.com/?16-Tips-to-Make-a-Great-First-Impression&id=2250755.

[16]Kelley, H. H. (1950). The Warm-Cold Variable in First Impressions of Persons. *Journal of Personality, 18,* 431–439.

[17]Wiseman, R. (2004). *The Luck Factor: The Four Essential Principles.* New York: Miramax.

[18]King, A. S. (1971). Self-Fulfilling Prophecies in Training the Hard-Core: Supervisors' Expectations and the Underprivileged Workers' Performance. *Social Science Quarterly, 52,* 369–378.

[19]Eden, D., & Shani, A. B. (1982). Pygmalion Goes to Boot Camp. *Journal of Applied Psychology, 67,* 194–199.

[20]Eden, D. (1990). Pygmalion Controlling Interpersonal Contrast Effects: Whole Group Gain from Raising Expectations. *Journal of Applied Psychology, 75,* 394–398.

[21]Oz, S., & Eden, D. (1994). Restraining the Golem: Boosting Performance by Changing the Interpretation of Low Scores. *Journal of Applied Psychology, 79,* 744–754; Livingston, J. S. (1969). Pygmalion in Management. *Harvard Business Review, 47,* 81–89.

[22]Oz, S. & Eden, D. (1994). Restraining the Golem: Boosting Performance by Changing the Interpretation of Low Scores. *Journal of Applied Psychology, 79,* 744–754.

[23]Eden, D., & Zuk, Y. (1995). Seasickness as a Self-Fulfilling Prophecy: Raising Self-Efficacy to Boost Performance at Sea. *Journal of Applied Psychology, 80,* 628–635.

[24]Eden, D. (1990). *Pygmalion in Management.* Lexington, MA: Lexington Books/D.C. Heath.

[25]Rosenthal, R., & Jacobson, L. (1968). *Pygmalion in the Classroom.* New York: Holt, Rinehart & Winston; Rosenthal, R. (1974). *On the Social Psychology of the Self-Fulfilling Prophecy: Further Evidence for Pygmalion Effects and Their Mediating Mechanisms.* New York: MSS Modular Publications.

[26]Rosenthal, R. (1993). Interpersonal Expectations: Some Antecedents and Some Consequences. In *Interpersonal Expectations: Theory, Research, and Applications,* ed. P. D. Blanck (pp. 3–24). Cambridge, UK: Cambridge University Press.

[27]Rosenthal, R. (1993). Interpersonal Expectations: Some Antecedents and Some Consequences. In *Interpersonal Expectations: Theory, Research, and Applications,* ed. P. D. Blanck (pp. 3–24). Cambridge, UK: Cambridge University Press.

[28]Eden, D. (1984). Self-Fulfilling Prophecy as a Management Tool: Harnessing Pygmalion. *Academy of Management Review, 9,* 64–73; Eden, D. (1990). *Pygmalion in Management.* Lexington, MA: Lexington Books/D.C. Heath.

[29]Weiner, B. (1974). *Achievement Motivation and Attribution Theory.* Morristown, NJ: General Learning Press; Weiner, B. (1980). *Human Motivation.* New York: Holt, Rinehart & Winston; Weiner, B. (1986). *An Attributional Theory of Motivation and Emotion.* New York: Springer-Verlag.

[30]Kelley, H. H. (1973, February). The Process of Causal Attribution. *American Psychologist,* 107–128.

[31]Lau, R. R., & Russell, D. (1980). Attributions in the Sports Pages. *Journal of Personality and Social Psychology, 39,* 29–38.

[32]Weiner, B. (1980). *Human Motivation.* New York: Holt, Rinehart & Winston; Weiner, B. (1986). *An Attributional Theory of Motivation and Emotion* (p. 362). New York: Springer-Verlag.

[33]Gilbert, D. T. (1995). Attribution and Interpersonal Perception. In *Advanced Social Psychology*, ed. A. Tesser (pp. 99–148). New York: McGraw-Hill.

[34]Rubin, Z., & Peplau, L. A. (1975). Who Believes in a Just World? *Journal of Social Issues, 31,* 65–88.

[35]Standing, C., Guilfoyle, A., Lin, C., & Love, P. E. D. (2006). The Attribution of Success and Failure in IT Projects. *Industrial Management and Data Systems, 106*(8), 1148–1165.

[36]Pressley, M., Borkowski, J. G., & Schneider, W. (1987). Cognitive Strategies: Good Strategy Users Coordinate Metacognition and Knowledge. In *Annals of Child Development,* eds. R. Vasta and G. Whilehurst (Vol. 4, pp. 80–129). Greenwich, CT: JAI Press.

[37]Martinko, M.J., Harvey, P. & Dasborough, M.T. (2011). Attribution Theory in the Organizational Sciences: A Case of Unrealized Potential, *Journal of Organizational Behavior,* 32(1), 144-149; Clifford, M. (1984). Thoughts on a Theory of Constructive Failure. *Educational Psychologist, 19,* 108–120.

[38]Martinko, M. J. (1995). *Attribution Theory: An Organizational Perspective.* Delray Beach, FL: St. Lucie Press.

[39]Schunk, D. H. (1983). Ability Versus Effort Attributional Feedback: Differential Effects on Self-Efficacy and Achievement. *Educational Psychology, 75,* 848–856.

[40]Martinko, M. J. (1995). *Attribution Theory: An Organizational Perspective.* Delray Beach, FL: St. Lucie Press.

[41]Lee, F., Peterson, C., & Tiedens, L. Z. (2004). Mea Culpa: Predicting Stock Prices from Organizational Attributions. *Personality and Social Psychology Bulletin, 30*(12), 1636–1649.

[42]Mendonca, L., & Miller, M. (2007, November). Crafting a Message That Sticks: An Interview with Chip Heath. *The McKinsey Quarterly.* Available online: http://www.mckinseyquarterly.com /Governance/Leadership/Crafting_a_message_that_sticks_An _interview_with_Chip_Heath_2062.

[43]Mendonca, L., & Miller, M. (2007, November). Crafting a Message That Sticks: An Interview with Chip Heath. *The McKinsey Quarterly.* Available online: http://www.mckinseyquarterly.com /Governance/Leadership/Crafting_a_message_that_sticks_An _interview_with_Chip_Heath_2062.

[44]Albert, R. D. (1983). The Intercultural Sensitizer or Culture Assimilator: A Cognitive Approach. In *Handbook of Intercultural Training,* eds. D. Landis and R. S. Brislin (Vol. 2, pp. 186–217). New York: Pergamon Press.

[45]Salzman, M. (1995). Attributional Discrepancies and Bias in Cross-Cultural Interactions. *Journal of Multicultural Counseling and Development, 23*(3), 181–193.

[46]Albert, R. A., & Triandis, H. C. (1979). Cross Cultural Training: A Theoretical Framework and Observations. In *Bilingual Multicultural Education and the Professional from Theory to Practice,* eds. H. Trueba and C. Barnett-Mizrahi. Rowley, MA: Newbury House.

[47]Salzman, M. (1995). Attributional Discrepancies and Bias in Cross-Cultural Interactions. *Journal of Multicultural Counseling and Development, 23*(3), 181–193.

[48]Matsumoto, D. & Juang. L. (2012). Culture and Psychology (5th ed.). Independence, KY: Wadsworth Publishing; Albert, R. A., & Triandis, H. C. (1979). Cross Cultural Training: A Theoretical Framework and Observations. In *Bilingual Multicultural Education and the Professional from Theory to Practice,* eds. H. Trueba and C. Barnett-Mizrahi. Rowley, MA: Newbury House.

[49]Miller, J. G. (1984). Culture and the Development of Everyday Social Explanation. *Journal of Personality and Social Psychology, 46,* 961–978.

[50]Morris, M. W., & Peng, K. (1994). Culture and Cause: American and Chinese Attributions for Social and Physical Events. *Journal of Personality and Social Psychology, 67,* 949–971.

[51]Markus, H. R., & Kitayama, S. (1991). Culture and the Self: Implications for Cognition, Emotion, and Motivation. *Psychological Review, 98,* 224–253.

[52]Greenberg, J. (1987). A Taxonomy of Organizational Justice Theories. *Academy of Management Review, 12,* 9–22.

[53]Lind, E. A., & Tyler, T. R. (1988). *The Social Psychology of Procedural Justice.* New York: Plenum.

[54]Cropanzano, R., Goldman, B., & Folger, R. (2004). Deontic Justice: The Role of Moral Principles in Workplace Fairness. *Journal of Organizational Behavior, 24*(8), 1019; Folger, R. (2001). Fairness as Deonance. In *Research in Social Issues in Management,* eds. S. Gilliland, D. D. Steiner, and D. P. Skarlicki (pp. 3–31). Greenwich, CT: Information Age; Folger, R., & Cropanzano, R. (1998). *Organizational Justice and Human Resource Management.* Thousand Oaks, CA: Sage; Folger, R., & Cropanzano, R. (2001). Fairness Theory: Justice as Accountability. In *Advances in Organizational Justice,* eds. J. Greenberg and R. Cropanzano (pp. 89–118). Stanford, CA: Stanford University Press; Folger, R., Cropanzano, R., & Goldman, B. (2005). What Is the Relationship Between Justice and Morality? In *Handbook of Organizational Justice,* eds. J. Greenberg and J. A. Colquitt (pp. 215–246). Mahwah, NJ: Erlbaum.

[55]Turillo, C. J., Folger, R., Lavelle, J. J., Umphress, E. E., & Gee, J. O. (2002). Is Virtue Its Own Reward? Self-Sacrificial Decisions for the Sake of Fairness. *Organizational Behavior and Human Decision Processes, 89,* 839–865.

[56]Folger, R., & Cropanzano, R. (1998). *Organizational Justice and Human Resource Management.* Thousand Oaks, CA: Sage; Folger, R., & Cropanzano, R. (2001). Fairness Theory: Justice as Accountability. In *Advances in Organizational Justice,* eds. J. Greenberg and R. Cropanzano (pp. 89–118). Stanford, CA: Stanford University Press.

[57]E.g., Greenberg, J. (1990). Employee Theft as a Response to Underemployment Inequity: The Hidden Costs of Pay Cuts. *Journal of Applied Psychology, 75,* 561–568; Greenberg, J. (1998). The Cognitive Geometry of Employee Theft: Negotiating "The Line" Between Taking and Stealing. In *Dysfunctional Behavior in Organizations,* eds. R. W. Griffin, A. O'Leary-Kelly, and J. M. Collins (Vol. 2, pp. 147–193). Stamford, CT: JAI; Greenberg, J. (2002). Who Stole the Money and When? Individual and Situational Determinants of Employee Theft. *Organizational Behavior and*

Human Decision Processes, 89, 985–1003; Colquitt, J., & Greenberg, J. (2003). Organizational Justice: A Fair Assessment of the State of the Literature. In *Organizational Behavior: The State of the Science,* ed. J. Greenberg (2nd ed., pp. 165–210). Mahwah, NJ: Lawrence Erlbaum.

[58]Wallace, J. C., Edwards, B. D., Mondore, S., & Finch, D. M. (2008). The Interactive Effects of Litigation Intentions and Procedural Justice Climate on Employee–Employer Litigation. *Journal of Managerial Issues, 20,* 313–326.

[59]Latham, G. P., & McCauley, C. D. (2005). Leadership in the Private Sector: Yesterday Versus Tomorrow. In *The Twenty-First Century Manager*, ed. C. Cooper. Oxford, England: Oxford University Press.

[60]Greenberg, J., & Bies, R. J. (1992). Establishing the Role of Empirical Studies of Organizational Justice in Philosophical Inquiries into Business Ethics. *Journal of Business Ethics, 11,* 97–108.

[61]Treviño, L. K., & Weaver, G. R. (2001). Organizational Justice and Ethics Program Follow Through: Influences on Employees' Helpful and Harmful Behavior. *Business Ethics Quarterly, 11*(4), 651–671.

[62]Treviño, L. K., & Weaver, G. R. (1998). Punishment in Organizations: Descriptive and Normative Perspectives. In *Managerial Ethics: Moral Management of People and Processes,* ed. M. Schminke (pp. 99–114). Mahwah, NJ: Lawrence Erlbaum.

[63]Treviño, L. K., Weaver, G. R., Gibson, D., & Toffler, B. (1999). Managing Ethics and Legal Compliance: What Works and What Hurts. *California Management Review, 41*(2), 131–151.

[64]For a more thorough discussion of organizational justice, see Colquitt, J. A., Greenberg, J., & Scott, B. A. (2005). Organizational Justice: Where Do We Stand? In *Handbook of Organizational Justice*, eds. J. Greenberg and J. A. Colquitt (pp. 589–620). Mahwah, NJ: Lawrence Erlbaum; Greenberg, J., & Cropanzano, R. (Eds.). (2001). *Advances in Organizational Justice.* Stanford, CA: Stanford University Press.

[65]Deutsch, M. (1975). Equity, Equality, and Need: What Determines Which Value Will Be Used as the Basis for Distributive Justice? *Journal of Social Issues, 31,* 137–149.

[66]Adams, J. S. (1965). Inequity in Social Exchange. *Advances in Experimental Social Psychology, 62,* 335–343.

[67]Carrell, M. R., & Dittrich, J. E. (1978). Equity Theory: The Recent Literature, Methodological Considerations, and New Directions. *Academy of Management Review, 3*(2), 202–210.

[68]Adams, J. S. (1965). Inequity in Social Exchange. *Advances in Experimental Social Psychology, 62,* 335–343.

[69]Carrell, M. R., & Dittrich, J. E. (1978). Equity Theory: The Recent Literature, Methodological Considerations, and New Directions. *Academy of Management Review, 3*(2), 202–210.

[70]Carrell, M. R., & Dittrich, J. E. (1978). Equity Theory: The Recent Literature, Methodological Considerations, and New Directions. *Academy of Management Review, 3*(2), 202–210.

[71]Sweeney, P. D. (1990). Distributive Justice and Pay Satisfaction: A Field Test of an Equity Theory Prediction. *Journal of Business and Psychology, 4*(3), 329–341.

[72]Gergen, K. J., Morse, S. J., & Bode, K. A. (1974, July–September). Overpaid or Overworked? Cognitive and Behavioral Reactions to Inequitable Rewards. *Journal of Applied Social Psychology, 4*(3), 259–274.

[73]McDowell, W. C., Boyd, N. G., & Bowler, W. M. (2007). Overreward and the Impostor Phenomenon. *Journal of Managerial Issues, 15,* 82–96.

[74]Bowditch, J. L., & Buono, A. F. (1997). *A Primer on Organizational Behavior* (4th ed.). New York: John Wiley & Sons.

[75]Singh, P. (2002). Strategic Reward Systems at Southwest Airlines. *Compensation and Benefits Review, 34*(2), 28–33.

[76]Leventhal, G. S. (1980). What Should Be Done with Equity Theory? New Approaches to the Study of Fairness in Social Relationships. In *Social Exchange: Advances in Theory and Research,* eds. K. Gergen, M. Greenberg, & R. Willis (pp. 27–55). New York: Plenum; Thibaut, J., & Walker, L. (1975). *Procedural Justice: A Psychological Analysis.* Hillsdale, NJ: Lawrence Erlbaum.

[77] Sources: Leventhal, G. S. (1976). The distribution of rewards and resources in groups and organizations. In L. Berkowitz & W. Walster (Eds.), *Advances in experimental social psychology* (Vol. 9, pp. 91–131). New York: Academic Press; Leventhal, G. S. (1980). What should be done with equity theory? New approaches to the study of fairness in social relationships. In K. Gergen, M. Greenberg, & R. Willis (Eds.), *Social exchanges: Advances in theory and research* (pp. 27–55). New York: Plenum; Thibaut, J., & Walker, L. (1975). *Procedural justice: A psychological analysis.* Hillsdale, NJ: Erlbaum.

[78]Leventhal, G. S. (1980). What Should Be Done with Equity Theory? New Approaches to the Study of Fairness in Social Relationships. In *Social Exchanges: Advances in Theory and Research,* eds. K. Gergen, M. Greenberg, and R. Willis (pp. 27–55, p. 44). New York: Plenum.

[79]See Lind, E. A., & Tyler, T. R. (1988). *The Social Psychology of Procedural Justice.* New York: Plenum.

[80]Keller, S., & Ailen, C. (2008). *The Inconvenient Truth About Change Management.* New York: McKinsey.

[81]Bies, R. J. (2001). Interactional (In)justice: The Sacred and the Profane. In *Advances in Organizational Justice,* eds. J. Greenberg and R. Cropanzano (pp. 89–118). Stanford, CA: Stanford University Press.

[82]Greenberg, J. (1990). Employee Theft as a Reaction to Underpayment Inequity: The Hidden Cost of Pay Cuts. *Journal of Applied Psychology, 75*(5), 561–568.

[83]Colquitt, J. A. (2001). On the Dimensionality of Organizational Justice: A Construct Validation of a Measure. *Journal of Applied Psychology, 86,* 386–400; Colquitt, J. A., Conlon, D. E., Wesson, M. J., Porter, C. O., & Ng, K. Y. (2001). Justice at the Millennium: A Meta-Analytic Review of 25 Years of Organizational Justice Research. *Journal of Applied Psychology, 86*(3), 425–445.

[84]Greenberg, J. (1993). The Social Side of Fairness: Interpersonal and Informational Classes of Organizational Justice. In *Justice in the Workplace,* ed. R. Cropanzano (Vol. 1, pp. 79–103). Hillsdale, NJ: Lawrence Erlbaum Associates.

[85]Aryee, S., Chen, Z., Sun, L., & Debrah, Y. (2007, January). Antecedents and Outcomes of Abusive Supervision: Test of a Trickle-Down Model. *Journal of Applied Psychology, 92*(1), 191–201.

[86]Baron, R. A., & Neuman, J. H. (1996). Workplace Violence and Workplace Aggression: Evidence on Their Relative Frequency and Potential Causes. *Aggressive Behavior, 22,* 161–173.

[87]Truxillo, D. M., Bodner, T. E., Bertolino, M., Bauer, T. N., & Yonce, C. A. (2009). Effects of Explanations on Applicant Reactions: A Meta-Analytic Review. *International Journal of Selection and Assessment, 17,* 346–361.

[88]McColl-Kennedy, J.R., Sparks, B.A. & Nguyen, D.T. (2011). Customer's Angry Voice: Targeting Employees or the Organization? *Journal of Business Research, 64*(7), 707–713.

[89]Blodgett, J. G., Hill, D. J., & Tax, S. S. (1997). The Effects of Distributive, Procedural and Interactional Justice on Postcomplaint Behavior. *Journal of Retailing, 73*(2), 185–210.

[90]Folger, R., Ford, R.C., Bardes, M. & Dickson, D. (2010) Triangle Model of Fairness: Investigating Spillovers and Reciprocal Transfers, *Journal of Service Management, 21*(4), 515–530.

[91]Mayer, R. C., Davis, J. H., & Schoorman, F. D. (1995). An Integrative Model of Organizational Trust. *Academy of Management Review, 20*(3), 709–734.

[92]Knowledge @ Wharton. (2006). Promises, Lies, and Apologies: Is It Possible to Restore Trust? Available online: http://knowledge .wharton.upenn.edu/article.cfm?articleid=1532&CFID=2057007 5&CFTOKEN=84396066&jsessionid=a83063faeb1404ef3119741 d49522353b445.

[93]Macneil, I. R. (1980). *The New Social Contract: An Inquiry into Modern Contractual Relations.* New Haven, CT: Yale University Press.

[94]Colquitt, J. A., Scott, B. A., & LePine, J. A. (2007). Trust, Trustworthiness, and Trust Propensity: A Meta-Analytic Test of Their Unique Relationships with Risk Taking and Job Performance. *Journal of Applied Psychology, 92*, 909–927.

[95]reputationRx. (2010). CEO Quotes. Available online: http:// www.reputationrx.com/Default.aspx/CEOREPUTATION /CEOQUOTES.

[96]McKnight, D. H., Cummings, L. L., & Chervany, N. L. (1998). Initial Trust Formation in New Organizational Relationships. *Academy of Management Review, 23,* 473–490.

[97]Davis, J. H., Schoorman, F. D., Mayer, R. C. & Tan, H. H. (2000). The Trusted General Manager and Business Unit Performance: Empirical Evidence of a Competitive Advantage. *Strategic Management Journal, 21,* 563–576.

[98]Barbian, J. (2002, June). Short Shelf Life. *Training,* 52.

[99]Tahmincioglu, E. (2004, December). Back from the Brink. *Workforce Management,* 32–37.

[100]Bernthal, P. (1997). *A Survey of Trust in the Workplace.* Pittsburgh, PA: DDI Center for Applied Behavioral Research.

[101]Frost, P. J. (2003). *Toxic Emotions at Work: How Compassionate Managers Handle Pain and Conflict.* Boston, MA: Harvard Business School Press.

[102]Tahmincioglu, E. (2006, January 16). On the Same Flight Plan. *Workforce Management,* 22–28.

[103]Tahmincioglu, E. (2006, January 16). On the Same Flight Plan. *Workforce Management,* 22–28.

[104]Nichols, J. (2005, October 2). New US Airways Making Sure Disparate Cultures Will Fly as 1. AZCentral.com. Available online: http://www.azcentral.com/arizonarepublic/business /articles/1002amwest-culture.html?&wired.

[105]Nichols, J. (2005, October 2). New US Airways Making Sure Disparate Cultures Will Fly as 1. AZCentral.com. Available online: http://www.azcentral.com/arizonarepublic/business /articles/1002amwest-culture.html?&wired.

[106]Argyris, C. (1960). *Understanding Organisational Behavior.* Homewood, IL: Dorsey Press.

[107]Makin, P., Cooper, C. L., & Cox, C. J. (1996). *Organizations and the Psychological Contract.* New York: Praeger.

[108]Prêt à Manger. (2010). Working as a Team Member. Pret.com. Available online: http://www.pret.com/jobs/working_shop/; Prêt à Manger. (2010). Working at Pret. Pret.com. Available online: http://www.pret.com/jobs/.

[109]Rousseau, D. M. (1989). Psychological and Implied Contracts in Organizations. *Employee Rights and Responsibilities Journal,* 2, 121–139; Schalk, R., & Rousseau, D. M. (2001). Psychological Contracts in Employment. In *Handbook of Industrial, Work and Organizational Psychology,* eds. N. Anderson, D. S. Ones, H. K. Sinangil, and C. Viswesvaran (Vol. 2, Organizational Psychology). Reprinted in Yochanan, A., Bournois, F., & Boje, D. (2008). *Managerial Psychology.* London: Sage.

[110]Robinson, S., & Rousseau, D. (1994). Violating the Psychological Contract: Not the Exception but the Norm. *Journal of Organizational Behavior, 16,* 289–298.

[111]Robinson, S., & Wolfe-Morrison, E. (1995). Psychological Contracts and Organizational Citizenship Behavior: The Effect of Unfulfilled Obligations on Civic Virtue Behavior. *Journal of Organizational Behavior, 16,* 289–298.

[112]Nicholson, N., & Johns, G. (1985). The Absence Culture and the Psychological Contract. *Academy of Management Review, 10,* 397–407.

[113]Morrison E. W., & Robinson, S. L. (1997). When Employees Feel Betrayed: A Model of How Psychological Contract Violation Develops. *Academy of Management Review, 22,* 226–256.

[114]Turnley, W. H., & Feldman, D. C. (1999). A Discrepancy Model of Psychological Contract Violations. *Human Resource Management Review, 9*(3), 367–386; Turnley, W. H., & Feldman, D. C. (1999). The Impact of Psychological Contract Violations on Exit, Voice, Loyalty and Neglect. *Human Relations, 52*(7), 895–922.

[115]Rousseau, D. M. (2001). The Idiosyncratic Deal: Flexibility Versus Fairness. *Organizational Dynamics, 29*(4), 260–273.

[116]Ang, S., Tan, M. L., & Ng, K. Y. (2000). Psychological Contracts in Singapore. In *Psychological Contracts in Employment: Cross-National Perspectives,* eds. D. Rousseau and R. Schalk. Newbury Park, CA: Sage.

[117]Robinson, S. L. (1996). Trust and Breach of the Psychological Contract. *Administrative Science Quarterly, 41,* 574–599.

[118]Cullen, K. (2009, March 12). A Head with a Heart. *The Boston Globe.* Available online: http://www.boston.com/news/local /massachusetts/articles/2009/03/12/a_head_with_a_heart/.

[119]Cooney, E. (2009). Sparing 450 Jobs at Beth Israel. *The Boston Globe.* Available online: http://www.boston .com/news/local/massachusetts/articles/2009/03/19/ sparing_450_jobs_at_beth_israel/.

[120]Cooney, E. (2009). Sparing 450 Jobs at Beth Israel. *The Boston Globe.* Available online: http://www.boston .com/news/local/massachusetts/articles/2009/03/19/ sparing_450_jobs_at_beth_israel/.

CHAPTER 7

Motivating Behavior

The Walt Disney Company strives to provide outstanding customer service in its theme parks. Disney tries to motivate employees to provide the four service basics of projecting a positive image and energy, being courteous and respectful to all guests, staying in character, and going beyond expectations.

KELLY-MOONEY PHOTOGRAPHY/CORBIS

REAL WORLD CHALLENGE

KEEPING DISNEY CAST MEMBERS MOTIVATED

After beginning in 1923 as an animation studio, The Walt Disney Company has become one of the biggest Hollywood studios. In addition, Disney owns a cruise line, and several television networks, including ABC and ESPN, and eleven theme parks known to millions worldwide.[1] The company strives to provide legendary customer service in its theme parks. Theme park employees are called "cast members" and are taught that the ultimate goal is guest happiness and that no matter what role they play, they are expected to smile, project a positive image, and be friendly.[2]

Disney wants to motivate its cast members to provide the four service basics of projecting a positive image and energy, being courteous and respectful to all guests, staying in character and play the part, and going above and beyond expectations, and asks you for suggestions. After reading this chapter, you should have some good ideas.

LEARNING OBJECTIVES

1. Describe what affects motivation.

2. Explain why different people are motivated by different things.

3. Discuss the challenges of motivating people from different cultures.

4. Describe how the motivational effects of goal setting can be maximized.

5. Discuss ethical issues in goal setting.

6. Give examples of when you would use different motivational techniques.

WHAT IS MOTIVATION?

As a manager and future professional, you should be concerned about motivation for at least three reasons. First, if you are in charge of achieving business goals or executing business strategies, you must be able to motivate the people who work with you to attain goals or execute strategies. Second, you must understand your own motivations because that is the first step to obtaining the things that you most value. This type of self-understanding will enable you to better manage your career. Third, understanding the needs, values, and motivations of your employees will help you to better recruit, select, train, retain, and develop your staff to perform their best.

So what does it mean to be motivated? When you plan to complete a class assignment, does it always go as you expect? Probably not—sometimes you may get distracted or find yourself unmotivated to finish the assignment. Effective managers understand that good plans and strategies are only the foundations of high performance. Strategies, plans, and organizational efforts are not translated into action without motivation. ***Motivation*** is the intensity of a person's desire to begin or to continue engaging in the pursuit of a goal. Understanding motivation is essential to effective management.

Why is motivation important? One reason is that motivated workers are more productive.[3] High performance requires both ability and motivation. Someone who is capable of performing a task will only do it well if she or he is motivated to do so. Higher employee motivation can also lead to faster and better quality work.[4] More motivated employees work more safely, provide more suggestions for improvement, and are less likely to quit.[5] Each of these factors can give a company a competitive advantage over other firms with less motivated workforces. As a manager, you will also have a much easier job supervising motivated rather than unmotivated workers. Clearly, both you and your organization can realize a number of benefits if you are able to increase employee motivation.

Anything that arouses, maintains, or channels a person's efforts toward a goal to fulfill unmet wants or needs affects motivation, as shown in Figure 7-1. As we discuss next, these factors come from a variety of sources in the individual, job, and work environment.

Think about current or past jobs you have held, or employees you have seen in various stores. Why did some employees come to work early, try hard, or take on additional work while others did the minimum amount to get by?

motivation

The intensity of a person's desire to begin or continue engaging in the pursuit of a goal

Figure 7-1
Basic Motivation Process

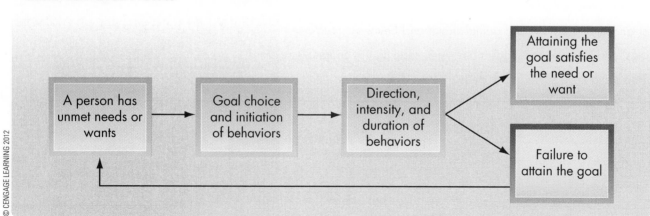

Understanding motivation helps managers to ensure that all employees do their best and work hard toward company goals. The purpose of this chapter is to show you how to use different theories of motivation, reinforcement, and rewards to motivate yourself and your employees, and to become a more effective leader and manager. It will also help you understand some of the different workplace behaviors you see others engage in.

FROM WHERE DOES MOTIVATION COME?

Understanding *why* people do what they do is an important part of motivating them. Motivation is influenced by the person, the job, and the work environment. We next discuss each of these.

Individual Characteristics

The reason two coworkers who do the same job can feel different levels of motivation is because people are not all the same. Different things motivate different people. People have different abilities, needs, personalities, values, and self-concepts—this is known in psychology as the *law of individual differences*. Because people are diverse, there is no one best way to motivate others.

What makes work motivating? Work can be motivating because it:

- Is interesting
- Is challenging
- Allows the development of new skills
- Provides a needed income or benefit such as health care
- Provides prestige and status
- Keeps us busy
- Provides social contact
- Is a way to give back to the community and help others

Work can be motivating in other ways as well. More junior employees might be motivated by the prospect of growth and career advancement, but this may have relatively little appeal to employees nearing retirement.[6] Senior employees may be motivated by mentoring others and having a chance to pass on their expertise. It is clear from the following conversation that the things that motivate these two workers are quite different.

Nancy: "I can't believe you quit your job. Your work seemed so interesting, and you always had a chance to learn new things. I like jobs that challenge me. Your new job sounds so boring that I'd go crazy."

Chris: "Well, it is tedious work, but it pays better than any other job around."

In this example, money is a strong motivator for Chris, but Nancy places higher value on challenging herself and doing a variety of tasks. This example highlights the fact that to motivate others, it is critical that you first understand what does and what does not motivate them.

An easy mistake to make when trying to motivate others is assuming that the same things that motivate you also motivate them. People are diverse in the personality, values, needs, abilities, cultures, and interests they bring to their jobs. These individual characteristics motivate us to work harder at some

law of individual differences
People have different abilities, needs, personalities, values, and self-concepts

SO WHAT

Good managers vary their motivational methods based on what works best for a particular employee and situation.

Table 7-1

Individual Characteristics Influencing Motivation

Goals	Needs and Values	Attitudes
Productivity	Achievement	Oneself
Quality	Friendship	Coworkers
Learning new things	Approval of others	Supervisor
Project accomplishment	Power	Job
Promotion	Hard work	Career
New product development	Ethical behavior	Work-life balance

things than at others. Individual characteristics are internal motivational factors that are a part of who we are and compel us to try harder and exert more effort toward reaching some goals as compared to others. Table 7-1 provides examples of different goals, needs and values, and attitudes that influence our motivation to do certain things.

The starting point for motivated employees is hiring people whose individual characteristics lead to high motivation on the job. A job requiring high-quality work will not be as motivating to someone who lacks attention to detail as it will to a conscientious, detail-oriented person. In your own career, finding a job that has the potential to fulfill your needs, meet your goals, and complement your attitudes can help you to maintain your motivation as well.

Theory X and Theory Y

Theory X
Belief that most people dislike work and will try to avoid it whenever possible

Theory Y
Belief that people can enjoy responsibility and work, and are able to make good decisions and exercise self-direction

Do you believe that in general other people are lazy or hardworking? Different people have different beliefs about the nature of other people. Watching how managers interact with their subordinates gave Douglas McGregor the idea that people hold either a generally negative view, called *Theory X*, or a generally positive view, called *Theory Y*, about others.[7] Theory X managers assume that most workers have little ambition, and believe that employees dislike work and will attempt to avoid it whenever possible. Not surprisingly, Theory X managers use coercion and threats to motivate employees to achieve the firm's goals. Theory Y managers, on the other hand, assume that the average person enjoys responsibility and can make good decisions. Theory Y managers motivate employees by giving them opportunities to develop their skills and abilities and to fulfill their potential.

McGregor personally subscribed to Theory Y and felt that participatory decision making, challenging and responsible jobs, and good workgroup relations maximize employees' motivation and effort. However, people differ in their work ethic, and effective managers have held both Theory X and Theory Y views. The important point is that although our personal characteristics can influence our own motivation to do things, understanding our alignment with Theory X or Theory Y can also influence how we view and motivate others. Being aware that we have this bias can help us to increase our objectivity in understanding ourselves and in choosing how best to motivate other people.

Consistent with Theory Y, some firms focus on creating a culture in which employees can flourish and find meaning in their work. Kimley-Horn is one of the nation's most comprehensive and best-respected engineering and land planning firms. It has won numerous awards for excellence and believes that its core purpose is "to provide an environment for our people to flourish."[8] Growing professionally, having fun with colleagues, and finding satisfaction in the work are central to the firm's culture and way of doing business.

Characteristics of the Job

Are there some tasks you just do not like to do and others that you enjoy? Think about why you dislike some and like others. The reasons you come up with probably include characteristics of the work—maybe certain types of work are dirty, repetitive, seem unimportant, or feel frustrating because you cannot tell how well you are doing. *Job characteristics* are attributes that describe the nature of the work. Doing a variety of tasks and getting feedback on your performance are job characteristics that many people find motivational. Some job characteristics are naturally more motivational than others. We will discuss a formal theory of job characteristics in more detail later in the chapter.

job characteristics
Attributes that describe the nature of the work

Characteristics of the Work Environment

The *work environment* is the constellation of an organization's rules, management practices, policies, and reward systems. Characteristics of the work environment can influence motivation. Things like supportive supervision and a fun work environment can be motivational. Some organizations create such a positive work environment that employees become passionate about working there. The strong sense of community, deep belief in people, and passion for great food and great service is very motivating to employees of Zingerman's Delicatessen in Ann Arbor, Michigan. As one employee said, "Working here has never felt like a job to me. I'm constantly learning about managing, about food, and about myself."[9]

Technology also influences the work environment by empowering employees—even in fairly low-level jobs.[10] Printer Wordsprint Inc. in Wytheville, Virginia, uses technology to give employees all the information they need to make many decisions without a supervisor.[11] Managers are still necessary, though, especially if employees lack experience, accountability, or motivation. Technology can help monitor employees' productivity and empower employees to make their own decisions, but employees still need to be motivated to do tasks well. Wordsprint motivates employees to take responsibility for decisions that might otherwise be made by a manager by basing a substantial portion

JEFF GREENBERG / ALAMY

Employees of Zingerman's Delicatessen in Ann Arbor, Michigan, are motivated by a strong sense of community, deep belief in people, and passion for great food and service.

"You have to have people who are willing to make decisions and [who] are interested in the big picture." —*Bill Gilmer, Owner of Wordsprint Inc.*

of their pay on individual, departmental, and company productivity. Staffing is essential in ensuring that employees are motivated by a company's work environment. Bill Gilmer, owner of Wordsprint, says, "You have to have people who are willing to make decisions and [who] are interested in the big picture."[12]

We next discuss ways employees' needs can be matched to the nature of the work.

INTERNAL MOTIVATION FACTORS

Remember the saying, "You can lead a horse to water, but you can't make it drink?" Motivation always comes, at least in part, from the individual. We all possess inner needs and are motivated by the desire to fulfill these needs. Next, we will discuss several needs-based theories of motivation and how you can use them to be a more effective manager.

Maslow's Hierarchy of Needs

Although it is of limited usefulness, Abraham Maslow's hierarchy of needs[13] is by far one of the most famous early theories of motivation. Maslow suggested that all people share a hierarchy of needs up which we progress. Basic physiological needs for food, water, and comfort must be met first, and then we address safety and security needs. We then pursue social needs for friendship and belonging, followed by self-esteem needs for self-respect and respect from others. Eventually, we pursue self-actualization needs, including self-fulfillment and the realization of our full potential.

Maslow proposed that once one need in the hierarchy is satisfied, it ceases to motivate behavior and the need at the next level up the hierarchy becomes our motivation. For example, when the basic need for food and clothing is satisfied, we aim for security needs, and so on.

Maslow intended the hierarchy to be a general theory of motivation, but some managerial theorists have enthusiastically adopted it for the workplace. The theory suggests that employees will always tend to want more from their employers. When jobs are secure, they will seek ways of satisfying social needs. If successful, they will then pursue the ultimate end of self-actualization.

Although it appeals to managers because it is simple and intuitive, academic research has not supported Maslow's theory.[14] It remains popular, perhaps because some of the terms such as *self-actualization* have been integrated into everyday language. It is also logical and actionable, giving managers a clear progression of employee needs to address. Nonetheless, little evidence supports the five-tier system, and it is not clear that our needs are activated in that order. We include this theory here because it identifies different categories of needs besides monetary rewards and because it is so popular with managers that you are certain to hear of it again at some point in your career. We want you to be prepared for this by understanding what the theory does and does not do well.

Despite the lack of empirical support for the theory, by identifying the importance of esteem and self-actualization, Maslow helped to increase managers' awareness of the motivating potential of giving employees greater responsibility, challenge, and continuous development—which is consistent with a Theory Y style of management. Maslow's work also has highlighted how needs for security can influence business strategy and performance.

In addition to their negative effects on the exiting employees,[15] downsizings and layoffs create fears about job security, which make it difficult for employees to attend to their jobs and customers. Several studies have shown that such restructuring practices do not yield long-term competitive advantage despite the costs initially saved.[16]

Alderfer's Existence-Relatedness-Growth (ERG) Theory

Clay Alderfer[17] suggests that there are three groups of individual needs:

- *Existence needs*: desires for physical and material well-being, including nutritional and material requirements (e.g., pay, benefits, and working conditions)
- *Relatedness needs*: desires for respect from and relationships with others
- *Growth needs*: a desire to make useful and productive contributions and to have opportunities for personal development

Alderfer's existence needs parallel Maslow's physiological and security needs, his relatedness needs parallel Maslow's social and esteem needs, and his growth needs parallel Maslow's self-actualization needs.

Despite the similarities, however, Alderfer's theory differs from Maslow's in a number of important respects. First, Alderfer believed that it was better to think in terms of a continuum rather than a hierarchy, and he argued that people can move along the continuum in either direction. While Maslow proposed that a satisfied need becomes less important to an individual, Alderfer argued that relatedness or growth needs become *more* important when satisfied. This means that work enriched by organizing employees into teams can continue to motivate employees.

Both Maslow's and Alderfer's theories were developed in the United States, and it is unlikely that the needs fall into the same order in all cultures and countries.[18] It is also unlikely that the order of the needs is the same in one country at different points in time—during periods of war or civil unrest, for example, security needs may take precedence over physiological needs. Different people are also likely to have different hierarchies when it comes to their own needs, as well as different thresholds for meeting their needs at one level. For example, some people may not feel financially secure until they have saved $10 million, while other people may feel quite secure with less than $1 million. These ambiguities make it difficult for managers to base specific actions on either theory.

Nonetheless, it can be helpful for managers to remember that people have different needs. Employees' motivation may be increased by meeting their various needs in creative ways. For example, some companies sponsor volunteer activities in the community or create mentoring programs with local schools, which can fulfill relatedness and growth needs. Umpqua Bank in Portland, Oregon, provides forty hours of paid time each year so that employees can volunteer or become involved in community service.[19] The organization strives to personally touch lives through the Connect Volunteer Network, Community Giving, and Wish Upon a Star programs.[20] Providing training and development programs can also help employees fulfill growth needs, as Verizon does to motivate its employees and enhance their skills. Verizon uses videos, podcasts, blogs, and its enterprise learning-management system to deliver needed information to employees whenever it is needed, wherever they are. The company offers over 14,000 courses in a variety of formats, from classroom to self-directed online learning.[21]

Herzberg's Two-Factor Theory

As early as the late 1950s, scholars recognized that economic rewards alone were insufficient to motivate employees to perform their best. Frederick Herzberg[22] theorized in his two-factor theory[23] that pay and supervisory style do not strongly impact worker satisfaction. At best they are what he called "maintenance" needs or *hygiene factors*. Although hygiene factors such as pay, status, and working conditions produce an acceptable working environment, they do not increase *satisfaction*. However, their absence causes *dissatisfaction*.

Think about this: If you like your supervisor, are you satisfied with your job? If your supervisor is mean, you would likely feel dissatisfied, but usually other factors must be present before you will feel satisfied—opportunities for growth, feelings of achievement, and enjoyable work perhaps. In other words, hygiene factors such as high pay, good supervision, and good working conditions are generally not enough to make us feel satisfied with our jobs. But if pay or working conditions are poor, then we feel dissatisfied. Hygiene factors correspond to Maslow's lower-level physiological, safety, and social needs and Alderfer's existence and relatedness needs.

Herzberg identified a second set of factors, which he called "satisfiers" or *motivators*, which are factors intrinsic to the job that can drive an employee to pursue excellence. Motivators include recognition, responsibility, and growth.[24] The presence of motivators leads to satisfaction and motivation, but their absence does not lead to dissatisfaction. That is, having responsibility and growth opportunities at work makes us feel satisfied, but if these factors are missing, we do not feel dissatisfied. Motivators correspond to Maslow's higher-level needs of esteem and self-actualization and Alderfer's growth needs.

Table 7-2 lists a sampling of motivators and hygiene factors.

Essentially, the two-factor theory draws upon the idea that motivation can be broken down into two distinct needs: *the need to avoid unpleasantness and discomfort* (addressed by hygiene factors) and *the need for personal development* (addressed by motivators). A shortage of the motivators that positively encourage employees will lower satisfaction and cause employees to focus on hygiene factors, which will produce feelings of dissatisfaction if they are missing. As shown in Figure 7-2, motivator factors can increase satisfaction but do not lead to dissatisfaction when absent, while hygiene factors can reduce dissatisfaction but do not lead to satisfaction or positive motivation when present. In other words, the opposite of both "satisfaction" and "dissatisfaction" is "neither satisfied nor dissatisfied." This differs from the traditional view of motivation that satisfaction is the opposite of dissatisfaction, as shown in Figure 7-2.

The most important contribution of Herzberg's two-factor theory of motivation is the idea that motivation comes from the intrinsic value and satisfaction the worker gets from the job itself, not from the conditions surrounding

hygiene factors
Factors such as pay, status, and working conditions that produce an acceptable work environment and whose absence leads to dissatisfaction

motivators
Factors intrinsic to the job that can drive an employee to pursue excellence and whose presence increases satisfaction

SO WHAT
Motivation can come from the intrinsic value of doing the job, not necessarily from the conditions surrounding the job.

Table 7-2

Herzberg's Motivators and Hygiene Factors

Motivators (Satisfiers)	Hygiene Factors (Maintenance Needs)
The work itself	Working conditions
Advancement	Pay
Achievement	Supervision
Responsibility	Status
Growth	Company policies and administration
Recognition	Interpersonal relations with colleagues

© CENGAGE LEARNING 2012

Figure 7-2

Traditional View and Herzberg's View of Motivation

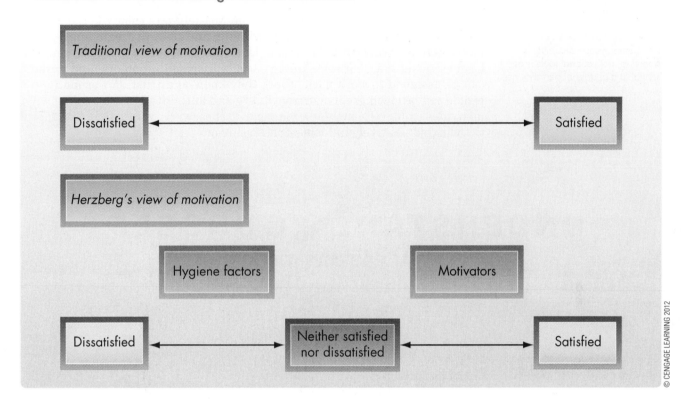

the job.[25] Even if pay and benefits are high, to be motivating a job must also be challenging, interesting, and have opportunities for feelings of achievement. Herzberg's two-factor theory thus highlights the importance of good job design and managers' attending to the motivator factors present in a job.

Although its intuitiveness and simplicity appeals to many managers, scholars have often criticized the two-factor theory.[26] One important issue is the fact that being satisfied and being motivated are different. For example, I might be satisfied with my pay but my pay may not motivate me to work harder. Despite the criticisms and lack of consistent research support, Herzberg's theory continues to influence management practitioners.[27]

McClelland's Needs for Achievement, Affiliation, and Power

David McClelland[28] divides motivation into three needs that influence both employee and leader performance:[29]

- *Need for affiliation*: Wanting to establish and maintain friendly and warm relations with others. People with a high affiliation need tend to be friendly and like to socialize with others. Their interpersonal skills often help them to resolve conflicts and facilitate cooperation within and between groups.
- *Need for achievement*: Wanting to do something better or more efficiently to solve problems, or to master complex tasks. People high in need for achievement prefer tasks of moderate difficulty, enjoy pursuing attainable goals, and like to be recognized.
- *Need for power*: Wanting to control and influence others, or to be responsible for others. People can express a need for power in ways that improve

organizations and societies (a *socialized* power orientation) or by manipulating and exploiting others (a *personalized* power orientation). A socialized power orientation is associated with effective motivation by inspiring others.

The core takeaway for managers from McClelland's theory is the need to first identify what motivates a subordinate, and then to create appropriate motivators for him or her. For example, achievement-motivated workers can be given goals and clear roles and responsibilities. Affiliation-oriented workers can be assigned to work with others they know and trust. Power-motivated people can be given greater responsibility and authority. Understanding what motivates employees enables a manager to choose motivators that will appeal to them and positively influence their behavior.

SO WHAT

There is no one best way to motivate employees—flexibility in applying motivational tools is essential to managerial performance.

UNDERSTAND YOURSELF

WHAT MOTIVATES YOU?

For each of the following fifteen statements, circle the number that most closely agrees with how you feel. Consider your answers in the context of your current job or past work experience.

	Strongly Disagree ←——→ Strongly Agree				
1. I work very hard to continually improve my work performance.	1	2	3	4	5
2. I enjoy competition. I like to win in sports and other things I do.	1	2	3	4	5
3. When working, I often chat with fellow employees about nonwork matters.	1	2	3	4	5
4. I enjoy difficult challenges. At work, I like to take on the hard jobs.	1	2	3	4	5
5. I enjoy being a manager. I like being in charge of things and people.	1	2	3	4	5
6. It is important to me to be liked by other people.	1	2	3	4	5
7. When I am working, I like to know how I am doing and how the work is progressing.	1	2	3	4	5
8. If I disagree with someone, I let them know it. I am not afraid of disagreement.	1	2	3	4	5
9. Many of my coworkers are also my friends. I enjoy spending my leisure time with them.	1	2	3	4	5
10. I typically set realistic goals and tend to achieve them.	1	2	3	4	5
11. It is important to me to get others to agree with my ideas.	1	2	3	4	5
12. I enjoy belonging to clubs, groups, and other organizations.	1	2	3	4	5
13. I enjoy the satisfaction of successfully completing a difficult job.	1	2	3	4	5
14. One of my important objectives is to get more control over events around me.	1	2	3	4	5
15. I would rather work with other people than work alone.	1	2	3	4	5

Scoring: Record your score for each of the fifteen statements on the appropriate line below, putting your response to the first statement on the top left line marked "1," your response to the second statement on the top middle line marked "2," and so on. Then add up each column to learn your achievement, power, and affiliation scores.

Achievement	Power	Affiliation
1. _____	2. _____	3. _____
4. _____	5. _____	6. _____
7. _____	8. _____	9. _____
10. _____	11. _____	12. _____
13. _____	14. _____	15. _____
TOTALS: _____	_____	_____

Question: How do you think your motivations influence the way that you lead or that you will lead in the future?

Source: Reprinted from *Journal of Vocational Behavior*, 9:2, Steers, R. & Braunstein, D. "A Behaviorally Based Measure of Manifest Needs in Work Settings", Pages 251–266, Copyright © 1976, with permission from Elsevier.

GLOBAL ISSUES

MOTIVATING A GLOBAL WORKFORCE

Effectively motivating employees located across the globe is a significant challenge. Managers must be sensitive to cultural differences in values and needs and understand that what is acceptable in one culture may be taboo in another.

The American culture is more individualistic and egocentric than many other cultures. Because American culture values individual achievement, Americans often have a desire to be singled out and praised. In some cultures, people would be embarrassed or even ashamed if they received the attention Americans strive for. In Japan, for example, there is a saying, "It's the nail that sticks up that gets pounded." Motivation and reward programs in the Far East also tend to be more paternal than in the United States. In Indonesia, if a company has a good year, bonuses are not a function of individual performance but rather of each employee's organizational loyalty as measured by the number of years worked with the company, plus the size of his or her family.[32]

Some motivation principles, like treating people with respect, apply equally well around the world. For example, Colgate-Palmolive operates in more than 170 countries and receives about 70 percent of its $7 billion revenues from overseas markets. A truly global company, Colgate expects managers everywhere to show respect for their employees. Colgate-Palmolive's performance-evaluation system, for instance, evaluates how managers exemplify and reinforce respect.[33] Employees from different cultures may differentially value things like equality and individualism, but being treated with fairness and respect resonates globally.

The above *Understand Yourself* feature will help you apply McClelland's theory to yourself and better understand what motivates you.

Motivation is strongly influenced by culture.[30] Most of the motivation theories put into practice today were developed in the United States and focus on Americans, or have been strongly influenced by U.S.-based theories. For example, the strong U.S. emphasis on individualism influenced the expectancy and equity theories of motivation. These theories emphasize rational, individual thought as the primary foundation of motivation rather than the social, collective, or quality-of-life values important in many Asian and Latin American cultures. It is important to remember that these motivation theories are not universal, and reflect primarily American values.[31] This chapter's *Global Issues* feature highlights some of the challenges faced by managers of global employees.

EXTERNAL MOTIVATION FACTORS

Whereas the theories we just discussed focus on which factors or needs *internal* to a person influence motivation, we now turn our attention to how and why different factors *external* to a person, such as job design, empowerment, goals, and reinforcement, influence motivation. Because managers can often influence these external factors, these theories are useful in generating ideas for increasing worker motivation.

Empowerment

One theme shared by the four internal motivation theories we just discussed is the idea that people are often motivated by a sense of achievement and responsibility. This corresponds with Maslow's self-actualization needs, Alderfer's growth needs, Herzberg's motivators, and McClelland's need for achievement. It is common to hear managers describe their employees as "empowered." Workgroups can even have a "culture of empowerment" that enhances their performance.[34]

Empowerment is the degree to which an employee has the authority to make and implement at least some decisions. Empowerment enables employees to use more of their potential, but it also requires a commitment on the part of managers to delegate not just some of their responsibilities, but some of their decision-making authority as well. Managers must then ensure that empowered employees have the skills, abilities, tools, and information to make good decisions. Empowerment is consistent with Theory Y.

The DVD rental company Netflix has high performance standards for its employees as it competes with Blockbuster, Redbox, and Apple to dominate online movie rentals. To keep its talented employees motivated, it pays them generously, focuses employees on clear goals, and empowers them to do what they need to do to reach their goals.[35] It even lets employees take as much vacation time as they want as long as it does not interfere with their work.[36] Patagonia also offers every employee a lot of empowerment, which helps improve employee loyalty.[37]

Technology has helped organizations to empower workers by making better and timelier information available to everyone in the organization. Although some employees are likely to feel more motivated when empowered, other employees may not react positively. Increased responsibility does not motivate everyone. Nonetheless, empowerment can be an important management tool to increase the motivation of many employees. Practical ways to empower others include:[38]

- Articulating a clear vision and goals
- Fostering personal mastery experiences to enhance self-efficacy and build skills
- Modeling successful behaviors
- Sending positive messages and arousing positive emotions in employees
- Connecting employees with the outcomes of their work and giving them feedback
- Building employee confidence by showing competence, honesty, and fairness

Job Design

Managers who have a clear appreciation for different types of employee needs can design jobs to provide different opportunities to fulfill those needs. For example, talented employees with a strong independence need can be given more opportunities to engage in autonomous decision making. Always remember, however, that different employees are motivated by different job characteristics.

So how can we design more motivating jobs? Scholars J. Richard Hackman and Greg R. Oldham developed the job characteristics model to answer this question.

Hackman and Oldham's Job Characteristics Model. Hackman and Oldham's job characteristics model[39] focuses on creating a good match between a person and a job. The ***job characteristics model*** suggests that objective characteristics of the job itself lead to job satisfaction. For example, perceiving that the work one is doing is important can improve motivation and performance.[40]

Hackman and Oldham[41] identified five characteristics on which jobs differ:

1. *Skill variety*: the degree to which the job requires a variety of activities, enabling the worker to use different skills and talents
2. *Task identity*: the degree to which the job requires the worker to complete a whole and identifiable piece of work
3. *Task significance*: the degree to which job performance is important and affects the lives or work of others
4. *Autonomy*: the degree to which the job gives the worker freedom, discretion, and independence in scheduling the work and determining how to do the work
5. *Task feedback*: the degree to which carrying out the job's required activities results in the individual's obtaining direct and clear information about the effectiveness of his or her performance

These five characteristics together determine a job's *motivating potential*.[42] A high motivating potential score alone does not mean that the job is more motivating for everyone. Not everyone wants more variety, responsibility, and so on—some people just want to do their jobs without having to think much about them or put in extra effort. For them, jobs that are stable, less complex, and less demanding (i.e., jobs with a lower motivating potential score) would be more motivating.

Our *growth need strength*, derived from our motivational preferences, such as desire for advancement, identifies the things that motivate us. We then compare a job's motivating potential to our growth need strength score to identify our *job-person match*. Ideally, the motivating potential of a job matches the growth needs of the individual. Managers can improve this match through hiring the right people and by changing the motivating potential of the job.

Hackman and Oldham suggest that if there is a good match between the needs of the person and the characteristics of the job, three critical psychological states can occur in employees:

1. Experienced meaningfulness of work
2. Experienced responsibility for work outcomes
3. Knowledge of results of work activities

According to Hackman and Oldham, these psychological states increase work motivation and job satisfaction. Figure 7-3 illustrates their model.

Although research has generally supported the existence of a positive relationship between the five job characteristics and job satisfaction and the role of growth need strength,[44] conceptual and methodological issues[45] in the research prevent firm conclusions from being drawn.[46] Nonetheless, the job characteristics model highlights the need for managers to be aware of the role of job redesign in addressing worker motivation problems. For example, when a U.S. printing company in the Midwest organized workers into semiautonomous teams to increase worker autonomy, employees put in greater effort, used more skills, and did a better job solving problems.[47]

Job Enrichment, Job Enlargement, and Job Rotation. For many people, complex work tends to be more motivating than simple, repetitive work. Task variety, task significance, and autonomy, characteristics of motivating work proposed by the job characteristics model, are much more likely to exist when a task is complex than when it is simplified.[48] Related to the notion of motivating potential, enriching and enlarging jobs can increase employee motivation for many employees.

Job enrichment is an approach to job design that increases a job's complexity to give workers greater responsibility and opportunities to feel a sense

job enrichment
An approach to job design that increases a job's complexity to give workers greater responsibility and opportunities to feel a sense of achievement

Figure 7-3
Job Characteristics Model[43]

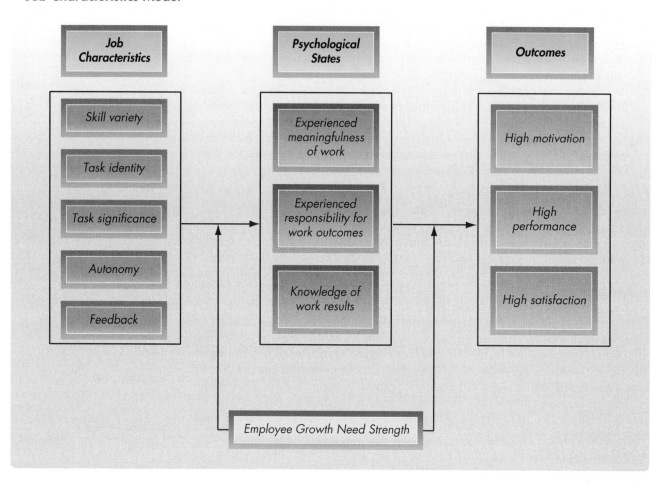

of achievement. Enriched jobs are typically expanded *vertically*—responsibilities previously performed by the supervisor are added to the enriched job. To enrich a job, a supervisor can introduce new or harder tasks, organize work in teams, or grant additional authority to employees. Job enrichment gives employees more autonomy and feelings of control, and can reduce the negative motivational effects of tasks that are repetitive or that require little autonomy.

For example, expanding a delivery driver's job responsibilities to include managing inventory, which was done by the supervisor, enriches the job. Merely adding more tasks at the same level of responsibility and skill related to an employee's current position (*horizontal* job expansion) is considered *job enlargement*. When a secretary's job responsibilities of receiving visitors and answering phones expand to include typing letters and sorting mail, this enlarges the job. Job enlargement is not the same as job enrichment, although it can help to keep workers from getting bored.

Although performing a variety of tasks can be motivating, be careful not to put too much into any one job. When UPS discovered that the high turnover rate among its drivers was due to the exhausting task of loading packages onto the vehicle, it redesigned the job. Now separate workers handle vehicle loading and drivers focus on making deliveries.[49]

Job rotation involves moving employees through a variety of jobs to increase their interest and motivation. For example, a workgroup of three secretaries may take turns answering the phones, sorting mail, and typing and

job enlargement

Adding more tasks at the same level of responsibility and skill related to an employee's current position

job rotation

Workers are moved through a variety of jobs to increase their interest and motivation

filing correspondence. *Cross-training* is usually required to give employees the skills they need to do multiple jobs. Because this enables employees to learn new skills, it can enhance motivation. Because it involves a horizontal rather than vertical expansion of job responsibilities, job rotation is a type of job enlargement rather than job enrichment.

It is important to remember that some workers actually prefer work with potentially low responsibility, autonomy, and variety to seemingly more stimulating jobs.[50] In addition to hiring workers likely to enjoy the work they will be doing, well-intentioned managers need to be careful when enriching or enlarging the jobs of people who like their jobs just the way they are.

Successful job enrichment efforts to improve employee motivation require an understanding of employee and management readiness for proposed changes, and an analysis of the job's suitability for enrichment. Although there is no guarantee that job enrichment will work as intended, job enrichment is likely to be more successful if:[51]

- An increase in satisfaction can be expected to improve productivity
- The benefits of job enrichment will compensate for lower task efficiencies due to less specialization
- Changes in job content are not too expensive
- Employees welcome changes in job content and work relationships
- Managers are knowledgeable about job enrichment and are experienced in implementing it
- Management realizes that substantial payoffs from job enrichment usually take one to three years

Goal Setting and Feedback

Edwin Locke and his colleagues[52] developed the theory of goal setting as a means of understanding motivation. Goal setting is perhaps the most consistently supported work motivation theory. Here is a summary of what we know about goal setting:[53]

- Participation in goal setting increases one's sense of control and fairness in the process.
- Performance is enhanced when goals are both difficult (challenging but attainable) and specific (a number rather than a range); for example, selling $1,000 worth of clothing in a shift or assembling fifteen parts per hour, rather than "do your best."
- A goal is most likely to be attained when people are strongly committed to it and are given feedback showing their progress toward the goal.
- People are most likely to set high goals and be committed to them when they have high self-efficacy (task-specific self-confidence) and believe they can reach the goals.
- Goals affect what people pay attention to, how hard they work, and how long they work, and motivate people to find and use appropriate task strategies.
- Goals work best on simpler and well-learned tasks than on complex and novel ones.

For the best business strategy execution, first translate business strategy into organizational goals. Then translate the organizational goals into business goals, department goals, team goals, and ultimately individual goals. Individual goals sometimes conflict with team or organizational goals, which can create ethical challenges for managers. For example, sales employees working

cross-training

Training employees in more than one job or in multiple skills to enable them to do different jobs

SO WHAT

Be careful in redesigning employees' jobs—not everyone wants an enriched or enlarged job.

SO WHAT

Setting specific, difficult, achievable goals that we are committed to is one of the best motivators.

on commission may not be as willing to help their coworkers serve other customers. For individual goals to be effective, they must be integrated with team and organizational goals and strategies.

Home Depot ensures that all senior store staff work toward the same goals by broadcasting a live twenty-five-minute show called "The Same Page" in stores every Monday. The show emphasizes the week's top priorities so that everyone shares the core goals of the business.[54] Bringing organizational goals, such as reducing greenhouse gas emissions by 20 percent, down to the individual level (e.g., turn off the computer, printer, and lights at night and do not use a space heater) helps individual employees understand their role in accomplishing the organization's larger goals.

Giving employees input into their goals can enhance their commitment to them. Employees given input into a company's environmental sustainability goals are more likely to stay with the company and see the goals realized.[55] Employees feeling bored due to repetitive work can also be motivated by goal setting.[56]

For goal setting to work, people must be *committed* to the goals and have *feedback* about their progress toward their goals. A goal will not increase motivation if employees do not care whether they achieve it or if they have no idea whether they need to do anything differently in order to reach it. Feedback must be balanced with the amount of exploration needed during practice to allow deep learning—if feedback is too specific too early, it can deter exploration and learning.[57]

Research has also found that goals can be manipulated subconsciously. One study found that viewing a large photo of a woman winning a race improved performance at a fundraising call center by raising employees' subconscious need for achievement and priming their subconscious goals.[58]

Some companies use technology to provide employees with real-time feedback about their performance. Computer technology lets Cisco employees have broad access to performance information, such as sales and customer satisfaction, to get a sense of whether they are accomplishing the goals on which they are measured.

Fast-food restaurant Chick-fil-A employees have a goal of completing orders within ninety seconds in the drive-through window and sixty seconds at the counter. Technology gives them constant feedback to help them reach this goal—a timer on the computer monitor flashes yellow if an order is cutting it close, and red if it runs over.[59] Not surprisingly, Chick-fil-A has ranked in the top five service times among all fast-food competitors.[60] Reaching such goals has an important impact on business execution and strategy. According to McDonald's former CEO Jack Greenberg, unit sales increase approximately 1 percent for every six seconds saved at the drive-through.[61]

"The way I believe you motivate people is to make it clear not only what goals the company is trying to achieve but also why the goals are important to society." —*S. Kenneth Kannappan, CEO of Plantronics*

Feeling that goals are important also enhances commitment to them and increases the motivation to do a job well. For example, S. Kenneth Kannappan, CEO of Plantronics, a $560 million maker of headsets and products for the hearing impaired, says, "The way I believe you motivate people is to make it clear not only what goals the company is trying to achieve but also why the goals are important to society. Our products, for example, help people drive safely while talking on mobile phones. That's a societal benefit we want our people to understand."[62] Explaining goal importance enhances feelings of task significance, which can also increase motivation according to the job characteristics model.

This chapter's *Improve Your Skills* feature gives you the opportunity to use goals as part of a planning process. You will identify your long-term and short-term goals, and develop an action plan to meet them.

JORGE RIOS/AGENCIA EL UNIVERSAL/EL UNIVERSAL DE MEXICO/NEWSCOM

Goal setting and feedback help employees including these assembly workers at a Plantronics plant in Tijuana, Mexico maintain appropriate productivity.

IMPROVE YOUR SKILLS

GOAL-SETTING WORKSHEET

One of the most effective motivational tools is setting goals. We can set goals for what we want to do in the next few minutes, the next few years, or for our lifetimes. In setting goals, it is important to also develop action plans to identify how best to pursue the goals. This *Improve Your Skills* feature will give you the opportunity to practice your goal-setting skills while planning for something important in your own future.

Goal-setting worksheets can help us to articulate our goals and what we will need to do to reach them. In the worksheet provided below, begin by writing today's date, the goal you want to achieve, and the target date by which you want to reach this goal. The goal could be something you want to accomplish in your education (like earning a certain course grade), in your career (like getting a particular job in a specific company), or in your personal life (like getting your desk better organized). Be sure to be as specific as possible in writing down the goal.

Next identify and record on your worksheet the potential benefits and downsides of achieving your goal. The benefits of reaching the goal should outweigh any downsides, and there should be a high probability that the achievement of your goal will lead to positive outcomes. Then identify and record the possible obstacles to reaching your goal, and solutions to them. Doing this in advance can increase your expectations of reaching your goal. These characteristics of goal setting (called *valence, instrumentality,* and *expectancy* in Vroom's VIE theory, which we discuss later in the chapter) are elements of the process that can increase your motivation to work hard toward your goal.Now you are ready to identify specific action steps and target dates for each goal. This step helps to break larger goals into subgoals. Accomplishing these subgoals is motivating and will move you closer to your ultimate goal. Target dates for subgoals will help to keep you on schedule in order to meet your overall goal by its target date.

Feel free to adapt the worksheet shown here to best meet your needs. For example, you might want to add more lines on a separate page.

Today's Date:	Target Date:	
Goal:		
Potential Benefits of Achieving Goal:		
1.		
2.		
3.		
4.		
Potential Downsides of Achieving Goal:		
1.		
2.		
3.		
4.		
Possible Obstacles	Solutions to Each Obstacle	
1.	1.	
2.	2.	
3.	3.	
4.	4.	
Action Steps		Target Date
1.		
2.		
3.		
4.		

Ethics and Goal Setting

In today's economy, organizations often face pressure to work faster with fewer resources. When challenging and motivating employees through high goals and tight schedules, managers must avoid setting unrealistic targets that may stimulate unethical behavior. Individuals who have goals—and are not on course to meet them—are more likely to act unethically than people who are trying to do their best. In particular, people whose performance is falling just short of a goal are the ones most likely to act unethically in order to collect a reward.[63]

Difficult economic times may also call more for realistic goals rather than stretch goals, according to William Conaty, the former head of human resources at General Electric. In a tough economic environment, Conaty says, "Somebody might say: 'If I don't make my numbers, I'm going to get fired, so I'm going to cut a few corners.' And that's where we all get into trouble."[64]

In the early 1990s, Sears, Roebuck, and Company set very difficult goals for its automotive service advisors. After a number of complaints, California state regulators investigated and found that unnecessary repairs had been performed 90 percent of the time. Sears' chairperson, Edward Brennan, later admitted that Sears' "goal setting process for service advisors created an environment where mistakes did occur."[65] Some experts also believe that stock options can misalign the goals of company executives. One study found that CEOs were more likely to manipulate firm earnings when they had more out-of-the-money stock options. The stock-based incentives misaligned the CEOs' personal goals with company goals, and led to unethical behavior.[66]

SO WHAT

Setting unrealistic goals can stimulate unethical behavior.

Goal setting has an important role in directing and motivating employees, but managers should be vigilant for unethical behavior when using goal setting, especially as the goal or deadline approaches. For example, the pursuit of productivity goals fueled the subprime mortgage crisis. To deter such behavior, managers must create an ethical climate so that employees feel comfortable bringing up conflicts. The pressure to reach high goals is often necessary to ensure that the company succeeds. Enhancing trust and teamwork reduces the pressure for unethical behavior and better equips employees to manage the pressure. Goals are most appropriate when the desired behaviors are clear, unethical behavior is unlikely, and goal pursuit will not compromise the attainment of other important goals.

Self-Efficacy

If you did not think that you could sell enough products to meet your quota, would you be motivated to try very hard? Because people are motivated in part by what they expect to be able to do, you would probably not be very motivated. *Self-efficacy* is a person's beliefs in his or her capabilities to do what is required to accomplish a task.[67] Self-efficacy influences an individual's effort and persistence in the face of challenges.[68] Self-efficacy beliefs have three dimensions:

self-efficacy

A person's confidence in his or her ability to organize and execute the courses of action necessary to accomplish a specific task

1. *Magnitude*: beliefs about how difficult a task can be accomplished
2. *Strength*: beliefs about how confident the person is that the task can be accomplished
3. *Generality*: beliefs about the degree to which similar tasks can be accomplished

Because self-efficacy perceptions are changeable, good managers proactively enhance subordinates' perceptions of their abilities. Managers can raise self-efficacy through coaching and encouragement, assuming the employee really does have the potential to perform better. If an employee fails at a task he or she should be able to do, the manager can express confidence in the employee and guide him or her through successful experiences. When an employee is successful, the manager can discuss how the success was due to the employee's skills and effort (rather than to luck) to enhance his or her self-efficacy.

Similarly, if you find yourself lacking the confidence that you can do a task, you can take steps to eliminate the performance barriers you identify. Perhaps more practice, seeking a coach, or watching others perform the task successfully will increase your self-efficacy and motivation. One of the most important determinants of motivation, and thus success, is whether you believe you can accomplish the things you are trying to do.

The lack of confidence resulting from low self-efficacy can interfere with task accomplishment.

COCO FLAMINGO/IMAGEZOO/GETTY IMAGES

Vroom's Valence, Instrumentality, and Expectancy (VIE) Theory

Is wanting a raise or promotion enough for you to feel motivated to do your job well? Not if you feel that your best efforts will not lead to a raise or promotion. This idea is at the core of Victor Vroom's valence, instrumentality, and expectancy (VIE) theory of motivation.[69] The VIE theory recognizes that motivation is the product of a three key factors: valence, instrumentality, and expectancy.

Valence is the perceived *value* of a given reward or outcome (in this case, the value of a raise or promotion). Instrumentality is the belief that performance will result in (be instrumental in) obtaining a particular reward (i.e., your belief that doing the job well will lead to a raise or promotion). If you do not expect a raise or promotional opportunity to be available for a long time, or if you feel that several coworkers are next in line for the raise or the job you want, your instrumentality will be low. Expectancy is the belief or *expectation* that effort will lead to performance (your belief that you will be able to do the job well). To summarize:

- *Valence*: Will the rewards I receive be things I care about? Remember that intrinsic rewards like job responsibility and having a sense of accomplishment can be as motivational to some people as extrinsic rewards like pay increases or promotions.[70]
- *Instrumentality*: If my performance is strong, will I receive any rewards? Believing that the policies and procedures used to make decisions are fair increases instrumentality by helping to reinforce employees' beliefs that if they engage in certain behaviors and perform at a certain level, they will receive rewards.
- *Expectancy*: If I work hard and put in a good effort, will I reach my desired performance?

Vroom proposed that the perception of a link between effort and reward is crucial to work motivation. A worker must believe that effort will lead to performance (expectancy), that performance will lead to rewards (instrumentality), and that the rewards will be desirable (valence). If the worker perceives valence, instrumentality, or expectancy to be low, then his or her motivation will also be low. Also, some outcomes can be negative (e.g., more hours worked after a promotion), and thus de-motivating. The total motivation is driven by the overall pattern of positive and negative outcomes, along with the valance (value), expectancies, and instrumentalities associated with each outcome. Interestingly, a high expectancy of success can sometimes reduce motivation. In most cases, a person will expend more effort when there is a moderate (rather than high or low) expectancy of success.[71]

The VIE theory has been criticized[72] in part because it focuses on only a few variables that are likely to influence motivation. The concept of instrumentality is also ambiguous and difficult to measure.[73] Although support for the theory is mixed, empirical research has shown that the strength of these three factors can influence a worker's effort and performance level.[74] The VIE theory is useful to managers because it highlights the role of employee perceptions in the motivation process. Because employees' perceptions determine valences, instrumentalities, and expectancies, managers can influence each of these factors by:

- Administering rewards that are highly valued (valence) by matching the reward to the employee, or giving workers their choice of reward when performance targets are met
- Linking rewards to performance (instrumentality) by creating easy-to-understand incentive plans and communicating employees' success stories in earning the rewards
- Enhancing employees' perceptions that they can perform well (expectancy) by ensuring that employees know what they are expected to do, that they know how to do it, and that they believe they can do it through training, coaching, and confidence building

Understanding the VIE theory can also help you to improve your motivation to do something you might not be motivated to do. Identifying valued rewards associated with doing the task, ensuring that successfully accomplishing the task will lead to the valued rewards, and increasing your expectancy by improving your skills and self-efficacy can boost your motivation and performance.

Fairness

How fairly we feel we are being treated influences our trust and motivation.[75] Fairness perceptions affect motivation, job performance, satisfaction, organizational commitment, withdrawal behaviors, and counterproductive behaviors such as stealing.[76] Fortunately, there are things managers can do to increase fairness perceptions and reduce negative reactions when people do feel that a situation is unfair. Many of these things are also inexpensive to do. Managers can improve fairness perceptions in two ways:

1. Change the fairness of the situation
2. Change how employees perceive the fairness of the situation

To change the fairness of the situation, managers can improve perceptions of the fairness of the outcomes employees receive by appropriately rewarding employees' contributions. Ensuring that the policies and procedures used in determining employee outcomes are objective and fair, treating employees with respect, and giving adequate explanations for why decisions are made also improve fairness perceptions.

Managers can change how employees perceive fairness by focusing on explaining the procedures and decision-making processes to employees so that they are clear and transparent. Employees should not wonder why some people get bonuses or get promoted and others do not—the requirements, procedures, and decision-making processes should be clear and understood and decisions thoroughly explained. Of course, managers should also always treat employees with sincerity and respect.

Managers must manage the perception of fairness in the mind of each employee. Even if you disagree with an employee's assessment, it will be difficult to motivate someone who thinks that you are treating her unfairly. This has important motivational implications for managers, especially when dealing with performance feedback and appraisals tied to rewards.

San Antonio–based Rackspace Managed Hosting is a highly awarded IT leader that delivers enterprise-class web infrastructure and hosting services to businesses of all sizes in Europe and the United States. Rackspace values transparency[77] and treats employees with respect—core values at Rackspace include "Keep Our Promises—Bad News First, Full Disclosure, No Surprises" and "Treat Fellow Rackers Like Friends and Family."[78] Obviously, fairness is important at Rackspace, and employees are passionate about working there. As one employee put it, "I've been searching for a company with positive energy that makes me want to come to work every day. I found that with Rackspace."[79]

This chapter's *Case Study* feature gives you the opportunity to learn more about how Aramark applied a variety of motivation theories and techniques to motivate its employees.

SO WHAT

Motivation can often be increased inexpensively by improving fairness perceptions.

CASE STUDY

Pride Building at Aramark

Aramark, a leader in professional services headquartered in Philadelphia, has approximately 250,000 employees serving clients in twenty-two countries.[80] Aramark wanted to better motivate its employees who clean airplanes for Delta and Southwest Airlines. Turnover of the low-paid staff of largely immigrant employees once exceeded 100 percent a year. Morale was low, and wallets and other valuable items that passengers left on planes had a tendency to disappear.

To turn things around, Aramark manager Roy Pelaez believed that he had to break some rules to get employees to feel motivated. "Managers are not supposed to get involved with the personal problems of their employees, but I take the opposite view," he says. "Any problem that affects the employee will eventually affect your account. If you take care of the employees, they will take care of you and your customer." Besides the typical "Employee of the Month" recognition programs, he brought in an English-language teacher to tutor employees twice a week on their own time, added Friday citizenship classes to help employees become U.S. citizens, and arranged for certified babysitters subsidized by government programs to keep single mothers showing up for work. He even created a small computer lab with three used computers so that employees could train each other in word processing and spreadsheets. "All of these things are important, because we want employees who really feel connected to the company," says Pelaez.

Employees who had perfect attendance over a six-month period or who turned in a wallet or pocketbook filled with cash and credit cards were rewarded with a day off with pay. Workers in the "Top Crew of the Month" were rewarded with movie passes, telephone calling cards, or "burger bucks." Turnover fell to 12 percent per year—amazing for jobs that pay only minimum wage to start. And crews started to recover large amounts of money from the airplanes, returning to passengers some 250 lost wallets with more than $50,000 in cash.[81]

In five years, Pelaez's efforts helped to increase Aramark's revenue in this area from $5 million to $14 million.[82] Since 1998, programs such as these have helped Aramark consistently rank as one of the top three most admired companies in its industry in *Fortune* magazine's list of "America's Most Admired Companies."[83]

Questions:

1. What motivation theories apply to the workers at Aramark?
2. If you were the manager of these employees, what would you do to motivate them? Be honest regarding your personal management style and beliefs rather than trying to be like Roy Pelaez.
3. What are some possible barriers to the effectiveness of your motivation ideas? What could you do to overcome them?

LEARNING AND REINFORCEMENT THEORIES OF MOTIVATION: THE ROLE OF CONSEQUENCES

learning

A relatively permanent change in behavior that occurs because of experience

Learning can be thought of as a relatively permanent change in behavior that occurs as a result of experience.[84] Throughout our lives, we learn cause and effect relationships both consciously and unconsciously. As children, we learn appropriate ways to behave as a result of our parent's smiles and reprimands in response to our actions. As adults, we learn what our bosses expect of us at work through the feedback and rewards we receive because of our performance. This type of learning tends to happen naturally and instinctively rather than because of deliberate thought.

Although several theories exist about how people learn, in this chapter we will focus on those involving reinforcement. Reinforcement theories address the role of consequences in shaping behavior.

Reinforcing Performance

Reinforcement theory is based on the work of psychologist Edward Thorndike[85] who discovered three laws:

1. *The law of effect*: People tend not to engage in behavior that does not result in a reward.
2. *The law of recency*: The most recent consequence of a behavior is likely to govern the recurrence of that behavior.
3. *The law of exercise*: Repetition strengthens the association between cause and effect.

The core of reinforcement theory is that behavior that is followed by positive consequences is likely to be repeated. B. F. Skinner expanded on Thorndike's work and found that many behaviors can be controlled using different types of reinforcers.[86] *Reinforcers* are anything that makes a behavior more likely to happen again. Reinforcers work best when they are immediate, sincere, and specific to an activity. There are four types of reinforcers, as shown in Figure 7-4:

reinforcers

Anything that makes a behavior more likely to happen again

1. *Positive reinforcement*: Use of rewards to increase the likelihood that a behavior will be repeated (like performance bonuses or praise).
2. *Negative reinforcement*: Removal of current or future unpleasant consequences to increase the likelihood that someone will repeat a behavior. In other words, avoidance or removal of something undesirable (like allowing an employee with a long commute to work from home one day a week as long as his or her performance stays high) is motivating.
3. *Punishment*: Application of negative outcomes to decrease the likelihood of a behavior (like cutting the work hours of low-performing employees).

Figure 7-4

Types of Reinforcers[87]

		Nature of the Stimulus	
		Positive	**Negative**
Action	**Present the Stimulus**	*Positive reinforcement*; increases the behavior	*Punishment*; decreases the behavior
	Remove the Stimulus	*Extinction*; decreases the behavior	*Negative reinforcement*; increases the behavior

Sources: Based on B. Lachman, F. Camm, & S. A. Resetar, Integrated Facility Environmental Management Approaches: Lessons from Industry for Department of Defense Facilities, 2001. Santa Monica, CA: RAND Corporation. http://www.rand.org/pubs/monograph_reports/MR1343/.

4. *Extinction*: Removal of any reinforcement (positive or negative) following the occurrence of the behavior to be extinguished to decrease the likelihood of that behavior (like no longer laughing at a coworker's inappropriate jokes).

Rewards can motivate a variety of work behaviors, including safety. Walt Disney World Resorts' Safety, Environment, Energy, and Security Committee presents a monthly award to the best-performing department and a "nonaward" to the worst-performing department in the categories including safety and security and the environment. If the nonaward-winning department improve improves within five days, the nonaward is taken away. Department managers must display the awards in their offices until the awards move to the next month's winners. For safety and security, the award is a statue of Donald Duck's uncle, Ludwig Von Drake, and the nonaward depicts a miniature broken crutch. For the environment, the award is a Jiminy Cricket statue, and the nonaward is a clear plastic case containing a hangman's rope with a dead rubber chicken. Because no one wants to have the rubber chicken nonaward in his or her office, environmental performance is often good enough that no department earns this award.[88]

For reinforcement to work, we must associate the reward with the behavior. In other words, we need to know exactly why we are receiving a reward. To best reinforce a behavior, the reward should come as quickly as possible after the behavior. The reward can be almost anything, and does not need to cost a lot of money, but it must be something desired by the recipient. Some of the most powerful rewards are symbolic—things that cost very little but mean a lot to the people who get them. Examples of symbolic rewards are things like plaques or certificates.

Rewards also impact ethical behavior choices. Although multiple studies have shown that incentives can increase unethical behavior,[89] the effects of rewards and punishments on ethical behavior are complex. Rewards do not always increase ethical behavior because the presence of the reward can undermine the intrinsic value of the ethical behavior.[90] Providing economic incentives for voluntary helping behavior undermines people's motivation for engaging in it.[91] Because the presence of sanctions makes it more likely that individuals will view a decision from a more narrow business-driven framework rather than an ethical decision-making framework, weak sanctions can undermine ethical behavior more than no sanctions at all.[92] Instead of choosing a course of action based on what is right, the decision becomes an evaluation of whether the unethical behavior is "worth" the risk of the punishment.

Behavior Modification

Behavior modification, based on the work of B. F. Skinner, gives managers a way to apply reinforcement theory to motivate workers. There are two basic issues in using behavior modification: the *type of reinforcement* (reward or punishment) and the *schedule of reinforcement*.

Types of Reinforcement. Managers must choose from among the four types of reinforcement listed above—positive reinforcement, negative reinforcement, punishment, and extinction. Each is best suited to a different type of situation:

1. *Positive reinforcement*: A manager can use positive reinforcement to motivate more of a certain behavior. For example, when a manufacturing employee wears safety gear, the manager can give the employee praise to increase the likelihood that the employee will wear the safety equipment in the future.

2. *Negative reinforcement*: Negative reinforcement is appropriate when an employee perceives something undesirable and the manager wants to increase the prevalence of certain types of behaviors. Removing whatever is undesirable motivates the employee to engage in the behavior. For example, negative reinforcement occurs if equipment sounds a loud buzzer upon being started and the buzzer continues until the seat belt is fastened. Because the employee wants to avoid hearing the unpleasant sound, she or he is motivated to engage in safe work behaviors (fastening the belt).

3. *Punishment*: Punishment focuses on decreasing the likelihood of current behaviors. It requires giving an employee an unpleasant consequence, such as a suspension, assigning an unpleasant task, or a reprimand. Company policies and procedures usually govern the use of punishment,[93] and it is generally less effective than the other methods of behavior modification.

4. *Extinction*: Extinction is appropriate when a manager realizes he or she has been rewarding the wrong thing and the manager wants to stop the behavior. For example, imagine that a manager used to laugh at an employee's teasing of coworkers, but now wants the employee to stop. The manager can begin ignoring the inappropriate comments. Over time, the lack of a positive reaction from the manager reduces the employee's motivation and the behavior is *extinguished*.

Schedule of Reinforcement. Behavior modification also requires attention to the schedule used to apply reinforcement. A *continuous* reinforcement schedule is one in which the desired behavior is reinforced each time that it occurs. A *partial* reinforcement schedule is one in which the desired behavior is reinforced only part of the time. There are four types of partial reinforcement schedules:

1. *Fixed-ratio*: Desired behavior is reinforced after a specified number of correct responses—for example, receiving pay bonuses for every ten error-free pieces made per hour.

2. *Fixed-interval*: Desired behavior is reinforced after a certain amount of time has passed—for example, receiving weekly paychecks.

3. *Variable-ratio*: Desired behavior is reinforced after an unpredictable number of behaviors—for example, a supervisor praises a call center representative after the third call, then the seventh call after that, and then the fourth call after that.

4. *Variable-interval*: Desired behavior is reinforced after an unpredictable amount of time has elapsed—for example, not knowing when a regional supervisor will visit your location for an inspection.

Fixed-ratio schedules produce a high, consistent rate of responding with desired behaviors but with fast extinction when the reinforcement stops. Fixed-interval schedules produce high performance near the end of the interval, but lower performance immediately after the reinforcement occurs. Variable-ratio schedules produce a high, steady rate of responding with desired behaviors and the behaviors are difficult to extinguish. With variable-interval schedules, the behavior of the individual does not influence the availability of reinforcement so it has a minimal effect on motivation.

Research suggests the following:

- The fastest way to get someone to learn is to use *continuous reinforcement* and reinforce the desired behavior every time it occurs. The downside to this approach is that as soon as the reward is stopped, the desired behavior decreases in frequency (extinction).

- The most effective schedule for sustaining a behavior is *variable reinforcement*. This requires reinforcing the desired behavior every few times it occurs, around some average number of times, rather than every time it occurs. Because performing the behavior could result in a reward at any time, this approach is a strong motivator of behavior. A good example of variable reinforcement is a slot machine—players know that their machine will eventually pay out, but they do not know when, so they are motivated to continue playing for a long time even when they are losing and not being reinforced.

Using Behavior Modification as a Manager. In terms of behavior modification, any behavior can be understood as being a result of its consequences. In other words, as a manager, you get whatever behaviors you are rewarding. If an employee continually comes to work late, it is because you are not providing the right positive consequences for coming to work on time, the negative consequences for coming in late are inappropriate, or both. To motivate the right behavior, an expert in behavior modification would identify the desired behaviors and then carefully reinforce them. This process involves five steps:[94]

1. Define the problem—what is it that could be improved?
2. Identify and define the specific behavior(s) you wish to change.
3. Record and track the occurrence of the target behavior.
4. Analyze the current negative consequences of the undesired behavior and arrange for more positive consequences to follow the desired behavior.
5. Evaluate whether the behavior has improved, and by how much.

REWARDING PERFORMANCE

Rewards are one of the most powerful motivational tools managers have at their disposal. The rewards offered by a job not only determine whether someone is willing to accept a job offer, but also how much effort he or she exerts. In organizations, workers exchange their time and effort for some set of rewards including pay, benefits, training opportunities, and so on. Organizations often use pay-for-performance or alternative rewards to motivate employees.

Pay for Performance

Although people are differentially motivated by money, pay can be a powerful motivator because it determines the degree to which people will be able to satisfy many of their needs and wants. In addition to base pay, employees can be rewarded for their individual performance as well as the performance of their workgroup or even the entire organization.

Merit pay is a salary increase, usually permanent, given because of an individual's past performance. Consistent with VIE theory, employee motivation is enhanced because good performance is expected to result in higher pay. Seeing clear links between effort, job performance, and the reward enhances motivation.

Spot awards are most consistent with reinforcement theory. Spot awards are given immediately, "on the spot," as soon as a desired behavior is seen.[95] Effective spot reward programs depend on discretion, timely acknowledgements, and obvious links between employee actions and recognition. A good example is consulting firm Decision Resources' spot award program that allows managers to give an award valued at $50 to $1,000 at any time to an employee who has performed in an extraordinary way.[96]

Pay-for-performance programs pay employees based on some specific measure of their performance. The amount employees produce or sell determines their pay—the higher their performance, the more money they make. The clear performance-reward link is consistent with VIE theory. In addition to job performance, rewards can also be linked to desirable work behaviors. For example, payroll processor Paychex gives employees rewards of $100 to $300 each year for healthy activities including getting flu shots and dental checkups, attending yoga or aerobics classes, biking to work, and running a 5K race.[97]

Some companies establish formal incentive programs to motivate employees and improve performance by providing positive reinforcement for engaging in certain behaviors or reaching certain performance or even attendance goals.[98] Technology is often used to enhance these positive reinforcement programs. For example, Sta-Dri, a forty-year-old plastics manufacturer based in Mankato, Minnesota, established an online scoreboard where sales representatives can check on their incentive points. "Having access, literally, twenty-four hours a day to see how they're progressing is important," says one expert, because they can say, "I'm doing great" or "I need to step it up because I'm really behind."[99]

Many Internet incentive sites exist, including incentivecity.com, maritz. com, hinda.com, premierchoiceaward.com, salesdriver.com, and loyaltyworks. com. In some cases, employees can specify the rewards they particularly want, adapting the rewards to be those most motivating to each employee, such as an extra day off for Jane and a flat screen TV for Miguel. Many incentive sites are point-based and work like airline frequent flier programs. Employees earn points for reaching certain goals or for doing certain things over a set period of time, and can cash the points in for a variety of trips and prizes.

Several different pay-for-performance programs are popular. *Variable-pay* plans are pay-for-performance plans that put a small amount of base pay at risk, in exchange for the opportunity to earn additional pay. For example, Indian information technology company Cognizant Technology Solutions Corp. makes 20 to 30 percent of its employees' salaries variable, linked to a combination of individual and company performance.[100]

Stock options are an incentive most often given to executives. It is assumed that managers offered the stock options will be motivated to increase the company's profitability and therefore its stock price. Stock options allow the holder to purchase a specific amount of the stock at a certain price, during a specific period. If the stock price is above this price, the resulting stock can be sold at a profit. If the stock price is below this price, the options are "underwater" and are worthless (although organizations can reprice the options to restore their value and motivating potential).

Criticisms of options include their motivating executives to manage the company for the short term rather than the long term. Another issue is that stock prices often are not directly under the control of managers, creating reinforcement problems or potentially reinforcing the wrong behaviors. For example, options can motivate executives to inflate earnings to maximize the value of their stock options. Nonetheless, they can be good performance motivators if properly managed.

Gainsharing is when a firm shares the value of productivity gains with the workforce. For example, if workers come up with ways to increase productivity 10 percent by lowering costs or increasing productivity, they receive some of the value of the 10 percent productivity gain. This clear link between performance and rewards is consistent with VIE theory and can motivate employees to improve productivity, since doing so will lead to financial rewards for them. Gainsharing can also increase employees' commitment to organizational goals by focusing their attention on cost and productivity.

SO WHAT

Technology can simplify the administration of pay-for-performance plans.

When it comes to compensation and rewards, it is important to remember that you get what you reward. Be sure to think through the possible unintended consequences of pay-for-performance programs, and evaluate the effects they have on employee behaviors and other outcomes. Tying traders' pay to the number of loans made or to the revenue they generated without sufficiently considering the risks associated with those activities contributed to the recent financial crisis.[101] As Treasury Secretary Timothy Geithner said, compensation practices were "designed in a way that people were able to benefit from the upside without being exposed to sufficient risk of loss on the downside. That is an untenable balance and it's something that has to change."[102]

Skill-Based Pay

Rather than paying employees for job performance, *skill-based pay* pays employees for the range and depth of their knowledge and skills. Broader skills make workers more flexible and enable them to contribute to the organization in a greater number of ways. When work is organized in teams, skill-based pay can encourage all team members to develop the skills needed to help the team be flexible and perform at its best. Research has found that skill-based pay plans are positively related to workforce flexibility and employee attitudes.[103]

An example of skill-based pay is when a General Mills plant implemented a plan that paid employees in several types of jobs based on their attained skill levels for their job.[104] Workers could attain three levels of skill in their job: *limited ability* (ability to perform simple tasks without direction); *partial proficiency* (ability to apply more advanced principles on the job); and *full competence* (ability to analyze and solve problems associated with that job). The company periodically tested workers to see if they had earned certification at the next higher skill level on their job. If they had, they received higher pay even though they kept the same job. The program increased employees' overall skill levels, and increased managers' ability to move employees from job to job as needed.

Skill-based pay plans are found predominantly in blue-collar environments because of the relative ease of understanding what skills are important to job performance. *Competency-based pay* is used to evaluate the skills and knowledge of other workers. Using salespeople as an example, the employer first learns what its best salespeople do well. It might be building relationships, tailoring the sales pitch to the client, or having good technical knowledge about the product. Once the elements that predict sales success are identified, all sales employees would be compensated based on how well they show those competencies.[105]

MONKEY BUSINESS IMAGES/SHUTTERSTOCK

Alternative rewards including telecommuting can improve both motivation and productivity. Allowing employees to work from home, even occasionally, saves employees some commuting time, can reduce the company's need for office space, and reduces greenhouse gas emissions.

Alternative Rewards

Besides money, employees also value recognition, appreciation, and help in balancing their work and family lives. Recognition and nonmonetary rewards are typically inexpensive, but can be effective motivators. Employee recognition methods include a personal thank-you note, a preferred parking space, public praise, a unique award, company picnics, and management doing something personal such as dressing in a crazy outfit if employees meet sales targets. Although their low cost makes alternative rewards particularly useful for firms following a low-cost business strategy, they can be effective in all organizations. Retailer Ann Taylor gives its more productive salespeople more favorable hours, which both rewards high-performing employees and motivates all sales employees to persuade shoppers to buy more things.[106]

Sometimes simple gestures can get great results. A Westinghouse sales manager agreed to pay for and cook lunch for all sixteen of his direct reports if they met their sales quotas. They subsequently outdid their goals in eighteen out of nineteen months. Corporate higher-ups volunteered to foot the bill for the luncheons, but the manager refused, saying that the incentive worked because he personally went to the supermarket to buy the steaks with his own money and because employees got a kick out of seeing the boss become a cook and a waiter.[107]

Employees have lives outside of work, and facilitating work-life balance can reward and motivate employees. Measurement company Agilent Technologies promotes employees' work-life balance by providing flexible work hours, telecommuting, dependent care resources, and other programs and activities to help employees balance their work and personal lives.[108]

Offering a *compressed workweek* allows employees to work a forty-hour week in less than five days. *Job sharing*, which allows two or more people to split a single job, is another option. One person might perform the job on Mondays and Tuesdays, the other person on Thursdays and Fridays, and both people might work on Wednesdays. Alternatively, one employee could work in the mornings and the other in the afternoons. This option requires finding compatible pairs of employees who are able to successfully share the responsibilities of one job, but can help motivate and retain skilled workers—for example, retirees and parents with young children.

Flextime is another scheduling option that lets employees decide when to go to work, within certain parameters. Companies typically establish a core set of work hours, say 9:00 A.M. to 3:00 P.M., during which time all employees need to be at work. Employees have flexibility to schedule their other two hours of work either before or after this core period. Flextime can increase the motivation of workers by helping them better match their work schedule to their personal needs and preferences.

When a PNC Financial Services Group operations center in suburban Philadelphia compressed the traditional five-day workweek schedule of a trial group of employees into four ten-hour days, the workers' productivity rose dramatically and their absenteeism and turnover declined. Now more than half of PNC's 23,000 employees take advantage of flex options, including staggering their start and stop times, the compressed workweek, and telecommuting.[109]

Telecommuting is another way employers can facilitate employees' work-life balance. Telecommuting allows employees to work from home and link to the company's offices via computer. This eliminates commuting time for employees, increases their ability to meet family demands, and can save the company money by reducing the company's need for office space. Telecommuting is also good for the environment. The 2.9 million U.S. telecommuters in 2011 saved an estimated 390 million gallons of gas and reduced greenhouse gas emissions by 3.6 million tons.[110]

Lifelong learning
A formal commitment to ensuring that employees have and develop the skills they need to be effective in their jobs today and in the future

learning
A relatively permanent change in behavior that occurs because of experience

In addition to motivating higher performance and lower turnover, alternative rewards such as telecommuting, flextime, and compressed workweeks may also promote ethical work behavior. One survey found that 91 percent of employed adults agreed that workers are more likely to behave ethically when they have a good work-life balance.[111]

Alternative rewards also include noncash rewards and recognition. Airline JetBlue trains managers to recognize and reward exemplary behavior in their departments. Southwest Airlines does not give employees monetary rewards. Instead, letters from the CEO are sent to employees' homes thanking them for their exemplary behavior. The letters are so valued that some employees keep the letter in their uniform pocket every day.[112]

Lifelong Learning

The skills and knowledge needed by employees change as new technologies are used and as the company's strategy changes to stay competitive. *Lifelong learning* is a formal commitment to ensuring that employees have and develop the skills they need to be effective in their jobs today and in the future. Lifelong learning programs include in-house training in basic skills such as English and math, courses on decision making and problem solving, leadership and technical skill development, and even tuition reimbursement for relevant college-level coursework. Because it increases employees' self-efficacy and expectancy, and provides an opportunity for employees to feel a sense of achievement and self-actualize, lifelong learning is inherently motivational for many people.

Rutgers University instituted a self-paced, computer-based continuous learning program for its facilities and maintenance operations staff by creating a computer room with sixteen terminals and developing courses that would enhance employees' math, computer-literacy, and supervisory skills. The targeted, self-paced approach to training not only improved worker morale, but also raised the skill levels of more than 300 workers.[113] This was not only motivational for employees, but improved their job performance as well.

It might not seem like lifelong learning can be an effective tool for motivating employees, but its motivational impact can be considerable. For many employees, pursuing educational opportunities outside of work can be difficult—particularly for people working two jobs or with family responsibilities. Things learned in these programs—for example, learning to read or improving computer skills—can also enrich employees' personal lives.

Because organizations must constantly adapt and change to succeed in an increasingly competitive and global business environment, and need employees to learn new skills to meet these challenges, lifelong learning is important to organizational success. One study found that organizational advantages of lifelong learning include productivity improvements, greater workforce flexibility, reduced material and capital costs, a better motivated workforce, and improved quality of the final product or service.[114]

SUMMARY AND APPLICATION

This chapter has covered a variety of methods managers can use to enhance employee motivation. Understanding *why* and *how* a motivational technique works helps managers better match motivational techniques with motivation opportunities, and enhances the likelihood of success. Table 7-3 lists a variety of common managerial challenges, and the motivational theories that can be applied to manage them.

Table 7-3

Applying Motivation Theories to Common Managerial Challenges

Managerial Challenges	Motivation Theories							
	Self-Efficacy	McClelland's Needs Theory	Herzberg's Two-Factor Theory	VIE Theory	Goal Setting	Equity Theory	Reinforcement	Nontraditional Rewards
Firm has a low-cost business strategy but needs to motivate employees	x	x	x	x	x	x	x	x
An employee feels he cannot meet his performance goals	x			x	x			
An employee feels underpaid relative to her coworkers			x			x		
An employee engages in inappropriate behavior (bullying, ridiculing coworkers)							x	
A talented employee is not feeling challenged at work		x	x	x	x			
Because the work is repetitive, some employees find it boring and hard to stay motivated		x	x		x			x

© CENGAGE LEARNING 2012

✓ TAKEAWAY POINTS

1. Anything that arouses, maintains, or channels a person's efforts toward a goal to fulfill unmet wants or needs affects motivation.
2. People are diverse in the personality, values, needs, abilities, cultures, and interests they bring to their jobs. These individual characteristics motivate us to work harder at some things than at others.
3. Effectively motivating employees located across the globe is a significant challenge. Managers must be sensitive to cultural differences in values and needs and understand that what is acceptable in one culture may be taboo in another.
4. For goal setting to work, people must be *committed* to the goal and have *feedback* about their progress toward their goal. Feeling that goals are important helps to increase goal commitment.

REAL WORLD RESPONSE

KEEPING DISNEY CAST MEMBERS MOTIVATED

To motivate cast members at Disney theme parks to provide exemplary customer service, the company begins by thoroughly training new hires in topics ranging from performance expectations to how to dress to how to anticipate guests' needs. Cast members are then rewarded daily by managers and cast members with verbal complements, written praise, and other monetary and non-monetary rewards. Because it is easiest to be motivated and perform well on a job we are good at, Disney also uses performance evaluations to put cast members in the best job for their unique talents.[115]

Disney believes that the key to rewards is the frequency and the immediacy with which they are administered. Disney tries to avoid time lags between when an employee does a good deed and the subsequent reward or recognition. Cast members are encouraged to give "Great Service Fanatic" cards to fellow Cast Members when they see each other going above and beyond to deliver outstanding service. After receiving a card, the Cast Member must have it signed by his/her manager to inform him or her of the praise. Disney believes that this type of praise is the key to building a highly motivated workforce and making guests happy.[116]

Whatever the reward given, Disney feels strongly that the purpose must be clear and motivational. Disney uses a variety of rewards including a numbered bottle of green tobasco sauce to an entry in a drawing for a family Disney cruise to motivate employees to maintain a high level of service quality and idea generation.[117]

5. When challenging and motivating employees through high goals and tight schedules, managers must avoid setting unrealistic targets that may stimulate unethical behavior. Individuals who have goals—and are not on course to meet them—are more likely to act unethically than people who are trying to do their best.

6. There is no single best motivational method. Peoples' needs, goal setting, feedback, fairness, reinforcement, and increasing employees' belief that performing certain behaviors or reaching a certain performance level will lead to valued rewards are all motivating. Because people differ, managers need a variety of motivational techniques in their toolbox, and the knowledge of which methods to apply in which situations.

DISCUSSION QUESTIONS

1. What motivates you at work? What do you find unmotivating at work? Are they opposites, or are there similar characteristics on each list?

2. How can managers use the various motivation theories you learned in this chapter to ensure that all employees do their best and work hard toward company goals?

3. How can technology make a manufacturing assembly task more motivating? How might it make the task less motivating? What theories from this chapter did you use in crafting your answer?

4. What can a manager do to increase employees' perceptions of instrumentality?

5. Can you think of any behavior at work that a person might engage in that is not rewarded in some way?

6. What are some advantages of using alternative rewards? What are some disadvantages?

7. How can pay for performance both support and undermine an organization's goals for ethical employee behavior?

EXERCISES

Managerial Motivation Skills

The goal of this exercise is to develop your managerial motivation skills. After you are assigned a partner, decide who will play the role of manager and who will play the role of the subordinate. The subordinate's task is to fold a paper airplane out of a single sheet of paper that flies farther than any other paper airplane made in the class. Your instructor will give the subordinate a confidential role assignment that is NOT to be shared with the manager. After reading the role sheet, the subordinate will act out the situation described in the role assignment. As the subordinate, DO NOT tell the manager what you will be doing—just act it out by behaving as a real employee would in the situation you have been assigned. The subordinate is responsible for folding the airplane under the supervision of the manager.

As the manager, your job is to identify the motivational problem, analyze the situation, and try different strategies to motivate the subordinate. As the subordinate, your job is to realistically portray the employee in the role description and respond realistically to the manager's attempts at increasing your motivation and changing your behavior.

When the instructor indicates, stop the role play. The subordinate should then show the manager his or her role assignment and talk about what the manager did well and less well in trying to analyze and improve the situation. Give honest, constructive feedback to help your partner improve his or her managerial skills.

Now switch roles, and the instructor will give the new subordinate a different role assignment. Repeat the process, including giving feedback to the manager when the exercise is complete.

Motivating Your Sales Staff

The goal of this exercise is to give you practice aligning individual and organizational goals, and thinking like a manager in managing employee motivation. After dividing into groups of four to five students, read the scenario below.

Imagine that you are the management team of a new high-end retail clothing store named Threads. Your company's business strategy is to provide high-quality customer service and to provide high-quality products. You are not the cheapest store in town, but you expect your employees to create a service-oriented atmosphere that customers will be willing to pay a little extra for.

You recognize that your sales staff will be essential to your store's success, and you want to create a system that motivates them to help create a competitive advantage for your business. Because this is the first store you have opened, you have some latitude to decide how to best motivate your staff. Market competitive starting salaries have already established, but you have decided to allocate 10 percent of the store's profits to use to motivate your sales staff in any way you see fit.

Working as a team, discuss your answers to the following questions. Be prepared to share your answers with the class.

Questions

1. What behaviors would you want from your sales staff?
2. What goals would you set for your sales staff, given your answer to question 1?
3. What type of system would you set up to reward these behaviors?
4. What challenges would you be on the lookout for? How would you proactively address these potential challenges to prevent them from happening?

Hilton@Home

More companies are allowing workers to telecommute, or work from home. Hilton Hotels' Hilton@Home program is one example of a work-from-home program. Not only does this decrease the company's need for office space, but it also improves the work-life balance of employees by decreasing or eliminating their commute time and increasing their scheduling flexibility.

As you have learned in this chapter, motivation is essential to employee and company performance. Motivating on-site employees can be challenging enough, but how do companies motivate employees who telecommute and work from home?

Questions

1. Why might productivity increase when these workers are allowed to telecommute?
2. What motivation challenges exist when workers like these telecommute?
3. How can Hilton keep its at-home workers motivated and connected to the rest of the company?

VIDEO CASES

Now What?

Imagine working in a group with two other members asked by your boss to brainstorm names for a new product. The other two members stop after quickly generating three to four weak ideas and want to quit. One group member doesn't see the point of the task. The other group member claims to not be good at this kind of creative stuff and would rather get back to work doing something else. *What do you say or do?* Go to this chapter's "Now What?" video, watch the challenge video, and choose a response. Be sure to also view the outcomes of the two responses you didn't choose.

Discussion Questions

1. Which aspects of motivation discussed in this chapter are illustrated in these videos? Explain your answer.
2. What do you feel is the biggest challenge facing this team in the challenge video?
3. As a manager, what motivational techniques would you apply in this situation?

Workplace | Flight 001: Motivating Employees

All retail jobs are not created equal. Just ask Amanda Shank. At a previous job, a storeowner bluntly told her, "You're just a number. You can be replaced at any time." Shank said, "When you're told something like that, why would you want to put any effort in?" That sort of callous treatment is hardly an incentive. Luckily, after landing a job at Flight 001, Shank started to feel motivated again.

Flight 001 co-founder Brad John frequently visits his New York stores to talk with staff about what's happening. While visiting Shank's Brooklyn store where she had recently been promoted to assistant store manager, John asked if customers were shopping differently after the airlines had added new fees for checked luggage. Shank confirmed John's suspicions and gave him a full report along with recommendations for how they might make adjustments in inventory and merchandising.

Shank is thrilled to have found a place where she can make a contribution and be challenged. "At this company they make an effort to show you you're appreciated; you have a say in what goes on. You're given compliments and feedback about what you could be better at," she explained.

Although growth opportunities might seem limited in retail, store leader Claire Rainwater involves crewmembers in projects that use their strengths. If someone excels at organization and operations, she asks that person to identify and implement an improvement that excites him or her. She gives visually talented associates free rein to create new

(Continued)

merchandising displays. Rainwater could easily provide direction on how to approach these tasks, but she allows her crewmembers the autonomy to determine how they want to approach and execute tasks, which ultimately creates a greater sense of empowerment and engagement.

Although retail offers careers, Crew Development Manager Emily Griffin says that the industry is temporary for many people. Most associates just want to make some money while pursuing other interests as students, photographers, musicians, etc. Usually Griffin can tell which associates are passing through and who might stick around. What is interesting is that when she started at Flight 001, Griffin thought she was passing through.

Discussion Questions

1. According to Maslow's hierarchy, which basic needs did Amanda Shank's old boss fail to meet?
2. How might feeling underpaid affect the work of a Flight 001 associate?
3. Speculate the possible reasons Griffin stayed at Flight 001 to pursue a career.

DO WHAT

CENGAGENOW™

CENGAGENOW™ includes **teaching and learning resources** to supplement the text, and is designed specifically to **help students "think like managers"** by engaging and challenging them to think critically about managerial situations. **CengageNOW uses today's technology to improve the skills** of tomorrow's managers.

END NOTES

[1]Company Overview, Disney, 2012. Available online: http://corporate.disney.go.com/corporate/overview.html.

[2]Barrett, Sarah (2011). Customer Service Secrets from Disney, The Locker Room, April 7. Available online: http://ggfablog.wordpress.com/2011/04/07/customer-service-secrets-from-disney/.

[3]Locke, E. A., & Latham, G. P. (2002, September). Building a Practically Useful Theory of Goal Setting and Task Motivation. *American Psychologist,* 705–717.

[4]Lo, T. Y. (2002). Quality Culture: A Product of Motivation Within Organizations. *Managerial Auditing Journal, 17*(5), 272–276.

[5]Makin, P. J., & Sutherland, V. J. (1994). Reducing Accidents Using a Behavioural Approach. *Leadership and Organization Development Journal, 15*(5), 5–10; Geller, E. S. (1997). *Understanding Behavior-Based Safety: Step-by-Step Methods to Improve Your Workplace.* Neenah, WI: J. J. Keller & Associates Inc.; Richer, S.

F., Blanchard, C., & Vallerand, R. J. (2002). A Motivational Model of Work Turnover. *Journal of Applied Social Psychology, 32,* 2089–2113.

[6]Kooij, D. T. A. M., De Lange, A. H., Jansen, P. G., Kanfer, R. & Dikkers, J. S. E. (2011). Age and Work-Related Motives: Results of a Meta-Analysis, *Journal of Organizational Behavior, 32*(2), 197–225.

[7]McGregor, D. (1960). *The Human Side of Enterprise.* New York: McGraw-Hill.

[8]Company Philosophy—Kimley-Horn and Associates, Inc. (2012). Available online: http://www.kimley-horn.com/about/our-philosophy

[9]Burlingham, B. (2003, January). The Coolest Small Company in America. *Inc.* Available online: http://www.inc.com/magazine/20030101/25036.html.

[10]Drucker, P. (1998, October 5). Management's New Paradigms. *Forbes*, 152–177.

[11]Henricks, M. (2005, January). Falling Flat? *Entrepreneur*. Available online: http://www.entrepreneur.com/magazine/entrepreneur/2005/january/74836.html.

[12]Henricks, M. (2005, January). Falling Flat? *Entrepreneur*. Available online: http://www.entrepreneur.com/magazine/entrepreneur/2005/january/74836.html.

[13]Maslow, A. (1954). *Motivation and Personality*. New York: Harper and Row.

[14]Lawler III, E. E., & Suttle, J. L. (1972, April). A Causal Correlational Test of the Need Hierarchy Concept. *Organizational Behavior and Human Decision Processes*, 265–287; Wahba, M. A., & Birdwell, L. G. (1976). Maslow Reconsidered: A Review of Research on the Need Hierarchy Theory. *Organizational Behavior and Human Decision Processes, 15,* 212–240.

[15]LaFarge, V., & Nurick, A. (1993). Issues of Separation and Loss in the Organizational Exit. *Journal of Management Inquiry, 2,* 356–365.

[16]Cascio, W. F. (2002). Strategies for Responsible Restructuring. *Academy of Management Executive, 16,* 80–91.

[17]Alderfer, C. P. (1972). *Existence, Relatedness and Growth*. New York: Free Press.

[18]Hofstede, G. (1980). Culture and Organizations. *International Studies of Management and Organization, 70*(4), 15–41.

[19]Levering, R., & Moskowitz, M. (2008, January 22). Top 50 Employers. Available online: http://money.cnn.com/galleries/2008/fortune/0801/gallery.bestcos_top50.fortune/13.html.

[20]Our Culture Makes it All Tick (2012). Available online: http://umpquabank.com/1.0/pages/culture.aspx?prodCAT=qCareers.

[21]Verizon's Employee Training Programs Ranked Tops in the U.S. Verizon, February 17, 2012. Available online: http://newscenter.verizon.com/press-releases/verizon/2012/verizons-employee-training.html.

[22]Herzberg, F. (1966). *Work and the Nature of Man*. Cleveland, OH: World Publishing Company; see also Herzberg, F., Mausner, B., & Snydermann, B. B. (1959). *The Motivation to Work*. New York: Wiley.

[23]Herzberg, F., Mausner, B., & Snydermann, B. B. (1959). *The Motivation to Work*. New York: Wiley.

[24]Herzberg, F. (1966). *Work and the Nature of Man*. Cleveland, OH: World Publishing Company.

[25]Dysvik, A. & Kuvaas, B. (2011). Intrinsic Motivation as a Moderator on the Relationship Between Perceived Job Autonomy and Work Performance, *European Journal of Work and Organizational Psychology, 20*(3), 367–387.

[26]King, N. (1970). Clarification and Evaluation of the Two-Factor Theory of Job Satisfaction. *Psychological Bulletin, 74,* 18–31.

[27]Steers, R. M., Porter, L. W., & Bigley, G. A. (1996). *Motivation and Leadership at Work*. New York: McGraw-Hill.

[28]McClelland, D. C. (1961). *The Achieving Society*. Princeton: Van Nostrand; McClelland, D. C. (1985). *Human Motivation*. Glenview, IL: Scott, Foresman; McClelland, D. C. (1975). *Power: The Inner Experience*. New York: Irvington.

[29]McClelland, D. C., & Boyatzis, R. E. (1982). Leadership Motive Pattern and Long-Term Success in Management. *Journal of Applied Psychology, 6,* 737–743; Collins, C. J., Hanges, P. J., & Locke, E. A. (2004). The Relationship of Achievement Motivation to Entrepreneurial Behavior: A Meta-Analysis. *Human Performance,*

17(1), 95–117; McClelland, D. C., & Burnham, D. H. (1976). Power Is the Great Motivator. *Harvard Business Review, 54*(2), 100–110.

[30]Taras, V., Steel, P. & Kirkman, B.L. (2011). *Organizational Dynamics, 40,* 189-198; Adler, N. J. (2008). *International Dimensions of Organizational Behavior* (5th ed.). Mason, OH: Thomson/South-Western.

[31]Erez, M., Kleinbeck, U., & Thiery, H. (Eds.). (2001). *Work Motivation in the Context of a Globalizing Economy*. Mahwah, NJ: Lawrence Erlbaum Associates; Illman, P.E. (1980). *Motivating the Overseas Work Force, in Developing Overseas Managers and Managers Overseas* (pp. 83–106). New York: AMACOM.

[32]Odell, P. (2005, November 9). Motivating Employees on a Global Scale: Author Bob Nelson. PROMO P&I. Available online: http://promomagazine.com/incentives/motivating_empolyees_110905/.

[33]Solomon, C. M. (1994, July). Global Operations Demand That HR Rethinks Diversity. *Personnel Journal, 73*(7), 40–50.

[34]Seibert, S. E., Silver, S. R., & Randolph, W. A. (2004). Taking Empowerment to the Next Level: A Multiple-Level Model of Empowerment, Performance, and Satisfaction. *Academy of Management Journal, 47,* 332–349.

[35]Whitney, K. (2008). Netflix Creates its Own Script for Talent Management, Talent Management, July 1. Available online: http://talentmgt.com/articles/view/netflix_creates_its_own_script_for_talent_management/1; Conlin, M. (2007, September 24). Netflix: Flex to the Max. *BusinessWeek*, 73–74.

[36]Workplacedemocracy. (2010, January 18). Netflix Takes a Vacation from Its Vacation Policy. Workplacedemocracy.com. http://workplacedemocracy.com/2010/01/18/netflix-takes-a-vacation-from-its-vacation-policy/.

[37] Henneman, T. (2011). Patagonia Fills Payroll With People Who Are Passionate, Workforce, November 7. Available online: http://www.workforce.com/article/20111104/NEWS02/111109975.

[38]Whetton, D. A., & Cameron, K. S. (2002). *Developing Management Skills* (pp. 426–427). Upper Saddle River, NJ: Prentice-Hall.

[39]Hackman, J. R., & Lawler, E. E. (1971). Employee Reactions to Job Characteristics. *Journal of Applied Psychology Monograph, 55,* 259–286; Hackman, J. R., & Oldham, G. R. (1975). Development of the Job Diagnostic Survey. *Journal of Applied Psychology, 60,* 159–170; Hackman, J. R., & Oldham, G. R. (1976). Motivation Through the Design of Work: A Test of a Theory. *Organizational Behavior and Human Performance, 16,* 250–279; Hackman, J. R., & Oldham, G. R. (1980). *Work Redesign*. Reading, MA: Addison-Wesley.

[40]Grant, A. M. (2008). The Significance of Task Significance: Job Performance Effects, Relational Mechanisms, and Boundary Conditions. *Journal of Applied Psychology, 93,* 108–124.

[41]Hackman, J. R., & Oldham, G. R. (1975). Development of the Job Diagnostic Survey, *Journal of Applied Psychology, 60,* 159–170. Reprinted by permission of APA.

[42]Hackman, J. R., & Oldham, G. R. (1980). *Work Redesign*. Reading, MA: Addison-Wesley.

[43]Adapted from J.R. Hackman & G.R. Oldham, "Development of the Job Diagnostic Survey," '*Journal of Applied Psychology*', 1975, 60, 2, pp. 159–170. Reprinted by permission of APA..

[44]Loher, B. T., Noe, R. A., Moeller, N. L., & Fitzgerald, M. P. (1985). A Meta-Analysis of the Relation of Job Characteristics to Job Satisfaction. *Journal of Applied Psychology, 70,* 280–289.

[45]Loher, B. T., Noe, R. A., Moeller, N. L., & Fitzgerald, M. P. (1985). A Meta-Analysis of the Relation of Job Characteristics to Job Satisfaction. *Journal of Applied Psychology, 70,* 280–289; Renn, R. W., & Vandenberg, R. J. (1995). The Critical Psychological States:

An Underrepresented Component in Job Characteristics Model Research. *Journal of Management, 21,* 279–303; Roberts, K. H., & Glick, W. (1981). The Job Characteristics Approach to Task Design: A Critical Review. *Journal of Applied Psychology, 66,* 193–217; Pierce, J. L., & Dunham, R. B. (1978). The Measurement of Perceived Job Characteristics: The Diagnostic Survey vs. the Job Characteristics Inventory. *Academy of Management Journal, 21,* 123–128.

[46]Grant, A.M., Fried, Y. & Juillerat, T. (2011). Work Matters: Job Design in Classic and Contemporary Perspectives. In S. Zedeck (Ed.), *APA Handbook of Industrial and Organizational Psychology, Vol. 1: Building and Developing the Organization* (pp. 417–453). Washington, DC: American Psychological Association; Kanfer, R. (1990). Motivation Theory and Industrial and Organizational Psychology. In *Handbook of Industrial and Organizational Psychology,* eds. M. D. Dunnette and L. M. Hough (2nd ed., Vol. 1, pp. 75–170). Palo Alto, CA: Consulting Psychologists Press; Renn, R. W., & Vandenberg, R. J. (1995). The Critical Psychological States: An Underrepresented Component in Job Characteristics Model Research. *Journal of Management, 21*(2), 279–303.

[47]Morgeson, F. P., Johnson, M. D., Campion, M. A., Medsker, G. J., & Mumford, T. V. (2006). Understanding Reactions to Job Redesign: A Quasi-Experimental Investigation of the Moderating Effects of Organizational Context on Perceptions of Performance Behavior. *Personnel Psychology, 59,* 333–363.

[48]Melamed, S., Ben-Avi, I., Luz, J., & Green, M. S. (1995). Objective and Subjective Work Monotony: Effects on Job Satisfaction, Psychological Distress, and Absenteeism in Blue-Collar Workers. *Journal of Applied Psychology, 80,* 29–42.

[49]Capelli, P. (2000). A Market-Driven Approach to Retaining Talent. *Harvard Business Review, 78*(1), 103–111.

[50]Molstad, C. (1986). Choosing and Coping with Boring Work. *Urban Life, 15,* 215–236; Forbes, J. B., & Barrett, G. V. (1978). Individual Abilities and Task Demands in Relation to Performance and Satisfaction on Two Repetitive Monitoring Tasks. *Journal of Applied Psychology, 63,* 188–196; Phillips, C. R., Bedeian, A. G., & Molstad, C. (1991). Repetitive Work: Contrast and Conflict. *Journal of Socio-Economics, 20,* 73–82.

[51]Herbert, T. T. (1976). *Organizational Behavior: Readings and Cases* (pp. 344–345). New York: Macmillan.

[52]Locke, E. A. (1968). Toward a Theory of Task Motivation and Incentives. *Organizational Behavior and Human Performance, 3,* 157–189; Locke, E. A., & Latham, G. P. (1990). *A Theory of Goals and Task Performance.* Englewood Cliffs, NJ: Prentice-Hall.

[53]Shalley, C. E., & Locke, E. A. (1996, October). Setting Goals to Get Innovation. *R&D Innovator, 5*(10), 1–6.

[54]Grow, B. (2006, March 6). Renovating Home Depot. *Business-Week,* 50–58.

[55]McClellan, J. (2008, June 27). Get Your Employees Excited About Sustainability. Society for Human Resource Management Online. Available online: http://www.shrm.org/hrdisciplines/ethics/articles/Pages/EmployeesAndSustainability.aspx.

[56]Phillips, J. (2008). The Role of Excess Cognitive Capacity in the Relationship Between Job Characteristics and Cognitive Task Engagement. *Journal of Business and Psychology, 23,* 11–24.

[57]Goodman, J. S., Wood, R. E., & Hendricks, M. (2004). Feedback Specificity, Exploration, and Learning. *Journal of Applied Psychology, 89,* 248–262.

[58]Shantz, A., & Latham, G.P. (2009). An Exploratory Field Experiment of the Effect of Subconscious and Conscious Goals on Employee Performance, *Organizational Behavior and Human Decision Processes, 109,* 9–17.

[59]Salter, C. (2006). Chick-fil-A's Recipe for Customer Service. *Fast Company.* Available online: http://www.fastcompany.com/resources/customer/chickfila.html.

[60]HM Electronics. (2005). How to Optimize Drive-Thru Operations with Profit-Driven Technologies. HM Electronics, Poway, CA. Available online: http://www.hme.com/collateral/Operations_2005.pdf.

[61]HM Electronics. (2005). How to Optimize Drive-Thru Operations with Profit-Driven Technologies. HM Electronics, Poway, CA. Available online: http://www.hme.com/collateral/Operations_2005.pdf.

[62]Mochari, I. (2001, June). In a Former Life: S. Kenneth Kannappan. *Inc.* Available online: http://www.inc.com/magazine/20010601/22711.html.

[63]Schweitzer, M., Ordonez, L., & Douma, B. (2004). Goal Setting as a Motivator of Unethical Behavior. *Academy of Management Journal, 47*(3), 422–432.

[64]McGregor, J. (2009, July 6). Straight Talk in a Slump. *Business-Week,* 52.

[65]Paine, L. S., & Santoro, M. A. (1993). Sears Auto Centers. Harvard Business School Case 9-394-010. Boston, MA: Harvard Business School Publishing.

[66]Zhang, X., Bartol, K. M., Smith, K. G., Pfarrer, M. D., & Khanin, D. M. (2008). CEOs on the Edge: Earnings Manipulation and Stock-Based Incentive Misalignment. *Academy of Management Journal, 51,* 241–258.

[67]Bandura, A. (1997). *Self-Efficacy: The Exercise of Control* (p. 3). New York: W.H. Freeman and Company.

[68]Judge, T. A., Jackson, C. L., Shaw, J. C., Scott, B. A., & Rich, B. L. (2007). Self-Efficacy and Work-Related Performance: The Integral Role of Individual Differences. *Journal of Applied Psychology, 92,* 107–127.

[69]Vroom, V. H. (1964). *Work and Motivation.* New York: John Wiley and Sons.

[70]Chiang, C. F., & Jang, S. (2008). An Expectancy Theory Model for Hotel Employee Motivation. *International Journal of Hospitality Management, 27,* 313–322.

[71]Atkinson, J. W. (1964). *An Introduction to Motivation.* New York: American Book-Van Nostrand-Reinhold.

[72]Walker, L. R., & Thomas, K. W. (1982). Beyond Expectancy Theory: An Integrative Model from Health Care. *Academy of Management Review, 7*(2), 187–194; Campbell, D., & Pritchard, R. (1976). Motivation Theory in Industrial and Organizational Psychology. In *Handbook of Industrial and Organizational Psychology,* ed. M. D. Dunnette (pp. 63–130). Chicago: Rand McNally; Van Eerde, W., & Thierry, H. (1996, October). Vroom's Expectancy Model and Work-Related Criteria: A Meta-Analysis. *Journal of Applied Psychology,* 575–586.

[73]Wahba, M. A., & House, R. J. (1974). Expectancy Theory in Work and Motivation: Some Logical and Methodological Issues. *Human Relations, 27,* 121–147.

[74]Mitchell, T. (1982). Expectancy-Value Models in Organizational Psychology. In *Expectations and Actions: Expectancy-Value Models in Psychology,* ed. N. T. Feather (pp. 293–312). Hillsdale, NJ: Erlbaum.

[75]Seppälä, T., Lipponen, J., Pirttilä-Backman, A.M. & Lipsanen, J. (2012). A Trust-Focused Model of Leaders' Fairness Enactment, *Journal of Personnel Psychology, 11(1),* 20-30; Greenberg, J., & Cropanzano, R. (Eds.). (2001). *Advances in Organizational Justice.* Stanford, CA: Stanford University Press.

[76]See Thibaut, J., & Walker, L. (1975). *Procedural Justice: A Psychological Analysis*. Hillsdale, NJ: Erlbaum; Greenberg, J., & Cropanzano, R. (2001). *Advances in Organizational Justice*. Stanford, CA: Stanford University Press; Greenberg, J., & Colquitt, J. A. (Eds.). (2005). *Handbook of Organizational Justice*. Mahway, NJ: Lawrence Erlbaum Associates; Colquitt, J. A., Conlon, D. E., Wesson, M. J., Porter, C., & Ng, K. Y. (2001). Justice at the Millennium: A Meta-Analytic Review of 25 Years of Organizational Justice Research. *Journal of Applied Psychology, 86*, 425–445.

[77]Levering, R., & Moskowitz, M. (2008, January 22). Top 50 Employers. Available online: http://money.cnn.com/galleries/2008 /fortune/0801/gallery.bestcos_top50.fortune/32.html.

[78]The Rackspace Core Values. (2008). Available online: http:// www.rackertalent.com/?page=corevalues.

[79]Straight from the Employee's Mouths. (2008). Available online: http://www.rackertalent.com/?page=testimonials.

[80]Company Snapshot. (2008). Available online: http://www .aramark.com/aboutaramark/.

[81]Byrne, J. A. (2003, August). How to Lead Now: Getting Extraordinary Performance When You Can't Pay for It. *Fast Company, 73*, 62.

[82]Byrne, J. A. (2003, August). How to Lead Now: Getting Extraordinary Performance When You Can't Pay for It. *Fast Company, 73*, 62.

[83]About Aramark. (2008). Available online: http://www.aramark .com/aboutaramark/.

[84]Ormrod, J. E. (2003). *Human Learning* (4th ed.). Upper Saddle River, NJ: Prentice-Hall.

[85]Thorndike, E. L. (1911). *Animal Intelligence*. New York: Macmillan.

[86]Skinner, B. F. (1950). Are Theories of Learning Necessary? *Psychological Review, 57*, 193–216; Skinner, B. F. (1953). *Science and Human Behavior*. New York: Macmillan; Skinner, B. F. (1954). The Science of Learning and the Art of Teaching. *Harvard Educational Review, 24*, 86–97.

[87]Lachman, B., Camm, F., & Resetar, S. A. (2001). *Integrated Facility Environmental Management Approaches: Lessons from Industry for Department of Defense Facilities*. Santa Monica, CA: RAND Corporation. Available online: http://www.rand.org/pubs /monograph_reports/MR1343/.

[88]Lachman, B. E., Camm, F., & Resetar, S. A. (2001). *Integrated Facility Environmental Management Approaches: Lessons from Industry for Department of Defense Facilities* (pp. 223–278). Santa Monica, CA: RAND.

[89]Ashkanasy, N. M., Windsor, C. A., & Treviño, L. K. (2006). Bad Apples in Bad Barrels Revisited: Cognitive Moral Development, Just World Beliefs, Rewards, and Ethical Decision Making. *Business Ethics Quarterly, 16*, 449–474; Treviño, L. K., & Youngblood, S. A. (1990). Bad Apples in Bad Barrels: A Causal Analysis of Ethical Decision Making Behavior. *Journal of Applied Psychology, 75*(4), 447–476.

[90]Treviño, L. K., & Youngblood, S. A. (1990). Bad Apples in Bad Barrels: A Causal Analysis of Ethical Decision Making Behavior. *Journal of Applied Psychology, 75*(4), 447–476.

[91]Frey, B. S., & Oberholzer-Gee, F. (1997). The Cost of Price Incentives: An Empirical Analysis of Motivation Crowding-Out. *American Economic Review, 87*(4), 746–755.

[92]Tenbrunsel, A. E., & Messick, D. M. (2004). Ethical Fading: The Role of Self-Deception in Unethical Behavior. *Social Justice Research, 17*(2), 223–235.

[93]Butterfield, K. D., Treviño, L. K., & Ball, G. A. (1996). Punishment from the Manager's Perspective: A Grounded Investigation and Inductive Model. *Academy of Management Review, 39*(6), 1479–1512.

[94]The following is based on: Connellan, T. (1978). *How to Improve Human Performance: Behaviorism in Business*. New York: Harper & Row; Miller, L. (1978). *Behavior Management: The New Science of Managing People at Work* (p. 253). New York: Wiley.

[95]Nelson, B. (1994). *1001 Ways to Reward Employees* (p. 19). New York: Workmen Publishing.

[96]Decision Resources (2012). Recognition. Available online: http:// decisionresources.com/Careers/Recognition. Accessed May 16, 2012.

[97]Unusual Perks: Paychex. (2010, January 21). *Fortune* online. Available online: http://money.cnn.com/galleries/2010/fortune/1001 /gallery.bestcompanies_unusual_perks.fortune/9.html.

[98]See Dermer, D. (2004, September). Selling Senior Execs on the Benefits of Online Incentives: Show Senior Managers How a Web-Based, Noncash Incentive Program Triggers Elevated Profits and Productivity in Their Area of Responsibility. *HR Magazine*.

[99]Hein, K. (2006, February 1). Anatomy of an Online Sales Incentive Program. *Incentive*. Available online: http://www.incentivemag .com/Incentive-Programs/Articles/Anatomy-of-an-Online -Incentive-Program/.

[100]Kandavel, S. (2012). Cognizant Rewards Employees With 200% Variable Payout, *The Economic Times*, March 13. Available online: http://articles.economictimes.indiatimes.com/2012-03-13 /news/31154016_1_performance-linked-bonus-payout-shankar-srinivasan-employee. Accessed May 16, 2012.

[101]Katz, I. (2010, April 22). Fed Tells Big Banks to Cut Risky Pay Incentives. *Bloomberg*. Available online: http://preview .bloomberg.com/news/2010-04-22/fed-supervisors-press-u-s -bank-executives-to-reduce-incentives-for-risk.html.

[102]Katz, I. (2010, April 22). Fed Tells Big Banks to Cut Risky Pay Incentives. *Bloomberg*. Available online: http://preview .bloomberg.com/news/2010-04-22/fed-supervisors-press-u-s -bank-executives-to-reduce-incentives-for-risk.html.

[103]Mitra, A., Gupta, N. & Shaw, J.D. (2011). A Comparative Examination of Traditional and Skill-Based Pay Plans, *Journal of Managerial Psychology, 26*(4), 278–296.

[104]Ledford Jr., G., & Bergel, G. (1991, March–April). Skill-Based Pay Case No. 1: General Mills. *Compensation and Benefits Review*, 24–38.

[105]Caudron, S. (1993, June). Master the Compensation Maze. *Personnel Journal, 2*(6), 64.

[106]O'Connell, V. (2008, September 10). Retailers Reprogram Workers in Efficiency Push. *The Wall Street Journal*, p. A1.

[107]Byrne, J. A. (2003, August). How to Lead Now: Getting Extraordinary Performance When You Can't Pay for It. *Fast Company, 73*, 62.

[108]Company Policy. Agilent Technologies, 2012. Available online: http://www.agilent.com/diversity/English/index .shtml?cmpid=4374.

[109]Gannon, J. (2005, November 8). Time Benders: Study Says Flextime Boosts Morale While Reducing Turnover. *Pittsburgh Post-Gazette*. Available online: http://www.post-gazette.com /pg/05312/602358.stm.

[110]Lister, K. & Harnish, T. (2011). The State of Telework in the U.S., Telework Research Network, June. Available online: http:// www.workshifting.com/downloads/downloads/Telework-Trends -US.pdf. Accessed May 16, 2012.

[111]Worthington, B. (2007, May 3). Work/Life Balance Influences Workplace Ethics. *Human Resource Executive Online.* Available online: http://www.hreonline.com/HRE/story .jsp?storyId=12614425.

[112]Morell, K. (2011, June 15). Employee Engagement Tips from JetBlue Co-Founder Ann Rhoades, Open Forum. Available online: http://www.openforum.com/articles/employee-engagement-tips -from-jetblue-co-founder-ann-rhoades.

[113]Dunn, K. (2000, May). Rutgers University Creates Culture of Lifelong Learning. *Workforce, 79*(5), 108–109.

[114]The Benefits of Lifelong Learning. (1997, February–March). *Journal of European Industrial Training,* 3.

[115]Kalogridis, G. (2010). Chain of Excellence. *Leadership Excellence , 27* (8), 7.

[116]Thomson, S. (2012). Encouraging and Motivating Leaders, Talking Point: The Disney Institute Blog, April 19. Available online: http://disneyinstitute.com/blog/blog_posting.aspx?bid=52 #.T7ENCOvLxNM.

[117]Ligos, M. (2009). How Mickey Makes Magic. *Successful Promotions, 42*(5), 44-47.

PART ③

Social Interactions

CHAPTER 8

Communication

Nokia's culture of innovation and collaboration is reinforced by keeping employees focused on the company's values.

ROBERT GALBRAITH/REUTERS /LANDOV

REAL WORLD CHALLENGE

VALUES IDENTIFICATION AND COMMUNICATION AT NOKIA[1]

Nokia Corporation, based in Espoo, Finland, is a leader in the world of mobile music, games, maps, photos, e-mail, and more. Named after the Nokia River in southern Finland and employing more than 100,000 people worldwide, Nokia has sold over a billion mobile phones in pursuit of its vision of a world where everyone is connected.[2] Nokia's strong culture is based on innovation and collaboration, and the company relies on its values to keep its employees focused and energized.

Nokia has long held strong, clear values that it regularly refreshes in various communications and initiatives. Recently, though, the company has realized that its values are no longer in the forefront of employees' minds. It seems like everything that could be said about Nokia's values has been said. Now employees are not talking about them as much, and the values seem old fashioned and less engaging.

Nokia knows that it needs to do something to modernize and reenergize its values among its employees. The company asks you for advice about how to effectively establish and communicate its core values to employees. After reading this chapter, you should have some good ideas about how Nokia can renew and refresh its values among its employees.

Source: This real world response is based on a telephone interview with Hallstein Moerk, Senior Vice President and Director of Human Resources, Nokia Corporation, June 26, 2009.

LEARNING OBJECTIVES

1. Describe the communication process.

2. Give three examples of noise that can interfere with effective communication.

3. Explain the difference between one-way and two-way communication.

4. Describe and explain four communication barriers.

5. Explain how the way we communicate can be more important to the meaning of a message than the words we actually say.

6. Explain how different communication media vary in richness and discuss why this is important.

Imagine what an organization would be like without social interactions. Managers could not manage, employees could not collaborate, and decisions would never get made. Social interactions and communication are the glue that holds organizations together—it is not an understatement to say that if these are done poorly, an organization cannot survive. In this part of the book, we turn our attention to social interactions in organizations, including communicating; decision making; power, influence, and politics; and conflict and negotiation. In this chapter we focus on communicating.

Organizations achieve their strategies, goals, and outcomes through communication. Organizational decision makers must communicate to plan and develop strategies. Making decisions requires the communication of information. Managers then communicate these strategies and decisions to employees, who communicate among themselves to execute them. Said Hmaidan, Senior Information Officer at The World Bank Group, stated, "Communication is the foundation of all conflict resolution and team building."[3] Managers also communicate with customers and suppliers and use communication to acquire information about the marketplace and competitors. In addition, communication is related to higher levels of employee engagement, which are related to higher shareholder return and increased market value.[4]

To be effective leaders, managers must have good communication skills, particularly during tough economic times. As former GE CEO Jack Welch said, in tough times, "you have to communicate like you've never communicated before. People must feel the excitement of tomorrow instead of the pain of today. You can only accomplish this by talking honestly about both."[5] When U.S. steelmaker Nucor was hit by the global recession, managers used communication to keep up morale. The CEO doubled the time he spent in the plants, and one plant's general manager sent weekly notes updating his 750-person staff on order volumes.[6]

> "Communication is the foundation of all conflict resolution and team building." —*Said Hmaidan, Senior Information Officer at The World Bank Group*

Communication is critical to employee motivation.[7] In this chapter, you will learn about the communication process, some of the basic issues in interpersonal communication, methods of communicating, and how information technology (IT) and the Internet have influenced organizational communications. We also discuss some specific communication skills, present some barriers to effective communication, and provide ways to overcome those barriers. This chapter should give you a good understanding of the communication process and help you to become a more effective communicator.

THE COMMUNICATION PROCESS

communication

The transmission of information from one person to another to create a shared understanding and feeling

Communication is the process of transmitting information from one person to another to create a shared understanding and feeling. The word *communication* actually comes from the Latin word *communicare*, meaning to share or make common.[8] Communication does not mean agreeing, only that information is transmitted and received as it was intended.

Figure 8-1 illustrates the communications process. The six parts of the model of the communication process are:

encoding

Converting a thought, idea, or fact into a message composed of symbols, pictures, or words

message

The encoded information

1. *Encoding* occurs when the message sender converts a thought, idea, or fact into a message composed of symbols, pictures, or words.
2. The *message* is the encoded information being sent. For example, a manager wants to communicate to her new employee Zack that he is doing well. The manager encodes that thought into words expressing that Zack's

Figure 8-1

The Communication Process

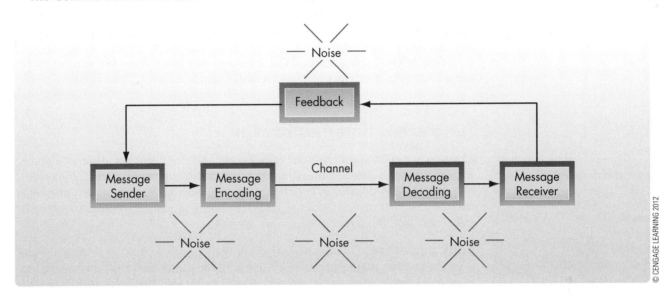

© CENGAGE LEARNING 2012

performance has been steadily increasing and that he is performing at 90 percent of his target level. These words are the message. The manager could also create a graph showing Zack's performance pattern and a line representing his target performance level.

3. The *channel* is the medium used to send the message to the receiver, including voice, writing, graphs, videos, intranets, the Internet, television, and body language.

4. When the message receiver sees, reads, or hears the message, it gets decoded. *Decoding* is the interpretation and translation of the message back into something understood by the receiver. The decoded information is hopefully the same as the information the sender intended to communicate, but this is not always the case.

5. *Feedback* is a check on the success of the communication. The message receiver sends a new message back to the original sender, and the original sender assesses if the receiver understood the original message as intended. Repeating or paraphrasing the original message, asking for clarification, and asking if your conclusion is correct are forms of feedback.

6. *Noise* is anything that blocks, distorts, or changes in any way the message the sender intended to communicate. For example, noise can be something physical in the environment, like a ringing bell or people talking, or it can occur because the sender or receiver are distracted and are unable to concentrate on the message being sent or received. Stereotypes, biases, and one's mood or psychological state can all serve as noise that distorts a message.

In other words, in the communication process the sender translates (encodes) information into words, symbols, or pictures and passes it to the receiver through some medium (channel). The sender then receives the message, retranslates (decodes) it into a message that is hopefully the same as what the sender intended. Noise can enter anywhere in the process, making the message received different from the one the sender intended. Feedback creates two-way communication that helps to check on the success of the communication and ensure that the received message was accurate.

channel
The medium used to send the message

decoding
Translating the message back into something that can be understood by the receiver

feedback
A check on the success of the communication

noise
Anything that blocks, distorts, or changes in any way the message the sender intended to communicate

As Hallstein Moerk, Executive Vice President of Human Resources at mobile communications leader Nokia, says, "Too many people say that they have written, said, or put something on video so that means that they have communicated. I don't care too much about that. What I want to know is what have you been able to get into the head of the receiver?"[9] Throughout the communication process, problems can arise that make the message ultimately received different from the one sent. These barriers can come from the sender or receiver, the organization, or noise. We will discuss some of these barriers next.

Nonverbal Communication

nonverbal communications
Communications that are not spoken or written but that have meaning to others

body language
A body movement such as a gesture or expression

The *way* we communicate—our nonverbal behaviors and vocal tone—is more important to a message's meaning than the words we actually say. *Nonverbal communications* are not spoken or written. Some of the strongest and most meaningful communications are nonverbal—a fire alarm, a smile, a red traffic light, or a look of anger on someone's face.

Body Language. *Body language* is a body movement such as a gesture or expression. For example, during a performance appraisal interview, an employee drumming his or her fingers on the table and fidgeting in the chair is communicating anxiety without saying a word.

According to noted nonverbal communications researcher Albert Mehrabian, in any face-to-face communication:[10]

- 7 percent of the total message is conveyed by the words.
- 38 percent of the total message is conveyed by vocal intonation.
- 55 percent of the total message is conveyed by facial and body expressions.

For communication to be effective and meaningful, all three parts of the message need to be congruent. If any of the three parts are incongruent, conflicting messages are being sent.[11]

SO WHAT
To communicate effectively, manage your vocal tone and nonverbal signals as well as the words you use.

Consciously controlling your body language is as important a managerial skill as knowing how to interpret others' body language. Controlling your nonverbal signals and vocal tone ensures that you reinforce your intended message. For example, in the United States (although not in all cultures), shifting your eyes and looking away while speaking makes people not trust your message. If you want people to see you as a leader, stand up straight, make eye contact, and smile—those signals project confidence and energy. Walking with slumped shoulders and with your head down, speaking in a flat tone, and fidgeting often communicates that you are indecisive, negative, or inexperienced.[12]

HELDER ALMEIDA/SHUTTERSTOCK.COM

Body language is a body movement such as a gesture or expression. What does this man's body language indicate?

Verbal Intonation. *Verbal intonation* is the emphasis given to spoken words and phrases. For example, the simple words, "May I speak with you?" can be interpreted very differently if said in a cheery, upbeat tone versus a strong or angry tone.

verbal intonation
The emphasis given to spoken words and phrases

Consider the statement, "Aiden earned a promotion" in Table 8-1. Emphasizing different words completely changes the meaning of the statement.

Remember the saying, "it's not what you say that matters but how you say it," every time you communicate. When body language is inconsistent with the spoken message, receivers are more likely to interpret your body language as the "true meaning."[13]

One-Way and Two-Way Communication

In *one-way communication*, information flows in only one direction. The sender communicates a message without expecting or getting any feedback from the receiver. For example, if a manager tells an employee to help a customer and the employee does so without saying a word or if a manager tells an employee that he is doing a good job and then leaves before hearing a response, one-way communication has occurred.

Once a receiver provides feedback to a sender, the sender and receiver have engaged in *two-way communication*. If a manager tells an employee to join a telephone conference and the employee says, "I'll be right there," this is two-way communication. Feedback enhances the effectiveness of the communication process by helping to ensure that the intended message is the one received. Have you ever sent an important e-mail and then waited and wondered if the receiver received and understood it? If so, you appreciate the value of two-way communication and feedback.

Task Interdependence

When one person or unit is dependent on another person for resources or information to get work done, communication needs increase. There are three types of interdependence, illustrated in Figure 8-2. *Pooled interdependence* is when employees work independently and their output is combined into group output. An example of pooled interdependence is a call center in which customer service agents act relatively independently in handling calls. Because employees work independently, pooled interdependence has low communication requirements.

Table 8-1

Changes in Meaning Depending on Emphasis

Aiden earned a promotion.	Aiden, not Jenna, earned the promotion.
Aiden *earned* a promotion.	Aiden earned the promotion; it was not political.
Aiden earned *a* promotion.	Aiden earned one promotion, not two, and it may not have been the only available promotion.
Aiden earned a *promotion*.	Aiden earned a promotion, not necessarily a raise or more vacation days.

Figure 8-2

Types of Task Interdependence

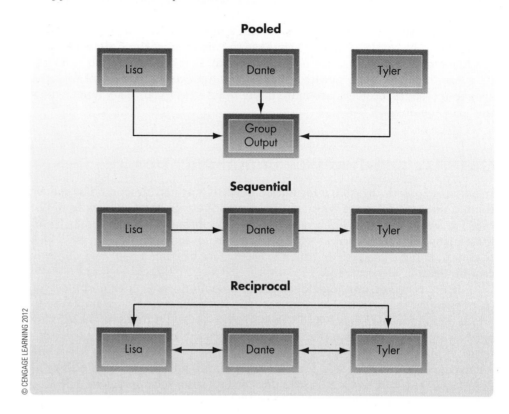

© CENGAGE LEARNING 2012

Sequential interdependence, like in an assembly line, requires tasks to be performed in a certain order. This increases the need for communication as individuals or groups are dependent on other individuals or groups for the resources they need to complete their own tasks. For example, in Figure 8-2, Lisa, Dante, and Tyler need to communicate to coordinate their work.

Reciprocal interdependence requires constant communication and mutual adjustment for task completion, such as a cross-functional research and development team, or an event planning team, and creates the highest potential for conflict. As shown in Figure 8-2, this is the most interdependent way of doing work and has the highest communication needs.

SO WHAT

When you send a message, don't assume that it is automatically received and understood.

Barriers to Effective Communication

A number of potential barriers to effective communication exist. Table 8-2 summarizes some of the most common barriers that can interfere with the accurate communication of a message.

Selective Perception. People tend not to hear things that they do not want to hear, and to hear things that are consistent with what they already believe. Selective perception occurs when we selectively interpret what we see based on our interests, expectations, experience, and attitudes rather than on how things really are. Sometimes people ignore conflicting information and focus only on the information that confirms what they already believe. Selective perception leads us to receive only the part of a message that is

Table 8-2

Communication Barriers

Barrier	Description
Selective perception	We selectively see and hear based on our expectations and beliefs.
Misperception	Messages are not always decoded by the receiver in the way the sender intended.
Filtering	Information is intentionally withheld, ignored, or distorted to influence the message that is ultimately received.
Information overload	It is possible to have so much information that it is impossible to process all of it.
Organizational barriers	A firm's hierarchical structure and culture can influence who is allowed to communicate what to whom, and may limit how messages can be sent.
Cultural barriers	Different national cultures have different ways of expressing things.
Noise	Anything that blocks, distorts, or changes the message the sender intended to communicate can create a barrier.

consistent with our expectations, needs, motivations, interests, and other personal characteristics.

For example, managers' functional expertise can influence how they perceive and solve complex problems.[14] Two managers given the same information about a problem may see the problem differently—a manager with a finance background may be more likely to see the problem as finance-based, while a manager with a production background may be more likely to see it as production-based. Each manager selectively perceives information that is consistent with his or her expertise and expectations, and does not pay as much attention to other types of information.

Misperception. *Misperception* occurs when a message is not decoded by the receiver in the way the sender intended. A misperception can occur because the sender's body language is inconsistent with the sender's words, and the receiver incorrectly interprets the body language to be the true message. A misperception can also be due to the receiver selectively perceiving favorable parts of the sender's message, distorting the message's meaning. Poor listening skills can also result in misperception.

misperception
When a message is not decoded by the receiver in the way the sender intended

Filtering. *Filtering* occurs when people receive less than the full amount of information due to the withholding, ignoring, or distorting of information. Filtering can happen when a sender manipulates information so that the receiver is more likely to perceive it in a favorable way. For example, to try to look good before a performance evaluation a manager might tell his or her boss about the things that are going well in the manager's unit and fail to mention the challenges she or he is facing.

filtering
Less than the full amount of information is received due to withholding, ignoring, or distorting information

Information Overload. Filtering can also occur when a receiver has too much information. When the amount of information available exceeds our ability to process it, we experience *information overload*. When faced with too much information, we have to use some sort of filtering strategy to reduce

information overload
The amount of information available exceeds a person's ability to process it

it to a manageable amount. For example, an executive who starts the day with 500 e-mails in her inbox will apply some sort of filter, such as the e-mail sender or the urgency conveyed by the sender, to decide which to read and which to delete or save to read later. Filtering is essential to managers because it helps to reduce the amount of noise in the communication process. Effective filtering amplifies relevant and accurate information and minimizes the rest.

Some companies use technology to reduce the filtering of messages as they move around the company. For example, to better manage its internal communications and encourage the free flow of information to better serve its clients, Medco Health Solutions built an internal broadcast facility to broadcast video with sound to all employee desktop computers in the country. The facility posts taped presentations to the company intranet, and hosts real-time interviews and panel discussions with company leaders. Employees can e-mail questions to the people in the studio, who can answer them in real time. This prevents lower-level employees from having to go through the company's hierarchy to get information about company issues. Medco also uses polling tools on its intranet and in the broadcast studio to quickly survey employees on important issues.

The broadcast facility enables Medco managers to go right to the source to get information that has not been filtered as it gets passed around and up the hierarchy. In addition, lower levels of the organization get faster resolution to their issues because the inefficient filtering and "managing up" that used to take place when the company relied on traditional linear communication channels are eliminated. An additional benefit of adopting the technology has been greater mutual visibility between the lower and higher levels of the organization, which helps to ensure that everyone shares the same goals and priorities.[15]

Organizational Barriers. Organizational barriers to communication come from the hierarchical structure and culture of the organization. Numerous hierarchical levels or department specializations can make communication across levels and departments difficult. Different hierarchical levels typically focus on different types of information, which can interfere with communication. Higher-level executives, for example, typically focus on information related to bigger picture issues and business strategy, while lower-level employees focus on customer issues, production, and deadlines.

Some organizational cultures encourage open communication while other cultures promote a limited sharing of information. Company spaces can reinforce an organization's communication culture. For example, when the music company Muzak moved from Seattle to Fort Mill, South Carolina, company leaders wanted to create more open communication paths. To do this, they designed the new workspace to be completely open with no cubicle walls. The open environment makes it easy for people to ask questions and offer ideas. This facilitates communication and allows the CEO to get ideas from people he never would previously have asked for input.[16]

Everything in the offices of animation company Pixar encourages collaboration. When designing the space, Steve Jobs even included only one set of bathrooms in the entire building to force interaction among the employees. Games, couches, and a variety of gathering areas help employees move around, communicate, and collaborate.[17]

ReThinkRewards, a web-based company that builds points-driven employee rewards and recognition programs, uses sessions called "Brutal Facts" to solicit employee feedback. One manager says that these sessions "create dialogue in an open environment with agreed-upon action items."[18]

Cultural Barriers. Words and gestures can mean different things in different cultures. For example, in much of the world the thumb-up sign means "okay." But in Nigeria, Afghanistan, Iran, and parts of Italy and Greece, it is an obscene insult and carries the same meaning as the middle finger does in the United States.

Dole, the world's largest producer and marketer of fresh fruit and vegetables, has 60,000 employees in 90 countries speaking 13 languages. Because of its global diversity, "even short, straightforward messages are complex and involved to communicate," said one company leader. When the company decided to go private, Dole conducted a mass communication campaign that included small and large group meetings, e-mails, newsletters, and the company's intranet. Since only one-tenth of Dole employees work at computers on the job, Dole ensured that its managers understood the change and communicated it to employees in person.[19]

Table 8-3 lists some marketing blunders due to cultural barriers.

In some cultures, people tend to say what they mean and to mean what they say, leaving little to subjective interpretation. These *low-context cultures* rely on the words themselves to convey meaning.[24] People in *high-context cultures* rely on nonverbal or situational cues or things other than words to convey meaning. For example, the Japanese tendency to say "I'll ask my boss" or "that could be difficult" when they mean "the answer is no" reflects their high-context culture. Sometimes it is what is *not* said that has the most meaning—like silence after you ask someone what she thinks of your idea.

Communicating in high-context cultures like Asian or Arab cultures requires more trust and a greater understanding of the culture. In high-context cultures, managers tend to make suggestions rather than give direct instructions. In low-context cultures like Germany, Switzerland, or North American cultures, communication tends to be more direct and explicit.

One informal survey of managers from fifteen countries identified lack of cultural understanding as the biggest challenge in communicating with people around the world. Other challenges (in order) were: "being through and very careful with interpretations," "careful audience research," "keeping communication simple," "respecting everyone," "using technology as an asset," and "knowing similarities as well as differences."[25] This chapter's *Global Issues* feature describes additional cultural issues in communication.

low-context cultures
Cultures that rely on words to convey meaning

high-context culture
Situational and nonverbal cues are used to convey meaning

SO WHAT
Cultural awareness will help you communicate more effectively.

Table 8-3

Cross-Cultural Marketing Blunders

- The Swedish furniture giant IKEA named a new desk "FARTFULL."[20]
- "Irish Mist" (an alcoholic drink), "Mist Stick" (a curling iron from Clairol), and "Silver Mist" (a Rolls Royce car) did poorly in Germany, as *mist* in German means dung/manure.[21]
- The Coors slogan "Turn It Loose" did not translate well into Spanish, where it was read as "Suffer from Diarrhea."[22]
- Traficante is an Italian brand of mineral water. In Spanish, it means drug dealer.[23]

GLOBAL ISSUES

CULTURAL DIFFERENCES IN COMMUNICATION

Because they are a part of culture, verbal and written communications vary around the world.[26] The international business communication process is filtered through a range of variables including language, environment, technology, social organization, social history, authority beliefs, and different nonverbal communication.[27] Problems in cross-cultural business communication often arise when participants from one culture are unable to understand the other person's communication practices, traditions, and thinking.

People generally perceive their own behavior as logical, and tend to generalize the values and practices of their culture to apply to everyone. For example, if your culture values promptness, then you probably assume that everyone you meet does too. But in many Hispanic cultures, not being on time is culturally acceptable. Because each culture has its own set of values, some of which are quite different from the values held in other cultures, the concepts of correct and incorrect, and even right and wrong, are often blurred. In international business, questions regularly arise regarding what is proper by each culture's values, what is wise by each culture's view of the world, and what is right by each culture's standards.[28]

Managing cultural differences is particularly important in cross-cultural teams because of the potential of these differences to reduce information sharing, create interpersonal conflict, or both. For example, Western norms for direct communication often clash with Asian norms of indirect communication. In describing the problems facing her team, one American manager leading a joint U.S. and Japanese

project said, "In Japan, they want to talk and discuss. Then we take a break and they talk within the organization. They want to make sure that there's harmony in the rest of the organization. One of the hardest lessons for me was when I thought they were saying yes but they just meant 'I'm listening to you.'"[29]

When the manager discovered flaws in the system that would significantly disrupt company operations, she e-mailed her American boss and the Japanese team members. Her Japanese colleagues were embarrassed because the manager had violated their norms. They probably would have responded better if she had pointed out the problems more indirectly—maybe by asking them what would happen if a certain part of the system was not functioning properly, even though she knew what was wrong. Because the typical Japanese response to direct confrontation is to isolate the norm violator, the American manager was isolated socially and physically. She explains, "They literally put my office in a storage room, where I had desks stacked from floor to ceiling and I was the only person there. So they totally isolated me, which was a pretty loud signal to me that I was not a part of the inside circle and that they would communicate with me only as needed."[30]

Effective managers understand how the perception of a given message changes depending on the viewpoint of those communicating. Because business is not conducted the same from culture to culture, business relations are enhanced when employees are trained to be aware of areas likely to create communication difficulties and conflict across cultures.[31]

Noise. As discussed earlier, noise is anything that blocks, distorts, or changes in any way the information the sender intended to communicate. It can enter anywhere in the communication process and interfere with the successful transmission and reception of a message. We will next discuss some of the most common sources of noise.

Interruptions, the sound of engines or machinery, dim computer screens, small font, or a receiver's headache are all *physical barriers* that create noise. *Loss of transmission* occurs when an Internet connection goes down, phone lines are full of static, or a videoconference link is dropped. *Competition* from other communication sources, such as employees checking their BlackBerrys or whispering to each other during a meeting, can also create noise.

Ambiguity is another source of noise in communication. *Ambiguity of meaning* occurs when the receiver is not sure what the sender meant. (Does "we need to do this" mean now or next year?) *Ambiguity of intent* means the receiver is uncertain about the message's consequences. (What am I supposed to be doing to "do this"?) The clearer a message, the less chance ambiguity will cloud its meaning.

Jargon, or technical language, can also create ambiguity when the receiver does not understand it. Consider this example of a CEO whose use of jargon prevented audiences from understanding exactly what his company did. He described his company as "a premier developer of intelligent semiconductor intellectual property solutions that dramatically accelerate complex SOC designs while minimizing risk." After some coaching, he more clearly communicated the same information in the statement, "Our technology makes cell phones that are smaller, more powerful, and last longer on a single charge."[32]

Semantics are another barrier that introduces noise into communications. Words mean different things to different people. *Soon* might mean immediately to one person and in a few days or weeks to another. Asking for feedback helps the sender ensure that his or her intended meaning is the same as the one ultimately received.

Some companies rely on technology to minimize the effect of these barriers to effective communication. For example, three locations of DreamWorks Animation often need to communicate, but traditional communication media is ineffective for communicating about animation, and adds noise that distorts messages.[33] CEO Jeffrey Katzenberg says, "We convey stories and ideas and emotions through pictures and words. . . . It's a science and an art, and a lot of it is nonverbal."[34] So Katzenberg created a videoconferencing room that resembles a typical boardroom. Physically present meeting participants sit on one side of the table, opposite their remote colleagues shown on three giant flat-screen monitors. A fourth screen allows participants to share documents, drawings, and animated sequences. The audio system even lets people talk over one another, just as they would in a "real" meeting, rather than waiting for a speaker to finish.

COMMUNICATION SKILLS

If you were a better communicator, how do you think you could perform better at work or at school? Communicating effectively is an important managerial skill, and a skill critical for effective leadership. Many barriers exist to good communications that are beyond your control, but improving your communication skills can help to overcome these barriers.

Listening Skills

Listening is not the same as hearing. *Hearing* is passive; *listening* is an active search for meaning. **Active listening** plays an important role in communication and is especially important for effective leadership. It requires becoming actively involved in the process of listening to what others are saying and clarifying messages' meaning. Both parties should engage in active listening until it is clear that each understands the final message.

Being an active listener requires concentration. When someone speaks to you, try to identify any ambiguous words, and any discrepancy between the words and nonverbal cues. Quickly compare the verbal and nonverbal messages to see if the messages are contradictory and to make sure you really understand the message being sent. Then reflect the message back to the sender, repeating the message in your own words. The person with whom you are speaking should either confirm your understanding or, if there is a misunderstanding, restate the message. This allows both parties to continue to work toward mutual understanding until you are both sure you understand each other.

active listening
Becoming actively involved in the process of listening to what others are saying and clarifying messages' meaning

Active listening requires the receiver to tune out noise and concentrate on the message. This is harder than it sounds—it can be as difficult to refrain from interrupting one speaker as it can be to keep your mind from wandering while listening to someone else. Ways to be an active listener include asking open-ended questions and sending the other person feedback to check that you understand the message. Making eye contact, nodding occasionally, and showing appropriate nonverbal behaviors also show the sender that you are listening.

Here is one expert's list of good listening skills. Good listeners:[35]

- Pay close attention to individual inferences, facts, and judgments and make useful and logical connections between what they have heard on multiple occasions.
- Give speakers clear nonverbal evidence that they are listening attentively, including leaning toward the speaker, maintaining eye contact, and not fidgeting.
- Give speakers clear verbal evidence that they are listening attentively, including giving constructive feedback, paraphrasing, and questioning for clarification and refinement.
- Show the speaker respect by not interrupting and using an inclusive, friendly, and sharing tone rather than an exclusionary, hostile, and condescending tone.
- Follow up on unusual or inconsistent communication cues from the speaker, such as changes in tone, vocabulary, and body language to determine the real message the speaker is trying to send.
- Use what the speaker says or infers to determine the speaker's motives, self-interest, and expectation(s) of listeners.
- Offer speakers honest, clear, timely, respectful, and relevant acknowledgment of what they have said.

This chapter's *Understand Yourself* feature will help you to better understand your own listening skills.

Writing Skills

From memos and business letters to e-mails, managers frequently need to communicate in writing.[36] Effective business writing is not just about grammar and punctuation—the style and tone also have to be appropriate for the audience.[37] Business writing needs to be professional and direct, and often needs to be persuasive. Always proofread your business communications, even if they are fairly short, and ensure that spelling and grammar are correct. Here are some guidelines for effective business writing:[38]

- *Write to express, not to impress.* Get to the point and use common language rather than jargon or difficult verbiage. For example, Mark Twain vowed never to write *metropolis* when paid the same for writing *city*.[39] Provide transitions between ideas.
- *Back up your assertions.* Support your points with statistics, examples, citation of authorities, and anecdotes. Footnote any ideas, phrases, sentences, and terms that are not your own.
- *Write for your audience.* Ensure that your language, length, and evidence suit your audience.
- *Edit and revise.* Correct grammar and spelling errors and stay focused.
- *Format for readability.* Make documents attractive and easy to read.
- *Use graphic aids and pictures where appropriate to highlight and express ideas.*
- *Write with energy and conviction.* Avoid passive voice.[40]

UNDERSTAND YOURSELF

LISTENING SELF-ASSESSMENT

Complete this fifteen-item questionnaire twice. The first time through, think about your behavior in recent meetings or social gatherings. Mark "yes" or "no" next to each question—and be honest! The second time through, mark a "+" next to your answer if you are satisfied with your response, or a "−" if you wish you had answered the question differently.

	Yes	No	+ or −

1. I frequently attempt to listen to several conversations at the same time.
2. I like people to give me only the facts and then let me make my own interpretations.
3. I sometimes pretend to pay attention to people.
4. I consider myself a good judge of nonverbal communications.
5. I usually know what another person is going to say before he or she says it.
6. I usually end conversations that do not interest me by diverting my attention from the speaker.
7. I frequently nod, frown, or whatever to let the speaker know how I feel about what he or she is saying.
8. I usually respond immediately when someone has finished talking.
9. I evaluate what is being said while it is being said.
10. I usually formulate a response while the other person is still talking.
11. The speaker's delivery style frequently keeps me from listening to content.
12. I usually ask people to clarify what they have said rather than guess at the meaning.
13. I make a concerted effort to understand other people's point of view.
14. I frequently hear what I expect to hear rather than what is being said.
15. Most people feel that I have understood their point of view when we disagree.

Scoring:
To determine your score based on listening theory, score your answers using the upside-down answer key at the bottom of this exercise, add up the number of incorrect answers, multiply that by 7, and subtract that total from 105.

Interpretation:
If you often marked "−" after a wrong answer, this suggests that you have some good insights about how you could improve your listening skills.

If you scored *between 91 and 105,* you have good listening habits! This skill will serve you well as a manager.

If you scored *between 77 and 90,* you have room for improving your listening skills. Refer to the behaviors in the questionnaire and practice some of these behaviors every day.

If you scored *below 76,* you are a poor listener and should work hard on improving this skill. Refer to the behaviors in the questionnaire and practice some of these behaviors every day.

Answers: (1) No (2) No (3) No (4) Yes (5) No (6) No (7) No (8) No (9) No (10) No (11) No (12) Yes (13) Yes (14) No (15) Yes.

Source: Reprinted by permission of the publisher from Supervisory Management © 1989 American Management Association, New York, NY. www.amanet.org

Composing effective electronic communications can be challenging. Because e-mail is not an interactive conversation, the rules for phone conversations are not appropriate. Neither are the rules for written correspondence, which is more formal and not instantaneous. Because e-mail falls in between a phone call and a letter, e-mail etiquette can be difficult. Table 8-4 provides some suggestions for effectively using e-mail at work.

Training in using all forms of electronic communication, including e-mail, instant messaging, blogs, and wikis, can help managers and employees reduce misunderstandings and enhance communication efficiency. For example, the New Jersey Hospital Association in Princeton, New Jersey, gives all new hires e-mail etiquette training that covers the basics including how to communicate quickly but with courtesy, what not to put in writing, and the importance of proofreading e-mails before sending them.

Table 8-4

E-Mail Tips

1. Deliver personal information in person or by telephone.
2. Avoid unprofessional e-mail addresses for business e-mails—have two e-mail accounts if necessary. This will avoid the embarrassment of having to tell a new boss that your e-mail address is partyon@isp.com.
3. Ensure that you are responding to every part of the e-mail that warrants a response.
4. Respond to e-mails quickly, preferably by the end of the same day. If you cannot do this, e-mail the person to let them know that you received their e-mail and cannot address their question right now, but you will get back to them soon with an answer.
5. Read your e-mails once or twice before sending them to check for clarity and readability.
6. Write concise and informative subject lines. For example, "We're meeting Wednesday at 9" sends a message without the recipient even opening the e-mail.
7. Do not criticize others via e-mail. This can make them feel belittled and disrespected, and if others forward your e-mail you could quickly regret ever sending it.
8. Do not use your inbox as a catchall folder. After reading an incoming item, answer immediately, delete it, or move it to a project-specific folder.
9. Agree on company acronyms for subject lines, such as "AR" for action required or "MFR" for monthly financial report. This both saves time and prevents confusion.
10. Send group mail only when useful to all recipients. Use "reply all" and "cc" sparingly.
11. Use the "out of office" feature and voice mail messages to let people know when you may not be able to respond quickly.
12. Before sending an attachment in a particular format, make sure the recipient can open it.
13. Because they are slow to download, avoid sending large attachments and graphics (especially to people who are traveling) unless it is necessary. Post large attachments on a wiki or portal instead.
14. Consolidate your messages in one organized e-mail rather than sending one message per thought.

Sources: Hyatt, M. (2007). Email Etiquette 101, MichaelHyatt.com. Available online: http://michaelhyatt.com/e-mailetiquette-101.html. Stanley, B. (2008). 5 Rules of Email Etiquette, February 10. Smartphonemag.com. http://www.smartphonemag.com/cms/blogs/27/5_rules_of_email_etiquette Andrea C. Poe, "Don't Touch that 'Send' Button! – e-mail messaging skills," HR Magazine, July, 2001, 46 (7) pp. 74–80.

Presentation Skills

Do you ever get the jitters when you are about to make a presentation? It is perfectly normal to feel nervous before speaking in front of a group, even if you have a lot of experience. Fortunately, the jitters tend to improve with practice; taking courses on public speaking is one way to get practice. Managers need effective presentation skills to present proposals to supervisors and to communicate with other managers and groups of subordinates.[40] Here are some suggestions for making effective presentations:[41]

- *Speak up and speak clearly.*
- *Quickly achieve rapport.* In the first few moments, show audience members that you feel comfortable with them.

- *Channel nervous energy into an enthusiastic delivery*; use gestures to express your ideas.
- *Move freely and naturally without pacing*; look at your audience.
- *Minimize notes and use them unobtrusively*. Notes work best as "thought triggers."
- *Highlight key ideas*. Use voice volume, graphic aids, pauses, and "headlining" (telling the audience that a point is particularly important).
- *Watch the audience for signs of comprehension or misunderstanding*. Tilted heads and furrowed brows can signal a need for clarification and review.
- *End with a bang*. Your concluding words should be memorable.

Meeting Skills

Because they lead groups and teams, another way that managers often communicate is through meetings. In addition to wasting time and money, poorly led meetings are often a source of frustration. One international survey found that employee well-being was related to whether meeting time was well spent, not to the amount of meeting time or number of meetings attended. Meeting effectiveness may be improved when people come prepared to meetings, an agenda is used, meetings are punctual (start and end on time), purposes are clear, and there is widespread participation.[42]

Leading meetings requires skills in organizing, eliciting input from meeting participants, and conflict management. Here are some suggestions for running effective meetings:[43]

- Have a good reason to meet in the first place, or do not meet.
- Have an agenda that clearly states the purpose of the meeting and key steps to satisfying that purpose by the end of the meeting.
- Ensure that participants receive the agenda in advance, know what you expect of them, and know how they should prepare.
- Be fully prepared for the meeting and bring any relevant outside information that might be needed.
- State a time frame at the beginning of the meeting and stick to it.
- Require that participants come prepared to discuss the topics on the agenda.
- Keep participants focused on the agenda items and quickly manage any interpersonal issues so that the meeting stays productive.
- Follow up on any outside assignments made to meeting participants.

This chapter's *Improve Your Skills* feature will help you to use the right body language when conducting the important managerial task of a job interview meeting.

COMMUNICATION MEDIA

Managers can choose from a variety of communication media. We next discuss some of the most popular forms.

The Internet

The Internet has fundamentally changed how many managers communicate.[44] Instead of filtering the information coming into an organization, they are now

IMPROVE YOUR SKILLS

IMPROVE YOUR INTERVIEW SKILLS

When conducting job interviews, good communication skills help you to best evaluate the job candidates and enable the candidates to do their best job in the interviews. Here are some tips to help you run an effective job interview meeting.

Do:

- Make any necessary accommodations if the candidate has a disability.
- Take the first two minutes to establish rapport and take control of the interview.
- Use open body language and present a straight, relaxed, confident posture; maintain good eye contact so that you look pleasant and engaged.
- Try to make the candidate feel relaxed; give the candidate the opportunity to ask you questions.
- Show sincerity in your vocal tone; speak at a suitable pace.
- Remember that in addition to evaluating the candidates, you also are selling them on the opportunity and trying to increase their interest in the position.

- Express interest in the candidates and their experiences; listen attentively and nod occasionally.
- Ask specific, job-relevant questions.

Avoid:

- Giving a weak or a bone-crushing handshake.
- Sitting across a table—the formality can make some candidates nervous.
- Standing too close—respect the candidate's personal space.
- Saying, "Tell me about yourself."
- Multitasking—focus on the candidate.

Sources: Adapted from Burges-Lumsen, A. (2005). Body language for successful HR, PersonnelToday.com, April 5, http://www.personneltoday.com/Articles/2005/04/05/29089/Body+ language+for+successful+HR.htm . New York State Department of Civil Service (2012). How to Conduct a Job Interview, March. http://www.cs.ny.gov/pio/interviewguide/ conductinterview .cfm. Office of Disability Employment Policy (2010). Accommodating Persons with Disabilities. United States Department of Labor. http://www.zurichna .com/internet/zna/SiteCollectionDocuments/en/ Products/workerscompensation/Interviewing%20People%20DCL.pdf.

---

responsible for aligning information with business goals and acting as facilitators by bringing the right people together to solve business problems as a collaborative community. Individuals using the Internet are able to select only the information they want using *information pull*.[45] Information pull occurs when someone receives requested information.

This contrasts with the broadcast technique of *information push* where people receive information without requesting it, just in case they need it. International retailer Target's career site provides information and videos about the company, its brand, and its careers and benefits. By making the site self-directed and providing only small amounts of information in each area, employees are empowered and engaged as they learn about the company's culture, procedures, and policies.[46]

Although technology should never replace all face-to-face interaction between leaders and subordinates, it can help the communication process by giving leaders more communication choices. For example, *e-mail* helps managers prioritize incoming communications and stay caught up while away from work. In many organizations, e-mail has evolved from an informal communication channel to become a primary and formal means of business correspondence.

Some companies have misused e-mail in communicating important or sensitive information. For example, RadioShack announced plans to cut about 400 jobs by notifying affected employees via e-mail rather than in person. This can be seen as dehumanizing by employees.[47]

Voice mail is similar to e-mail but instead of writing, a spoken message is digitized and sent to someone to be retrieved and listened to later. Like e-mails, voice mails can be saved or sent to others to hear.

Instant messaging enables users to see who is logged on and to chat with them in real time rather than e-mailing and waiting for a response. This allows employees to get in touch with each other immediately to get input or ask questions. At Medco Health Solutions, instant messaging is available companywide and is used constantly to provide high-quality customer service. Most managers are rarely without their wirelessly connected laptops. Because meeting customer needs is Medco's priority, managers are even expected to respond to customer-oriented instant messages during meetings. Although this can create some distractions, managers have become skilled at multitasking and handling the multiple communication channels simultaneously open to them.[48]

Managers can also use various software tools to meet with staff without being face-to-face. *Videoconferencing* can enable leaders to communicate effectively with employees and customers. By allowing the parties to see as well as hear each other, teleconferencing can be a very effective form of communication.

At the Global Outsourcing Group at Unisys Corporation, leaders regularly use teleconferencing to stay in touch with telecommuting staff. Any employee can schedule a telephone meeting over Unisys' phone system.[49]

Sometimes, face-to-face communication simply is not possible. That is the case at Alpine Access, a provider of outsourced call-center services based in Golden, Colorado. Nearly all of the company's 7,500 employees work from home and are located around the country—senior executives at the company rarely see them. Hiring, training, day-to-day management, and strategic planning are done electronically or over the phone. "There's no opportunity to look into someone's eyes to make sure they understand what's being said," says cofounder Jim Ball. So the company developed three rules to boost the effectiveness of e-mail at any company.

First, clarity is a priority. Important messages, such as word that everyone needs to work harder to meet a monthly target, are checked by several people for everything from grammar to nuance. Second, employees must acknowledge receipt of every e-mail and can immediately ask questions. Managers seek feedback by regularly checking that employees are on track and not missing any critical information. Third, telephone calls are made for truly difficult conversations, such as performance reviews. "You can be just as empathetic over the phone as you would be in person," a company leader insists. "It's more difficult, but it can be done."[50]

Telework is work conducted in a location other than a central office or production facility with communications between coworkers and supervisors occurring via electronic communication systems.[51] There are four major types of telework:[52]

1. *Home-based telecommuting* includes people who work at home for some period on a regular basis, but not necessarily every day.
2. *Satellite offices* are offices situated to be more convenient for employees and/or customers. These offices are located away from what would normally be the main office location.
3. *Neighborhood work centers* provide office space for the employees of more than one company in order to save commutes to central locations.

JON FEINGERSH/BLEND IMAGES/JUPITER IMAGES

Videoconferencing can enable leaders to communicate effectively with employees and customers.

4. *Mobile work* refers to work completed by traveling employees who use technology to communicate with the office as necessary from places such as client offices, airports, cars, and hotels.

Telecommuting allows organizations to reduce the amount of office space they own or rent, and decreases employees' need to commute to work. IBM saves more than $100 million a year in real estate costs because its telecommuting employees do not need offices.[53] If telecommuting employees sometimes need to work at the company's location, the company can set up a *hoteling* space for them. This gives visiting telecommuting employees who do not have dedicated office space at the company's location a cubicle or office in which to set up their laptop computer, log in, and be immediately connected to the company's intranet. They can then work effectively at the company's location when they need to.

Collaboration Software

Computer software such as Microsoft's SharePoint allows members of workgroups and teams to share information to improve their communication, efficiency, and performance. *Collaborative software*, also called *groupware*, enhances the collaborative abilities of group or team members by providing an electronic meeting site. It essentially integrates work being done on a single project simultaneously by several users at different computers located anywhere in the world.

Collaborative writing systems allow group members to work simultaneously on written documents through a network of interconnected computers. As team members work on different sections of the document, each member has access to the entire document and can modify his or her section to be compatible with the rest of it.

A *group scheduling system* lets group members input their daily schedules into a common scheduling database. This makes it faster and easier to identify the best times for meetings and to schedule them quickly.

Workflow automation systems use technology to facilitate and speed up work processes. These systems send documents, information, or tasks to the right people or places based on the established procedure. For example, imagine a nurse ordering medication for a hospital patient. A workflow automation system sends the prescription request to a doctor, and then forwards the prescription to the pharmacy. If the pharmacy does not have the medicine in stock, the system can notify the nurse that the prescription cannot be filled. If the medicine is dispensed, the system records it in the medicine dispense record and updates the pharmacy's inventory. The system can also immediately update the patient's medical record.

Decision support systems are interactive, computer-based systems that help decision-making teams find solutions to unstructured problems that require judgment, evaluation, and insights.[54] Team members can meet in the same room or in separate locations and interact via their computers. Software tools including electronic questionnaires, brainstorming tools, idea organizers, and voting tools to weight and prioritize recommended solutions help the group make decisions and complete projects. A decision support system can reduce the likelihood that one member will dominate the discussion, and helps groups avoid many of the barriers that face-to-face groups encounter.

Intranets

An *intranet* is a type of centralized information clearinghouse. At its simplest, an intranet is a website stored on a computer that is connected to other company computers by an internal network. Employees reach the intranet site with standard web-browser software such as Netscape or Microsoft Explorer. An intranet can be connected to the Internet at large so that suppliers and customers can visit using company-issued passwords. In such cases, firewall software can be installed to act as a barrier between the internal systems and unauthorized outsiders.

Because they centralize data in an easy-to-access way, intranets are a good idea when a company's employees need to reach the same company information. Intranets give employees controlled access to the information stored on a company's network, which can reduce the need for paper versions of documents such as manuals and company forms. Intranets are not useful if many employees do not use or have access to computers, or if no one has the expertise to set up and manage the intranet.

Portals are similar to intranets but tend to be more project-focused. Portals strongly resemble Internet sites like Yahoo.com and AOL.com. Users interact with them with a standard computer browser like Internet Explorer or Netscape, but instead of containing links to news and weather, the links lead you to sites on the company's private intranet.

Portals can make project status continually visible to managers through real-time reports and visual cues such as red-yellow-green traffic signals or digital dashboards. Portals allow managers to use their browser to get a high-level summary of project status at any time. Some portals also provide visual comparisons and metrics between projects within a program.[55]

Project managers use portals to manage schedules and any issues that arise. By centralizing a variety of information, portals allow managers to track progress and identify any problems early on. Managers can also use portals to quickly disseminate information (documents, processes, notices, etc.) to all of their team members, wherever they are located, and solicit input and feedback in a controlled manner.[56]

Portals allow team members to easily share news and ideas, enhancing collaboration and project implementation efficiency. Project managers can delegate responsibilities down to individual team members, yet still retain control of the project.[57] Portals are often customizable, allowing employees to subscribe only to the information they need.

Portals can be integrated with other applications. For example, one button on a portal might call up yesterday's production charts, another lets employees check their 401(k) balance, and a third lets employees tell colleagues about how they solved important customer problems. Portals also let everyone in a company share databases, documents, calendars, and contact lists. They make it possible to collaborate easily with coworkers in remote locations and even conduct instant employee opinion polls. By consolidating information and connecting employees with each other, they help companies function as a single unit, rather than as individual entities.[58]

© CENGAGE LEARNING 2014

Corporate intranets, including this example from publisher Cengage Learning, make it easy for employees to obtain information and stay updated on company news.

Sperry Marine, a business unit of the global aerospace and defense giant Northrop Grumman, implemented a project management portal to create virtual "war rooms" for collaborating on requests for proposals and resulting projects. The portal also provides a centralized, visible location for coordinated document storage, information, schedule tracking, and status information. One manager says, "Before using the portal, people had to e-mail back and forth or call to stay informed. The wrong version of a document could be passed to somebody and team members might miss information if they missed meetings. Now everyone gets general information from the portal's home pages, reviews an up-to-date notice board, checks documents in and out, accesses process and risk information, and views live schedule and milestone reports."[59] This facilitates communication and ensures that everyone is on the same page.

Until recently, portals were strictly for big businesses due to their prohibitive cost. Their complexity also required a team of computer specialists to set up and administer them. But intranets have become more common as software vendors like IBM, Microsoft and Oracle, Plumtree, and SAP have developed packaged portal solutions to suit almost every size business and meet almost every business need.[60]

In addition to portals for their customers to use in interacting with the company and employee portals to facilitate work, companies are using specialized portals to meet specific goals. For example, to help control health care premiums, insurance brokerage Keenan & Associates of Torrance, California, created a web-based portal to encourage employees to eat right and exercise more. The service, KeenanFit, offers customized fitness, nutrition, and self-improvement plans for employees and their families. The portal also allows employees to complete self-assessments to monitor specific health risks.[61]

Webcasts are live or prerecorded video segments that are broadcast over a company's intranet and archived for employees to view later. They can help higher levels of management communicate with more employees and communicate messages more effectively because the executive is able to use voice and even video to express the message through intonation and body language.

To ensure that employees are all on the same page, once a quarter Lucent's CEO and the executive leadership team webcast what the company has done in the prior quarter and what needs to be done going forward. These webcasts are then archived on Lucent's website, making it possible for employees globally to view the messages at a time that is most convenient for them. Clips of Lucent leaders reflecting on pivotal moments or discussing important topics such as innovation and taking a risk are also posted weekly on the MyLucent site.

As Bill Price, Lucent's Director of Corporate Communications, says, "Employees want more candor in communications—they want to hear the real voice of what is going on in the business. While we try to reflect this in our written communications, employees often interpret this as 'the company line.' When it's the executive's own voice, the message is given much more credibility."[62] The webcast medium has been so well received by employees that Lucent leaders now do their own webcasts and archive them for their teams to view when it fits their schedules.

> "Employees want more candor in communications—they want to hear the real voice of what is going on in the business." —*Bill Price, Lucent's Director of Corporate Communications*

Wikis are searchable, archivable websites that allow people to comment on and edit one another's work in real time. The user-edited *Wikipedia* encyclopedia (Wikipedia.org) is one of the most popular online wikis. Wikis are well suited for collaborative writing because they allow users to quickly and easily add and edit content. Wikis are essentially a simplified system of creating webpages combined with a system that records and catalogs all revisions. This allows entries to be changed to a previous state at any time. A wiki system may also include tools designed to provide users with an easy way to monitor the constantly changing state of the wiki. A place to discuss and resolve any issues or disagreements over wiki content is also common.

Wikis are easy to use and inexpensive. Because real-time project information is located in one easy-to-access place, project completion times can be greatly reduced. Unlike a portal or intranet, wikis have no inherent structure. Some popular wiki features are an automatically generated list of pages recently changed and an index of all the wiki's pages.[63] Access can be restricted to a limited group of people and even require passwords. Disney, Kodak, and Motorola have all found ways to use wikis.[64]

Information technology and the Internet have made it easier for organizations to communicate with people outside the organization. When Intuit wanted to connect with more tax professionals, it created a free wiki called TaxAlmanac.org, where thousands of professors, authors, and tax attorneys contributed thousands of articles as a tax law resource.[65]

Blogs are individuals' chronicles of personal thoughts and interests. Some blogs function as online diaries. A typical blog combines text, images, and links to other blogs, webpages, and other media related to its topic. In some cases, a CEO will create a blog to communicate more directly with employees and stakeholders.

When the investment bank Dresdner Kleinwort Wasserstein wanted to make it easier for its employees to collaborate, it used blogs and wikis. Now that its 1,500 employees create, comment, and revise projects in real time, meeting times have been cut in half, and productivity has increased.[66] When online shoe retailer Zappos had to cut staff by 8 percent, CEO Tony Hsieh used his popular blog to reassure employees and outline the steps the company would take.[67] Hotelier Marriott International's CEO Bill Marriott sometimes uses video clips to supplement his blog, "Marriott on the Move."[68]

Better software and greater network bandwidth have made video presentations much easier and more effective at communicating with employees. Some firms are giving senior executives Flip video cameras to let them shoot short videos and easily upload clips.[69] Even smaller firms can use free or low-cost online tools, such as setting up a private area in YouTube for corporate videos.[70]

Southwest Airlines' blog, Nuts About Southwest, gives new employees the opportunity to communicate with each other and also to receive important information from the company. The links to social and interactive media encourage employees to interact, form their own interest groups, and form relationships that enable them to become more personally invested in the company. The RSS feed allows employees to know instantly when new information is posted to the site. This can help keep communication flowing during emergencies, or when important meetings are posted or changed.[71]

Oral Communication

Despite the speed and convenience of technology-based message channels, many of them promote one-way communication and decrease feedback opportunities. If used improperly, this can increase the chances of miscommunication because the receiver has less opportunity to ask questions or get clarification. It can also decrease the quality of decisions if it is harder for employees to make suggestions or share concerns.

Technology has certainly changed the ways many managers communicate, but there will always be a need for managers to communicate verbally. One expert advises people to use electronic communication only for transmitting and confirming simple information, and to have actual conversations for anything that could possibly be sensitive.[72]

During its restructuring, Avon Products engaged in a large communication effort to facilitate the changes. The CEO, president, and others addressed Avon's top 150 managers to explain the rationale for the restructuring. Company leaders then went region to region to tell the same story to the top 1,000 leaders around the world. Reflecting Avon's values, they wanted employees to hear the good and bad news directly from them and from their own managers rather than through e-mails or communications bulletins. This honesty, respect, and transparency created a lot of trust among employees, who responded positively to the leaders' appeal for support.[73]

Communicating in person is important to building credibility and trust. One DreamWorks representative says that despite the technology, face-time is still critical, especially early in a project. "When you meet someone, there's that instinctive, involuntary chemical reaction, where you decide what you think and whether you trust them."[74] To be perceived as competent communicators, managers must share and respond to information in a timely manner, actively listen to other points of view, communicate clearly and succinctly, and utilize a variety of communication channels.[75]

Media Richness

Communication media can be classified in terms of their *richness*, or the media's ability to carry nonverbal cues, provide rapid feedback, convey personality traits, and support the use of natural language.[76] The richness of a medium depends on four things:

1. Interactivity, or the availability of *feedback*. Immediate feedback allows senders to adjust their messages. Richer media provide faster feedback.
2. The ability to transmit *multiple cues*, such as physical presence, voice inflection, nonverbal cues, and pictures. Richer media allow the communication of multiple cues.
3. *Language variety* for conveying a broad set of concepts and ideas. For example, ideas about a new advertising campaign cannot be expressed in as many ways in a letter as they can in a face-to-face conversation. Richer media allow for greater language variety.
4. The *personal focus* of the medium, or the degree to which it allows the expression of emotions and other social cues. Richer media allow for more personal focus.

The more a medium displays these attributes, the richer it is; the less it displays these attributes, the leaner it is. Face-to-face is the richest medium because it has the capacity for immediate feedback, carries multiple cues, and uses natural language.

When communicating, managers must choose the media that best matches the information richness required of the task or communication.[77] The more ambiguous and uncertain a task is, the richer the media should be that supports it. For example, text-based computer messaging is a good fit for generating ideas, but not for negotiating conflicts. Videoconferencing is a good fit for decision-making tasks but is not rich enough for negotiating. Table 8-5 describes how different media compare in terms of their richness.

Sometimes the extra expense of face-to-face communication is worth the cost because of the richness of the communication it enables as well as the respect and sincerity it conveys. After Luxottica Group acquired rival Cole National, Luxottica human resource officials made constant weeklong trips from

Table 8-5

Media Richness of Various Managerial Communications

Media	Richness	Feedback Availability	Number of Cues	Language Variety	Personal Focus
Face-to-face	High	High	High	High	High
Videoconferences	High	High	High	High	High
Telephone	Moderate	Moderate	Moderate	Moderate	High
Instant messaging[78]	Moderate	High	Low	Low	Moderate
E-mail	Moderate	Moderate	Low	Low	Moderate
Personal written correspondence	Low	Low	Low	Low	Low
Formal written correspondence	Low	Low	Low	Low	Low

their North American headquarters in Mason, Ohio, to the central Cole office in Twinsburg, Ohio. The visits were part of a broad effort to prevent a culture clash from undermining the merger from the start. Robin Wilson, senior director of human resources technology and analytics at Luxottica, and about a dozen HR officials made the journey to make sure that approximately 600 former Cole employees in Twinsburg understood that they mattered and could get their questions answered. Luxottica also set up a call center exclusively to field questions from former Cole employees. "It was all designed to ensure that we demonstrated a culture of inclusiveness," Wilson says.[79]

This chapter's *Case Study* feature describes how Cisco effectively matched the communication media it used with the need for information richness in training its employees on ethics and social responsibility.

SO WHAT

Match your communication media to the targeted receiver and to the message being sent.

CASE STUDY

Communicating Ethics at Cisco

Technology provider Cisco Systems Inc. puts a high value on ethics and corporate social responsibility. Cisco is one of only three companies to appear on the business ethics publication *Corporate Responsibility Officer*'s "100 Best Corporate Citizens" list every year in the list's first nine years. So it was no surprise that company leaders were concerned when an employee survey revealed that ethics and compliance issues training was seen as boring and dry. Cisco realized that it had been cramming ethics and compliance information down employees' throats. Because many of Cisco's employees are tech-savvy engineers who are more comfortable figuring things out for themselves, the old model of in-person PowerPoint-based training clearly was not working.

Accordingly, Cisco decided to revamp the ethics and compliance program for its 65,000 worldwide employees to make the training interesting, engaging, and fun. The company developed "Ethics Idol," a cartoon-based parody of the television reality show *American Idol,* to engage employees in ethical decision making. Featured on Cisco's intranet, employees view four cartoon "contestants," each of whom sings the tale of a different, complicated ethical situation. The three judges then give their decisions as in *American Idol.*

(Continued)

The themes of the song parodies include international trade regulations and chain-of-command issues when reporting malfeasance or harassment. The parodies are purposely vague to make employees really think about the ethical issues. After viewing the judges' decisions, employees vote on which of the three judges gave the most appropriate response to each situation, and instantly see how their vote matches up companywide. Cisco's ethics office then weighs in at the end of each episode to give the correct answer based on the company's official ethics and compliance standards.

Thanks to its ability to easily change the language in which it is broadcast, Ethics Idol is being rolled out to Cisco employees globally. The Ethics Idol program not only got Cisco employees to learn more about ethics and compliance, but it also gave the company momentum when it decided to rewrite its Code of Business Conduct in more simple and clear language. Cisco's new code was introduced shortly after Ethics Idol was rolled out, and within ten weeks, 99.6 percent of Cisco employees certified that they had received and read the new document. A survey of employees found that 94 percent agreed that the new code was easy to read, and 95 percent agreed that it was easy to comprehend.

Ethics Idol has been a hit among the technology-loving employees at Cisco. As one expert says, "You cannot teach people morality, but you can teach them how to deal with the ethical problems they encounter in the hopes they will make a good decision."[81] Ethics Idol has done just that by matching the communication medium to the audience and making learning fun.

Questions:

1. What are the advantages of Ethics Idol as an ethics training communication medium over in-person PowerPoint training?
2. Would you enjoy this type of training program? Why or why not?
3. Can you think of other ways ethics and corporate social responsibility information could be communicated in an engaging way?

Sources: Based on O'Brien, M. (2009). 'Idol'-izing Ethics, May 16. http://www.hreonline.com/HRE/story.jsp?storyId=209480118. Singer, A. (2008). Cisco Transmits Ethics to a 'Wired' Workforce, Ethikos, November/December. http://www.singerpubs.com/ethikos/html/cisco.html.

ORGANIZATIONAL COMMUNICATION

organizational communication
The exchange of information among two or more individuals or groups in an organization that creates a common basis of understanding and feeling

Organizational communication is the exchange of information among two or more individuals or groups in an organization that creates a common basis of understanding and feeling. Organizational communication can move in a variety of directions, and be formal or informal in nature. Figure 8-3 illustrates downward, upward, horizontal, and diagonal communication paths in organizations.

Downward Communication

Downward communication occurs when higher-level employees communicate to those at lower levels the organization—for example, from a manager to a subordinate. Downward communication typically consists of messages about how to do a job, performance goals, the firm's policies, and how the company is performing.

Technology now gives many executives real-time feedback on employees' and the company's performance, but getting those executives' decisions

Figure 8-3

Communication Paths in Organizations

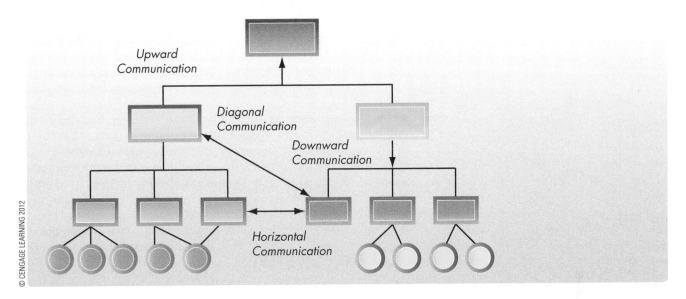

© CENGAGE LEARNING 2012

communicated to employees often takes longer. Setting up procedures and creating a culture that enables the uninhibited flow of information is the foundation of effective communication.[80] As a senior leader of Tata Consultancy Services in Mumbai, India, says, "From communicating key organizational policies and initiatives to establishing a direct connection between the CEO, senior management and the employees, technology can help dissolve geographic and hierarchical barriers."[82]

Management by wandering around is a face-to-face management technique in which managers get out of their offices and spend time talking informally to employees throughout the organization.[83] Being actively engaged in the day-to-day operations of the business gives managers a feel for what is really going on in the company. For example, in the first six months after Gary Kusin became CEO of Kinko's Inc, he went into each of Kinko's twenty-four markets in the United States, visited more than 200 stores, and met with more than 2,500 team members to learn what the company needed to do to continue evolving.[84]

Information technology and the Internet have given managers more choices in how to communicate downward, including e-mail, instant messaging, intranets, portals, wikis, blogs, and webcasts in addition to traditional verbal and written communication. In this chapter's opening Real World Challenge you learned about some of the ways Nokia is using technology to reinforce its values. One manager at technology provider Cisco Systems says, "Between videos and blogs, we are engaging with employees in a way that causes them to think, not just absorb things in a stale or static manner."[85]

Lucent uses a variety of technologies to communicate with employees around the world and gathers employee feedback to identify what is and is not working. Through this feedback Lucent has learned how to use satellite broadcasts, e-mail messages, and Internet publications to share information with employees. A Lucent executive says, "Global communication becomes almost instantaneous when posted to the website. We can send out an internal press release and ensure that employees are getting accurate information as quickly as possible."[86] When big news hits, Lucent quickly posts audio files on its intranet so that employees can listen to the leader's message.

Upward Communication

Upward communication occurs when lower-level employees communicate with those at higher levels—for example, when a subordinate tells a manager about a problem employees are having meeting a customer's request. Encouraging upward communication can help managers check that subordinates understand their goals and instructions, keep managers informed of employee challenges and complaints, and cultivate acceptance and commitment by giving employees the opportunity to express ideas and suggestions.[87]

Despite its potential benefits, getting subordinates to give upward feedback can be challenging. Subordinates often filter bad news, fearing that their boss does not really want to hear it. Being approachable, accessible, and creating a culture of trust and openness can help subordinates feel more comfortable giving upward feedback. Managers should avoid overreacting, becoming defensive, or acting blameful, and should respect confidentiality when a subordinate shares potentially controversial or negative information. Attitude surveys, an open-door policy, and regular face-to-face meetings with subordinates can also foster upward communication. One of the best ways to make subordinates comfortable sharing information may be sympathetically listening to them during your daily informal contacts with them in and outside of the workplace.[88] This can build the trust required for subordinates to share their ideas and honestly communicate negative information.

Technology tools such as wikis can enhance bottom-up communication in organizations. By creating an open-source workspace, all employees can be part of the brainstorming and problem-solving process. For example, when a manager at an investment bank wanted an analysis of how to double profits on a particular trade, he put the problem on a wiki page where other employees could comment, brainstorm, and edit in real time. In two days, the manager had analytics that otherwise would have taken two weeks to acquire.[89]

Horizontal Communication

Horizontal communication occurs when someone in an organization communicates with others at the same organizational level. Managers often depend on each other to help get the job done, and communication is necessary for them to coordinate resources and workflow. Although horizontal communication occurs between peers, as in all organizational communications, it is best to stay professional and avoid confrontational words and negative body language.

Managers can facilitate horizontal or interdepartmental communication by appointing liaison personnel or creating interdepartmental committees or task forces to facilitate communication and coordination and solve common problems. Technology also can help.

Kraft Foods gives employees many communication tools to use in communicating with each other. KraftCast is a quarterly podcast featuring an interview with a company executive or newsmaker. On Ask the KET (short for Kraft executive team), employees ask questions about anything from recipe changes to how the financial crisis is affecting Kraft. Online videos, blogs, wikis, and discussion boards can be made available to all employees or to a particular workgroup. An online notice board even lets employees congratulate each other or thank coworkers for their help.[90]

Diagonal Communication

When employees communicate across departments *and* levels, they are engaging in *diagonal communication*. For example, if Ryan's subordinate Owen contacts Ryan's peer in a different department, diagonal communication has occurred. Diagonal communication is common in cross-functional project teams composed of people from different levels drawn from different departments.

Diagonal communication allows employees in different parts of an organization to contribute to creating a new product or solving a problem. Diagonal communication also helps to link groups and spread information around the firm. Almost all successful managers use these informal communication networks to monitor employee communication and to communicate quickly with employees.[91] A long-standing practice at General Motors is its "diagonal slice meetings" in which top executives seek feedback from white-collar people at all levels of the company.[92]

Diagonal communication can be inappropriate depending on the situation and the people involved. Subordinates who engage in diagonal communication may alienate their direct supervisor who might feel "out of the loop" and punish the subordinate for disrespecting the chain of command.

Information technology and the Internet can facilitate horizontal and diagonal communication through the company's intranet, portals, and wikis. By creating a central location where employees can post questions and help solve problems other employees are dealing with, communication can occur among employees who would be unable to communicate without the use of technology. For organizations with multiple locations, IT and the Internet can create employee networks that allow employees located around the world to work together and share knowledge.

Formal and Informal Communication

Formal communications are official, organization-sanctioned communications. They can be upward, downward, horizontal, or diagonal. Formal communication channels typically involve some sort of written communication that provides a permanent record of the exchange. Formal communication is usually interpreted accurately.

Informal communication is anything that is not official. Informal communications include gossip and answering another employee's question about how to do something. The grapevine is an example of an informal communication channel. The grapevine can promote the spread of gossip or rumors, which can be destructive and interfere with the functioning of the company, particularly if they are untrue.[93] You should not avoid the grapevine, but be sure to evaluate the credibility of the source before you believe what you hear.[94] If a rumor does not make sense or is inconsistent with other things you know or have heard, seek more information before reacting.

As a manager, being aware of current office gossip can help to keep you informed of what is on employees' minds and prevent rumors from growing out of control. It is best to prevent rumors from starting by establishing clear communication channels, building trust with your employees, and providing employees adequate facts and information. If a rumor does start to spread, *neutralize* it by consistently and honestly communicating with employees about the issue. Not making a comment is usually seen as confirmation of a rumor.[95]

SO WHAT

To minimize damage, including a loss of trust and a tarnished reputation, neutralize rumors quickly.

Social Networking

social network

The set of relationships among people connected through friendship, family, work, or other ties

SO WHAT ?

Social networks will make you more effective in your career by improving the professional and career-related information and expertise available to you.

A *social network* is the set of relationships among people connected through friendship, family, work, or other ties. People form social networks in organizations that allow for an exchange of information from one employee to another, or even to people outside the company. These informal networks can be helpful—they give employees access to people who can help solve problems and get work done. It is often recommended that new employees try to tap into existing social networks to learn how to successfully do their work.[96]

Our social networks consist of both formal and informal ties. *Formal ties* refer to relationships with coworkers, bosses, and others we know because of the roles we hold. Employees have formal ties with their bosses and subordinates. *Informal ties* are relationships based on friendship and choice. If an accounting employee and a production employee create a tie between them because they want to discuss work issues or develop a friendship, and not because they have to, this tie is an informal one.

Some people's social networks have many ties, making them central in an organization's social network. The employee who everyone goes to with a question, or who seems to know everything about everyone else, is central to that company's social network.

The pattern of relationships in a company influences its communication patterns and information flow. If employees tend to be connected to many other employees, as shown in Figure 8-4, communication is more open and information flows more freely. If employees tend to be connected to very few other employees, as shown in Figure 8-5, or if employees tend to be connected only to their managers, the network is more closed and information tends to flow only to the central person.

Personal contacts are essential to the success of salespeople and managers alike. Social networking Internet sites take these personal relationships online. Hundreds of companies worldwide, including Saturn and Smart Car, use internal social networks to boost productivity and encourage collaboration. LinkedIn's service, Company Groups, digitally gathers all of a company's employees into a single, private web forum where they can talk, share ideas, and ask company-related questions. More than 1,000 companies have signed up for the service.[97] Facebook also has a service that lets people sharing company e-mail addresses join the same group.

Figure 8-4

Social Network Reflecting Open Communication

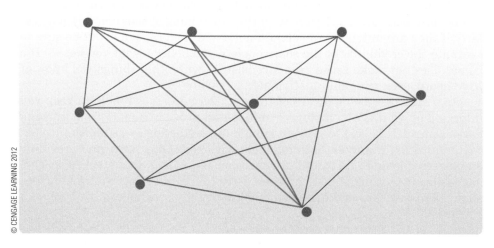

© CENGAGE LEARNING 2012

© CENGAGE LEARNING 2012

Figure 8-5

Social Network Reflecting Less Open Communication

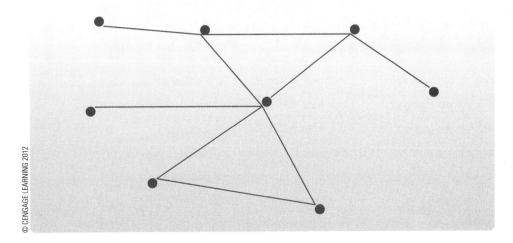

Social networking has a potential downside. If employees and customers are satisfied, these networks can help build loyalty. If not, employees and customers will communicate and amplify every complaint through these networks.

Both employees and managers need to be careful about what they post on Internet social networking sites like Facebook, LinkedIn, and MySpace. This information will be available for others to view for many years, and many hiring managers look at Facebook and other sites to learn more about job candidates.[98] You can use this to your advantage by posting information that reinforces and further explains your qualifications and accomplishments, rather than photos and other information that might frame you in a negative light.[99]

SO WHAT

Use online social networking sites to reinforce your professional accomplishments and image.

SUMMARY AND APPLICATION

In the communication process, the sender translates (encodes) information into words, symbols, or pictures and passes it to the receiver through some medium (channel). The sender then receives the message, and retranslates (decodes) it into a message that is hopefully the same as what the sender intended. Noise can enter anywhere in the process, making the message received different from the one the sender intended. Feedback creates two-way communication that helps to check on the success of the communication and ensure that the received message is accurate.

Writing, speaking, and meeting management skills are all important to effective communication. Organizational communication can move in a variety of directions, and be formal or informal in nature. Communication paths can be downward, upward, horizontal, or diagonal. Social networks help to establish communication patterns in organizations.

Managers need to fit the media to the message, use appropriate body language and nonverbal cues, and ensure that subordinates understand the meaning of the messages sent. It is also a good idea to understand how employees like to be communicated with and seek their feedback about how different communication channels are working.

VALUES IDENTIFICATION AND COMMUNICATION AT NOKIA

Employees had stopped referring to Nokia's values as energizing. Because of the importance of its values to its strong culture of innovation and teamwork, Nokia wanted to reenergize employees around its core values. Nokia understands that the core of communication is getting your message into the heads of the receivers, and that the best way to do this is to engage them.

To engage employees in identifying and living the company's values, Nokia began by conducting a worldwide series of two-day workshops called Value Cafés. Over six months, 2,500 employees from all organizational levels and around the world discussed what values Nokia should have to achieve its strategic goals and how to best communicate them. Nokia then sent representatives from the Value Cafés to Helsinki to hold a Global Value Café to synthesize the input and identify what Nokia's values should look like. They then presented their ideas to Nokia's Group Executive Board, which loved them. The new values were:

1. *Engaging you*: "You" refers to the whole ecosystem of all key stakeholders—customers, suppliers, partners, communities, employees, and so on, rather than just the customer.

2. *Achieving together*: This value emphasizes the fact that teamwork and collaboration are essential to Nokia's success.

3. *Passion for innovation*: Nokia's success depends on innovation, which is encouraged and expected throughout the company.

4. *Very human*: Nokia is focused on creating very human technology with a customer-friendly human interface; this value also reflects its values when dealing with people internally.

engaging you
My six-year-old son has been eagerly learning how to take photos. If you look closely, you can see the delight in his eyes. What you can't see is the pride in mine.

NOKIA

NOKIA INC

This is one of the winning photos from Nokia's photo contest reinforcing its core values.

One of the Value Café representatives then presented the new values during a gathering of about 250 of Nokia's top managers, and received standing ovations. Nokia next held a forty-eight-hour online jam session to put the new values and strategies on the Internet and to get employees to discuss, chat, and debate them. More than 15,000 employees participated, including all of Nokia's top executives who showed their interest and answered questions.

To further engage all of its employees, Nokia held a photo contest encouraging employees to use their mobile phones to take pictures about things at Nokia that reflected the company's values. Employees then voted on the best pictures, which were given prizes. A third-party expert who was unaware of the values was given a subset of the pictures to analyze and identify what the pictures reflected. The expert identified the four values from the pictures. The contest was very popular among employees, and Nokia received many outstanding pictures they could later use in company communications to further reinforce the company's values. The photo contest was so well received that Nokia held a similar video contest, which also was energizing and fun for employees.

Nokia understands that the ownership of values lies with its employees. By involving them in defining and capturing the company's values, employees became actively involved and engaged. In the process of taking photos and shooting videos, Nokia employees were implementing Nokia's values. The popularity of the contests ensured that almost all employees developed an idea of what the values mean to them. This made the communication of the new values thorough and personal by engaging employees, rather than simply telling them what the new values would be.

After the values initiative, Nokia saw positive trends on its next employee survey regarding values. Employees' excitement about Nokia's values and their expectations that Nokia live by them went up substantially. Whenever Nokia makes companywide decisions, the leaders always get feedback from employees about how the decisions fit with the company's values. Nokia's employees are again actively talking excitedly about the company's values.

Source: This real world response is based on a telephone interview with Hallstein Moerk, Senior Vice President and Director of Human Resources, Nokia Corporation, June 26, 2009.

✔ TAKEAWAY POINTS

1. In the communication process, the sender translates (encodes) information into words, symbols, or pictures and passes it to the receiver through some medium (channel). The sender then receives the message, and retranslates (decodes) it into a message that is hopefully the same as what the sender intended. Noise can enter anywhere in the process, making the message received different from the one the sender intended. Feedback creates two-way communication that helps to check on the success of the communication and ensure that the received message is accurate.

2. Distractions, physical barriers, loss of transmission, competition from other communications, ambiguity of meaning or intent, jargon, and semantics are all types of noise that can interfere with effective communication.

3. In one-way communication, information flows in only one direction. The sender communicates a message without expecting or getting any feedback from the receiver. Once a receiver provides feedback to a sender, the sender and receiver have engaged in two-way communication.

4. Communication barriers include body language, verbal intonation, selective perception, filtering, information overload, organizational barriers, cultural barriers, and noise.

5. Some of the strongest and most meaningful communications are nonverbal—for example, an alarm, a flashing police light, or a look of happiness on someone's face. The most common nonverbal interpersonal communications are body language and intonation.

6. The richness of a communication media reflects the media's ability to carry nonverbal cues, provide rapid feedback, convey personality traits, and support the use of natural language. The richness of a medium depends on the availability of feedback, the ability to transmit multiple cues, language variety, and personal focus. The more a medium displays these attributes, the richer it is. When communicating, managers must choose the media that best matches the information richness required of the task or communication. The more ambiguous and uncertain a task is, the richer the media should be that supports it. For example, text-based computer messaging is a good fit for generating ideas, but not for negotiating conflicts. Videoconferencing is a good fit for decision-making tasks, but is not rich enough for negotiating.

DISCUSSION QUESTIONS

1. What are your preferred methods of receiving information? Does your answer differ depending on the type of information being sent?
2. What are the implications of organizational diversity on the communication media the company should use?
3. What are some of the most common sources of noise when others try to talk to you? What can you do to reduce their effects?
4. Think of a time when you have been persuaded by someone to do something. Why was the other person able to change your attitude or behavior?
5. If you had to tell your boss bad news, what communication media would you use?
6. If you were about to be fired, how would you want to hear the news? Why? How would you least want to hear the news? Why?
7. Which do you think is more important for organizations: downward communication or upward communication?
8. Which do you think is more important for organizations: formal or informal communication?
9. What role, if any, do you feel the grapevine plays in organizations?

EXERCISES

Active Listening

Form groups of at least four people. Each group then selects one of the following workplace scenarios:

___1. An employee asking for a raise
___2. A supervisor explaining a new vacation policy to an employee
___3. A new employee asking a coworker about the company's culture
___4. Two new employees generating potential solutions to a problem

After selecting a scenario, each group has twenty minutes to prepare two three-minute skits. The first skit, performed by team members one and two, should show the interaction without active listening techniques. The second skit, performed by team members three and four, should duplicate the conversation while clearly using active listening techniques.

*We thank Professor Jim Gort at Davenport University for suggesting this exercise.

Overcoming Barriers to Diversity

You have just taken your most challenging job yet. You are the new Chief Operations Officer of a restaurant chain that has been successfully sued by former employees for racial and gender discrimination seven times in the last five years. The company's last CEO is seen as the source of many of the problems. He frequently communicated his discriminatory views to his managers, and expected them to hire and promote white males above everyone else.

The company's poor image has started to hurt business. Employee turnover has increased dramatically among women and minorities, and some employees are threatening to sue if conditions do not improve. The restaurant chain's workforce is currently two-thirds women, of which half are women of color. Twenty-five percent of the male workforce is men of color. Middle management and above are all white males.

Last month the Board of Directors replaced the CEO with a talented young Latina to try to change the company and its image. She has asked you to help her implement a diversity program to reach all aspects of the company's operations, and needs your report by the end of next week.

Assignment: In a group of four to six people, discuss the following questions. Be sure to take notes and identify who will share your group's ideas with the class.

Questions

1. What communications might you use as you research your report? Given your tight deadline, what information will you gather and how will you collect it in time to meet the deadline?
2. What types of communication would you suggest the CEO use to most effectively reach employees with a new diversity message?
3. What cautions might you give the new CEO about how to avoid making communication mistakes during her transition and establishment of a new diversity culture at the company?

Communication at Southwest Airlines

Southwest Airlines feels that communication is important in keeping its employees connected to the company. As you learned in this chapter, there are many different methods of communicating. Point your browser to http://www.southwest.com/careers/freedom_connected.html and read about the various communication methods the company uses. Then answer the following questions.

Questions

1. What communication problems might exist at a company such as Southwest Airlines?
2. Which of Southwest's communication methods are one-way? Which are two-way? How do the goals of its one-way versus two-way methods differ?
3. If you were an employee, which communication methods would you prefer to use? Why?

Writing Conciseness

Read the following customer complaint. Write a paragraph describing the business representative's goals in responding to the complaint. Then play the role of the company representative and compose a business letter in response. Provide a solution, a reason for not complying with the complainer's request, or whatever you deem appropriate. You should use a clear, concise, business style and format your letter professionally.

Emil Tarique
101 Main Street
Chicago, IL 60610

October 17, 2013

Computer Kingdom
Consumer Complaint Division
2594 Business Drive
Tallahassee, FL 32301

Dear Sir or Madam:
Re: Account #29375403

On April 15, I bought a store-brand laptop computer at your Michigan Avenue store. Unfortunately, the computer has not performed well because of hardware issues. I am disappointed because I need the machine to do my work, and have had to take it in for repairs twice in the short time I have owned it. This has cost me time as well as decreased my productivity. I don't trust the machine, and am constantly worried about losing more data even though it has supposedly been repaired.

To resolve the problem, I would appreciate your exchanging this computer for a new one in good working order. Enclosed is a copy of my purchase receipt as well as the receipts for the two repairs.

I look forward to your reply and a resolution to my problem and will wait until August 30 before seeking help from a consumer protection agency or the Better Business Bureau. Please contact me at the above address or by e-mail at: myfakeemail.gmail.com.

Sincerely,

Emil
Enclosure(s)

VIDEO CASES

Now What?

Imagine having a tight deadline requiring you to focus on writing a report for the rest of the day in order to get it done on time. A worried looking subordinate enters your office and ineffectively tries to communicate a hurried message. *What do you say or do?* Go to this chapter's "Now What?" video, watch the challenge video, and choose a response. Be sure to also view the outcomes of the two responses you didn't choose.

Discussion Questions

1. How are verbal and nonverbal communication illustrated in these videos?
2. How do these videos illustrate active listening?
3. Which other aspects of communicating discussed in this chapter are illustrated in these videos? Explain your answer.

Workplace | Greensburg Public Schools: Communication

Greensburg superintendent Darrin Headrick was driving home the night the tornado hit town. He stopped at Greensburg High School principal Randy Fulton's house to take cover. He soon discovered the entire school system was wiped out. Every building was gone. Textbooks were scattered all over town, and computers were destroyed.

Along with 95 percent of the town's 1,500 residents, Headrick was homeless. With only four months to restore Greensburg Unified School District No. 422, Headrick went to work. All he had to work with was his laptop and cell phone, so he got in his truck and started looking for a wireless signal.

For the first three months after the tornado, no one could live in Greensburg. Because the tornado had affected telephone service, no one had a home telephone; people were either in shelters or staying with friends and family out of town. Everyone was eager to reconnect and get information. The Federal Emergency Management Agency (FEMA) provided primary crisis communications by distributing flyers, but residents had to come to town to get them.

Unable to access the school's normal communication channels, Headrick took a lesson from his students who preferred to communicate via text messaging because of its capacity for rapid exchange. Headrick realized text messaging was the perfect new channel for disseminating formal school communications. Few people had computers or landlines, but most folks had cell phones. Headrick set up a centralized network in which families were able to subscribe to a text service and receive important updates instantly wherever they were.

(Continued)

When things stabilized, Headrick set up forums at which students, parents, and teachers could participate in two-way, face-to-face communication. The text service was fabulous, but it didn't allow for real feedback or personal dialogue.

Rebuilding will take several years, but thanks to a temporary campus of trailers, the Greensburg schools started on time that fall. Communications within the school have continued to change. Every Greensburg High student now has a laptop and hands in assignments via e-mail. Teachers provide instant feedback on homework through instant messaging. The administration, teachers, students, and parents of Greensburg schools still talk to each other in person when it makes sense. The rest of the time, they happily communicate using the latest technologies.

Discussion Questions

1. Describe the advantages of text messaging as the preferred communication channel in Greensburg after the tornado.
2. Describe the disadvantages of text messaging as the preferred communication channel in Greensburg after the tornado.
3. What lessons can managers take from this story?

DO WHAT CENGAGENOW™

CENGAGENOW™ includes **teaching and learning resources** to supplement the text, and is designed specifically to **help students "think like managers"** by engaging and challenging them to think critically about managerial situations. **CengageNOW uses today's technology to improve the skills** of tomorrow's managers.

END NOTES

[1] This real world response is based on a telephone interview with Hallstein Moerk, Senior Vice President and Director of Human Resources, Nokia Corporation, June 26, 2009.

[2] The Nokia Story, 2012. Available online: http://www.nokia.com/global/about-nokia/about-us/story/the-nokia-story/.

[3] Bauer, R. (2009). 10 Annoying Employee Work Behaviors and What to Do About Them. Available online: http://ezinearticles.com/?10-Annoying-Employee-Work-Behaviors-and-What-to-Do-About-Them&id=570168.

[4] Watson Wyatt. (2010). 2009/2010 Communication ROI Study Report: Capitalizing on Effective Communication. Watson Wyatt. Available online: http://www.towerswatson.com/research/670.

[5] Welch, J. (2009, June 28). Keynote address at the 2009 SHRM 61st Annual Conference and Exposition, Seattle, WA.

[6] Byrnes, N. (2009, April 6). A Steely Resolve. *BusinessWeek*, 54.

[7] Welch, M. (2011). The Evolution of the Employee Engagement Concept: Communication Implications, *Corporate Communications: An International Journal, 16*(4), 328–346; Mayfield, J. R., Mayfield, M. R., & Kopf, J. (1998). The Effects of Leader Motivating Language on Subordinate Performance and Satisfaction. *Human Resource Management, 37*, 235–248.

[8] Bell, A., & Smith, D. (1999). *Management Communication* (p. 19). New York: John Wiley.

[9]Telephone interview with Hallstein Moerk, Senior Vice President and Director of Human Resources, Nokia Corporation, June 26, 2009.

[10]Mehrabian, A. (1968). Communication Without Words. *Psychology Today, 2*(9), 52–55.

[11]Mehrabian, A. (1971). *Silent Messages*. Belmont, CA: Wadsworth; see also Mehrabian, A. (1981). *Silent Messages: Implicit Communication of Emotions and Attitudes* (2nd ed.). Belmont, CA: Wadsworth; Mehrabian, A. (1972). *Nonverbal Communication*. Chicago, IL: Aldine-Atherton.

[12]Warfield, A. (2001, April). Do You Speak Body Language? *Training and Development,* 60.

[13]Warfield, A. (2001, April). Do You Speak Body Language? *Training and Development,* 60.

[14]Dearborn, D. C., & Simon, H. A. (1958). Selective Perception: A Note on the Departmental. Identification of Executives. *Sociometry, 21,* 140–144; Beyer, J. M., Chattopadhyay, P., George, E., Glick, W. H., Ogilvie, D. T., & Pugliese, D. (1997). The Selective Perception of Managers Revisited. *Academy of Management Journal, 40*(3), 716–737.

[15]Dessler, G., & Phillips, J. M. (2008). *Managing Now!* New York: Houghton-Mifflin.

[16]Lawrence, P. (2005). Designing Where We Work. *Fast Company.* Available online: http://www.fastcompany.com/resources/learning/lawrence/050205.html.

[17]Herrington, A. (2011). PIXAR is Inspiration for Modea's New Headquarters, Modea, September 19. Available online: http://www.modea.com/blog/pixar-is-inspiration-for-modeas-new-headquarters. Accessed May 16, 2012.

[18]Grensing-Pophal, L. (2008). Focus on Conversation, Not Data, for Best Employee Feedback. Society for Human Resource Management. Available online: http://www.shrm.org/hrdisciplines/employeerelations/articles/Pages/FocusonConversation.aspx.

[19]Marquez, J. (2009). Private Concerns. *Workforce Management Online.* Available online: http://www.workforce.com/archive/feature/24/54/77/index.php?ht=.

[20]Kwintesesential. (2010). Cross Cultural Marketing Blunders. Available online: http://www.kwintessential.co.uk/cultural-services/articles/crosscultural-marketing.html.

[21]Kwintesesential. (2010). Cross Cultural Marketing Blunders. Available online: http://www.kwintessential.co.uk/cultural-services/articles/crosscultural-marketing.html.

[22]Digital Dreams (2010, March 10). Famous Marketing Blunders. Available online: http://www.digitaldreams.com.ar/english/empresa/marketing_blunders.htm.

[23]Marketing Translation Mistakes. (2010). Available online: http://www.i18nguy.com/translations.html.

[24]Hall, E. T. (1976). *Beyond Culture.* New York: Doubleday.

[25]Geddie, T. (1998, April–May). Moving Communication Across Cultures. *Communication World, 16*(5), 37–41.

[26]Martin, J. S., & Chaney, L. H. (2006). *Global Business Etiquette: A Guide to International Communication and Customs.* New York: Praeger.

[27]Cross-Cultural/International Communication. (2009). Small Business Encyclopedia. Available online: http://www.answers.com/topic/cross-cultural-international-communication.

[28]Cross-Cultural/International Communication. (2009). Small Business Encyclopedia. Available online: http://www.answers.com/topic/cross-cultural-international-communication.

[29]Brett, J., Behfar, K., & Kern, M. C. (2006, November). Managing Multicultural Teams. *Harvard Business Review,* 86.

[30]Brett, J., Behfar, K., & Kern, M. C. (2006, November). Managing Multicultural Teams. *Harvard Business Review,* 87.

[31]Brett, J., Behfar, K., & Kern, M. C. (2006, November). Managing Multicultural Teams. *Harvard Business Review,* 84–91.

[32]Gallo, C. (2005, December 1). Lose the Jargon or Lose the Audience. *BusinessWeek Online.* Available online: http://www.businessweek.com/stories/2005-11-30/lose-the-jargon-or-lose-the-audience.

[33]Kirsner, S. (2006, January). DreamWorks Animation Couldn't Find a Videoconferencing System That Made CEO Jeffrey Katzenberg Happy—So It Built Its Own. *Fast Company,* 90.

[34]Kirsner, S. (2006, January). DreamWorks Animation Couldn't Find a Videoconferencing System That Made CEO Jeffrey Katzenberg Happy—So It Built Its Own. *Fast Company,* 90.

[35]Petress, K. C. (1999). Listening: A Vital Skill. *Journal of Instructional Psychology, 26*(4), 261–262.

[36]Dwyer, J. (2011). The Business Communicatin Handbook, 8th ed. New York: Pearson.

[37]Tyler, K. (2003, March). Toning Up Communications: Business Writing Courses Can Help Employees and Managers Learn to Clearly Express Organizational Messages. *HR Magazine,* 87–89.

[38]Adapted from Bell, A. H., & Smith, D. M. (1999). *Management Communication* (p. 14). New York: Wiley.

[39]Twainquotes.com. Available online: http://www.twainquotes.com/Word.html.

[40]Stockard, O. (2011). *The Write Approach: Techniques for Effective Business Writing.* Bingley, UK: Emerald Group.

[41]Adapted from Bell, A. H., & Smith, D. M. (1999). *Management Communication* (p. 14). New York: Wiley.

[42]Rogelberg, S. G., Leach, D. L., Warr, P. B., & Burnfield, J. L. (2006). "Not Another Meeting!" Are Meeting Time Demands Related to Employee Well-Being? *Journal of Applied Psychology, 91,* 86–96.

[43]Walters, J. (2003, January). Was That a Good Meeting, or a Bad One? *Inc.* Available online: http://www.inc.com/articles/2003/01/25007.html.

[44]Bloom, N., Garicano, L., Sadun, R. & Van Reenen, J. (2009). *The Distinct Effects of Information Technology and Communication Technology on Firm Organization.* NBER Working Paper No. 14975, May.

[45]Gonzalez, J. S. (1998). *The 21st-Century INTRANET.* Upper Saddle River, NJ: Prentice-Hall.

[46]Impastato, J. (2009, January). Integrate Web 2.0 into the On-Boarding Experience. *Talent Management,* 18–20.

[47]*USA Today.* (2007, March 2). RadioShack Lays Off Employees Via E-Mail. Available online: http://www.usatoday.com/tech/news/2006-08-30-radioshack-email-layoffs_x.htm.

[48]Dessler, G., & Phillips, J. M. (2008). *Managing Now!* New York: Houghton-Mifflin.

[49]Mayor, T. (2001). Remote (Worker) Control. *CIO Magazine.* Available online: http://www.cio.com/article/30100/Management_Remote_Worker_Control_.

[50]Wellner, A. S. (2005, September). Lost in Translation. *Inc.,* 37.

[51]Martin, B.H. & MacDonnell, R. (2012). Is Telework Effective for Organizations? A Meta-Analysis of Empirical Research on Perceptions of Telework and Organizational Outcomes, *Management Research Review, 35*(7).

[52]Kurland, N. B., & Bailey, D. E. (1999). Telework: The Advantages and Challenges of Working Here, There, Anywhere, and Anytime. *Organizational Dynamics, 28*(2), 53–67.

[53]Stark, B. (2007, August 27). The Future of the Workplace: No Office, Headquarters in Cyberspace. ABC World News with Dianne Sawyer. Available online: http://abcnews.go.com/WN/story?id=3521725&page=1.

[54]Laudon, K.. & Laudon, J. (2006). Management Information Systems: Managing the Digital Firm (9th ed., p. 436). Upper Saddle River, NJ: Prentice-Hall.

[55] Nielsen Norman Group (2011). Usability of Intranet Portals, Fremont, CA: Nielsen Norman Group.

[56] Nielsen Norman Group (2011). Usability of Intranet Portals, Fremont, CA: Nielsen Norman Group.

[57] Nielsen Norman Group (2011). Usability of Intranet Portals, Fremont, CA: Nielsen Norman Group.

[58]Howard, N. (2009). Information Please! *Inc.com.* Available online: http://www.inc.com/partners/businessinsights/content/Intranet.html.

[59] Nielsen Norman Group (2011). Usability of Intranet Portals, Fremont, CA: Nielsen Norman Group.

[60]Howard, N. (2009). Information Please! *Inc.com.* Available online: http://www.inc.com/partners/businessinsights/content/Intranet.html. An example of a portal can be found at http://en.wikipedia.org/wiki/Wikipedia:Community_Portal.

[61]Workforce Management. (2006, March 19–25). Get Fit. *Workforce Week: Management,* 7(12). Available online: www.workforce.com.

[62]Dessler, G., & Phillips, J. M. (2008). *Managing Now!* (p. 447). New York: Houghton-Mifflin.

[63]Wiki. (2012). Wikipedia. Available online: http://en.wikipedia.org/wiki/Wiki..

[64]Goodnoe, E. (2005, August 8). How to Use Wikis for Business. *InternetWeek.* Available online: http://www.informationweek.com/news/global-cio/showArticle.jhtml?articleID=167600331&pgno=1.

[65]Pacesetters: Collaboration. (2005, November 21). *Business Week,* 92.

[66]Pacesetters: Collaboration. (2005, November 21). *BusinessWeek,* 92.

[67]Robb, D. (2009, February). From the Top. *HR Magazine,* 61–63.

[68]Robb, D. (2009, February). From the Top. *HR Magazine,* 61–63.

[69]Robb, D. (2009, February). From the Top. *HR Magazine,* 61–63.

[70]Robb, D. (2009, February). From the Top. *HR Magazine,* 61–63.

[71]Impastato, J. (2009, January). Integrate Web 2.0 into the On-Boarding Experience. *Talent Management,* 18–20.

[72]Wellner, A. S. (2005, September). Lost in Translation, *Inc.,* 37.

[73]Phone interview with Lucien Alziari, Senior Vice President of Human Resources at Avon, Jean Phillips, June 8, 2009.

[74]Kirsner, S. (2006, January). DreamWorks Animation Couldn't Find a Videoconferencing System That Made CEO Jeffrey Katzenberg Happy—So It Built Its Own. *Fast Company,* 90.

[75]Madlock, P. E. (2008). The Link Between Leadership Style, Communicator Competence, and Employee Satisfaction. *Journal of Business Communication, 45,* 61–78.

[76]Daft, R. L., & Lengel, R. H. (1986). Organizational Information Requirements, Media Richness and Structural Design. *Management Science, 32*(5), 554–571; Daft, R. L., & Lengel, R. H. (1984). Information Richness: A New Approach to Managerial Behavior and Organization Design. In *Research in Organizational Behavior,* eds. B. M. Staw and L. L. Cummings (Vol. 6, pp. 191–233). Greenwich, CT: JAI Press.

[77]McGrath, J. E., & Hollingshead, A. B. (1993). Putting the Group Back in Group Support Systems: Some Theoretical Issues About Dynamic Processes in Groups with Technological Enhancements. In *Group Support Systems: New Perspectives,* eds. L. M. Jessup and J. S. Valacich (pp. 78–96). New York: Macmillan; Suh, K. S. (1999). Impact of Communication Medium on Task Performance and Satisfaction: An Examination of Media-Richness Theory. *Information & Management, 35*(5), 295–312.

[78]Trevino, L, K., Lengel, R. H., Bodensteiner, W., Gerloff, E., & Muir, N. (1990). The Richness Imperative and Cognitive Style: The Role of Individual Differences in Media Choice Behavior. *Management Communication Quarterly, 4,* 176–197.

[79]Frauenheim, E. (2007, March 26). Luxottica Group: Optimas Award Winner for Managing Change. *Workforce Management,* 29.

[80]Nazari, J.A., Herremans, I.M., Isaac, R.G., Manassian, A. & Kline, J.B. (2011). Organizational Culture, Climate, and IC: An Interaction Analysis, *Journal of Intellectual Capital, 12*(2), 224–248.

[81]Kincaid, C. (2009, April 6). Corporate Ethics Training: The Right Stuff. *Training,* 46, 34–36.

[82]Robb, D. (2009, February). From the Top. *HR Magazine,* 61.

[83]Peters, T. J., & Waterman, Jr., R. H. (1982). *In Search of Excellence.* New York: Harper & Row; Bell, C. R. (2000). Managing by Wandering Around. *Journal for Quality and Participation, 23,* 42–44.

[84]Overholt, A. (2002, May). New Leaders, New Agenda. *Fast Company,* 52.

[85]O'Brien, M. (2009, May 16). "Idol"-izing Ethics. Available online: http://www.hreonline.com/HRE/story.jsp?storyId=209480118.

[86]Dessler, G., & Phillips, J. M. (2008). *Managing Now!* (p. 447). New York: Houghton-Mifflin.

[87]Dessler, G. (1993). *Winning Commitment: How to Build and Keep a Competitive Workforce.* New York: McGraw-Hill.

[88]Plenty, E., & Machaner, W. (1977). Stimulating Upward Communication. In *Readings in Organizational Behavior,* eds. J. Gray and F. Starke (pp. 229–240). Columbus, OH: Charles Merrill.

[89]Conlin, M. (2005, November 28). E-Mail Is So Five Minutes Ago. *BusinessWeek,* 111.

[90]Robb, D. (2009, February). From the Top. *HR Magazine,* 61–63.

[91]Wilson, D. O. (1992). Diagonal Communication Links Within Organizations. *Journal of Business Communication, 29*(2), 129–143.

[92]Welch, D. (2009, October 5). GM: His Way or the Highway. *BusinessWeek,* 62–63.

[93]Michelson, G., & Mouly, S. (2000). Rumour and Gossip in Organizations: A Conceptual Study. *Management Decision, 38*(5), 339–346.

[94]Burke, L., & Wise, J. (2003). The Effective Care, Handling, and Pruning of the Office Grapevine. *Business Horizons, 46*(3), 71–76.

[95]Difonzo, N., Bordia, P., & Rosnow, R. (1994). Reigning in Rumors. *Organizational Dynamics, 23*(1), 47–62.

[96]Abrams, L. C., Cross, R., Lesser, E., & Levin, D. Z. (2003, November 17). Nurturing Interpersonal Trust in Knowledge-Sharing Networks. *Academy of Management Executive, 17*(4), 64–77.

[97]Swartz, J. (2008, October 8). Social Networking Sites Help Companies Boost Productivity. Available online: http://www.usatoday.com/tech/products/2008-10-07-social-network-work_N.htm.

[98]Roberts, C. (2009, July 14). Hey Kids, Facebook Is Forever. *NYDailyNews.com*. Available online: http://www.nydailynews.com/money/2009/07/14/2009-07-14_hey_kids_facebook_is_forever.html.

[99]Schepp, D. (2012). 1 in 3 Employers Reject Applicants Based on Facebook Posts, AOL Jobs, April 18. Available online: http://jobs.aol.com/articles/2012/04/18/one-in-three-employers-reject-applicants-based-on-facebook-posts/.

CHAPTER 9 Making Decisions

Decision making is at the core of many ethical challenges. What would you do if you had to choose between disclosing information that risks the demise of your company and possibly endangering customer safety by not disclosing the information?

REAL WORLD CHALLENGE

AN ETHICAL CHALLENGE

The CEO of a $20 million aircraft engine repair company just received a troubling fax. An airline is reporting that eight jets repaired by his company were just grounded because the turbines no longer worked. The airline claims that the CEO's company's parts are the cause of the problem. Within two hours, more calls come in and a total of eleven planes are grounded because of what the airline claims are problems with his company's parts. Although word has not yet reached the press, the FAA has been notified of the problem. The CEO fears that if his lenders learn of the accusation, the company's loans might be pulled. Not only would this be bad for the company, but it would jeopardize his own financial stake in the firm. Because the FAA has begun an investigation, he reasons, the only thing to do is sit tight until more details are revealed.

Unfortunately, the company is also in the middle of its annual audit. As part of the process, the CEO has to sign a letter stating that the auditors have been informed of any outstanding circumstances that more than likely could have a negative financial impact on the company. Disclosing the FAA investigation could mean the financial demise of his company. The CEO states, "In my industry, there's a very tight code of ethics about the use of drugs or alcohol by a manufacturer's employees. But there's nothing that tells you how you're supposed to deal with reporting information like this."[1]

Imagine that the CEO asks you how to decide what to do. Should he disclose the information and risk the jobs of hundreds of employees and his own financial stake in the company? Or should he stay quiet until he has more information? After reading this chapter, you should have some good advice for him.

MONTY RAKUSEN/JUPITER IMAGES

As Napoleon Bonaparte said, "Nothing is more difficult, and therefore more precious, than to be able to decide." Decision making is one of the most important things people do in organizations. Decisions made throughout all organization levels can impact the firm's opportunities and performance. Management expert Peter Drucker explained, "Most discussions of decision making assume that only senior executives make decisions or that only senior executives' decisions matter. This is a dangerous mistake. Decisions are made at every level of the organization, beginning with individual professional contributors and frontline supervisors."[2]

Even seemingly small decisions can have a financial impact. When warehouse retailer Costco decided to change the packaging of cashews from a round to a square canister CEO Jim Sinegal said, "It sounds crazy, but we saved something like 560 truckloads a year of that one product. That's significant savings."[3]

> "Nothing is more difficult, and therefore more precious, than to be able to decide." —*Napoleon Bonaparte, Historic French Military and Political Leader*

Clearly, making better decisions gives any organization a competitive advantage in its industry. Because so many organizational processes and outcomes depend on making good decisions, including business strategy, product design, and customer interactions, understanding how to make the best decisions will make you a more effective professional and manager.

So how are decisions made in organizations? This seemingly simple question is actually quite complicated. Thinking and debating about how to best make decisions goes back at least 2,500 years to Plato and the Greek pursuit of logical debate and reasoning. Yet despite all of the thought that has gone into it, it is still difficult for many managers and organizations to make the best decisions. Understanding common decision-making errors and techniques for overcoming them will help you to improve your decision-making skills.

In this chapter, we first discuss different types of decisions and describe a model of how decisions should be made along with some of the barriers to using this ideal process. We then explain how decisions are actually made by individuals and by groups. We also discuss ethical decision making and some of the ethical situations you might deal with throughout your career. We end the chapter with a discussion of creative decision making.

TYPES OF DECISIONS

Managers make many types of decisions including how to allocate a budget, who to hire or fire, and how to handle a disgruntled customer. They also decide when and how to introduce new products, when to buy new equipment, and how to best motivate subordinates. All decisions are essentially choices—even choosing to not do something or to not pursue an opportunity is a choice. Some decisions are made to determine whether we want to pursue an opportunity or not, and in what way. Other decisions are made to address a problem. Decisions can be described in three ways: programmed or non-programmed, strategic or operational, and top-down or bottom-up. Let's further explore what these distinctions mean.

Programmed versus Non-programmed Decisions

programmed decisions
Routine decisions that address specific problems and result in relatively structured solutions

Programmed decisions are routine decisions that address specific problems and result in relatively structured solutions. Programmed decisions follow a set of policies, procedures, or rules developed through past experience with similar decisions.[4] The information needed to make a programmed decision is readily available, and the problem is highly structured. Deciding how to handle a subordinate's overtime request or how to discipline an employee are examples of programmed decisions—rules and procedures exist that must be followed. Programmed decisions can sometimes be delegated to subordinates or others who understand the predetermined decision rules.[5]

Non-programmed decisions are novel decisions that require unique solutions. Introducing a new product, like when Apple introduced the iPad, and developing an advertising campaign for a new service are examples of non-programmed decisions. Non-programmed decisions are unstructured, and require managers to use creativity rather than experience to find good solutions. The information used to make non-programmed decisions is usually incomplete or ambiguous, and the solution relies on judgment or creativity. Because non-programmed decisions require customized solutions, managers are generally unable to delegate them.

non-programmed decisions
Novel decisions that require unique solutions

The same decision can be a programmed decision for one organization or manager and a non-programmed decision for another. For example, how to handle a broken manufacturing machine may be a programmed decision in a large company with established rules and standard operating procedures for handling the broken machine. The same decision might be a non-programmed decision for a small start-up company that has never experienced a breakdown in the machine. Experienced managers are more likely to have experienced similar decisions before, making many decisions programmed for them but non-programmed for more junior managers.

Non-programmed decisions, including who to hire, whether to expand or shut down a business, and whether to take out a loan, are some of the most difficult decisions managers have to make. Managers have to make these decisions without the ability to replicate previous decisions. Table 9-1 highlights some of the most difficult decisions managers face.

Strategic versus Operational Decisions

Strategic decisions address the long-term direction and focus of the organization. Deciding how to increase profitability, market share, and product quality are all strategic decisions. Determining what businesses to enter, what products or services to offer to what markets, and what talent and other resources will be needed to execute these plans are also strategic decisions. Strategic decisions are usually made by executive-level managers and the CEO.

strategic decisions
Address the long-term direction and focus of the organization

Table 9-1

The Toughest Managerial Decisions

Finance and investment

Staff issues including hiring and firing

Opening a business

Closing or selling a business

Expanding or relocating

Supplier and customer issues

Issues with business partners

Source: National Australia Bank (2006), What is the Toughest Decision You've Had to Make? Available online at: http://www.nab.com.au/wps/wcm/connect/nab/nab/home/About_Us/8/5/33/33.

operational decisions

Focus on the day-to-day running of the company

Operational decisions focus on the day-to-day running of the company. Determining work schedules, equipment utilization, and production schedules as well as handling unexpected absenteeism and equipment failures are common managerial operational decisions. Operational decisions require faster decision making than do strategic decisions. Operational decisions are made by the middle- and lower-level managers responsible for the daily operations of the business.

Top-Down versus Decentralized Decisions

top-down decisions

Directive decisions made solely by managers who then pass them down to lower-level employees for implementation

decentralized decisions

Employees, not managers, make decisions about their work, including staffing, production scheduling, and resource allocation

Top-down decisions are directive decisions made solely by managers who then pass them down to lower-level employees for implementation. Market share goals and companywide budget decisions are top-down decisions in organizations.

In contrast, *decentralized decisions* (or bottom-up decisions) occur when employees, not managers, make decisions about their work, including staffing, production scheduling, and resource allocation. Motorola was one of the first companies to facilitate decentralized decision making through its quality improvement teams.

Decentralized decision making empowers employees to make decisions themselves, rather than having to always go to a manager. How are involvement and empowerment different? Involvement gives subordinates influence in the decision being made; empowerment gives subordinates the ability and authority to make the decision themselves. In today's challenging business environment, empowerment lets leaders spend more time running the business rather than micromanaging employees. Participation in decision making can also have positive effects on employee performance and satisfaction.[6]

SO WHAT

Letting others participate in decision making can improve their performance and satisfaction and improve decision quality.

THE RATIONAL DECISION-MAKING PROCESS

rational decision-making process

Assumes that we make decisions systematically to maximize our expected utility

expected utility

All the objective and subjective outcomes associated with a decision

The *rational decision-making process* assumes that we use a systematic decision-making process and consistently try to maximize our expected utility. *Expected utility* includes all the objective (e.g., economic gain) and subjective (e.g., being ethical) outcomes associated with a decision. The process has six stages:

1. Define the problem or opportunity.
2. Set goals and identify evaluation criteria.
3. Identify alternatives.
4. Evaluate alternatives based on the evaluation criteria.
5. Choose the best alternative.
6. Implement the decision and monitor the results.

Figure 9-1 illustrates the rational decision-making process. Let's break down this process and discuss the strengths of each part of it as well as various barriers, biases, and errors that interfere with it at each of the stages.

Define the Problem or Opportunity

The first step in the rational decision-making process is the identification of a problem or opportunity. What will we be making a decision about? Perhaps a

Figure 9-1

The Rational Decision-Making Process

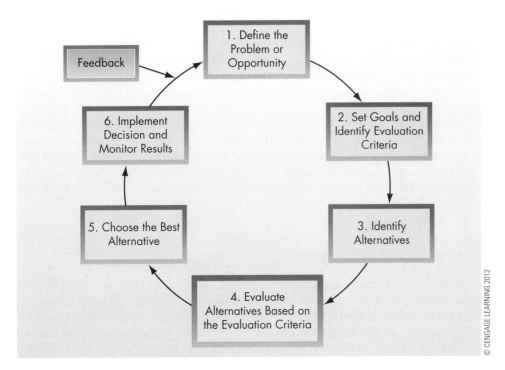

© CENGAGE LEARNING 2012

broken production machine means that our biggest client's order will not get filled in time, and we need to decide what to do. We might frame the problem in terms of quickly fixing or replacing the machine, or we might focus more broadly on the need to get the order filled and to the customer as soon as possible in order to keep the customer satisfied. Because the second problem definition is broader, it leads us to consider a wider set of alternatives. In addition to repairing or replacing the machine, alternatives include outsourcing the work to complete the order, asking the client for an extension, and doing the work without the machine, if possible. Because overly narrow problem definitions restrict our options for a solution, appropriately defining the problem or opportunity is an important foundation for making effective decisions.[7]

It is often difficult to identify the real problem or opportunity in a situation. If we do not understand the root cause of a situation, obviously it will be difficult to make a good decision about how to manage it. Not all problems or opportunities are clear and unambiguous, nor are the possible evaluation criteria. It can also be difficult to recognize when a decision needs to be made at all. The *status quo bias* reflects our tendency to not change what we are doing unless the incentive to change is compelling.[8] Similarly, identifying all the relevant evaluation criteria can be challenging, particularly when decisions need to be made quickly.

SO WHAT

Try not to define a problem too narrowly to ensure that you consider an appropriate variety of possible solutions.

status quo bias

Our tendency to not change what we are doing unless the incentive to change is compelling

Set Goals and Identify Evaluation Criteria

Once we have identified the problem or opportunity, we need to determine our goals for the decision outcome and identify the characteristics a good solution must have. In the case of the delayed order due to a broken machine, we might identify customer satisfaction and retention, speed, cost, quality, and other

SO WHAT

Unintended consequences can be minimized by spending appropriate time identifying the possible outcomes of a decision.

factors as criteria to use in evaluating alternatives. We also establish weights for the various criteria—we give goals and criteria that are more important than others greater weight in the final decision.

If some criteria must be met at a certain level (e.g., below a certain cost or at a certain speed or level of quality), these levels should be identified at this stage. For example, if the order must be filled within a month, taking more time than that is not an option. Because each decision alternative will later be evaluated and compared based on these goals and criteria, and this information will be used to persuade others to adopt or support the ultimate decision, it is important to be thorough.

Because unintended consequences can undermine the effectiveness of any decision, it is important to think through all the possible important consequences and set goals for them. It could be very damaging, for example, to make a decision based on speed and cost, only to lose business because the outcome of that decision was lower-quality products, a consequence that was not considered.

Identify Alternatives

After identifying and weighting the decision criteria, we next identify alternatives to solve the problem or to determine if the opportunity is worth pursuing. If we are considering buying a new production machine, we need to learn what machines are available that meet our needs. If we are considering outsourcing the production work, we need to identify other companies able to do the work quickly, at the right cost, and to our quality specifications. Because only alternatives that are included on the list that is evaluated in the next stage can be ultimately chosen as our decision, it is important to not be too critical of alternatives at this stage.

It is difficult to identify all the possible alternative solutions to a decision problem. It is also impossible to know when all possible alternatives have been identified. Involving multiple people and even outside consultants can improve the generation of alternatives. When insurance company Aflac wanted a new advertising campaign to increase its name recognition among consumers, it invited several advertising agencies to deliver pitches at the same time in a creative shoot-out. After reviewing at least twenty different concepts, Aflac invited the top two agencies to submit five ads each for testing.[9]

Evaluate the Alternatives

The next step is to evaluate each of the alternatives we identify based on each criterion we identified earlier. It is rare to find an optimal solution—alternatives often involve trade-offs among different goals. The purpose of this stage is to try to thoroughly understand the strengths and limitations of each alternative. Alternatives that do not meet minimum criteria (e.g., are too expensive or too low in quality) are removed from the list, as they are not viable alternatives.

Making a table with the surviving alternatives in the rows and the various goals and objectives in the columns as shown in Table 9-2 can help summarize this information. In Table 9-2, the four alternatives include two different machines and two different outsourcing options. The three goals of the decision, maximizing speed and quality at the lowest cost, are in the columns and are equally weighted, and rated on a scale from 1 (worst possible score) to 10 (best possible score). The last column contains the totals of the values of

Table 9-2

Evaluating Alternatives with Criteria of Equal Weight

Alternative	Speed	Cost	Quality	Total
Machine A	8	4	6	18
Machine B	7	7	8	22
Outsourcing A	9	5	7	21
Outsourcing B	10	2	4	16

Table 9-3

Evaluating Alternatives with Unequally Weighted Criteria

Alternative	Speed (.5)	Cost (.3)	Quality (.2)	Total
Machine A	8	4	6	19.2
Machine B	7	7	8	21.6
Outsourcing A	9	5	7	22.2
Outsourcing B	10	2	4	19.2

the different criteria. Table 9-2 shows that when speed, cost, and quality are equally weighted, Machine B is the best choice because it has the highest total value in the far-right column.

Then note what happens when the criteria of speed, cost, and quality are unequally weighted, as is often the case. As illustrated in Table 9-3, when speed becomes the most important factor (weighted 50 percent), followed by cost (weighted 30 percent) and then quality (weighted 20 percent), the best decision changes to Outsourcing A.

We tend to have difficulty objectively evaluating decision outcomes. To optimize the identification and evaluation of alternatives, some companies control the order in which participants voice their opinions or ban purely anecdotal arguments.[10] Time pressure also detracts from our ability to generate a thorough list of alternatives. Many errors and biases can occur during this stage of the decision-making process. We next discuss some of the most common ones and summarize them in Table 9-4.

Escalation of Commitment. Imagine that you buy tickets to a movie only to learn that it is horrible. Since you already bought the tickets, you are much more likely to still see the movie than if you had won or been given the tickets. A more rational decision would be to not go based on your low interest in seeing the movie. But because you paid for the tickets, you have a sunk cost that prevents you from evaluating the decision to watch the movie on its own merits. This *escalation of commitment* causes you to persist with a failing course of action.

escalation of commitment
Persisting with a failing course of action

Escalation of commitment has been blamed for the loss of thousands of lives and billions of dollars.[11] Managers who initiate a project are less likely to perceive that it is failing, are more committed to it, and are more likely to continue funding it than are managers assuming leadership after a project has started.[12] Leaders are also more likely to continue to invest in a failing course of action if they have a strong need to save face and avoid looking bad.[13]

Table 9-4

Common Errors in Evaluating Alternatives

Escalation of commitment:	persisting with a failing course of action
Framing:	describing or framing a decision as a loss or a gain influences our evaluation of alternatives
Overconfidence:	the tendency to be overoptimistic
Availability bias:	when we can readily remember past instances of an event, we tend to overestimate the likelihood that such an event will occur again
Representativeness:	we overestimate what we are familiar with, and underestimate things with which we are not familiar or that we do not remember as well
Anchoring and adjustment:	making assessments by starting with, or anchoring onto, a familiar starting value and then adjusting it based on other elements of the decision problem to arrive at a final decision
Halo bias:	drawing a general impression about something or someone based on a single (typically good) characteristic

SO WHAT

Rewarding employees for ending failing projects in a reasonable period of time can help to counter escalation of commitment.

framing

How a situation is described or framed influences the decision we make

loss aversion

Tendency to experience losses more strongly than gains

Expectations that leaders "stay the course" in the face of challenges contribute to escalation of commitment. Also, because managers are often punished for failure, they are more likely to persist in the face of negative results. Creating reward systems that reinforce a faster recognition of failing projects can help to reduce the effects of escalation of commitment.

Framing. *Framing* reflects the influence of how a situation is described or framed (e.g., as a winning or losing proposition) on the decision we make. We tend to feel the pain of losses more strongly than the pleasure of gains.

Loss aversion, our tendency to experience losses more strongly than gains, is one of the biggest threats to objectively evaluating alternatives and making effective decisions. Loss aversion leads people to prefer avoiding losses to making gains. Loss aversion often leads to inaction and undercommitment, frequently affecting investment decisions. As one expert put it, "More money has probably been lost by investors holding a stock they really did not want until they could 'at least come out even' than from any other single reason."[14]

In one famous study, participants were given the following anecdote:[15]

Imagine that the United States is preparing for the outbreak of an unusual Asian disease, which is expected to kill 600 people. Two alternative programs to combat the disease have been proposed. Assume that the exact scientific estimates of the consequences of the programs are as follows: If program A is adopted, 200 people will be saved. If program B is adopted, there is a one-third probability that 600 people will be saved and a two-thirds probability that no people will be saved. Which of the two programs would you favor?

Seventy-eight percent of participants chose program A, and 22 percent chose program B. However, when the researchers changed the wording so that the anecdote referred instead to the number of deaths (e.g., if program A is adopted, 400 people will die) but the consequences remained the same, the results were nearly reversed.[16] As a manager, it is important to understand the effect that the simple framing of a problem as a gain or a loss can have on evaluating alternatives and on subsequent decisions.

Organizational incentives magnify the effects of loss aversion on the career-motivated self-censorship of "risky" proposals.[17] In one example, a manager at a large manufacturing company decided not to propose an investment that had a 50–50 chance of either losing the entire $2 million or returning $10 million. The chance for a 5:1 gain should have attracted him to pursue the investment. Instead, he worried that his reputation and career prospects would be hurt if the investment failed, and he did not expect to be punished if the investment was not pursued. This framed the decision as a potential loss, triggering the executive's natural loss aversion, which was then magnified by his career concerns.[18]

Overconfidence. Compared to your classmates, how do you think you compare as a student? Are you in the top third, bottom third, or about average? Whenever we ask this of a class, well over half usually rate themselves in the top third, although clearly only one in three students actually does rank in the top third, and very few choose the bottom third, though one in three would belong there. Why is this? When evaluating the likelihood of potentially positive outcomes, we have a strong tendency to be overoptimistic or overconfident, believing that the future will be great, especially for us. When making decisions, this optimism not only leads to unrealistic expectations about positive outcomes, but also leads us to underestimate the likelihood of future problems and challenges. Overconfidence affects our judgments of probability and often leads to overcommitment.

One way of tempering our natural optimism is to track the outcomes of our past decisions. Few managers get regular feedback about the results of their decisions. Without this, it is natural to assume that our past decision-making methods and choices worked. By providing frequent, rapid, and clear feedback to subordinates, effective managers also reduce the effects of overconfidence in their staff. Getting a second opinion on the merits of the alternatives under consideration is another strategy. Many companies do this by assigning important decisions to committees (e.g., budget committees). Some organizations regularly take a systematic and fresh look at past decisions. At some private equity firms, after a partner has supervised a company for a few years, a different partner evaluates it. Someone looking with a fresh pair of eyes and no emotional connections can sometimes see things that escape the attention of the current decision makers.[19]

Availability Bias. When we can readily remember past instances of an event, like a failed product launch or a successful marketing strategy that doubled the product's market share, we tend to overestimate the likelihood that a similar event will

SO WHAT
In order to reduce the effects of loss aversion, be careful not to punish failure too severely.

SO WHAT
Seek feedback on the accuracy of your past decisions to reduce overconfidence.

Getting a second opinion can help to reduce the risk of overconfidence influencing a decision.

availability bias

When we can readily remember past instances of an event, we tend to overestimate the likelihood that such an event will occur again

occur again.[20] The *availability bias* operates on the notion that if we can think of it, it must be important.[21] This results in an underestimation of the probability of occurrence of events that have never happened, because we do not tend to think of them, and an overestimation of the probability of occurrence of events that we remember, such as rare negative events like environmental disasters that receive extensive media coverage and are thus easily remembered. The availability bias is easily seen when people use an anecdote ("I know of one employee who . . .") to support a decision rather than data or statistical probability.

representativeness bias

Occurs when we overestimate what we are familiar with, and underestimate things with which we are not familiar or that we do not remember as well

Representativeness Bias. The *representativeness bias* happens when we overestimate what we are familiar with, and underestimate things with which we are not familiar or that we do not remember as well.[22] For managers, the representativeness bias can result in placing too much emphasis on a subordinate's recent performance during a performance appraisal intended to capture the employee's performance over the previous year.

Anchoring and Adjustment. It is common for decision makers to make assessments by starting with, or anchoring onto, a familiar starting value and then adjusting it based on other elements of the decision problem to arrive at a final decision. This bias is called *anchoring and adjustment*.[23]

anchoring and adjustment

Making assessments by starting with, or anchoring onto, a familiar starting value and then adjusting it based on other elements of the decision problem to arrive at a final decision

One study by Nobel prize winning decision-making researchers Amos Tversky and Daniel Kahneman found that when asked to guess the percentage of African nations that are members of the United Nations, people who were asked "Is it more or less than 45 percent?" guessed lower values than those who were asked if it is more or less than 65 percent.[24] This pattern has held in other experiments for a wide variety of subjects. A different study asked an audience to first write the last two digits of their social security number, and then submit mock bids on items such as wine and chocolate. The half of participants with higher two-digit numbers submitted bids between 60 and 120 percent higher than the other half. Simply thinking of the first number strongly influenced the second, even though there was no connection between them.[25] This suggests that to maximize negotiation outcomes, you should begin from an extreme initial position and ask for more from the other side than you are willing to ultimately accept.

halo effect

Drawing a general impression about something or someone based on a single (typically good) characteristic

Halo Effect. Many decisions are undermined by a bias known as the *halo effect*, which occurs when we form a general impression about something or someone based on a single (typically good) characteristic.[26] If we learn that something is on sale for a very low price, we may evaluate its other attributes more favorably than we otherwise would. This bias increases the favorability of our evaluation of the other criteria and increases the likelihood that we will choose it.

Choose the Best Alternative

Pulling the trigger on a decision can be difficult, especially if it involves a lot of resources or the loss of peoples' jobs. As General George S. Patton said, "Be willing to make decisions. That's the most important quality in a good leader. Don't fall victim to what I call the 'ready-aim-aim-aim-aim syndrome.' You must be willing to fire." As former Intel CEO Andy Grove put it, "None of us has a real understanding of where we are heading. But decisions don't wait for the picture to be clarified. So you take your shots and clean up the bad ones later."[27]

After evaluating each alternative, a decision is made that best meets all of the criteria. No perfect alternative may exist, making trade-offs among the criteria necessary. For example, higher quality usually comes at a higher cost, and faster speed often results in lower quality. Equally weighting the criteria is often not ideal. As illustrated in Tables 9-2 and 9-3, appropriately weighting the criteria to reflect their relative importance is critical—equal weighting is usually not optimal. Typically, the alternative with the highest score is chosen because it maximizes the outcomes.

"Be willing to make decisions. That's the most important quality in a good leader. Don't fall victim to what I call the 'ready-aim-aim-aim-aim syndrome.' You must be willing to fire." —*George S. Patton, General in World War II*

If no single best solution is clear, the decision needs to be made that maximizes the most important goals. Sometimes no solutions are identified that meet the minimum standards for being chosen. In this case, returning to the problem or opportunity identification stage of the process can help. Sometimes redefining the problem more broadly can lead to alternatives that were not previously considered.

A critical aspect of bounded rationality is the fact that we are limited in the amount of information we can process. Miller's Law, named after the psychologist who developed it, states that the number of objects the average person can hold in working memory is seven, plus or minus two.[28] Although people differ in their ability to process information,[29] there is usually so much information available about possible solutions that it can be difficult for anyone to process it all completely in making a final choice.

Implement and Monitor the Decision

Once a decision is made, the decision must be implemented. We then monitor the outcomes of the decision and use the feedback to ensure that the original problem is solved and the goals have been met. If the decision did not work, the problem remains to be solved. Sometimes a failed decision creates a new problem to solve. If the replacement machine does not arrive in time to meet the customer's order deadline, your biggest customer might be lost. This can create a new problem if your firm's remaining business is not enough to justify as many employees, machines, or inventory.

SO WHAT
When all goals cannot be met, make the decision that maximizes as many outcomes as possible.

When Facebook decided to revise its terms of use and received a backlash from users with privacy and other concerns, it changed back to its previous terms of use as it resolved the issues that were raised.[30]

We often have difficulty recognizing when our decisions have failed. We also tend to succumb to *post-decisional justification*, which makes us more likely to remember our decisions as better than they actually were.[31] When we base future decisions on the outcomes of decisions we previously have made, this bias can distort our evaluation of the alternatives.

post-decisional justification
Remembering our decisions as better than they actually were

In one study, participants chose which of two job candidates to hire. Both candidates had four positive and four negative attributes. When later asked to recall the attributes of the two candidates, participants recalled more positive attributes of the candidate of their choice and more negative attributes of the candidate they had rejected.[32] This bias can obviously hamper our ability to learn from previous decisions.

Hindsight bias describes how our impression of how we acted or would have acted changes when we learn the outcome of an event.[33] Hindsight bias can occur when we make a decision and are later asked to recall our choice. If we have learned the correct decision in the interim, our memory of our

hindsight bias
How our impression of how we acted or would have acted changes when we learn the outcome of an event

decision may become biased toward the new information. For instance, suppose a manager was asked to estimate the likely market share of a new product a year after being launched. If before the launch the manager estimated 20 percent, and then learned that the actual figure was 40 percent, the manager may later recall that his answer was 30 percent.

Any feedback or correct information we receive after making an initial judgment updates the knowledge base underlying our initial decision. If we cannot remember our initial judgment, we reconstruct it from what we currently know, which is the updated version that includes the correct information. So while feedback does not directly affect our memory for the original response, it indirectly affects our memory by updating the knowledge we use to reconstruct the response.[34]

HOW ARE DECISIONS REALLY MADE IN ORGANIZATIONS?

The rational decision-making process is very logical, and seems easy enough to follow. However, real decision making rarely resembles this model. The main limitations to the model are that people are not efficient and logical information processors and that the assumptions of the rational decision-making process are rarely met. Decision makers also often lack the time and money needed to fully execute all of the steps in the model. Decisions influenced by a desire to save time and money may have contributed to the 2010 Deepwater Horizon drilling rig blowout and resulting catastrophic oil spill in the Gulf of Mexico.[35]

Rather than being rational decision makers, often our rationality is limited by the amount of information, time, and resources available. These factors create *bounded rationality*.[36] This leads us to engage in *satisficing*, or making satisfactory rather than optimal decisions. Satisficing leads us to select the first acceptable alternative we consider, even though better alternatives may exist.[37] The rational decision-making model also ignores the many errors and biases that interfere with our decision-making process. People are just not as rational as assumed by the rational decision-making model.

The Abilene Paradox is a classic example of bad decision making:[38]

bounded rationality
Our rationality is limited by the amount of information, time, and resources available.

satisficing
Making a satisfactory rather than optimal decision

In a small town near Abilene, Texas, a couple and the wife's parents are sitting comfortably on a porch in 104-degree heat. They are engaging in as little motion as possible, drinking lemonade, and occasionally playing dominoes. At some point, the wife's father suggests they drive to Abilene to eat. The son-in-law thinks this is a crazy idea but doesn't see any need to upset the apple cart since the others seem to want to go, so he goes along with it, as do the two women. The air conditioning in their car is broken, but they all get in and drive an uncomfortable fifty-three miles through a dust storm to Abilene. They eat a mediocre lunch at a cafeteria and return exhausted, hot, and generally unhappy with the experience. It is not until they return home that they learn that none of them really wanted to go to Abilene—they were just going along because they thought the others were eager to go. Even the person who suggested it only did so because he thought (mistakenly) that the others were bored.

Even if the process is imperfect, effective decision making is logical and consistent, focuses on what is important, and maximizes our expected outcomes. It involves the efficient gathering of relevant information and expert opinion, and only as much information and analysis as is necessary. It is also straightforward and easy to use in a wide variety of decision situations.

Let's next explore the role of intuition, emotions, and culture in making decisions.

Intuition

Rational analysis plays a crucial role in decision making, especially when you have clear criteria and extensive high-quality, quantitative data. Yet in many business situations, following the rational decision-making model is impractical or impossible. *Intuition* is knowing something instinctively based on expertise and experience solving similar problems.

Intuition is not the opposite of rationality, nor is it guessing. Intuition evolves from experience and learning over time[39] and becomes a sophisticated form of expert reasoning honed throughout years of job-specific experience and problem solving.[40] Because it enables rapid decision making, effective managers often use intuition in making decisions.[41] As Jonas Salk, discoverer of the polio vaccine, noted, "if we combine our intuition and our reason, we can respond in an evolutionary sound way to our problems."[42]

As the business world becomes less structured and more dynamic, intuition has gained increasing recognition as an important decision-making tool. You have probably heard of experienced executives who are able to directly recognize the best option or course of action in many tricky situations. The solution just comes to them, instead of resulting from a lengthy process of deliberation. This is the result of years of experience and decision making. Nonetheless, intuition is generally not trusted on its own. As some experts have noted, "Managers often combine gut feel with systematic analysis, quantified data, and thoughtfulness."[43]

Intuition is obviously most useful for experts. Intuition is also most helpful when change is rapid and fast decisions are needed, the problem or decision-making rules are unclear, and available information is incomplete. Table 9-5 summarizes when intuition can be most useful.

The Role of Emotions in Decision Making

Emotions often interfere with optimal decision making. One manager may be elated about the birth of a grandchild and subsequently overestimate the value of a possible business acquisition. Another manager may be angry about

Table 9-5

When Is Intuition Most Useful?

Intuition can be most useful when:
- Fast decision making is required
- Change is rapid
- The problem is novel or poorly structured
- Decision-making rules are unclear
- Available information is ambiguous, conflicting, or incomplete
- The decision maker is an expert and has experience making similar decisions

recently losing money in the stock market and underestimate the potential value of launching a new product line. Emotions can distort our rationality and receptiveness to advice.

We also tend to base complicated decisions on how we feel. Making a complicated decision like "Should we hire this person?" or "Should we divest this business?" requires considering a lot of factors and comparing a lot of complex things, so often we use the simple summary metric of how we feel about the job candidate or the business. Doing that, however, opens us to the possibility of making a mistake based on emotion. One study found that mood swings induced by prior large trading gains or losses negatively interfered with traders' decision making.[44] This chapter's *Understand Yourself* feature gives you the opportunity to understand more about the role emotions tend to play in your own decision making.

SO WHAT

Because emotions interfere with our ability to make good decisions, try not to make important decisions when you are feeling strong emotions.

Cultural Differences

The decision-making process used by a manager is influenced by his or her cultural background.[45] In different cultures, decision problems are defined and framed differently, different alternatives may be identified, evaluation criteria may be differentially weighted, and even the importance of being rational may differ. The degree to which decisions should be made top-down or made by empowered employees also differs across cultures.[46]

UNDERSTAND YOURSELF

EMOTION-BASED DECISION MAKING

Using the scale below, write the number from 1 to 6 that reflects your agreement or disagreement with the statements below. When you are finished, follow the scoring instructions at the bottom to interpret your score.

strongly disagree	moderately disagree	slightly disagree	slightly agree	moderately agree	strongly agree
1	2	3	4	5	6

___1. I listen to my feelings when making important decisions.
___2. I base my goals in life on inspiration, rather than logic.
___3. I plan my life based on how I feel.
___4. I plan my life logically.
___5. I believe emotions give direction to life.
___6. I believe important decisions should be based on logical reasoning.
___7. I listen to my brain rather than my heart.
___8. I make decisions based on facts, not feelings.

Scoring: For questions 4, 6, 7, and 8, change your score as follows: 1 = 6; 2 = 5; 3 = 4; 4 = 3; 5 = 2; 6 = 1. Cross out your old response so that you can clearly see the replacement number. Now add up your responses to the eight items.

Interpretation: If you scored *36 or above,* you tend to rely heavily on your feelings when making decisions. This could mean that you try to make decisions too quickly. You might try to recognize the role that emotions tend to play in your decisions, and consciously take more time to identify and consider the facts before deciding.

If you scored *between 24 and 35,* you tend to use a balance of logic and emotion when making decisions. Although intuition can be helpful when making complex decisions, try to remain fact- rather than emotion-focused.

If you scored *23 or less,* you tend to use logic over emotions when making decisions. This can lead to effective decisions, although it also can lead to slower decision making.

Source: International Personality Item Pool: A Scientific Collaboratory for the Development of Advanced Measures of Personality Traits and Other Individual Differences. http://ipip.ori.org

In the United States, for example, managers tend to view most situations as opportunities for improvement through change. Other cultures, including those of Indonesians, Thais, and Malays, are more likely to accept life as it is and tend to see no need for change.[47] Cultures also vary in the extent to which they are comfortable using intuition. Managers in the United States, for example, are more likely to use fact-oriented, empirical evidence while their Israeli counterparts are more intuitive.[48] Managers in the United States also pride themselves on being fast decision makers. Many other cultures, including Egyptians, downplay time urgency, and even view slow decisions as having more value.[49]

SO WHAT

Don't expect people from other cultures to make decisions the same way that you do.

GROUP DECISION MAKING

Decision making by groups and teams can provide many benefits over individual decision making. Not only do more people generally identify more possible alternatives, the diversity of perspectives offered by a group can also provide a more thorough evaluation of each alternative. In addition, groups have the benefit of creating a shared responsibility for the decision and its successful implementation, increasing the chances that the decision will be implemented successfully.

University of Iowa Leadership Styles

Kurt Lewin and his colleagues at the University of Iowa[50] explored three types of leadership styles relevant to group decision making: autocratic, democratic, and laissez-faire. A leader who centralizes authority, makes decisions alone, and expects followers or subordinates simply to follow instructions uses an *autocratic leadership style*.

A leader who shares decision making with others and encourages subordinates to be involved in setting goals uses a *democratic leadership style*. A democratic leader may be *consultative*, seeking input from others but making the final decision alone, or *participative*, giving employees a say in the decision.

A *laissez-faire leadership style* is an extremely hands-off approach. Employees are given discretion to make decisions and perform their work any way they want. A laissez-faire leader exercises little or no control over the group and may not even participate in discussions.

So which style is best? Not surprisingly, the laissez-faire style consistently underperforms the democratic and autocratic styles. Jimmy Cayne, former CEO of Bear Stearns, expected his team of superstars to

autocratic leadership style
Centralizing authority, making decisions alone, and expecting followers or subordinates simply to follow instructions

democratic leadership style
Sharing decision making with others and encouraging subordinates to be involved in setting goals

consultative
Seeking input from others but making the final decision alone

participative
Giving employees a say in the decision

laissez-faire leadership style
Employees are given discretion to make decisions and perform their work any way they want

Leaders differ in the extent to which they share decision making with others or make decisions alone and expect subordinates to simply follow their instructions.

handle any problems that might appear in the firm's highly leveraged, mortgage-related hedge funds. When they did not, Cayne's hands-off management style left him in the dark and unable to manage the subsequent liquidity crisis.[51] Management expert Peter Cappelli says that too many managers simply choose not to lead. He claims that managers mistakenly believe that if they hire smart people and provide huge financial incentives for individual results, management of the firm will take care of itself.[52] Clearly, leaders must be ready and able to make decisions regardless of the talents of their staff.

Although employees' satisfaction is generally higher when working with a democratic leader than an autocratic one,[53] research comparing the two has been inconclusive. Because more employee-centered decision making tends to produce greater motivation, decision quality, morale, and teamwork, managers should involve employees in decisions whenever possible.[54]

When Should Groups Participate in Decision Making?

Tannenbaum and Schmidt[55] identified three forces that influence the appropriateness of subordinate participation in decision making:[56]

1. *Manager factors*: personal values, tolerance for ambiguity, confidence in subordinates, and the leadership behaviors the manager is comfortable engaging in
2. *Subordinate factors*: need for independence, willingness to take responsibility, tolerance for ambiguity, problem-solving interest, comprehension of goals and commitment to them, relevant knowledge and experience, expectations about participating
3. *Situation factors*: time constraints, ability of the group to work together, organizational type, nature of the problem

Based on an assessment of these factors, leaders choose a decision-making style along a continuum ranging from autocratic, when the leader makes a decision alone and announces it to the group, to delegative, where the manager permits employees to function autonomously within defined limits.

Tannenbaum and Schmidt stressed to leaders the importance of being honest with subordinates and making clear what kind of leadership behavior is being used.[57] If the manager intends to make a certain decision alone, but the group expects or has the impression that this authority should be delegated to them, considerable confusion and resentment will likely result. These authors also warned against using a "democratic façade" to conceal the fact that the leader has already made a decision that she or he hopes the group will accept as its own.[58]

Although members' diverse perspectives and expertise can improve the quality of decision making, groups and teams do make decision making more complicated. Effective managers often want to involve the appropriate perspectives to improve the quality of a decision and acceptance of it, but group decision making often leads to conflict and underperformance.[59]

Group Decision-Making Errors

In this section we discuss some common team decision-making errors and some ways technology can help reduce their effects.

Group Polarization. When working in groups, people tend to be more extreme in their decisions. This results in *group polarization*. People who tend to make more risky decisions as individuals will make even riskier decisions in a group.[60] This effect is called *risky shift*. As a manager, you can use this information to your advantage. If you want to get risky decisions made, you will be more successful if you put people in the decision-making group who tend toward risk. If you prefer to maintain the status quo or make a more conservative decision, staff the team with more conservative people.

Groupthink. *Groupthink* occurs when group members try to minimize conflict and reach consensus without critically analyzing and evaluating alternatives. It has been described as "a mode of thinking that people engage in when they are deeply involved in a cohesive in-group, when the members' strivings for unanimity override their motivation to realistically appraise alternative courses of action."[61]

Irving Janis identified eight symptoms of groupthink:[62]

1. *Illusions of invulnerability* that create excessive optimism and encourage risk taking
2. *Rationalizing warnings* that might challenge the group's assumptions
3. An *unquestioned belief* in the morality of the group, causing members to ignore the consequences of their actions
4. *Stereotyping* anyone who is opposed to the group as weak, evil, biased, spiteful, or stupid
5. *Direct pressure* to conform placed on any member who questions the group, couched in terms of "disloyalty"
6. *Self-censorship* of ideas that deviate from the apparent group consensus
7. *Illusions of unanimity*—silence is viewed as agreement
8. *Mindguards*—self-appointed members who shield the group from conflicting information

Groupthink obviously results in suboptimal decision making. It has been argued that groupthink was responsible for many examples of faulty decision making, including the failure of the large United Kingdom bank Northern Rock. Groupthink was also blamed in part for the Penn State pedophilia scandal.[63] The role of groupthink in the recent financial crisis is described in this chapter's *Case Study*.

Irving Janis did not believe that groupthink is inevitable in decision-making groups and devised seven ways of preventing it:[67]

1. Leaders should assign the role of "critical evaluator" to each group member to allow each member to freely voice objections and doubts.
2. Leaders should not express an opinion when assigning a task to a group.
3. The organization should set up several independent groups, working on the same problem.
4. All effective alternatives should be examined.
5. Each member should discuss the group's ideas with trusted people outside of the group.
6. The group should invite outside experts to their meetings. Group members should be allowed to discuss the problem with and question the outside experts.
7. At least one group member (a different person for each meeting) should be assigned the role of devil's advocate to intentionally challenge the group's assumptions and conclusions.

group polarization
The tendency of people to make more extreme decisions in a group than when alone

risky shift
People who tend to make more risky decisions as individuals will make even riskier decisions in a group

groupthink
A mode of thinking that people engage in when they are deeply involved in a cohesive in-group, when the members' strivings for unanimity override their motivation to realistically appraise alternative courses of action

CASE STUDY

The Role of Groupthink in the Financial Crisis

When an organization's leaders and members allow themselves to be captured by their own beliefs, they see only what they want to see. When coupled with ambition and greed, a feedback loop develops that increasingly biases the interpretation of information and distorts reality. Group members may rationalize or ignore warning signs that are in conflict with closely held beliefs and develop illusions of invulnerability. Many historians now feel that aspects of these processes are a core explanation for the excessive credit expansion that fuelled the 2007 subprime mortgage meltdown and subsequent financial crisis.

In the years leading up to the financial crisis, clear warnings of impending problems were ignored. The revered chairman of the U.S. Federal Reserve Bank, Alan Greenspan, was a strong advocate of the free market and supported minimal market intervention. He was also known to be unwelcoming to challenges to his ideas. As William White, the chief economist for the central bank of all central bankers, the Bank for International Settlements, recalls, "Greenspan always demanded respect."[64] And who could question Greenspan? He was an economic superstar and everything was going well. As White further states, "When you are inside the bubble, everybody feels fine. Nobody wants to believe that it can burst." [65]

White was the only central banker in the world willing to challenge or criticize Greenspan and his ideas. White predicted the approaching financial crisis years before it happened and presented a paper to the central bankers that contradicted everything Greenspan believed. Despite White's and his team's persistent criticism of the mortgage securitization business, explanations of the perils of risky loans, and provision of evidence about the rating agencies' lack of credibility, few in the highly secretive world of central banking listened. As White later said, "Somehow everybody was hoping that it wouldn't go down as long as you don't look at the downside."[66]

All the ingredients of the financial crisis were known by the central bankers more than two years before the crisis began. The Mortgage Insurance Companies of America, a trade association of U.S. mortgage providers, even sent a letter to Alan Greenspan expressing its strong concerns about risky mortgage lending practices and speculating that the Fed might be using incorrect data. But the data and warnings were ignored because the economy was doing well and billions in bonuses were being awarded on Wall Street. No one was anxious to break up the party. When Ben Bernanke succeeded Greenspan in early 2006, he also ignored the warnings. Even as the financial crisis began, Bernanke downplayed the risk of the troubles spreading further. We now know that the troubles and concerns highlighted by White and others rocked the foundations of the global economy.

To decrease the chances of groupthink undermining the financial industry again, some experts have suggested increasing the diversity of senior management and among those developing products that affect the risks in the financial system. Because similar people (age, race, education, gender, etc.) tend to think in the same way, perhaps people from different backgrounds would be more willing to question ideas and counter the effects of groupthink.

Questions:

1. How were the elements of groupthink illustrated in the financial crisis?
2. What could be done to reduce the effects of groupthink in the future?
3. Do you think that increasing the diversity of the financial companies' leadership would reduce groupthink? Why or why not?

Groupware and Group Decision Support Systems

Many team meetings are poorly run, take too long, and accomplish too little. *Meeting management software* can facilitate meetings by creating a record of the ideas presented, comments made, votes taken, and action items identified. It allows people to meet while sitting at their own desks, wherever they are in the world, eliminating travel expense and wasted time. Meeting management software allows people to contribute ideas, to view other people's ideas anonymously, and to comment and vote on them. Everybody can see everything, but because contributions can be anonymous, it can promote greater participation and idea sharing.

Effective communication is critical for groups to make good decisions, yet group members are not always in the same location. Because communication for many groups occurs at least in part through technology, group members have to consciously diagnose both the verbal and nonverbal elements of communications. Technology can facilitate communication among team members, and support team decision making as well. Electronic whiteboards and collaborative document editors allow members located anywhere in the world to see where others are pointing. Revisions and comments appear on all users' screens at the same time and changes are tracked and saved automatically. Document management systems provide index and search-engine capabilities to prevent companies from being overwhelmed by the proliferation of messages created by groupware.

Instant poll capabilities allow teams to quickly assess member opinions.[68] Instant messaging allows for fast, personal communication. The company intranet can also contain discussion threads and a place to store shared documents. Technology-based meeting aids also include a silent-voting function to assess consensus among meeting participants and a raise-hands function for asking questions during a virtual presentation.

Using group support systems can take some getting used to. In one hospital, teams developing plans to improve customer service within a hospital tried using group support systems instead of their usual face-to-face meetings, but found the technology-based meeting process uncomfortable and reverted to their traditional verbal discussion-based process. They then found the traditional processes to be uncomfortable after their experience with the technology, and went back to using more electronic communication-based processes.[69]

Videoconferencing is also an important component of groupware. It gives team members a richer medium through which to communicate when necessary. Group video can link meeting rooms in multiple locations and participants can see who is in each room, who is talking, and who has entered or left the meeting—providing, in effect, a virtual meeting space.

One of the key lessons is that for collaboration to work well, it has to be between people, not just machines. Management experts say digital workspaces cannot completely replace more traditional interactions, especially in the creative process. In-person communication can be important for training and building relationships. For example, Land O' Lakes builds trust and helps virtual teams sort out their problems by requiring face-to-face meetings every quarter.[70]

The goal of the World Health Organization's (WHO's) "Health InterNetwork" is to improve global public health by giving health professionals, researchers, and policy makers in developing countries access to high-quality, relevant, and timely health information using the Internet.[71] WHO's challenge is to keep its worldwide project teams both productive and on track, while minimizing the expense and time associated with coordinating such a global effort. To coordinate and support its widely dispersed project teams, WHO

SO WHAT

Technology can facilitate group decision making when members are together or when they are apart.

uses Project.net to facilitate the teams' global collaboration. WHO invites relevant experts and consultants worldwide to participate in the project, and they then work together in a web-based "virtual forum." Team members can participate at times and places convenient to them, and the software helps manage processes and documentation, and provides tools to track and archive completed work. Using Project.net, WHO now works with health experts in more than twenty countries on this important health initiative for the world's underserved populations.

Enhancing Group Decision-Making Effectiveness

A number of methods can enhance group decision-making effectiveness. This section discusses some of these methods and describes how they work.

brainstorming

A process for developing creative solutions

Brainstorming. *Brainstorming* is a process for developing creative solutions. When normal team meetings and deliberations fail to generate acceptable ideas and alternatives, brainstorming can help focus group members' creativity and discover novel solutions. The purpose of brainstorming is to generate new and creative ideas—the ideas will be analyzed and discussed afterward. Here are some general steps to follow when brainstorming:

1. Write down a brief description of the problem and ensure that all brainstorming participants understand the challenge. Participants should come from a wide range of disciplines, backgrounds, and experiences to maximize the group's creativity.
2. Collect as many ideas as possible from all participants. Do not allow any criticisms or judgments while ideas are being generated. Be creative but stay focused on the problem. Welcome all ideas no matter how silly or far out they seem—the more ideas the better because at this point you do not know what might work.
3. Absolutely no discussion or evaluation should take place during the brainstorming activity. This will occur after brainstorming is complete.
4. Do not allow participants to criticize, judge, frown, scowl, or laugh at any idea. All ideas are equally valid at this stage.
5. Encourage participants to build on each other's ideas.
6. Record all ideas so the whole group can easily see them.
7. Set a time limit (e.g., thirty minutes) for the brainstorming exercise.

Brainstorming can be an effective way to generate new and creative ideas, but the freewheeling nature of the interaction and the fact that only one person can speak at a time can result in some participants dominating the process. This can lead to the suppression of some participants' input, and restrict the ideas generated. The nominal group technique, discussed next, was created to address these limitations.

nominal group technique

A structured variation of a small-group discussion to reach consensus

Nominal Group Technique. The *nominal group technique* is a structured variation of a small-group discussion to reach consensus. The steps in the nominal group technique are:[72]

1. *Generating ideas*: Each group member silently generates ideas and writes them down.
2. *Recording ideas*: Group members engage in a round-robin feedback session while a facilitator concisely records each idea.
3. *Discussing ideas*: The group discusses each recorded idea to obtain clarification and evaluation.

4. *Voting on ideas*: Individuals vote privately to prioritize the ideas, and the group decision is determined based on these ratings. The idea rated highest by the group as a whole becomes the group's collective preferred idea.

Because ideas are first generated silently and independently and recorded in writing, more ideas are often generated than through brainstorming. The process also prevents the domination of the discussion by a single person, encourages all group members to participate, and results in a set of prioritized solutions or recommendations that represent the group's preferences.

The nominal group technique is useful when gaining consensus is important, and works best for addressing a single decision.[73] It has been successfully used to improve team processes, identify a unit's core strengths, and even identify the challenges associated with different restructuring alternatives.[74]

Delphi Method. The *Delphi method* assumes that group judgments are superior to individual judgments. The technique was developed to obtain the opinion of experts without having to bring them together face-to-face. The success of the Delphi method depends on the expertise of the members and their communication skills. In the Delphi method, experts' judgments gathered through successive iterations of a questionnaire result in a decision by consensus. A group of experts sends their individual answers to a questionnaire to a facilitator who compiles the responses, filters out irrelevant content, identifies areas of convergence and divergence, and redistributes it to the group. The process continues until consensus is reached.

The Delphi method protects the anonymity of participants until the final report is issued to prevent some members from dominating the discussion because of their personality or expertise. Open critique and free expression of opinions is encouraged, as well as revising earlier judgments over the course of the communications with the facilitator. This eliminates the possible negative group dynamics that could result from a face-to-face discussion.

When a decision depends on the subjective judgment of experts rather than structured analysis, the Delphi method can enhance decision-making effectiveness. In one case the Delphi method predicted the sales of a new product during the first two years within one percent of actual sales. Quantitative methods produced errors of 10 to 15 percent, and traditional unstructured forecast methods had errors of about 20 percent.[75]

Delphi method
Experts' judgments gathered through successive iterations of a questionnaire result in a decision by consensus

CREATIVE DECISION MAKING

Most successful managers are skilled at solving problems rationally. Often, though, they pass up opportunities to look at problems from a more creative viewpoint. This can mean that they limit the alternatives they have to choose from and may fail to capitalize on some good opportunities.[76] Creativity has become increasingly valued across a variety of tasks and jobs because of its importance in generating novel and competitive products and processes. As one expert says, "Most managers would agree that there is room, in almost every job, for employees to be more creative."[77] Non-programmed decisions in particular can benefit from creativity.

Model of Creativity

Creative does not mean crazy. Business creativity requires ideas that are useful and actionable and that positively influence the way business gets done.[78]

Figure 9-2

Three-Component Model of Creativity[79]

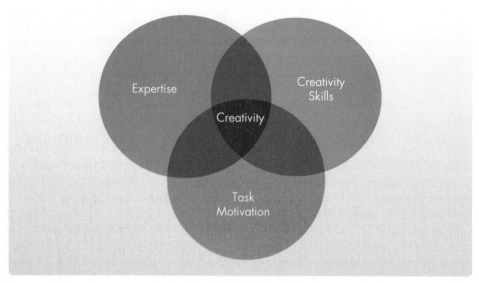

Source: Amabile, T. "Motivating Creativity in Organizations: On Doing What You Love and Loving What You Do", © 1997, California Management Review, 40, 39. Reproduced with permission of University of California Press.

Creativity expert Teresa Amabile's Three-Component Model of Creativity, shown in Figure 9-2, describes what influences creativity.

Creative thinking skills determine how well people can imaginatively approach problems. Some people are naturally more creative than others, although creative ideas can come from just about anyone. Being around creative people and being in a positive mood enhance creativity, suggesting that staffing and leadership can enhance employees' creative thinking potential. Creative thinking is also enhanced by personality and style characteristics including self-discipline, tolerance for ambiguity, perseverance in the face of frustration, and a low concern for social approval.[80]

Expertise is all the relevant technical, procedural, and intellectual knowledge that we bring to a creative effort. Expertise is the foundation for creativity. Someone with a limited knowledge of biology would obviously have a hard time being a creative developer of pharmaceutical drugs.

Task motivation reflects a drive to solve the challenge at hand. This intrinsic motivation can stimulate creativity more than monetary or other external rewards. When Arthur Schawlow, winner of the Nobel Prize for physics in 1981, was asked what he thought made the difference between highly creative and less creative scientists, he replied, "The labor of love aspect is important. The most successful scientists often are not the most talented. But they are the ones who are impelled by curiosity. They've got to know what the answer is."[81]

Although managers can influence all three of these components, motivation is the easiest one to manipulate. Matching employees with the expertise and creative thinking requirements of their jobs increases intrinsic motivation. Giving employees the freedom to do tasks in their preferred ways when possible also sparks creativity. Let's explore some other things managers can do to enhance creativity.[82]

Enhancing Creativity

To support creativity, supervisors should be encouraging and supportive of employees.[83] Negative feedback from leaders inhibits creativity.[84] Leaders can also model the types of behaviors that are more likely to lead to creativity.

Hiring employees with a greater predisposition to be creative boosts creativity. When placing employees in different jobs, leaders can consider their fit with the job and the level of creativity required by that job. In addition, managers can make sure that employees who need to be more creative receive training in creative problem solving and any other skills they need to be more creative in their jobs.[85]

Another way to encourage creativity is to set goals involving creativity, for example, that an individual's output should be creative (i.e., novel and appropriate) or that the employee should attempt to engage in activities that could lead to more creative outcomes (e.g., flexible thought, playing with ideas, and data gathering). When we know that creativity is important, we are more likely to be creative.[86] On the other hand, if there are goals for other aspects of performance, such as production quantity, but not for creativity, then creative performance is less likely to occur.[87]

Failures should not be punished. At one chemical company, instead of punishing a research scientist for spending a great deal of time on an ultimately unsuccessful experiment, the company gave him a company award as an outstanding scientist for his consistently creative work.[88]

Time pressure decreases creativity.[89] Because creativity takes hard work and mental energy, time is a critical resource that managers need to give to their employees. It takes more time to generate multiple alternatives and look at problems in a different manner. However, by engaging in creative activities, the quality of decisions and judgments should be better. Sufficient time to think creatively, explore different perspectives, and play with ideas is important for creativity in research and development (R&D).[90] Uninterrupted time is critical for engineers working on new technologies.[91] Scientists and R&D professionals at 3M are encouraged to spend 15 percent of their work time thinking creatively, trying new products, and learning new ideas or processes that contribute to their being creative.[92]

Brainstorming, delaying judgment about the relevance of information to a decision, and consciously suspending judgment and staying open-minded and receptive to new ideas can enhance decision-making creativity. Playing devil's advocate and taking time to discuss ideas that a group would normally reject can lead to a new and more creative frame of reference for evaluating alternatives.[93] Organizational challenges including poor communication and protection of the status quo can stifle creativity. Teams with diverse members, enthusiastic and open-minded managers, and challenging projects enhance the creativity of decisions.[94] Managers can also enhance creativity by giving employees a sense of control and removing negative stressors such as bureaucracy, role conflict, and time pressure.[95]

Some companies even create physical spaces that promote creativity. When AOL felt that a standard conference room was insufficient to spark creativity at their headquarters in Dulles, Virginia, they created creativity centers with oversize cartoon murals, leopard-print walls, and giant paint cans that appear to spill over.[96]

SO WHAT

Encouraging creativity involves time, encouragement, setting appropriate goals, and accepting that projects do not always succeed.

The Aflac duck, now recognized by millions worldwide, came from a creative moment in a meeting.

AFLAC INCORPORATED

Creativity is often the product of interactions among coworkers. When the insurance company Aflac hired an ad agency to improve their name recognition, even the ad agency employees had trouble remembering the name of the company they were pitching. When one of them asked another for a reminder of what the company's name was, the employee replied, "Aflac—Aflac—Aflac—Aflac." Someone said that he sounded like a duck, and the idea was born.[97] The white duck and the name Aflac are now recognized by millions of people worldwide.

Although coming up with creative ideas is not the same as commercializing them, creativity is often the first step to bringing an innovative product to market.[98] This chapter's *Improve Your Skills* feature describes how to make creative decisions by borrowing ideas from the solutions to similar problems in other areas.

MAKING DECISIONS ETHICALLY

Ethics refers to standards of behavior about how people ought to act in different situations. But often the right decision is not clear. For example, should you accept sporting event tickets from a vendor? Should you be forthcoming with all relevant information when providing a reference? Should you tell an employee who is preparing to purchase a new home that she is about to be laid off? As you can tell from this chapter's real world challenge, company codes of ethics and ethical training programs often do not cover all possible ethical situations.

IMPROVE YOUR SKILLS
CREATIVE DECISIONS THROUGH BORROWING IDEAS

Creative decisions are novel and useful, and borrowing ideas from other areas is often a foundation of the creative decision-making process.[99] Johannes Gutenberg's idea for a movable type printing press was inspired by the technology of the screw-type wine presses of France's Rhine Valley. It was there in 1440 that Gutenberg created his printing press, in which ink was rolled over the raised surfaces of moveable hand-set block letters held within a wooden form which was then pressed against a sheet of paper.[100] He creatively combined his knowledge of goldsmithing, linen, and presses used for other things to arrive at an innovative solution. More recently, Steve Jobs of Apple recognized Amazon's Kindle as an inspiration for the iPad.

Rather than being out of touch for most people, creative decision making can follow a deliberate process in pursuit of an existing idea that solves a related problem in some other area. It is still difficult—the borrowed ideas only provide the raw material. Noted author David Kord Murray provides six simple steps that you can practice to improve your own creativity:[101]

1. *Defining*: Define the problem you are trying to solve. How you define the problem will determine how you solve it. Mistakes often result from defining problems too narrowly or too broadly.

2. *Borrowing*: Borrow ideas from places that have faced a similar problem. One tactic is to start with your competitors, then other industries, and then outside business and to nature, the sciences, or entertainment to see how they solve similar problems.

3. *Combining*: Combine the borrowed ideas. This is the essence of creativity, as in Gutenberg's printing press.

4. *Incubating*: Give your subconscious mind time to work and listen to the ideas it generates. This can involve sleeping on it or putting it away for a little while. Sometimes not thinking at all is the most effective thinking.

5. *Judging*: Identify the strengths and weaknesses of the decision.

6. *Enhancing*: Tweak your decision to contain more positives and fewer negatives. Evolve your decisions through trial and error and make appropriate adjustments.

Sources: Muray, D.K. (2009). Borrowing Brilliance: The Six Steps to Business Innovation by Building on the Ideas of Others. New York: Gotham; Murray, D.K. (2009). What are the Six Steps? Available online at: http://www.borrowingbrilliance.com/sixsteps.html. Accessed August 31, 2009; Harry Ransom Center (2009). Adapting Technology, Harry Ransom Center at the University of Texas at Austin. Available online at: http://www.hrc.utexas.edu/educator/modules/gutenberg/invention/adapting/. Accessed August 28, 2009; Lienhard, J.H. (1988). No. 753: Johann Gutenberg. Available online at: http://www.uh.edu/engines/epi753.htm. Accessed August 31, 2009.

Ethical Standards

There are five different types of ethical standards, each of which can help us evaluate the ethics of a decision:

1. The *utilitarian standard*: the ethical decision is the one that provides the most good or does the least harm, or that essentially strikes the best balance of good over harm. When Southwest Airlines cut all employees' pay rather than laying anyone off, it followed a utilitarian standard.

2. The *rights standard*: the ethical decision is the one that best respects and protects the moral rights of all those affected by the decision. Moral rights may include the right to be told the truth, to not be injured, and to privacy. If a supervisor tells an employee that she can leave work at 2:00 instead of 5:00, the employee has a right to leave at 2:00.

3. The *fairness standard*: the ethical decision treats all people equally, or at least fairly based on some defensible standard. The debate over the appropriateness of CEO salaries that are hundreds of times larger than the pay of the average employee reflects the fairness standard.

4. The *common good standard*: the ethical decision shows respect and compassion for all others, especially the most vulnerable. Ensuring that suppliers do not use illegal labor or provide unhealthy working conditions is an example of applying the common good standard.

5. The *virtue standard*: the ethical decision is consistent with certain ideal virtues, including honesty, courage, compassion, fairness, and generosity. This standard asks, "Is this action consistent with my acting at my best?" Quickly recalling products that might be defective because the company values honesty reflects the virtue standard.

These five different types of ethical standards may not lead to the same preferred decision choice. Decision makers may not even agree on the content of some of the approaches, such as the same set of moral rights. Nonetheless, each standard provides insights we can use to make the most ethical choice in a given decision-making situation. Table 9-6 describes some of the ethical decisions you are likely to face throughout your career.

utilitarian standard
The ethical decision is the one that strikes the best balance of good over harm

rights standard
The ethical decision is the one that best respects and protects the moral rights of all those affected by the decision

fairness standard
The ethical decision treats all people equally, or at least fairly based on some defensible standard

common good standard
The ethical decision shows respect and compassion for all others, especially the most vulnerable

virtue standard
The ethical decision is consistent with certain ideal virtues, including honesty, courage, compassion, fairness, and generosity

Table 9-6

Typical Ethical Decisions Faced by Managers

- Taking credit for subordinates' work
- Showing favoritism in employment decisions
- Inconsistency in discipline
- Not doing what you tell others to do
- Padding your expense account
- Harassment or disrespectful treatment of employees
- Choosing not to act when observing unethical behavior by others in the organization
- Choosing to carry out your supervisor's orders or decisions that you believe are wrong
- Presenting false or misleading data to meet goals, quality standards, or deadlines
- Breaches of confidentiality
- Avoiding extra work
- Stealing office supplies for personal use
- Doing personal business on company time or on company computers

Ethical decisions can be influenced by cultural norms and values, the lack of checks and balances in the organization, pressures or threats from supervisors, and unrealistic goals.[102] Toyota's slow decision in 2010 to recall cars affected by a faulty gas pedal design reflected the company's norms in handling safety concerns.[103] Executives can improve their ethical decision making by becoming aware of systematic cognitive biases that affect how individuals process information. For example, overcoming the tendency to reduce the number of consequences considered is critical to improving ethical decision making.[104] Also, incorrect theories and stereotypes about social groups such as women and minorities often result in ethnocentric decisions.[105] Explicit corporate policies that make decisions more concrete, systematic, and objective can improve the ethics of decisions.

Individuals' theories about themselves can also interfere with effective ethical decision making. For example, people tend to view themselves as highly ethical people who are in control of their lives.[106] This might decrease their openness to fully recognizing ethical issues when making decisions. Researchers have found that professionals gradually become morally compromised over time, a process facilitated by unconscious thought processes.[107] Potential safeguards include basing decisions on data, using a devil's advocate to question decisions, and consciously expanding the analysis to include consequences for multiple stakeholders.[108]

Many techniques are available to help you make ethical decisions. Management guru Peter Drucker recommends the "mirror test"—asking, "What kind of person do I want to see when I shave . . . or put on my lipstick in the morning?"[109] The former CEO of Lockheed Martin, Norman Augustine, uses four questions to help determine a course of action: (1) Is it legal? (2) Would you think it was fair if someone else did it to you? (3) Would you be content if it appeared on the front page of your hometown newspaper? (4) Would you like your mother to see you do it? Augustine says, "If you can answer yes to all four questions, then whatever you are about to do is probably ethical."[110]

Ethical Awareness

ethical awareness

The identification of an ethical issue

The first and most critical step in making ethical decisions is *ethical awareness*, or the identification of an ethical issue.[111] This involves an interpretive process through which we recognize that an ethical problem exists, or that an ethical standard or principle is relevant to the situation. This stage is critical because once we become aware of an ethical issue, we are more likely to consider any ethical issues more closely in making a decision.

Ethical awareness is influenced by personal factors including nationality and culture and ethical experience.[112] This chapter's *Global Issues* feature discusses the role of nationality in ethical awareness in greater detail.

Moral Disengagement

Personal standards tend to guide ethical behavior and deter misconduct that would violate those standards.[116] However, we are capable of detaching from these self-regulatory processes through anticipatory moral disengagement that free us from the self-sanctions and guilt that would normally accompany violation of our ethical standards. Once we are morally disengaged, unethical behavior is more likely.

How do we become morally disengaged? Albert Bandura proposed some ways in which this can happen, each of which can manifest itself in multiple ways:[117]

1. *Cognitively reconstructing behavior*: moral justification, euphemistic labeling, and advantageous comparison; for example, "It is okay to pad my expense account because I spend a lot of extra time doing work I'm not paid for."
2. *Minimizing one's role in harmful behavior*: displacement of responsibility, diffusion of responsibility, and disregarding or distorting of the consequences; for example, "These extra charges are nothing given what the company spends on travel every year."
3. *Focusing on the targets' unfavorable acts*: dehumanization and attribution of blame;[118] for example, "It's the company's fault—someone should have more clearly stated that these expenses weren't appropriate to claim."

Being aware of these tendencies can help us to stay focused on the ethical issues involved in the decisions we are faced with.

SO WHAT

Because ethics is not always straightforward, staying focused on your ethical standards can help to prevent you from disengaging your morals when making decisions.

GLOBAL ISSUES

CULTURE AND NATIONALITY INFLUENCES ON ETHICAL AWARENESS

If we do not recognize ethical issues in a situation, we are unlikely to attend to them in making subsequent decisions. Research has found that both culture and nationality influence the recognition of ethical issues. One study found that Taiwanese sales agents were more likely to perceive ethical issues associated with their companies' or competitors' agents while U.S. sales agents were more likely to perceive ethical issues with their colleagues' behavior.[113]

A second study compared the ethical awareness Australians and Americans, argued to be "cultural cousins" because of their similar cultures. Despite having similar cultures, Americans were more likely than the Australians to identify an ethical problem in scenarios involving the withholding of information and the misleading of an appraiser.[114]

A third study asked managers from around the world to decide what they would do next in the following situation:[115]

You are riding in a car driven by a close friend. He hits a pedestrian. You know he was going at least thirty-five miles-per-hour in an area of the city where the maximum allowed speed is twenty miles-per-hour. There are no witnesses. His lawyer says that if you testify under oath that he was only driving twenty miles-per-hour, it might save him from serious consequences.

1. What right has your friend to expect you to protect him?
   a. My friend has a definite right as a friend to expect me to testify to the lower figure.
   b. He has some right as a friend to expect me to testify to the lower figure.
   c. He has no right as a friend to expect me to testify to the lower figure.
2. What do you think you would do in view of the obligations of a sworn witness and the obligations to your friend?
   a. Testify that he was going twenty miles an hour.
   b. Not testify that he was going twenty miles an hour.

Managers' responses to this situation differed widely. More than 90 percent of managers in Canada (96 percent), the United States (95 percent), Switzerland (94 percent), and Sweden (93 percent) said that because society's rules were made for everyone, their friend had no right to expect them to testify falsely. Consequently, they would not testify that their friend was driving at twenty miles-per-hour. In contrast, fewer than half of the managers from South Korea (26 percent), Venezuela (34 percent), Russia (42 percent), and China (48 percent) would refuse to support their friend.

AN ETHICAL CHALLENGE[119]

Did the CEO of the aircraft engine repair company disclose the pending claim that his company's parts were the possible cause of the grounding of eleven airplanes and risk the jobs of hundreds of employees and his own stake in the company? Or did he stay quiet until he had more information? The right choice is not always clear—this type of decision is typical of many of the tough decisions managers have to make.

In this case, the CEO considered that the bankers might call the company's loans and company investors might lose their money if word of the FAA investigation got out. He also worried about the effect on his employees if the banks started pulling loans and the company had to lay off workers. But he did not consider whether he had any responsibility to passengers regarding the situation to enable them to make their own decisions about their safety. Years later, he acknowledged that passengers' safety never crossed his mind when making the decision.

The CEO ultimately decided not to disclose the information and signed the audit papers. Eventually the FAA found that it was impossible to identify who was at fault for the engine failures. The company's name was never publicly disclosed as being a possible factor in the grounding of the airplanes.

SUMMARY AND APPLICATION

Decision making is obviously critical to your individual and to organizational success. Although the rational decision-making process describes an ideal way of making decisions, many barriers exist to following this model. Understanding the biases and obstacles we all face in decision making can improve your skills in this important area. Although it is difficult to make perfect decisions, we can still recognize the merits of rational decision making and strive for the best decisions possible.

Group decision making has the potential to outperform individual decision making, but it can take longer and has its own set of challenges. Being aware of common issues including groupthink and group polarization can help you keep your teams on track to make the best decisions. Brainstorming, the nominal group technique, and the Delphi technique can also improve team decision-making effectiveness.

Making ethical decisions is more difficult than it may seem. Recognizing ethical issues, understanding different ethical standards, and being aware of the ethical decision-making process can improve the ethics of your own decision making.

TAKEAWAY POINTS

1. Programmed decisions are routine decisions that address specific problems using an existing set of rules and result in relatively structured solutions. Non-programmed decisions are unstructured, novel decisions that require unique solutions. Strategic decisions address the long-term direction and focus of the organization. Operational decisions require faster decision making and focus on the day-to-day running of the company.

Top-down decisions are directive decisions made solely by managers who then pass them down to lower-level employees for implementation. Decentralized decisions are made by employees, not managers.

2. The rational decision-making process begins with the identification of a problem or opportunity. We then determine the characteristics a good solution must have and the weight each of these should carry. After that, we gather and process the information we need to identify alternatives to solve the problem or to determine if the opportunity is worth pursuing. The next step is to list and evaluate each of the alternatives based on each criterion. A decision is then made and implemented, and we monitor the results of the decision to ensure the problem has been solved. Our rationality is limited by the amount of information, time, and resources available, which can lead us to satisfice, or make satisfactory rather than optimal decisions. Emotions also can interfere with our ability to make the best decisions. Our status quo bias leads us to avoid changing what we are doing unless the incentive to change is compelling. In addition, we have a strong tendency to be overoptimistic or overconfident. We also experience losses more acutely than gains, and when we can readily remember past instances of an event, we tend to overestimate the likelihood that such an event will occur again. We tend to overestimate what we are familiar with, and underestimate things with which we are not familiar or that we do not remember as well.

3. Emotions often interfere with effective decision making. Emotions can distort our rationality and receptiveness to advice.

4. Culture influences our perception of ethical issues, as well as our response to ethical decision situations.

5. Decision-making groups face several challenges. Group polarization reflects the tendency of people to make more extreme decisions in a group than when alone. This leads to risky shift when people who tend to make more risky decisions as individuals make even riskier decisions in a group. Groupthink happens when people are deeply involved in a cohesive in-group and members' strivings for unanimity override their motivation to realistically evaluate alternative courses of action.

6. The five types of ethical standards are:
   - *The utilitarian standard:* The ethical decision is the one that strikes the best balance of good over harm.
   - *The rights standard:* The ethical decision is the one that best respects and protects the moral rights of all those affected by the decision.
   - *The fairness standard:* The ethical decision treats all people equally, or at least fairly based on some defensible standard.
   - *The common good standard:* The ethical decision shows respect and compassion for all others, especially the most vulnerable.
   - *The virtue standard:* The ethical decision is consistent with certain ideal virtues including honesty, courage, compassion, fairness, generosity, and so on.

7. Managers can enhance decision-making creativity by encouraging brainstorming, delaying judgment about the relevance of information to a decision, and staying open-minded and receptive to new ideas. Playing devil's advocate and taking the time to discuss ideas that the group would normally reject can also help. Reducing organizational challenges to creativity, including poor communication and protection of the status quo, as well as staffing teams with diverse members, hiring enthusiastic and open-minded managers, and assigning challenging projects are other ways to enhance creativity. Physical spaces can even be designed in ways that promote creativity.

DISCUSSION QUESTIONS

1. When do you feel you are more likely to make decisions rationally instead of emotionally? Why?
2. Which decision-making biases are the biggest challenges for you? Why?
3. As the manager of a multicultural team, what could you do to minimize possible negative cultural effects on the team's decision-making process?
4. If you were the CEO in this chapter's real world challenge, what would you have done? Why? Did the CEO violate any ethical standards in making his decision?
5. Identify a decision you faced in which you were ethically challenged. What did you do? Would you do anything differently if you had it to do over?
6. As a manager, what can you do to enhance the ethics of your staff's decisions?
7. Think of a time when you made a particularly creative decision. What elements of the decision-making process you used most influenced your creativity?

EXERCISES

Making a Rational Decision

Select a personal decision that you are currently making or that you will need to make soon. It might be picking a major, buying a car, renting an apartment, choosing a job, or something else. Now apply the rational decision-making process to it by identifying criteria and goals, assigning weights to the criteria, generating and evaluating alternatives, ranking the alternatives, and making a decision.

Next, compare the outcome of this decision with the outcome you would have reached by following a more intuitive or emotional process. Are the outcomes different? Which process do you feel led you to the best decision? Why?

*We would like to thank Professor Carolyn M. Youssef of Bellevue University for providing this exercise.

Performance Management and Rewards

In a group of four to five students, assume the role of the executive management team for a large pharmaceutical company such as Merck or Pfizer. You have been charged with the task of devising a new performance management and reward system for your research staff charged with developing new cancer drugs. This group is comprised of people with education levels ranging from B.A. to Ph.D degrees and with a wide range of years of experience with your company. These people are essential to your company's future performance, and you want to be sure you are ethical in how you evaluate and reward them.

As a group, your job is to:

1. Discuss what type of performance evaluation and reward system would be best for this group of employees under each of the five ethical standards discussed in this chapter:

   - The utilitarian standard
   - The rights standard
   - The fairness standard
   - The common good standard
   - The virtue standard

Your recommendations are likely to differ based on each of the five perspectives.

2. After considering the challenge from each of these perspectives, identify which performance evaluation and reward system you would recommend that the company adopt. Be prepared to explain to the class why you chose it over the other alternatives.

Discovery Communications

Discovery Communications is a media company reaching more than 1.5 billion cumulative subscribers in more than 170 countries through its 100-plus world-wide networks including Discovery Channel, TLC, Animal Planet, and The Science Channel. The company believes that offering its employees a variety of programs helps to meet employees' needs and to attract and retain top talent.

Point your browser to http://corporate.discovery.com/discovery-news/discovery-open-onsite-childcare-center/ to learn about the company's decision to open an on-site childcare facility at the company's global headquarters. Then answer the following questions.

Questions

1. Is the decision to open an on-site childcare facility an example of a programmed or non-programmed decision? Why?
2. What other alternatives might Discovery Communications have considered to address its goal of meeting the needs of its working parents?
3. What is your opinion of the ethics of the decision to open the new childcare center? Which ethical standard(s) did you use in forming this opinion?

Superheroes

Each student should pick his or her favorite superhero. Now assume that a large earthquake just hit a populated island. How could your superhero assist the island? Take five minutes to write down your ideas.

Now form groups of five to six students. Share which superhero you chose and the ideas you generated based on your superhero's special abilities (e.g., Batman could use his gadgets and tools to help free people trapped in rubble). The group should then work together to identify true possible solutions based on the ideas generated for the superheroes (e.g., Batman's grappling hook might be adapted for use in moving large obstacles during rescues).

*We would like to thank Professor Jim Gort of Davenport University for suggesting this exercise.

VIDEO CASES

Now What?

Imagine being part of a group with three other coworkers trying to make a decision about whether to discontinue funding an underperforming product. The group has been working together on the product line for three years, but the product is clearly a failure. When you start to question where the decision is headed you are called disloyal and told to go with the team and give the product more time. One of the team members calls for a final vote on the group's decision, which appears to be to continue funding a clearly awful and doomed-to-fail product. What do you say or do? Go to this chapter's "Now What?" video, watch the challenge video, and choose a response. Be sure to also view the outcomes of the two responses you didn't choose.

Discussion Questions

1. How is groupthink illustrated in these videos? Explain your answer.
2. How is stereotyping illustrated in these videos? Explain your answer.
3. How else might you handle this situation?

Workplace | Greensburg, Kansas: Decision Making

It's almost impossible to assign credit or blame to any one person for Greensburg's decision to rebuild the small Kansas town as a model green community after a tornado decimated 95 percent of its buildings. Many folks in Greensburg would assert that whoever made the decision, made a good one. Other residents make a different case.

Former mayor Lonnie McCollum expressed interest in exploring the possibilities of running Greensburg's municipal buildings on solar and wind power well before the EF5 tornado hit in May 2004. After the storm, he saw the tragedy as an opportunity to reinvent the dying town and put it back on the map. But McCollum was not the sole decision maker; instead, he was the leader of a small community facing endless uncertainties. Ultimately, the Greensburg City Council would have to vote on this matter.

After multiple rounds of community meetings in which residents engaged in rigorous debate, Greensburg's City Council voted in favor of rebuilding the town using green methods and materials. And when the council members voted on the specifics of implementation, they decided to build all municipal buildings to the Leadership in Energy and

Environmental Design (LEED) Platinum standard, which is the highest nationally accepted benchmark for the design, construction, and operation of high-performance green buildings.

But residents were divided over the decision, and the town meetings generated rancor and politicking. Mayor McCollum eventually resigned, city administrators dug in, and many residents checked out. But the rebuilding plan went forward, and today a collaborative effort among business and nonprofit groups is putting Greensburg back on the map.

There is no way to convince every Greensburg resident that going green was a good decision. Perhaps all the City Council can hope for is support from a majority of residents. In their minds, what were the alternatives? The town was dying. But Greensburg is rebuilding thanks to generous corporate sponsorships and government grants. The town also stars in a TV show on Planet Green. The TV show is aptly named, *Greensburg*.

Discussion Questions

1. Cite reasons for and against rebuilding Greensburg as a "green town." Which reasons do you find most convincing and why?
2. Do you think Greensburg's decision-making process was effective? Explain.
3. What prevented the City of Greensburg from making purely rational decisions?

DO WHAT CENGAGENOW™ includes **teaching and learning resources** to supplement the text, and is designed specifically to **help students "think like managers"** by engaging and challenging them to think critically about managerial situations. **CengageNOW uses today's technology to improve the skills** of tomorrow's managers.

END NOTES

[1]Seglin, J. L. (2005, April). How to Make Tough Ethical Calls. *Harvard Management Update, 3.*

[2]Drucker, P. (2004, June 1). What Makes an Effective Executive? *Harvard Business Review, 82*(6), 61.

[3]Chu, J., & Rockwood, K. (2008, October 13). CEO Interview: Costco's Jim Sinegal. *Fast Company.* Available online: http://www.fastcompany.com/magazine/130/thinking-outside-the-big-box.html?page=0%2C2.

[4]March, J. G. (1994). *A Primer on Decision Making: How Decisions Happen.* New York: Free Press.

[5]Akanbi, P.A. (2011). Managerial Decision Making in an Organization: A Theoretical Framework, *Journal of Management and Corporate Governance, 3,* 38–52.

[6]Cotton, J. L., Vollrath, D. A., Froggatt, K. L., Lengnick-Hall, M. L., & Jennings, K. W. (1988). Employee Participation: Diverse Forms and Different Outcomes. *Academy of Management Review, 13,* 8–22.

[7]Bazerman, M. H. (2002). *Judgment in Managerial Decision Making* (5th ed.). New York: John Wiley.

[8]Samuelson, W., & Zeckhauser, R. J. (1988). Status Quo Bias in Decision Making. *Journal of Risk and Uncertainty, 1,* 7–59.

[9]Amos, D. P. (2010, January–February). How I Did It: AFLAC's CEO Explains How He Fell for the Duck. *Harvard Business Review*. Available online: http://hbr.org/2010/01/how-i-did-it-aflacs-ceo-explains-how-he-fell-for-the-duck/ar/1.

[10]Lovallo, D. (2006, February). Distortions and Deceptions in Strategic Decisions. *The McKinsey Quarterly*. Available online: http://www.mckinseyquarterly.com/Strategy/Strategic_Thinking/Distortions_and_deceptions_in_strategic_decisions_1716.

[11]McNamara, G., Moon, H., & Bromiley, P. (2002). Banking on Commitment: Intended and Unintended Consequences of an Organization's Attempt to Attenuate Irrational Commitment. *Academy of Management Journal, 45,* 443–452; Ross, J., & Staw, B. M. (1993). Organizational Escalation and Exit: Lessons from the Shoreham Nuclear Power Plant. *Academy of Management Journal, 36,* 701–732.

[12]Calantone, R. J. (2002). Escalation of Commitment During New Product Development. *Journal of the Academy of Marketing Science, 30,* 103–118.

[13]Brockner, J., Rubin, J. Z., & Lang, E. (1981). Face Saving and Entrapment. *Journal of Experimental Social Psychology, 17,* 68–79.

[14]Fisher, P. A. (1997). *Common Stocks and Uncommon Profits* (p. 91). New York: John Wiley.

[15]Kahneman, D., & Tversky, A. (2000). *Choices, Values, and Frames* (p. 4). New York: Cambridge University Press.

[16]Tversky, A., & Kahneman, D. (1981). The Framing of Decisions and the Psychology of Choice. *Science, 211,* 453–458.

[17]Lovallo, D. (2006, February). Distortions and Deceptions in Strategic Decisions. *The McKinsey Quarterly*. Available online: http://www.mckinseyquarterly.com/Strategy/Strategic_Thinking/Distortions_and_deceptions_in_strategic_decisions_1716.

[18]Lovallo, D. (2006, February). Distortions and Deceptions in Strategic Decisions. *The McKinsey Quarterly*. Available online: http://www.mckinseyquarterly.com/Strategy/Strategic_Thinking/Distortions_and_deceptions_in_strategic_decisions_1716.

[19]Lovallo, D. (2006, February). Distortions and Deceptions in Strategic Decisions. *The McKinsey Quarterly*. Available online: http://www.mckinseyquarterly.com/Strategy/Strategic_Thinking/Distortions_and_deceptions_in_strategic_decisions_1716;Gino,F., & Schweitzer, M. (2008). Blinded by Anger or Feeling the Love: How Emotions Influence Advice Taking. *Journal of Applied Psychology, 93*(5), 1165–1173.

[20]Tversky, A., & Kahneman, D. (1974). Judgments Under Uncertainty: Heuristics and Biases. *Science, 185,* 1124–1131.

[21]Esgate, A., & Groome, D. (2004). *An Introduction to Applied Cognitive Psychology*. New York: Psychology Press.

[22]Tversky, A., & Kahneman, D. (1974). Judgment Under Uncertainty: Heuristics and Biases. *Science, 185,* 1124–1131.

[23]Tversky, A., & Kahneman, D. (1974). Judgment Under Uncertainty: Heuristics and Biases. *Science, 185,* 1124–1131.

[24]Tversky, A., & Kahneman, D. (1974). Judgment Under Uncertainty: Heuristics and Biases. *Science, 185,* 1124–1131.

[25]Ariely, D., Loewenstein, G., & Prelec, D. (2003). Coherent Arbitrariness: Stable Demand Curves Without Stable Preferences. *Quarterly Journal of Economics, 118,* 73–105.

[26]Thorndike, E. (1920). A Constant Error in Psychological Rating. *Journal of Applied Psychology, 4,* 25–29.

[27]Pfeffer, J., & Sutton, R. I. (2006, June 29). Why Managing by Facts Works. Strategy+Business. Available online: http://www.strategy-business.com/article/06114?pg=0.

[28]Miller, G. A. (1956). The Magical Number Seven, Plus or Minus Two: Some Limits on our Capacity for Processing Information. *Psychological Review, 63,* 81–97.

[29]Henry, W. A. (1980). The Effect of Information-Processing Ability on Processing Accuracy. *Journal of Consumer Research, 7,* 42–48.

[30]Zuckerberg, M. (2009). Update on Terms. Facebook. Available online: http://blog.facebook.com/blog.php?post=54746167130.

[31]Mather, M., Shafir, E., & Johnson, M. K. (2000). Misrememberance of Options Past: Source Monitoring and Choice. *Psychological Science, 11,* 132–138.

[32]Mather, M., Shafir, E., & Johnson, M. K. (2000). Misrememberance of Options Past: Source Monitoring and Choice. *Psychological Science, 11,* 132–138.

[33]For additional information about hindsight bias, see Guilbault, R. L., Bryant, F. B., Brockway, J. H., & Posavac, E. J. (2004). A Meta-Analysis of Research on Hindsight Bias. *Basic and Applied Social Psychology, 26,* 103–117.

[34]Hoffrage, U., Hertwig, R., & Gigerenzer, G. (2000). Hindsight Bias: A By-Product of Knowledge Updating? *Journal of Experimental Psychology: Learning, Memory, and Cognition, 26*(3), 566–581.

[35]Mufson, S. (2010, May 25). Pressure to Save Time, Money May Have Contributed to Oil Disaster. *The Washington Post*. Available online: http://www.washingtonpost.com/wp-dyn/content/article/2010/05/25/AR2010052502293.html.

[36]Simon, H. A. (1957). *Administrative Behavior*. New York: Free Press; Simon, H. A. (1960). *The New Science of Management Decision*. New York: Harper & Row.

[37]March, J. G., & Simon, H. A. (1958). *Organizations*. New York: John Wiley.

[38] Adapted from Harvey, J. B. (1988). *The Abilene Paradox and Other Meditations on Management*. San Francisco: Jossey-Bass. The original publication of *The Abilene Paradox* appeared as: The Abilene Paradox: The Management of Agreement. *In Organizational Dynamics (Summer* 1974).

[39]Simon, H. A. (1987, February). Making Management Decisions: The Role of Intuition and Emotion. *Academy of Management Executives,* 57–64; Parikh, J. (1994). *Intuition: The New Frontier of Management*. Oxford, UK: Blackwell Business; Sinclair, M. & Ashkanasy, N.M. (2005). Intuition: Myth or a Decision-Making Tool, *Management Learning, 36 (3),* 353-370.

[40]Prietula, M. J., & Simon, H. A. (1989). The Experts in Your Midst. *Harvard Business Review, 67*(1), 120–124.

[41] Eisenhardt, K. (1989). Making Fast Strategic Decisions in High-Velocity Environments. *Academy of Management Journal, 32*(3), 543–576.

[42]Cited in Ray, M., & Myers, R. (1990). Practical Intuition. In *Intuition in Organizations,* ed. W. H. Agor (pp. 247–262, p. 249). Newbury Park, CA: Sage.

[43]Bell, D. E., Raiffa, H., & Tversky, A. (1988). *Decision Making: Descriptive, Normative, and Prescriptive Interactions* (p. 531). New York: Cambridge University Press.

[44]Fenton-O'Creevy, M., Soane, E., Nicholson, N., & Willman, P. (2011). Thinking, Feeling, and Deciding: The Influence of Emotions on the Decision Making and Performance of Traders, *Journal of Organizational Behavior, 32*(8), 1044–1061.

[45]Weber, E.U. & Morris, M.W. (2010). Culture and Judgment and Decision Making: The Constructivist Turn, *Perspectives on Psychological Science, 5*(4), 410–419.

[46]Adler, N. J. (2008). *International Dimensions of Organizational Behavior*. Mason, OH: Thomson/South-Western.

[47]Adler, N. J. (2008). *International Dimensions of Organizational Behavior*. Mason, OH: Thomson/South-Western.

[48]Adler, N. J. (2008). *International Dimensions of Organizational Behavior*. Mason, OH: Thomson/South-Western.

49Adler, N. J. (2008). *International Dimensions of Organizational Behavior*. Mason, OH: Thomson/South-Western.

50Lewin, K., & Lippitt, R. (1938). An Experimental Approach to the Study of Autocracy and Democracy: A Preliminary Note. *Sociometry 1, 292–300; Lewin, K. (1939). Field Theory and Experiment in Social Psychology: Concepts and Methods. *American Journal of Sociology, 44,* 868–896; Lewin, K., Lippitt, R., & White, R. (1939). Patterns of Aggressive Behaviour in Experimentally Created "Social Climates." *Journal of Social Psychology, 10,* 271–299.

51Cascio, W. F., & Cappelli, P. (2009, January). Lessons from the Financial Services Crisis. *HR Magazine, 47–50.*

52Eyes on the Wrong Prize: Leadership Lapses That Fueled Wall Street's Fall. (2008, September 17). Knowledge@Wharton. Available online: http://knowledge.wharton.upenn.edu/article .cfm?articleid=2048.

53Bass, B. M. (1981). *Stogdill's Handbook of Leadership*. New York: Free Press.

54Tannenbaum, R., &. Schmidt, W. H. (1958, March–April). How to Choose a Leadership Pattern. *Harvard Business Review, 36,* 95–101. (Reprinted in May–June 1973 issue.)

55Tannenbaum, R., & Schmidt, W. H. (1958, March–April). How to Choose a Leadership Pattern. *Harvard Business Review, 36,* 95–101. (Reprinted in May–June 1973 issue).

56Tannenbaum, R., & Schmidt, W. H. (1958, March–April). How to Choose a Leadership Pattern. *Harvard Business Review, 36,* 95–101. (Reprinted in May–June 1973 issue.)

57An exhibit from Tannenbaum, R., & Schmidt, W. H. (1973, May–June). How to Choose a Leadership Pattern. Copyright © 1973 by the President and Fellows of Harvard College; all rights reserved.

58Tannenbaum, R., & Schmidt, W. H. (1958, March–April). How to Choose a Leadership Pattern. *Harvard Business Review*, 36, 95–101. (Reprinted in May–June 1973 issue).

59Kerr, N., & Tindale, R. S. (2004). Group Performance and Decision Making. *Annual Review of Psychology, 55,* 623–655.

60Moscovici, S., & Zavalloni, M. (1969). The Group as a Polarizer of Attitudes. *Journal of Personality and Social Psychology, 12,* 125–135; Myers, D. G., & Arenson, S. J. (1972). Enhancement of Dominant Risk Tendencies in Group Discussion. *Psychological Science, 6,* 10–19.

61Janis, I. L. (1972). *Victims of Groupthink* (p. 9). Boston: Houghton Mifflin.

62Janis, I. L., & Mann, L. (1977). *Decision Making*. New York: Free Press.

63How Groupthink Sacked Penn State, Veritas, November 16, 2011. Available online: http://theveritasgroup.com/2011/11/16 /how-groupthink-sacked-penn-state/.

64Balzli, B., & Schiessl, M. (2009, July 8). Global Banking Economist Warned of Coming Crisis. *Spiegel Online*. Available online: http://www.spiegel.de/international /business/0,1518,druck-635051,00.html.

65Balzli, B., & Schiessl, M. (2009, July 8). Global Banking Economist Warned of Coming Crisis. *Spiegel Online*. Available online: http://www.spiegel.de/international /business/0,1518,druck-635051,00.html.

66Balzli, B., & Schiessl, M. (2009, July 8). Global Banking Economist Warned of Coming Crisis. *Spiegel Online*. Available online: http://www.spiegel.de/international /business/0,1518,druck-635051,00.html.

67Janis, I. L. (1972). *Victims of Groupthink*. Boston: Houghton Mifflin.

68This section is based on Malhotra, A., & Majchrzak, A. (2005, Winter). Virtual Workspace Technologies. *MIT Sloan Management Review, 46*(2), 11–14.

69Dennis, A. R., & Garfield, M. J. (2003, June). The Adoption and Use of GSS in Project Teams: Toward More Participative Processes and Outcomes. *MIS Quarterly, 27*(2), 289–323.

70Keenan, F., & Ante, S. E. (2002, February 18). The New Teamwork. *BusinessWeek*, e.Biz Supplement, pp. EB12–EB16. Available online: http://www.businessweek.com/magazine /content/02_07/b3770601.htm.

71Aronson, B. (2002). WHO's Health InterNetwork Access to Research Initiative (HINARI), Health Information & Libraries Journal, *19*(3), 164–165.

72Delbecq, A. L., Van de Ven, A. H., & Gustafson, D. H. (1975). Group Techniques for Program Planning: A Guide to Nominal Group and Delphi Processes. Glenview, IL: Scott, Foresman and Company; Dunham, R. (1998). Nominal Group Technique: A User's Guide. University of Wisconsin. Available online: http://www. peoplemix.com/documents/general/ngt.pdf.

73Dunham, R. Nominal Group Technique: A User's Guide. University of Wisconsin. Available online: http://www.peoplemix.com /documents/general/ngt.pdf.

74Sy, T., & D'Annunzio, L. S. (2005, March). Challenges and Strategies of Matrix Organizations: Top-Level and Mid-Level Managers' Perspectives. *Human Resource Planning*. Available online: http://www.entrepreneur.com/tradejournals/article/131500184. html.

75Basu, S. & Schroeder, R. G. (1977). Incorporating Judgments in Sales Forecasts: Application of the Delphi Method at American Hoist & Derrick. *Interfaces, 7,* 18–27.

76Gilson, L. L. (2007). Why Be Creative? A Review of the Practical Outcomes Associated with Creativity at the Individual, Group, and Organizational Levels. In *Handbook of Organizational Creativity*, eds. C. Shalley and J. Zhou (pp. 303–322). Mahwah, NJ: Lawrence Erlbaum.

77Shalley, C. E., & Gibson, L. L. (2004). What Leaders Need to Know: A Review of Social and Contextual Factors That Can Foster or Hinder Creativity. *The Leadership Quarterly, 15,* 33.

78Amabile, T. M. (1998, September–October). How to Kill Creativity. *Harvard Business Review,* 77–87.

79Amabile, T. "Motivating Creativity in Organizations: On Doing What You Love and Loving What You Do", © 1997, *California Management Review*, 40, 39. Reproduced with permission of University of California Press.

80Barron, F. (1955). The Disposition Toward Originality. *Journal of Abnormal and Social Psychology, 51,* 478–48; Feldman, D. (1980). *Beyond Universal in Cognitive Development*. Norwood, NJ: Ablex; Golann, S. E. (1963). Psychological Study of Creativity. *Psychological Bulletin, 60,* 548–565.

81Going for the Gaps. (1982, Fall). Interview in *The Stanford Magazine*, 42.

82Amabile, T. M. (1998, September–October). How to Kill Creativity. *Harvard Business Review,* 77–87.

83Andrews, F. M., & Farris, G. F. (1967). Supervisory Practices and Innovation in Scientific Teams. *Personnel Psychology, 20,* 497–575; Tierney, P., & Farmer, S. M. (2002). Creative Self-Efficacy: Potential Antecedents and Relationship to Creative Performance. *Academy of Management Journal, 45,* 1137–1148.

84Andrews, F. M., & Gordon, G. (1970). Social and Organizational Factors Affecting Innovation Research. *Proceedings for the American Psychological Association, 78,* 570–589.

85Amabile, T. M. (1998, September–October). How to Kill Creativity. *Harvard Business Review,* 77–87.

86Shalley, C. E. (1995). Effects of Coaction, Expected Evaluation, and Goal Setting on Creativity and Productivity. *Academy of Management Journal, 38,* 483–503.

[87]Shalley, C. E. (1991). Effects of Productivity Goals, Creativity Goals, and Personal Discretion on Individual Creativity. *Journal of Applied Psychology, 76,* 179–185.

[88]Amabile, T. M. (1998, September–October). How to Kill Creativity. *Harvard Business Review, 77–87.*

[89]Amabile, T. M., Mueller, J. S., Simpson, W. B., Hadley, C. N., Kramer, S. J., & Fleming, L. (2003). Time Pressures and Creativity in Organizations: A Longitudinal Field Study. HBS Working Paper 02-073.

[90]Amabile, T. M., & Gryskiewicz, S. (1987). Creativity in the R&D Laboratory. Technical Report 30. Greensboro, NC: Center for Creative Leadership.

[91]Katz, R., & Allen, T. J. (1988). Project Performance and Locus of Influence in the R&D Matrix. In *Managing Professionals in Innovative Organizations: A Collection of Readings,* ed. R. Katz (pp. 469–484). Cambridge, MA: Ballinger.

[92]Amabile, T. M. (1998, September–October). How to Kill Creativity. *Harvard Business Review, 77–87.*

[93]DeBono, E. (1990). *Lateral Thinking: Creativity Step by Step.* New York: Perennial Library.

[94]Amabile, T. M., Conti, R., Coon, H. Lazenby, J., & Herron, M. (1996). Assessing the Work Environment for Creativity. *Academy of Management Journal, 39,* 1154–1184.

[95]Byron, K., Khazanchi, S., & Nazarian, D. (2010). The Relationship Between Stressors and Creativity: A Meta-Analysis Examining Competing Theoretical Models. *Journal of Applied Psychology, 95,* 201–212.

[96]Dessler, G., & Phillips, J. (2008). *Managing Now!* (pp. 164–165). New York: Houghton-Mifflin.

[97]Amos, D. P. (2010, January–February). How I Did It: AFLAC's CEO Explains How He Fell for the Duck. *Harvard Business Review.* Available online: http://hbr.org/2010/01/how-i-did-it-aflacs-ceo-explains-how-he-fell-for-the-duck/ar/1.

[98]Govindarajan, V. (2010). Innovation is Not Creativity, HBR Blog Network, August 3. Available online: http://blogs.hbr.org/govindarajan/2010/08/innovation-is-not-creativity.html.

[99]Akande, A. (1991). How Managers Express Their Creativity. *International Journal of Manpower, 12,* 17–19.

[100]Bellis, M. (2009). Johannes Gutenberg and the Printing Press. About.com. Available online: http://inventors.about.com/od/gstartinventors/a/Gutenberg.htm

[101]Muray, D. K. (2009). *Borrowing Brilliance: The Six Steps to Business Innovation by Building on the Ideas of Others.* New York: Gotham.

[102]For a more detailed discussion of ethical decision making, see O'Fallon, M. J., & Butterfield, K. D. (2005). A Review of the Empirical Decision-Making Literature: 1996–2003. *Journal of Business Ethics, 59,* 375–413.

[103]Maynard, M. (2010, April 11). Toyota Delayed a U.S. Recall, Documents Show. *The New York Times.* Available online: http://www.nytimes.com/2010/04/12/business/12gap.html.

[104]Messick, D. M., & Bazerman, M. H. (1996). Ethical Leadership and Psychology of Decision Making. *Sloan Management Review, 37,* 9–22.

[105]Messick, D. M., & Bazerman, M. H. (1996). Ethical Leadership and Psychology of Decision Making. *Sloan Management Review, 37,* 9–22.

[106]Messick, D. M., & Bazerman, M. H. (1996). Ethical Leadership and Psychology of Decision Making. *Sloan Management Review, 37,* 9–22.

[107]Moore, D. A., Tetlock, P. E., Tanlu, L., & Bazerman, M. H. (2006). Conflicts of Interest and the Case of Auditor Independence: Moral Seduction and Strategic Issue Cycling. *Academy of Management Review, 31,* 10–49.

[108]Messick, D. M., & Bazerman, M. H. (1996). Ethical Leadership and Psychology of Decision Making. *Sloan Management Review, 37,* 9–22.

[109]Seglin, J. L. (2005, April). How to Make Tough Ethical Calls. *Harvard Management* Update. Case No. U0504C.

[110]Seglin, J. L. (2005, April). How to Make Tough Ethical Calls. *Harvard Management Update,* 3. Case No. U0504C.

[111]Rest, J. R. (1986). *Moral Development: Advances in Research and Theory.* New York: Praeger.

[112]Tenbrunsel, A. E., & Smith-Crowe, K. (2008). Ethical Decision Making: Where We've Been and Where We're Going. *Academy of Management Annals, 2,* 545–607.

[113]Blodgett, J. G., Lu, L. C., Rose, G. M., & Vitell, S. J. (2001). Ethical Sensitivity to Stakeholder Interests: A Cross-Cultural Comparison. *Academy of Marketing Science Journal, 29*(2), 190–202.

[114]Singhapakdi, A., Karande, K., Rao, C. P., & Vitell, S. J. (2001). How Important Are Ethics and Social Responsibility? A Multinational Study of Marketing Professionals. *European Journal of Marketing, 35*(1–2), 133–152.

[115]Trompenaars, F., & Hampden-Turner, C. (1998). *Riding the Waves of Culture: Understanding Cultural Diversity in Business* (2nd ed.). New York: McGraw-Hill.

[116]Bandura, A. (1999). Moral Disengagement in the Perpetration of Inhumanities. *Personality and Social Psychology Review, 3,* 193–209.

[117] Bandura, A. (1999). Moral Disengagement in the Perpetration of Inhumanities. Personality and *Social Psychology Review*, 3, 193–209.

[118]Bandura, A. 1986. *Social Foundations of Thought and Action: A Social Cognitive Theory.* Englewood Cliffs, NJ: Prentice-Hall.

[119]Based on Seglin, J. L. (2005, April). How to Make Tough Ethical Calls. *Harvard Management Update.* Case No. U0504C.; Seglin, J. (1998, July 1). Would You Lie to Save Your Company? *Inc.* http://www.inc.com/magazine/19980701/961.html; Seglin, J. (2009). The Right Thing: "Without You, We Wouldn't Be Where We Are Today." http://jeffreyseglin.blogspot. com/2009/03/right-thing-without-you-we-wouldnt-be.html.

CHAPTER 10

Power, Influence, and Politics

Bob Davies, CEO of Church and Dwight, used a variety of influence tactics and reward power to maintain employee engagement during an organizational restructuring.

REAL WORLD CHALLENGE

INFLUENCING ACCEPTANCE OF CHANGE AT CHURCH & DWIGHT[1]

Church & Dwight Company, Inc., founded in 1846, is a leading consumer packaged goods company headquartered in Princeton, New Jersey. With subsidiary locations around the world, Church & Dwight's brands include Arm & Hammer, Trojan, and OxiClean.

After a corporate review of its business, company leaders realized that without new successful product launches, the company would lack organic growth. To spur the creation of significant, consumer-meaningful products and to effectively market them worldwide, the company created a new strategic plan focused on generating consistent organic growth.

One key part of the new strategy was splitting the marketing department into two parallel marketing organizations. One marketing group would now focus on new products and the other would focus on the base marketing of the company's current brands to best execute the company's new strategy.

Although Church & Dwight's leaders knew that this was the right strategy for the company, an important obstacle remained. Most marketing employees felt that the most exciting part of their job was new product development. The company's marketing professionals enjoyed doing market research, spending time with consumers, and working on new product ideas. Under the new structure, base marketing employees would have to give this up and become responsible for what many saw as the more mundane, tactical execution of base

LEARNING OBJECTIVES

1. Explain the difference between position and personal power.

2. Explain which types of power are most effective.

3. Describe what you can do to increase your power in an organization.

4. Explain how involvement and empowerment differ.

5. Describe how organizational subunits gain power.

6. Describe which influence tactics are the most and least effective.

7. List the six primary upward influence tactics.

8. Describe which upward influence style is the most and least effective.

9. Describe some of the factors that influence political behavior in organizations.

10. Explain why impression management is relevant to power, influence, and politics.

marketing. Church & Dwight knew that its marketing talent drives the company's performance, and wanted to keep them engaged.

Church & Dwight's leaders ask you for advice on how to best influence its key marketing talent to support the new strategy and embrace their new responsibilities. After reading this chapter, you should have some good ideas.

The word *power* often conjures up a variety of thoughts, both good and bad. When used effectively, power and influence are essential to every manager's performance. When used inappropriately, power can result in unethical behavior and be damaging to employees and organizations. Effectively using power and influence is a skill, and misusing either can quickly derail your career. Conflict in organizations is often about power and influence, and the way power is manifested in the organization and across workgroups. Understanding what power and influence are and how to effectively use them will enhance your success in any organization.

Politics is closely related to power and influence. In addition to impacting your own success as a manager, politics is important to understand due to its negative effects on firm performance.[2] In this chapter, we discuss the nature of power, influence, and politics. After reading this chapter, you should have a good idea of how to effectively use them in advancing your career and managing more effectively.

POWER

power

A person or group's potential to influence another person's or group's behavior

Power refers to a person or group's potential to influence another person or group to do something that would not otherwise have been done.[3] Power is held by individuals as well as by groups. People tend to respond differently when they gain power. Although some people use power altruistically, others use it for more selfish motives.[4]

need for power

Wanting to control and influence others, or to be responsible for others

leadership motive pattern

A high need for power (with high impulse control) and a low need for affiliation

Noted power researcher David McClelland initially expected effective leadership to be grounded in the need to achieve, but he found that the real driver of a leader's performance was the leader's *need for power*,[5] or wanting to control and influence others or to be responsible for others. He found that an individual's power need could be directed positively if the leader could postpone immediate gratification and not act impulsively. He later called this the *leadership motive pattern*: a high need for power (with high impulse control) and a low need for affiliation.[6] The leadership motive pattern is grounded in a need for power, and is generally associated with high managerial performance.[7]

There are seven types of power, summarized in Table 10-1.

Table 10-1

Types of Power

Legitimate	Power due to the position of authority held
Reward	Power due to control over rewards
Coercive	Power due to control over punishments
Expert	Power due to control because of knowledge, skills, or expertise
Informational	Power due to control over information
Referent	Power due to control because subordinates respect, admire, and identify with the leader
Persuasive	Power due to the ability to use logic and facts to persuade

Legitimate, reward, and coercive powers come from the position one holds in an organization. The levels of these powers are greater for employees in higher organizational levels. Expert, informational, referent, and persuasive powers are types of personal powers. The levels of these powers depend on characteristics unique to each person. We next discuss these sources of position and personal power in greater detail, and provide tips on using them most effectively.

Position Power

Managers' power stems in part from organizational authority. Managers typically have formal authority because of their position, which gives them a legitimate right to ask employees to do things that are part of their job descriptions. Organizational authority gives a manager *position power*, which is power based on one's position in the organization. For example, the president of a company, dean of a school, or manager of a sports team has certain forms of control that come with each position. We next discuss the three types of position power: power due to one's job, power due to control over rewards, and power due to control over punishments.

position power

Based on one's position in the organization influence tactics

Legitimate Power. *Legitimate power* is a position power based on a person's holding of a managerial position rather than anything the manager is or does as a person.[8] Legitimate power is the formal authority the firm gives a manager to hire new employees, assign work, monitor employees' work, and enforce organizational rules. Subordinates comply because they believe that the managerial position gives the manager the right to make certain requests of them. For example, nurses will show up for their shifts as assigned by a supervisor, even if those shifts are not those they prefer. Because the scheduling manager has the legitimate power to assign shifts, employees accept the final work schedule.

legitimate power

A position power based on a person's holding of the managerial position rather than anything the manager is or does as a person

In using legitimate power effectively, it is important to follow the proper channels of communication and to be responsive to subordinates' concerns. Your requests should be made politely but confidently, and your authority to make the request should be clearly communicated.

Reward Power. *Reward power* is a position power that involves the use of both tangible (e.g. pay raises or preferred work assignments) and intangible (e.g. praise) rewards to influence and motivate followers.[9] Students comply with instructor instructions and deadlines because they want to receive the reward of a good grade. Rewards are one of the strongest tools used by managers to inspire high performance. This chapter's *Real World Response* describes how Church & Dwight used reward power to influence its marketing talent to embrace the changes made to their job responsibilities.

reward power

A position power that involves the use of rewards to influence and motivate followers

Because rewards are such strong motivators, it is important to monitor the positive and negative impacts they have on employee behavior. For example, the manager of a hair salon wanted to motivate his stylists to sell more beauty products. The manager began offering a monthly prize to the stylist who sold the most products. Because one stylist's customers always tended to buy more products than did the other stylists' customers, the other stylists felt that there was no way they could win the prize. Rather than trying harder to sell products, they stopped trying at all, and overall product sales and revenues fell. Clearly, if rewards are improperly used, they can decrease the motivation of employees who do not expect to receive them.

SO WHAT

Rewards are only motivating to those expecting to receive them.

To effectively use your reward power, offer attractive rewards (which may differ across employees), make reasonable requests, and ensure that the rewards you offer are viewed as ethical and not as bribes.

Coercive Power. If a manager has the ability to punish subordinates, she or he can use position power to "coerce" subordinates to comply out of fear or because people want to avoid being punished. This is *coercive power*.[10] Punishment could be any undesired or negative consequence, including a reduction in work hours, undesirable shifts, or a written or verbal reprimand. If an instructor threatens to deduct points from a paper assignment for poor grammar, this is the use of coercive power.

Threatening punishment can have negative side effects on employees, including stress, resentment, decreased morale, and retaliation[11] and can even cost the manager his or her job. William J. Fife, former CEO of Giddings and Lewis, Inc, a company that manufactures factory equipment, was fired because of his abuse of coercive power. Fife destructively used punishments such as verbally criticizing, attacking, and embarrassing top managers in meetings. After investigating managers' complaints, the board of directors asked Fife to resign.[12]

Although it can produce behavior change, use coercion only when absolutely necessary—for example, if an employee is engaging in unsafe behaviors. Informing subordinates about rules and punishments for violations, giving subordinates sufficient warning prior to the punishment and giving them a chance to improve, and using punishment only when you are certain of a violation helps to decrease employee resentment and retaliation. To most effectively use coercive power, it is also important to administer appropriate punishment promptly and consistently, avoid appearing hostile, and give warnings and punishment notifications in private.

Personal Power

Position power does not guarantee that employees will fully cooperate with you. For example, employees of an unpopular supervisor may do the minimum amount possible to meet the requirements of their jobs. A manager's ability to influence others to give their full effort depends on the power or capability she or he has to influence other people's behavior or attitudes. Personal influence gives a manager *personal power*, which is based on the characteristics of that individual and stays with the individual regardless of where that person works.

We next discuss the four types of personal power that are based on a person's unique characteristics and that are independent of one's formal position in an organization: power based on an individual's expertise, power due to control over information, power based on the respect of others, and power due to the ability to persuade.

Expert Power. *Expert power* is based on an individual's expertise in some area.[13] When Warren Buffet, nicknamed the "Sage of Omaha," speaks on the economy, for example, many people listen intently to what he has to say. People respond to expert power because of their belief in the person's knowledge, skills, or expertise. For example, some sales managers may have specialized knowledge of certain market segments or customers, giving them expert power among other managers and employees.

Because an individuals' knowledge is the foundation of expert power, it is a personal power and can exist at any level in an organization. To enhance

---

coercive power

A position power based on fear or a desire to avoid punishment

personal power

Based on the person's individual characteristics; stays with a person regardless of his or her job or organization

expert power

A personal power based on an individual's knowledge or expertise your own expert power, try to identify the technical expertise that is important in your organization. Then enhance your own expertise in this area through formal training or on-the-job learning. Become an expert in your company's industry, products, services, and systems. Maintaining credibility by telling the truth, acting confident, and staying current in your field will also enhance others' perceptions of your expert power.

Informational Power. Control over information is *informational power*. In addition to experts with specialized knowledge, some people in an organization have or are able to control access to important information. These *gatekeepers* are able to exert power over others by providing or withholding information that others need. For example, managers with extensive personal networks may have access to information few others have. Once shared, however, the informational power that information provided is lost. Managers who depend on informational power must therefore continually replenish their supply of hard-to-get information.

Referent Power. *Referent power* is another type of personal power based on a manager's charisma or attractiveness to others. Subordinates "refer" to the manager as a role model and comply out of respect, admiration, and liking. They behave as the manager does and wants because they seek his or her approval.[14] Consistent ethical behavior can increase your reputation and thus your referent power.

Referent power is not limited to high-visibility leaders. All managers can use referent power effectively by displaying respect for subordinates, modeling behaviors consistent with the organization's culture, and being effective role models. By consistently "walking the walk" and "talking the talk," managers can use their referent power to promote the attitudes and behaviors they desire in employees. For example, when Walmart founder Sam Walton was worth more than $25 billion, he still drove his own pickup truck to work. His modeling of frugality permeated the company and promoted the behaviors and values that made Walmart consistently profitable.[15]

Persuasive Power. *Persuasive power* is due to the ability to use logic and facts to persuade others to adopt one's ideas or perspectives. Good listening skills and identifying and appealing to the goals and motivations of the other person can enhance your persuasive power.

informational power
Power derived from control over information

SO WHAT
Consistent ethical behavior can increase your power.

referent power
A personal power based on a manager's charisma or attractiveness to others

persuasive power
Power due to the ability to use logic and facts to persuade

WORLDFOTO / ALAMY

The charisma of Amazon.com President Jeff Bezos increases his referent power.

When Is Each Type of Power Appropriate?

It is important to adjust your use of power to the situation and person you are trying to influence. Because the effects of referent and expert power rely on the employee's *internal motivation* and voluntary compliance, they are always appropriate. However, these types of power are not always effective—if they do not motivate employee behavior, then either legitimate or reward organizational power might be appropriate. Although you may lack some types of power, you should assess what types of power you do have and strategically choose which to assert in a particular situation.

Legitimate, reward, and coercive power rely on *external motivation* and obligatory obedience. Legitimate and reward power are frequently employed as methods of influence by managers, but coercive power is rarely appropriate and should be reserved for only the most extreme situations. Effective leaders tend to rely on expert and referent power more than legitimate, reward, or coercive power.[16] Using legitimate, reward, and coercive powers to influence others is using power rather than leadership. Leadership is more effective to the degree that followers' behaviors toward the leader's goals are voluntary and not coerced.

Through your speech and actions, you can use your power to motivate subordinates by arousing appropriate motives in them. For example, when competitive follower behavior is required, you might arouse followers' need for power. When you want to inspire exceptional efforts to attain difficult goals, you might arouse followers' need for achievement.[17]

SO WHAT

Because coercive power decreases motivation and commitment, it is rarely used by effective leaders.

Acquiring and Using Power

So how can you increase your power in your organization? How can you get a good raise and a promotion? How can you avoid abusing your power? This section will help to answer these questions and give you some ideas about how you might best acquire and use power in your own career.

Acquiring Power. It is important to recognize that you have different levels of each type of power, and to understand when each type of power is appropriate to use. Your power is greater if the things you control are important, rare, and cannot be substituted for by something else.[18] If you have expertise that is important to your company, that not many other people in your field have, and that cannot be substituted for by something else, then you will have more power than if you could be easily replaced and do not contribute much value to your workgroup or organization. Table 10-2 gives you the opportunity to understand the amount of power you hold in your own organization.

Developing your expertise and performing well can increase your power. In addition to technical expertise, becoming an expert on your own company can make you a valuable and powerful employee. Learn your company's history, strategy, and what is on its website. Learn how each department contributes to other departments and to the company as a whole. Identify emerging trends that will influence your industry or the economy as a whole. Persuade management to let you present these important issues to key people elsewhere in the company. Be sure that your work is relevant to important organizational problems and that you and your work are visible to the people who control raises and promotions. Network inside and outside your organization to develop positive relationships with people who can be helpful to you throughout your career.[19]

SO WHAT

Developing positive relationships and performing well can increase your power.

Table 10-2

Are You Powerful?

As you have learned in this chapter, power is greater among individuals who control scarce resources that are important to others. This assessment measures the importance and scarcity of your contributions to your supervisors and coworkers. Use the following scale to respond to the questions below.

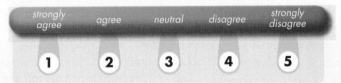

___1. I do not think that my department/area would function well if my job was not done properly.

___2. If I were to leave, my manager would have a difficult time finding someone with my skills and abilities as a replacement.

___3. It seems that a lot of other people in this department/area depend on me to do my job well.

___4. My manager knows that I do things in my job that not very many other people can do.

___5. My manager depends on me a lot.

___6. My manager is aware that I have pretty unique job-related skills and abilities.

Scoring: To calculate your perceived power in your organization, add up your answers to the six questions. Your total should be between 6 and 30. Place your score on this continuum:

5——10——15——20——25——30

Low perceived power   High perceived power

Interpretation: The higher your perceived power, the more successful your influence attempts are likely to be. You can rely on your expert, referent, and informational power to increase the success of your influence attempts. If you have low power and would like to increase it, try to identify ways you can develop skills and expertise that would be useful to your workgroup and that other group members do not already have. You might also try to develop your listening and persuasion skills.

Source: JOURNAL OF MANAGERIAL ISSUES 7, 92–108, Hospital Professionals' Use of Upward Influence Tactics, by Boss, R. W.

Abuse of Power. Power in itself is neither good nor bad—what matters is how the power is used. An important point to make about power is the potential for its abuse. The *abuse of power* is using any type of power to demean, exploit, or take advantage of another or influencing someone to do something the person later regrets. Disrespecting individual dignity and interference with job performance or deserved rewards are abuses of power.[20] It is easy to think of news stories where people have abused their power. In addition to financial damage, the results of the abuse of power may include decreased employee satisfaction and helping behaviors,[21] increased employee deviance,[22] and increased turnover.

It is important to remember that having power does not mean that you must use it. Being able to fire a subordinate if he does not follow formal work rules does not mean that you have to do so. Having power also does not guarantee that using it will be effective in influencing desired behavior. If you have the power to punish a subordinate if she does not work a particular shift, the subordinate can still refuse the extra shift and quit. The greater the importance that others place on the resources or outcomes that you control, the greater the power you have in that relationship. If you do not have something that another person wants, you have no power over him or her.

abuse of power

Using any type of power to demean, exploit, or take advantage of another or influencing someone to do something the person later regrets

Unchecked authority can result in the abuse of power. Managers should not have free reign to do whatever they want—managers' power should match their responsibilities. For example, a manager responsible for subordinates' performance should possess some sort of reward power such as allocating merit pay awards. But the power given to a manager should generally not exceed what is required to do his or her job.

Regularly reviewing managers' behaviors and performance and holding them accountable for their actions is important. Even CEOs report to a board of directors, and legislation like the Sarbanes-Oxley Act of 2002 limits the unchecked authority of CEOs.

Perhaps the best known types of power abuse are bullying, abusive supervision, and sexual harassment (involving unwanted advances, requests, communication, or contact with the threat of punishment for noncompliance). When managers do not know how to persuade or influence through more effective tactics, they may resort to the use of fear, threats, and intimidation because that is all they know how to do.[23]

Mark Cuban, owner of the Mavericks NBA basketball team, is a good example of how power alone is insufficient in securing desired outcomes. Cuban has position power as the owner of five businesses, and many people look up to him due to his referent power. He has coercive power, which he used in firing the Mavericks' coach, and is considered an expert in business. He is well connected with other influential people, and has high information power. Nonetheless, Cuban's behavior has cost him respect as well as a lot of money. He has stormed into locker rooms and cursed players when his team lost, and he has berated referees. Although he would like to own more professional sports teams, he has stated that he knows other sports leagues might not consider his bids for ownership due to his poor NBA behavior.[24]

SO WHAT

People who do not know how to effectively influence or persuade others often resort to the use of fear, threats, and intimidation.

Empowerment

The degree to which power is shared and an employee has the authority to make and implement at least some decisions is *empowerment*.[25] Empowerment may be organization-wide and embedded in an organization's culture, or it may be something created by individual managers. Empowering employees to improve quality, cut costs, and improve their work efficiency is becoming more common in organizations as computerized technologies increasingly give employees the feedback they need to manage themselves. If trained employees have important, accurate, and timely information, they can often handle situations and spot opportunities without a manager's intervention. This can increase the flexibility and responsiveness of organizations.

empowerment

Sharing power with employees and giving them the authority to make and implement at least some decisions

Essentially, empowerment requires two things: (1) that managers allow those beneath them to have more power and control over their work, and (2) that managers provide training, resources, and coaching to give them the skills and confidence to act empowered. Just telling an employee that he or she is empowered is not enough. Employees must have the skills to do what they are empowered to do and believe that they can successfully do it. The authors saw this when consulting for a manufacturing facility. Newly empowered employee teams had the authority to spend up to $500 to improve their teams' processes without having to consult with a manager. At first, none of the teams were willing to spend anything, fearing that they would make a bad choice. Not until the teams went through a hands-on training program teaching decision making, communication, and problem-solving skills did they have the confidence to act empowered.

Because your good reputation for ethical behavior decreases a supervisor's concern that you might behave inappropriately, it also can increase your supervisor's willingness to give you more responsibility and empowerment. A reputation for ethical behavior increases the influence you are given because you are not seen as someone trying to advance a personal agenda.[26]

Being an ethical leader is a source of power because it eliminates hidden agendas and builds trust. Ethics also increases our resistance to attempts by others to influence us because it keeps us focused, thus decreasing the power others have over us.[27]

Technology can empower employees to solve problems themselves. For example, knowing that to receive her quarterly bonus she must consistently meet call volume targets, Pat uses the digital dashboard to check her performance. The color-coded display shows that she is below target. She knows that she has been getting to work on time and that she is productive. So why is her performance below her target? Pat sees that her call volume has been consistently low for the last month, always just after lunch. This reveals the root cause of the problem. Her afternoon shift starts at exactly the time her lunch break ends, and although she hurries through lunch, she is getting back from lunch ten minutes after her scheduled start each afternoon. Pat requests a minor schedule change that gives her ten more minutes to get from the cafeteria to her workstation.[28] The digital dashboard helped to empower Pat to solve her performance problem without needing the help of a supervisor, other than for approval of the minor schedule change.

How Subunits Obtain Power

We now shift our attention away from individual power to how subunits acquire the power that allows them greater influence in organizational decisions. A workgroup's, department's, or subunit's power is derived either from its control of resources or through its strategic power.[29] The more desirable and important the resources controlled by a group (budget, space, etc.), the greater the group's *resource power*. Groups that occupy a central role in decision making wield greater *strategic power* by influencing higher-level decisions. Key subunits that influence the performance of other subunits have greater power. We next discuss several conditions that enhance a subunit's power.

Resource Scarcity. When resources are scarce, power differences across subunits are likely to be magnified. Power is greater for subunits that control scarce resources that are vital to the organization as a whole. When resources are plentiful, subunit power differences are often reduced.

Centrality. A subunit's activities are central to the extent that they influence the work of many other subunits (e.g., budget approval power), when their impact is more immediate (e.g., a performance decline in that unit would be felt faster by the organization as a whole), and when the subunit has a critical impact on the firm's key product or service. This is one reason why production and marketing departments tend to have greater power than human resource departments.

Substitutability. A subunit's power is reduced to the extent that others inside or outside of the organization can also perform its responsibilities. The labor market has a big influence on substitutability—when a subunit's skills become scarce in the labor market, the power of that subunit increases. If a subunit's work can be outsourced, that unit's power decreases because the threat of outsourcing can counter its influence attempts.

⌐ **Uncertainty.** Organizations do not like surprises or uncertainties. Accurate planning, financing, budgeting, and staffing all depend on a reasonably predictable future. The subunits most capable of coping with uncertainty or of guiding the organization through a period of increased uncertainty tend to have greater power.

INFLUENCE

Influential people have power, but not all powerful people have influence. For example, employees are often more responsive to the social influence of their peers than to the control and incentives of management.[30] Leadership is in large part an influence process that involves the use of various powers or interpersonal styles to affect the behaviors and attitudes of others. But whether a leader's use of power to influence someone will be successful depends on whether the other person allows him- or herself to be influenced. How much formal power or authority a manager has is not nearly as important as the amount of influence the manager has over subordinates. If you lack the respect of subordinates because of unethical behavior or perceptions that you are unqualified, you will not effectively motivate your subordinates to work their hardest toward the firm's goals.

Influence Tactics

influence tactics

How people translate their power to affect the behavior of others

People apply their power to influence the behavior of others through *influence tactics*. Influence tactics increase the likelihood that others will respond favorably to your requests. What might be different for you at work if you had a greater ability to influence your bosses and coworkers? What might be different for you at school if you were better able to influence your classmates and instructor?

Influence tactics should be matched to the situation and to the person being influenced, and can be learned with practice.[31] Responses to influence attempts are not always positive, however. Table 10-3 summarizes some influence tactics along with the possible responses to them.

Of the various influence tactics, rational persuasion, inspirational appeals, and consultation have been found to be the most effective, and pressure is the least effective.[34] Using more than one influence tactic at the same time can increase your effectiveness as long as the tactics are compatible.[35] For example, ingratiation could enhance the effectiveness of a personal appeal. Rational persuasion can be combined with any of the other tactics. Pressure, on the other hand, undermines the feelings of friendship that are the foundation of personal appeals and ingratiation.

Influence tactics are most effective when they are compatible with the influencer's power relative to the target person and with the interpersonal relationship between the two people. When the influencer and target person have mutual trust and shared objectives, rational persuasion, consultation, and collaboration are often effective. A moderate degree of friendship is usually necessary for personal appeals to work. Assertiveness is not likely to be effective with a superior.

Influence attempts are often unsuccessful on the first try and require the skilled use of a sequence of tactics over time. Initial influence attempts

Table 10-3

Influence Tactics and Responses to Them

Influence Tactics

Coalition tactics	Engaging the help of others to persuade someone to do something; referring to the support of others to convince someone to agree to a proposal or to change his or her attitude toward something
- Consultation	Requesting someone's advice to solve a problem or mutually setting goals to increase a follower's commitment to the leader's decision; being willing to modify the goals or solution based on the person's concerns and suggestions to sustain commitment
Exchange	Offering to exchange something of value now or in the future for someone's cooperation; usually used after other tactics have failed due to the higher cost
Ingratiation	Flattering or praising someone to put them in a good mood or to make them more likely to want to help (e.g., complimenting your manager's outfit before asking for additional project funding), or using humor;[32] seen as more credible when used early rather than after other influence attempts have failed
- Inspirational appeals	Appealing to someone's aspirations, values, and ideals to gain his or her commitment, or increasing people's confidence that they can do something in order to increase motivation; for example, Wayne Hale, Chairman of NASA's Space Shuttle Mission Management Team during the space shuttle Discovery's Return to Flight mission, stated, "So the fundamental question remains, do we have those qualities that made our ancestors successful? Do we have the judgment to weigh it all in the balance? Do we have the character to dare great deeds? History is watching."[33]
Legitimating tactics	Enhancing one's formal authority to make a certain request by referring to rules, precedents, or official documents; should be used early if doubts about the request's legitimacy are expected
Personal appeals	Asking someone to do something "because we're friends" or asking for a personal favor
Pressure	Using coercion or persistent follow-up or reminders to gain influence; risks undesirable side effects such as resentment
- Rational persuasion (or reason)	Using logic and facts to persuade someone

Responses to Influence Attempts

Commitment	Endorsing and becoming an actively involved participant as a result of the influence attempt
Compliance	Going along with what the influencer wants without being personally committed
Passive resistance	Rejecting the influence attempt but not getting in the way of what the influencer is trying to do
Active resistance	Rejecting the influence attempt and actively trying to stop the influencer from doing what she or he is trying to do, or trying to change the influencer's attitudes

Source: Gary A. Yukl, Table 6.8, p. 172, *"Leadership in Organizations"*, 7th ed., © 2010.

with subordinates or peers often begin with a simple request or with a weak form of rational persuasion because these techniques are easy and relatively low in personal cost (such as a weakened friendship). Anticipated resistance may be met with a stronger form of rational persuasion and softer tactics including consultation, personal appeals, inspirational appeals, and collaboration. Continued resistance is then countered with harder tactics or abandoning the effort if the request does not warrant the risks of escalation.[36]

This chapter's *Case Study* feature illustrates the use of different influence tactics among employees trying to influence a leader's decision.

CASE STUDY

Influencing Decisions

Imagine that you are a manager responsible for choosing which new project to support. Your budget is limited, and you can support only one new project. You must make a decision by tomorrow morning. Your staff just finished presenting their ideas to you, and you are finding it difficult to choose. Each project has merit, and you feel that they all have an equal chance of success. As the meeting comes to a close, your team members each make a last-minute appeal to win your support.

Jose: "You are a great leader and have always made great decisions for the team. I'm sure you'll choose the best one this time, too!"

Kira: "You've always said we should aim high. I think my idea will help our company reach new markets and raise us to the next level."

John: "I think my idea has the highest chance for a good return on our investment with the least risk. My market research is solid, and I think my idea is our best choice."

Sandy: "I talked to the folks in marketing and they said that we were really onto something with my idea. I think they really support this project and hope you choose it."

Questions:

1. What influence tactics did each staff member use?
2. Which influence tactic do you think would best persuade you to choose that person's idea? Why?
3. Which influence tactic do you think would be least effective in persuading you to choose that person's idea? Why?

Role of National Culture in Influence Effectiveness

Your ability to effectively influence others is enhanced by high cultural intelligence, or your ability to function effectively in culturally diverse environments. Understanding diverse cultures, values, and perspectives enhances your sensitivity to what is important to others and how to best influence them.

Influence tactics are also most effective when they are consistent with the social values in the national and organizational cultures. For example, consultation is likely to be a more effective influence tactic in a country with strong democratic traditions than in a country in which obedience to leaders is a strongly held cultural value.[37] This chapter's *Global Issues* feature describes the importance of understanding the appropriateness of using different influence tactics in different national cultures.

SO WHAT

For the most success, match the influence tactic you use to the context and to the person you are trying to influence.

Persuasion Skills

Influencing others often requires persuading them to do or to believe something. Because persuasion gets people to do things differently because they *want* to, not because they have been ordered to, it is a more effective way to lead. The manager who wants more resources, the supervisor who wants to keep a key employee from leaving, and the company president who wants to sell her idea to the board of directors all need to be persuasive. Because most people are resistant to altering their habits, managers need to use persuasion skills whenever they need to create change.[44]

GLOBAL ISSUES

EFFECTIVENESS OF DIFFERENT INFLUENCE TACTICS DEPENDS ON NATIONAL CULTURE

Although rational persuasion and consultation have been found to be effective influence tactics in many countries,[38] national culture can affect the appropriateness of different influence tactics.[39] For example, consider Hong Kong and Taiwanese managers. Managers from both cultures believe that exchange and rational persuasion are the most effective influence tactics. However, Taiwanese managers tend to use inspirational appeals and ingratiation more than do Hong Kong managers, who feel that pressure is a more effective tactic.[40] Direct, task-oriented influence tactics are seen as more effective by western managers than by Chinese managers, who prefer tactics involving personal relations, avoidance, or an informal approach.[41] Understanding these differences is important to employees working as expatriates as well as to anyone who works in a multicultural workplace.

Matching your influence technique to the context and to the person you are trying to influence is important for upward as well as downward influence. One study found that host-country managers who demonstrate upward influence tactics that are culturally appropriate to the parent company's national culture will be more promotable than those who do not. Exchanging benefits and coalition are more likely to be associated with promotability in German firms than in domestic Ecuadorian firms.[42] Upward-appeal assertiveness is more likely to be associated with promotability in American firms than in domestic Ecuadorian firms.[43] Being aware not only of your sources of power, but also of the receptiveness of the other person to different influence tactics will improve your effectiveness as a manager.

Persuasion requires thorough and careful preparation, the compelling framing of arguments, the presentation of vivid supporting evidence, and finding the correct emotional match with the audience. It is much more than a sales skill. As one expert says, "Many businesspeople misunderstand persuasion, and more still underutilize it."[45]

Here are some recommendations for being more persuasive:

- *Build credibility* based on both your skills and your relationships. Using good posture and an appropriate tone of voice, and showing a sense of confidence will increase the chances that others will quickly see you as credible.[46]
- *Do not begin with a hard sell.* This gives potential opponents something to resist and fight against.[47]
- *Search for shared ground and be willing to compromise.* Every audience is different, and it is important not to come across as if you have already made up your mind. Communicate in words the audience easily understands and relates to, and incorporate values and beliefs they share.[48]
- *Develop compelling positions* based on only a few convincing arguments, rather than overwhelming people with facts and information.
- *Connect with people emotionally* rather than relying solely on logical arguments.
- *Create a continuous feedback loop* from the audience to yourself. Incorporate the audience's perspective back into your own arguments.[49]
- *Be patient*—people are rarely persuaded on the first try.[50]

Upward Influence

In addition to using influence to guide the behavior of subordinates, *upward influence* can also be used to influence superiors. When Jack

upward influence
Influencing superiors

Welch was the CEO of General Electric, he realized that the web was going to transform business. He recognized that GE's younger, "webified" employees had better Internet skills and e-business knowledge than did GE's older and higher-ranking executives. He decided to pair Internet-savvy employees with GE's 600 worldwide executives to share their expertise about the new technology. In addition to building the e-business capabilities of his managers, this unique "mentoring up" program made managers at all levels more comfortable with upward influence in the company.[51]

Upward influence is an important aspect of influence and contributes substantially to individual effectiveness in organizations.[52] There are six primary upward influence tactics:[53]

1. *Ingratiation*: using flattery and acting polite, friendly, or humble to put the supervisor in a good mood
2. *Exchange*: offering to trade favors or rewards for compliance
3. *Rationality*: using logic, planning, reason, and compromise
4. *Assertiveness*: using aggression, nagging, and verbal confrontations or giving orders
5. *Coalition formation*: seeking the support of other organization members to show a united front
6. *Upward appeals*: making informal or formal appeals to organizational superiors for intervention

Your source(s) of power generally determines which upward influence tactics you tend to use. An employee with referent power might use integration, for example, and someone with expert power might prefer rationality. It is also important to adjust your influence tactic to suit the boss you are trying to influence.[54] The self-assessment in this chapter's *Understand Yourself* feature gives you the opportunity to learn more about your preferred upward influence tactics.

The six upward influence tactics can be used alone, but are often used in combination with each other in what are called ***upward influence styles***. People tend to have a preferred upward influence style that they use when trying to influence their managers. The four upward influence styles are:[55]

upward influence styles

Combinations of upward influence tactics that tend to be used together

1. *Shotgun*: This style uses the most influence and emphasizes assertiveness and bargaining. Shotgun managers tend to have less job tenure and the greatest needs to obtain personal benefits and "sell" their ideas about how the work should be done.[56] Shotgun managers attempt to obtain what they want by using many different tactics.[57] This style is associated with the highest levels of job tension and personal stress.[58]
2. *Tactician*: This style uses an average amount of influence and emphasizes reason. Tactician managers tend to direct organizational subunits involved in nonroutine work that gives them a skill and knowledge power base. Tacticians tend to have considerable influence in their organizations over budgets, policy, and personnel and rely heavily on reason and logic to gain compliance.[59] This style is associated with the lowest levels of job tension and personal stress[60] and with more favorable individual outcomes than the more forceful shotgun style.
3. *Bystander*: This style uses little influence with superiors. Bystander managers tend to direct organizational units doing routine work and generally have little organizational power (i.e., little control over budgets, policy, or personnel matters). Because they also tend to have few personal or organizational objectives that require compliance from others, they generally

UNDERSTAND YOURSELF

UPWARD INFLUENCE SCALE

People use a variety of tactics when attempting to influence their bosses. Please use the following scale to record how often you engage in each of the following behaviors when influencing your boss. Be honest—there are no right or wrong answers.

never	occasionally	frequently	almost always
1	2 3 4	5 6	7

___1. Act very humbly while making my request.

___2. Make my boss feel good about me before making my request.

___3. Act in a friendly manner before making my request.

___4. Remind my boss of past favors I have done for him/her.

___5. Offer an exchange (e.g., if you do this for me, I will do something for you).

___6. Offer to make a personal sacrifice (e.g. work late) if he/she will do what I want.

___7. Use logic to convince him/her.

___8. Explain the reasons for my request.

___9. Present my boss with information supporting my point of view.

___10. Have a showdown in which I confront my boss face-to-face.

___11. Express my anger verbally.

___12. Use a forceful manner: try things like making demands, setting deadlines, and expressing strong emotion.

___13. Obtain the support of coworkers to back up my request.

___14. Obtain the support of my subordinates to back up my request.

___15. Mobilize other people in the organization to help me in influencing my boss.

___16. Obtain the informal support of higher-ups.

___17. Make a formal appeal to higher levels to back up my request.

___18. Rely on the chain of command—on people higher up in the organization who have power over my boss.

Scoring:

Ingratiation: Add up your scores to statements 1–3 ____

Exchange: Add up your scores to statements 4–6 ____

Rationality: Add up your scores to statements 7–9 ____

Assertiveness: Add up your scores to statements 10–12 ____

Coalitions: Add up your scores to statements 13–15 ____

Upward appeal: Add up your scores to statements 16–18 ____

Interpretation: Rank the upward influence tactics from highest to lowest based on your scores. The tactics with the highest scores are your preferred influence tactics. Do you agree with the ranking? Which other tactics do you think you should try using more frequently in the future? Why?

Source: Table 4 (adapted) from Kipnis, D., Schmidt, S. M., and Wilkinson, I. (1980). Intraorganizational influence tactics: Explorations in getting one's way. Journal of Applied Psychology, 65(4), 440–452.
Text excerpts (adapted scale items), from Schriesheim, C. A., & Hinkin, T. R. (1990). Influence tactics used by subordinates: A theoretical and empirical analysis and refinement of the Kipnis, Schmidt, and Wilkinson subscales. Journal of Applied Psychology, 75(3), 246–257.

exert little influence.[61] Between 30 and 40 percent of managers are classified as bystanders.[62]

4. *Ingratiator:* This style primarily uses a friendliness strategy but also uses the other influence strategies to some extent. The name of this style reflects the dominant mode by which these managers exercise influence.[63] Research has found that top managers who use ingratiation behaviors toward their CEO, including flattery, expressing confirming opinions, and performing favors, are more likely to receive board appointments at firms where their CEO is either director or knows members of the board.[64]

ORGANIZATIONAL POLITICS

organizational politics

Social influence attempts directed at those who can provide rewards that will help promote or protect the self-interests of the actor

SO WHAT

The core of effective politics is influencing others through persuasion, generating support, and inspiring trust.

In organizations, people differ in their ability to influence others and influence work processes. Accordingly, people differ in what they can do to protect and promote their own interests. *Organizational politics* are social influence attempts directed at people who can provide rewards that will help promote or protect the self-interests of the actor.[65] At some point everyone needs to influence others to follow their ideas or preferred courses of action, and doing that requires the use of politics. Effectively influencing others through persuasion, generating support, and inspiring trust are the core of effective politics.

Politics are a fact of life in work organizations—virtually every employee in America can describe a political incident in which he or she was directly or indirectly involved.[66] Employees who have been negatively affected by politics tend to perceive politics to be a negative influence in organizations, whereas those whose interests were advanced through political means tend to view it as a useful tool.[67] Because employees act based on their perceptions, recognizing and understanding employees' perceptions of politics is important to managing effectively.[68]

Organizational politics are the result of both individual employees and the culture of the organization.[69] Some cultures permit and even promote certain types of political behaviors. Political behaviors are most likely to occur when there is a reasonably high degree of ambiguity or uncertainty in the work environment.[70] Some organizations proactively seek to eliminate political behavior. For example, new hires at the software company Success Factors agree in writing to fourteen "rules of engagement." Rule 14 starts out, "I will be a good person to work with—not territorial, not be a jerk." One of the company's founding principles is that "our organization will consist only of people who absolutely love what we do, with a white-hot passion. We will have utmost respect for the individual in a collaborative, egalitarian, and meritocratic environment—no blind copying, no politics, no parochialism, no silos, no games—just being good!" Employees are not expected to be perfect, but when they lose their cool or belittle colleagues, inadvertently or not, they are expected to apologize.[71]

Eugene McKenna identified these common political tactics in organizations:[72]

1. *Controlling information*: restricting information to certain people
2. *Controlling lines of communication*: establishing gatekeepers to restrict access to information
3. *Using outside experts*: outside consultants may seem neutral, but are paid and directed by management to "do their bidding"
4. *Controlling the agenda*: to ensure only certain topics are discussed
5. *Game playing*: leaking information, getting only friends to provide feedback, and so on
6. *Image building*: enlisting "spin doctors" to project a desirable image
7. *Building coalitions*: befriending powerful others or starting small subgroups to promote specific aims
8. *Controlling decision parameters*: trying to influence decisions before they are made
9. *Eliminating political rivals*: this may even mean getting them promoted to get them out of the way

When politics are constructive rather than destructive, they are unnoticeable. When politics are used to advance self-serving causes, employees tend to perceive the workplace as more highly political. The more political employees perceive a work environment to be, the greater their job anxiety and intentions to leave, and the lower their job and supervisor satisfaction and organizational commitment.[73] Individuals' perceptions about the political nature of their work environment impact employees' productivity, satisfaction, and intent to leave.[74] They also determine how political the environment will actually be. Employees who perceive that others get ahead by acting politically engage in more political behaviors themselves.[75] Organizational culture is thus influenced by the perceived degree of political activity and how the employees in that organization react to these perceptions.[76]

Political skill involves having interpersonal influence as well as social astuteness, which involves showing respect for others' ways of thinking. Developing a strong network and being perceived by others as sincere also reflects high political skill.[77] Political skill has been found to be positively related to job performance.[78] The self-assessment in Table 10-4 gives you the chance to better understand your political skill.

Causes of Political Behavior

Conflict is at the core of organizational politics.[79] Because political behavior is self-serving, it has the potential to threaten the self-interests of others. When a perceived threat is followed by retaliation, conflict arises.[80] Uncertainty increases political behavior. Lacking specific rules and policies for guidance, employees develop their own rules for acceptable behavior that are often self-serving. Decisions made under uncertainty are particularly susceptible to political influence.[81]

Scarcity of valued resources (e.g., transfers, raises, office space, budgets) also promotes political behavior. Jockeying for a position to receive a valued but scarce resource is classic political behavior.[82] This is why organizations with limited resources tend to have more political environments. Understanding why resources are limited can help to predict who is likely to be the target of the political activities, as well as how strong the political behavior is likely to be. Anyone who controls critical resources that cannot be secured elsewhere is a probable target of political influence tactics.[83]

Some individuals desire to avoid conflict, and therefore tend not to resist others' influence attempts. Although this may appear to be nonpolitical, it is actually a form of political behavior. It has been suggested that the distinction between political and nonpolitical behavior in organizations can be made on the basis of intent.[84] That is, if a behavior is enacted specifically to advance one's own self-interests (including conflict avoidance), then the individual is acting politically.[85] Because employees who "don't rock the boat" are not viewed as threatening opponents, they may be welcomed into the "in-group" and receive valued outcomes simply for not interfering with a politically acting individual's or group's agenda. Inaction, or going along to get ahead, can be a reasonable and profitable approach to take in order to advance one's own self-interests when working in a political environment.[86]

Organizational policies sometimes reward and perpetuate political behavior.[87] In particular, compensation policies may inadvertently reward individuals who engage in influence behaviors and penalize those who do not. Individually oriented rewards induce individually oriented behavior, which is often self-interested and political in nature. When this type of behavior is rewarded or reinforced, the tactics used to secure the reward will likely be repeated. This can lead to cultures that foster and reward political behavior. Rewarding political behavior can induce those who have not acted politically in the past to do so in the future. Individuals who perceive themselves as inequitably rewarded relative to others who engage in organizational politics may begin engaging in political behaviors to increase their own rewards.[88]

SO WHAT

Conflict and resource scarcity are at the core of organizational politics.

Table 10-4

Political Skill Inventory

This self-assessment gives you the opportunity to better understand your political skill. Be honest in responding to the statements below using the following scale:

strongly disagree	disagree	slightly disagree	neutral	slightly agree	agree	strongly agree
1	2	3	4	5	6	7

___ 1. I spend a lot of time and effort at work networking with others.

___ 2. I am able to make most people feel comfortable and at ease around me.

___ 3. I am able to communicate easily and effectively with others.

___ 4. It is easy for me to develop good rapport with most people.

___ 5. I understand people very well.

___ 6. I am good at building relationships with influential people at work.

___ 7. I am particularly good at sensing the motivations and hidden agendas of others.

___ 8. When communicating with others, I try to be genuine in what I say and do.

___ 9. I have developed a large network of colleagues and associates at work who I can call on for support when I really need to get things done.

___10. At work, I know a lot of important people and am well connected.

___11. I spend a lot of time at work developing connections with others.

___12. I am good at getting people to like me.

___13. It is important that people believe I am sincere in what I say and do.

___14. I try to show a genuine interest in other people.

___15. I am good at using my connections and network to make things happen at work.

___16. I have good intuition and am savvy about how to present myself to others.

___17. I always seem to instinctively know the right things to say or do to influence others.

___18. I pay close attention to people's facial expressions.

Scoring: Add up your responses to the eighteen statements. This is your overall political skill score. Scores *over 72* are considered high and scores *below 36* are considered low. To calculate your score for the four dimensions of political skill, add up your responses to the following subsets of statements:

Social Astuteness	Interpersonal Influence	Networking Ability	Apparent Sincerity
5 ___	2 ___	1 ___	8 ___
7 ___	3 ___	6 ___	13 ___
16 ___	4 ___	9 ___	14 ___
17 ___	12 ___	10 ___	
18 ___		11 ___	
		15 ___	

Total Score: _____ /126
Subset Scores:
Social Astuteness: _____ /35   Interpersonal Influence: _____ /28
Networking Ability: _____ /42   Apparent Sincerity: _____ /21

Interpretation: The higher your score, the stronger your political skill in that area.

Source: Ferris, G.R., Davidson, S.L., Perrewé, P.L. (2005). Political Skill at Work: Impact on Work Effectiveness. Mountain View, CA: Davies-Black, p. 23.

IMPROVE YOUR SKILLS

RECOGNIZING POLITICS

Political behavior can be placed in three main categories: general political behavior, which includes the behaviors of individuals who act in a self-serving manner to obtain valued outcomes; going along to get ahead, which consists of a lack of action by individuals (e.g., remaining silent) in order to secure valued outcomes; and pay and promotion policies, which involve the organization behaving politically through the policies it enacts.[90] Rating the following set of statements based on the scale shown below will help you to assess the political environment that exists in your organization.

strongly disagree	disagree	slightly disagree	neutral	slightly agree	agree	strongly agree
1	2	3	4	5	6	7

___ 1. People in this organization attempt to build themselves up by tearing others down.

___ 2. There has always been an influential group in this department that no one ever crosses.

___ 3. Agreeing with powerful others is the best alternative in this organization.

___ 4. It is best not to rock the boat in this organization.

___ 5. Sometimes it is easier to remain quiet than to fight the system.

___ 6. Telling others what they want to hear is sometimes better than telling the truth.

___ 7. It is safer to think what you are told than to make up your own mind.

___ 8. None of the raises I have received are consistent with the policies on how raises should be determined.

___ 9. When it comes to pay raise and promotion decisions, policies are irrelevant.

___ 10. Promotions around here are not valued much because how they are determined is so political.

Scoring: Add up the numbers you assigned to the ten statements. Your total should be between 10 and 70. Place your score on this continuum:

10——20——30——40——50——60——70
Not Political   Extremely Political

Sources: Adapted from: Kacmar, K.M. and Ferris, G.R. (1991), Perceptions of Organizational Politics Scale (POPS): Development and Construct Validation. *Educational and Psychological Measurement, 51,* 193–205. Kacmar, K.M. & Carlson, D.S. (1997), Further Validation of the Perceptions of Politics Scale (POPS): A Multiple Sample Investigation. Journal of Management, 23, 627–658.

This chapter's *Improve Your Skills* feature (above) lets you hone your ability to assess the degree to which politics is a factor in your organization.

Managing Organizational Politics

Centuries ago, the philosopher Plato knew the importance of managing politics. He advised, "Those who are too smart to engage in politics are punished by being governed by those who are dumber." A modern expert advises, "Even if you are a person who takes no active part in [office] politics, knowing how the game is played means that you stand a good chance of surviving the depredations of those who undertake the lifestyle of cubicle warfare."[91] A survey of 150 executives of major U.S. companies found that they waste 19 percent of their time—at least one day per week—dealing with company politics.[92] The executives surveyed said they spent a bulk of that time dealing with internal conflicts, rivalry disputes, and other volatile situations at work. Because politics is pervasive and because political skill has been found to decrease job stress[89] it is worth developing your skills in this area.

"Those who are too smart to engage in politics are punished by being governed by those who are dumber." —*Plato, Philosopher*

Because political behaviors are enhanced by organizational factors including scarce resources, ambiguous roles and goals, centralization,[93] and complexity,[94] formal rules and procedures can help to reduce the occurrence of political behavior.[95] Clarifying job expectations; opening the communication process; confronting employees acting inefficiently, unethically, or irresponsibly; and serving as a good role model can all decrease political behavior.[96]

Keeping the number of employees assigned to each manager at a reasonable level is another way to decrease political behavior. In large workgroups, the amount of attention a supervisor is able to devote to each employee decreases. This can increase ambiguity and uncertainty, promoting a more political environment.[97]

Managing politics is about managing power. As one expert states, "Being a good office politician means that you know how to turn individual agendas into common goals."[98] If you understand the motivations and aspirations of your subordinates, you can help them to attain what they most want without resorting to politics or the inappropriate use of power. Building trust and openness to allow employees to freely discuss their feelings, fears, and opinions without fear of retaliation decreases the need for political behavior.[99]

To reduce political behavior and promote creativity at the innovation factory IDEO, company leaders have created an idea-friendly environment that minimizes the amount of corporate posturing associated with trying to guess what answer the boss is hoping for. As a result, IDEO employees tend to speak their minds, regardless of whether a "boss" is in the room.[100]

IMPRESSION MANAGEMENT

impression management

The process of portraying a desired image or attitude to control the impression others form of us

Being perceived positively by others is related to greater power and influence. It may also help employees succeed in political environments. ***Impression management*** is the process of portraying a desired image or attitude to control the impression others form of us.[101] This does not mean that the presented image is accurate, although misrepresenting your image can backfire if others later learn that the image is false.

Impression management is not inherently a bad thing[102]—in fact, most people regularly engage in some form of interpersonal deception. Research has found that 61.5 percent of people's natural conversation involves some form of deception,[103] and people tend to average sixteen white lies over a two-week period.[104]

self-monitoring

Having a high concern with others' perceptions of us and adjusting our behavior to fit the situation

People who are higher in the personality trait of ***self-monitoring***, which reflects having a high concern with others' perceptions of us and adjusting our behavior to fit the situation,[105] are more likely to engage in impression management behaviors.[106] High self-monitors are good at reading situations and adjusting their behavior accordingly to maintain their desired image. Low self-monitors tend to present consistent images of themselves regardless of the situation.

People who engage in impression management often take great care to be perceived in a positive light.[107] Impression management techniques are commonly used by job applicants in interviews with positive results.[108] In particular, impression management techniques related to self-promotion[109] and ingratiation[110] tend to work well in job interviews. Self-promotion may not work as well on the job, however, because the supervisor

NEUSTOCKIMAGES/ISTOCKPHOTO.COM

Making eye contact, smiling, and giving a firm handshake helps us to make a good impression on people we meet.

Table 10-5

Detecting Impression Management Behaviors

Although it can take a lot of experience and practice to be able to interpret them correctly, individuals engaging in impression management often display the following involuntary cues resulting from the emotions and cognitive effort required to manage their self-presentation:

1. *Elevated speaking pitch*—speaking at a higher pitch as compared to someone telling the truth[113]
2. *Speech errors*—interspersing words with uh, ah, or um[114]
3. *Speech pauses*—allowing greater periods of silence while engaged in a conversation[115]
4. *Negative statements*—using words like *no, not, can't,* and *won't*[116]
5. *Eye shifting*—looking away rather than at the person to whom they are speaking[117]
6. *Increased pupil dilation*—pupils tend to widen as they would in dim lighting[118]
7. *Blinking*—more frequent blinking[119]
8. *Tactile manipulation*—fondling or manipulating objects with the hands[120]
9. *Leg fidgeting*—leg twitches, foot tapping, and swiveling or rocking when sitting[121]
10. *Less hand gesturing*—"speaking" less with the hands and keeping the head relatively still[122]

SO WHAT

Nonverbal cues are most indicative of deception and impression management.

has a better opportunity to observe what you can really do. In fact, self-promotion is related to lower performance evaluations.[111]

As a manager, being able to detect others' impression management and deception is obviously useful. Because nonverbal cues are most indicative of deception, focusing on the person's body language is particularly helpful.[112] Table 10-5 presents some tips for detecting impression management and deception on the part of others.

SUMMARY AND APPLICATION

When used properly, power, influence, and politics are essential tools for managerial success. When used improperly, power, influence, and politics can undermine trust, result in unethical behavior, and create a toxic organization. Understanding these tools and how to use them effectively will help you to be a more successful manager.

TAKEAWAY POINTS

1. Position power (legitimate, reward, and coercive powers) is derived from the position one holds in an organization. Personal power (expert, informational, referent, and persuasive powers) comes from the unique characteristics of individuals regardless of their position in the organization.
2. Because leadership is more effective to the degree that followers' behaviors toward the leader's goals are voluntary and not coerced, effective leaders tend to rely on expert and referent power more than legitimate, reward, or coercive power.

REAL WORLD RESPONSE

INFLUENCING ACCEPTANCE OF CHANGE AT CHURCH & DWIGHT

Church & Dwight knew that its marketing talent was likely to resist the change to two parallel marketing organizations, one focused on current brands and one focused on new product development. To keep its marketing talent engaged, the company ensured that its current brand team would still be involved in new product development even though the new product development team would run it and be accountable for it. The company also applied rational persuasion and showed the current brand team that the new arrangement would give them dedicated resources to use to do more with their own brands. The current brand team saw the logic of having dedicated resources to innovation and subsequent organic growth.

As expected, there was some resistance at beginning when the company carved some of the marketing people out and moved them into the new roles. To maintain job excitement, management used inspirational appeals linking the new structure and strategy to the company's success. Church & Dwight leaders also used legitimating tactics by making it clear that the change would happen and needed to happen quickly. Reward power also was used when all incentives were aligned around the new structure and objectives. This exchange of rewards for cooperation reflected the exchange influence tactic as well.

Church & Dwight's Executive Vice President of Global New Products Innovation, Steve Cugine, said that the results of the change "have been remarkable." Within three years the organic growth rate from new product development doubled to just under 6 percent. The effectiveness of current brand marketing also increased, helping the company to achieve record organic growth of close to 10 percent for the consumer domestic U.S. business. The change has been so successful that Church & Dwight is expanding the new structure to the rest of its global locations.

Sources: This real world response is based on a telephone interview with Steve Cugine, Executive Vice President of Global New Products Innovation, Church & Dwight Co.,October 2, 2009.

3. Developing your technical expertise and high performance can increase your power in an organization. Becoming an expert in your own company can make you a valuable and powerful employee. Ensuring that your work is relevant to important organizational problems and that you and your work are visible to the people who control raises and promotions will also increase your power.

4. Involvement gives subordinates influence in the decision being made; empowerment gives subordinates the ability and authority to make the decision themselves.

5. Organizational subunits are more powerful when they control resources that are important but scarce, when they are central to the organization, when they cannot be substituted for, and when they help the organization successfully manage uncertainty.

6. Rational persuasion, inspirational appeals, and consultation are the most effective influence tactics, and pressure is the least effective.

7. The six primary upward influence tactics are ingratiation, exchange, rationality, assertiveness, coalition formation, and upward appeals.

8. The tactician's upward influence style relies heavily on reason and logic to gain compliance. This style is associated with the lowest levels of job tension and personal stress and with more favorable individual outcomes than the more assertive shotgun style.

9. Uncertainty, scarcity of valued resources, and organizational policies can influence political behavior.

10. Impression management involves the communication of a desired image or attitude to influence the image others form of us. Being perceived positively by others is related to greater power and influence. It may also help employees succeed in political environments.

DISCUSSION QUESTIONS

1. What power(s) does your instructor have?
2. What influence tactics does your instructor use to motivate you to learn?
3. Describe a time in the last week that someone influenced you to do something you would not otherwise have done. What influence tactic(s) did she or he use?
4. Is another person's ethics important to you in your decision to allow that person to influence you? Why or why not?
5. How can you ethically use power, influence, and politics to get a promotion?
6. Have you ever tried to influence your boss to do something? What upward influence tactics did you try? Were you successful? Why or why not?
7. Are office politics bad? Why or why not?
8. How do you use impression management at work?

EXERCISES

Influencing Your Instructor

Form groups of four to six students and identify your group's spokesperson. Using what you learned in this chapter, come up with a strategy to influence your instructor to change the evaluation criteria for this course (although it is likely too late in the semester for any changes to actually be made). Identify the influence tactics you will use, as well as the sources of power you will draw from. Now make a brief presentation to the class and instructor. The class will vote on which group is the most persuasive.

Influencing an Ethical Decision

Working alone or in a small group, read the following situation and complete the assignment below.

Soon after you begin a new job, you receive a troubling report from the company's new 401(k) provider. Several social security numbers do not match the names of the employees who provided them, which suggests that these individuals may be illegal and ineligible to work in the United States. You begin an investigation, but your boss quickly orders you to stop, explaining that the company cannot afford to terminate those employees even if they are illegal because that would leave the company shorthanded. When you express your concern about this deliberate violation of federal immigration laws, the company's leadership is unworried. They have reasoned that the Immigration and Naturalization Service has bigger fish to fry, and that even if they are caught, the fine would be an acceptable business expense, since the company is making huge profits due to the cheap labor.

Assignment: Using what you have learned in this chapter, describe what you would do to change the company's policy toward employing illegal workers. How effective do you think you would be? Why?

Empowerment at Nucor Steel

Nucor Steel is famous for empowering its employees to innovate and help the company perform well. Visit http://www.nucor.com/careers/ to learn how Nucor Steel empowers its employees. Look around Nucor's career center to learn more about how Nucor employees have wide latitude to make changes to their job and decisions about their work. Then answer the following questions.

Questions

1. In what ways does Nucor empower its employees?
2. How do employees react to this level of empowerment?
3. How does empowering employees contribute to Nucor's success?

VIDEO CASES

Now What?

Imagine learning that your boss is trying unsuccessfully to influence a peer of yours to organize the company picnic again this year. When you are asked to try to influence the stubborn subordinate to agree to plan the picnic, *what do you say or do?* Go to this chapter's "Now What?" video, watch the challenge video, and choose a response. Be sure to also view the outcomes of the two responses you didn't choose.

Discussion Questions

1. Which aspects of organizational behavior discussed in this chapter are illustrated in these videos? Explain your answer.
2. Which influence tactics do you think were the most effective in these videos? Why?
3. How else might you persuade your coworker to organize the picnic?

Workplace | Numi Organic Tea: Managing the Value Chain, Information Technology, and E-Business

Numi is the tea maker of choice for high-end restaurants, hotel chains, colleges, and cruise lines. As pioneer of green marketing, the organic beverage company is dedicated to sustainability, fair trade, and a small carbon footprint. Unlike most businesses, Numi has a three-fold bottom line of "people, planet, and profit," which requires managers to evaluate performance on a range of criteria, including the overall "greenness" of supply chain operations.

But maintaining an eco-friendly business isn't easy. Many international businesses don't share Numi's perspectives on social responsibility, waste management, and workers' rights. Some don't even speak the same ethical language. While some disagreements are acceptable, others require shrewd political calculation and pressure to resolve.

Fortunately for Numi, the technical side of managing partnerships has become easier through information technology. Whether the task involves inventory, packaging, or transport, Numi's high-tech enterprise resource planning system (ERP) enables efficient coordination with strategic partners around the globe. An ERP is a computer system that processes vast organization data and provides real time information on specific companywide operations. Since members of Numi's supply chain—mostly growers, mills, and factories—are linked to the same computer system, the tea maker is able to monitor global operations from its headquarters in Oakland, California. "We're managing our inventories in multiple countries through the same software program," says Brian Durkee, director of operations. "All we do now is simply go into the system and push a button to say we want to make a particular product, and the system pulls all the lots and materials for us and allocates the inventory."

Despite the cultural and ethical differences between Numi and certain overseas partners, managers are committed to achieving a common vision through a variety of tactics, both political and technological. The tea maker's pursuit of an ethical and sustainable supply chain reduces waste in energy and natural resources. As a result, Numi's organic tea products not only taste great, but they are good for the planet as well.

Discussion Questions

1. Describe the power relationship between Numi and its supply chain partners.
2. In the video, what issues with China-based suppliers require Numi's managers to use influence and persuasion tactics?
3. How does Numi get suppliers to comply with its policies?

DO WHAT

CENGAGENOW™

CENGAGENOW™ includes **teaching and learning resources** to supplement the text, and is designed specifically to **help students "think like managers"** by engaging and challenging them to think critically about managerial situations. **CengageNOW uses today's technology to improve the skills** of tomorrow's managers.

END NOTES

[1]This vignette is based on a telephone interview with Steve Cugine, Executive Vice President of Global New Products Innovation, Church & Dwight Co.,October 2, 2009.

[2]Eisenhardt, K., & Bourgeois, L. J. (1988). Politics of Strategic Decision Making in High Velocity Environments: Toward a Mid-Range Theory. *Academy of Management Journal, 31,* 737–770.

[3]Cartwright, D., & Zander, A. (1968). *Group Dynamics.* New York: Harper & Row; Richmond, V. P., McCroskey, J. C., Davis, L. M., & Koontz, K. A. (1980). Management Communication Style and Employee Satisfaction: A Preliminary Investigation. *Communication Quarterly, 28,* 37–46.

[4]For a more detailed discussion of power and influence, see Schriesheim, C., & Neider, L. (2006). *Power and Influence in Organizations: New Empirical and Theoretical Perspectives* (Vol. 5). Greenwich, CT: Information Age Publishing.

[5]McClelland, D. C. (1975). *Power: The Inner Experience.* New York: Irvington.

[6]McClelland, D. C., & Boyatzis, R. E. (1982). Leadership Motive Pattern and Long-Term Success in Management. *Journal of Applied Psychology, 6,* 737–743.

[7]McClelland, D. C. (1975). *Power: The Inner Experience.* New York: Irvington.

[8]French, Jr., J. R. P., & Raven, B. H. (1968). The Bases of Social Power. In *Studies of Social Power,* ed. D. Cartwright. Ann Arbor, MI: Institute for Social Research.

[9]French, Jr., J. R. P., & Raven, B.H. (1968). The Bases of Social Power. In *Studies of Social Power,* ed. D. Cartwright. Ann Arbor, MI: Institute for Social Research.

[10]French, Jr., J. R. P., & Raven, B. H. (1968). The Bases of Social Power. In *Studies of Social Power,* ed. D. Cartwright. Ann Arbor, MI: Institute for Social Research.

[11]Inness, M., Barling, J., & Turner, N. (2005). Understanding Supervisor-Targeted Aggression: A Within-Person, Between-Jobs Design. *Journal of Applied Psychology, 90*(4), 731–739; Zellars, K. L., Tepper, B. J., & Duffy, M. K. (2002). Abusive Supervision and Subordinates' Organizational Citizenship Behavior. *Journal of Applied Psychology, 87,* 1068–1076; Williams, S. (1998). A Meta-Analysis of the Relationship Between Organizational Punishment and Employee Performance/Satisfaction. *Research and Practice in Human Resource Management, 6,* 51–64.

[12]Rose, R. L. (1993, June 22). After Turning Around Giddings and Lewis, Fife Is Turned Out Himself. *The Wall Street Journal,* A1.

[13]French, Jr., J. R. P., & Raven, B. H. (1968). The Bases of Social Power. In *Studies of Social Power,* ed. D. Cartwright. Ann Arbor, MI: Institute for Social Research.

[14]French, Jr., J. R. P., & Raven, B. H. (1968). The Bases of Social Power. In *Studies of Social Power,* ed. D. Cartwright. Ann Arbor, MI: Institute for Social Research.

[15]Tracy, B. (2005, November 21). Seven Keys to Growing Your Business. Entrepreneur.com. Available online: http://www.entrepreneur.com/startingabusiness/startupbasics/article81128.html.

[16]Yukl, G. (1998). *Leadership in Organizations* (4th ed.). Englewood Cliffs, NJ: Prentice Hall.

[17]House, R. J. (1977). A 1976 Theory of Charismatic Leadership. In *Leadership: The Cutting Edge*, eds. J. G. Hunt and L. L. Larson (pp. 189–207). Carbondale, IL: Southern Illinois University Press; Shamir, B., House, R. J., & Arthur, M. B. (1993). The Motivational Effects of Charismatic Leadership: A Self-Concept Based Theory. *Organization Science, 4,* 577–594.

[18]Emerson, R. M. (1962). Power-Dependence Relations. *American Sociological Review, 27,* 31–41.

[19]McIntosh, P. & Luecke, R.A. (2011). *Increase Your Influence at Work*. New York: American Management Association.

[20]Vredenburgh, D., & Brender, Y. (1998). The Hierarchical Abuse of Power in Work Organizations. *Journal of Business Ethics, 17,* 1337–1347.

[21]Zellars, K. L., Tepper, B. J., & Duffy, M. K. (2002). Abusive Supervision and Subordinates' Organizational Citizenship Behavior. *Journal of Applied Psychology, 87,* 1068–1076.

[22]Tepper, B. J., Henle, C. A., Lambert, L. S., Giacalone, R. A., & Duffy, M. K. (2008). Abusive Supervision and Subordinates' Organization Deviance. *Journal of Applied Psychology, 93,* 721–732.

[23]Furnham, A. (2005). *The Psychology of Behaviour at Work: The Individual in the Organization.* New York: Psychology Press.

[24]Lussier, R. N., & Achua, C. F. (2009). *Leadership: Theory, Application, & Skill Development* (4th ed.). Mason, OH: South-Western.

[25]Conger, J. A. (1989). Leadership: The Art of Empowering Others. *Academy of Management Executive, 3,* 17–24; Conger, J. A., & Kanungo, R. N. (1988). The Empowerment Process: Integrating Theory and Practice. *Academy of Management Review, 13,* 471–482.

[26]Deluca, J. M. (1999). *Political Savvy: Systematic Approaches to Leadership Behind the Scenes.* Berwyn, PA: EBG.

[27]Deluca, J. M. (1999). *Political Savvy: Systematic Approaches to Leadership Behind the Scenes.* Berwyn, PA: EBG.

[28]Based on An Analytical Approach to Workforce Management. *CRM Today.* Available online: http://www.crm2day.com/content/t6_librarynews_1.php?id=EplVpulFAusyoHEmpq.

[29]Greenberg, J., & Baron, R. A. (2003). *Behavior in Organizations* (8th ed.). Upper Saddle River, NJ: Prentice Hall.

[30]Henslin, J. M. (2008). *Sociology: A Down to Earth Approach* (9th ed.). Upper Saddle River, NJ: Pearson.

[31]Lewis-Duarte, M. & Bligh, M.C. (2012). Agents of "Influence": Exploring the Usage, Timing, and Outcomes of Executive Coaching Tactics, *Leadership & Organization Development Journal, 33*(3), 255–281.

[32]Cooper, C. (2005). Just Joking Around? Employee Humor Expression as an Ingratiatory Behavior. *Academy of Management Review, 30,* 765–776.

[33]Hale, W. (2005, April 3). NASA Internal Memo from Wayne Hale: What I Learned at ISOS. Available online: http://www .spaceref.com/news/viewsr.html?pid=16028.

[34]Yukl, G. (2002). *Leadership in Organizations* (5th ed., pp. 141–174). Upper Saddle River, NJ: Prentice Hall; Higgins, C.A., Judge, T. A., & Ferris, G. R. (2003). Influence Tactics and Work Outcomes: A Meta-Analysis. *Journal of Organizational Behavior, 24,* 89–106.

[35]Falbe, C. M., & Yukl, G. (1992). Consequences for Managers of Using Single Influence Tactics and Combinations of Tactics. *Academy of Management Journal, 35,* 638–653.

[36]Conger, J. A., & Riggio, R. E. (2006). *The Practice of Leadership: Developing the Next Generation of Leaders.* New York: Jossey-Bass.

[37]Conger, J. A., & Riggio, R. E. (2006). *The Practice of Leadership: Developing the Next Generation of Leaders.* San Francisco: Jossey-Bass.

[38]Kennedy, J. C., Fu, P. P., & Yukl, G. (2003). Influence Tactics Across Twelve Cultures. *Advances in Global Leadership, 3,* 127–147.

[39]Duyar, I., Aydin, I., & Pehlivan, Z. (2009). Analyzing Principal Influence Tactics from a Cross-Cultural Perspective: Do Preferred Influence Tactics and Targeted Goals Differ by National Culture? *International Perspectives on Education and Society, 11,* 191–220.

[40]Fu, P. P., Peng, T. K., Kennedy, J. C., & Yukl, G. (2004, February). A Comparison of Chinese Managers in Hong Kong, Taiwan, and Mainland China. *Organizational Dynamics,* 32–46.

[41]Yukl, G. A., Fu, P. P., & McDonald, R. (2003). Cross-Cultural Differences in Perceived Effectiveness of Influence Tactics for Initiating or Resisting Change. *Applied Psychology: An International Review, 52,* 68–82.

[42]Herrmann, P., & Werbel, J. D. (2007). Promotability of Host-Country Nationals: A Cross-Sectional Study. *British Journal of Management, 18,* 281–293.

[43]Herrmann, P., & Werbel, J. D. (2007). Promotability of Host-Country Nationals: A Cross-Sectional Study. *British Journal of Management, 18,* 281–293.

[44]Garvin, D. A., & Roberto, M. A. (2005, February). Change Through Persuasion. *Harvard Business Review,* 104–112.

[45]Conger, J. A. (1998, May–June). The Necessary Art of Persuasion. *Harvard Business Review,* 85–95.

[46]Conger, J. (1998). *Winning 'Em Over: A New Model for Management in the Age of Persuasion.* New York: Simon & Schuster.

[47]Conger, J. A. (1998, May–June). The Necessary Art of Persuasion. *Harvard Business Review,* 85–95.

[48]Conger, J. (1998). *Winning 'Em Over: A New Model for Management in the Age of Persuasion.* New York: Simon & Schuster.

[49]Conger, J. (1998). *Winning 'Em Over: A New Model for Management in the Age of Persuasion.* New York: Simon & Schuster.

[50]Conger, J. A. (1998, May–June). The Necessary Art of Persuasion. *Harvard Business Review,* 85–95.

[51]Breen, B. (2001, November). Trickle-Up Leadership. *Fast Company, 52,* 70.

[52]Pelz, D. (1952). Influence: A Key to Effective Leadership in the First Line Supervisor. *Personnel, 29,* 3–11; Kanter, R. M. (1977). *Men and Women of the Corporation.* New York: Basic Books.

[53]Kipnis, D., Schmidt, S. M., & Wilkinson, I. (1980). Intra-Organizational Influence Tactics: Explorations of Getting One's Way. *Journal of Applied Psychology, 65,* 440–452.

[54]Botero, I.C., Foste, E.A., & Pace, K.M. (In press). Exploring Differences and Similarities in Predictors and Use of Upward Influence Strategies in Two Countries, *Journal of Cross-Cultural Psychology, 43*(4).

[55]Kipnis, D., & Schmidt, S. M. (1988). Upward-Influence Styles: Relationship with Performance, Evaluations, Salary, and Stress. *Administrative Science Quarterly, 33,* 528–542.

[56]Schriesheim, C. A., & Hinkin, T. R. (1990). Influence Tactics Used by Subordinates: A Theoretical and Empirical Analysis and Refinement of the Kipnis, Schmidt, and Wilkinson Subscales. *Journal of Applied Psychology, 75,* 246–257.

[57]Kipnis, D., & Schmidt, S. (1983). An Influence Perspective on Bargaining. In *Negotiating in Organizations*, eds. M. Bazerman and R. Lewicki (pp. 303–319). Beverly Hills, CA: Sage.

[58]Kipnis, D., & Schmidt, S. M. (1988). Upward-Influence Styles: Relationship with Performance, Evaluations, Salary, and Stress. *Administrative Science Quarterly, 33,* 528–542.

[59]Kipnis, D., & Schmidt, S. (1983). An Influence Perspective on Bargaining. In *Negotiating in Organizations*, eds. M. Bazerman and R. Lewicki (pp. 303–319). Beverly Hills, CA: Sage.

[60]Kipnis, D., & Schmidt, S. M. (1988). Upward-Influence Styles: Relationship with Performance, Evaluations, Salary, and Stress. *Administrative Science Quarterly, 33,* 528–542.

[61]Kipnis, D., & Schmidt, S. (1983). An Influence Perspective on Bargaining. In *Negotiating in Organizations,* eds. M. Bazerman and R. Lewicki (pp. 303–319). Beverly Hills, CA: Sage.

[62]Kipnis, D., & Schmidt, S. M. (1988). Upward-Influence Styles: Relationship with Performance, Evaluations, Salary, and Stress. *Administrative Science Quarterly, 33,* 528–542.

[63]Kipnis, D., & Schmidt, S. M. (1988). Upward-Influence Styles: Relationship with Performance, Evaluations, Salary, and Stress. *Administrative Science Quarterly, 33,* 528–542.

[64]Westphal, J. D., & Stern, I. (2006). The Other Pathway to the Boardroom: Interpersonal Influence Behavior as a Substitute for Elite Credentials and Majority Status in Obtaining Board Appointments. *Administrative Science Quarterly, 51,* 1–28.

[65]Cropanzano, R. S., Kacmar, K. M., & Bozeman, D. P. (1995). Organizational Politics, Justice, and Support: Their Differences and Similarities. In *Organizational Politics, Justice and Support: Managing Social Climate at Work,* eds. R. S. Cropanzano and K. M. Kacmar (pp. 1–18). Westport, CT: Quorum Books.

[66]Kacmar, K. M., & Carlson, D. S. (1997). Further Validation of the Perceptions of Politics Scale (POPS): A Multiple Sample Investigation. *Journal of Management, 23,* 627–658.

[67]Ferris, G. R., & Kacmar, K. M. (1992). Perceptions of Organizational Politics. *Journal of Management, 18,* 93–116.

[68]Lewin, K. (1936). *Principles of Topological Psychology.* New York: McGraw-Hill; Porter, L. W. (1976). Organizations as Political Animals. Presidential address, Division of Industrial-Organizational Psychology, 84th Annual Meeting of the American Psychological Association, Washington, DC.

[69]For a more detailed discussion of organizational politics, see Vredenburgh, D. J., & Maurer, J. G. (1984). A Process Framework of Organizational Politics. *Human Relations, 37,* 47–65.

[70]Ferris, G. R., Fedor, D. B., Chachere, J. G., & Pondy, L. R. (1989). Myths and Politics in Organizational Contexts. *Group & Organization Studies, 14,* 83–103; Fandt, P. M., & Ferris, G. R. (1990). The Management of Information and Impressions: When Employees Behave Opportunistically. *Organizational Behavior and Human Decision Processes, 45,* 140–158.

[71]Sutton, R. (2007, May). Building the Civilized Workplace. *The McKinsey Quarterly.* Available online: http://www.mckinseyquarterly.com/Organization/Talent/Building_the_civilized_workplace_1963.

[72]McKenna, E. F. (2000). *Business Psychology and Organisational Behavior: A Student's Handbook.* Hove, UK: Psychology Press.

[73]Chang, C. S., Rosen, C. C., & Levy, P. E. (2009). The Relationship Between Perceptions of Organizational Politics and Employee Attitudes, Strain, and Behavior: A Meta-Analytic Examination. *Academy of Management Journal, 52,* 779–801; Anderson, T. P. (1994). Creating Measures of Dysfunctional Office and Organizational Politics: The DOOP and Short Form DOOP Scales. *Psychology, 31,* 24–34; Cropanzano, R. S., Howes, J. C., Grandey, A. A., & Toth, P. (1997). The Relationship of Organizational Politics and Support to Work Behaviors, Attitudes, and Stress. *Journal of Organizational Behavior, 18,* 159–181.

[74]Ferris, G. R., & Kacmar, M. K. (1992). Perceptions of Organizational Politics. *Journal of Management, 18,* 93–116.

[75]Ferris, G. R., Fedor, D., Chachere, J. G., & Pondy, L. (1989). Myths and Politics in Organizational Contexts. *Group & Organizational Studies, 14,* 88–103.

[76]Kacmar, K. M., & Carlson, D. S. (1997). Further Validation of the Perceptions of Politics Scale (POPS): A Multiple Sample Investigation. *Journal of Management, 23,* 627–658.

[77]Ferris, G. R., Treadway, D. C., Perrewé, P. L., Brouer, R. L., Douglas, C., & Lux, S. (2007). Political Skill in Organizations. *Journal of Management, 33,* 290–320.

[78]Kapoutsis, I., Papalexandris, A., Nikolopoulos, A., Hochwarter, W.A., & Ferris, G.R. (2011). Politics Perceptions as Moderator of the Political Skill-Job Performance Relationship: A Two-Study, Cross-National, Constructive Replication, *Journal of Vocational Behavior, 78*(1), 123–135.

[79]Drory, A., & Romm, T. (1990). The Definition of Organizational Politics: A Review. *Human Relations, 43,* 1133–1154.

[80]Porter, L. W., Allen, R. W., & Angle, H. L. (1981). The Politics of Upward Influence in Organizations (pp. 109–149). In *Research in Organizational Behavior,* eds. L. L. Cummings and B. M. Staw (Vol. 3). Greenwich, CT: JAI Press.

[81]Drory, A., & Romm, T. (1990). The Definition of Organizational Politics: A Review. *Human Relations, 43,* 1133–1154.

[82]Farrell, D., & Peterson, J. C. (1982). Patterns of Political Behavior in Organizations. *Academy of Management Review, 45,* 403–412; Kumar, P., & Ghadially, R. (1989). Organizational Politics and Its Effect on Members of Organizations. *Human Relations, 42,* 305–314.

[83]Frost, P. J. (1987). Power, Politics, and Influence. In *Handbook of Organizational Communication,* eds. F. Jablin, L. Putnam, K. Roberts, & L. Porter. Beverly Hills, CA: Sage.

[84]Drory, A., & Romm, T. (1990). The Definition of Organizational Politics: A Review. *Human Relations, 43,* 1133–1154.

[85]Frost, P. J. (1987). Power, Politics, and Influence. In *Handbook of Organizational Communication,* eds. F. Jablin, L. Putnam, K. Roberts, & L. Porter. Beverly Hills, CA: Sage.

[86]Kacmar, K. M., & Ferris, G. R. (1991). Perceptions of Organizational Politics Scale (POPS): Development and Construct

Validation. *Educational and Psychological Measurement, 51,* 193–205. Shortened in Kacmar, K. M., & Carlson, D. S. (1997). Further Validation of the Perceptions of Politics Scale (POPS): A Multiple Sample Investigation. *Journal of Management, 23,* 627–658.

[87]Ferris, G. R., Fedor, D., Chachere, J. G., & Pondy, L. (1989). Myths and Politics in Organizational Contexts. *Group & Organizational Studies, 14,* 88–103; Ferris, G. R., & King, T. R. (1991). Politics in Human Resource Decisions: A Walk on the Dark Side. *Organizational Dynamics, 20,* 59–71; Kacmar, K. M., & Ferris, G. R. (1993). Politics at Work: Sharpening the Focus of Political Behavior in Organizations. *Business Horizons, 36,* 70–74.

[88]Ferris, G. R., Russ, G. S., & Fandt, P. M. (1989). Politics in Organizations. In *Impression Management in the Organization,* eds. R. A. Giacalone and P. Rosenfeld (pp. 143–170). Hillsdale, NJ: Lawrence Erlbaum; Kacmar, K. M., & Ferris, G. R. (1993). Politics at Work: Sharpening the Focus of Political Behavior in Organizations. *Business Horizons, 36,* 70–74.

[89]Jam, F.A., Khan, T.I., Zaidi, B.H., & Muzaffar, S.M. (2011). Political Skills Moderates the Relationship between Perception of Organizational Politics and Job Outcomes, *Journal of Educational and Social Research, 1*(4), 57–70.

[90]Kacmar, K. M., & Carlson, D. S. (1997). Further Validation of the Perceptions of Politics Scale (POPS): A Multiple Sample Investigation. *Journal of Management, 23,* 627–658.

[91]In Martinez, M. N. (2009). Politics Come with the Office. Graduating Engineer. Available online: http://www.graduatingengineer.com/articles/20010928/Politics-Come-With-the-Office

[92]In Martinez, M. N. (2009). Politics Come with the Office. Graduating Engineer. Available online: http://www.graduatingengineer.com/articles/20010928/Politics-Come-With-the-Office.

[93]Eisenhardt, K. M., & Bourgeois, L. J. (1988). Politics of Strategic Decision Making in High Velocity Environments: Toward a Midrange Theory. *Academy of Management Journal, 31,* 737–770.

[94]Greenberg, J., & Baron, R. A. (2003). *Behavior in Organizations* (8th ed.). Englewood Cliffs, NJ: Prentice Hall.

[95]Mintzberg. H. (1979). Organizational Power and Goals: A Skeletal Theory. In *Strategic Management: A New View of Business Policy and Planning,* eds. D. Schendel and C. Hofer (pp. 143–171). Boston: Little, Brown.

[96]Greenberg, J., & Baron, R. A. (2003). *Behavior in Organizations* (8th ed.). Englewood Cliffs, NJ: Prentice Hall.

[97]Ferris, G. R., & Kacmar, M. K. (1992). Perceptions of Organizational Politics. *Journal of Management, 18,* 93–116.

[98]In Martinez, M. N. (2009). Politics Come with the Office. Graduating Engineer. Available online: http://www.graduatingengineer.com/articles/20010928/Politics-Come-With-the-Office.

[99]Cohen, A., & Bradford, D. L. (2005). Influence Without Authority (2nd ed.). New York: Wiley.

[100]Wiscombe, J. (2007, January). IDEO: The Innovation Factory. *Workforce Management Online.* Available online: http://www.workforce.com/section/09/feature/24/73/71/index.html.

[101]Schlenker, B. R. (2003). Self-Presentation. In *Handbook of Self and Identity,* eds. M. R. Leary and J. P. Tangney (pp. 492–518). New York: Guilford.

[102]Bolino, M. C., Kacmar, K. M., Turnley, W. H., & Gilstrap, J. B. (2008). A Multi-Level Review of Impression Management Motives and Behaviors. *Journal of Management, 34,* 1080–1109.

[103]Turner, R. E., Edgley, C., & Olmstead, G. (1975). Information Control in Conversations: Honesty Is Not Always the Best Policy. *Kansas Journal of Sociology, 11,* 69–89.

[104]Camden, C., Motley, M. T., & Wilson, A. (1984). White Lies in Interpersonal Communication: A Taxonomy and Preliminary

Investigation of Social Motivations. *Western Journal of Speech Communication, 48,* 309–325.

[105]Snyder, M. (1974). Self-Monitoring of Expressive Behaviour. *Journal of Personality and Social Psychology, 30,* 526–537.

[106]Turnley, W. H., & Bolino, M. C. (2001). Achieving Desired Images While Avoiding Undesired Images: Exploring the Role of Self-Monitoring in Impression Management. *Journal of Applied Psychology, 86,* 351–360.

[107]Stevens, C. K., & Kristof, A. L. (1995). Making the Right Impression: A Field Study of Applicant Impression Management During Job Interviews. *Journal of Applied Psychology, 80,* 587–606.

[108]Higgins, C. A., & Judge, T. A. (2004). The Effect of Applicant Influence Tactics on Recruiter Perceptions of Fit and Hiring Recommendations: A Field Study. *Journal of Applied Psychology, 89,* 622–632.

[109]Stevens, C. K., & Kristof, A. L. (1995). Making the Right Impression: A Field Study of Applicant Impression Management During Job Interviews. *Journal of Applied Psychology, 80,* 587–606.

[110]Higgins, C. A., Judge, T. A., & Ferris, G. R. (2003). Influence Tactics and Work Outcomes: A Meta-Analysis. *Journal of Organizational Behavior, 24,* 89–106.

[111]Higgins, C. A., Judge, T. A., & Ferris, G. R. (2003). Influence Tactics and Work Outcomes: A Meta-Analysis. *Journal of Organizational Behavior, 24,* 89–106.

[112]Forrest, J. A., & Feldman, R. S. (2000). Detecting Deception and Judge's Involvement: Lower Task Involvement Leads to Better Lie Detection. *Personality and Social Psychology Bulletin, 26,* 118–125.

[113]Streeter, L. A., Krauss, R. M., Geller, V., Olson, C., & Apple, W. (1977). Pitch Changes During Attempted Deception. *Journal of Personality and Social Psychology, 35,* 345–350.

[114]Cody, M. J., Marston, P. J., & Foster, M. (1984). Deception: Paralinguistic and Verbal Leakage. In *Communication Yearbook*, eds.

R. N. Bostrom and B. H. Westley (pp. 464–490). Beverly Hills, CA: Sage; deTurck, M. A., & Miller, G. R. (1985). Deception and Arousal: Isolating the Behavioral Correlates of Deception. *Human Communication Research, 12,* 181–201.

[115]Cody, M. J., Marston, P. J., & Foster, M. (1984). Deception: Paralinguistic and Verbal Leakage. In *Communication Yearbook,* eds. R. N. Bostrom and B. H. Westley (pp. 464–490). Beverly Hills, CA: Sage.

[116]Mehrabian, A. (1967). Orientation Behaviors and Nonverbal Attitude Communication. *Journal of Communication, 17,* 324–332; Wiener, M., & Mehrabian, A. (1968). *Language Within Language: Immediacy, a Channel in Verbal Communication.* Englewood Cliffs, NJ: Prentice Hall.

[117]Hocking, J. E., Bauchner, J. E., Kaminski, E. P., & Miller, G. R. (1979). Detecting Deceptive Communication from Verbal, Visual and Paralinguistic Cues. *Human Communication Research, 6,* 33–46.

[118]O'Hair, H. D., Cody, M. J., & McLaughlin, M. L. (1981). Prepared Lies, Spontaneous Lies, Machiavellianism, and Nonverbal Communication. *Human Communication Research, 7,* 325–339.

[119]Ekman, P., Friesen, W. V., O'Sullivan, M., & Scherer, K. R. (1980). Relative Importance of Face, Body, and Speech in Judgments of Personality and Affect. *Journal of Personality and Social Psychology, 38,* 270–277; Riggio, R. E., & Friedman, H. S. (1983). Individual Differences and Cues to Deception. *Journal of Personality and Social Psychology, 45,* 899–915.

[120]Ekman, P., & Friesen, W. V. (1972). Hand Movements. *Journal of Communication, 22,* 353–374; McClintock, C. C., & Hunt, R. G. (1975). Nonverbal Indicators of Affect and Deception in an Interview Setting. *Journal of Applied Social Psychology, 5,* 54–67.

[121]Buller, D. B., & Aune, R. K. (1987). Nonverbal Cues to Deception Among Intimates, Friends and Strangers. *Journal of Nonverbal Behavior, 11,* 269–290.

[122]Ekman, P., & Friesen, W. V. (1974). Detecting Deception from the Body or Face. *Journal of Personality and Social Psychology, 29,* 288–298.

CHAPTER 11

Managing Conflict and Negotiating

MARKS & SPENCER SIMPLY FOOD

Marks & Spencer tries to handle workplace conflicts and disputes responsibly and ethically. Doing so helps to create a safe and productive work environment.

IAN HAMILTON/MAXIAN/ISTOCKPHOTO.COM

REAL WORLD CHALLENGE

RESOLVING DISPUTES AT MARKS & SPENCER[1]

Global clothing, home products, and food retailer Marks & Spencer employs over 78,000 people around the world and has over 700 stores in the United Kingdom alone. Marks & Spencer understands that workplace conflicts and disputes are inevitable, and wants to handle them responsibly and ethically. The company also knows that the managerial time spent on disputes as well as damaged coworker relationships can distract employees from focusing on their jobs and performing their best.

Marks & Spencer wants to give its employees the opportunity to find fair, mutually agreed upon, constructive solutions in a safe environment and enable them to move forward after a conflict positively and confidently. Imagine that the company's management team approaches you for suggestions. What advice would you give them? After reading this chapter you should have some good ideas.

LEARNING OBJECTIVES

1. Describe the difference between dysfunctional and constructive conflict.

2. Explain what causes conflict.

3. Describe the conflict escalation process.

4. Describe how conflict can be de-escalated.

5. List the five interpersonal conflict management strategies.

6. Explain why culture is important to conflict resolution.

7. Describe some of the best and worst conflict resolution behaviors.

8. Describe the difference between distributive and integrative negotiation.

9. List the three types of alternative dispute resolution.

Conflict is the inevitable result of interdependencies among people, workgroups, and organizations.[2] Given that all organizations are interdependent systems, organizations without conflict do not exist.[3] Indeed, mid-level managers spend approximately 25 percent of their time managing conflict.[4] Your ability to effectively manage conflict will influence both your individual success and organizational performance.

Although many people feel that conflict is inherently destructive, in fact some conflict is beneficial and desirable. Conflict can certainly have negative consequences in the short run, such as when a manager and staff have a conflict over customer needs or when two employees disagree about how to do something. Conflict can undermine decision quality when either or both parties withdraw and refuse to cooperate.[5] It can also lead to the departure of valued employees, as happened in the fashion company Gianni Versace when CEO Giancarlo Di Risio resigned after a conflict with Donatella Versace over creative control.[6]

In the long run, however, conflict can lead to positive outcomes including better decisions, more motivated employees, and happier customers. When it is well managed, conflict can improve problem solving and innovation, increase employee involvement and commitment, and clarify work processes and goals. How conflict is managed is the biggest determinant of whether a conflict has positive or negative outcomes. For example, compared with a no-conflict situation, conflict can improve decision quality when it is managed through cooperative problem solving. Constructive change is typically the result of well-managed conflict.

Negotiation is an important skill in managing and resolving conflicts, and is a part of all managers' jobs. After reading this chapter, you should have a good understanding of what conflict is, its role in organizations, and how to manage it. You will also understand how to be a more effective negotiator.

CONFLICT

conflict

A disagreement through which two or more parties perceive a threat to their interests, needs, or concerns

Conflict is a disagreement through which two or more parties perceive a threat to their interests, needs, or concerns. Conflict can be both constructive and destructive.[7] Conflict resolution theory pioneer Morton Deutsch claimed that whether conflict is positive or negative is determined by the parties' response to the conflict rather than by the conflict itself.[8] Focusing on the conflict management process, not just the outcomes desired by the parties, is thus a key to realizing the potential benefits of a conflict. Mismanaged conflict helps to explain why so few family businesses make it to the third generation. A survey of 1,002 family-business owners revealed that the potential for conflict increases significantly as family businesses age.[9]

dysfunctional conflict

Destructive conflict focused on emotions and differences between the two parties

Behaviors that escalate a conflict until the conflict seems to take on a life of its own generate *dysfunctional conflict*. Dysfunctional conflicts focus on emotions and differences between the two parties and can degenerate to the extent that the parties forget the substantive issues and focus on getting even, retaliating, or even hurting the other party.

Not only can dysfunctional conflict negatively influence employee, workgroup, and company performance, but it also can lead to employee depression, absenteeism, turnover, burnout, and negative emotional states.[10] It is characterized by feelings of contempt and at least one of the parties withdrawing from communicating.[11] No one is satisfied with the outcome of dysfunctional conflict, potential gains from the conflict are not realized, and the negative feelings at the end of one conflict are carried over to the next conflict, creating a negative spiral. As a result, dysfunctional conflict often becomes separated from the initial issue and continues even after the original conflict becomes irrelevant or is forgotten.

Have you ever ended a disagreement feeling better about something? When it is effectively managed, conflict can be healthy. Interpersonal conflict can lead to greater learning, flexibility, and creativity.[12] Behaviors that are adaptive and responsive to the situation, person, and issues create *constructive conflict*. Constructive conflicts, also called functional conflicts, balance the interests of both parties to maximize mutual gains and the attainment of mutual goals. Constructive conflicts contain elements of creativity, adaptation, and a desire to discover a mutually acceptable outcome. Constructive conflict can lead to the identification of new alternatives and ideas.[13] Constructive conflict is a natural, inevitable, and creative force, and can be beneficial to employees and their organizations.[14]

constructive conflict
Adaptive, positive conflict (also called functional conflict)

What Causes Conflict?

SO WHAT?
Conflict should not necessarily be avoided—when managed properly, it can have many positive outcomes.

What creates conflict? The short answer is that conflict can be caused by anything that leads to a disagreement. We next discuss nine of the most common sources of conflict, and summarize them in Table 11-1.

Differing Task Goals. *Task conflict* is a disagreement about the task or goals. A moderate amount of task conflict is beneficial in the early stages of a project because it increases innovation and generates more alternatives from which to choose. However, task conflict is more likely to be detrimental over time when tasks are complex.[15] Task conflict can be very productive if handled correctly. For example, marketing employees want to provide product variety to maximize sales whereas production employees focus on efficiencies and cost and prefer long, economical production runs of a limited number of

task conflict
A disagreement about the task or goals

Table 11-1

Sources of Conflict

Differing task goals	disagreements over what is to be accomplished
Differing process goals	disagreements over how to accomplish tasks or goals
Interpersonal differences	differences in motivation, aspirations, or personality
Resource constraints	incompatible needs or competition over perceived or actual resource constraints
Change	the uncertainty of change often creates conflict and changes the relative importance of different organizational groups
Differing values	perceived or actual incompatibilities in beliefs about what is good or bad, right or wrong, or fair or unfair
Poor communication	when people lack necessary information, are misinformed, interpret information differently, or disagree about which data is relevant
Task interdependence	when one person or unit is dependent on another for resources or information, the potential for conflict increases
Organizational structure	conflict (either horizontal or vertical) can result from structural or process features of the organization

products. Resolving this task conflict balances the organization's need for cost efficiencies with its goal of maximizing sales. Task conflict also occurs when employees disagree about which packaging design is best or whether quality or quantity is more important.

Compensation systems often create differing task goals within an organization. For example, if marketing employees are compensated based on the number of units the company sells but production employees are compensated based on the average cost per unit, conflict between them is understandable. Holding marketing and production employees jointly accountable for both sales and cost gives them common goals and reduces their conflict. Focusing employees, workgroups, and departments on a common enemy such as a competitor or even a challenging economy can also unite employees in their pursuit of a common goal and reduce the negative effects of conflict.

Differing Process Goals. Have you ever wanted to do a task one way but someone else preferred a different strategy? Even when we agree about what we are trying to accomplish, we can still disagree about how we should accomplish it. *Process conflict* reflects conflict about how to accomplish a task, who is responsible for what, or how things should be delegated.[16] Role ambiguity increases process conflict. If a manager does not clearly assign work tasks to employees, employees may experience process conflict as they jockey with each other to do the most desirable assignments and avoid the least desirable tasks.

process conflict

Conflict about how to accomplish a task, who is responsible for what, and how things should be delegated

Interpersonal Differences. Have you ever had trouble working with someone because you just did not like the person? Conflicts can arise from interpersonal differences in motivation, aspirations, or personality. Interpersonal differences are a common trigger of *relationship conflict*, which is the result of incompatibility or differences between individuals or groups. Relationship conflict can also be triggered by personality, particularly the personality traits of dogmatism and power motivation. Relationship problems often fuel disputes and lead to an unnecessary escalating spiral of dysfunctional conflict.

relationship conflict

Conflict due to incompatibility or differences between individuals or groups

Relationship conflict is rarely a good thing. In fact, it is consistently recognized as a primary source of stress for employees of all ages, cultures, and occupations. Twenty-five percent of employees from a wide range of occupations identified interpersonal issues as the most vexing stressor at work.[17] In another study, negative social interactions at work accounted for 75 percent of all work situations that employees described as detrimental.[18]

Relationship conflict is fueled primarily by emotions (usually anger and frustration) and by perceptions about the other party's personality, character, or motives. Some conflicts occur because people ignore their own or others' feelings and emotions. Other conflicts occur when feelings and emotions differ over a particular issue. Because relationship conflict is personalized, it tends to become more extreme. In a privately held $12 million company, the relationship between the CEO and COO deteriorated to the point that they avoided each other in the hallway, seldom talked, and communicated primarily through other people.[19]

Because relationship conflict is not about concrete issues, neither party is really interested in solving the problem and may even try to create new problems. If relationship conflict cannot be converted to task conflict, it almost always gets worse because each person acts as if the other is untrustworthy, looks for and finds more problems, and gets angrier. Sometimes moving one or more team members to another team to separate the employees experiencing relationship conflict is necessary.

Effective project teams tend to have low but increasing levels of process conflict, moderate levels of task conflict in the middle of the project, and low levels of relationship conflict that increase toward the end of the project.[20] Creating a culture of respect and supporting the safe and balanced expression of perspectives and emotions can help to suppress relationship conflict. Intel trains all new employees in how to constructively manage conflict. Employees learn how to deal with others in a positive manner, use facts rather than opinion when persuading others, and focus on the problem rather than the people involved.[21]

Resource Constraints. The availability and allocation of scarce resources is a major source of conflict in organizations. Incompatible needs and competition over perceived or actual resource constraints can create *conflicts of interest*.[22] Conflicts of interest occur when someone believes that to satisfy his or her own needs, the needs and interests of someone else must be sacrificed. This is particularly problematic when dividing resources (like money or time) is a zero-sum game in which one party's gain is the other party's loss. Conflicts of interest can occur over:

conflicts of interest
Conflict due to incompatible needs or competition over perceived or actual resource constraints

- *Substantive issues* including time, money, and physical resources
- *Procedural issues* involving the way the conflict will be handled
- *Psychological issues* including perceptions of fairness, trust, or interest in participating

Conflicts of interest are best resolved by jointly addressing both parties' interests. If a scarce resource can be expanded, for example, say through a bigger budget or by adding more office space, a conflict can be resolved to both parties' satisfaction. Resolving conflicts of interest often increases creativity and innovation and stimulates performance.[23]

Change. Change causes conflict. Indeed, it has been said that change is not possible without conflict.[24] One of the primary drivers of conflict is uncertainty. Organizational changes, including reorganization, downsizing, and changing business strategies, increase uncertainty and opportunities for resource conflicts. External changes can also trigger conflict if regulations or changing market conditions change the relative importance of different organizational groups. For example, if a strong new competitor enters a company's market, the firm's marketing and advertising departments may get resources previously available to the research and development or human resources departments. A big lawsuit filed against the company is likely to elevate the relative status and resources given to the legal department.

Apple Computer's shift in focus from the Apple II computer to the Macintosh PC illustrates the conflict that can accompany change. When Apple's cofounder Steve Jobs presented the new computer in the company's auditorium, Mac Division employees watched from front-row seats. Meanwhile, Apple II employees watched Jobs's presentation on closed-circuit TV in another room. This differential treatment clearly communicated Jobs's view that the Mac was the future of the company and the Apple II was much less important. Much internal conflict followed as the differential treatment prompted Apple cofounder and Apple II inventor Steve Wozniak to resign and the morale of the Apple II employees to plummet.[25]

Differing Values. People differ in their values and worldviews. These differences are the source of *values conflict*, or conflict arising from perceived or actual incompatibilities in beliefs about what is good or bad, right or wrong, and fair or unfair. Values conflicts can arise when people or groups have different values or a different understanding of the world. For example, if some

values conflict
Conflict arising from perceived or actual incompatibilities in belief systems

employees feel that the organization should be focused on maximizing the firm's profits while other employees feel that the firm should be focused on doing the maximum good for the maximum number of people, the two groups of employees are experiencing values conflict.

What violates someone's values differs across national cultures. Different events can trigger conflict in various cultural contexts due to different core concerns. For example, rights violations trigger greater anger in the United States, whereas violations over duties and face cause greater anger among Koreans.[26] In the United States, Americans perceive conflicts to be more about winning and violations to individual rights, whereas Japanese view the same conflicts to be about compromise and violations to duties and obligations.[27]

Poor Communication. Remember, uncertainty is one of the primary drivers of conflict. Poor communication increases uncertainty, and can thus increase the potential for conflict. *Information conflict* occurs when people lack important information, are misinformed, interpret information differently, or disagree about which information is relevant.

If a manager tells only some subordinates about strategy changes or upcoming scheduling changes, this increases the opportunity for conflict between the employees who have this important information and those who lack the information. Because e-mail restricts the richness of communication and increases the chances for misunderstanding, conflicts are more likely to escalate when people communicate via e-mail compared to face-to-face or over the telephone.[28]

Task Interdependence. When one person or unit is dependent on another for resources or information, the potential for conflict increases. Imagine writing a class paper with a partner. If you divide the assignment in half and each of you completes your section independently, there is less potential for conflict than if your ability to do a good job writing your section of a paper depends on the quality of the other student's section.

Organizational Structure. *Structural conflict* is the result of structural or process features of the organization. Structural conflict can be horizontal or vertical. *Horizontal* conflict occurs between groups at the same organizational level, such as between line and staff employees or between departments such as production and marketing. A classic example is the marketing-production conflict between marketing's longer-term view of sales and production's shorter-term goal of cost efficiency. Because the realities of employees in each department are aligned with their identification with these dimensions, conflict is a perfectly justified response to "those people in that other department."[29]

Vertical conflict occurs across different hierarchical levels in the organization, including conflicts over wage issues or control. Union-management relationships are a classic example of vertical conflict.

Because structural conflict is due to organizational design, adjusting the design often reduces or eliminates the structural conflict. Matching a department's structural design with its needs given its environment improves its effectiveness. Structural interventions should focus on creating a moderate amount of constructive task conflict and minimal relationship conflict by addressing the sources of these conflicts for that particular unit.

How Does Conflict Escalate?

Conflict escalation happens when one party involved in a conflict (individuals, small groups, departments, or entire organizations) first uses an aggressive tactic or begins using more aggressive tactics.[30] When

SO WHAT?

Because of differing cultural values, a decision might trigger conflict in one culture but not in another.

information conflict

Conflict that occurs when people lack necessary information, are misinformed, interpret information differently, or disagree about which information is relevant

structural conflict

Conflict resulting from structural or process features of the organization

KATHY WILLENS/APIMAGES

Escalating conflicts can involve substantial amounts of money. In 2012, Ron Perelman, pictured here, sued Ira Rennert for over $100 million in a dispute over loans.

constructive approaches to conflict resolution are unsuccessful and break down, the conflict escalates. The farther the conflict escalates, the more difficult it is to reverse. Friedrich Glasl's nine-stage model of conflict escalation is summarized in Table 11-2.[31]

Table 11-2

Glasl's Nine-Stage Model of Conflict Escalation

Stage	Main Conflict Issues	Behaviors	Trigger to Move to the Next Level
1. Hardening	Objective issues	Discussion	Argumentation tactics
2. Debate	Objective issues Superiority/inferiority	Verbal confrontation Argumentation Emotional pressure Debates	Action without consultation
3. Action over Words	Objective issues Self-image Proving one's mastery	One side gets frustrated and takes action without consulting the opponent Blocking opponent's goals and forcing opponent to yield Decreased verbal and increased nonverbal communication	Covert attacks aimed directly at opponent's identity
4. Images and Coalitions	Shift from focus on issues to personalization of the conflict "Win or lose" mentality Save own reputation	Coalition formation Attacks on opponent's core identity Exploitation of gaps in norms	Loss of face
5. Loss of Face	Fundamental values Restore own dignity Expose opponent Distrust of opponent	Attacking opponent's public face Restoring own prestige	Strategic threats Ultimatums
6. Threat as a Strategy	Control opponent	Extending conflict Presenting threats and ultimatums that restrict future alternatives	Execute ultimatums or threats
7. Limited Attempts to Overthrow	Hurt opponent more than self Survival	Limited attempts to overthrow opponent Opponent not seen as a person	Effort to shatter opponent by attacking core
8. Fragmentation of the Enemy	Winning is no longer possible Survival, outlasting opponent Malice	Acts intended to shatter opponent Annihilate opponent by destroying power base No real communication	Abandon self-preservation Total war
9. Together into the Abyss	Annihilation at any cost, including personal destruction	Unlimited war with limitless violence Accept own destruction if opponent is also destroyed	

Sources: Glasl, F. (1982) The Process of Conflict Escalation and Roles of Third Parties (1982). In G. B. J. Bomers and R. B. Peterson, (eds) *Conflict management and industrial relations,* (pp. 119–140) The Hague: Kluwer Nijhoff Publishing; Glasl, F. (1992). Konfliktmanagement. *Ein Handbuch für Führungskräfte und Berater.* 2nd Ed., Stuttgart: Bern; Glasl, F. & Kopp, P. (1999). *Confronting Conflict: A First-Aid Kit for Handling Conflict.* Binghamton, NY: Hawthorn Press.

In the first stage of conflict escalation, *hardening*, each side's opinion hardens and the two opponents adopt a collision course. The disagreement is recognized but each side believes that the issue can be resolved through discussion. In the second stage, *debate*, each side's opinion becomes polarized and emotions rise. Each side begins thinking in terms of black and white and adopts a viewpoint of self-superiority and opponent-inferiority. Constructive conflicts are generally resolved by the second stage. The third stage, *action over words*, sees a decrease in empathy for the opponent, and the idea that "talking no longer helps" emerges. The conflict becomes increasingly destructive in this stage. In the fourth stage, *images/coalitions*, negative rumors are spread and stereotypes are formed as each side prepares for a fight and conducts a search for supporters. The fifth stage, *loss of face*, marks the beginning of open and direct aggression intended to cause the opponent's loss of public face. In the sixth stage, *threat as a strategy*, threats and counterthreats increase. As ultimatums are made, conflict escalation accelerates. In the seventh stage, *limited attempts to overthrow*, the opponent is no longer viewed as a person. Slight personal damage is considered acceptable as a consequence of limited attempts to overthrow the opponent. In the eighth stage, *fragmentation of the enemy*, the goal becomes the destruction and dissolution of the system. This goal is pursued aggressively. The ninth and final stage, *together into the abyss*, sees the descent into total confrontation with no way back. Extermination of the opponent at the price of self-extermination is seen and accepted.[32]

The later stages of this conflict escalation model might sound extreme, but unfortunately workplace aggression and violence do happen. Table 11-3 summarizes some of the factors associated with an increased risk of workplace violence resulting from conflict. It is obviously a good idea to be especially vigilant for potential conflicts in these situations, and to manage them quickly when they do occur. Generating feelings of empathy and sympathy and keeping both parties focused on common goals also helps to de-escalate conflict. Fairness and the appearance of fairness often decrease the risk of workplace violence when conflicts do occur.[33]

SO WHAT?

Because it is increasingly difficult to manage a conflict as it escalates, it is important to manage conflict at its earliest stages.

Table 11-3

Coworker Violence Risk Factors

- Supervising others
- Working in a high-stress environment
- Personality conflicts
- Understaffed workplaces
- Economic downturns

De-Escalating Conflict

Even if it does not escalate quickly, unresolved conflict drains employees' energy and reduces their performance. It is obviously easier to manage conflict escalation in the early stages of a conflict. Unfortunately, conflicts are often hard to detect in their early stages. Because the conflict is still minimal, the parties also have little motivation to invest their time and energy in preventing further escalation.

If you are involved in a conflict, one of the best ways to prevent further escalation is to react equivalently to the other party and not overreact. Sometimes underreacting can trigger de-escalation of the conflict. By being aware of the dynamic and setting personal behavior limits at the beginning of the conflict, you can often avoid being caught up in the conflict escalation process.

As a manager, you can reduce conflict escalation by modeling de-escalation processes, and by setting and enforcing limits on conflict escalation (prohibiting threats or violence, for example). Managers can serve as a conflict resolution facilitator as well. Referring to Glasl's nine-stage model of conflict escalation discussed above can help you to assess how far a conflict has progressed and how best to respond. It is also important to continue to monitor conflicts to ensure that they do not reemerge. After Ina Drew, chief investment officer at JPMorgan Chase, contracted Lyme disease and had to miss periods of work, her absences allowed tensions and relationship conflicts among her subordinates to flare up again. These issues are credited in part with JPMorgan Chase's trading loss of over $3 billion in 2012.[34]

Table 11-4 summarizes what to do and some things to avoid in de-escalating conflict.

Table 11-4

De-Escalating Conflict

Do	Avoid
Be an empathetic listener	Communicating hostility verbally or through body language
Focus your attention on the other person	Rejecting all requests from the start
Use delay tactics to create time to diffuse emotions	Challenging, threatening, or daring
Control your body language—relax, uncross legs and arms, and make eye contact	Raising your voice
Remind both parties that a win-win solution can be found	Blaming either party or saying anything that would cause the parties to lose face
Stay focused on issues, not emotions	Minimizing the situation or the conflict

After a conflict is resolved, it is important to re-establish a sense of justice and trust among the parties. Strengthening shared goals and shared identities can help to reduce the potential for future conflict. It is also important to remember that you do not always have to intervene in a conflict, particularly if it is not affecting job performance. Letting employees learn to work out their differences and resolve conflicts on their own through training and experience will decrease their dependence on you to resolve their conflicts.

SO WHAT?

After a conflict is resolved, trust must often be re-established.

Role of Emotion in Conflict

When we are in conflict we feel emotionally charged.[35] In fact, we are often unaware that we are in conflict until we recognize that we are emotional about something.[36] There is an important distinction between perceiving conflict and feeling conflict—conflict is often not recognized until it is felt.[37] One expert observes that "emotions are an important element of conflict. They define individuals' subjective interpretations of reality and reactions to current situations."[38] Even though the emotional component is most evident in relationship conflict, task and process conflict also can contain high levels of emotion.[39]

Many people let their feelings and emotions influence how they deal with conflict. Controlling your emotions and staying focused on the issues can help to prevent a conflict from escalating. Assessing and acknowledging the emotions of the other party can also help you to more effectively manage the conflict.

SO WHAT?

Managing your emotions and staying focused on the issues involved can help prevent a conflict from escalating.

Interpersonal Conflict Management Strategies

Once you understand the source of a conflict you are engaged in, you need to identify the best strategy for addressing it. We next discuss five conflict management strategies that differ in their concern for others and concern for your own interests.[40]

collaborating

A conflict management style reflecting a desire to give both parties what they want

Collaborating. *Collaborating* reflects a high concern for your own interests and a high concern for the interests of the other party. This conflict management style emphasizes problem solving and pursues an outcome that gives both parties what they want. Saying, "Let's see if we can find a solution that meets both of our needs" reflects a collaborating conflict management style.

Collaborating helps to build commitment to the outcome, although the communication required to reach a solution can take substantial time and energy. Even though there is a risk that one party may take advantage of the other party's trust and openness, collaboration is generally regarded as the best approach for managing most conflicts. The objective of collaboration is to fulfill both parties' needs with a goal of "I win / you win."

compromising

A conflict management style in which each side sacrifices something in order to end the conflict

Compromising. *Compromising* is a conflict management style in which each side sacrifices something in order to end the conflict. This middle-ground style reflects a moderate concern for your own interests and a moderate concern for the interests of the other party. Saying, "Maybe we can meet in the middle" or "I'm willing to reconsider my initial position" reflects a compromising style.

A compromising style is often used to achieve temporary solutions, to avoid destructive power struggles, or when a conflict must be resolved quickly. The goal of compromising is "I win some and lose some / you win some and lose some."

competing

Pursuing one's own interest at the expense of the other party

Competing. *Competing* is a conflict management style resulting from a high concern for your own interests and low concern for the other party. This approach is generally used when the conflict issue is important or to set a precedent. However, because one party is trying to dominate the other, this conflict management style can escalate the conflict and the loser may try to retaliate. A person who uses threats or ultimatums is using a competing conflict management style. Saying, "If you don't accept this offer the deal is off" reflects a competing style. The goal of competing is "I win / you lose."

accommodating

A cooperative conflict management style

Accommodating. *Accommodating* is a cooperative conflict management style. Accommodating reflects a low concern for your own interests and a high concern for the interests of the other party. This conflict management style is generally used when the issue is more important to the other party than it is to you. This style is also appropriate when you recognize that you are wrong. Saying, "I'll go along with whatever is best for you" reflects an accommodating style. The goal of accommodating is "I lose / you win."

Avoiding. *Avoiding* is a passive conflict management style involving ignoring the conflict or denying that it exists. This style reflects a low concern for your own interests and a low concern for the interests of the other party. When this strategy is used to manage trivial conflicts no damage may be done, but it can result in maximum damage when important issues are involved. Avoidance is also used when more information is needed or when addressing the conflict has the potential to create more problems (perhaps the other party is known to be aggressive). The primary drawback to an avoidance style is that the decision may not be optimal to you and your interests. The goal of avoiding is "no winners / no losers." Because conflict is often uncomfortable, members of workgroups often resort to passive forms of conflict management such as avoidance.[41]

avoiding
Ignoring the conflict or denying that it exists

Figure 11-1 illustrates how these five styles of managing interpersonal conflict compare in their focus on others and on pursuing one's self-interests.

This chapter's *Understand Yourself* feature gives you a chance to assess your preferred conflict management style.

In general, each style of handling interpersonal conflict is appropriate and ethical in some situations as long as it is used to attain the organization's proper goals.[43] Remember, because people differ in their preferred conflict management styles, it is important to adapt your own style accordingly. What is most important is that you proactively manage workplace conflict. Research has found that conflict leads to stress and emotional exhaustion.[44] Cultural values can influence preferred conflict management styles, as you will learn in this chapter's *Global Issues* feature.

SO WHAT

Adapt your conflict management style to the situation and to the other person involved in the conflict.

Figure 11-1

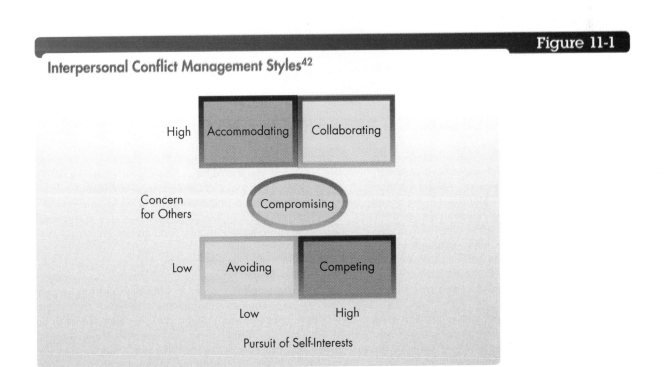

Interpersonal Conflict Management Styles[42]

UNDERSTAND YOURSELF

YOUR PREFERRED CONFLICT MANAGEMENT STYLE

People tend to use a subset of the possible conflict management styles based on their personal comfort with conflict and personal management style. Understanding your preferred conflict management style can help you to reflect on how you might better use other styles when they are more appropriate.

To help you understand your conflict management style, rank order the five conflict management styles based on how often you tend to use each one:

_____ Competing
_____ Collaborating
_____ Compromising
_____ Avoiding
_____ Accommodating

The styles with the lowest numbers reflect your preferred conflict management styles. Do you think this accurately reflects you? When might this style be most appropriate? When might it be least appropriate? What can you do to improve your comfort and skill with some of the other styles?

If you would like to complete a self-assessment to help analyze your conflict management style, go to: http://academic.engr. arizona.edu/vjohnson/ConflictManagementQuestionnaire/ConflictManagementQuestionnaire.asp.

Source: Adapted from T.L.P. Tang (1992), "The Meaning of Money Revisited", 'Journal of Organizational Behavior', 13, 197–202; J.A. Roberts and C.J. Sepulveda, "Demographics and Money Attitudes: A Test of Yamauchi and Templer's (1982) Money Attitude Scale in Mexico," Personality and Individual Differences, 27 (July 1999), pp. 19–35; K. Yamauchi and D. Templer, "The Development of a Money Attitudes Scale," Journal of Personality Assessment, 46 (1982), pp. 522–528.

GLOBAL ISSUES

CONFLICT MANAGEMENT DIFFERENCES ACROSS CULTURES

Reflecting variations in cultural values, individuals from different cultures adopt different conflict resolution strategies.[45] For example, compared to U.S. managers, Asian managers avoid explicitly discussing a conflict. Managers in the United States tend to prefer a style of dominance and assertively competing to see who can convince the other of their preferred resolution of the conflict.[46] Chinese managers favor compromise and avoidance, whereas British executives favor collaboration and competition.[47] Arab Middle Eastern executives use more of an integrating and avoiding style in handling interpersonal conflict.[48]

As another example, an employee from a culture in India who considers you a superior may be hesitant to give you direct feedback to save face for both of you. Instead, the person may tell you what he or she thinks you want to hear, especially when others are around. Because Indians may communicate only the positives when asked to give constructive feedback, you should listen carefully for what they do *not* say.[49] A desire to maintain one's own public face is related to a greater use of a dominating conflict style, and a desire to maintain the face of the other party is related to a greater use of the avoiding, integrating, and compromising styles of conflict management.[50]

Members of collective cultures also perceive and manage conflict differently from those in individualistic cultures.[51] Collectivism emphasizes group harmony and interdependence. Individualism emphasizes individual rights and independence. The Chinese culture is collective and the U.S. culture is individualistic. Collective societies tend to avoid open conflict—any conflict that emerges must be resolved in inner circles before it becomes serious enough to justify public involvement.[52]

The Conflict Process

Putting it all together, the conflict process is summarized in Figure 11-2. After a potential conflict is triggered, it is perceived by both parties. The true disagreement may differ from the perceived disagreement—conflict is often accompanied by misunderstandings that exaggerate the perceived disagreement. If neither party experiences emotion in reaction to the potential conflict, it does not escalate. For example, if Ryan disagrees with his boss about how to do something but Ryan does not mind doing it the boss's way, neither party experiences emotion over the disagreement and the conflict ends. On the other hand, if Ryan feels strongly that his way is better or that the boss's way will not work, emotion may be felt. In this case, the conflict will begin to escalate.

Figure 11-2

The Conflict Process

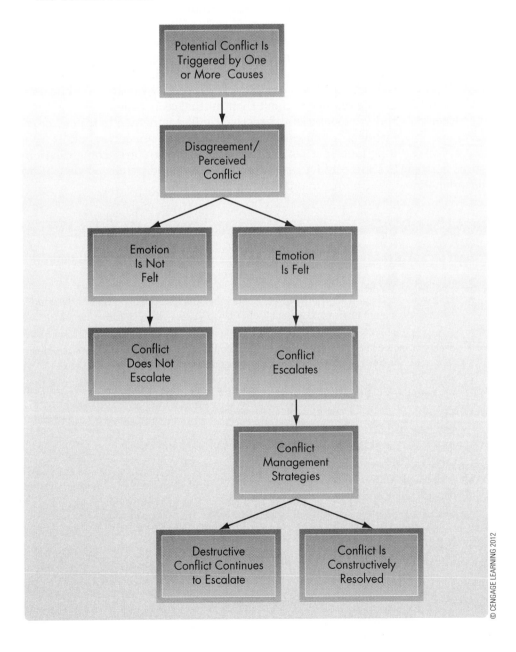

Both sides will then implement one or more conflict management strategies that either will end the conflict constructively or allow the conflict to continue to escalate, perhaps to the point of becoming destructive.

Conflict Management Skills

The good news is that almost everyone can learn the necessary skills for effective conflict management. Professionals in conflict resolution training suggest four areas of skill development:[53]

1. Listening (including eye contact, rephrasing, and summarizing what each side tells you to show them that you understand each side's position)
2. Questioning
3. Communicating nonverbally
4. Mediating

If you are mediating a conflict, ask open rather than leading questions, and use nonverbal cues to show that you are sincerely trying to help. Read nonverbal cues to learn additional information. Mediation skills include open-mindedness, staying nonjudgmental and calm, demonstrating empathy and sensitivity, remaining neutral, respecting confidentiality, and showing flexibility and resiliency.[54] Try to identify and communicate a super ordinate goal shared by both parties that cannot be reached without their mutual cooperation.

A person's ability to successfully resolve conflict is related to his or her effectiveness as a leader.[55] Managers with poor conflict management skills hit a promotional ceiling much earlier in their careers.[56] There are strong relationships between certain conflict resolution behaviors and perceived suitability for promotion,[57] which are summarized in Table 11-5.

SO WHAT

Learning to effectively manage conflicts will increase your leadership effectiveness.

Table 11-5

Best and Worst Conflict Resolution Behaviors for Career Advancement

Best Conflict Resolution Behaviors:

- *Perspective taking*: Try to put yourself in the other person's position and understand that person's point of view.
- *Focusing on interests rather than positions*: Interests could include better serving clients or increasing the clarity of work expectations. By focusing on the outcome, the root cause of the conflict is more likely to be addressed.
- *Creating solutions*: Brainstorm with the other person or group, ask questions, and try to create solutions to the problem.
- *Expressing emotions*: Talk honestly with the other person and express your thoughts and feelings.
- *Reaching out*: Reach out to the other party, make the first move, and try to make amends.
- *Documenting*: Document areas of agreement and disagreement to ensure common understanding and clear communication.
- *Smoothing*: Playing down the differences between the two sides while emphasizing common interests.
- *Asking the parties involved in a conflict to identify three or four specific actions they would like the other party to take*: An example of this would be saying, "I would like you to send me the report by noon on Wednesday so that I can meet my deadline of 10 A.M. Friday."

Worst Conflict Resolution Behaviors:

- *Avoiding the conflict*: Avoiding or ignoring the conflict, hoping it will pass, is rarely successful.

- *Winning at all costs*: Arguing vigorously for your own opinion, refusing to consider changing your position, and trying to win regardless of the interpersonal costs are approaches that do not make for speedy or satisfying conflict resolution.

- *Displaying anger*: Expressing anger, raising your voice, and using harsh, angry words will make the other person defensive and will slow down or prevent any resolution of the conflict.

- *Demeaning the other party*: Laughing at the other person, ridiculing the other's ideas, and using sarcasm are both disrespectful and not conducive to resolving conflict.

- *Retaliating*: Obstructing the other person, retaliating against the other person, and trying to get revenge are unprofessional and disrespectful behaviors and will not promote conflict resolution.

- *Meeting separately with the people in conflict*: Because the sole goal of each employee involved in a conflict is to convince you of the merits of their own case, the parties are likely to become more committed to their positions rather than committed to resolving the conflict if you talk to each party in private.

Sources: Delahoussaye, M. (2002). Don't Get Mad, Get Promoted, *Training*, June, 39, 20; Heathfield, S.M. (2009). Workplace Conflict Resolution: People Management Tips. About.com. Available online at: http://humanresources. about.com/od/managementtips/a/conflict_solue.htm. Accessed October 27, 2009; Susskind, L. & Cruikshank, J. (1987). *Breaking the Impasse: Consensual Approaches to Resolving Public Disputes.* New York, NY: Basic Books.

Creating Constructive Conflict

As management guru Warren Bennis put it, "Leaders do not avoid, repress, or deny conflict, but rather see it as an opportunity."[58] You have learned that conflict can lead to better decisions, better relationships, and other positive outcomes. However, most people dislike conflict. It is seen as easier, less stressful, and less risky to one's career to avoid conflict and suppress dissenting opinions, despite their effectiveness in stimulating more creative and effective ideas and solutions. Often we are unsure of whether or not we are correct, and we also may fear ridicule or rejection.[59] Yet organizations that avoid conflict will have an increasingly difficult time competing successfully in a global environment. So what can managers do to increase the positive outcomes of conflict?

> "Leaders do not avoid, repress, or deny conflict, but rather see it as an opportunity." —*Warren Bennis, Management Expert*

The successful design company IDEO printed the three rules of brainstorming on the wall. These rules are: (1) concentrate on the quantity of ideas; (2) don't criticize others' ideas; and (3) elaborate and build on others' ideas.[60] Emerson Electric Co. makes conflict a fundamental element of its strategic planning process, creating an atmosphere of vigorous debate.[61] Hewlett Packard awards a medal of defiance for continuing work on an idea contrary to management's views.[62] General Electric uses workout groups to allow employees to voice their dissenting opinions.[63] The hotelier Marriott even has a policy that if managers cannot explain why they are asking an employee to do something, the employee does not have to do it.[64]

To successfully create constructive conflict, organizations often punish conflict avoiders. Rewarding employees who engage in constructive conflict can help to reduce employees' fears of ridicule or rejection. A simple "thank you" for voicing a dissenting opinion can signal to employees that it is okay to speak up. Hiring employees who are comfortable with constructive conflict and who tend to use effective conflict management strategies can also enhance constructive conflict and improve organizational performance.

SO WHAT

Investing in building a culture that supports constructive conflict and discourages destructive conflict improves organizational performance.

Assigning one or more employees to play the role of devil's advocate can help to generate constructive conflict by providing a safer environment for the introduction of different perspectives. The dialectical method in which multiple groups discuss issues separately and then together to better synthesize different viewpoints into a common framework can help to reduce conflict by ensuring that multiple perspectives are incorporated into decisions.

NEGOTIATION

Everyone is a negotiator.[65] Often we experience conflicts with other people in which we must negotiate to reach a solution. Negotiation skills thus are not only critical for managers, but also improve the effectiveness of all employees.

Negotiating Skills

negotiation

A process in which two or more parties make offers, counteroffers, and concessions in order to reach an agreement

Negotiation is a process in which two or more parties make offers, counteroffers, and concessions in order to reach an agreement. Most managers do a lot of negotiating as part of their jobs. Job offers and contracts with customers and suppliers have to be negotiated, resources have to be secured and shared with other departments, and agreements have to be made with bosses and subordinates.

There are two types of negotiation, distributive and integrative. *Distributive negotiation* occurs under zero-sum conditions, where any gain to one party is offset by an equivalent loss to the other party.[66] Distributive negotiation essentially *distributes* resources among the parties involved. Because distributive negotiation structures the conflict in a win-lose way, it tends to be competitive and adversarial. For example, every dollar one manager gets from the company's total budget is a dollar another manager does not get.

distributive negotiation

Any gain to one party is offset by an equivalent loss to the other party

Yahoo! CEO Jerry Yang is widely faulted for his failed negotiations with Microsoft in 2008. Yang's behavior during negotiations indicated that he misinterpreted his bargaining position in pursuing a distributive negotiation strategy. High-tech analyst Rob Enderle explains that Yang "kept saying we

AP PHOTO/SUSAN WALSH

Senator Barbara Boxer reports on a bipartisan transportation bill resulting from integrative negotiation between Republicans and Democrats.

should get more money, we should get more money, and not realizing how precarious their position was."[67] Yang was ultimately terminated by Yahoo!'s board of directors.

Integrative negotiation is a win-win negotiation in which the agreement involves no loss to either party.[68] In general, integrative bargaining is better than distributive bargaining because when it is over neither party feels that they have lost. Integrative bargaining helps to build good long-term relationships, and minimizes grudges between the parties. This is particularly beneficial when the parties have to work together on an ongoing basis once the negotiations are finished.

A classic example of integrative bargaining involves a dispute over an orange. Two people take the position that they want the whole orange. The moderator of the dispute gives each person one half of the orange. However, if the parties' interests were considered, there could have been a different, win-win outcome. One person wanted to eat the meat of the orange, but the other just wanted the peel to use in baking cookies. If the mediator had understood their interests, they could have both gotten all of what they wanted, rather than just half.[69]

The four fundamental principles of integrative negotiation are:[70]

1. *Separate the people from the problem.* Separate relationship issues (or "people problems" such as emotions, misperceptions, and communication issues) from substantive issues, and deal with them independently.
2. *Focus on interests, not positions.* Negotiate about things that people really want and need, and not what they say they want or need.
3. *Invent options for mutual gain.* Look for new solutions to the problem that will allow both sides to win, rather than just fighting over the original positions that assume that for one side to win, the other side must lose.
4. *Insist on objective fairness criteria.* Outside, objective fairness criteria for the negotiated agreement are ideal if they exist (like the terms of another company's union-management contract).

As illustrated in this chapter's *Real World Response*, ITT Senior Vice President and Director of Human Resources Scott Crum focuses on integrative bargaining in which both parties satisfy their interests without compromising. To do this, Crum focuses on establishing trust through his negotiating style and tactics. He first asks the parties to state their interests, not their demands. Identifying desired outcomes not only improves his understanding of each side's needs, but builds trust as well. Crum feels that respect builds trust, which leads to openness, which is critical to achieving lasting, final, win-win solutions.[71]

It is also helpful to research and understand the individual with whom you will be negotiating. The better you understand the person's background, interests, and negotiating style, the more effective you will be. Try to begin with a positive exchange, create an open and trusting environment, and emphasize win-win situations. Be sure to prepare well, listen actively, and think through your alternatives. The more options you feel you have, the better a negotiating position you will be in.[72]

Here are some suggestions for being an effective negotiator:[73]

- *Do not look at a deal as an either/or proposition.* Negotiating is about compromise.
- *Make sure each side knows the other's perception of the issues and each other's interests.*
- *Identify what you can and cannot part with.* If you are negotiating an employment contract, identify the things most important to you (e.g., more vacation, a signing bonus) and those things that are less important (e.g., a prestigious job title). Act like everything is important, and grudgingly

integrative negotiation
A win-win negotiation in which the agreement involves no loss to either party

SO WHAT
To negotiate effectively, prepare well, listen actively, and understand your alternatives.

concede ground on the things that matter less to you. The other party will count these concessions as a victory and might yield on things you value more.

- *Try to identify and use sources of leverage.* Leverage consists of anything that can help or hinder a party in a bargaining situation. For example, a seller who must sell is at a disadvantage, and if the other party needs to move quickly you might be able to make a tougher offer. Competing offers can also increase one party's leverage over the other.

- *Show the other side that you understand their position.* Help the other person to see you as an ally by mirroring their emotions. If the other person appears frustrated, let him or her know that you recognize he or she is frustrated. The other person may respond with, "I sure am frustrated!" and now you're agreeing on something. Empathizing with the other party helps to preserve a cordial and productive atmosphere.

- *Suppress your emotions.* Negotiations can become tense and stir emotions. Constantly reminding yourself of your goal can help you to maintain an appropriate level of detachment and continue to see the deal clearly. Stay rationally focused on the issue being negotiated, and take a break if emotions start to flare up. Also, be careful not to show too much desire for something, or your bargaining power will be reduced. If the other side can tell that you emotionally want something, this weakens your bargaining power.

- *Know your BATNA.* The acronym BATNA stands for "best alternative to a negotiated agreement." It is what you could have done had no negotiation taken place, or what you will do if you cannot reach an agreement with the other party. The purpose of negotiations is to see if you can get your interests better met by negotiating an agreement with the other party, compared to this best alternative. If the BATNA is not compared to the agreement being negotiated, negotiators can make agreements that are worse than not making an agreement at all.[74] If negotiations stall, letting the other side know that you are prepared to proceed with your backup plan can also help to get the process started up again.

This chapter's *Improve Your Skills* feature gives you some tips for improving your negotiation skills.

Cultural Issues in Negotiations

Different national cultures have different preferred negotiation styles. For example, Russians tend to ignore deadlines and view concessions as a sign of weakness.[75] Some cultures, like the French, are more comfortable with conflict than other cultures. Although they also value tact or diplomacy, the French can be very direct and frequently question and probe into the other side's arguments.[76] In Saudi Arabia, saving face is essential. Causing embarrassment to the other party may be disastrous to a negotiation. Maintaining cordial relationships is also crucial to Saudi Arabians.[77] In India's group-oriented culture, asserting individual preferences may be less effective than having a sense of belonging to a group, conforming to its norms, and maintaining harmony among group members.[78] Iraqis attend more to how something is said than to what is actually said. Messages spoken in a calm manner are not given the same weight or credibility as those communicated with emotion.[79] Because Americans' desire to be liked is known in other cultures, skilled negotiators from other cultures use this to their advantage by making friendship conditional on the final outcome of the negotiation.[80]

When people believe they have been treated disrespectfully as a result of differing cultural norms, the whole project can blow up. In one Korean-U.S.

IMPROVE YOUR SKILLS

IMPROVING YOUR NEGOTIATION SKILLS

Do:

Prepare well

Use silence to your advantage

Offer a warm greeting and build rapport

Understand your position and what you can and cannot part with

Maintain a confident posture, lean forward, and smile

Maintain good eye contact

Ask good-quality, open questions

Speak in a clear, measured manner

Show empathy

Display controlled energy

Avoid:

Constantly making eye contact

Ignoring members of the group

Celebrating a victory in the presence of the other party

Coldness or harshness in your voice

Closed body language (arms folded, head down, avoiding eye contact)

---

negotiation, the American team was having difficulty getting information from their Korean counterparts. They nearly destroyed the deal by complaining directly to higher-level Korean management. The higher-level managers were offended because the Korean culture strictly adheres to hierarchy. Their own lower-level people, not the U.S. team members, should have been the ones to come to them with a problem. The Korean team members were also mortified that the Americans involved their bosses before they themselves could brief them. The crisis was resolved only when high-level U.S. managers made a trip to Korea, conveying appropriate respect for their Korean counterparts.[81]

Clearly, intercultural negotiation requires paying attention to issues beyond what is being negotiated. The appropriateness of different negotiation tactics, the emphasis to put on developing relationships, how to respond to deadlines, and even where the negotiation should be held are all influenced by national culture. Preparation is particularly important when engaging in cross-cultural negotiations.

Alternative Dispute Resolution

Sometimes two parties are unable to reach an acceptable settlement through direct negotiations with each other. In such cases, the parties may involve a third party to overcome the stalemate. This process is sometimes called *alternative dispute resolution*. There are three types of alternative dispute resolution:

1. *Conciliation*: A third party builds a positive relationship between the parties, improves their communication, and directs them toward a satisfactory settlement; the conciliator may give guidance to the parties but they are free to reject the proposed resolution.
2. *Mediation*: An impartial third party (the mediator) facilitates a discussion using persuasion and logic, suggesting alternatives, and establishing each side's priorities; the mediator suggests a settlement that does not have to be accepted.
3. *Arbitration*: A third party is involved and usually has the authority to impose a settlement on the parties.

alternative dispute resolution
Involving a third party in a negotiation to overcome a stalemate between the parties

conciliation
A third party builds a positive relationship between the parties and directs them toward a satisfactory settlement

mediation
An impartial third party (the mediator) facilitates a discussion using persuasion and logic, suggesting alternatives, and establishing each side's priorities

arbitration
A third party is involved and usually has the authority to impose a settlement on the parties

Conciliation is often the first step in the alternative dispute resolution process. Its goal is to get the parties to better communicate and resolve the problem on their own, although the conciliator may suggest a resolution that the parties can accept or reject. Arbitration and mediation also pursue the ideal of a fair outcome.

Mediation is a voluntary and nonbinding process, whereas the results of arbitration are legally binding. If the conflict has not escalated too much and both sides are motivated to resolve their conflict through bargaining, mediation can be very effective. If the mediator is not perceived as neutral, he or she is not likely to be effective.

Arbitration may be required by a contract or by law, or may be voluntary if the parties agree to it. The negotiating parties can establish rules for the arbitrator, such as restricting the arbitrator to one of the negotiators' final offers or freeing the arbitrator to make any judgment he or she wishes. Although arbitration, unlike mediation, always results in a settlement, it has greater potential to leave at least one party dissatisfied, which could cause the conflict to resurface later.

An ***ombudsman*** is someone who investigates complaints and mediates fair settlements between aggrieved parties. Universities often have ombudsmen to resolve conflicts between students and the institution, and large companies often have them to mediate conflicts with consumers. Ombudsmen help to resolve disputes while they are relatively small. This chapter's *Case Study* feature illustrates how ombudsmen can help companies resolve various types of internal conflicts.

ombudsman

Someone who investigates complaints and mediates fair settlements between aggrieved parties

CASE STUDY

Ombudsman to the Rescue

A growing number of small and midsize businesses are enlisting ombudsmen to handle internal conflicts. Alan Siggia, cofounder of Sigmet, a Massachusetts data processor design company that is now a part of Vaisala Group,[82] and his cofounder Richard Passarelli did their best to manage employee squabbles, but became overwhelmed. Even small coworker disagreements could lead to a grudge match. Siggia says, "The struggles people were having were beyond what a well-intentioned but untrained person like me could handle."[83]

To better deal with the internal conflicts, the partners hired an ombudsman to spend a few hours a week at Sigmet. The ombudsman asks how things are going and counsels upset employees. She listens to employees' problems, asks questions, and helps devise solutions. An employee fed up with a colleague's unsolicited opinions, for example, might be walked through a hypothetical conversation asking the colleague to stop the behavior. The sessions are confidential, encouraging honesty, unless there is an imminent risk of harm to the company or a person. Employees wanting even more privacy can arrange an outside meeting. The ombudsman also helps the company to identify company policies that create conflicts. For instance, vague job descriptions were fueling a turf war, so the owners are crafting clear job descriptions and reviving performance reviews.[84]

Sigmet is now enjoying better communication, less stress, and less conflict. Having a neutral person to help resolve conflicts has made a real difference—senior management has gained 30 percent more time, and colleagues are working together more efficiently. Office morale also has improved dramatically.[85]

Questions:

1. How has the ombudsman decreased conflicts at Sigmet?
2. Would you feel comfortable using an ombudsman to resolve a conflict with a coworker? Why or why not?
3. What could companies do to maximize the effectiveness of an ombudsman?

REAL WORLD RESPONSE

RESOLVING DISPUTES AT MARKS & SPENCER[87]

U.K.-based retailer Marks & Spencer wanted a process for its employees to use in identifying fair, mutually agreed upon, constructive conflict solutions in a safe environment. It also wanted to enable employees to move forward after a conflict positively and confidently. To accomplish these goals Marks & Spencer decided to train a team of accredited mediators to provide dispute resolution support to employees and to embed mediation and informal dispute resolution in the company's culture. The commitment of the company's CEO, Sir Stuart Rose, to mediation process was essential to the adoption of mediation as the primary dispute resolution process throughout the company.

The mediation process involves each party first separately talking with the mediator about the dispute. They then meet with the mediator a second time to discuss what they will say to each other and how they will respond during the meeting. The mediator focuses on coaching each party to help them reach a successful outcome and de-escalating strong emotions. After a lunch break the parties meet to discuss and resolve the dispute.

Mediation allows workplace problems to be addressed as early as possible to prevent escalation, and helps to make dispute resolution less adversarial. By bringing the people involved in a dispute together to explore what went wrong and what impact it had, employees' relationships with each other can even be strengthened as a result of the mediation process. By training a number of skilled mediators able to promote and offer mediation as an alternative to traditional formal grievance processes, a more healthy conflict resolution culture developed at Marks & Spencer.

SUMMARY AND APPLICATION

Conflict is a natural part of organizational life. It can lead to positive outcomes including better quality decisions, but it also has the potential to lead to negative outcomes if it is not properly handled. Emotion helps to convert a disagreement into a conflict. A variety of conflict management strategies can be used to help keep a conflict from escalating. Organizational effectiveness is enhanced through an appropriate diagnosis and management of conflict.[86]

Negotiation is one of the best ways to dissipate potential conflict. Integrative negotiation practices seeking to meet the needs of both parties are generally best for establishing long-term solutions that maintain a healthy relationship between the two parties. Alternative dispute resolution can be used when the negotiating parties are unable to negotiate a solution by themselves.

 **TAKEAWAY POINTS**

1. Constructive conflict results in positive outcomes including creativity and better decisions. Dysfunctional conflict is destructive and focuses on emotions and the differences between the two parties.
2. Conflict is caused by anything that leads to a disagreement. This includes differing task or process goals, interpersonal differences, resource constraints, change, task interdependence, organizational structure, value differences, and poor communication.
3. Conflict begins with a disagreement that is recognized and first approached with discussion, and then verbal confrontation over objective issues. The focus then shifts to blocking the opponent and winning. As distrust grows and loss of face is experienced, the parties make threats and attempt to overthrow each other. Eventually, the conflict becomes such that personal destruction is accepted as long as the other party is destroyed as well.
4. Underreacting, modeling de-escalation processes, and setting and enforcing limits on conflict escalation (e.g., prohibiting threats or violence) can help to de-escalate conflict. Generating feelings of empathy and sympathy and keeping both parties focused on common goals also helps.
5. The five interpersonal conflict management strategies are: collaborating, compromising, competing, accommodating, and avoiding.
6. Collectivism and individualism, among other cultural factors, influence how people manage conflict. The importance of maintaining face also differs across cultures and influences the appropriateness of different conflict management strategies.
7. Some of the best conflict resolution behaviors are perspective taking, creating solutions, expressing emotions, reaching out, and documenting areas of agreement and disagreement. Some of the worst conflict management behaviors are avoiding the conflict, winning at all costs, displaying anger, demeaning the other party, and retaliating.
8. Distributive negotiation focuses on win-lose solutions. Any gain to one party is offset by an equivalent loss to the other party. Integrative negotiation focuses on win-win solutions. The final agreement involves no loss to either party.
9. The three types of alternative dispute resolution are: conciliation, mediation, and arbitration.

DISCUSSION QUESTIONS

1. Have you ever experienced a constructive conflict? What happened? How was the disagreement resolved?
2. Have you ever experienced a dysfunctional conflict? What happened? Why was the conflict not resolved earlier?
3. How can managers promote constructive conflict?
4. Which of the conflict causes do you feel is most challenging to a manager? Why?

5. Think about a current conflict you are experiencing with a coworker, friend, or family member. Which of Glasl's conflict stages are you in? What can you do to keep the conflict from escalating to the next level?

6. If two of your subordinates were experiencing relationship conflict, what would you do to manage it? Why?

7. If two of your subordinates were experiencing task conflict, what would you do to manage it? Why?

8. What could you do to minimize the potential for negative outcomes in cross-cultural negotiations?

9. What would have to happen for you to fully accept and cooperate with a mediator's recommended settlement?

EXERCISES

Negotiate a Job Offer

In this exercise you will role-play a job offer negotiation. Your instructor will provide you and your partner with goals for your role and a payoff matrix to help you prioritize your issues.

Win as Much as You Can!

Directions: For ten successive rounds, each team will select either an "X" or a "Y" and submit their choice to the instructor on a small piece of paper with their team name on it. The "payoff" for each round is determined by the patterns of choices made by the other teams as described below:

Choice Pattern	Payout
4 Xs	Lose $1 each
3 Xs	Win $1 each
1 Y	Lose $3
2 Xs	Win $2 each
2 Ys	Lose $2 each
1 X	Win $3
3 Ys	Lose $1 each
4 Ys	Win $1 each

Task: In each round, teammates confer and make a joint decision. Before rounds 5, 8, and 10, the teams will have a chance to confer with each other for three minutes before conferring with teammates for one minute and making a decision. Note the three bonus rounds, where the payoff is multiplied.

Round	Time Allowed	Confer with Other Teams	Your Choice	$ Won	$ Lost	Balance	Bonus?
1	2 min	No					No
2	1	No					No
3	1	No					No
4	1	No					No
5	3 + 1	Yes					*Bonus 3X*
6	1	No					No
7	1	No					No
8	3 + 1	Yes					*Bonus 5X*
9	1	No					No
10	3 + 1	Yes					*Bonus 10X*

Conflict at GSK

GlaxoSmithKline is a pharmaceutical company whose mission statement is "to improve the quality of human life by enabling people to do more, feel better, and live longer."[88] Point your favorite browser to http://www.gsk.com/responsibility/index.htm. Then answer the following questions.

Questions

1. As a pharmaceutical firm researching and developing new pharmaceuticals, what type of conflict do you think is most common at GlaxoSmithKline?
2. How does GSK want its employees to manage this conflict?
3. How else can GSK encourage its employees to manage conflict in the best way for its employees and customers?

Union Conflict

Point your favorite browser to http://www.lasvegassun.com/news/2008/jun/28/toxic-feud-seius-top-ends-resignations/ to learn what happened when the conflict between the top two leaders of a union got out of hand. Then answer the following questions.

Questions

1. What type of conflict(s) existed between the two leaders? Explain your answer.
2. What did the two union leaders do to resolve their conflict?
3. In hindsight, what might have been done to resolve the conflict before it escalated so far?

VIDEO CASES

Now What?

Imagine being part of a team of two other coworkers experiencing negative task conflict as they try to finalize the design of a new toy before an imminent deadline. One team member is focused on making the toy of maximum quality and the other is focused on the conflicting goal of making the toy at the lowest cost. One of the team members is getting frustrated and feels that the team should be making better progress. The coworker asks you if there is anything the team can do to be more effective. *What do you say or do?* Go to this chapter's "Now What?" video, watch the challenge video, and choose a response. Be sure to also view the outcomes of the two responses you didn't choose.

Discussion Questions

1. What type(s) of conflict is (are) the team experiencing in the challenge video?
2. Which other aspects of organizational behavior discussed in this chapter are illustrated in these videos? Explain your answer.
3. As a manager, how else might you handle this situation? Why?

Workplace | Maine Media Workshops-Building a Contingent Workforce

Since 1973, Maine Media Workshops has seen some of the most talented filmmakers, photographers, and writers pass through its doors. The program began as a summer camp for amateur and professional artists wanting to hone their skills along the beautiful coast of Rockport, Maine. Over the years, the workshops have allowed students to work alongside some of Hollywood's heavy-hitters, including Vilmos Zsigmond (*The Black Dahlia*), Alan Myerson (*Boston Public*), and Gene Wilder (*Willy Wonka & the Chocolate Factory*).

Staff selection is difficult for Maine Media Workshops. From January through November, the organization hires instructors to teach weeklong classes for approximately 500 courses. With the exception of a few full-timers, the organization is staffed with temporary week-to-week instructors. In the time it takes new hires to get their employee handbook and complete W2 forms, most instructors at the Maine Media Workshops have finished their course and are moving on.

Job requirements workshops instructors are unique. Instructors act as mentors and coaches who dine with students, participate in social events, teach, and discuss assignments and careers. "What makes a good teacher is someone who is generous enough and open enough to share her life, her experience, her career and her knowledge 24/7 with students," said Elizabeth Greenburg, director of education.

(Continued)

Keeping courses staffed requires constant recruitment, and there is no time for training. As a result, the HR department seeks people who, like Elizabeth Greenburg, were once students. That way a new hire already understands what it takes to perform according to the Maine Media Workshops standard.

Surprisingly, compensation is not an issue. Although the Maine Media Workshops pays a fair wage, the real compensation doesn't come in a check. "No one comes here for the money," said Mimi Edmunds, film program manager. "They come here because they love it."

Discussion Questions

1. What is the primary problem that education directors face when recruiting instructors to teach at Maine Media Workshops?
2. What sources of conflict are hampering recruitment at Maine Media Workshops?
3. What might Maine Media Workshops do to help resolve its ongoing staffing conflicts?

DO WHAT **CENGAGENOW**™ includes **teaching and learning resources** to supplement the text, and is designed specifically to **help students "think like managers"** by engaging and challenging them to think critically about managerial situations. **CengageNOW uses today's technology to improve the skills** of tomorrow's managers.

END NOTES

[1] Papakostis, P. (2012). Marks & Spencer Case Study, The TCM Group, January 24. http://www.thetcmgroup.com/news/327-http-www-thetcmgroup-com-news/?p_view=all; Sir Stuart Rose Supports the Benefits of Mediation in the Workplace (2009). Globis Mediation Group, October 9. http://www.globis.co.uk/news/2009/10/09/sir-stuart-rose-supports-the-benefits-of-mediation-in-the-workplace/; Company Overview, Marks & Spencer, 2012. Available online: http://corporate.marksandspencer.com/aboutus/company_overview.

[2] Rahim, A. (2000). *Managing Conflict in Organizations* (3rd ed.). Westport, CT: Quorum Books.

[3] Pfeffer, J. (1997). *Managing with Power: Politics and Influence in Organizations.* Boston: Harvard Business Press.

[4] Thomas, K. W., & Schmidt, W. H. (1976). A Survey of Managerial Interests with Respect to Conflict. *Academy of Management Journal, 19,* 315–318.

[5] De Dreu, C. K. W., & Gelfand, M. J. (2008). Conflict in the Workplace: Sources, Dynamics, and Functions Across Multiple Levels of Analysis. In *The Psychology of Conflict and Conflict Management in Organizations,* eds. C. K. W. De Dreu and M. J. Gelfand (pp. 3–54). New York: Lawrence Erlbaum.

[6] Forden, S. G. (2009). Versace Said Likely to Fire CEO Today After Conflict. Bloomberg. Available online: http://www.bloomberg.com/apps/news?pid=newsarchive&sid=awNvtXtoyJ9w.

[7] Pruitt, D. G., & Kim, S. H. (2004). *Social Conflict: Escalation, Stalemate, and Settlement* (3rd ed.). New York: McGraw-Hill.

[8] Deutsch, M. (1973). Conflicts: Productive and Destructive. In *Conflict Resolution Through Communication,* ed. F. E. Jandt. New York: Harper & Row.

[9] Fenn, D. (1995, July). Benchmark: Sources of Conflict in Family Businesses. *Inc.* Available online: http://www.inc.com/magazine/19950701/2343.html; Massachusetts Mutual Life Insurance Co. (1994). Telephone Survey, Springfield, MA.

[10] Dormann, C., & Zapf, D. (1999). Social Support, Social Stressors at Work, and Depressive Symptoms: Testing for Main and Moderating Effects with Structural Equations in a Three-Wave Longitudinal Study. *Journal of Applied Psychology, 84,* 874–884; Spector, P. E., Dwyer, D. J., & Jex, S. M. (1988). Relation of Job

Stressors to Affective, Health, and Performance Outcomes: A Comparison of Multiple Data Sources. *Journal of Applied Psychology, 73,* 11–19.

[11]Wilmot, W. W., & Hocker, J. L. (1998). *Interpersonal Conflict* (5th ed.). Boston: McGraw-Hill.

[12]Schulz-Hardt, S., Mojzisch, A., & Vogelgesang, F. (2007). Dissent as a Facilitator: Individual- and Group-Level Effects on Creativity and Performance. In *The Psychology of Conflict and Conflict Management in Organizations,* eds. C. K. W. De Dreu and M. Gelfand (pp. 149–177). Hillsdale, NJ: Lawrence Erlbaum.

[13]Pondy, L. R. (1992). Reflections on Organizational Conflict. *Journal of Organizational Behavior 13,* 257–262.

[14]Pondy, L. R. (1992). Reflections on Organizational Conflict. *Journal of Organizational Behavior 13,* 257–262.

[15]De Dreu, C. K. W., & Weingart, L. R. (2003). Task Versus Relationship Conflict: Team Performance, and Team Member Satisfaction: A Meta-Analysis. *Journal of Applied Psychology, 88,* 741–749.

[16]Jehn, K. A. (1997). A Qualitative Analysis of Conflict Types and Dimensions in Organizational Groups. *Administrative Science Quarterly, 42,* 530–557.

[17]Smith, C. S., & Sulsky, L. (1995). An Investigation of Job-Related Coping Strategies Across Multiple Stressors and Samples. In *Job Stress Interventions,* eds. L. R. Murphy, J. J. Hurrell, S. L. Aauter, and G. P. Keita (pp. 109–123). Washington, DC: American Psychological Association.

[18]Schwartz, J. E., & Stone, A. A. (1993). Coping with Daily Work Problems: Contributions of Problem Content, Appraisals, and Person Factors. *Work and Stress, 7,* 47–62.

[19]Frank, W. S. (2005, June 24). How to Resolve Conflict Between Two Warring Executives. *Denver Business Journal.* Available online: http://denver.bizjournals.com/denver/stories/2005/06/27/smallb3.html.

[20]Jehn, K. A., & Mannix, E. A. (2001). The Dynamic Nature of Conflict: A Longitudinal Study of Intergroup Conflict and Group Performance. *Academy of Management Journal, 44,* 238–251.

[21]Sutton, R. I. (2007). *The No Asshole Rule: Building a Civilized Workplace and Surviving One That Isn't.* New York: Grand Central Publishing.

[22]De Dreu, C. K. W., & Gelfand, M .J. (2008). Conflict in the Workplace: Sources, Dynamics, and Functions Across Multiple Levels of Analysis. In *The Psychology of Conflict and Conflict Management in Organizations,* eds. C. K. W. De Dreu and M. J. Gelfand (pp. 3–54). New York: Lawrence Erlbaum.

[23]Van de Vliert, E., & De Dreu, C. (1994). Optimizing Performance by Conflict Stimulation, *International Journal of Conflict Management, 5,* 211–222.

[24]Coser, L. (1956). *The Functions of Social Conflict.* Glencoe, IL: Free Press.

[25]Wise, D. C., & Lewis, G. C. (1985, March 11). A Split That's Sapping Morale at Apple. *Business Week,* 106–107; Nee, S. (1985, July 29). Sculley Confirms Rift with Jobs. *Electronic News,* 22.

[26]Shteynberg, G., Gelfand, M. J., & Kim, H. G. (2005, April). The Cultural Psychology of Revenge. Paper presented at the annual conference of the Society for Industrial and Organizational Psychology, Los Angeles, CA.

[27]Gelfand, M. J., Nishii, L. H., Holcombe, K., Dyer, N., Ohbuchi, K., & Fukumo, M. (2001). Cultural Influences on Cognitive Representations of Conflict: Interpretations of Conflict Episodes in the U.S. and Japan. *Journal of Applied Psychology, 86,* 1059–1074.

[28]Friedman, R. A., & Curall, S. C. (2003). Conflict Escalation: Dispute Exacerbating Elements of E-Mail Communication. *Human Relations, 56,* 1325–1347.

[29]Banner, D. K., & Gagné, E. T. (1994). *Designing Effective Organizations: Traditional & Transformational Views* (p. 402). New York: Sage.

[30]Pruitt, D. G. (2007). Conflict Escalation in Organizations. In *The Psychology of Conflict and Conflict Management in Organizations,* eds. C. K. W. De Dreu and M. J. Gelfand (pp. 245–265). Hillsdale, NJ: Lawrence Erlbaum.

[31]Glasl, F. (1982). The Process of Conflict Escalation and Roles of Third Parties (1982). In *Conflict Management and Industrial Relations,* eds. G. B. J. Bomers and R. B. Peterson (pp. 119–140). The Hague: Kluwer Nijhoff; Glasl, F. (1992). *Konfliktmanagement. Ein Handbuch für Führungskräfte und Berater* (2nd ed.). Stuttgart: Bern; Glasl, F., & Kopp, P. (1999). *Confronting Conflict: A First-Aid Kit for Handling Conflict.* Binghampton, NY: Hawthorn Press.

[32]Glasl, F. & Kopp, P. (1999). *Confronting Conflict: A First-Aid Kit for Handling Conflict.* Binghampton, NY: Hawthorn Press.

[33]Neuman, J. H., & Baron, R. A. (1998). Workplace Violence and Workplace Aggression: Evidence Concerning Specific Forms, Potential Causes, and Preferred Targets. *Journal of Management, 24,* 391–419; Jawahar, I. M. (2002). A Model of Organizational Justice and Workplace Aggression. *Journal of Management, 6,* 811–834; Kriesberg, L. (1998). De-Escalating Conflicts. In *Constructive Conflicts* (pp. 181–222). Lanham, MD: Rowman & Littlefield.

[34]Silver-Greenberg, J. & Schwartz, N.D. (2012). Discord at Key JPMorgan Unit is Faulted in Loss, The New York Times, May 19. Available online: http://www.cnbc.com/id/47489227.

[35]Bodtker, A. M., & Jameson, J. K. (2001). Emotion in Conflict Formation and Its Transformation: Application to Organizational Conflict Management. *International Journal of Conflict Management, 12*(3), 259–275.

[36]Nair, N. (2008). Towards Understanding the Role of Emotions in Conflict: A Review and Future Directions. *International Journal of Conflict Management, 19,* 359–381.

[37]Pondy, L. R. (1967). Organizational Conflict: Concepts and Models. *Administrative Science Quarterly, 12,* 296–320.

[38]Jehn, K. A. (1997). A Qualitative Analysis of Conflict Types and Dimensions in Organizational Groups. *Administrative Science Quarterly, 42,* 532.

[39]Jehn, K. A. (1997). A Qualitative Analysis of Conflict Types and Dimensions in Organizational Groups. *Administrative Science Quarterly, 42,* 530–557.

[40]Rahim, M., & Bonoma, T. (1979). Managing Organizational Conflict: A Model for Diagnosis and Intervention. *Psychological Reports, 44,* 1323–1344; Blake, R. R., & Mouton, J. S. (1964). *The Managerial Grid.* Houston, TX: Gulf Publishing.

[41]Ayoko, O. B., Hartel, C. E. J., & Cullen, V. J. (2002). Resolving the Puzzle of Productive and Destructive Conflict in Culturally Heterogeneous Work Groups: A Communication-Accommodation Approach. *International Journal of Conflict Management, 13,* 165–195.

[42]Based on Rahim, M.A. & Blum, A.A. (Eds.) (1994). *Global Perspectives on Organizational Conflict.* Westport, CT: Praeger, p. 5.

[43] Rahim, M. A., Garrett, J. E., & Buntzman, G. F. (1992). Ethics of Managing Interpersonal Conflict in Organizations. *Journal of Business Ethics, 11,* 423–432.

[44]Jaramillo, F., Mulki, J.P., & Boles, J.S. (2011). Workplace Stressors, Job Attitude, and Job Behaviors: Is Interpersonal Conflict the Missing Link? *Journal of Personal Selling and Sales Management, 31*(3), 339-356; Ilies, R., Jhnson, M.D., Judge, T.A., & Keeney, J. (2011). A Within-Individual Study of Interpersonal Conflict as a Work Stressor: Dispositional and Situational Moderators. *Journal of Organizational Behavior, 21*(1), 44–64.

[45]Kirkbride, P. S., Tang, F. Y., & Westwood, R. I. (1991). Chinese Conflict Preferences and Negotiating Behaviour: Cultural and Psychological Influences. *Organization Studies, 12,* 365–386.

[46]Morris, M. W., Williams, K. Y., Leung, K., Larrick, R., Mendoza, M. T., Bhatnagar, D., Li, J., Kondo, M., Luo, J., & Hu, J. (1998). Conflict Management Style: Accounting for Cross-National Differences. *Journal of International Business Studies, 29,* 729–747; Tse, D. K., Francis, J., & Walls, J. (1994). Cultural Differences in Conducting Intra- and Intercultural Negotiation: A Sino-Canadian Comparison. *Journal of International Business Studies, 3,* 537–555.

[47]Tang, S. F. Y., & Kirkbride, P. S. (1986). Developing Conflict Management Skills in Hong Kong: An Analysis of Some Cross-Cultural Implications. *Management Learning, 17,* 287–301.

[48]Elsayed-Ekhouly, S., & Buda, R. (1996). Organizational Conflict: A Comparative Analysis of Conflict Styles Across Cultures. *International Journal of Conflict Management, 1,* 71–81.

[49]Katz, L. (2007). *Negotiating International Business—The Negotiator's Reference Guide to 50 Countries Around the World.* Dallas, TX: Booksurge.

[50]Ting-Toomey, S., Gao, G., Trubisky, P., Yang, Z., Kim, H. S., Lin, S. L., & Nishida, T. (1991). Culture, Face Maintenance, and Styles of Handling Interpersonal Conflict: A Study in Five Cultures. *International Journal of Conflict Management, 2,* 275–296.

[51]Ting-Toomey, S. (1988). Intercultural Conflicts: A Face-Negotiation Theory. In *Theories in Intercultural Communication,* eds. Y. Kim and W. Gudykunst (pp. 213–235). Newbury Park, CA: Sage.

[52]Ting-Toomey, S. (1988). Intercultural Conflicts: A Face-Negotiation Theory. In *Theories in Intercultural Communication,* eds. Y. Kim & W. Gudykunst (pp. 213–235). Newbury Park, CA: Sage; Tse, D. K., Francis, J., & Walls, J. (1994). Cultural Differences in Conducting Intra- and Intercultural Negotiation: A Sino-Canadian Comparison. *Journal of International Business Studies, 3,* 537–555.

[53]Ramsey, R. D. (1996, August). Conflict Resolution Skills for Supervisors. *Supervision, 57*(8), 9–12.

[54]Ramsey, R. D. (1996, August). Conflict Resolution Skills for Supervisors. *Supervision, 57*(8), 9–12.

[55]In Delahoussaye, M. (2002, June). Don't Get Mad, Get Promoted. *Training, 39*(6), 20.

[56]Delahoussaye, M. (2002). Don't Get Mad, Get Promoted. *Training,* June, 39, 20; Heathfield, S.M. (2009). Workplace Conflict Resolution: People Management Tips. About.com. Available online at: http://humanresources.about.com/od/managementtips/a/conflict_solue.htm.

[57]Delahoussaye, M. (2002, June). Don't Get Mad, Get Promoted, *Training, 39*(6), 20; Heathfield, S. M. (2009). Workplace Conflict Resolution: People Management Tips. About.com. Available online: http://humanresources.about.com/od/managementtips/a/conflict_solue.htm; Susskind, L., & Cruikshank, J. (1987). *Breaking the Impasse: Consensual Approaches to Resolving Public Disputes.* New York: Basic Books.

[58]Bennis, W. (1989). *Why Leaders Can't Lead: The Unconscious Conspiracy Continues* (p. 153). San Francisco: Jossey-Bass.

[59]Nemeth, C. J., Endicott, J., & Wachtler, J. (1977). Increasing the Size of the Minority: Some Gains and Some Losses. *European Journal of Social Psychology, 1,* 11–23.

[60]Paulus, P. B., & Nijstad, B. A. (2003). *Group Creativity: Innovation Through Collaboration.* New York: Oxford University Press.

[61]Lagace, M. (2005, June 6). Don't Listen to "Yes." *Harvard Business School Working Knowledge.* Available online: http://hbswk.hbs.edu/item/4833.html.

[62]Sommerfield, F. (1990, May). Paying the Troops to Buck the System. *Business Month,* 77–79.

[63]Cabana, S., & Fiero, J. (1995). Motorola, Strategic Planning and the Search Conference. *Journal for Quality and Participation, 18,* 22–31.

[64]Cabana, S., & Fiero, J. (1995). Motorola, Strategic Planning and the Search Conference. *Journal for Quality and Participation, 18,* 22–31.

[65]Fisher, R., & Ury, W. L. (1991). *Getting to Yes: Negotiating Agreement Without Giving In.* New York: Penguin.

[66] Korda, P. (2011). *The Five Golden Rules of Negotiation.* J. M. Phillips and S.M. Gully, Eds., New York: Business Expert Press.

[67]Arnoldy, B. (2008, November 19). Why Yahoo!'s Jerry Yang Stepped Down. Available online: http://www.csmonitor.com/Money/2008/1119/p02s01-usec.html.

[68]Fisher, R., Ury, W., & Patton, B. (1991). *Getting to Yes: Negotiating Agreement Without Giving In* (2nd ed.). New York: Houghton Mifflin.

[69]De Dreu, C. K. W. (2005, June). A PACT Against Conflict Escalation in Negotiation and Dispute Resolution. *Current Directions in Psychological Science, 14,* 149.

[70]Based on Fisher, R. & Ury, W. & Patton, B. (1992). *Getting to Yes: Negotiating Agreement Without Giving In,* 2nd ed. New York: Houghton Mifflin.

[71]This vignette is based on a telephone interview with Scott Crum, Senior Vice President and Director of Human Resources at ITT, June 8, 2009.

[72]Walker, R. (2003, August). Take It or Leave It: The *Only* Guide to Negotiating You Will Ever Need. *Inc.,* 75.

[73]Watkins, M. (2002). *Breakthrough Business Negotiation: A Toolbox for Managers.* New York: Jossey-Bass; Kaplan, M. (2005, May). How to Negotiate Anything. Money, 34(5), 116–119; Stansell, K. (2000, October 1). Practice the Art of Effective Negotiation. Inc. Available online: http://www.inc.com/articles/2000/10/20856.html.

[74]Fisher, R., Ury, W., & Patton, B. (1991). *Getting to Yes: Negotiating Agreement Without Giving In* (2nd ed.). New York: Houghton Mifflin.

[75]Glenn, E. S., Witmeyer, D., & Stevenson, K. A. (1977). Cultural Styles of Persuasion. *Journal of Intercultural Relations,* 52–66.

[76]Katz, L. (2007). *Negotiating International Business—The Negotiator's Reference Guide to 50 Countries Around the World.* Dallas, TX: Booksurge.

[77]Katz, L. (2007). *Negotiating International Business—The Negotiator's Reference Guide to 50 Countries Around the World.* Dallas, TX: Booksurge.

[78]Katz, L. (2007). *Negotiating International Business—The Negotiator's Reference Guide to 50 Countries Around the World.* Dallas, TX: Booksurge.

[79]Triandis, H. C. (1994). *Culture and Social Behavior.* New York: McGraw-Hill.

[80]Harris, P. R., & Moran, R. T. (1999). *Managing Cultural Differences* (5th ed.). Houston: Gulf Publishing.

[81]Brett, J., Behfar, K., & Kern, M. C. (2006, November). Managing Multicultural Teams. *Harvard Business Review,* 84–91.

[82]Sigmet. (2009). Sigmet Product Line. Available online: http://www.vaisala.com/weather/products/sigmet.html.

[83]Gill, J. (2005, November 1). Squelching Office Conflicts. *Inc.* Available online: http://www.inc.com/magazine/20051101/handson-managing.html.

[84]Gill, J. (2005 November 1). Squelching Office Conflicts. *Inc.* Available online: http://www.inc.com/magazine/20051101/handson-managing.html.

[85]Lynch, D. B. (2005, December 2). Say No to Office Conflict. PR Web. Available online: http://www.prweb.com/releases/2005/12/prweb317075.htm.

[86]Rahim, M. A. (2002). Toward a Theory of Managing Organizational Conflict. *International Journal of Conflict Management, 13,* 206–235.

[87]Papakostis, P. (2012). Marks & Spencer Case Study, The TCM Group, January 24. http://www.thetcmgroup.com/news/327-http-www-thetcmgroup-com-news/?p_view=all; Sir Stuart Rose Supports the Benefits of Mediation in the Workplace (2009). Globis Mediation Group, October 9. http://www.globis.co.uk/news/2009/10/09/sir-stuart-rose-supports-the-benefits-of-mediation-in-the-workplace/; Company Overview, Marks & Spencer, 2012. Available online: http://corporate.marksandspencer.com/aboutus/company_overview.

[88]GlaxoSmithKline. (2010). Our Values and Behaviors. Available online: http://www.gsk.com/responsibility/our-people/our-values-and-behaviours.htm.

PART 4

Groups, Teams, and Leadership

CHAPTER **12**

Group Behavior and Effective Teams

Starbucks culture values equality and teamwork. This posed a challenge when it expanded into countries that value hierarchy and power distance.

LEARNING OBJECTIVES

1. Describe how groups are different from teams.

2. Describe the stages of team development.

3. Describe the three components of team effectiveness.

4. Explain the difference between process gain and process loss.

5. Describe cohesiveness and discuss whether it is always good for a team to be cohesive.

6. Describe groupthink and discuss how it can be avoided.

7. Explain why emotional intelligence is important in teams.

8. Describe some of the challenges to managing virtual teams.

9. List four mechanisms for cross-team integration.

10. Explain how diversity can both help and hinder team performance.

REAL WORLD CHALLENGE

TEAMWORK AT STARBUCKS

Coffee giant Starbucks believes that teamwork is essential to its strategic execution and ultimate success.[1] Reinforcing this belief, Starbucks' core values include teamwork, diversity, and equal participation. Employees are called by their first names and are referred to as "partners" rather than by hierarchical titles. Teamwork is seen as so important to the company's success that new hires spend several days learning how to be part of the Starbucks team. Employees also work together on the front line, eliminating the distance between different statuses.[2]

When Starbucks started planning for its expansion into South Korea it realized that the country's culture valued hierarchical relationships and power distance, which were inconsistent with the company's equality and teamwork values. Starbucks had to decide if it wanted to change its organizational structure in South Korea to better fit the country's national culture, or stay the same to maintain its core values.[3]

Imagine that Starbucks asks for your advice on how it should handle its expansion into South Korea. After reading this chapter, you should have some good ideas.

AP PHOTOS/KEVIN P. CASEY

Quick—think of as many organizations as you can that do not use any teams. Your list is likely to be quite short, if not empty. Of the many trends in business, perhaps the best documented has been the increased use of teams in organizations.[4] One reason why organizations have increasingly relied on teams is the belief that they can be more creative, productive, and efficient than individuals working alone. In fact, few managers seem to question the potential benefits of work teams.[5] Despite this optimism, the fact remains that teams often fail to live up to their potential.[6]

In this part of the book we shift our attention to the performance and leadership of groups and teams. When tasks require multiple skills and expert judgment, or when tasks must be completed faster than an individual can do alone, teams typically outperform individuals.[7] Good teams are not a result of luck—they are a product of careful planning, effective leadership, and support from the broader organization. Companies like Hewlett-Packard use technology to promote effective teamwork by making it easy to express information visually, share data freely, and promote open communication.[8] In this chapter you will learn the difference between groups and teams, and learn about different types of teams. In addition to discussing the drivers of team effectiveness, we will discuss virtual teams and methods of building effective teams.

GROUPS AND TEAMS

teams

An interdependent collection of at least two individuals who share a common goal and responsibility for specific outcomes

What are teams? The definition that we will use is that **teams** are an interdependent collection of at least two individuals who share a common goal and responsibility for specific outcomes.[9] A key part of this definition is that team members are *interdependent* with respect to information, resources, and skills. As tasks become more complex, they require greater coordination among team members. Team members' roles become interdependent, increasing the need for teamwork, reciprocal communication, and feedback. Communication and collaboration demands also increase dramatically.[10]

A group of people at work is not necessarily a team. Teams differ from groups in six key ways, as summarized in Table 12-1. First, members of workgroups have low *task interdependence* and individual *goals*. Second, group members are *accountable* for their individual performance. Members of teams, on the other hand, are interdependent, have shared goals, and share accountability for the team's as well as their own performance. Workgroups and teams both require members to be *competent* at doing their required tasks, but teams also require social skills.

Table 12-1

Differences Between Workgroups and Work Teams

Workgroups		Teams
Low	Interdependence	High
Individual	Goals	Shared
Individual	Accountability	Individual and group
Task	Competencies	Task and social
Individual/leader	Decision making	Shared
Fixed	Leadership	Fixed, shared, or rotates

Groups also have a clear, formal leader or manager who makes *decisions* for the group. Group members may make decisions for themselves as individuals, but not for the group as a whole. Teams, on the other hand, engage in shared decision making, and have a shared or rotating *leadership role*. Because of these differences, managing teams is more challenging than managing groups. Teams are not always the best way of organizing work. When work can be done best by individuals or workgroups, it is usually better not to use teams.

Types of Teams

There are many different types of teams. Each type of team is composed of different members and responsible for different types of tasks. The members of *functional teams* come from the same department or functional area. A team of marketing employees and a team of finance employees are examples of functional teams.

functional teams
Members come from the same department or functional area

Cross-functional teams have members from different departments or functional areas. This is one of the most common types of work teams. An example of a cross-functional team is a top management team with members representing different functions or units of the organization. Some organizations are organized such that the company's core work is done in cross-functional teams.

cross-functional teams
Members come from different departments or functional areas

For example, IDEO, a product innovation and design company, believes that interdisciplinary teamwork boosts innovation and creativity.[11] Teams share and improve ideas, building on their members' skills and providing more opportunities for problem solving. Steelcase; IDEO; Hammel, Green, and Abrahamson, Inc.; and the Mayo Clinic formed a cross-functional team that worked together to integrate technology to improve patient care at the Mayo Clinic.[12]

Cross-functional teams have several strengths. In addition to getting things done faster, particularly customer service and new product development, they can increase creativity. Cross-functional teams also improve a firm's ability to solve complex problems by bringing different skill sets, perceptions, and experiences together. Because they bring diverse people from different functional areas together, they also increase employees' knowledge about other areas of the organization. The same diversity that can be a strength for cross-functional teams can also be a weakness if this diversity is not properly managed and conflicts are not effectively handled.

Problem-solving teams are teams established to solve problems and make improvements at work. The core strength of problem-solving teams is that because employees are the ones actually *doing* the work, they usually know the job best. Putting employees on teams responsible for solving problems puts this expertise to work. For example, Colgate and JM Huber, a raw material supplier, jointly assembled a multidisciplinary team to identify ways to reduce costs. The team ultimately realized savings of hundreds of thousands of dollars.[13] Quality circles can exist for long periods whereas suggestion teams are short-lived and assembled to address specific issues. Problem-solving teams can also increase employees' commitment to decisions because they were involved in making them.

problem-solving teams
Teams created to solve problems and make improvements

Organizations are increasingly turning to outside teams to help them solve important problems. When online movie rental site Netflix sponsored a contest to improve the accuracy of its movie recommendation system, more than 40,000 teams from 186 countries formed to vie for the million dollar prize.[14]

Because self-directed teams handle responsibilities that are usually reserved for team leaders or managers, members must have strong self-management and teamwork skills.

YURI ARCURS/SHUTTERSTOCK.COM

self-directed teams
Set their own goals and pursue them in ways defined by the team

venture teams
Teams that operate semi-autonomously to create and develop new products, processes, or businesses

virtual teams
Teams whose members are linked by technology

Self-directed teams set their own goals and pursue them in ways defined by the team. Team members are responsible for tasks typically reserved for team leaders or managers, including scheduling work and vacations, ordering supplies, and evaluating their performance. At 3M, self-directed work teams have made improvements in products, services, and processes while increasing customer responsiveness, lowering operating costs, increasing productivity, and decreasing cycle times.

Self-directed teams can improve commitment, quality, and efficiency. Cross-trained team members also help to increase the flexibility of the team during staffing shortages. Self-directed teams are difficult to implement, however, as they require specific self-management and team skills that many employees lack.

Venture teams are teams that operate semi-autonomously to create and develop new products (product development teams), processes (process design teams), or businesses (venture teams).[15] Separating a team from the formal structure of the rest of the organization can enhance its innovativeness and speed up cycle time.

A classic example illustrating the pros and cons of venture teams is the IBM team created to develop IBM's first personal computer.[16] The team had its own budgets and leader, and the freedom to make decisions without the constraints of many of the typical IBM rules and policies. The team successfully developed the new PC and brought it to market in less than two years, which was much faster than it would have been with IBM's usual hierarchical, "check with me first" approach. However, the team's autonomy also let it avoid IBM's traditional requirement of using only IBM parts. The team used Microsoft for the computer's disk operation system and Intel for its processor. This allowed Microsoft and Intel to sell these same parts to other PC manufacturers, leading to increased competition from low-priced IBM clones.[17] Clearly, although team autonomy can have advantages, appropriate controls are needed.

Virtual teams are teams of geographically and/or organizationally dispersed coworkers who communicate using telecommunications and information technologies.[18] Some virtual team members may never see each other face-to-face. Many organizations use virtual teams to accomplish a variety of goals. For example, PricewaterhouseCoopers, one of the world's largest accounting firms with more than 130,000 employees in 148 countries, uses virtual teams to bring employees from around the globe "together" for a week or two to prepare work for a particular client. Whirlpool Corporation used a virtual team composed of experts from the United States, Brazil, and Italy during a two-year project to develop a chlorofluorocarbon-free refrigerator.[19] You will learn more about virtual teams later in this chapter.

The U.S.-based engineering department of Aventis, a world leader in pharmaceuticals and agriculture, used to be composed of many isolated technical units that reported to different organizations and different businesses. There was no consistency in work quality, no practical standards, and minimal cross-group cooperation. To improve this, Aventis created five virtual technical service groups developed around process technologies and customer needs. The engineers in each group can be located anywhere in North America. This new virtual organization is more mobile, better focused on customer needs, and more strongly aligned with business goals.[20]

Global teams have members from different countries. Global teams can be virtual or meet face-to-face. Procter & Gamble, a multinational manufacturer of family, personal, and household care products, uses global teams to allow employees at its Cincinnati headquarters to collaborate with employees and suppliers all over the world. Bosch und Siemens Hausgeräte GmbH (BSH) is a global company that operates thirty-one production sites and forty-three factories in fifteen countries across Europe, Asia, the United States, and Latin America. The company sells household appliances under brand names including Bosch and Siemens, and uses global teams of employees from Spain, China, and Latin America to develop technologies and concepts for new products.

These team types are summarized in Table 12-2.

global teams
Face-to-face or virtual teams whose members are from different countries

How Groups Become Teams

Teams typically progress through a series of developmental stages before performing effectively. Many models of team development exist, but most are a

Table 12-2

Types of Teams

Functional teams	members come from the same department or functional area
Cross-functional teams	members come from different departments or functional areas
Problem-solving teams	teams created to solve problems and make improvements
Self-directed teams	set their own goals and pursue them in ways defined by the team *Venture teams*: teams that operate semi-autonomously to create and develop new products, processes, or businesses
Virtual teams	teams of geographically and/or organizationally dispersed coworkers who communicate using telecommunications and information technologies
Global teams	face-to-face or virtual teams whose members are from different countries

Table 12-3	

How Groups Become Teams

Forming	Team members learn about each other and about the team's purpose, goals, and life span, and begin to identify each member's strengths and potential contribution to the team.
Storming	Team members begin establishing goals, work processes, and individual roles, and test how the team will respond to differences among team members and to conflict.
Norming	The team becomes more cohesive and clarifies members' roles and responsibilities and team goals; team processes and members' expectations of each other are established.
Performing	The team is cohesive, productive, and makes progress toward its goals; cohesiveness and goal commitment are high.
Adjourning	The team disbands.

variation of the basic five-stage model developed by Bruce W. Tuckman in the 1960s and refined in the 1970s.[21] Teams vary in how they proceed through the stages, but Tuckman's stages, summarized in Table 12-3, are useful guideposts for leaders and team members.

During the first stage, ***forming***, team members get to know each other; learn the team's purpose, goals, and life span; and begin to identify each member's strengths and potential contribution to the team. Members typically ask the leader questions about the team's purpose and goals, establish their identity in the team, and test what types of behaviors are acceptable. The purpose of the forming stage of team development is to create a team with clear structure, goals, and roles so that members begin to trust each other and feel like a team. Managers can facilitate this process by providing a good orientation to the team, clarifying the team's mission and goals, and establishing expectations about the team's processes and outcomes.[22]

The ***storming*** stage is characterized by conflict as team members begin establishing goals, work processes, and individual roles, and test how the team will respond to differences among team members and to conflict. *Constructive conflict* is over work goals and processes. Constructive conflict is a positive type of conflict—through addressing it, the team identifies the goals and processes that will best work for it.

Dysfunctional conflict focuses on personalities and conflicts between individual group members. Dysfunctional conflict fosters distrust and cynicism, and can undermine team effectiveness. The team leader needs to keep team members focused on their goals, roles, and tasks to avoid members' becoming distracted by the frustrations and conflicts developing among the team members. At the end of the storming stage, team goals and leadership are clear.

During the ***norming*** stage the team clarifies roles and responsibilities and reaches agreement about team goals and processes. Cohesiveness increases as team members accept their teammates' differences and recognize that the diversity of member opinions and perspectives strengthens the team. Goal commitment is strong. At the end of the norming stage, team processes and members' expectations of each other are established.

During the fourth stage of team development, ***performing***, the team has a shared understanding of why it is doing what it is doing. At this stage the

forming

First stage of team development in which members learn about each other and the team's goals, purpose, and life span

storming

A stage of conflict in which team members begin establishing goals, work processes, and individual roles

norming

The team becomes more cohesive and clarifies members' roles and responsibilities, team goals, and team performing

performing

The team is cohesive, productive, and makes progress toward its goals

team is cohesive, productive, and makes progress toward its goals. Disagreements in the team are positively resolved and there is a focus on goal achievement. Team members are also able to attend to relationship and process issues that arise. As team members master their roles, team roles may become more flexible, with members taking on various roles and responsibilities as needed. Cohesiveness and goal commitment are high, and the team makes significant progress toward its goals.

Although teams become high performing during the performing stage, this stage is not the end of the team's development needs. The team needs to be able to adapt to any changes in its environment or goals. The team also needs to address membership changes—each new member requires the team to cycle back to an earlier stage to incorporate the new member and find ways to fill the roles left by the departing member. A team that does not take the time to socialize a new member and modify the team's roles and processes does not allow a newcomer to contribute maximally to the team.

If membership and environmental changes are recognized and addressed, teams can remain in this stage indefinitely. Technology can facilitate and speed up the integration of new team members. By keeping everything a new team member needs to know on a website, Deloitte Consulting says it can bring a new team member up to speed on a project in a day or two, compared to three weeks without it.[23]

The fifth stage of team development is **_adjourning_**, or the breakup of the team. This stage is less relevant to managing and developing a team, but is important to members who have formed an attachment to the team. Ideally, the team is ending because it has accomplished its goals and everyone feels good about what it has achieved. If members of the team have become friends and enjoyed the team experience, it can be beneficial to recognize their sense of loss and give them a sense of closure. It is also a good idea to address members' anxiety over the uncertainty of their next assignment in the organization. This is the time to evaluate what the team did well and poorly to learn how to make future teams more effective.

adjourning
When the team disbands

Holding a closing celebration that acknowledges the contributions of each team member and the accomplishments of the team as a whole formally ends the existence of the team. This is a good time to evaluate the team's processes and outcomes in order to identify "lessons learned" that can be passed on to other team leaders.

Although research has supported the idea that teams tend to develop in this five-stage sequence, not all teams do. Teams develop in different ways and at their own speeds. Some teams never get out of the storming stage while others are able to advance rapidly to the performing stage. Some teams perform effectively at the storming and norming stages, depending on the nature of the task and the team members. It is best to consider Tuckman's sequence as a general framework, and not expect teams to rigidly follow each stage.

ENHANCING TEAM EFFECTIVENESS

As illustrated in Figure 12-1, team effectiveness has three components: *a quality team product, an improved ability to work together effectively in the future,* and *a team experience that is meaningful and satisfying for its members.*[24] Teams that deliver on all three of these components are the most effective.

Figure 12-1

Effective Teams

© CENGAGE LEARNING 2012

No single leadership or coaching style works best for all teams. It is the leader's job to flexibly create the conditions needed for a team to be successful. Noted teams expert J. Richard Hackman believes that teams perform best when leaders create five conditions that allow teams to manage themselves effectively. The five conditions he has identified as necessary for effective teams are:[25]

1. *The team must be a real team, rather than a team in name only*. The team needs to have a real team task requiring interdependence that is neither too large nor too small for the team to accomplish and find energizing. Teams need to have the authority to manage their own work processes, and membership needs to be reasonably stable.

2. *The team needs compelling direction*. A challenging and clear direction can orient, energize, and engage team members. Essentially, setting direction for the team means the leader is authoritative and insistent about the team's goals, but does not specify how the team should go about achieving those goals. Leaders must strike a balance between giving teams too much direction (e.g., telling them exactly what to do and how to do it) and too little (e.g., providing a broad vision statement and letting the team work out the details).

3. *The team must have an enabling structure that facilitates teamwork*. A team's work should provide meaningfulness, responsibility, and knowledge of results to maximize team members' motivation. The team also needs to develop appropriate norms and be an appropriate size. The team must have members with an appropriate mix of skills, including interpersonal skills. Hackman refers to team structure as "the shell of the team . . . the shaping structure within which [the team] comes to life."[26] He states that, "those who create teams have two quite different but equally important responsibilities: to make sure that a team has the best structure that can be provided, and to help members move into that structure and competently launch themselves onto a course of their own."[27]

4. *The team should operate within a supportive organizational context*. The rest of the organization's policies and practices need to support teamwork. For example, a reward system that recognizes and rewards individual performance rather than team excellence is not supportive of work teams. Technology must

provide teams with the necessary information, at the appropriate time, in the appropriate format. Leaders also must ensure that team members acquire needed technical and interpersonal skills. The extent to which these systems are supportive of team efforts reflects the extent to which an organization's culture truly supports a team-based approach to effective operations. Without cultural support for teams, team efforts are not likely to be successful.

5. *The team needs effective teamwork coaching*. Acquiring teamwork skills often takes some coaching. Leaders can promote team effectiveness by helping team members develop the skills required to work interdependently with others. Coaching with well-timed suggestions can influence team members' motivation and effort, the levels of knowledge and skills team members can apply to team tasks, and teams' performance strategies.

"If one of us stumbles for the second time in ten minutes, there's no question about what needs to be done: Somebody reaches into that person's pack and takes out some weight, and then we all just move on." —*Robert Nagle, Founder of Team EcoInternet*

Creating Effective Teams

People working together have the potential to produce more or higher-quality outputs than would have resulted if the individual efforts of team members were later combined. *Process gain* refers to the performance improvements that occur because people work together rather than independently. Process gain is the goal of working in teams—people working together doing more and doing it better than would be possible working alone.

Unfortunately, many teams do not realize process gain and instead experience *process loss* Process loss occurs when a team of people working together performs worse than the individual members would have if they had worked alone. Process loss can be reduced by making clear role and task assignments and not tolerating free riders. Free riders do not contribute because they rely on the work of others. Paying attention to *how* a team does its work can help you to identify and remedy many of the factors contributing to process loss.

Develop Team Efficacy. *Team efficacy* is a team's shared belief that it can organize and execute the behaviors necessary to reach its goals.[28] Team efficacy is strongly related to team performance, particularly when team interdependence is high.[29]

Develop Cohesiveness. *Cohesiveness* refers to the degree to which members are attracted to the team and to its members, and how loyal team members are to the team and to each other. Members of a highly cohesive team are motivated to stay in the team, contribute as much as they can, and conform to team norms. Because members of teams that lack cohesiveness are not strongly committed to the team or its goals and do not contribute to their full potential, team performance is compromised.[30]

High cohesiveness can actually interfere with team effectiveness if it encourages the wrong norms and goals. For example, a highly cohesive team that pursues its own goals of having fun and socializing rather than accomplishing organizational goals is not effective. Factors that promote cohesiveness include a smaller team size, team success, the effective management of conflict, and friendly competition with other teams.

Create Trust. Trust is our confidence that other people will honor their commitments, especially when it is difficult to monitor or observe the other people's behavior.[31] Trust is the glue that holds teams together. Teams build trust through

process gain
The performance improvements that occur because people work together rather than independently

process loss
When a team of people working together performs worse than the individual members would have if they had worked alone

team efficacy
A team's shared belief that it can organize and execute the behaviors necessary to reach its goals

cohesiveness
The degree to which members are attracted to the team and to its members, and how loyal team members are to the team and to each other

social loafing

When people put less effort into a task when working with a team than they do when working alone

social facilitation

An increase in effort by a person working in a group

roles

The behaviors and tasks each team member is expected to perform because of their position

groupthink

When decision-making groups do not consider all alternatives and value unanimity rather than quality decisions

repeated positive experiences, commitment to shared goals, and an understanding of team members' needs, motives, and ideas. Because the lack of trust in a team can undermine any team activity, building trust is an important managerial task. Giving frequent task feedback and interpersonal contact can help diverse teams utilize their diversity to their advantage and create process gain.[32]

Mutual trust is the foundation of the entire team strategy of Team EcoInternet, an adventure racing team. The team can progress only as fast as its current weakest member, and because the grueling race lasts several days, every team member is the weakest link at some point. Team founder Robert Nagle says, "If one of us stumbles for the second time in ten minutes, there's no question about what needs to be done: Somebody reaches into that person's pack and takes out some weight, and then we all just move on."[33] Team members do not feel heroic for helping each other, nor do they feel like they are letting the team down if they need help. Team members trust their teammates and know that in a while, the person whose stuff they are carrying is likely to be carrying theirs.

Prevent Social Loafing. *Social loafing* occurs when people put less effort into a task when working with a team than they do when working alone.[34] Social loafing is a primary cause of process loss. Research has supported the occurrence of social loafing,[35] particularly for trivial to moderately important tasks. Social loafing is less common with very important tasks,[36] and with smaller teams.[37] Social loafing often occurs because team members feel that their individual contributions will not be evaluated or because they expect others in the team to do tasks so they choose not to do them.[38]

An opposite behavior occurs when people actually work harder and are more motivated when others are present than when they are working alone. *Social facilitation* happens when people are motivated to look good to others and want to maintain a positive self-image. It happens when people are working alone, but in the presence of an audience. People sometimes increase their effort when working in a group simply because others are present[39] or because of evaluation apprehension.[40]

Keeping team size small, clarifying what the team expects each member to do, and making individual contributions to the team identifiable can help reduce social loafing and encourage social facilitation.[41] For example, giving a team member the responsibility for ensuring that meeting notes are shared with the team within two days of a meeting makes it more likely that notes will be taken and distributed. Letting team members choose which tasks they will be responsible for can also increase their motivation for getting them done.

Establish Clear Roles. *Roles* define the behaviors and tasks each team member is expected to perform because of the position they hold. One of the primary outcomes of the forming, storming, norming, and performing process of team development is the establishment of clear roles in the team. Understanding what your teammates expect you to do and what you can expect your teammates to do reduces conflict and enables smooth team performance. Making team roles and expectations clear helps to reduce process loss.

Two important roles must be performed in any team.[42] The *task specialist* role keeps the team moving toward goal accomplishment, and is played by people with more advanced job-related skills and abilities. The *team maintenance specialist* role creates and maintains team harmony. Team maintenance specialists boost morale, show concern for members' well-being, and provide support and humor. Any member of the team can perform these roles, and over time, different team members are likely to play both roles.

Prevent Groupthink. Irving L. Janis coined the term *groupthink* to explain a type of faulty decision making that he observed in groups. *Groupthink* occurs when decision-making groups do not consider all alternatives and value unanimity rather than quality decisions.[43] Janis said that groupthink can be found whenever institutions make difficult decisions, and that it reflects the triumph of agreement over good sense and authority over expertise. The escalation of the Vietnam War, the Bay of Pigs,[44] and the space shuttle Columbia disaster[45] are famous examples of groupthink. The three conditions Janis identified as antecedents of groupthink are (1) high group cohesiveness, (2) leader preference for a particular decision, and (3) group insulation from outside opinions.[46]

Symptoms of groupthink include the group believing it is invincible, group members pressuring other group members to conform, rationalizing poor decisions, and maintaining an illusion of unanimity.[47] Self-appointed *mindguards* who protect the group and its leader from negative information are an additional symptom of groupthink.

Social pressures often encourage conformity to group opinions rather than expressing a different opinion and risking conflict. Using outside experts, having a group member play devil's advocate to question the group's assumptions and ideas, making it clear that all opinions are welcome, and not punishing anyone for speaking up can help to discourage groupthink.

Establish Positive Norms. *Norms* are shared rules, standards, or guidelines for team member behavior and performance. By helping team members know what to expect from each other, norms help to ensure high performance. An example of a positive team norm is arriving to meetings prepared and on time, and participating fully. Team members comply with team norms (1) to avoid punishments and receive rewards; (2) to imitate team members who they like and admire; and (3) because they have internalized the norm and believe it is the appropriate way to behave.[48]

norms
Shared rules, standards, or guidelines for team member behavior and performance

Team norms can also be negative, such as not producing more than the team's quota, not thoroughly checking product quality to save time, or not wearing safety equipment. The team leader establishes norms to ensure that the team benefits from the best talents of each member by setting a positive emotional tone, modeling appropriate behavior, and using positive images, optimistic interpretations, and culture-building norms and leadership styles.[49] Managers can also help to establish positive team norms by leading discussions about how the team can best function to achieve both the team's and the team members' objectives. Clear and mutually agreed-upon norms, work processes, and rules are important for effective teams. When a problem arises, effective teams have an open discussion and find a solution.[50]

Create Shared Team Goals and Provide Feedback. High-performing teams have clear and challenging goals that all team members are committed to, and create subgoals and milestones against which they measure themselves. If performance is lagging, feedback helps the team quickly adjust its behavior and processes to reach its goals.[51] As featured in this chapter's real world response, in South Korea Starbucks created shared team goals around tasks typically performed by females to encourage its male employees to perform these tasks as well.[52]

Provide Appropriate Rewards. Team rewards motivate effective teamwork behaviors. Tying team rewards to team performance motivates team members to pursue team goals rather than individual goals.[53] Teams require firms to shift the

NASA ARCHIVE / ALAMY

The space shuttle Columbia disaster is attributed to groupthink and a faulty decision making culture at NASA.

emphasis of their compensation and rewards programs from individual to team rewards. Any remaining individual rewards should acknowledge people who are effective team players—people who freely share their expertise, help when needed, and challenge their teams to improve. A "star" system that rewards only individual performance undermines team effectiveness. Some individual rewards may be appropriate for those who make particularly critical individual contributions to the team, but the bulk of rewards need to be made at the team level.

Southwest Airlines is an example of a company that relies heavily on collective rewards such as profit sharing and stock ownership to promote teamwork. Unlike other airlines, when reporting the cause of flight delays, Southwest allows flight crews to identify "team delay" to avoid wasting time assessing and placing blame for problems instead of solving them.[54]

At Men's Wearhouse, CEO George Zimmer rewards team selling because its customers want to have a positive total store experience. To encourage collaboration, Men's Wearhouse tracks the sales performance of each "wardrobe consultant." Having substantially more sales than one's coworkers is taken as a sign that the person is hogging rather than sharing customers. Team selling is taken so seriously that the company even terminated one of its most successful salespeople because he refused to conform to the firm's cultural values. After the salesperson was fired, no one matched his individual sales figures but the store's total sales volume increased significantly.[55]

Use an Appropriate Team Size. Jeff Bezos of Amazon.com believes that if you cannot feed a team with two pizzas, the team is too big and will be hindered by bureaucracy.[56] The insight that teams can get bogged down if they are too big is a good one. Although larger teams technically have more resources available, members of smaller teams are better able to interact and share information, tend to be more motivated and satisfied, and can more clearly identify their contributions to the team. Imagine working on a project or exercise for this class on a team of twenty-five people versus a team of five people. It would be difficult for everyone to fully participate and effectively communicate with each other on such a large team. A team should be only large enough to contain the expertise it needs to get its work done without compromising individual and team productivity. Generally teams should have fifteen or fewer members; the ideal number is about seven.

Integrate New Team Members. Team member turnover compromises team effectiveness as new members must be proactively integrated and socialized.[57] Leaders are critical to this newcomer integration and socialization process. New team member integration involves motivating all team members by promoting shared goal commitment, positive affect, and shaping team processes. Team socialization creates affective bonds that connect members to the team and its mission, and helps build trust and a sense of community. If current team members do not take the time to incorporate new members into the fabric of the team, the team will be less cohesive, new members will not be able to contribute to their full potential, and new members are likely to be less committed to the team.

Use Emotional Intelligence. Another characteristic that is important for team members to have is *emotional intelligence*, or an interpersonal capability that includes the ability to perceive and express emotions, to understand and use them, and to manage emotions in oneself and other people.[58] Setting the right ground rules for a team and maintaining positive team processes require an emotionally intelligent leader. The best leaders pay attention to and act on their sense of what is going on in the team. This helps teams naturally develop positive norms and expectations about how to work with each other[59] and internalize the team's vision.[60]

emotional intelligence

An interpersonal capability that includes the ability to perceive and express emotions, to understand and use them, and to manage emotions in oneself and other people

Emotional intelligence is important for team members as well as team leaders.[61] Teams with less well-defined emotional intelligence climates experience increased task and relationship conflict and increased conflict intensity.[62] The U.S. Air Force and L'Oreal use emotional intelligence training to improve team performance. This chapter's *Understand Yourself* feature will help you to evaluate and understand your emotional intelligence skills.

UNDERSTAND YOURSELF

ARE YOU EMOTIONALLY INTELLIGENT?

Emotional intelligence will help you to be a more effective team member, and increase your effectiveness in many other areas as well. The following sixteen questions will help you to assess yourself on four aspects of emotional intelligence. Please answer each question honestly using the following scale. Write the number from 1 to 7 that corresponds to your answer on the scale in the space to the left of each item number.

strongly disagree	disagree	slightly disagree	neutral	slightly agree	agree	strongly agree
1	2	3	4	5	6	7

___ 1. I have a good sense of why I have certain feelings most of the time.
___ 2. I have a good understanding of my own emotions.
___ 3. I really understand what I feel.
___ 4. I always know whether or not I am happy.
___ 5. I can always distinguish my friends' emotions from their behavior.
___ 6. I am a good observer of others' emotions.
___ 7. I am sensitive to the feelings and emotions of others.
___ 8. I have a good understanding of the emotions of people around me.
___ 9. I always set goals for myself and then try my best to achieve them.
___10. I always tell myself I am a competent person.
___11. I am a self-motivating person.
___12. I would always encourage myself to try my best.
___13. I am able to control my temper so that I can handle difficulties rationally.
___14. I am quite capable of controlling my own emotions.
___15. I can always calm down quickly when I am very angry.
___16. I have good control of my own emotions.

Scoring and Interpretation: Each score is out of a maximum score of 28. The accuracy and usefulness of your score depends on the accuracy of your self-perceptions.

Your *self-emotion appraisal* score is your total score for statements 1 to 4: _____
A score *above 23* reflects high self-emotion appraisal and means that you have a good understanding of your own emotions.

Your *others' emotion appraisal* score is your total score for statements 5 to 8: _____
A score *above 22* reflects high others' emotion appraisal and means that you are sensitive to what others are feeling.

Your *use of emotion* score is your total score for statements 9 to 12: _____
A score *above 22* reflects high use of emotion and means that you are able to use your emotions to drive positive behavior.

Your *regulation* of emotion score is your total score for statements 13 to 16: _____

A score *above 23* reflects high regulation of emotion and means that you control your emotions effectively.
It is important to remember that the usefulness of your scores depend on the accuracy of your self-perceptions.

Source: Reprinted from The Leadership Quarterly, 13/3, Wong, C.S. & Law, K.S.,The Effects of Leader and Follower Emotional Intelligence on Performance and Attitude: An Exploratory Study, 243–274, Copyright © 2002, with permission from Elsevier.

Staff the Team Appropriately. In addition to staffing the team with needed knowledge and skills, it is a good idea to also ensure that team members are effective working in team-based settings. Not everyone is effective in a team setting due to personality, values, work style, and a desire to be an individual contributor. If someone is not effective in team settings, it is obviously best to assign that person to individual contributor roles whenever possible.

Table 12-4 gives you the chance to self-assess your teamwork attitude.

Teams higher in general mental ability, conscientiousness, agreeableness, extraversion, and emotional stability tend to perform better than teams lower in these characteristics.[63] Interestingly, research suggests that the variability in the personality characteristics of team members may be more important than the team's average level.[64] Greater personality variability tends to be related to lower team performance. This could be because personality differences can be a source of interpersonal conflict, which can decrease team performance. Imagine a highly conscientious person working with a teammate low in conscientiousness. The highly conscientious person is likely to feel some frustration with his or her teammate's lack of attention to detail or missing deadlines.

Table 12-4

What Is Your Preference for Teamwork?

One important characteristic team members should have is a positive teamwork attitude. Believing that the team is unlikely to be effective lowers team efficacy, which decreases team member effort and ultimately lowers performance. This self-assessment gives you the chance to assess your teamwork attitude.

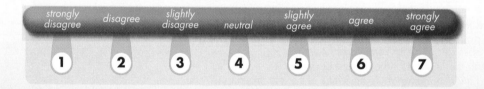

strongly disagree	disagree	slightly disagree	neutral	slightly agree	agree	strongly agree
1	2	3	4	5	6	7

Using the scale above, and thinking about yourself and how you normally feel, rate the following statements to show the extent to which you agree with each of them.

_____1. I generally prefer to work as part of a team.

_____2. I am eager to be working with other employees in a team.

_____3. I find that working as a member of a team increases my ability to perform effectively.

_____4. I feel that, given a choice, I would prefer to work in a team rather than work alone.

_____5. I support the use of teams.

Scoring: Add up your responses to the five statements. This is your preference for teamwork score.

Interpretation: The higher your score, the more comfortable you are in work teams and the more positive your attitude about them. Scores *above 28* reflect an above-average preference for teamwork. You might become more positive about teamwork as you have more successful experiences in teams. Try to seek out opportunities to work in groups and teams to sharpen your teamwork skills and practice what you learn in this chapter.

Sources: Adapted from: Kirkman, B.L. & Shapiro, D.L. (2001). The Impact of Cultural Values on Job Satisfaction and Organizational Commitment in Self- Managing Work Teams: The Mediating Role of Employee Resistance. *Academy of Management Journal, 44,* 557–69. Campion, M.A., Medsker, G.J., and Higgs, C. (1993). Relations Between Work Group Characteristics and Effectiveness: Implications for Designing Effective Work Groups. *Personnel Psychology, 46,* 823–50. Kiffin-Petersen, S.A., Cordery, J.L. (2003). Trust Individualism and Job Characteristics as Predictors of Employee Preference for Teamwork. *International Journal of Human Resource Management, 14,* 93–116.

Diagnosing Team Issues. One of the most important skills team leaders and team members can have is the ability to diagnose team issues and take appropriate steps to correct them. This chapter's *Improve Your Skills* feature gives you some tips to use in diagnosing the problems facing a team.

Virtual Teams

Managing virtual teams can be difficult.[65] Virtual team members are frequently separated by both geographic space and time, increasing the challenges of working together effectively. In such environments, team members are often isolated from one another and find it difficult to feel connected to their team.[66] It is hard enough to lead teams who see each other, and whose members share common language and culture, but these challenges multiply when teams "go virtual" and communication is via technology and involves team members with far different cultures and life experiences.[67]

Virtual teams allow organizations to access the most qualified individuals for a particular job regardless of their location, enable organizations to respond faster to increased competition, and provide greater flexibility to individuals working from home or on the road. In some cases, some members of the team may be free agents or alliance partners and not be employees of the organization. In some teams, members may never even meet face-to-face. Many virtual teams operate within a particular organization, but increasingly they cross organizational boundaries as well.[68] Hewlett-Packard, Motorola, and Bank of Boston rely on virtual teams to execute their strategies.[69]

Keeping team members engaged and connected to the team requires additional effort in virtual teams. IBM created a social networking site called

IMPROVE YOUR SKILLS

DIAGNOSING TEAM PROBLEMS

Here are some questions you can ask in diagnosing team issues.

1. *Clear direction*
   - Can team members each articulate the purpose that the team exists to achieve?
2. *A real team task*
   - Is the team assigned collective responsibility for all of its customers and major outputs?
   - Does the team make collective decisions about work strategies (rather than leaving it to individuals)?
   - Are team members willing and able to help each other?
   - Does the team get team-level feedback about its performance?
3. *Team rewards*
   - Are more than 80 percent of all rewards available to teams only, and not to individuals?
4. *Basic material resources*
   - Does the team have its own meeting space?
   - Can the team easily get the basic materials it needs to do its work?

5. *Authority to manage the work*
   - Do team members have the authority to decide the following without first receiving special authorization?
   - How to meet client demands
   - Which actions to take, and when
   - Whether to change their work strategies when they deem necessary
6. *Team goals*
   - Can team members articulate specific and shared team goals?
7. *Improvement norms*
   - Do team members encourage each other to detect and solve problems?
   - Do members openly discuss differences in what members have to contribute to the team?
   - Do members encourage experimentation with new ways of operating?
   - Does the team actively seek to learn from other teams?

Source: Wageman, R. (1997). Critical Success Factors for Creating Superb Self-Managing Teams," *Organizational Dynamics,* Summer, Vol 26, Issue 1, p. 59.

SocialBlue where employees post pictures and personal information about themselves. Informal online networks of virtual IMB employees also share ideas and moral support, just like cubicle mates. Employee surveys have shown that being able to work far from colleagues without losing touch has increased the retention of top talent and boosted employee satisfaction, productivity, and teamwork.[70]

Virtual Team Leadership Skills. The effective leadership of teams whose members are linked by technology and whose members often do not see each other requires unique skills and behaviors compared to managing and leading teams located in the same place.[71] Working from different locations introduces challenges with communication, collaboration, and the integration of the team members with the rest of the team and the broader organization. When team members rarely see each other or other employees, it can be difficult for them to feel part of the team and organizational community.

One of the most important things a virtual team leader can do is to establish a communication climate that is characterized by openness, trust, support, mutual respect, and risk taking. This helps the team establish positive working relationships, share information openly, reduce the formation of in-groups and out-groups, and avoid misinterpreting communications.[72]

One expert identified five categories of important leadership skills in virtual project team or distance management situations:[73]

1. *Communicating effectively and matching technology to the situation:* Collaborative online tools help virtual teams manage files, meetings, and task assignments.
2. *Building community among team members based on mutual trust, respect, affiliation, and fairness:* Effective leaders solicit and value the contributions of all team members, and consistently treat all team members with respect and fairness.
3. *Establishing a clear and motivating shared vision, team purpose, goals, and expectations:* Subtle messages, such as quietly reminding someone not to attack ideas during a brainstorming session, are powerful tools in shaping virtual team norms.
4. *Leading by example and focusing on measurable results:* Effective virtual leaders set clear goals and make clear task assignments. The leaders then hold team members accountable for them.
5. *Coordinating and collaborating across organizational boundaries:* Virtual team leaders need to work effectively with people in multiple organizations and with free agents and alliance partners who are not employees of the leader's organization.

Leader Behaviors. The lack of face-to-face contact with virtual team members makes it difficult for leaders to monitor team member performance and to implement solutions to work problems. It is also difficult for virtual team leaders to perform typical mentoring, coaching, and development functions. The challenge for virtual team leaders is that these tasks must be accomplished by empowering the team to perform these functions itself without the leader being physically present.[74]

For example, members of virtual teams are usually chosen for their expertise and competence, and for their prior virtual team experience. They are expected to have the technical knowledge, skills, abilities, and other attributes to be able to contribute to team effectiveness and to operate effectively in a virtual environment. Thus, the need for virtual team leaders to monitor or develop team members may not be as crucial. In addition, virtual team leaders can distribute aspects of these functions to the team itself, making it more of a self-managing team.[75]

Virtual team leaders need to provide a *clear, engaging direction for the team*[76] along with *specific individual goals*. Clear direction and goals allow team members to monitor and evaluate their own performance.[77] Although this is relevant in all teams, virtual team leaders need to be more proactive and structuring. Virtual team leaders need to develop team processes that become the way the team naturally behaves.

One way virtual team leaders can do this is by developing appropriate *routines and procedures* early on in the team's lifecycle.[78] Routines create consistent patterns of behavior that occur even in the leader's absence. Leaders can define desired routines (e.g., standard operating procedures), train members in them, and provide motivational incentives sufficient to ensure compliance with them. Leaders can also establish *rules and guidelines* that specify appropriate team member behavior. For example, computer-mediated communication tends to lead to more uninhibited individual behavior, such as strong and inflammatory expressions.[79] Therefore, virtual team leaders may need to develop standard operating procedures that specify appropriate and inappropriate computer-mediated communication. Because virtual team members are more detached from the overall team environment, it is also important for leaders to *monitor the environment* and inform team members of any important changes.[80]

Groupware and Group Decision Support Systems. Synchronous and asynchronous information technologies support members of virtual teams.[81] Synchronous technologies such as videoconferencing, instant messaging, electric meetings, and even conference calls allow real-time communication and interaction. Asynchronous technologies such as e-mail, wikis, and some electronic meetings delay the communication of the message. Many virtual teams rely on both types of information technology and use the one best suited to the message being communicated and task being performed. Bausch & Lomb found that a web-based collaboration tool increased synergy by decreasing the number of meetings, giving people more free work time to get things done.[82]

Many team meetings are poorly run, take too long, and accomplish too little. *Meeting management software, electronic whiteboards*, and *collaborative document editors* facilitate meetings by allowing team members to contribute ideas, to view other people's ideas anonymously, and to comment and vote on them. Computer-mediated communication enhances team performance by helping team members communicate more effectively with each other.[83]

The right technology is critical to making virtual teams work. Office furniture maker Steelcase relies on its cross-functional, cross-office, and even cross-company virtual teams to do business every day.[84] To reduce travel costs and to increase team productivity and efficiency, the company uses software to support its virtual teams and enable them to work together as if they were in the same location. The collaboration software connects virtual teams with members in locations around the world and helps structure the meeting process. Teams can share files, manage projects, and coordinate business processes by marking up documents and showing PowerPoint presentations within secure workspaces synchronized across all team members' PCs. Team members communicate via instant messaging, chat, or voiceover-IP using the virtual meeting tool. A meeting wizard facilitates the process of creating a meeting and inviting team members. Once a meeting is created, any participant can easily add agenda topics, create action items, attach files, and record minutes.[85]

SO WHAT

Leading virtual teams requires setting clear individual and team goals, establishing rules and guidelines, maintaining a supportive group communication climate, and monitoring the environment for any changes.

SO WHAT

Effective communication technology is critical for virtual teams' performance.

Cross-Team Integration

liaison roles
One or more team members are responsible for regularly communicating with other teams and coordinating the teams' activities as needed

Teams often need to coordinate and communicate with other teams. This can be done by assigning one or more team members to serve in *liaison roles* in which they are responsible for regularly communicating with other teams and coordinating the teams' activities as needed. This makes some team members boundary spanners who serve in a relatively informal integrating role across teams, managing resources and keeping teams informed of other teams' activities and accomplishments.

overlapping team membership
One or more team members is also a formal member of another team

Another method of cross-team integration is by creating *overlapping team membership*, making one or more team members a formal member of another team. Serving as a member of two teams can be challenging unless there are clear expectations about how the individual will divide his or her time and neither team makes inappropriate demands. Overlapping membership helps to decrease inter-team competition, since the person is an actual member of both teams. Figure 12-2 illustrates overlapping team membership.

cross-team integrating teams
A team member serves on a work team and a second team with the function of integrating multiple teams

Cross-team integrating teams also rely on having a team member serve on a work team and a second team called a cross-team integrating team whose function is to integrate multiple teams. Team members essentially comprise a team that integrates and coordinates multiple teams. This is different from *management teams* in which a higher-level team of managers manages lower-level cross-team integration. Figure 12-3 illustrates these cross-team integration mechanisms.

management teams
A higher-level team of managers manages lower-level cross-team integration

Many organizations focus their team training and development activities on intra-team dynamics and performance. Although this is certainly important, it is also necessary to enable teams to coordinate and communicate with each other to reduce competition and maximize cooperation.

Figure 12-2

Overlapping Team Membership

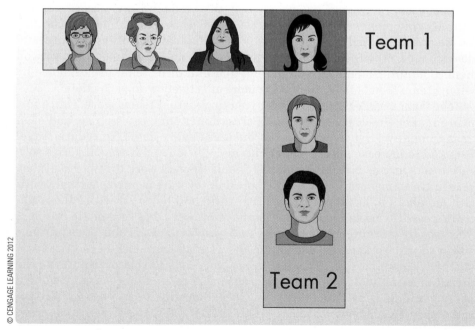

© CENGAGE LEARNING 2012

A team member serves on two teams simultaneously

Figure 12-3

Cross-Team Integration Mechanisms

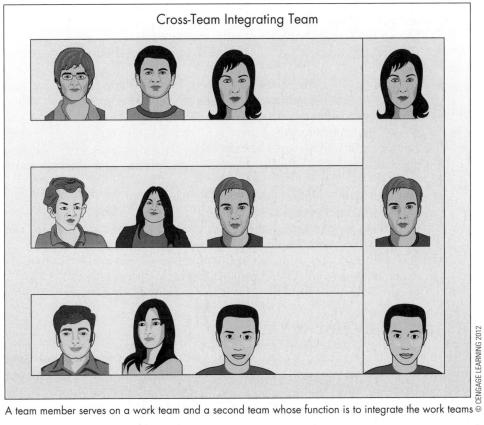

Cross-Team Integrating Team

A team member serves on a work team and a second team whose function is to integrate the work teams © CENGAGE LEARNING 2012

BUILDING EFFECTIVE TEAMS

As a manager you will inevitably be called upon to build and lead an effective team. In addition to the team effectiveness factors you just learned about, you will also need to staff the team with people likely to be effective team players and likely to behave ethically in a team context.

Teamwork Competencies

One of the foundations of an effective team is the nature of the people chosen to be in the team. Staffing teams with people who have the interpersonal skills and competencies to contribute to task performance but who are also able to work well in team settings is critical. Some of the teamwork abilities you should look for are:[86]

- *Conflict resolution abilities*
  - The ability to recognize and encourage desirable and discourage undesirable team conflict
  - The ability to recognize the type and source of conflict confronting the team and implement an appropriate resolution strategy
  - The ability to employ an integrative (win-win) negotiation strategy, rather than the traditional distributive (win-lose) strategy

- *Collaborative problem-solving abilities*
  - The ability to identify situations requiring participative group problem solving and to utilize the proper degree and type of participation
  - The ability to recognize the obstacles to collaborative group problem solving and implement appropriate corrective actions
- *Communication abilities*
  - The ability to communicate openly and supportively
  - The ability to listen objectively and to appropriately use active listening techniques
  - The ability to maximize the congruence between nonverbal and verbal messages and to recognize and interpret the nonverbal messages of others
  - The ability to engage in small talk and ritual greetings and a recognition of their importance
- *Goal-setting and self-management abilities*
  - The ability to help establish specific, challenging, and accepted team goals
  - The ability to provide constructive feedback
- *Planning and task coordination abilities*
  - The ability to coordinate and synchronize activities, information, and tasks between team members
  - The ability to help establish task and role assignments for individual team members and ensure proper balancing of workload

Ethical Behavior in Teams

The more frequently and intensely we interact with peers, the stronger their influence on our own behavior.[87] Other people's ethical behavior influences our own ethical behavior.[88] This is particularly true for managers, highlighting the importance of consistently setting a good example as a manager.[89] Four ethical issues are especially important in teams:

team contract

Written agreement among team members establishing ground rules about the team's processes, roles, and accountabilities

1. How do teams fairly distribute work?
2. How do teams assign blame and award credit?
3. How do teams ensure participation, resolve conflict, and make decisions?
4. How do teams avoid deception and corruption?

A **team contract** is a written agreement among team members establishing ground rules about the team's processes, roles, and accountabilities. Team members must communicate and negotiate in order to identify the quality of work they all wish to achieve, how decisions will be made, and the level of participation and individual accountability they all feel comfortable with. Team contracts help to reduce the potential for team conflict stemming from an unequal division of resources and deter free riding. By enhancing personal accountability and creating clear rules and expectations, team contracts can promote ethical team behavior and improve team performance and team member satisfaction.

SO WHAT

Creating team contracts can enhance role and goal clarity, increase team member commitment and satisfaction, and promote ethical behavior.

DIVERSITY IN TEAMS

Diversity can both help and hinder team effectiveness. Diversity can be a source of creativity and innovation that can create a competitive advantage[90] and improve a team's decision making.[91] Innovative companies intentionally use heterogeneous teams to solve problems.[92]

Despite its potential for improving team performance, diversity can be a two-edged sword.[93] Diversity can create misunderstandings and conflict that can lead to absenteeism, poor quality, low morale, and loss of competitiveness[94] as well as lowered workgroup cohesiveness.[95] Diverse groups are less able to provide for all of their members' needs and tend to have less integration and communication and more conflict than do homogeneous groups.[96] This chapter's *Case Study* feature describes the role of teamwork at design company IDEO.

We next discuss two types of team diversity, and how each contributes to team effectiveness.

Types of Team Diversity

Informational diversity, or diversity in knowledge and experience, has a positive impact on team performance. Because team members' unique knowledge enlarges the team's knowledge resources and can enhance the options it is able to consider, it can enhance creativity and problem solving. Richard Gabriel, a distinguished engineer at Sun Microsystems, looks for a range of interests and skills when building a team. "What I look for is diversity. People who are diverse in their talents. People who are used to failure. People who are used to revision. . . . Creativity is largely a matter of triggers. You need a diverse amount of material and a diverse group that can respond without ego."[97]

Demographic diversity often has a negative impact on performance. Team conflict tends to increase and teams tend to perform lower as they become more demographically diverse.[101] Increasing demographic diversity can result in work teams having more difficulty utilizing their informational diversity because team members are not able to work effectively with different others. When this happens, the potential for demographically diverse work teams to perform more effectively is lost.[102]

informational diversity
Diversity in knowledge and experience

demographic diversity
Diversity in age, gender, race, and other demographic characteristics

CASE STUDY

Teamwork at IDEO

IDEO is a global award-winning design firm.[98] Every year teams of people including psychologists, mechanical engineers, biologists, and industrial designers work on projects ranging from Apple's first computer mouse to heart defibrillators to the Neat Squeeze toothpaste tube.

IDEO's corporate philosophy is that teamwork improves innovation and creativity. Group brainstorming is used to spark a lot of new ideas at once. Project teams share and improve ideas by leveraging members' skills and solving problems together. The company believes that the diversity of interdisciplinary teams allows higher quality, faster innovation.[99]

Regardless of the project, IDEO teams use the same process. First they identify similar products and experiences, then they observe people using them. The teams then visualize, evaluate, refine, and implement innovative solutions to their clients' problems drawing from their research and observations. IDEO team members lack status or formal titles, and every team member is given equal respect.[100]

Questions:

1. How does teamwork influence innovation at IDEO?
2. How does diversity influence the effectiveness of teamwork at IDEO?
3. What characteristics would you look for in staffing a project team at IDEO?

"What I look for is diversity. People who are diverse in their talents. People who are used to failure. People who are used to revision." —*Richard Gabriel, Distinguished Engineer at Sun Microsystems*

To leverage the potential benefits of diversity, many companies take steps to proactively staff their teams with informational diversity and with people who are comfortable with diversity and with teamwork. Effectively managing diversity in teams has as much to do with the attitudes of team members toward diversity as it does with the diversity of the team itself.

Multicultural Team Challenges

Multicultural teams can create frustrating dilemmas for managers. Cultural differences can create substantial obstacles to effective teamwork, but they may be difficult to recognize until significant damage has been done.[103] It is easy to assume that challenges in multicultural teams are just due to differing communication styles, but differing attitudes toward hierarchy and authority and conflicting norms for decision making can also create barriers to a multicultural team's ultimate success.[104] We next elaborate on all three of these factors.

Direct versus Indirect Communication. Communication in Western cultures is typically direct and explicit, and a listener does not have to know much about the context or the speaker to interpret it. In many other cultures, meaning is embedded in the way the message is presented. For example, people in the West obtain information about other people's preferences and priorities by asking direct questions, such as "Do you prefer option A or option B?" In cultures using indirect communication, people often have to infer preferences and priorities from changes, or the lack of them, in the other person's counterproposal. In cross-cultural settings, the non-Westerner can easily understand the direct communications of the Westerner, but the Westerner often has difficulty understanding the indirect communications of the non-Westerner.[105]

Communication challenges create barriers to effective teamwork by reducing information sharing, creating interpersonal conflict, or both. Because accepted communication patterns differ across cultures, it is a good idea to familiarize yourself with the communication patterns and norms of any other cultures with which you will be interacting.

Differing Attitudes toward Hierarchy and Authority. By design, teams have a rather flat structure. But team members from cultures in which people are treated differently according to their status in an organization are often uncomfortable on flat teams. If they defer to higher status team members, their behavior will be seen as appropriate by team members from hierarchical cultures, but they may damage their credibility if most of the team comes from egalitarian cultures. For example, in multicultural teams, engineers from the culture in India are not culturally comfortable arguing with the team leader or with older people.[111] This decreases the ability of the team to secure everyone's input.

Conflicting Decision-Making Norms. Cultures differ substantially when it comes to how quickly decisions should be made and how much analysis is required. Compared with managers from other countries, U.S. managers like to make decisions very quickly and with relatively little analysis. A Brazilian manager at an American company made these comments about a negotiation, "On the first day, we agreed on three points, and on the second day, the

GLOBAL ISSUES

INCREASING THE EFFECTIVENESS OF MULTICULTURAL TEAMS

So what should you do to increase the effectiveness of multicultural teams? The best solution seems to be to make minor concessions on process—learn to adjust to and even respect another approach to decision making. For example, global American managers have learned to keep impatient bosses away from team meetings and give them frequent updates. A comparable lesson for managers from other cultures is to be explicit about what they need—saying, for example, "We have to see the big picture before we will be ready to talk about details."[106]

Four strategies for dealing with the challenges of multicultural teams are:

1. *Adaptation*: seeing a problem as a cultural difference, and not a personality issue. This works when team members are willing and able to identify and acknowledge their cultural differences and to assume responsibility for figuring out how to live with them.
2. *Structural intervention*: changing the shape of the team. Social interaction and working can be structured to engage everyone on the team.
3. *Managerial intervention*: setting norms early or bringing in a higher-level manager. This usually works best early in a team's life. In one case, a manager set norms of respect by telling his new team that no one had been chosen for English skills; each member was chosen because

he or she was technically the best person for the job, so get over the accents.[107]

4. *Exit*: removing a team member when other options have failed. If emotions get too high and too much face has been lost, it can be almost impossible to get a team to work together effectively again.[108]

As one expert says:

The most fundamental thing is to be a role model for respect. It rubs off on the other members of the team. Helping team members see that problems are due to cultural differences and not personality helps a lot. And if you're able to help the team see that the behavior that's so frustrating and annoying is due to culture, then people get curious: How do they get anything done in that culture? And when you unleash curiosity, that inspires learning. The last thing is, don't intervene too swiftly. If they can always bring a problem to your door and you solve it, they don't learn to solve it themselves.[109]

Managers and multicultural team members must find ways to utilize each member's strengths while minimizing coordination losses resulting from communication problems, language differences, varying work styles, and misunderstandings.[110]

company wanted to start with point four. But the Koreans wanted to go back and rediscuss points one through three. My boss almost had an attack."[112]

This chapter's *Global Issues* feature gives you some tips on improving the effectiveness of multicultural teams.

SUMMARY AND APPLICATION

Groups and teams are an important part of organizations. Groups tend to follow a predictable pattern as they move from the forming to the performing and adjourning stages of development. Achieving process gain depends on factors including developing team trust and cohesiveness, goal setting and feedback, appropriate staffing and rewards, and emotional intelligence. Using appropriate technology can facilitate team effectiveness, especially in virtual teams.

Managers must understand how to diagnose team issues and how to build and maintain effective teams. Doing this requires skill in managing multicultural teams and flexibility in leadership style. Staffing teams with members who value diversity and teamwork, and facilitating the development of team contracts also can improve team effectiveness.

REAL WORLD RESPONSE

TEAMWORK AT STARBUCKS

Starbucks expansion into South Korea posed a challenge. Should the company change its teamwork and equality culture to better fit South Korea's hierarchical natural culture that valued hierarchical distance between employees or should it stay the same and reinforce its own values in South Korea?

Starbucks decided to stay true to its culture and values, but to be sensitive to the cultural needs and expectations of its South Korean employees. Because South Korean employees were uncomfortable calling each other by their first names rather than by traditional hierarchical titles, Starbucks' managers gave every South Korean employee an English name to use at work. This made employees more comfortable using first names while preserving Starbucks' equality values.[113]

Another teamwork issue emerged because South Korean men typically do not do "housework" chores including washing dishes and cleaning toilets. However, this type of work is expected of everyone in Starbucks' stores. To help its male employees overcome the psychological barrier to cleaning, Starbucks leveraged the South Korean cultural affinity for imitating leaders' behaviours. The international director for Starbucks' headquarters personally did all of the cleaning activities and even hung a picture of him cleaning the toilet. Because lower-level employees imitate the behavior of top leaders this helped them overcome this cultural obstacle to teamwork.[114]

TAKEAWAY POINTS

1. Teams and groups are different in their interdependence, goals, accountability, competencies, decision making, and leadership. All teams are groups, but groups are not necessarily teams.
2. The five stages of team development are forming, storming, norming, performing, and adjourning.
3. Effective teams (1) produce an acceptable team product, (2) enhance their capacity to work together effectively in the future, and (3) satisfy all team members.
4. Process gain is the improved performance resulting from people working together rather than independently. Process loss occurs when a team of people working together performs worse than the individual members would have if they had worked alone.

5. Cohesiveness is the degree to which members are attracted to the team and to its members, and how loyal team members are to the team and to each other. If cohesiveness encourages the wrong norms and goals, it can be detrimental to team performance.

6. Groupthink happens when decision-making groups conform to group opinions rather than expressing a different opinion and risking conflict. Using outside experts, assigning a devil's advocate to question the group's assumptions and ideas, welcoming all opinions, and not punishing anyone for speaking up can help to discourage groupthink.

7. Emotional intelligence is the ability to understand and manage one's own emotions and moods and those of other people. Setting the right ground rules for a team and maintaining positive team processes requires an emotionally intelligent leader.

8. Virtual team members are frequently separated by both geographic space and time, increasing the challenges of working together effectively. In such environments, team members are often isolated from one another and find it difficult to feel connected to their team.

9. Four mechanisms for cross-team integration are liaison roles, overlapping membership, cross-team integrating teams, and management teams.

10. Diversity can improve a team's creativity and decision quality, but diverse groups are less able to provide for all of their members' needs and tend to have less integration and communication and more conflict than do homogeneous groups. Multicultural teams have additional challenges in managing different communication styles, decision-making norms, and attitudes toward hierarchy and authority.

DISCUSSION QUESTIONS

1. Think about an effective team you have been on. What made it effective?
2. Think about an underperforming team you have been on. Why was it underperforming?
3. This chapter stated that effective teams (1) produce an acceptable team product, (2) enhance their capacity to work together effectively in the future, and (3) satisfy all team members. Do you agree that team effectiveness should have all three components? If you had to eliminate one of the components, which do you think should be removed? Why?
4. What factors do you think have most contributed to process loss in groups you have been in?
5. If you were staffing a team, what would you look for in team members? Why?
6. Which do you feel is more important to team performance, goals and feedback or rewards? Why?
7. Do you think a team contract would improve the effectiveness of teams? Why or why not?
8. Which do you feel is more important to team performance, informational diversity or demographic diversity? Why? Do multicultural teams increase this type of diversity? If so, how?

EXERCISES

Write a Team Contract

Form groups of three to five students. Based on what you learned in this chapter, write a team contract to maximize the effectiveness of your group if you were a new product development team. Be sure to address how the team will handle disagreements, how you will make decisions, and how the team will ensure that all team members' ideas are shared. Think about the different aspects of team effectiveness and ways of promoting team effectiveness as you draft your contract.

Team Training

In this exercise your team will play the role of a training team in an organization charged with developing a team exercise illustrating some aspect of team effectiveness to other employees in the organization (the rest of your class). Your team will have approximately thirty minutes to develop a team exercise about cohesiveness, trust, team efficacy, team formation, conflict management, goal setting and feedback, or any other topic covered in this chapter. Every ten minutes your instructor will ask your group to pause, reflect on your team's performance and processes, and give each other constructive feedback to improve the team's effectiveness.

Form teams of approximately five people and decide who will be the team secretary. This person will ultimately share your team's ideas with the class. Your team then needs to:
1. Decide which team effectiveness construct to illustrate or develop in your trainee teams.
2. List the key learning objectives of your exercise.
3. Describe the resources and time needed to do the exercise.
4. Describe the exercise and how the learning objectives will be met.
5. Determine the potential challenges to the effectiveness of the exercise as a learning tool.

Weyerhaeuser's Teams

Weyerhaeuser wanted to reorganize its residential wood products division to better compete in a rapidly consolidating home building industry. Rather than start with the organizational chart, the firm focused on identifying all the things that needed to be done in sales and other critical areas. It then formed six cross-functional teams of experts from different areas of the company. Each team was told to work in confidence and to be creative in developing a proposal for redesigning sales, manufacturing, or another function of the new venture.

About ten different options were identified for how sales could be organized, each of which was then evaluated against a set of criteria to determine which provided the best return. The five leaders of the affected businesses evaluated the final proposals along with other key company leaders. It was sometimes an uncomfortable process because the five leaders all had long careers running successful businesses and had a lot of stake in tearing down the business walls and reassembling them into one integrated business.[115]

Based on what you read in this chapter, what advice would you give to Weyerhaeuser on maximizing the effectiveness of the leadership team making the final reorganization decisions?

VIDEO CASES

Now What?

Imagine being part of a group meeting with two coworkers and the boss to discuss a situation with a customer who wants a 30 percent discount on an order because it will be a week late. The team can't agree on whether to give the discount to keep the good customer happy or not give the discount to make more money on the sale, and is having trouble making a decision. *What do you say or do?* Go to this chapter's "Now What?" video, watch the challenge video, and choose a response. Be sure to also view the outcomes of the two responses you didn't choose.

Discussion Questions

1. What type(s) of conflict is (are) the team experiencing in the challenge video?
2. Which other aspects of organizational behavior discussed in this chapter are illustrated in these videos? Explain your answer.
3. As a manager, how else might you handle this situation? Why?

Workplace | Evo: Teamwork

For years Evo has supported athletic teams, but only recently did the Seattle-based e-commerce company launch a formal workplace team. Like many organizations, the online retailer of snowboard, ski, skate, and wake gear used team metaphors loosely to describe anything involving random groups of employees. But Evo got an education on real work teams when the company formed a team for its creative services employees.

The new group, which is comprised of a photographer, designer, and copywriter, is responsible for producing Evo's magazine ads, promotions, and website content. Although the individuals' roles are not generally interchangeable, photographer Tre Dauenhauer might dabble in design, graphic designer Pubs One may write a few lines of copy, and copywriter Sunny Fenton might snap photos on occasion. Most team projects require a combination of eye-grabbing photos, clever words, and a compelling design, and the teammates are committed to a common purpose.

When the creative services team launched, group members moved into their own space, away from Evo's chaotic, open-plan work areas. Being together every day enabled the team members to become better acquainted and move through the "forming" stage more quickly. But even with close

(Continued)

VIDEO CASES (continued)

quarters, Dauenhauer, One, and Fenton needed help navigating the conflict-ridden, storming stage of their team's development. Before joining the team, they functioned individually and weren't used to sharing power or making decisions as a group. To help the members learn to work together, Nathan Decker, director of e-commerce, became the team leader. As a skilled negotiator, Decker makes sure his talented trio steers clear of dysfunction and delivers the goods. Any time the team finishes a project, Decker brings members together for a postmortem discussion—a method of reviewing what was learned, and how things could be executed differently. It's here that the team members identify new routines and rituals to incorporate into their process for future improvement.

Due to Decker's leadership and skillful negotiation of conflicts, members of the creative services team are learning how to communicate in ways never before possible. Having a skilled leader to facilitate work processes has helped build team cohesiveness and deliver a collective output that is greater than the sum of its parts.

Discussion Questions

1. What organizational dilemma was hurting Evo's creative output, and how did management resolve the problem using teams?
2. How might Nathan Decker lead effectively as the team starts "norming"?
3. What conflicts have team members encountered at Evo, and how are those conflicts being resolved?

DO WHAT CENGAGENOW

CENGAGENOW™ includes **teaching and learning resources** to supplement the text, and is designed specifically to **help students "think like managers"** by engaging and challenging them to think critically about managerial situations. **CengageNOW uses today's technology to improve the skills** of tomorrow's managers.

END NOTES

[1]Strauss, S. (2002). How to Be a Great Place to Work, USA Today, May 20. Available online:.

[2]Jargon, J. (2009). Latest Starbucks Buzzword: 'Lean' Japanese Techniques, *The Wall Street Journal*, August 5. Available online: http://online.wsj.com/article/SB124933474023402611.html.

[3]Chen, X. & Tsui, A. S. (2006). An Organizational Perspective on Multi-Level Cultural Integration: Human Resource Management Practices in Cross-Cultural Contexts, in Francis J. Yammarino & Fred Dansereau (ed.) *Multi-Level Issues in Social Systems (Research in Multi Level Issues, Volume 5)*, Emerald Group Publishing Limited, 81–96.

[4]Cohen, S. G., & Bailey, D. E. (1997). What Makes Teams Work? Group Effectiveness Research from the Shop Floor to the

Executive Suite. *Journal of Management, 23,* 239–290; Ilgen, D. R. (1999). Teams Embedded in Organizations: Some Implications. *American Psychologist, 54,* 129–139; Kozlowski, S. W. J., & Bell, B. S. (2003). Work Groups and Teams in Organizations. In *Comprehensive Handbook of Psychology,* eds. W. C. Borman, D. R. Ilgen, and R. J. Klimoski (Vol. 12, pp. 333–375). New York: Wiley; Kirkman, B. L., Tesluk, P. E., & Rosen, B. (2001). Assessing the Incremental Validity of Team Consensus Ratings over Aggregation of Individual Level Data in Predicting Team Effectiveness. *Personnel Psychology, 54,* 645–667.

[5]Sundstrom, E. (1999). The Challenges of Supporting Work Team Effectiveness. In *Supporting Work Team Effectiveness: Best Management Practices for Fostering High Performance,* ed. E. D. Sundstrom (pp. 3–23). San Francisco, CA: Jossey-Bass; Thompson, L. L.

(2004). *Making the Team: A Guide for Managers* (2nd ed.). Upper Saddle River, NJ: Pearson Education.

[6]Smolek, J., Hoffman, D., & Moran, L. (1999). Organizing Teams for Success. In *Supporting Work Team Effectiveness: Best Management Practices for Fostering High Performance,* ed. E. Sundstrom (pp. 24–62). San Francisco, CA: Jossey-Bass.

[7]Salas, E., Bowers, C. A., & Edens, E. (Eds.). (2001). *Improving Teamwork in Organizations: Applications of Resource Management Training.* Mahwah, NJ: Lawrence Erlbaum.

[8]Hewlett-Packard Case Study. Microsoft TechNet. Available online: http://technet.microsoft.com/en-us/library/cc751328.aspx.

[9]Sundstrom, E., DeMeuse, K. P., & Futrell, D. (1990). Work Teams: Applications and Effectiveness. *American Psychologist, 45*(2), 120–133; Thompson, L. L. (2004). *Making the Team: A Guide for Managers* (2nd ed.). Upper Saddle River, NJ: Pearson Education.

[10]Hollingshead, A. B., McGrath, J. E., & O'Connor, K. M. (1993). Group Task Performance and Communication Technology: A Longitudinal Study of Computer-Mediated Versus Face-to-Face Work Groups. *Small Group Research, 24*(3), 307–333; Hollingshead, A. B., & McGrath, J. E. (1995). Computer-Assisted Groups: A Critical Review of the Empirical Research. In *Team Effectiveness and Decision Making in Organizations,* eds. R. Guzzo and E. Salas (pp. 46–78). San Francisco, CA: Jossey-Bass; Thompson, L. L. (2004). *Making the Team: A Guide for Managers* (2nd ed.). Upper Saddle River, NJ: Pearson Education.

[11]Inventors' Stories: IDEO Innovative Product Design Team. Smithsonian.org. Available online: http://invention.smithsonian.org/centerpieces/iap/inventors_ide.html.

[12]Case Study: Mayo Clinic SPARC Innovation Program. Steelcase. Available online: http://www.oneworkplace.com/images/dynamic/case_studies/MayoClinic.pdf.

[13]Global Procurement Mission and Goals. Colgate. Available online: http://www.colgate.com/app/Colgate/US/Corp/ContactUs/GMLS/MissionAndGoals.cvsp.

[14]Lohr, S. (2009, July 27). Netflix Competitors Learn the Power of Teamwork. *The New York Times.* Available online: http://www.nytimes.com/2009/07/28/technology/internet/28netflix.html?_r=2; Dybwad, B. (2009). Netflix Million Dollar Prize Ends in Photo Finish. Mashable. Available online: http://mashable.com/2009/09/21/netflix-prize-winners/.

[15]Olson, P. (1990, January–February). Choices for Innovation Minded Corporations. *Journal of Business Strategy,* 86–90.

[16]Dessler, G. (2004). *Management: Principles and Practices for Tomorrow's Leaders.* Upper Saddle River, NJ: Pearson/Prentice Hall.

[17]Successful venture teams are sometimes spun off into their own divisions or even independent companies. Some organizations create new venture divisions devoted exclusively to new product development. See, for example, Bart, C. (1988, Summer). New Venture Units: Use Them Wisely to Manage Innovation. *Sloan Management Review,* 35–43; Burgelman, R. (1985). Managing the New Venture Division: Research Findings and Implications for Strategic Management. *Strategic Management Journal, 6,* 39–54.

[18]Townsend, A. M., DeMarie, S. M., & Hendrickson, A. R. (1998). Virtual Teams: Technology and the Workplace of the Future. *Academy of Management Executive, 12*(3), 17–29, p. 17.

[19]Geber, B. (1995). Virtual Teams. *Training, 32*(4), 36–42.

[20]Pang. L. (2001). Understanding Virtual Organizations. *Information Systems Control Journal,* 6. Available online: http://www.isaca.org/Journal/Past-Issues/2001/Volume-6/Pages/Understanding-Virtual-Organizations.aspx.

[21]Tuckman, B. W. (1965). Developmental Sequence in Small Groups. *Psychological Bulletin, 63,* 384–399; Tuckman, B. W.,

& Jensen, M. A. C. (1977). Stages of Small-Group Development Revisited. *Group & Organization Studies, 2,* 419–427.

[22]Roussin, C. J. (2008). Increasing Trust, Psychological Safety, and Team Performance Through Dyadic Leadership Discovery. *Small Group Research, 39*(2), 224–248.

[23]Keenan, F., & Ante, S. E. (2002, February 18). The New Teamwork. *BusinessWeek.* e.Biz Supplement, EB12–EB16. Available online: http://www.businessweek.com/magazine/content/02_07/b3770601.htm.

[24]Hackman, J. R. (1987). The Design of Work Teams. In *Handbook of Organizational Behavior,* ed. J. Lorsch. Englewood Cliffs, NJ: Prentice Hall; Hackman, J. R. (2002). *Leading Teams: Setting the Stage for Great Performances.* Boston: Harvard Business School Press.

[25]See Hackman, J. R. (2002). *Leading Teams: Setting the Stage for Great Performances.* Boston: Harvard Business School Press.

[26]Hackman, J. R. (2002). *Leading Teams: Setting the Stage for Great Performances* (p. 129). Boston: Harvard Business School Press.

[27]Hackman, J. R. (2002). *Leading Teams: Setting the Stage for Great Performances.* Boston: Harvard Business School Press.

[28]Bandura, A. (1997). Collective Efficacy. In *Self-Efficacy: The Exercise of Control,* ed. A. Bandura (pp. 477–525). New York: Freeman.

[29]Gully, S. M., Joshi, A., Incalcaterra, K. A., & Beaubien, J. M. (2002). A Meta-Analysis of Team-Efficacy, Potency, and Performance: Interdependence and Level of Analysis as Moderators of Observed Relationships. *Journal of Applied Psychology, 87*(5), 819–832; Jung, D. I., & Sosik, J. (2003). Group Potency and Collective Efficacy: Examining Their Predictive Validity, Level of Analysis, and Effects of Performance Feedback on Future Group Performance. *Group and Organization Management, 28*(3), 366–391.

[30]Gully, S. M., Devine, D. J., & Whitney, D. J. (1995). A Meta-Analysis of Cohesion and Performance: Effects of Levels of Analysis and Task Interdependence. *Small Group Research, 26*(4), 497–520.

[31]Thompson, L. L. (2004). *Making the Team: A Guide for Managers* (2nd ed., p. 93). Upper Saddle River, NJ: Pearson Education.

[32]Watson, W. E., Johnson, L., Kumar, K., & Critelli, J. (1998). Process Gain and Process Loss: Comparing Interpersonal Processes and Performance of Culturally Diverse and Non-Diverse Teams Across Time. *International Journal of Intercultural Relations, 22,* 409–430.

[33]Dahle, C. (1999, November). Xtreme Teams. *Fast Company, 29,* 310; Thompson, L. L. (2004). *Making the Team: A Guide for Managers* (2nd ed.). Upper Saddle River, NJ: Pearson Education.

[34]Comer, D. R. (1995, June). A Model of Social Loafing in Real Work Groups. *Human Relations, 48*(6), 647–667; George, J. M. (1992). Extrinsic and Intrinsic Origins of Perceived Social Loafing in Organizations. *Academy of Management Journal, 35,* 191–202; Shepperd, J. A. (1993). Productivity Loss in Performance Groups: A Motivation Analysis. *Psychological Bulletin, 113,* 67–81; Thompson, L. L. (2004). *Making the Team: A Guide for Managers* (2nd ed.). Upper Saddle River, NJ: Pearson Education.

[35]Horowitz, I. A., & Bordens, K. S. (1995). *Social Psychology.* Mountain View, CA: Mayfield.

[36]Karau, S. J., & Williams, K. D. (1993). Social Loafing: A Meta-Analytic Review and Theoretical Integration. *Journal of Personality and Social Psychology, 65,* 681–706.

[37]Kerr, N. L. (1989). Illusions of Efficacy: The Effects of Group Size on Perceived Efficacy in Social Dilemmas. *Journal of Experimental Social Psychology, 25,* 287–313.

[38]Williams, K. D., Harkins, S. G., & Latané, B. (1981). Identifiability as a Deterrent to Social Loafing: Two Cheering Experiments. *Journal of Personality and Social Psychology, 40,* 303–311.

[39]Zajonc, R. (1965). Social Facilitation. *Science, 149,* 269–274.

[40]Cottrell, N. B. (1972). Social Facilitation. In *Experimental Social Psychology,* ed. C. G. McClintock. New York: Holt, Rinehart & Winston.

[41]Williams, K., Harkins, S., & Latane, B. (1981). Identifiability as a Deterrent to Social Loafing: Two Cheering Experiments. *Journal of Personality and Social Psychology, 40,* 303–311; Latane, B. (1986). Responsibility and Effort in Organizations. In *Designing Effective Work Groups,* ed. P. S. Goodman. San Francisco, CA: Jossey-Bass.

[42]Bales, R. F. (1950). *Interaction Process Analysis: A Method for the Study of Small Groups.* Reading, MA: Addison-Wesley.

[43]Janis, I. (1972) *Victims of Groupthink.* Boston: Houghton Mifflin.

[44]Janis, I. (1972) *Victims of Groupthink.* Boston: Houghton Mifflin.

[45]Schwartz, J., & Wald, M. L. (2003, March 9). "Groupthink" Is 30 Years Old, and Still Going Strong. *The New York Times,* 5; Ferraris, C., & Carveth, R. (2003). NASA and the Columbia Disaster: Decision-Making by Groupthink? Proceedings of the 2003 Association for Business Communication Annual Convention, Association for Business Communication.

[46]Janis, I. (1972) *Victims of Groupthink.* Boston: Houghton Mifflin.

[47]Janis, I. (1972) *Victims of Groupthink.* Boston: Houghton Mifflin.

[48]Hackman, J. R. (1992). Group Influences on Individuals in Organizations. In *Handbook of Industrial and Organizational Psychology,* eds. M. D. Dunnette and L. M. Hough (2nd ed., Vol. 3). Palo Alto, CA: Consulting Psychologists Press.

[49]Goleman, D., McKee, A., & Boyatzis, R. (2002). *Primal Leadership: Realizing the Power of Emotional Intelligence.* Boston: Harvard Business School Press.

[50]MacGregor, D. (1960). *The Human Side of Enterprise.* New York: McGraw-Hill.

[51]Katzenbach, J. R., & Smith, D. K. (1994). *The Wisdom of Teams: Creating the High-Performance Organization.* New York: HarperBusiness.

[52]Chen, X. & Tsui, A. S. (2006). An Organizational Perspective on Multi-Level Cultural Integration: Human Resource Management Practices in Cross-Cultural Contexts, in Francis J. Yammarino & Fred Dansereau (ed.) *Multi-Level Issues in Social Systems (Research in Multi Level Issues, Volume 5),* Emerald Group Publishing Limited, 81–96.

[53]Parker, G., McAdams, J., & Zielinski, D. (2000). *Rewarding Teams: Lessons from the Trenches.* San Francisco, CA: Jossey-Bass.

[54]Sinton, P. (2000, February 23). Teamwork the Name of the Game for IDEO. *San Francisco Chronicle.* Available online: http://www.sfgate.com/business/article/Teamwork-the-Name-of-the-Game-for-Ideo-3304722.php.

[55]Sinton, P. (2000, February 23). Teamwork the Name of the Game for IDEO. *San Francisco Chronicle.* Available online: http://www.sfgate.com/business/article/Teamwork-the-Name-of-the-Game-for-Ideo-3304722.php.

[56]Lidsky, D. (2004, November). Fast Forward 2005. *Fast Company,* 69.

[57]Levine, J. M., & Moreland, R. L. (1989). Newcomers and Oldtimers in Small Groups. In *Psychology of Group Influence,* ed. P. Paulus (2nd ed., pp. 143–186). Hillsdale, NJ: Erlbaum; Levine, J. M., & Moreland, R. L. (Eds.). (2006). *Small Groups.* Philadelphia: Psychology Press.

[58]Mayer, J. D., & Salovey, P. (1993). The Intelligence of Emotional Intelligence. *Intelligence, 17,* 433–442; Mayer, J. D., & Salovey, P. (1997). What Is Emotional Intelligence? In *Emotional Development and Emotional Intelligence,* eds. P. Salovey and D. J. Sluyter. New York: Basic Books.

[59]Goleman, D., McKee, A., & Boyatzis, R. (2002). *Primal Leadership: Realizing the Power of Emotional Intelligence.* Boston: Harvard Business School Press.

[60]Hur, Y., Van Den Berg, P.T., & Wilderom, C.P.M. (2011). Transformational Leadership as a Mediator Between Emotional Intelligence and Team Outcomes, *The Leadership Quarterly,* 22(4), 591–603.

[61]Rowe, A., Cherbosque, J., & Gardenswartz, L. (2009). Coaching Teams for Emotional Intelligence in Your Diverse Workplace, American Society for Training and Development, February. Available online: http://www.astd.org/Publications/Magazines/TD/TD-Archive/2009/02/Coaching-Teams-for-Emotional-Intelligence-in-Your-Diverse-Workplace.

[62]Ayoki, O. B., Callan, V. J., & Hartel, C. E. J. (2008). The Influence of Team Emotional Intelligence Climate on Conflict and Team Members' Reactions to Conflict. *Small Group Research,* 39(2), 121–149.

[63]Barrick, M. R., Stewart, G. L., Newbert, M. J., & Mount, M. K. (1998). Relating Member Ability and Personality to Work-Team Processes and Team Effectiveness. *Journal of Applied Psychology, 83,* 377–391; O'Neill, T.A. & Allen, N.J. (2011). Personality and the Prediction of Team Performance, *European Journal of Personality, 25*(1), 31–42.

[64]Barrick, M. R., Stewart, G. L., Newbert, M. J., & Mount, M. K. (1998). Relating Member Ability and Personality to Work-Team Processes and Team Effectiveness. *Journal of Applied Psychology, 83,* 377–391; Pieterse, A.N., van Knippenberg, D., & van Ginkel, W.P. (2011). Diversity in Goal Orientation, Team Reflexivity, and Team Performance, *Organizational Behavior and Human Decision Processes, 114*(2), 153–164.

[65]Berry, G.R. (2011). Enhancing Effectiveness on Virtual Teams: Understanding Why Traditional Team Skills are Insufficient, *Journal of Business Communication,* 48(2), 186–206.

[66]Bhappu, A. D., Griffith, T. L., & Northcraft, G. B. (1997). Media Effects and Communication Bias in Diverse Groups. *Organizational Behavior and Human Decision Processes, 70,* 199–205.

[67]Gibson, C., & Cohen, S. (2003). *Virtual Teams That Work: Creating Conditions for Virtual Team Effectiveness.* San Francisco, CA: Jossey-Bass.

[68]Cascio, W. F. (2000). Managing a Virtual Workplace. *Academy of Management Executives, 14*(3), 81–90.

[69]Lipnack, J., & Stamps, J. (1997). *Virtual Teams: Reaching Across Space, Time, and Organizations with Technology.* New York: John Wiley.

[70]Fisher, A. (2009, December 10). How to Build a (Strong) Virtual Team. *Fortune.* Available online: http://money.cnn.com/2009/11/16/news/companies/ibm_virtual_manager.fortune/index.htm.

[71]Bell, B. S., & Kozlowski, S. W. J. (2002). A Typology of Virtual Teams: Implications for Effective Leadership. *Group and Organization Management, 27*(1), 14–49.

[72]Gibson, C. B., & Gibbs, J. L. (2006). Unpacking the Concept of Virtuality: The Effects of Geographic Dispersion, Electronic Dependence, Dynamic Structure, and National Diversity on Team Innovation. *Administrative Science Quarterly, 51,* 451–495.

[73]Thompsen, J. A. (2000, September). Leading Virtual Teams. *Quality Digest.* Available online at http://www.qualitydigest.com/sept00/html/teams.html.

[74]Bell, B. S., & Kozlowski, S. W. J. (2002). A Typology of Virtual Teams: Implications for Effective Leadership. *Group and Organization Management, 27*(1), 14–49.

[75]Manz, C., & Sims, H. P. (1987). Leading Workers to Lead Themselves: The External Leadership of Self-Managing Work Teams. *Administrative Science Quarterly, 32,* 106–128.

[76]Hackman, J. R., & Walton, R. E. (1986). Leading Groups in Organizations. In *Designing Effective Work Groups,* eds. Paul S . Goodman & Associates. San Francisco, CA: Jossey-Bass.

[77]Kozlowski, S. W. J. (1998). Training and Developing Adaptive Teams: Theory, Principles, and Research. In *Decision Making Under Stress: Implications for Training and Simulation,* eds. J. A. Cannon-Bowers and E. Salas (pp. 115–153). Washington, DC: APA Books; Smith, E. M., Ford, J. K., & Kozlowski, S. W. J. (1997). Building Adaptive Expertise: Implications for Training Design. In *Training for a Rapidly Changing Workplace: Applications of Psychological Research,* ed. M. A. Quinones and A. Ehrenstein (pp. 89–118). Washington, DC: APA Books.

[78]Gersick, C. J. G., & Hackman, J. R. (1990). Habitual Routines in Task-Performing Teams. *Organizational Behavior and Human Decision Processes, 47,* 65–97.

[79]Siegel, J., Dubrovsky, V., Kiesler, S., & McGuire, T. W. (1986). Group Processes in Computer-Mediated Communication. *Organizational Behavior and Human Decision Processes, 37,* 157–187; Strauss, S. G., & McGrath, J. E. (1994). Does the Medium Matter? The Interaction of Task Type and Technology on Group Performance and Member Reactions. *Journal of Applied Psychology, 79,* 87–97; Thompson, L. L. (2004). *Making the Team: A Guide for Managers* (2nd ed.). Upper Saddle River, NJ: Pearson Education.

[80]Bell, B. S., & Kozlowski, S. W. J. (2002). A Typology of Virtual Teams: Implications for Effective Leadership. *Group and Organization Management, 27*(1), 14–49.

[81]Duarte, D. L., & Snyder, N. T. (1999). *Mastering Virtual Teams.* San Francisco, CA: Jossey-Bass.

[82]Rosencrance, L. (2005, January). Meet Me in Cyberspace. *Computerworld.* Available online: http://www.computerworld.com.au /article/1636/meet_me_cyberspace/?relcomp=1.

[83]http://careers.jnj.com/careers/global/index.htm.

[84]Purdum, T. (2005, May 4). Teaming, Take 2. *Industry-Week.* Available online: http://www.industryweek.com/articles /teaming_take_2_10179.aspx.

[85]Rosencrance, L. (2005, January 3). Meet Me in Cyberspace. *Computerworld.* Available online: http://www.computerworld .com.au/article/1636/meet_me_cyberspace/?relcomp=1.

[86]From Stevens, M. J., & Campion, M. A. (1994). The Knowledge, Skill, and Ability Requirements for Teamwork: Implications for Human Resource Management. *Journal of Management, 20,* 505.

[87]Zey-Ferrell, M., & Ferrell, O. C. (1982). Role-Set Configuration and Opportunity as Predictors of Unethical Behavior in Organizations. *Human Relations, 35*(7), 587–604.

[88]Treviño, L. K., Weaver, G. R., & Reynolds, S. J. (2006). Behavioral Ethics in Organizations: A Review. *Journal of Management, 32,* 951–990.

[89]Treviño, L. K., Weaver, G. R., & Reynolds, S. J. (2006). Behavioral Ethics in Organizations: A Review. *Journal of Management, 32,* 951–990.

[90]Bassett-Jones, N., & Lloyd, G. (2005). The Paradox of Diversity Management. *Journal of Creativity and Innovation Management, 14,* 169–175.

[91]Williams, K. Y. (1998). Demography and Diversity in Organizations: A Review of 100 Years of Research. In *Research in Organizational Behavior,* eds. B. M. Staw and L. L. Cummings (Vol. 20, pp. 77–140). Greenwich, CT: JAI Press.

[92]Moss-Kanter, R. (1983). *The Change Masters.* New York: Simon and Schuster.

[93]Millikin, F. J., & Martins, L. L. (1996). Searching for Common Threads: Understanding the Multiple Effects of Diversity in Organizational Groups. *Academy of Management Review, 21,* 402–433.

[94]See Bassett-Jones, N., & Lloyd, G. (2005). The Paradox of Diversity Management. *Journal of Creativity and Innovation Management, 14,* 169–175.

[95]See Jackson, S. E., Stone, V. K., & Alvarez, E. B. (1992). Socialization Amidst Diversity: The Impact of Demographics on Work Team Old-Timers and Newcomers. In *Research in Organizational Behavior,* L. L. Cummings and B. M. Staw (Vol. 15, pp. 45–109). Greenwich, CT: JAI.

[96]Williams, K. Y., & O'Reilly III, C. A. (1998). Demography and Diversity in Organizations: A Review of 40 Years of Research. *Research in Organizational Behavior, 20,* 77–140.

[97] Moore, T. (2003, February 22). It's the People Skills! Say Entrepreneurs. *Stanford GSB News.* Available online: http://www.gsb .stanford.edu/news/headlines/2003entrepreneurshipconf.shtml . Accessed March 19, 2009.

[98]About IDEO, 2012. Available online: http://www.ideo.com /about/.

[99]Innovative Product Design Team, *Invention at Play,* 2012. Available online: http://inventionatplay.org/inventors_ide.html.

[100]Dawson, I. (2012). Teamwork and Innovation the IDEO Way, *Dare Dreamer Magazine,* May 28. Available online: http:// daredreamermag.com/2012/05/28/teamwork-and-innovation-the -ideo-way/.

[101]Jehn, K., Northcraft, G., & Neale, M. (1999). Why Differences Make a Difference: A Field Study of Diversity, Conflict, and Performance in Workgroups. *Administrative Science Quarterly, 44*(4), 741–763.

[102]Bhappu, A. D., Zellmer-Bruhn, M., & Anand, V. (2001). The Effects of Demographic Diversity and Virtual Work Environments on Knowledge Processing in Teams. *Advances in Interdisciplinary Studies of Work Teams, 8,* 149–165.

[103]Brett, J., Behfar, K., & Kern, M. C. (2006, November). Managing Multicultural Teams. *Harvard Business Review,* 84–91.

[104]Behfar, K., Kern, M., & Brett, J. (2006). *Managing Challenges in Multicultural Teams: Research on Managing Groups and Teams* (Vol. 9, pp. 233–262). New York: Elsevier.

[105]Brett, J., Behfar, K., & Kern, M. C. (2006, November). Managing Multicultural Teams. *Harvard Business Review,* 84–91.

[106]Melymuka, K. (2006, November 20). Managing Multicultural Teams. *Computerworld.* Available online: http://www.computerworld .com/s/article/271169/Managing_Multicultural_Teams.

[107]Brett, J., Behfar, K., & Kern, M. C. (2006, November). Managing Multicultural Teams. *Harvard Business Review,* 84–91.

[108]Brett, J., Behfar, K., & Kern, M. C. (2006, November). Managing Multicultural Teams. *Harvard Business Review,* 84–91.

[109]Melymuka, K. (2006, November 20). Managing Multicultural Teams. *Computerworld.* Available online: http://www. computerworld .com/s/article/271169/Managing_Multicultural_Teams.

[110]Melymuka, K. (2006, November 20). Managing Multicultural Teams. *Computerworld.* Available online: http://www.computerworld .com/s/article/271169/Managing_Multicultural_Teams.

[111]Melymuka, K. (2006, November 20). Managing Multicultural Teams. *Computerworld*. Available online: http://www.computerworld .com/s/article/271169/Managing_Multicultural_Teams.

[112]Behfar, K., Kern, M., & Brett, J. (2006). *Managing Challenges in Multicultural Teams: Research on Managing Groups and Teams* (Vol. 9, pp. 233–262). New York: Elsevier.

[113]Chen, X. & Tsui, A. S. (2006). An Organizational Perspective on Multi-Level Cultural Integration: Human Resource Management Practices in Cross-Cultural Contexts, in Francis J. Yammarino & Fred Dansereau (ed.) *Multi-Level Issues in Social Systems (Research in Multi Level Issues, Volume 5)*, Emerald Group Publishing Limited, 81–96.

[114]Chen, X. & Tsui, A. S. (2006). An Organizational Perspective on Multi-Level Cultural Integration: Human Resource Management Practices in Cross-Cultural Contexts, in Francis J. Yammarino & Fred Dansereau (ed.) *Multi-Level Issues in Social Systems (Research in Multi Level Issues, Volume 5)*, Emerald Group Publishing Limited, 81–96.

[115]Huff, C. (2006, May 8). Weyerhaeuser's Speedy Workforce Overhaul. *Workforce Management, 1,* 28–36.

CHAPTER 13

Leading

Costco co-founder Jim Senegal's leadership philosophy is that great businesses can be made and sustained on the back of a set of core values. Sinegal believes that good, happy employees are more productive and are the backbone of Costco's success.

REAL WORLD CHALLENGE

ETHICAL LEADERSHIP AT COSTCO[1]

Warehouse retailer Costco has over $50 billion in sales from its more than 500 outlets in several countries, and employs more than 120,000 workers. Costco competes by giving customers the best value at the best price. The maximum mark-up at Costco is 15 percent, which means that customers never pay more than 15 percent over what Costco paid for the item. Costco's cofounder and CEO, Jim Sinegal, believes in treating employees with respect. He also knows that acting ethically and never losing sight of the purpose of the business is critical to his leading Costco into the future.

At the core of Sinegal's leadership philosophy is the idea that great businesses can be made and sustained on the back of a set of core values. As Costco continues to grow and become even more multinational, Sinegal wants to maintain the central role of ethics in his leading of the company. However, Wall Street analysts have long criticized Sinegal for paying high wages and keeping employees around too long, which increases salary and benefits costs.

NEWSCOM

Source: Career Opportunities for You, Costco.com, 2012. http://shop.costco.com/About/Costco-Employment; Q&A with Jim Sinegal Founder of Costco. (2009, March). SmallBizBee. http://smallbizbee.com/index/2009/03/19/ qa-jim-sinegal-founder-costco/; Machan, D. (2008, March 27). CEO Interview: Costco's James Sinegal. SmartMoney. http://www.smartmoney.com/investing/stocks/ceointerview-costcos-james-sinegal-22782/; Chu, J., & Rockwood, K. (2008, October 13). CEO Interview: Costco's Jim Sinegal. Fast Company. http://www.fastcompany.com/ magazine/130 /thinking-outside-the-big-box.html?page=0%2C2; Goldberg, A. B., & Ritter, B. (2006, August 2). Costco CEO Finds Pro-Worker Means Profitability. ABC News 20/20. http:// abcnews.go.com/2020/Business/story?id=1362779; Wadhwa, V. (2009, August 17). Why Be an Ethical Company? They're Stronger and Last Longer. BusinessWeek. http://www.businessweek.com/stories/2009-08-17/whybe- an-ethical-company-theyre-stronger-and-last-longerbusinessweek- business-news-stock-market-and-financial-advice; Lamm, G. (2008, December 19). 2008 Executive of the Year. Enterprise Seattle. http://www .enterpriseseattle.org/index. php?option=com_content=view=210=104=2009-10-01

LEARNING OBJECTIVES

1 Describe how leadership differs from management.

2 Discuss the role of traits and skills in leadership emergence and effectiveness.

3 Explain what determines the effectiveness of a leader.

4 Describe the core activities done by all leaders.

5 Describe ethical leadership.

6 Describe e-leadership and how technology influences what effective leaders do.

7 Describe how technology can help new leaders become effective more quickly.

Sinegal knows that good, happy employees are more productive and believes that they are the backbone of Costco's success. Sinegal attributes Costco's success to a team effort, not the work of any individual. Assume that Sinegal asks you for advice on how to effectively lead Costco into the future. After reading this chapter, you should have some good ideas.

Think of the best boss you have ever had. Now think of the worst boss you have ever had. What made the two so different? The chances are good that you described aspects of each person's leadership style and skills.

Strategies, resources, and good products are not enough to make an organization successful. Even with the right organizational systems and dedicated employees, little will happen without leadership. Effective leadership converts an organization's potential into high performance. Weak or ineffective leadership depletes a firm's resources and erodes its competitive edge. The high-profile failures of Merrill Lynch CEO John Thain, who was upset that he would not receive a bonus after his firm lost billions,[2] and Enron CEO Ken Lay, who was willing to do almost anything to protect his company from disclosures that might lower its stock price,[3] spotlight the importance of having effective leadership in place.

What exactly is leadership? In many ways leadership is the effective use of organizational behavior principles. Effective leadership involves influencing others to work toward common objectives, which requires a variety of OB skills including communication, motivation, and influence. The better you can master the tools provided by a thorough knowledge of organizational behavior, the better a leader you will be.

There is no one best way to lead—leadership requires different styles and behaviors in different situations. As leadership expert Stephen D. Reicher states, "The leader needs to be multifaceted and emphasize different facets at different times. Those who fail to do that have a limited shelf life."[4] Leaders can and must do a variety of things—including motivate, communicate, and build culture, confidence, and trust.

> "The leader needs to be multifaceted and emphasize different facets at different times. Those who fail to do that have a limited shelf life." —*Stephen D. Reicher, Leadership Expert*

In this chapter you will learn about how leading differs from managing, as well as what characteristics leaders tend to possess. We also discuss what leaders do, what makes leaders effective, and how to be an ethical leader. After studying this chapter, you should have a variety of tools at your disposal to help you become a better leader.

WHAT IS LEADERSHIP?

leadership
Guiding and influencing others to work willingly toward the leader's objectives

Leadership means guiding and influencing others to work willingly toward the leader's objectives. Leaders set team goals, train team members, provide feedback, manage resources, support the team, and perform a variety of other roles.[5] Leadership can have both positive and negative effects in organizations. At its best, leadership inspires and motivates employees to work hard toward organizational objectives and help the organization succeed. At its worst, leadership can reduce the performance of individual employees as well as the entire organization, and even result in unethical behavior and organizational collapse.

Is Leadership Different from Management?

Confusion around the question of whether leadership and management mean the same thing is common. One way to think about whether they are different is to answer the question, "Are all managers leaders?" Most people can think of someone, perhaps a former boss, who they would not describe as being a leader despite the person holding a position of authority. Most people can also think of someone they would consider a leader despite that person not being in a formal position of authority. Therefore, the answer must be that the two are different.

Management is an important *function* in every organization. Management exists to establish and implement the procedures, processes, and practices that help the firm function smoothly. Managers are also responsible for goal attainment.[6] Because of their position in the organization, managers have formal authority to reward and punish. They obtain, coordinate, and distribute the human and material resources the firm needs,[7] and ensure that what employees do is consistent with the organization's rules and regulations.

Leadership, on the other hand, is a *relationship* between the leader and the led.[8] Leadership is the behavioral and interpersonal aspect of what managers do. Leaders may or may not have a formal leadership position—anyone in a firm can and should engage in leadership behaviors. Leaders often can influence the behaviors of others without the use of reward or punishment. Leaders help devise strategies for the attainment of organizational goals and they help others understand their role in the implementation of those strategies. Table 13-1 summarizes the differences between managers and leaders.

Because accomplishing organizational goals requires both leadership and management, both leadership and managerial skills are important.[9] Leadership experts Warren Bennis and Burt Nanus put it this way: "Management controls, arranges, does things right; leadership unleashes energy, sets the vision so we do the right thing."[10]

Must all managers be leaders? Because leadership can help all managers be more effective, managers should ideally have leadership skills. Managers who are not leaders can still get the job done, but at its best, managing involves leading. As a manager, if you can only influence the behavior of subordinates by using rewards or punishments, you simply will not be as effective as a manager who inspires subordinates to do their best and work hard toward company goals.

Must all leaders be managers? The reality is that everyone in an organization from the CEO to those at the entry level can and should exhibit leadership regardless of their job titles. The leadership displayed by a store employee who inspires her coworkers to provide better customer service and the leadership shown

SO WHAT

Because leadership enables the attainment of managerial goals, both managerial and leadership skills are important to organizational performance.

"Management controls, arranges, does things right; leadership unleashes energy, sets the vision so we do the right thing." — *Warren Bennis and Burt Nanus, Leadership Experts*

Table 13-1

Management versus Leadership

Management	Leadership
A function	A relationship
Planning	Building culture
Acquiring resources	Motivating
Evaluating	Coaching
Attaining goals	Building trust

by a warehouse employee who inspires everyone to work more safely both have positive consequences for the firm. And leadership matters—one study found that companies with more rigorous leadership development programs tend to outperform their competitors.[11] Successful organizations develop leadership skills in all of their employees, encouraging employees to set a positive example for their coworkers and continually work toward the accomplishment of the firm's goals.

Effective Leadership

Throughout human history, kings, pharaohs, and generals must have wondered, "Why are some people more effective leaders than others?"[12] Yet only in the last seventy years or so have behavioral scientists addressed this question. Briefly stated, experts' current thinking is that effective leadership reflects a balance of (1) a leader's traits and skills and (2) a leader's style or behaviors, (3) combined in a way that best fits the followers and is most appropriate for the situation at hand.[13] The idea that leadership is a function of the leader, the followers, and the situation is shown in Figure 13-1.

Essentially, effective leadership depends on who the leader "is" in terms of his or her traits and skills, how the leader behaves, and the appropriateness of the two given the situation the leader is facing. The situation refers to anything from the task being done to the environment the group is facing. Followers' perceptions of the leader and their willingness to let the leader influence them also determine leadership effectiveness. No one can be a leader without followers, and only the followers determine whether someone will lead them.

Because it took some time for researchers to identify and assemble these three pieces of the puzzle, many theories of leadership have been developed. Because effective leadership is contingent on many different things, leadership theories tend to build on previous theories. To understand modern thinking on leadership, we will review the importance of leaders' characteristics, the importance of what leaders do, and what ultimately influences a leader's effectiveness.

Figure 13-1

Three Contingencies of Effective Leadership

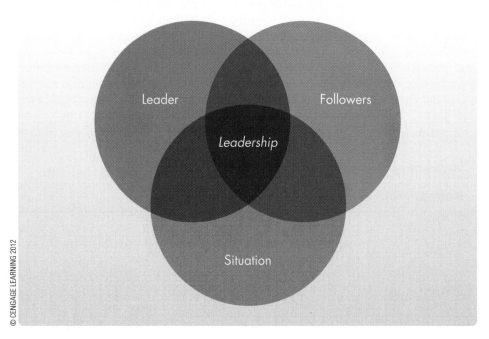

© CENGAGE LEARNING 2012

DO LEADERS SHARE CERTAIN CHARACTERISTICS?

Think for a moment about several people who you consider to be great leaders. How would you describe them? Do they share any traits, skills, or other characteristics? When researchers first started studying leadership, they began by asking similar questions. So are there any traits, skills, or other characteristics that tend to be associated with leadership?

Are Certain Traits or Skills Associated with Leadership?

When asked to name people they consider leaders, most people can easily come up with names such as Martin Luther King Jr., Margaret Thatcher, Mahatma Gandhi, and Oprah Winfrey. But why are these people considered leaders? When asked, many people explain that these leaders have charisma, intelligence, a strong vision, and a determination to achieve their goals. But do personality traits or skills really predict who will become a leader?

Because people differ in so many ways, it is natural to think that some people have certain characteristics or special gifts that enhance their abilities to lead. The first systematic research studies on leadership investigated individual *traits*, or a person's unchanging characteristics that predispose them to act in a certain way, including intelligence, birth order, socioeconomic status, and child-raising practices.[14] These early attempts to isolate specific leadership traits were generally unsuccessful and led to the tentative conclusion that no single characteristic distinguishes leaders from anyone else. In fact, the search for universal leadership traits failed because the most desirable leadership traits depend on the nature of the group being led.[15]

Later research on leadership traits and skills focused on broader characteristics and had better success in identifying some traits and skills relevant to successful leadership. Leaders seem to have higher internal control orientation, emotional maturity,[16] intelligence, self-confidence, determination, integrity, and interpersonal skill.[17] Although research has found that trait-like individual differences including creativity, charisma, self-confidence, integrity, and energy as well as skills including oral and written communication skills, interpersonal skills, administrative skills, and problem-solving and decision-making skills are consistent predictors of effective leadership, the effects tend to be modest.[18] Indeed, it is hard to imagine someone without these characteristics being a successful leader. Table 13-2 describes these and other leadership traits and skills.

Southwest Airlines CEO Herb Kelleher was famous among Southwest employees for "walking the walk, not just talking the talk." Kelleher helped gate crews every time he traveled, participated in a wide range of company events, spoke often with customers and employees of all ranks, and paid special attention to hiring and promoting the right people. As one union leader stated, "How many CEOs do you know who come into a cleaner's break room at 3 a.m. on a Sunday passing out doughnuts or putting on a pair of overalls to clean a plane?"[19]

HP executive vice president Ann Livermore believes that the best leaders excel at six skills. They have a winning attitude, a passion for customers, an ability to collaborate across boundaries, a global mindset, an ability

traits

A person's unchanging characteristics that predispose them to act in a certain way

Table 13-2

Traits and Skills of Leaders

Determination:	Leaders overcome obstacles and achieve their goals through initiative, drive, dominance, and a motivation to achieve.
Flexibility:	Effective leaders use different styles and motivational techniques depending on the situation and the person being led.
Emotional maturity:	Effective leaders control their emotions rather than letting their emotions control them.
Energy levels:	Leaders have the energy to work hard toward their goals and can create excitement and enthusiasm in others.
Integrity:	Leaders who behave honestly and earn the trust of followers are more effective at motivating them.
Intelligence:	Leaders must scan, interpret, and integrate large amounts of information; identify patterns; and devise courses of action based on the information.
Internal control orientation:	Leaders tend to believe that they are able to control their environment rather than merely reacting to things that happen around them.
Job-relevant knowledge:	Leaders make decisions and set appropriate goals and strategies based on their understanding of how their unit and firm work.
Self-confidence:	Leaders who demonstrate self-confidence and a belief that their chosen course of action is correct develop followers who are more committed.
Sociability and interpersonal skill:	Leaders who are good communicators are able to build trusting relationships with followers

Source: Based on Zaccaro, S.J., Kemp, C. & Bader, P. (2004). Leader Traits and Attributes, In Antonakis, J., Cianciolo, A.T. & Sternberg, R.J. (Eds.), *The Nature of Leadership,* 101–125 London: Sage; Northouse, P.G. (2000). *Leadership: Theory and Practice, 2nd Ed.,* London: Sage; and Yukl, G. (2002). *Leadership in Organizations, (5th Ed.),* Upper Saddle River, NJ: Prentice Hall.

WILLIAM THOMAS CAIN/ GETTY IMAGES NEWS / GETTY IMAGES

Southwest Airlines CEO Herb Kelleher was famous among Southwest employees for "walking the talk." He helped gate crews, participated in company events, and spoke with customers and employees of all ranks.

to leverage diversity, and a talent for finding the right balance point between overly rapid decision making and paralysis by analysis. With those skills, "great leaders can make an organization work like a system. They can pick a direction; excite people to move in that direction and turn individual stars into a high-performing team, like a sports team. Then you get a really powerful group."[20]

Is Gender Important to Leadership?

Despite making up more than 45 percent of the U.S. workforce, women led only eighteen Fortune 500 companies in 2012.[21] Excuses that have been offered as to why so few women reach the top in organizations include: women not being in managerial positions long enough, lacking managerial experience, being less suited to demanding jobs, and not being sufficiently qualified. Research has not supported these excuses.[22] So why are most women managers having trouble breaking into the top ranks?

One constraint facing women in management may stem from *institutional biases*, or patterns of preferences inherent in organizations that create barriers. For example, managers often prefer hiring and promoting people who are similar to themselves. Because most managers are male, they tend to prefer that other managers also be male. Whether conscious or unconscious, this type of bias contributes to the glass ceiling effect by restricting women's access to managerial jobs.

Women leaders often emphasize inaccurate gender *stereotypes* as a key barrier to their advancement.[23] Stereotypes are generalizations people make to differentiate groups of people, such as believing that men are better leaders than women. However, men and women are much more similar in personality, communication, ability, and leadership than commonly believed.[24] Several reviews of studies of gender differences in leadership have found many more similarities than differences across males and females,[25] although research does suggest that males tend to punish subordinates more harshly than women.[26] It is important to note that while males and females may differ in respect to participative management and punishment tendencies, research has found males and females to be equally effective as leaders.

Another problem may be that people frequently compare women to an *ideal leadership style* that favors autocratic men. It is common for both men and women to view competitive (stereotypically masculine) characteristics as managerial, and cooperative and communicative (stereotypically feminine) characteristics as nonmanagerial.[27] Because men are more likely to exhibit the masculine characteristics thought to reflect better managerial and leadership skills, they are more likely than women to be viewed as appropriate leaders.

Research does suggest that many women use a more participative style and have better interpersonal skills than many males.[28] It is interesting to note, however, that a more participative style may actually be *more* appropriate for today's challenges of managing diversity and leading empowered teams. As Rosabeth Moss Kanter put it, "women get high ratings on exactly those skills needed to succeed in the global Information Age, where teamwork and partnering are so important."[29] Rather than changing how women lead, it may be more appropriate to change perceptions about what it means to be an effective leader and what characteristics and styles are required to become one.

WHAT DO LEADERS DO?

If leaders cannot easily be identified by their traits, perhaps we can identify leaders by what it is that they *do*. It is important to note that perceptions of how managers should lead differ internationally.[30] French managers, for example, view their work as an intellectual challenge depending on brain power. This contrasts with the Western view of management as an interpersonally demanding role requiring ideas and plans to be "sold" upward and downward using interpersonal skills.[31]

After the early leadership researchers ran out of steam in their search for traits, attention turned to what leaders did and how they behaved, especially toward followers. This led to the identification of various *leadership behaviors and styles*. We now turn our attention to understanding leadership styles and behaviors.

Ohio State and University of Michigan Studies

In the 1950s, Ralph Stogdill and his Ohio State University colleagues[32] and Rensis Likert and his team at the University of Michigan's Survey Research Center[33] identified two dimensions of leadership style: concern for task results and concern for people.

Concern for task results emphasizes the achievement of concrete goals. Leaders look for ways to organize people and activities that will best accomplish these goals. Concern for task results includes planning, organizing, and defining the required tasks. Setting goals and clearly communicating them to the group is one example. When Steve Ballmer took the reins of Microsoft, he initiated structure by implementing an online performance appraisal system (there had previously been no formal performance appraisal process).[34]

Concern for people emphasizes the social and emotional needs of individuals. Leaders with a high concern for people generate trust, respect, work satisfaction, and self-esteem by being respectful and friendly.

The Leader Behavior Description Questionnaire (LBDQ) was developed to measure these two styles. One of the major research findings was that effective leaders address both the task and the human aspects of their organizations. Although people tend to be more satisfied when working with people-oriented leaders,[35] task performance is not necessarily better.[36] And although leaders high in concern for task results tend to have higher-performing groups, this is not always true. Subordinates of leaders who are very task-oriented can have lower morale unless the leader is also high in concern for people.[37]

Like Costco's Jim Sinegal, featured in this chapter's *Real World Challenge*, the first two CEOs at McDonald's, Ray Kroc and Fred Turner, demanded a lot from their employees. But these leaders never considered themselves too important to perform even the lowest task, including picking up trash. That leadership style helped make both of these companies successful, and it is still an important part of their cultures.[38]

Leaders must take a balanced approach in their concern for task results and concern for employees. The best-performing supervisors focus on the human aspects of their subordinates' problems and on building effective workgroups with high performance goals. Higher-performing managers are also more facilitative than directive, and use a participative style in making decisions that take recommendations from the team into account.[39]

Blake and Mouton's Managerial Grid

Robert Blake and Jane Mouton[40] developed a two-dimensional *managerial grid* that has become a classic way to illustrate the behavioral approach to leadership. The grid diagrams leadership styles based on the leader's concern for people and concern for task results.

Figure 13-2 shows the grid. "Concern for people" is on the vertical axis and "concern for production" (concern for results) is on the horizontal axis. Both have a range of 0 to 9. Concern for people reflects the leader's consideration of team members' needs and preferences when deciding how to best accomplish a task. Concern for production reflects a leader's focus on efficiency, productivity, and goals when deciding how to best accomplish a task.

Each cell of the grid contains a numerical rating reflecting the manager's concern for results and concern for people, which are independent of each other. For example, a manager high in concern for production and low in concern for people would be considered a controlling leader. General Motors Chairman Edward E. Whitacre, Jr., can be considered this type of leader. In describing Whitacre, CEO Bob Lutz says, "He cajoles, motivates, and uses the occasional veiled threat to induce fear."[41]

Although Blake and Mouton considered the ideal to be a 9, 9-oriented manager who integrates a high concern for both task and people, there is little evidence supporting this style as most effective in all situations.[42] Effective leadership requires more than the use of a particular style regardless of the context—the nature of the followers and the situation are important as well.

Figure 13-2

Blake and Mouton's Managerial Grid[43]

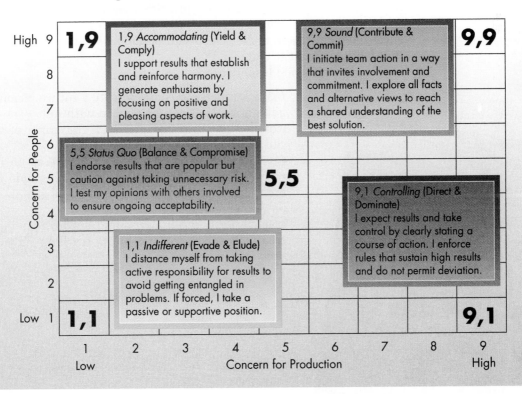

As a new manager you can use this grid to understand how you tend to lead, and identify skills you can further develop. Do you always focus on how to most efficiently accomplish each task without considering the preferences of your staff? Or do you tend to be more concerned about group harmony and focus on assigning tasks based on the preferences of your staff? The grid illustrates how placing too much emphasis on one or the other can compromise team effectiveness. Sometimes, however, there are crises in which being high in both concern for people and concern for production is not ideal, and a focus on either people or task results is necessary.

Transformational and Transactional Leadership

transformational leadership

Leadership that inspires followers to adopt the values and goals of the leader and put aside their own self-interests for the good of the organization

Another way to think about leadership is to consider what the leader is trying to accomplish. Some leaders focus on making incremental improvements to the status quo. Other leaders focus on making large-scale revolutionary changes to an organization. Organizations requiring change can benefit from *transformational leadership*[44] that changes the values and priorities of followers, motivating them to achieve more by doing things in new ways. Transformational leaders inspire followers through a clear mission, optimism, enthusiasm, and emotional appeals.

When Steve Jobs told his team at Apple that they were making a dent in the universe, they believed they were making a dent in the universe.[45] Transformational leaders provide personal support and encouragement, set a good personal example, and behave ethically. Followers then connect deeply to the mission and seek ways to improve their performance. John F. Kennedy and Gandhi are good examples of transformational leaders.

Transformational leadership affects a wide range of employee factors (including motivation, satisfaction, and commitment) and organizational outcomes (including business unit performance).[46] Transformational leaders can influence followers to change their priorities, set new goals, and develop confidence in their abilities by giving subordinates developmental work experiences, inspiring them to do their best, and demonstrating positive behaviors that followers want to emulate.[47]

Transformational leaders are:[48]

1. *Inspirational* and communicate a future vision of the organization that can be shared with followers. Visionary explanations help to depict what the employee workgroup can accomplish.
2. *Considerate* and treat each employee as an individual rather than simply as a member of the group. A transformational leader tries to bring out the strengths of each individual employee.
3. *Intellectually stimulating* and encourage employees to creatively solve problems by approaching old and familiar problems in new ways.

NASA ARCHIVE / ALAMY

John F. Kennedy is commonly cited as a transformational leader who inspired change.

Transactional leadership is based on a transaction or exchange of something of value that the leader possesses or controls and that the follower wants in return for his or her services. Transactional leaders rely on a transaction or exchange process in which organizational resources are used to obtain desired employee behaviors. By offering jobs in exchange for work done, or bonuses in exchange for extra effort or good performance, leaders are able to influence and motivate others.

transactional leadership
Leadership based on a reciprocal exchange of something of value

With transactional leadership, employees comply because of contingent reinforcement, but with transformational leadership, employees comply because they are personally committed to the leader's goals. In many ways transactional leadership reflects the practice of management whereas transformational leadership reflects the practice of leadership.

Transformational leadership and transactional leadership complement each other,[49] and the choice of which to use depends on the situation. The best leaders are both transformational and transactional.[50] The transactional style can work well for short-term goals when both leader and followers understand and are in agreement about which tasks are important. Because transformational leadership results in employees' adopting the leader's mission, vision, and goals as their own, it is more effective for long-term goals and organizational change. If transformational leaders are unsuccessful in gaining compliance by appealing to the values of the followers or peers, they may resort to a transactional style to get things done.[51]

SO WHAT
Effective leaders use both transactional and transformational leadership depending on the situation.

Early leadership research focused on transactional leadership.[52] But as one expert stated, "Transactional leaders do not generate passion and excitement, and they do not empower or inspire individuals to transcend their own self-interest for the good of the organization."[53] Today, researchers are devoting more time to understanding transformational leadership.[54]

Charismatic Leadership

Charismatic leaders[55] are idealized by followers who develop strong emotional attachments to them. Charismatic leaders try to increase followers' commitment to ideological goals and also their commitment to the leader.[56] Charisma helps leaders to gain followers' respect, pride, trust, and confidence. Inspirational motivation is used to communicate high expectations and focus efforts on important objectives.

charismatic leaders
Leaders idealized by followers who develop strong emotional attachments to them

Charismatic leaders are self-confident, dominant, extraverted, and possess strong convictions in their beliefs and moral righteousness.[57] Charismatic leaders articulate a vision and are willing to take personal risks in the name of their beliefs. They also attract followers through a combination of personality, charm, and behaviors that show sensitivity to each follower's needs and to the environment.[58] Charismatic leaders exercise strong social influence over others through their values, beliefs, and behaviors.[59]

Charismatic leadership during the early stages of a group's life can influence the group's belief that it will be successful, enhancing the likelihood that it will perform well.[60] Although substantial research has found charismatic leadership to spur high performance and follower satisfaction,[61] it is not always needed. Charisma appears to be most influential when the environment has a high degree of uncertainty with accompanying stress or when the followers' task is ideological in some way.[62] Transformational leaders can be charismatic, but unlike transformational leaders who want to create change, charismatic leaders may not want to change anything.

Level 5 Leadership

Level 5 leadership requires a leader to use a combination of transformational and transactional leadership styles and channel their ambition away from themselves and into the goal of building a great company. It requires a combination of personal humility and strong professional determination.[63] Level 5 leaders are humble and willing to take the blame for failure while simultaneously setting high standards and demonstrating an unwavering resolve to do whatever it takes to produce the best long-term results.

When Bob Moore, founder of Oregon-based Bob's Red Mill Natural Foods, gave the company to his 209 employees after more than thirty years in business, he said, "It's the only business decision that I could make. I don't think there's anybody worthy to run this company but the people who built it."[64]

David Maxwell spent nine years turning around and leading financial services company Fannie Mae. When he retired, his retirement package, which had grown to be worth $20 million because of Fannie Mae's strong performance, drew the attention of Congress (Fannie Mae operates under a government charter). Maxwell responded by writing a letter to his successor expressing concern that the future of the company could be jeopardized and asked that the remaining $5.5 million balance be contributed to the Fannie Mae foundation for low-income housing.[65] This type of leadership has gained popularity among executives, and some consider it to be the ultimate leadership style.

Ethical Leadership

Ethical leadership is "the demonstration of normatively appropriate conduct through personal actions and interpersonal relationships, and the promotion of such conduct to followers through two-way communication, reinforcement, and decision making."[66] How are followers influenced by leaders' ethical behavior? Leaders set an example for others whether they intend to or not. Employees pay attention to company leaders and the ethical standards they set (or fail to set) in part because leaders are prominent authority figures able to gain employees' attention and hold them accountable to ethical standards.[67]

Leaders differ in the extent to which they focus on the ethics of their behaviors. Google cofounder Sergey Brin said, "Obviously everyone wants to be successful, but I want to be looked back on as being very innovative, very trusted and ethical and ultimately making a big difference in the world."[68]

Because ethical leaders are caring and fair, followers' relationships with them are built upon social exchange and reciprocity norms.[69] An ethical leader's followers want to reciprocate the leader's supportive treatment with their own ethical behavior.[70] Research has found that employees' perceptions of their supervisors' ethical leadership are positively related to their willingness to report problems to management, job commitment, and satisfaction with their supervisor.[71]

WHAT INFLUENCES A LEADER'S EFFECTIVENESS?

As we have seen, an effective leader does not rely on a single preferred style. Leadership is more complex—good leaders adapt to the situation, take into account the motivation and capability of followers, evaluate the challenges of the task, and consider the organizational environment. A good manager uses many different leadership styles over the course of a day depending on the nature of the problem and the people being led.

Many of the early writers on leadership styles argued that greater decision participation made followers more satisfied. But this idea did not hold up in practice.[72] There were many inconsistencies between studies, and it was hard to say that any particular style of leadership always enabled groups to work better. Perhaps the biggest problem, though, was one shared with those who looked for traits: ignoring the context or setting in which the style was used. The same leadership style is not likely to work equally well in a corporate boardroom, on a construction site, and in a hospital emergency room. The influence of the followers and the situation made the search for any "one best way to lead" futile. Leadership effectiveness is clearly contingent on the leader's traits, the followers, and the situation.

Researchers eventually began to pursue the idea that leadership needs differ depending on the situation. Researchers began to believe that different contexts required particular types of leadership. This meant that leaders had to develop an ability to work in different ways, and change their style to be contingent on the situation and the followers. We next discuss various *contingency theories of leadership* that acknowledge that the appropriateness of any leadership style depends on the nature of the followers and the situation.

contingency theories of leadership Leadership theories that acknowledge that the appropriateness of any leadership style depends on the nature of the followers and the situation

Fiedler's Leader Match Model

Fred Fiedler[73] argued that leader effectiveness depends on two interacting factors: *leadership style* and the *degree to which the situation gives the leader control and influence*. The *leader match model* proposes that a person's leadership style is part of who that person is and cannot be changed. Fiedler did not believe that leaders can adopt different styles in different situations. Instead, he proposed two ways to make leaders more effective: *match* them to the situation to which they are best suited, or *change the context* to suit the leader's style.

Three things are important in understanding the context:

1. *Leader-follower relations*. Fiedler felt that this was the key: "A leader who is liked, accepted, and trusted by his members will find it easy to make his [or her] influence felt."[74]
2. *Task structure*. If the goals, methods, and performance standards of a task are clear, then it is more likely that leaders will be able to exert influence.
3. *Position power*. If an organization or group confers powers on the leader to get the job done, then this may well increase the influence of the leader.

According to Fiedler's model, effective leadership is contingent on matching the leader's style to the setting, and certain styles will be effective in certain situations. Task-oriented leaders will do well when the situation is extremely favorable or extremely unfavorable for the leader (where leader-member relations, task structure, and leader position power are all very high or very low), and relationship-oriented leaders will do well in more moderate situations. In favorable situations, the leader can get away with focusing solely on the task, and in unfavorable situations, the leader has no choice but to focus on the task. A more people-oriented leader is appropriate in the middle range where these three contextual factors are mixed.

Fiedler thought of leadership style as a continuum, with task motivation at one end and relationship motivation at the other. He developed the least-preferred coworker (LPC) scale to assess a leader's style. Leaders describe their least preferred coworker using a list of adjectives. Leaders who describe their least preferred coworker favorably (pleasant, friendly, enthusiastic) are considered "high LPC" and are more people-oriented. Leaders who describe their least preferred coworker unfavorably (inefficient, gloomy, uncooperative) are considered "low LPC" and are more task-oriented. Moderate LPC leaders are not clearly addressed in the model. Fiedler states that middle LPC individuals must "determine for themselves which LPC fits them best."[75] This chapter's *Improve Your Skills* feature provides an opportunity for you to self-assess your leadership style according to Fiedler's LPC scale. Table 13-3 will help you apply your score to understand where you might be most effective as a leader according to Fiedler's model.

Fiedler's leader match model has been criticized because it does not explain why some people are more effective in different situations. It is also not entirely clear what the LPC scale actually measures. For example, some people may have had very different experiences with their LPC than others and this can influence responses to the measure. A fair amount of research has produced mixed results. Although popular in management training programs, the usefulness of the leader match model, including its more recent variants, remains uncertain although generally positive.[76]

So how would you apply Fiedler's ideas? As Fiedler once said, "If you learn to avoid situations in which you are likely to fail, you're bound to be a success."[77] Since he views a leader's abilities as fixed, group performance can be improved in only two ways: replace the leader or change the situation. The leader can be changed to fit the situation, much as a baseball coach changes pitchers to match the next batter. Leaders could be assigned to groups best led by their task- and relationship-orientation profile. Alternatively, the situation could be changed to fit the current leader's profile. Increasing task structure or giving the leader more or less power to control salary increases, discipline, or promotions could improve the group's performance.

Hersey's Situational Leadership Model

Paul Hersey and Kenneth Blanchard[79] first published the 'Life Cycle' theory of leadership in 1969 to help leaders decide how to adapt their balance of task- and relationship-oriented behaviors to a given situation. The sole variable considered by this theory was team members' 'maturity.' Maturity did not refer to team members' age or emotional stability, but to the ability to act independently, desire for achievement, willingness to accept responsibility, and task related ability and experience. The theory focused on developing team members' leadership skills.

Subsequently, the Center for Leadership Studies improved the theory to support the development of leadership skills that addressed the demands of the accelerating global business environment. Rather than using 'maturity' for diagnosis, the Center discovered that the simplest and most easily quantifiable method to assess the performance needs of an individual or group could be distilled into what Hersey called 'performance readiness,' or the amount of willingness and ability demonstrated while performing a specific task.

Willingness is composed of varying degrees of confidence, commitment, and motivation. All three components must be present before the person or group can move forward into performance readiness. For example, imagine Carlos, who is completely committed to the job, quality, and the organization. Carlos may be motivated to do well and at the same time be insecure about being able to do the job. Even though Carlos' commitment and motivation are strong, his insecurity will have to be addressed before he can move forward in performance readiness. The most common error in diagnosing willingness is to view

UNDERSTAND YOURSELF

LEAST PREFERRED COWORKER SCALE

Think of the person *with whom you can work least well*. This may be a person you currently work with or someone you knew in the past. This person is not necessarily the person you like least well, but he or she should be the person with whom you had the most difficulty in getting a job done.

The following questionnaire asks you to describe this person as she or he appears to you. Look at the words at both ends of the line before you mark one box with an "x." Please remember that there are *no right* or wrong answers. Work quickly; your first answer is usually the most accurate. Do not omit any items, and mark only one answer for each item. When you are finished, add the numbers appearing under each line you marked with an "x." Scoring instructions are at the bottom of the table.

Pleasant	8	7	6	5	4	3	2	1	Unpleasant
Friendly	8	7	6	5	4	3	2	1	Unfriendly
Rejecting	1	2	3	4	5	6	7	8	Accepting
Helpful	8	7	6	5	4	3	2	1	Frustrating
Unenthusiastic	1	2	3	4	5	6	7	8	Enthusiastic
Tense	1	2	3	4	5	6	7	8	Relaxed
Distant	1	2	3	4	5	6	7	8	Close
Cold	1	2	3	4	5	6	7	8	Warm
Cooperative	8	7	6	5	4	3	2	1	Uncooperative
Supportive	8	7	6	5	4	3	2	1	Hostile
Boring	1	2	3	4	5	6	7	8	Interesting
Quarrelsome	1	2	3	4	5	6	7	8	Harmonious
Self-assured	8	7	6	5	4	3	2	1	Hesitant
Efficient	8	7	6	5	4	3	2	1	Inefficient
Gloomy	1	2	3	4	5	6	7	8	Cheerful
Open	8	7	6	5	4	3	2	1	Guarded

Scoring and Interpretation: Those with scores *above 78* are considered high LPCs and are more people-oriented, while those with scores *below 29* are considered low LPCs and are more task-oriented.

Source: Fiedler, F.E., "*A Theory of Leadership Effectiveness*" (New York: McGraw-Hill, 1967), p. 41. Reproduced with permission of the author.

Table 13-3

Matching the Leader to the Situation Using the LPC Score

Labor-Management Relations	Task Structure	Position Power	Best Leader LPC For This Situation
Good	Structured	Strong	Low
Good	Structured	Weak	Low
Good	Unstructured	Strong	Low
Good	Unstructured	Weak	Low
Poor	Structured	Strong	High
Poor	Structured	Weak	High
Poor	Unstructured	Strong	High
Poor	Unstructured	Weak	High

someone who is insecure or apprehensive as unmotivated. Given the dramatically different approaches a manager would take to increase motivation as opposed to insecurity, it is critical to get this diagnosis correct.

Ability is determined by the amount of knowledge, experience, and demonstrated skill the individual or group brings to the task. The actual display of ability is what matters—performance readiness should not be diagnosed based on the leader's beliefs of what the individual or group should know. A frequent leadership error is to assume that knowledge exists and hold the group or individual accountable for skills they have not had an opportunity to fully learn and demonstrate.

It was with these changes that Hersey's Situational Leadership® Model was born in 1980. Since then Hersey's Situational Leadership® Model has continued to undergo refinement. Figure 13-3 illustrates the current model. As the follower moves from low to moderate and high performance readiness, the best leader influence behaviors move from telling to selling to participating, and ultimately to delegating.

- *Telling:* making the decision and telling the group what to do. This style works best when followers lack confidence or don't know how to do something. The leader must be directive and task focused in order to accomplish the task. Abercrombie and Fitch CEO Mike Jeffries is known for interviewing every model who will appear in the company's catalog, approving all merchandise, and even describing how clothes should be folded in stores.[80]
- *Selling:* making the decision alone, but explaining to the group the reasons for the decision, then helping followers to achieve task completion by persuading them and providing opportunities to learn more about the task. This style works well when followers have minimal competence but are confident and willing to do the job.
- *Participating:* asking group members for input but making the final decision alone. This style is most effective when followers have the ability to do something but are insecure and therefore require emotional support. The leader doesn't have to show followers how to do the task but must encourage commitment to it.
- *Delegating:* letting group members decide what to do. This style works best when followers are confident and know how to do it so they only need to be asked to accomplish it. Phil Knight, the founder of Nike, has been described as the ultimate delegator, often giving his executives the freedom to make decisions that can dramatically affect the company. [81]

CASE STUDY

Leading a Police Force Transformation

When Melvin Wearing obtained the Chief of Police position he had been dreaming of for 28 years, he stepped into a huge challenge. His predecessor had undermined the department's credibility. Morale was terrible, and communication between the chief's office and the officers was often through union grievances.

Wearing had previously been an assistant chief, and the other officers respected him and called him "compassionate," "humanistic," and "a source of inspiration and pride." On his first day, Wearing visited each of the day's four lineups (the roll call of officers that begins each shift), wearing his dress blues for the occasion. He wanted to show his pride in police work and support of the officers. He also clearly communicated to his officers that he did not want them to even *think* about messing around. This was not just a matter of restoring the force's credibility; as the department's first Black chief, he knew that he too would be under special scrutiny. He quickly moved to upgrade the department's technology, installed air conditioning and laptops in cruisers, and upgraded office equipment.

Wearing also raised standards in the training academy and increased the department's diversity. By 2002, women and minorities made up 51 percent of New Haven's sworn personnel, up from 24 percent in 1990. In 1997, New Haven logged 13,950 major crimes; in 2001, the city had only 9,322. The department has even earned four national and international awards for community policing. Chief Wearing understands that he has to keep making an impact: "The real challenge for me is to sustain this over a long period of time."[78]

Questions:

1. Explain how Chief Wearing can exhibit a transformational leadership style in his role as police chief.
2. Describe the environment facing Chief Wearing in terms of leader-member relations, task structure, and position power. Using Fiedler's model, what leadership style do you think is most appropriate given the situation you just described? Does this style match Chief Wearing's?
3. If you were Chief Wearing, how might you use the information you learned in this chapter to enhance the diversity of the police force?

Figure 13-3

Situational Leadership Model[83]

	FOLLOWER READINESS		
LOW	MODERATE		HIGH
Incapable and insecure followers	Incapable but confident followers	Capable but insecure followers	Capable and confident followers

TELLING	SELLING	PARTICIPATING	DELEGATING
Give specific instructions and supervise closely	Clarify and explain decisions as needed	Share ideas with followers and facilitate their decision making	Empower followers to make the decisions

	TELLING	SELLING	PARTICIPATING	DELEGATING
Task Behaviors	High	High	Low	Low
Relationship Behaviors	Low	High	High	Low

Although research support has been limited,[82] Hersey's Situational Leadership Model is logical and intuitively appealing. It is also widely used in management training and development programs. The idea that leaders should change their style to best fit the current situation and the needs of followers is a good one. The idea that leaders should develop both followers' skills and confidence is also important. Using the correct style in lower-readiness situations can develop followers' confidence and abilities and allows leaders to be less directive as followers mature. Delegating is also a critical leadership skill. James Cash Penney once said, "The surest way for an executive to kill himself is to refuse to learn how, and when, and to whom to delegate work."

Path-Goal Theory. As Microsoft Australia chief executive Steve Vamos said, "The role of the leader is to create environments where others can do great work—and then to get out of the way." Path-goal theory emphasizes that the leader's job is to help followers attain their goals and to provide appropriate direction and support to ensure that followers' goals are consistent with those of the group and organization.[84] *Path-goal theory* is based on the expectancy theory of motivation, which proposes that motivation to exert effort is based on a person's belief that (1) he or she has the *ability* to accomplish a goal, (2) goal accomplishment will lead to *rewards*, and (3) these rewards are attractive or *valued*.

> "The role of the leader is to create environments where others can do great work—and then to get out of the way." —*Steve Vamos, Microsoft Australia Chief Executive*

By addressing all three components, leaders can clarify subordinates' path to the goal. Path-goal theory reflects the belief that effective leaders increase the personal rewards subordinates receive for attaining goals and clarify the path to these goals by reducing roadblocks. The core assumption is that subordinates will be motivated if they think they can do their work and get a favorable outcome for doing so.

Path-goal theory originally focused on the leadership dimensions of concern for the task and concern for people.[85] It now focuses on four leadership styles:[86]

1. *Directive leadership*: letting subordinates know what the leader expects of them, giving specific guidance as to what to do and how to do it, and scheduling the work to be done.
2. *Supportive leadership*: being "friendly and approachable" and showing concern for the status and well-being of subordinates.
3. *Participative leadership*: soliciting subordinates' suggestions and input. When Anne Mulcahy, chair at Xerox, took over the company, it was $18 billion in debt and the shareholders wanted to sell it in pieces because it did not seem "fixable." She spent a year asking everyone—including other companies' heads, her salespeople, the engineers, and customer service employees—what they thought should be done.[87]
4. *Achievement-oriented leadership*: setting challenging goals, expecting subordinates to perform at their highest level, continuously seeking improvements in performance, and showing confidence that subordinates will assume responsibility.[88]

The leader's job is to help subordinates reach their goals by providing the guidance, coaching, support, and rewards lacking in the environment that are necessary for effective and satisfying performance.[89] Based on (1) task structure, (2) employee morale, and (3) employee self-confidence, the theory suggests which style is most appropriate for leaders.

Essentially, to be effective a leader has to structure ambiguous tasks, be supportive and considerate when employees lack confidence or are demoralized, and always clarify how job effort will lead to rewards. The idea is that if employees do not know what to do, think they cannot do it, or do not see how effort leads to rewards, they will not be motivated to do the job.

Despite making a lot of intuitive sense, research on path-goal theory has yielded mixed results.[90] Supportive leadership tends to have a positive relationship regardless of the task, and the results for directive leadership generally have not supported the theory. Research is insufficient to draw conclusions about the situational factors influencing the effectiveness of participative and achievement-oriented leadership.[91]

Leader-Member Exchange Theory

Managers behave quite differently toward different subordinates, depending on the quality of their relationship. *Leader-member exchange theory* (LMX) describes how leaders develop different relationships with different subordinates over time.[92] LMX theory proposes that leaders usually develop a special relationship with a subset of subordinates (the *in-group*). Members of the in-group serve as trusted advisors and assistants and have greater influence, autonomy, and tangible benefits in exchange.

Members of the *out-group* have less or no input into group decisions, and are primarily influenced with position power. Out-group members exchange their compliance with formal role requirements and legitimate requests from the leader for the standard benefits of employment and compensation. Being an out-group member can lead to lower rewards, less autonomy, and less influence.

Leader-member relationships develop over time as the leader interacts with the follower. The leader's perceptions of a follower ultimately determine whether the follower becomes part of the in-group or out-group.[93] When a new employee enters the organization, the leader assesses his or her talents and abilities and assigns the employee a role in the group. The employee then negotiates that role in a role-making process that develops respect and trust. This could explain why employees with a more proactive personality tend to establish higher-quality exchange relationships with their supervisors.[94] Ultimately, a pattern of exchange with the leader becomes routine.

The follower's abilities, interpersonal compatibility with the leader, and ingratiation behaviors all influence the relationship development process and ultimate LMX. The leader's liking and trust of the employee also contribute to LMX. Figure 13-4 illustrates LMX.

LMX theory is more descriptive than prescriptive, and is unclear how desirable it is to have sharply differentiated in-groups and out-groups. Although the theory does not specify what pattern of exchange relationships is optimal for effective leadership, research has shown that in-group members do have greater loyalty and higher performance than out-group members.[95] Members of a clear out-group are likely to feel resentment, withdraw effort and participation,[96] and are more likely to quit.[97] The quality of leader-member relations also influences the degree to which managers are willing to empower workers.[98]

It is clear that supervisors do form different quality relationships with their subordinates.[99] All organizations have "in" and "out" groups, and it is not necessary for leaders to treat all subordinates the same—effective leaders relate differently to various people and give them different amounts of influence. But each team member should feel important and respected rather than feeling like a "second-class citizen."[100]

Figure 13-4

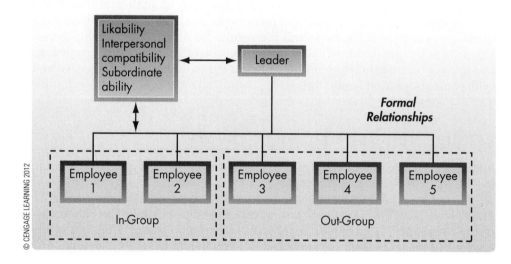

Leader-Member Exchange (LMX)

© CENGAGE LEARNING 2012

As a leader, having the loyal support of a trusted in-group can be nice, but it may cause you to miss out on the potential contributions of the out-group members. As Andy Pearson, CEO of Tricon Global Restaurants, Inc., the largest restaurant chain in the world, commented, "If I could only unleash the power of everybody in the organization, instead of just a few people, what could we accomplish? We'd be a much better company."[101] Research has found that group effectiveness decreases when leaders treat individuals within the group differently.[102]

Substitutes for Leadership

Leadership substitutes theory[103] proposes that the importance of formal leaders is reduced by aspects of the situation called *substitutes* and *neutralizers*. **Leadership substitutes** are factors that make leadership unnecessary, such as empowered or highly competent employees. For example, a high-performing call center team that has been together for years may not need a leader to provide instruction or set goals for the team. **Leadership neutralizers** are factors that make leadership impossible, such as a union contract that prohibits a supervisor from giving workers incentives for higher performance.

leadership substitutes
Factors that make leadership unnecessary

leadership neutralizers
Factors that make leadership impossible

Substitutes for leadership can come from subordinates (e.g., their abilities and need for independence), the task (e.g., if it is routine or intrinsically satisfying), and the organization (e.g., cohesive workgroups or a high degree of formalization or inflexibility). Research has supported the idea that intrinsically satisfying work and task-provided performance feedback prevent a leader's supportive behaviors from making a difference in task performance.[104] It is likely that substitutes exist for some but not all leader activities.

A good example of leadership substitutes occurred in the Coast Guard after hurricane Katrina in 2005. While Coast Guard employees usually specialize in certain types of operations, they are cross-trained so that they can do other jobs. This allows teams to form quickly in emergencies, with everyone knowing what each job entails and how it fits into overall operations. After Katrina, Coast Guard crews rescued more than 33,000 people in Louisiana, Mississippi, and Alabama, despite a nearly complete loss of connectivity for extended periods between Air Station New Orleans and the chain of command. The complex operation successfully continued because of the employees' clear objectives, united effort, and flexibility. These factors served as leadership substitutes and reduced the need for centralized leadership.[105]

Leadership substitutes can be particularly useful if you are a higher-level leader and are unable to find talented managers to hire for lower-level positions. By incorporating some of the leadership substitutes, you may be able to at least partially compensate for the lack of leadership at lower organizational levels.

Followership

When we think about leadership, we tend to describe only the leader. But successful leadership depends on dedicated followers.[106] Leaders and followers exist in a reciprocal, interdependent relationship, and each exists only because of the other. Although we defined leadership early in this chapter as "guiding and influencing others to work willingly toward the leader's objectives," it also can be thought of as "followers' willing compliance with the goals or vision of the leader."[107] The two statements reflect the two sides of the leadership coin, and illustrate the importance of followership to leadership. Leaders cannot lead if the followers refuse to follow.

How can leaders use the idea of followership to be more effective? Leaders cannot simply walk into a group and expect members to immediately embrace them and their plans. Leaders must first build a support base by winning followers' respect. It appears that leaders do this by accumulating *idiosyncrasy credits*—psychological "brownie points" that allow the leader to take the group in new directions.[108] Studies have found that elected leaders (who have group member backing) are more likely to challenge poor group decisions than are appointed leaders.[109] Without followers' backing, leaders seem to be unable to display genuine leadership in their management of the group, decreasing the group's performance.[110]

Effective followers are important to effective leadership. Because leaders depend on their followers for good information, one of the most important follower characteristics is a willingness to tell the truth.[111]

Followers sometimes share the blame for the effects of damaging leaders. Overly loyal followers have been blamed in part for Merck's turning a blind eye to any study of its blockbuster drug Vioxx that was ultimately linked to increased risk of serious cardiovascular events.[112]

Leadership Effectiveness in Different Cultures

Much of the leadership literature has an American bias. However, cultural factors influence the effectiveness of different leadership styles.[113] For example, some cultures are more individualistic and others focus more on preserving group harmony. Since no one berates an Indonesian in public, when an American oil rig supervisor in Indonesia shouted at an employee to take a boat to shore, a mob of outraged workers chased the supervisor with axes.[114]

Different cultures have different norms and expectations about what is appropriate leader behavior, and about the use of power and influence. It is important to understand the impact of culture on leadership effectiveness not only because companies are increasingly operating in multiple countries, but also because increasing diversity in the workplace means that most Western businesses (even those based in one location) employ people from many cultural backgrounds.[115]

SO WHAT
Formal leaders are not always necessary for high performance.

Consider China as an example of how culture influences the exercise of leadership. In China *guanxi*, which literally means social relationships or social connections, defines in-group and out-group people. Like LMX, *guanxi* determines how individuals treat others—in-group people are benefited and protected while out-group people may be rejected.[116] Followers expect Chinese leaders to have personal contact with subordinates and show their awareness of their subordinates' personal problems and sentiments to gain their loyalty and support.[117] Not only is a manager responsible for business success, but the manager also is supposed to act as a "father" and take care of employees' personal lives.[118] The effective model for leadership in the Chinese system is thus the wise and loving father, which results in a *paternalistic* managerial style[119] in which the leader will take care of subordinates in exchange for responsible behavior and performance. This clearly calls for a different leadership style than would be found in most Western cultures.

A recent large-scale, eleven-year study of global leadership effectiveness investigated the leadership beliefs of people in sixty-two different societal cultures.[120] One of the goals of the research was to identify the ways in which middle managers worldwide distinguish between effective and ineffective leadership. The GLOBE team identified many leader attributes universally seen as being at least somewhat responsible for a leader's effectiveness or ineffectiveness. They also identified a large number of *culturally contingent* attributes, whose effects on leadership effectiveness differed across different cultures. A summary of the effect of culture on perceptions of leaders' attributes is in this chapter's *Global Issues* feature.

HOW DOES TECHNOLOGY INFLUENCE THE PRACTICE OF LEADERSHIP?

Technology is rapidly altering how leaders must engage followers. Leaders must manage work through telecommuting relationships, communicate with employees through e-mail and web-based portals, and support virtual teams that may have members around the world. We next discuss e-leadership and how technology can help new leaders.

E-Leadership

E-leadership addresses the human interactions that now occur through information technology.[121] E-leaders use technology to enhance, improve, and refine relationships in an organization's structure and environment.[122] For example, a participative leader may set up chat rooms to solicit input on an important decision. Anonymous commenting during meetings can encourage honest input, and electronic polls can take the pulse of current opinions.[123]

Like traditional leadership, e-leadership can be inspiring and transformative, even if it takes place through website postings, e-mail, or large-scale web-conferencing. So how is e-leadership different from traditional leadership? Emerging trends in leadership and concerns expressed by current mid- and high-level executives provide some clues.[124]

GLOBAL ISSUES

EFFECT OF CULTURE ON PERCEPTIONS OF LEADERS' ATTRIBUTES

Universal *Positive* Leader Attributes	Universal *Negative* Leader Attributes	*Culturally Contingent* Leader Attributes
Trustworthy	Irritable	Cunning
Dependable	Dictatorial	Sensitive
Excellence-oriented	Uncooperative	Evasive
Honest	Ruthless	Risk taker
Motivating	Egocentric	Ruler

Source: Based on House, R.J. Hanges, P.J., Javidan, M., Dorfman, P.W. & Gupta, V. (2004). *Culture, Leadership, and Organizations: The GLOBE Study of 62 Societies.* London: Sage Publications; Avolio, B.J. & Dodge, G.E. (2000). E-Leadership: Implications for theory, research, and practice. *Leadership Quarterly.* 11(4), 615–668.

First, e-leaders must use more participative styles to address both global and local situational demands of decision making. E-leaders must use technology to gather and distribute information around the globe so that others with specific knowledge or expertise can provide insights about emerging issues. Shell Global Solutions International, the consultancy arm of the energy giant Shell, found that most task- as well as relationship-oriented behaviors are even more important in virtual settings.[125]

Second, e-leaders must become more comfortable with developing, managing, and maintaining relationships without having direct personal control and oversight. A manager of telecommuting call center employees must use technology to keep abreast of employee attitudes, maintain effective working relationships, and evaluate current levels of productivity. This requires a different set of skills than a leader who has an office inside a call center filled with employees. Hiring employees who are able to self-lead,[126] set their own goals, and self-motivate can facilitate the leading of remote employees.

Third, e-leaders must be able to build relationships and trust with and among team members. Because team members do not see each other regularly, opportunities to build trust are limited in virtual teams. It is critical that team members trust the leader as well as each other. E-leaders can build trust by encouraging and considering the input of every team member, and by building the team's belief in its collective ability to accomplish its goals.[127]

Fourth, e-leaders must become increasingly comfortable with using technology to communicate, influence, motivate, and inspire others.[128] Although the vast majority of leaders use e-mail to communicate at least once a day, more sophisticated technologies (such as videoconferencing, web-conferencing, instant messaging, chat rooms, blogs, and wikis) are used less frequently.

SO WHAT

Because virtual teams rarely meet face-to-face, e-leaders must facilitate group processes and relationships through technology.

Blogs are web-logs, or online diaries, that can provide information to a particular subscriber audience. A wiki is a type of website that allows users to easily and collaboratively add and edit content. Wikis are especially well suited for collective writing and collaborative problem solving.

Technology gives managers the opportunity to communicate with employees in a variety of ways. Sometimes technology can enhance a leader's effectiveness, but sometimes it can get in the way.[129] This chapter's *Improve Your Skills* feature gives you some tips for deciding when technology is an appropriate medium of communication.

Let's now look at how technology can help new leaders become effective more quickly.

How Can Technology Help New Leaders?

New leaders often have a lot to learn before they can get down to the business of leading. They have to learn what their new goals and responsibilities are and who it is that they are responsible for leading. Both new and existing leaders often benefit from training in coaching and leadership skills. Technology can help get new leaders get up to speed in a variety of ways.[130]

CD-ROMs. Many companies, including Dell Computer, are putting new-hire and new-leader information on *CD-ROMs*, including hyperlinks to important company intranet pages; videos featuring corporate leaders and corporate spaces, manufacturing facilities, and product lines; and information about the company's history, mission, and culture. Unlike formal training programs that require leaders to be in a particular place at a particular time to learn the information, the leader can watch a CD-ROM when he or she has the time to devote to it or when the leader needs the information. Because CD-ROMs do not require an Internet connection, they are more flexible than intranets.

· · · · · · · · · · · · · · · · IMPROVE YOUR SKILLS · · · · · · · · · · · · · · · ·

NETIQUETTE TIPS FOR MANAGERS

- Never use e-mail to fire employees or deliver bad news. Because it contains no body language, facial expression, and intonation, e-mail is the worst way to deliver bad news to employees. A one-on-one meeting is better.

- Do not use e-mail to discuss an employee's performance with other managers. Hold these discussions privately.

- Be careful when writing e-mail messages. Like written performance reviews and other documents, e-mails can be subject to discovery and subpoena. E-mail is also not always secure, and sometimes unintended readers receive confidential information.

- Do not rely on e-mail to the exclusion of personal contact. Even in the age of IT, relationship skills are the heart of long-term business success. Supplement your e-mails with periodic face-to-face staff, customer, and supplier meetings, even if they must occur through videoconferencing.

- Do not use e-mail when there is any chance of the message being misunderstood. Use a telephone call or a face-to-face meeting if a message is complex, technical, or in any danger of being misinterpreted.

PDAs. Some companies provide incoming leaders with *personal digital assistants* (PDAs) preloaded with important contact information in the organization, key tasks to complete, and even pictures of staff and others that the new leader needs to know. Important meeting dates can also be preloaded to help the new leader schedule his or her time.

Web-Based Tool Kits. Some companies create *web-based tool kits* or "survival guides" that contain information leaders regularly refer to, including company information about ethics, performance management, and processes and procedures.

Communities of Practice. Leaders and others are encouraged to visit online chat rooms and bulletin boards to form *communities of practice* where members ask questions and share answers. This can be particularly helpful for a new leader who wants advice on how to handle certain situations or challenges.

Online Leadership Development. Web-based coaches and tools can support leadership development. For example, Boeing's web-based leadership development tool called Waypoint helps leaders develop their leadership and management competence. Waypoint allows leaders to engage in self-directed learning using an interactive website that allows them to take assessment tests, devise personal development plans, and identify training and stretch assignments. Reading materials and other learning resources facilitate their continued development.[131]

Mixed Modes of Training and Development. Some companies use learning programs that incorporate technology to help leaders quickly get up to speed and develop new skills. For example, Xerox partnered with the Center for Creative Leadership to create the Emerging Leaders Program, a five-month program that combines web-based conferencing with face-to-face sessions along with web-based learning modules, personal executive coaching, and internal mentoring.[132]

Using the Intranet to Build Culture. Leaders can use the intranet to build culture and reinforce organizational culture in virtual teams. The intranet can reinforce the company's vision, mission, and cultural values. It can also serve as a hub where employees can share information, ask and answer questions, and applaud employees' successes. Team leaders can be held responsible for keeping their sections updated, and team members can be held responsible for visiting and contributing to the site.

SUMMARY AND APPLICATION

As the great Chinese philosopher Lao-Tzu said, "As for the best leaders, the people do not notice their existence. The next best, the people honour and praise. The next, the people fear, and the next the people hate. When the best leader's work is done, the people say, 'we did it ourselves!'" Effective leaders balance their own traits and skills and their leadership styles or behaviors in a way that best fits the followers and is most appropriate for the situation at hand. Effective leaders are flexible, and adapt their style to the follower and to the situation.

ETHICAL LEADERSHIP AT COSTCO

Costco's CEO Jim Sinegal responds to the criticisms of Wall Street analysts that he pays employees too much and keeps them too long by saying that keeping good employees is strategic for Costco's long-term success and growth. He backs up this claim with per-employee sales that are notably higher than those found at rivals such as Sam's Club.

To keep his employees happy and productive, Sinegal tries not to distance himself from his employees. Sinegal asks his employees to refer to him as "Jim, the CEO." He wears a name tag that simply says "Jim." When touring stores, he could easily be mistaken for a stock clerk. From the very beginning he wanted to create a company in which everyone is on a first-name basis.

The culture of the company flows downward from Sinegal, who has an open-door policy at Costco headquarters. It is actually more of a no-door policy, since he had an entire wall removed from his office when Costco moved into a new office building. Costco regularly improves its product mix due to alert employees in the warehouses who feed the latest information up to headquarters. Costco enjoys an extremely low turnover rate of below 6 percent among employees who have been there at least a year and has some of the lowest shrinkage (unexplained disappearances of merchandise) in the industry at one-tenth of 1 percent.

Sinegal believes the leaders should model what is expected from employees. When he goes to a Costco store and takes the time to pick up a piece of trash on the ground, employees immediately know it is important and therefore do it themselves. He likes to visit as many of the stores as he can every year and likes employees to think that he might show up anytime. When Sinegal walks into one of his stores, he is treated like a celebrity. He says, "The employees know that I want to say hello to them, because I like them. . . . No manager and no staff in any business feels very good if the boss is not interested enough to come and see them."[133]

Sinegal also gets a compensation package far below what most CEOs receive, with a combined salary and bonus of less than $600,000 (plus stock options, but even so his total compensation is low compared with peers). "I figured that if I was making something like twelve times more than the typical person working on the floor, that that was a fair salary," he said.[134] An expert on corporate governance was shocked to discover that Sinegal's employment contract is only a page long. She says, "Of the 2,000 companies in our database, he has the single shortest CEO employment contract. And the only one which specifically says he can be—believe it or not—'terminated for cause.' If he doesn't do his job, he is out the door."[135]

As Costco continues to grow internationally, Sinegal intends to continue following his code of ethics. He says, "Our code of ethics says we have to obey the law. We have to take care of our customers, take care of our people. And if we do those things, we think that we'll reward our shareholders."[136]

Source: Smallbizbee (2009). Q&A with Jim Sinegal Founder of Costco. SmallBizBee, March. http://smallbizbee. com/index /2009/03/19/qa-jim-sinegal-founder-costco/. Machan, D. (2008). CEO Interview: Costco's James Sinegal, SmartMoney, March 27. http://www.smartmoney.com/investing/stocks/ceo -interview-costcos-james-sinegal-22782/. Chu, J. & Rockwood, K. (2008). CEO Interview: Costco's Jim Sinegal. Fast Company, October 13. http://www. fastcompany.com/magazine/130 /thinking-outside-the-big-box. html?page=0%2C2. Goldberg, A.B. & Ritter, B. (2006). Costco CEO Finds Pro-Worker Means Profitability, ABC News 20/20, August 2. http:// abcnews.go.com/2020/Business/story?id=1362779. Wadhwa, V. (2009). Why Be an Ethical Company? They're Stronger and Last Longer, BusinessWeek, August 17. http://www .businessweek.com/technology/content/aug2009 /tc20090816_435499.htm. Lamm, G. (2008). 2008 Executive of the Year, Enterprise Seattle. December 19. http:// www.enterpris-eseattle.org/index.php?option=com_content&task=view&id=210&It emid=104&date=2009-10-01

✓ TAKEAWAY POINTS

1. Leadership and management differ from one another. Management is a function that exists to establish and implement the procedures, processes, and practices that help the firm function smoothly. Managers have formal authority to reward and punish. Leadership, on the other hand, is a relationship between the leader and the led—leadership is the behavioral and interpersonal aspect of what managers do. Leaders may or may not have a formal leadership position.

2. Although most traits and skills do not differentiate leaders from followers, leaders do seem to have higher energy levels, higher internal control orientation, emotional maturity, intelligence, self-confidence, determination, integrity, and interpersonal skills.

3. Effective leadership depends on who a person "is" in terms of traits and skills, how the person behaves, and the appropriateness of the two given the situation the leader is facing. Followers' perceptions of the leader and their willingness to let the leader influence them determine leadership effectiveness.

4. To varying degrees, all leaders organize work tasks and develop productive work relationships with their subordinates and among subordinates. Leaders also use a variety of styles, depending on the situation and on the people being led.

5. Ethical leadership involves demonstrating appropriate conduct through personal actions and interpersonal relationships, and promoting that conduct to followers through two-way communication, reinforcement, and decision making.

6. E-leadership addresses the human interactions that now occur through technology. Technology influences what effective leaders do because e-leaders must manage telecommuting relationships, communicate with employees through e-mail and web-based portals, and support virtual teams that may have members distributed around the world.

7. Technology can help new leaders become effective more quickly by providing on-demand access to a variety of organizational and leadership-oriented material. Online material, information preloaded onto a PDA or CD-ROM, and other technology-based learning resources facilitate leaders' continued development.

DISCUSSION QUESTIONS

1. Describe an effective leader with whom you are familiar. Now describe an ineffective leader with whom you are familiar. How do they differ? What could the ineffective leader do to be more effective?
2. Should all managers be leaders? Why or why not?
3. When would transactional leadership be preferred to transformational leadership?
4. What are some common barriers preventing leaders from behaving ethically? How can these barriers be overcome?
5. When should leaders focus on the task and not on the people doing the task?
6. Do you feel that it is possible for leadership substitutes to be effective? Why or why not?
7. What advice would you give a leader on managing people from multiple cultures?

EXERCISES

What Is Your Leadership Potential?

For each pair of statements below, distribute 5 points based on how characteristic each statement is of you. If the first statement is totally like you and the second is not like you at all, give 5 points to the first and 0 to the second. If it is the opposite, use 0 and 5. If the statement is usually like you, then the distribution can be 4 and 1, or 1 and 4 if it is not usually like you. If both statements tend to be like you, the distribution should be 3 and 2, or 2 and 3. Remember, the combined score for each pair of statements must equal 5. There are no right or wrong answers—be honest in answering the questions, so that you can better understand yourself and your behavior as it relates to leadership.

Here are the possible scoring distributions for each pair of statements:

0-5 or 5-0	One of the statements is totally like you; the other is not like you at all.
1-4 or 4-1	One statement is usually like you; the other is not.
3-2 or 2-3	Both statements are like you, although one is slightly more like you.

1. _____ I'm interested in and willing to take charge of a group.
   _____ I want someone else to be in charge of the group.
2. _____ When I'm not in charge, I'm willing to give input to the leader to improve performance.
   _____ When I'm not in charge, I do things the leader's way, rather than offer my suggestions.
3. _____ I'm interested in and willing to get people to listen to my suggestions and to implement them.
   _____ I'm not interested in influencing other people.

4. _____ When I'm in charge, I want to share management responsibilities with group members.

   _____ When I'm in charge, I want to perform the management functions for the group.

5. _____ I want to have clear goals and to develop and implement plans to achieve them.

   _____ I like to have very general goals and take things as they come.

6. _____ I like to change the way my job is done, and to learn and do new things.

   _____ I like stability, or to do my job in the same way; I don't like learning and doing new things.

7. _____ I enjoy working with people and helping them succeed.

   _____ I don't really like working with people and helping them succeed.

Scoring: To calculate your leadership potential score, add up your scores (0 to 5) for the first statements in each pair; ignore the numbers for the second statements. Your total should be between 0 and 35. Place your score on this continuum:

0----------5----------10----------15----------20----------25----------30----------35

Low leadership   High leadership

potential   potential

Interpretation: Generally, the higher your score, the greater your potential to be an effective leader. Because the key to leadership success is not simply potential, but also persistence and hard work, you can develop your leadership ability by applying the principles and theories you learn from studying this book to your personal and professional lives. One good place to start is to look at the effective leadership statements to which you gave a low score and practice engaging in those behaviors.

Source: Adapted from Lussier, R.N., & Achua, C.F., *Leadership: Theory, application and skill development*. © 2001 Cengage Learning.

Tasty Beverages

Working alone or in a small group, imagine that you are the CEO or the executive team of soft-drink maker Tasty Beverages. The company's performance has been slipping and you have decided that the company should add a line of snack foods including pretzels and potato chips to your product line. This is a big change for your company, and you know that you will need the full support of your employees to make the new strategy work. Using what you learned in this chapter, how would you lead Tasty Beverages through this change? What leadership style(s) would you use? Why? There is more than one way to be an effective leader; be honest regarding your personal leadership style and beliefs.

VIDEO CASES

Now What?

Imagine that your boss is delegating parts of a project to you and to another team member. Because the other team member has a longer work history with the boss and is highly trusted, you are assigned the unchallenging portions of the project. *What do you say or do?* How can you improve your relationship with your boss to get more challenging assignments and eventually earn a promotion? Go to this chapter's "Now What?" video, watch the challenge video, and choose a response. Be sure to also view the outcomes of the two responses you didn't choose.

Discussion Questions

1. What leadership style is the boss exhibiting in the challenge video?
2. Which aspects of leadership discussed in this chapter are illustrated in these videos? Explain your answer.
3. If this were you, what would you do to improve your relationship with your boss to get assignments that are more challenging and eventually earn a promotion?

Workplace | City of Greensburg, Kansas: Leadership

After working in Oklahoma City as a parks director, Steve Hewitt wanted to run an entire town. A smaller community seemed the perfect place to get hands-on leadership experience before tackling a bigger city, so Hewitt took the city administrator position in his hometown, Kansas (population: 1,500). But on May 4, 2007, while staring into a dark sky from the tattered remains of his kitchen, Hewitt realized that he got more than he'd bargained for—a tornado had struck the town.

The morning after the powerful EF-5 tornado whipped through the area, everyone knew Greensburg was gone—perhaps forever. But in a subsequent press conference, Mayor Lonnie McCollum announced that the town would rebuild as a model green community, and he convinced the city it needed a full-time administrator to make big changes. Hewitt was the man for the job.

Intense and fast-talking, Steve Hewitt provided the perfect complement to McCollum's humble, measured demeanor. Daniel Wallach, executive director of Greensburg GreenTown, describes the young leader as "the kind of guy you want taking the last shot in a basketball game." Indeed, Hewitt had the ambition and confidence necessary to get the community back on its feet. While Mayor McCollum offered a vision for rebuilding Greensburg, it is Hewitt who stepped up to ensure that the vision became a reality.

Hewitt quickly went to work on a plan for rebuilding. He took a crash course on interpersonal influence tactics, increased his staff from twenty to thirty-five people, and established full-time fire, planning, and community development departments. To keep Greensburg on everyone's radar, Hewitt spent hours each week conducting interviews with news media. The press attention kept Greensburg on the map even though it lay in ruins.

City workers give Hewitt high marks for his handling of the crisis. "He has been very open as far as information," said recovery coordinator Kim Alderfer. "He's very good about delegating authority. He gives you the authority to do your job. He doesn't have time to micromanage."

Like most good leaders, Hewitt hasn't been afraid to ruffle feathers as needed. When certain residents opposed the strict environmental building codes, Hewitt found the courage and moral leadership, to say, "No. You're going to build it right and you're going to do it to code." Asked about his management of conflict in the middle of a crisis, Hewitt answered, "I'm dumb enough not to care what people say, and young enough to have the energy to get through it."

Discussion Questions

1. Where does Hewitt's leadership fall on the Managerial Grid discussed in the chapter? Explain.
2. Would Steve Hewitt be considered a Level 5 leader? Explain.
3. Is Hewitt's leadership style appropriate for Greensburg's situation? Explain your answer using insights drawn from Fiedler's leader match model.

DO WHAT

CENGAGENOW™ includes **teaching and learning resources** to supplement the text, and is designed specifically to **help students "think like managers"** by engaging and challenging them to think critically about managerial situations. **CengageNOW uses today's technology to improve the skills** of tomorrow's managers.

END NOTES

[1]Career Opportunities for You, Costco.com, 2012. http://shop.costco.com/About/Costco-Employment; Q&A with Jim Sinegal Founder of Costco. (2009, March). SmallBizBee. http://smallbizbee.com/index/2009/03/19/ qa-jim-sinegal-founder-costco/; Machan, D. (2008, March 27). CEO Interview: Costco's James Sinegal. SmartMoney. http://www.smartmoney.com/investing/stocks/ceointerview-costcos-james-sinegal-22782/; Chu, J., & Rockwood, K. (2008, October 13). CEO Interview: Costco's Jim Sinegal. Fast Company. http://www.fastcompany.com/ magazine/130/thinking-outside-the-big-box.html?page=0%2C2; Goldberg, A. B., & Ritter, B. (2006, August 2). Costco CEO Finds Pro-Worker Means Profitability. ABC News 20/20. http://abcnews.go.com/2020/Business/story?id=1362779; Wadhwa, V. (2009, August 17). Why Be an Ethical Company? They're Stronger and Last Longer. BusinessWeek.

http://www.businessweek.com/stories/2009-08-17/whybe-an-ethical-company-theyre-stronger-and-last-longerbusinessweek-business-news-stock-market-and-financial-advic

[2]Baldoni, J. (2008, December 17). If They Gave Awards for Poor Leadership. HarvardBusiness.org. Available online: http://blogs.harvardbusiness.org/baldoni/2008/12/and_the_awards_for.html.

[3]Fisher, D. (2006, July 5). Ken Lay's Legacy. Forbes.com. Available online: http://www.msnbc.msn.com/id/13720384/.

[4]Reicher, S. D., Platow, M. J., & Haslam, S. A. (2007, July 31). The New Psychology of Leadership. *Scientific American.* Available online: http://www.scientificamerican.com/article.cfm?id=the-new-psychology-of-leadership.

[5]Morgeson, F. P., DeRue, D. S., & Karam, E. P. (2010). Leadership in Teams: A Functional Approach to Understanding Leadership Structures and Processes. *Journal of Management, 36,* 5–39.

[6]Spangler, W. D., House, R. J., & Palrecha, R. (2004). Personality and Leadership. In *Personality and Organizations,* eds. B. Schneider and D. B. Smith (pp. 251–290). Mahwah, NJ: Lawrence Erlbaum.

[7]Ubben, G. C., & Hughes, L. (1987). *The Principal: Creative Leadership for Effective Schools.* Boston: Allyn & Bacon.

[8]Macoby, M. (2000, January–February). Understanding the Difference Between Management and Leadership. *Research & Technology Management,* 57–59.

[9]Yukl, G., & Van Fleet, D. D. (1976). Theory and Research on Leadership in Organizations. In *Handbook of Research in Industrial and Organizational Psychology,* eds. Marvin D. Dunnete and Leaetta M. Hough (Vol. 3, pp. 147–197). Palo Alto, CA: Consulting Psychologists Press.

[10]Bennis, W., & Nanus, B. (1985). *Leaders: The Strategies for Taking Charge* (p. 21). New York: Harper & Row.

[11]Effron, M., Greenslade, S., & Salbo, M. (2005). Growing Great Leaders: Does It Really Matter? *Journal of The Human Resource Planning Society, 28,* 18–23.

[12]See Waldman, D., Ramirez, G., House, R. J., & Puranam, P. (2001). Does Leadership Matter? CEO Leadership Attributes and Profitability Under Conditions of Perceived Incremental Uncertainty. *Academy of Management Journal, 44,* 134–143.

[13]See Yukl, G. (2002). *Leadership in Organizations* (5th ed.). Upper Saddle River, NJ: Prentice Hall; Northouse, P. G. (2000). *Leadership: Theory and Practice* (2nd ed.). London: Sage; Phillips, J. M. (1995). Leadership Since 1975: Advancement or Inertia? *Journal of Leadership Studies, 2,* 58–79.

[14]Bass, B. M. (1960). *Leadership, Psychology and Organizational Behavior.* New York: Harper; Stogdill, R. (1948). Personal Factors Associated with Leadership. A Survey of the Literature. *Journal of Psychology, 25,* 35–71; Stogdill, R. (1974). *Handbook of Leadership: A Survey of the Literature.* New York: Free Press.

[15]Reicher, S. D., Platow, M. J., & Haslam, S. A. (2007, July 31). The New Psychology of Leadership. *Scientific American.* Available online: http://www.scientificamerican.com/article.cfm?id=the-new-psychology-of-leadership.

[16]Yukl, G. (2002). *Leadership in Organizations* (5th ed.). Upper Saddle River, NJ: Prentice Hall.

[17]Northouse, P. G. (2000). *Leadership: Theory and Practice* (2nd ed.). London: Sage.

[18]Hoffman, B.J., Woehr, D.J., Maldagen-Youngjohn, R., & Lyons, B.D. (2011). Great Man or Great Myth? A Quantitative Review of the Relationship Between Individual Differences and Leader Effectiveness, *Journal of Occupational and Organizational Psychology, 84*(2), 347–381.

[19]Singh, P. (2002). Strategic Reward Systems at Southwest Airlines. *Compensation and Benefits Review, 34*(2), 28–33.

[20]HP and Patagonia: Two Similar, Yet Different, Leadership Styles. (2005, March 30). Knowledge@Wharton. Available online: http://knowledge.wharton.upenn.edu/article.cfm?articleid=1153.

[21]Hoare, R. (2012). Meet Fortune 500's Female Powerbrokers, CNN, May 9. Available online: http://edition.cnn.com/2012/05/08/business/f500-leading-women/index.html.

[22]Indvik, J. (2000). Women and Leadership. In *Leadership: Theory and Practice,* ed. P. G. Northouse (2nd ed., pp. 265–300). London: Sage.

[23]Catalyst. (2004). *Women and Men in U.S. Corporate Leadership: Same Workplace, Different Realities?* New York: Catalyst.

[24]Hyde, J. S. (2005). The Gender Similarities Hypothesis. *American Psychologist, 60*(6), 581–592.

[25]Eagly, A. H., & Johannessen-Schmidt, M. C. (2001). The Leadership Styles of Women and Men. *Journal of Social Issues, 57,* 781–797; Eagly, A. H., & Carli, L. L. (2003). The Female Leadership Advantage: An Evaluation of the Evidence. *Leadership Quarterly, 14,* 807–834; Eagly, A. H., & Carli, L. L. (2003). Finding Gender Advantage and Disadvantage: Systematic Research Integration Is the Solution. *Leadership Quarterly, 14,* 851–859; Hyde, J. S. (2005). The Gender Similarities Hypothesis. *American Psychologist, 60*(6), 581–592.

[26]Bass, B. M. (1985). *Leadership and Performance Beyond Expectations.* New York: Free Press.

[27]See, for example, Bowditch, J., & Buono, A. (1994). *A Primer on Organizational Behavior* (p. 238). New York: John Wiley.

[28]Indvik, J. (2000). Women and Leadership. In *Leadership: Theory and Practice,* ed. P. G. Northouse (2nd ed., pp. 265–300). London: Sage.

[29]Sharpe, R. (2000, November 20). As Leaders, Women Rule. *BusinessWeek,* 74–84.

[30]Fatehi, K. (2007). *Managing Internationally: Succeeding in a Culturally Diverse World.* New York: Sage.

[31]Barsoux, J. L., & Lawrence, P. (1991, July–August). The Making of a French Manager. *Harvard Business Review,* 58–67.

[32]Stogdill, R., & Kooonz, A. E. (1957). *Leader Behavior: Its Description and Measurement.* Columbus: Bureau of Business Research, Ohio State University. See also Bass, B. M. (1990). *Bass & Stogdill's Handbook of Leadership: Theory, Research, & Managerial Applications* (3rd ed.). New York: Free Press.

[33]Likert, R. (1961). *New Patterns of Management.* New York: McGraw-Hill; Likert R. (1967). *The Human Organization: Its Management and Value.* New York: McGraw-Hill.

[34]Schlender, B. (2004, January 26). Ballmer Unbound: How Do You Impose Order on a Giant, Runaway Mensa Meeting? Just Watch Microsoft's CEO. *Fortune,* 117–124.

[35]Valenzi, E., & Dessler, G. (1978). Relationships of Leader Behavior, Subordinate Role Ambiguity and Subordinate Job Satisfaction. *Academy of Management Journal, 21,* 671–678.

[36]Yukl, G. (1971, July). Towards a Behavioral Theory of Leadership, Organizational Behavior and Human Performance (pp. 414–440). See also Yukl, G. (1989). *Leadership in Organizations* (2nd ed.). Englewood Cliffs, NJ: Prentice Hall.

[37]Blake, R., & Mouton, J. (1964). *The Managerial Grid.* Houston, TX: Gulf Publishing.

[38]Facella, P. (2008). *Everything I Know About Business I Learned at McDonald's: The 7 Leadership Principles That Drive Break Out Success.* New York: McGraw-Hill.

[39]Likert, R. (1967). *New Patterns of Management.* New York: McGraw-Hill.

[40]Blake, R. R., & Mouton, J. S. (1964). *The Managerial Grid.* Houston, TX: Gulf.

[41]Welch, D. (2009, October 5). GM: His Way or the Highway. *BusinessWeek*, 62.

[42]Larson, L. L., Hunt, J. G., & Osburn, R. N. (1976). The Great Hi-Hi Leader Behavior Myth: A Lesson from Occam's Razor. *Academy of Management Journal, 19*, 628–641; Nystrom, P. C. (1978). Managers and the Hi-Hi Leader Myth. *Academy of Management Journal, 21*(2), 325–331.

[43]Adapted from Blake, R. R., & Mouton, J. S. (1985). *The Managerial Grid III: The Key to Leadership Excellence* (3rd ed.). Houston, TX: Gulf Publishing; The Leadership Grid. Grid International, Inc.

[44]Bass, B. M. (1998). *Transformational Leadership: Industrial, Military, and Educational Impact.* Mahwah, NJ: Lawrence Erlbaum; Burns, J. M. (1978). *Leadership.* New York: Harper & Row.

[45]Bennis, W. (2004, December 1). Putting Passionate People to Work. CIO Insight. Available online: http://www.cioinsight.com/c/a/Past-Opinions/Putting-Passionate-People-to-Work/.

[46]Bass, B. M. (1998). *Transformational Leadership: Industrial, Military, and Educational Impact.* Mahwah, NJ: Lawrence Erlbaum.

[47]Kirkpatrick, S. A., & Locke, E. A. (1996). Direct and Indirect Effects of Three Core Charismatic Leadership Components on Performance and Attitudes. *Journal of Applied Psychology, 81*, 36–51.

[48]Based on Bass, B. (1985). *Leadership and Performance Beyond Expectations.* New York: Free Press; Deluga, R. (1988, December). Relationship of Transformational and Transactional Leadership with Employee Influencing Strategies. *Group and Organizational Studies*, 457–458; Podsakoff, P. M., MacKenzie, S. B., & Bommer, W. H. (1996). Transformational Leader Behaviors as Determinants of Employee Satisfaction, Commitment, Trust, and Organizational Citizenship Behaviors. *Journal of Management, 22*(2), 259–298; Avolio, B. J. (1999). *Full Leadership Development.* Thousand Oaks, CA: Sage; Yamarino, F., & Bass, B. (1990). Transformational Leadership and Multiple Levels of Analysis. *Human Relations, 43*, 975–995.

[49]Bass, B. M. (1985). *Leadership and Performance Beyond Expectations.* New York: Free Press.

[50]Bass, B. M. (1985). *Leadership and Performance Beyond Expectations.* New York: Free Press; Waldman, D. A., Bass, B. M., & Yammarino, F. J. (1990). Adding to Contingent-Reward Behavior: The Augmenting Effect of Charismatic Leadership. *Group & Organizational Studies, 15*, 381–394.

[51]Waldman, D. A., Bass, B. M., & Yammarino, F. J. (1990) Adding to Contingent-Reward Behavior: The Augmenting Effect of Charismatic Leadership. *Group & Organizational Studies, 15*, 381–394.

[52]Fatehi, K. (2007). *Managing Internationally: Succeeding in a Culturally Diverse World.* New York: Sage.

[53]Gomez-Mejia, L. R., Balkin, D. B., & Cardy, R. L. (2005). *Management: People, Performance, Change* (pp. 559–560). Boston: McGraw-Hill.

[54]Bass, B. M. (1999). Two Decades of Research and Development in Transformational Leadership. *European Journal of Work and Organizational Psychology, 8*, 9–32.

[55]For a further understanding of charisma, see Conger, J. A., & Kanungo, R. N. (1998). *Charismatic Leadership in Organizations.* Thousand Oaks, CA: Sage.

[56]Musser, S. J. (1987). *The Determination of Positive and Negative Charismatic Leadership.* Grantham: PA: Messiah College.

[57]House, R. J. (1999). Weber and Neo-Charismatic Leadership Paradigm: A Response to Beyer. *Leadership Quarterly, 10*, 563–574.

[58]Conger, J. A., & Kanungo, R. N. (1998). *Charismatic Leadership in Organizations.* Thousand Oaks, CA: Sage.

[59]House, R. J. (1999). Weber and Neo-Charismatic Leadership Paradigm: A Response to Beyer. *Leadership Quarterly, 10*, 563–574.

[60]Lester, S. W., Meglino, B. M., & Korsgaard, A. M. (2002). The Antecedents and Consequences of Group Potency: A Longitudinal Investigation of Newly Formed Work Groups. *Academy of Management Journal, 45*(2), 352–368.

[61]Waldman, D. A., & Yammarino, F. J. (1999). CEO Charismatic Leadership: Levels of Management and Levels of Analysis Effects. *Academy of Management Review, 24*, 266–268.

[62]House, R. J., & Aditya, R. N. (1997). The Social Scientific Study of Leadership: Quo Vadis? *Journal of Management, 23*, 409–473.

[63]Collins, J. (2001, January). Level 5 Leadership. *Harvard Business Review*, 73.

[64]Brozyna, C. (2010, February 18). American Heart: Owner of Multi-Million Dollar Company Hands Over Business to Employees. ABC World News with Diane Sawyer. Available online: http://abcnews.go.com/WN/owner-multi-million-dollar-company-hands-business-employees/story?id=9875038#.UFCp4I1lSbE.

[65]$5.5 Million Declined by Ex-Official. (1992, January 22). *Washington Post*, Fl.

[66]Brown, M. E., Treviño, L. K., & Harrison, D. A. (2005). Ethical Leadership: A Social Learning Perspective for Construct Development and Testing. *Organizational Behavior and Human Decision Processes, 97*, 120.

[67]Bandura, A. (1986). *Social Foundations of Thought and Action: A Social Cognitive Theory.* Englewood Cliffs, NJ: Prentice Hall.

[68]afterQuotes. (2010). Available online: http://www.afterquotes.com/great/quotes/success.htm.

[69]Blau, P. M. (1964). *Exchange and Power in Social Life.* New York: John Wiley. Read more about this topic at: http://family.jrank.org/pages/1595/Social-Exchange-Theory-Major-Contemporary-Concepts.html#ixzz0RTRBXCjC.

[70]Treviño, L. K., & Brown, M. E. (2004). Managing to Be Ethical: Debunking Five Business Ethics Myths. *Academy of Management Executive, 19*, 69–81.

[71]Brown, M. E., Treviño, L. K., & Harrison, D. A. (2005). Ethical Leadership: A Social Learning Perspective for Construct Development and Testing. *Organizational Behavior and Human Decision Processes, 97*, 117–134.

[72]Sadler, P. (1997). *Leadership: Styles, Role Models, Qualities, Behaviors.* London: Coopers & Lybrand.

[73]Fiedler, F. E. (1967). *A Theory of Leadership Effectiveness.* New York: McGraw-Hill.

[74]Fiedler, F. E. (1967). *A Theory of Leadership Effectiveness* (p. 143). New York: McGraw-Hill.

[75]Fiedler, F. & Chemers, M. (1984). Improving Leadership Effectiveness: The Leader Match Concept, 2nd ed. New York: Wiley, 21.

[76]See, for example, House, R. J., & Singh, J. V. (1987). Organizational Behavior: Some New Directions for I/O Psychology. *Annual Review of Psychology, 38*, 669–718; Peters, L. H., Hartke, D. D., & Pohlmann, J. T. (1985). Fiedler's Contingency Theory of Leadership: An Application of the Meta-Analytic Procedures of Schmidt and Hunter. *Psychological Bulletin, 97*, 274–285; Vecchio, R. T. (1990, April). Theoretical and Empirical Examination of Cognitive Resource Theory. *Journal of Applied Psychology*, 141–147; Vecchio, R. (1992). Cognitive Resource Theory: Issues for Specifying a Test of the Theory. *Journal of Applied Psychology, 7*, 375–376.

[77]Fiedler, F. & Chemers, M. (1984). Improving Leadership Effectiveness: The Leader Match Concept, 2nd ed. New York: Wiley, 176.

[78]Tischler, L. (2002, September). Sudden Impact. *Fast Company, 62*, 106.

[79]Hersey, P., & Blanchard, K. H. (1969). *Management and Organizational Behavior—Utilizing Human Resources. New Jersey: Prentice* Hall.

[80]Berner, R. (2005). Flip-Flops, Torn Jeans—and Control, *BusinessWeek,* May 30, 68–70.

[81] Roth, D. (2005). Can Nike Still Do It Without Phil Knight? Fortune, April 4. Available online at: http://money.cnn.com /magazines/fortune/fortune_archive/2005/04/04/8255930/index.htm.

[82]Graeff, C. L. (1983). The Situational Leadership Theory: A Critical View. *Academy of Management Review, 8,* 285–291.

[83]Adapted from Hersey, P. (1985). *Situational Selling.* Escondido, CA: Center for Leadership Studies, 19.

[84]House, R. J. (1995). *Leadership in the Twenty-First Century. In The Changing Nature of Work,* ed. A. Howard. San Francisco, CA: Jossey-Bass; Evans, M.G. (1996). R.J. House's "A Path-Goal Theory of Leader Effectiveness." *Leadership Quarterly,* 7(3), 305–309.

[85]Dessler, G. (1972). An Investigation of a Path-Goal Theory of Leadership, Ph.D. Dissertation, City University of New York.

[86]House, R. J. (1971, September). A Path-Goal Theory of Leader Effectiveness. *Administrative Science Quarterly,* 321–338; House, R. J., & Mitchell, T. (1974, Autumn). Path-Goal Theory of Leadership. *Journal of Contemporary Business, 3,* 81–97; reprinted in White, D. (1982). *Contemporary Perspectives in Organizational Behavior* (pp. 228–235). Boston: Allyn & Bacon.

[87]McKee, J. (2007). The Best Managers Are Not Afraid of Looking Dumb. TechRepublic. Available online: http://blogs.techrepublic .com.com/career/?p=97.

[88]House, R. J., & Mitchell, T. (1974, Autumn). Path-Goal Theory of Leadership. *Journal of Contemporary Business, 3,* 81–97; reprinted in White, D. (1982). *Contemporary Perspectives in Organizational Behavior* (pp. 228–235). Boston: Allyn & Bacon.

[89]House, R. J., & Dessler, G. (1974). The Path-Goal Theory of Leadership: Some Posthoc and A Priori Tests. In *Contingency Approaches to Leadership,* eds. J. G. Hunt and L. L. Larson (pp. 29–55). Carbondale, IL: Southern Illinois University Press.

[90]Howell, J., & Costley, D. (2001). *Understanding Behavior for Effective Leadership.* Upper Saddle River, NJ: Prentice Hall.

[91]Yukl, G. (2002). *Leadership in Organizations* (5th ed.). Upper Saddle River, NJ: Prentice Hall.

[92]Graen, G. B., & Cashman, J. F. (1975). A Role Making Model of Leadership in Formal Organizations: A Developmental Approach. In *Leadership Frontiers,* eds. J. G. Hunt and L. L. Larson. Kent, OH: Kent State University Press.

[93]Dansereau, Jr., F., Graen, G., & Haga, W. J. (1975). A Vertical Dyad Linkage Approach to Leadership Within Formal Organizations: A Longitudinal Investigation of the Role Making Process. *Organizational Behavior and Human Performance, 13,* 46–78; Graen, G., & Cashman, J. F. (1975). A Role Making Model of Leadership in Formal Organizations: A Developmental Approach. In *Leadership Frontiers,* eds. J. G. Hunt and L. L. Larson (pp. 143–165). Kent, OH: Kent State University Press.

[94]Li, N., Liang, J., & Crant, J. M. (2010). The Role of Proactive Personality in Job Satisfaction and Organizational Citizenship Behavior: A Relational Perspective. *Journal of Applied Psychology, 95,* 395–404.

[95]Graen, G. B., Novak, M. A., & Sommerkamp, P. (1982). The Effects of Leader-Member Exchange and Job Design on Productivity and Satisfaction: Testing a Dual Attachment Model. *Organizational Behavior and Human Performance, 30,* 109–131; Vecchio, R. V., & Gobdel, B. C. (1984). The Vertical Dyad Linkage Model of Leadership: Problems and Prospects. *Organizational Behavior and Human Performance, 34,* 5–20.

[96]McClane, W. E. (1991). Implications of Member Role Differentiation: Analysis of a Key Concept in the LMX Model of Leadership. *Group and Organization Studies, 16,* 102–113; Phillips, J. M. (2001). The Role of Decision Influence and Team Performance in Member Self-Efficacy, Withdrawal, Satisfaction with the Leader, and Willingness to Return. *Organizational Behavior and Human Decision Processes,* 84(1), 122–147; Yukl, G. (1989). *Leadership in Organizations* (2nd ed.). Englewood Cliffs, NJ: Prentice Hall.

[97]Graen, G. B., Liden, R. C., & Hoel, W. (1982). Role of Leadership in the Employee Withdrawal Process. *Journal of Applied Psychology, 67,* 868–872.

[98]Gomez, C., & Rosen, B. (2001). The Leader-Member Exchange as a Link Between Managerial Trust and Employee Empowerment. *Group and Organization Management,* 26(1), 53–69.

[99]Liden, R .C., & Graen, G. (1980). Generalizability of the Vertical Dyad Linkage Model of Leadership. *Academy of Management Journal, 23,* 451–465.

[100]Yukl, G., & Van Fleet, D. D. (1976). Theory and Research on Leadership in Organizations. In *Handbook of Research in Industrial and Organizational Psychology,* eds. M. D. Dunnete and L. M. Hough (Vol. 3, p. 163). Palo Alto, CA: Consulting Psychologists Press.

[101]Dorsey, D. (2001, July 31). Andy Pearson Finds Love. *Fast Company.* Available online: http://www.fastcompany.com /magazine/49/pearson.html.

[102]Wu, J. B., Tsui, A. S., & Kinicki, A. J. (2010). Consequences of Differentiated Leadership in Groups. *Academy of Management Journal, 53,* 90–106.

[103]Howell, J. P., Bowen, D. E., Dorfman, P. W., Ker, S., & Podsakoff, P. M. (1990). Substitutes for Leadership: Effective Alternatives to Ineffective Leadership. *Organizational Dynamics, 19,* 21–38; Kerr, S., & Jermier, J. M. (1978). Substitutes for Leadership: Their Meaning and Measurement. *Organizational Behavior and Human Performance, 22,* 375–403.

[104]Kerr, S., & Jermier, J. M. (1978). Substitutes for Leadership: Their Meaning and Measurement. *Organizational Behavior and Human Performance, 22,* 375–403.

[105]Arnone, M. (2005, September 1). Katrina Smashes Coast Guard IT. *Federal Computer Week.* Available online: http://fcw. com/articles/2005/09/01/katrina-smashes-coast-guard-it.aspx?sc_ lang=en; Barr, S. (2005, September 6). Coast Guard's Response to Katrina a Silver Lining in the Storm. *Washington Post,* B02.

[106]Hollander, E. (2008). *Inclusive Leadership: The Essential Leader-Follower Relationship.* New York: Routledge Academic.

[107]Reicher, S. D., Platow, M. J., & Haslam, S. A. (2007, July 31). The New Psychology of Leadership. *Scientific American.* Available online: http://www.scientificamerican.com/article .cfm?id=the-new-psychology-of-leadership.

[108]Reicher, S. D., Platow, M. J., & Haslam, S. A. (2007, July 31). The New Psychology of Leadership. *Scientific American.* Available online: http://www.scientificamerican.com/article .cfm?id=the-new-psychology-of-leadership.

[109]Hollander, E. P., & Julian, J. W. (1970). Studies in Leader Legitimacy, Influence, and Innovation. In *Advances in Experimental Social Psychology,* ed. L. L. Berkowitz (Vol. 5, pp. 33–69). New York: Academic Press.

[110]Haslam, S. A. (2004). *Psychology in Organizations: The Social Identity Approach* (2nd ed.). New York: Sage.

[111]Bennis, W. (1993). *An Invented Life: Reflections on Leadership and Change.* New York: Addison-Wesley.

[112]Culp, D. R., & Berry, I. (2007). Merck and the Vioxx Debacle: Deadly Loyalty. *St. John's Journal of Legal Commentary, 22,* 1–34.

[113]Lankau, M. J., & Chung, B. G. (2009). A Comparison of American and International Prototypes of Successful Managers. *Journal of Leadership Studies, 3,* 7–18.

[114]Payne, N. (2004). The Costly (and Humorous) Impact of Cultural Blunders. Culturosity.com. Available online: http://www.culturosity.com/articles/culturalblunders.htm.

[115]Harris, P. R., Moran, R. T., & Moran, S. V. (2004). *Managing Cultural Differences: Leadership Strategies for a New World of Business* (6th ed.). Boston: Elsevier.

[116]Chang, H., & Holt, R. G. (1991). More Than Relationship: Chinese Interaction and the Principle of Kuan-His. *Community Quarterly, 39,* 251–271; Hui, H. C., & Graen, G. (1997). Guanxi and Professional Leadership in Contemporary Sino-American Joint Ventures in Mainland China. *Leadership Quarterly, 8,* 451–465.

[117]Child, J. (1994). *Management in China During the Age of Reform.* Cambridge: Cambridge University Press.

[118]Krone, K., Carrett, M., & Chen, L. (1992). Managerial Communication Practices in Chinese Factories: A Preliminary Investigation. *Journal of Business Communication, 29,* 229–243.

[119]Bond, M. H. (1991). Beyond the Chinese Face: Insights from Psychology. Hong Kong: Oxford University Press.

[120]House, R. J., Hanges, P. J., Javidan, M., Dorfman, P. W., & Gupta, V. (2004). *Culture, Leadership, and Organizations: The GLOBE Study of 62 Societies.* London: Sage.

[121]Avolio, B.J., & Kahai, S.S. (2003). Adding the "E" to E-Leadership: How it May Impact Your Leadership, *Organizational Dynamics, 31*(4), 325–338.

[122]Avolio, B. J., & Dodge, G. E. (2000). E-Leadership: Implications for Theory, Research, and Practice. *Leadership Quarterly, 11*(4), 615–668.

[123]Avolio, B. J., & Kahai, S. S. (2003). Adding the "E" to E-Leadership: How It May Impact Your Leadership. *Organizational Dynamics, 31*(4), 325–338.

[124]Martin, A. (2005). *The Changing Nature of Leadership: A CCL Research Report.* Centers for Creative Leadership. Available online: http://www.ccl.org/leadership/pdf/research/NatureLeadership.pdf; Hernez-Broome, G., & Hughes, R. L. (2004). Leadership Development: Past, Present, and Future. *Human Resource Planning, 27*(1), 24–32.

[125]Zimmermann, P., Wit, A., & Gill, R. (2008). The Relative Importance of Leadership Behaviours in Virtual and Face-to-Face Communication Settings. *Leadership, 4,* 321–337.

[126]Anderson, J. S., & Prussia, G. E. (1997). The Self-Leadership Questionnaire: Preliminary Assessment of Construct Validity. *Journal of Leadership & Organizational Studies, 4,* 119–143; Prussia, G. E., Anderson, J. S., & Manz, C. C. (1998). Self-Leadership and Performance Outcomes: The Mediating Influence of Self-Efficacy. *Journal of Organizational Behavior, 19,* 523–538.

[127]Roebuck, D. B., Brock, S. J., & Douglas R. (2004). Using a Simulation to Explore the Challenges of Communicating. *Business Communication Quarterly, 67,* 359.

[128]Wang, V.C.X. (2011). E-Leadership in the New Century, Adult Vocational Education and Technology, 2(1), 50–59.

[129] Avolio, B. J., Walumbwa, F. W., & Weber, T. J. (2009). Leadership: Current Theories, Research, and Future Directions. *Annual Review of Psychology, 60,* 421–449.

[130]This section is based in part on Hartley, D. E. (2004, March). Technology Kicks Up Leadership Development: Bam! Some Basic Technologies Can Help Leverage Leadership Development in Your Organization. *T+D,* 22–24.

[131]Gary, L. (2003). Pulling Yourself Up Through the Ranks. *Harvard Management Update, 8*(10). Available online: http://hbswk.hbs.edu/archive/3806.html.

[132]Xerox Corporation: Blended Learning Prepares Leaders Around the World. (2005). Center for Creative Leadership. Available online: http://www.ccl.org/leadership/pdf/solutions/Xerox_Corporation.pdf.

[133]Goldberg, A.B., & Ritter, B. (2006, August 2). Costco CEO Finds Pro-Worker Means Profitability. ABC News 20/20. Available online: http://abcnews.go.com/2020/Business/story?id=1362779.

[134]Goldberg, A. B., & Ritter, B. (2006, August 2). Costco CEO Finds Pro-Worker Means Profitability. ABC News 20/20. Available online: http://abcnews.go.com/2020/Business/story?id=1362779.

[135]Goldberg, A. B., & Ritter, B. (2006, August 2). Costco CEO Finds Pro-Worker Means Profitability. ABC News 20/20. Available online: http://abcnews.go.com/2020/Business/story?id=1362779.

[136]Goldberg, A. B., & Ritter, B. (2006, August 2). Costco CEO Finds Pro-Worker Means Profitability. ABC News 20/20. Available online: http://abcnews.go.com/2020/Business/story?id=1362779.

PART 5

Organizational Design, Organizational Change, and Career Management

CHAPTER 14

Organizational Structure and Design

American Airlines relied on a comprehensive restructuring to reduce costs. The company tried to be as fair as possible to employees during the restructuring process.

REAL WORLD CHALLENGE

RESTRUCTURING AMERICAN AIRLINES[1]

American Airlines needs to cut 13,000 employees from its work force of more than 72,000 and reduce labor cost $1.25 billion a year to be competitive in the airline industry. After entering bankruptcy to cut labor costs and shed debt, American wants to identify an additional $1.75 billion a year in other cost savings and increase revenue by $1 billion a year to emerge successfully from bankruptcy.

To do this, the company decides to restructure to spread the effects of cost savings as broadly and evenly as possible. The company knows that the restructuring will be difficult on its employees, and identifies three principles to guide its approach:

- Commitment to success by reducing costs by at least $3 billion, including annual employee-related costs of more than $1.25 billion

- Being fair and equitable by reducing total costs by 20 percent for all workgroups, including management

- Rewarding performance and recognizing employees for their contributions through a profit sharing plan that pays awards totaling 15 percent of all pre-tax income

What advice would you give American Airlines? After reading this chapter, you should have some good ideas.

LEARNING OBJECTIVES

1. Describe the difference between organizational design, organizational structure, and organizational charts.

2. List and define the four characteristics of organizational structure.

3. Explain why delegation is important in any organizational structure.

4. Explain what influences an organization's structure.

5. Describe the difference between prebureaucratic and bureaucratic structures.

6. Explain when network organizations are appropriate.

7. Describe how mechanistic and organic structures differ.

8. Explain what communities of practice are and why they are important.

In this section of the book we shift our attention to organizational design, organizational change, and managing your career. Once an organization decides how it wants its members to behave, what attitudes it wants to encourage, and what it wants its members to accomplish, it can then design an appropriate structure and develop appropriate supporting cultural values and norms. The right organizational structure can give an organization a competitive advantage by enabling it to best execute its business strategy.[2]

An organization's structure affects its performance by influencing how it operates.[3] The wrong organizational structure can hamper communication and slow work processes. Effective organizational structures improve the working efficiency of the organization, motivate employees rather than frustrate them, and facilitate working relationships among employees and across organizational units. An organization's structure also influences how it operates, how employees communicate, and how they are expected to behave.

Effective organizational structures improve efficiency and facilitate positive working relationships. Ineffective organizational structures block communication and cooperation, and drain employee motivation. Organizational structure is related to employee satisfaction, commitment,[4] and turnover.[5]

In this chapter we first discuss organizational structure and organizational charts. After discussing factors that influence organizational structure, we identify different types of structures and when they are most appropriate. We also discuss virtual organizations and ways of integrating employees in any organizational structure to enhance collaboration and knowledge transfer. After studying this chapter, you should have a good understanding of how to use organizational design to support a firm's business strategy and encourage desired employee behaviors.

ORGANIZATIONAL STRUCTURE

organizational design
The process of selecting and managing aspects of organizational structure and culture to enable the organization to achieve its goals

organizational structure
The formal system of task, power, and reporting relationships

Organizational design is the process of selecting and managing aspects of organizational structure and culture to enable the organization to achieve its goals. Designing and redesigning the organization in response to internal and external changes is a key managerial function.

One of the most important outcomes of organizational design is *organizational structure*, or the formal system of task, power, and reporting relationships. Organizational structure is the core of what coordinates, controls, and motivates employees to cooperate toward the attainment of organizational goals. When the organizational structure is aligned with organizational needs, it results in greater organizational efficiencies and less conflict.

Organizational structures influence employee behavior by enabling or restricting communication, teamwork, and cooperation as well as intergroup relationships. Imagine the difference between working in an organization comprised of independent work teams given the authority to make their own decisions compared to a highly centralized bureaucratic organization in which decisions are made solely by the CEO. Your autonomy, influence, and work variety would differ greatly in each firm. Each type of structure can be effective depending on the nature of the organization and its environment, but each creates very different patterns of communication and levels of individual responsibility.

Imagine that you start a business selling homemade chocolates. You start by yourself, and your business quickly takes off. You land some big contracts and realize that there is just too much work for you to do alone. So you hire people to help you make, market, sell, and ship your candy. When they all

SO WHAT
Effective managers use organizational structure to coordinate, control, and motivate employees.

report for their first day of work, what do you do next? You organize them to best get the work done in the way you want and need it done. You may even create an *organizational chart* like the one shown in Figure 14-1 to illustrate the chain of command and reporting relationships in your company. Higher levels in an organizational chart supervise and are responsible for the activities and performance of the levels beneath them.

organizational chart
Diagram of the chain of command and reporting relationships in a company

It is a common mistake to believe that a person's location in the organizational chart reflects their importance to the company and its performance. But what usually matters most is what each person contributes, and people at all levels of an organization can make meaningful contributions. Think of the salespeople at a retail chain like The Gap. They may be low on the organizational chart, but imagine what would happen to The Gap's performance if its salespeople were poorly trained, poorly motivated, and poorly managed. Salespeople have a huge impact on The Gap's performance despite their position at the bottom of the organizational chart. As an executive vice president for global shipper FedEx said of its drivers, "If I don't come to work, we're OK. If *they* don't come to work, we're . . . out of luck."[6]

Characteristics of Organizational Structure

Organizational structures reflect the company's division of labor, span of control, hierarchy, formalization, and centralization. Different structures have different levels of each of these characteristics. Table 14-1 summarizes these characteristics.

Division of Labor. In addition to illustrating the chain of command, organizational charts show the *division of labor*, which reflects the degree to which employees specialize or perform a variety of tasks as generalists. Highly specialized firms have a greater proportion of "specialists" who focus their attention on a well-defined set of tasks (market research, pricing, accounting, etc.). Lower levels in an organization tend to be more specialized than higher levels. The division of labor is reflected in the number of job titles in an organization,[7] or by the extent to which specialist roles exist within each functional area.[8]

division of labor
The degree to which employees specialize

Figure 14-1

Organizational Chart—Narrow Span of Control

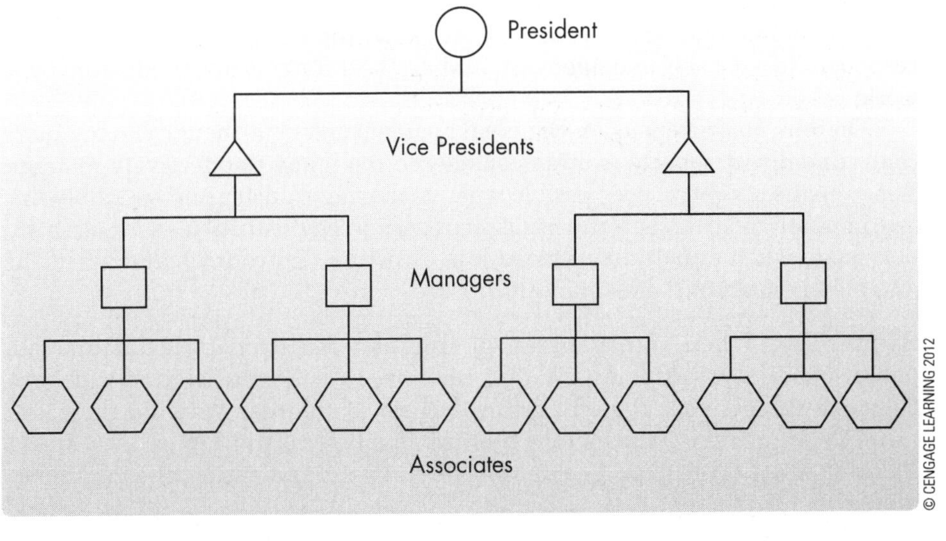

© CENGAGE LEARNING 2012

Table 14-1

Characteristics of Organizational Structure

Division of labor: the extent to which employees specialize or generalize

Span of control: the number of people reporting directly to an individual

Hierarchy: the degree to which some employees have formal authority over others

Formalization: the extent to which organizational rules, procedures, and communications are written down and closely followed

Centralization: the degree to which power and decision-making authority are concentrated at higher levels of the organization rather than distributed

SO WHAT

Although employing generalists can reduce costs, specialists can make faster decisions and better respond to environmental changes.

Dividing work into specialized jobs increases work efficiency.[9] Specialized employees can learn their jobs faster and with less training, and because their jobs are focused they waste little time changing tasks. Division of labor also makes it easier to assess job candidates for the specific talents needed to do each job. Because specialists are experts, they often have greater autonomy and decision-making authority, which increases the firm's ability to respond quickly to environmental changes.

On the downside, employees tend to be more isolated when division of labor is high. This can make it difficult for different divisions in the company to understand each other's priorities and needs, and can increase the potential for conflict. The increased specialization of employees in each division also decreases organizational flexibility.

Because generalists are often less expensive than specialists, organizations employing a greater proportion of generalists may be able to reduce costs. Because they are not experts, however, generalists often need more time to make decisions and to respond to environmental changes because they need to do additional research.

span of control
The number of people reporting directly to an individual

Span of Control. The number of people reporting directly to an individual is that person's *span of control*. Figure 14-2 illustrates a flatter organizational structure with a wider span of control than the structure shown earlier in Figure 14-1. The lowest-level supervisor in Figure 14-2 supervises seven rather than the three employees in the taller structure in Figure 14-1. Clearly, narrow spans of control are more costly, but they also provide closer supervision and more coaching. Narrower spans of control are necessary for novel and complex tasks. Wider spans of control give subordinates greater autonomy and responsibility for self-management, and are best for routine, production-type work.

There is no consensus on the ideal span of control, although having more than nine direct reports is often considered too many to effectively manage. Wider spans of control are possible when technology (such as an assembly line or computerized call center management technology) substitutes for close supervision, when subordinates need less direction and control, and when the jobs being supervised are similar.

hierarchy
The degree to which some employees have formal authority over others

Hierarchy. When an organization creates a *hierarchy*, it outlines supervision relationships by giving some employees authority over others. Hierarchy establishes the tallness or flatness of an organizational chart. For example, Figure 14-1 shows four hierarchical layers, and Figure 14-2 shows a flatter three-layer firm. The more layers in an organization, the greater its hierarchy.

Figure 14-2

Organizational Chart—Wide Span of Control

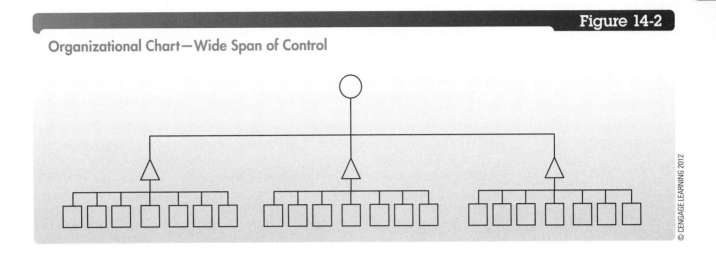

© CENGAGE LEARNING 2012

Although hierarchy can facilitate the coordination of different departments, organizations clearly should not have more hierarchical levels than are necessary. Not having enough levels can also create problems—when work activities require control and coordination, middle management layers can facilitate work processes. Hierarchy can give too much power to a few people at the top of the organization, which can increase the risk of unethical behavior. Because hierarchy creates a clear chain of command, it can also restrict the interaction and communication among employees.

To better compete in a fast-changing, global marketplace, organizations are increasingly restructuring to reduce their hierarchy and improve speed and efficiency. Revlon recently delayered, or flattened, its organizational structure to increase its performance. This change improved its effectiveness and removed several layers of management.[10]

Grouping employees into self-managed work teams decreases hierarchy because the teams incorporate some of the roles previously held by higher layers of management. Even in this case, though, managers are important. Although Hewlett-Packard is considered a high employee-involvement organization with minimal hierarchy, it still has eight organizational levels that coordinate its tens of thousands of employees.[11]

Formalization. Formalization reflects the extent to which organizational rules, procedures, and communications are written down.[12] In highly formalized firms, little flexibility exists in making decisions, and both procedures and rewards follow explicit rules. Formalization is not necessary for high performance—Google and Internet shoe retailer Zappos are known for having low formalization. Because formalization increases job and role clarity, it can increase employee commitment.[13] Without role clarity, dissatisfaction, anxiety, and lower performance can result.[14] If employees perceive that organizational rewards are consistently allocated based on formal rules and procedures, their confidence that they are being compensated appropriately is increased.

Centralization. When organizations are first formed, including your hypothetical chocolate business earlier in this chapter, they are typically very *centralized organizations* concentrating power and decision-making authority at higher levels of the organization. The two subcomponents of centralization are *participation in decision making* and *hierarchy of*

centralized organizations
Concentrate power and decision-making authority at higher levels of the organization

authority.[15] When you first started your chocolate company, you made all the decisions and did a variety of tasks. Centralization creates clear lines of communication and responsibility, and the implementation of decisions tends to be straightforward. Centralization is best in noncomplex, stable environments.

Whereas centralized organizations concentrate authority at higher levels of the organization, flatter *decentralized organizations* give lower levels more authority and autonomy for making decisions.[16] Decentralized organizations tend to have flatter structures than centralized organizations because employees' greater autonomy decreases the need for middle management. Flatter structures promote innovation and increase the speed of decision making, and can save money as a result of fewer management layers. Decentralization is best when the organization performs nonroutine tasks in complex environments because it empowers the managers closest to the environment to make decisions and quickly implement them.

decentralized organizations
The authority for making decisions affecting an organization is distributed

If employees have appropriate information and are allowed to make decisions relevant to their task, there are often benefits for both the organization and the employees.[17] Employee involvement and participation (traits of decentralization) are important managerial tools in achieving increased organizational effectiveness and positive employee attitudes.[18] Decentralization increases organizational commitment through greater involvement in the organization and identification with the organization's mission and values.[19]

"No person will make a great business who wants to do it all himself or get all the credit." —*Andrew Carnegie, American Capitalist Icon and Philanthropist*

Organizations do not have to be fully centralized or decentralized. Centralization is best thought of as a continuum, and different functions in a company can have different degrees of centralization. When Lou Gerstner led IBM's turnaround in the 1990s, he said, "Let's decentralize decision making wherever possible, but . . . we must balance decentralized decision making with central strategy and common customer focus."[20]

SO WHAT

Although it can be difficult to give up control, delegation is essential to managerial performance because one person cannot do everything effectively.

Centralizing authority can lead many managers to feel that they are solely responsible for completing their job tasks and responsibilities. In reality, you are setting yourself up to fail if you hold onto the belief that you must do everything yourself. As Andrew Carnegie said, "No person will make a great business who wants to do it all himself or get all the credit." Delegating tasks to others not only frees you to focus on more important tasks, but also develops skills in the recipient, increases trust, and can even lead to a higher-quality product. This chapter's *Improve Your Skills* feature gives you some tips for delegating more effectively.

RONDA CHURCHILL/BLOOMBERG/GETTY IMAGES

Internet shoe retailer Zappos. com is known for having low formalization.

IMPROVE YOUR SKILLS

DELEGATION SKILLS

In any organization structure, it is important to occasionally relinquish control and delegate tasks and responsibilities to others. If you consistently work longer hours than other employees and have trouble completing your primary responsibilities, it may help to reflect on how much (or how little) you are delegating. It is often difficult for managers to relinquish control over tasks, but doing so is essential to managerial performance. Here are some tips to help you delegate more effectively:

1. *Delegate only when appropriate*: If recipients lack the skills, capability, and information to complete a task, then they are unlikely to successfully complete it; if the task is critical to long-term success (e.g., hiring), you should probably stay involved—you are still responsible for the final product.

2. *Provide a thorough explanation and expectation*: Explain what you are asking the recipients to do and why it is important; be clear about what is expected as a final product.

3. *Delegate the authority to complete the task*: If you want people to do a job, you must give them the authority to get it done; do not micromanage.

4. *Provide the necessary tools and information*: Without the needed resources and information, recipients are just being set up to fail.

5. *Try to create a win-win situation*: Delegate in a way that recipients can get some benefit from the delegated task; for example, assign the task to someone who can learn new skills by doing it.

6. *Respect recipients' workload*: You are not the only busy person—be sure recipients' workload enables them to take on the extra work.

Mechanistic and Organic Structures

Organizational structures can be thought of as being either more mechanical and machine-like or more biological and organic. *Mechanistic organizations* are rigid, traditional bureaucracies with centralized power and hierarchical communications. Job descriptions are uniform, and formal rules and regulations guide decision making. More mechanistic organizations may minimize costs, but fit best with a relatively stable or slow-changing environment. When new opportunities present themselves, mechanistic organizations usually move too slowly to capitalize on them.

mechanistic organizations
Rigid, traditional bureaucracies with centralized power and hierarchical communications

In contrast, *organic organizations* are flexible, decentralized organizations with less clear lines of authority, decentralized power, open communication channels, and a focus on adaptability in helping employees accomplish their goals.[21] Organic organizations benefit from faster awareness of and response to market and competitive changes, better customer service, and faster decision making. Organic forms like teams and other flatter structures have typically been associated with increased job satisfaction,[22] affective commitment,[23] and learning.[24]

organic organizations
Flexible, decentralized structures with less clear lines of authority, decentralized power, open communication channels, and a focus on adaptability in helping employees accomplish goals

For many years Nordstrom's extremely organic structure was reflected in its employee handbook, shown in Figure 14-3. For years new employees received a simple gray card with these seventy-five words on it. Although employees now receive additional material summarizing more specific rules and legal regulations, Nordstrom's low formality and high emphasis on customer service continues.

Note that mechanistic and organic structures represent ends of a continuum, not a dichotomy.[26] No organization is perfectly organic or completely mechanistic. Firms usually display some characteristics of both forms along a mechanistic/organic continuum, as shown in Figure 14-4.

This chapter's *Understand Yourself* feature gives you the opportunity to identify whether you prefer to work in a more organic or mechanistic organizational structure.

Figure 14-3

Nordstrom's Employee Handbook[25]

Welcome to Nordstrom

We're glad to have you with our Company. Our number one goal is to provide outstanding customer service. Set both your personal and professional goals high. We have great confidence in your ability to achieve them.

Nordstrom Rules: Rule #1: Use good judgment in all situations. There will be no additional rules.

Please feel free to ask your department manager, store manager, or division general manager any question at any time.

Source: Spector, R. (2000). Lessons from the Nordstrom Way: How Companies Are Emulating the #1 Customer Service Company. NewYork: John Wiley

Figure 14-4

Mechanistic/Organic Continuum[27]

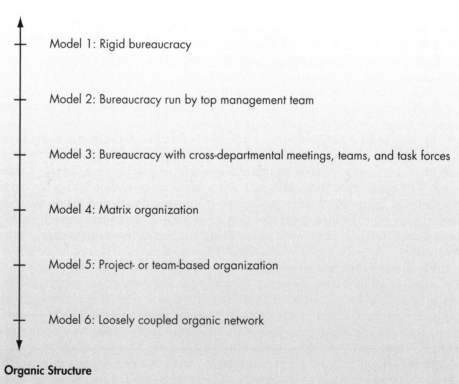

Mechanistic Structure

Model 1: Rigid bureaucracy

Model 2: Bureaucracy run by top management team

Model 3: Bureaucracy with cross-departmental meetings, teams, and task forces

Model 4: Matrix organization

Model 5: Project- or team-based organization

Model 6: Loosely coupled organic network

Organic Structure

UNDERSTAND YOURSELF

WHAT IS YOUR PREFERRED TYPE OF ORGANIZATIONAL STRUCTURE?

People differ in their preference for different types of organizational structures. This self-assessment will give you some insight into your preferred structure. Rate the fifteen statements using the scale below, and then follow the scoring instructions.

strongly disagree	disagree	slightly disagree	neutral	slightly agree	agree	strongly agree
1	2	3	4	5	6	7

I prefer to work in an organization in which:

___ 1. Goals are defined by those at higher levels.

___ 2. Clear job descriptions exist for every job.

___ 3. Top management makes the important decisions.

___ 4. Promotions and pay increases are based as much on length of service as on performance level.

___ 5. Clear lines of authority and responsibility are established.

___ 6. My career is pretty well planned out for me.

___ 7. I have a great deal of job security.

___ 8. I can specialize.

___ 9. My boss is readily available.

___ 10. Organization rules and regulations are clearly specified.

___ 11. Information rigidly follows the chain of command.

___ 12. There is a minimal number of new tasks for me to learn.

___ 13. Workgroups incur little member turnover.

___ 14. People accept the authority of a leader's position.

___ 15. I am part of a group whose members' training and skills are similar to mine.

Scoring: Add up your responses to all fifteen items. Remember that this assessment enables you to better understand your work preferences and is *not* an evaluation of yourself.

Interpretation: *Scores above 75* suggest that you prefer stable, rule-driven, hierarchical, and bureaucratic organizations and would be most comfortable in a more mechanistic organization. You are likely to feel frustrated in an organization that is flatter, more flexible, and more innovative.

Scores below 45 suggest a preference for a more organic structure that is innovative, flexible, and team-based. This tends to characterize smaller organizations. You are likely to feel frustrated by overly rigid organizational structures with a lot of hierarchy and rules.

Scores between 45 and 75 reflect no clear preference for a mechanistic or organic structure.

Source: Veiga, J.F. & Yanouzas, J.N. (1979). *The Dynamics of Organization Theory: Gaining a Macro Perspective.* St. Paul, MN: West Publishing Company, 158–160.

What Influences Organizational Structure?

The most appropriate structure for an organization depends on many things, as summarized in Table 14-2. Let's discuss each influence in more detail.

Business Strategy. One of the most important factors influencing the appropriateness of different organizational structures is the *business strategy*.[28] Simple designs are appropriate for simple strategies, and more complex designs are necessary when strategies require more complex processes and interactions. Matching organizational structure to the business strategy leads to higher firm performance.[29] For example, an innovation strategy is best supported by low formalization and centralization and high specialization. A low-cost strategy would be best executed in a structure with moderate formalization, centralization, and specialization.

External Environment. Another important factor is the company's *external environment*. Rapidly changing environments require more flexible structures to deal effectively with the constant changes. This usually means that authority needs to be decentralized in some way to process relevant information and adjust to the changing environment.

Table 14-2

What Influences Organizational Structure?

Influence	Example
Business strategy	Being a low-cost producer would require a more hierarchical, rigid structure than would pursuing an innovation strategy.
External environment	A rapidly changing environment requires a more flexible structure than a more stable environment.
Nature of the organization's talent	If workers have professional skills (e.g., lawyers, scientists, etc.) and need to work together, then a flatter, team-based structure would be more appropriate than a taller, bureaucratic structure.
Organizational size	Larger organizations tend to have greater specialization, greater hierarchy, and more rules than do smaller firms.
Expectations of how employees should behave	If employees are expected to follow explicit rules and procedures, a more hierarchical, centralized structure would be called for.
Organization's production technology	If the firm uses unit production and makes custom products, a flatter structure with a low managerial span of control is most appropriate.
Organizational change	As the environment and business strategies change, organizational structures change too.

Firms facing a highly differentiated environment usually create different business units to best serve each market segment. For example, because consumer preferences for cars differ around the world, car manufacturers including Honda often create different business units to serve each market segment. Organizations are also sometimes able to impose elements of organizational structure on their suppliers. Walmart and General Motors impose accounting systems and cost controls on their suppliers.

Nature of the Organization's Talent. A third factor influencing organizational structure is the nature of the organization's *talent*. For example, a flexible structure is more appropriate if highly skilled workers, who often have professional norms guiding their behavior and decisions (e.g., doctors or lawyers), need to work in flatter, team-based structures to get the work done most effectively. Advertising and marketing firms are often organized into teams.

Organizational Size. An organization's size also influences its structure.[30] Smaller organizations tend to be less bureaucratic than larger firms. Larger organizations tend to have greater specialization and departmentalization, greater hierarchy, and more rules than do smaller firms. Larger firms also benefit from lower costs due to economies of scale. The larger an organization and its subunits, the taller the hierarchy, the greater the centralization, and the more bureaucratically it operates, and the greater the chances of conflict between managers and employees.[31]

It is impossible to identify an optimal organizational size. Many firms tend to start with a more organic form, but after a firm employs about 1,000 people, it usually adopts many mechanistic features to manage its increasing coordination and communication needs. As organizations grow larger, they become more bureaucratic and are often seen as less personable and harder to identify with, decreasing employee commitment.[32] Nonetheless, even some large firms including Google manage to retain elements of more organic structures.

To capitalize on the flexibility, adaptability, and decision-making speed of smaller sizes and the economies of scale of larger sizes, many firms including Johnson and Johnson—whose slogan is "small-company environment, big-company impact"—strive to create smaller units within the larger organization.

Behavioral Expectations. A fourth important factor influencing organizational structure is the *organization's expectations of how employees should behave*, and what attitudes it wants to encourage or suppress. This decision is based in part on the company's values. If employees are to be encouraged to make decisions and work collaboratively, a more decentralized and flatter structure is appropriate. If employees are expected to follow explicit rules and procedures, a more hierarchical, centralized structure would be called for. Because power plants and pharmaceutical manufacturing facilities need employees to follow explicit rules and procedures, they tend to be very centralized and hierarchical.

Production Technology. A fifth factor influencing organizational structure is the organization's *technology*, or primary production system. When a firm uses **unit production**, it produces in small batches or makes one-of-a-kind custom products. Employees' talents are more important than the machines being used, and it is difficult to specify rules and procedures in advance. In this case, a flatter structure with a low managerial span of control is most appropriate. Advertising agencies and consulting firms typically use unit production.

When a firm uses **mass production**, it makes large volumes of identical products, typically using assembly lines and machines. In this case, a taller, bureaucratic structure with a larger managerial span of control would be appropriate. Hershey and Sam Adams Brewery are examples of companies that use mass production.

When a firm uses **continuous production**, machines constantly make the product and employees monitor the machines and plan changes. At the bottom of the organization, continuous production requires a more mechanistic structure and low levels of supervision because machines do most of the work. The structure of a firm using continuous production is often tall and thin, or even an inverted pyramid. Dow Chemical and Exxon Mobil use continuous production.

Organizational Change. As organizations change their strategies and adapt to changing environments, they often modify and change their structures to support the changes. Samsung recently adopted a more centralized structure and created a new chief operating officer position to expedite decision making and improve efficiency.[33] Avaya's CEO appointed a chief restructuring officer to lead their restructuring to support its new business strategy.[34]

TYPES OF ORGANIZATIONAL STRUCTURES

In new or young organizations, the entrepreneur or founding group makes the decisions, and most communication is one-on-one because of the small organization size. This type of early organizational structure is called *prebureaucratic* and is highly centralized and lacking task standardization. This type

---

SO WHAT
Creating smaller units within a larger organization can increase flexibility, adaptability, and decision-making speed.

unit production
Producing in small batches or making one-of-a-kind custom products

mass production
Producing large volumes of identical products

continuous production
Machines constantly make the product

prebureaucratic structure
Smaller organizations with low standardization, total centralization, and mostly one-on-one communication

of structure is best for simple tasks and entrepreneurial organizations as the founder is able to control the organization's decisions and growth.

The founder's personal characteristics and values drive many of a company's prestructural characteristics, which often stay with the firm as it grows.[35] Indeed, other things being equal, it is the founder's personality that determines organizational structure and strategy.[36] Bill Gore's values and beliefs influenced the structure at W. L. Gore, the $2.4 billion high-tech materials company that manufactures Gore-Tex fabric.[37]

bureaucratic structure

An organizational structure with formal division of labor, hierarchy, and standardization of work procedures

As small companies grow, they typically adopt greater standardization and taller structures and develop a *bureaucratic structure* with greater standardization. In a bureaucratic structure, there is a formal division of labor, hierarchy, and standardization of work procedures, and employee behaviors follow written rules.[38] The greater importance placed on employees higher in the structure is reflected in centralized decision making and a strict chain of command. Bureaucracies are most appropriate in larger organizations when work tasks are well-understood and it is possible to specify the best way to execute them.

As they grow, organizations must decide how to carve employees into subunits. This usually means grouping people in a way that somehow relates to the tasks they perform. Here are six common bases for grouping employees:

1. *Employee knowledge and skills*: Employees are grouped by what they know; for example, pharmaceutical organizations have departments like oncology and genetics.
2. *Business function*: Employees are grouped by business function; for example, many organizations have departments of human resources, marketing, and research and development.
3. *Work process*: Employees are grouped based on the activities they do; for example, a retailer may have different retail store and online departments reflecting two different sales processes.
4. *Output*: Employees are grouped based on the products or services they work on; for example, Colgate-Palmolive has two business divisions: oral, personal, and home care and pet nutrition.
5. *Client*: Employees are grouped based on the type of clients they serve; for example, Dell Computer has different departments supporting home, medium and small business, the public sector, and large business customers.
6. *Location*: Employees are grouped based on the geographical areas they serve; for example, many retailers including Lowe's Home Improvement divide employees by regions.

Now let's discuss some of the structures that arise from these different groupings.

Functional Structure

functional structure

An organizational structure that groups people with the same skills, or who use similar tools or work processes, together into departments

A *functional structure* groups people with the same skills, or who use similar tools or work processes, together into departments. For example, a marketing department is staffed solely with marketing professionals. When Cisco Systems changed from a decentralized structure to a functional structure, it decreased the duplication and greater standardization of its products and process designs and reduced costs.[39]

Functional structures tend to work well for organizations in stable environments selling only a few products or services because of the increased economies of scale. Career paths within each function are clear, and employee

GLOBAL ISSUES

MULTINATIONAL ORGANIZATIONAL STRUCTURES

Multinational organizations have additional challenges in creating an effective structure to support their business strategies. There are four primary organizational structures that support global business:

1. *Global product division structure* (e.g., McDonald's): All functional activities are controlled by a product group at headquarters; local managers do not usually provide input into product decisions and are involved only in local administrative, legal, and financial affairs. This structure is appropriate when the benefits of global integration are large and local differences are small.

2. *Global area division structure* (e.g., Frito Lay): Regional and/or country managers are given substantial autonomy to adapt strategies to fit local situations. This structure is appropriate when local differences are large and the benefits of global integration are small.

3. *Global transnational division structure* (e.g., Kraft Foods[40]): A balanced, matrixed relationship between local managers and headquarters with a two-way flow of ideas, resources, and employees between the two locations. This structure works best when both global integration and local responsiveness are needed.

4. *Regional headquarters structure* (e.g., Coca-Cola and Sony): A regional headquarters is established in major geographical areas (often North America, Asia, Latin America, and Europe) that works collaboratively with the product divisions to give the local units clearer operational goals and directions than typically happens under the global transnational division matrix structure. This structure is best when a balance of global integration and local responsiveness is needed.

---

skill development tends to be in-depth but focused on a particular function. The possible disadvantages of a functional structure include poor coordination and communication across functions and a lack of clear responsibility for the delivery of a product or service. There is also an increased risk of conflict if employees develop a narrow perspective relevant to their function and not the organization as a whole.

Divisional Structure

A *division* is a collection of functions organized around a particular geographic area (*geographic structure*), product or service (*product structure*), or market (*market structure*). Divisional structures are common among organizations with many products or services, geographic areas, and customers.

When companies are global, they might put different divisions in charge of different geographic regions. Alternatively, if similar products are sold in different geographic regions, the firm might keep most of the functional work at home but set up divisions in different regions to market the product. This chapter's *Global Issues* feature discusses some of the organizational structures used by multinational organizations.

Divisional structures improve coordination across functions and enable flexibility in responding to environmental changes because employees' expertise is focused on specific products, customers, and/or geographic regions. These structures can also help organizations grow or downsize as needed because divisions can be added or deleted as required. The possible disadvantages of a divisional structure are that rivalries and conflict might emerge across divisions, economies of scale are reduced because resources and skills are duplicated across divisions, and employees may become focused on divisional rather than organizational goals.

division

A collection of functions organized around a particular geographic area, product or service, or market

Matrix Structure

matrix structure

Employees report to both a project or product team and to a functional manager

Can you imagine having two bosses at the same time? When employees report to both a project or product team and to a functional manager, they are working in a **matrix structure**.[41] Employees represent their function in their work team, which allows the team to house all of the skills and expertise it needs to perform effectively and make good decisions. Project managers coordinate the different functional contributions to the project and are held accountable for the team's performance. An organizational chart for a matrix structure is shown in Figure 14-5.

Matrix structures generate complex reporting relationships because a matrixed employee essentially has two bosses: the project or product boss and his or her functional manager. Adjusting to a dual reporting relationship can be challenging, but as long as communication is open and expectations and goals are shared, the problems can be minimized. Costs tend to be higher due to the addition of program managers in addition to the functional managers, and power struggles may result from the two-boss system.

Matrix organizations are good at providing quality customer service, are very flexible, and can respond quickly to changes because the work units contain all of the needed functional expertise to make decisions. They are best suited to complex activities in uncertain environments, and work well when one affiliation is permanent (typically functional) and the other is temporary, such as a specific project—for example, assigning a production specialist in

Figure 14-5

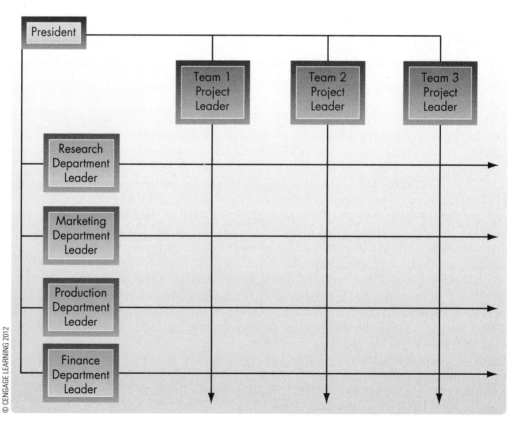

Organizational Chart—Matrix Structure

© CENGAGE LEARNING 2012

your chocolate company to a Valentine's Day project for three months and then to a Six Flags project for four months.

If project managers share organizational financial and human resources and cooperate, the matrix structure is more effective.[42] The distributed expertise, enhanced communication, and faster decision making enabled by a matrix structure decrease employees' protectionism of their functions, enabling more collaboration and more effective decision making.

Team-Based Structure

Organizations with a *team-based structure* create horizontal or vertical teams that can define part or all of the organization. Unlike matrix teams, in a team-based structure, performance team members from different functions are permanently assigned to the project or product team and do not report to a second functional manager. Whole Foods Market, the largest natural-foods grocer in the United States, has an average of ten self-managed teams in each store. Team leaders in each store and in each region are also a team.[43] Team-based structures are best when collaboration and inputs from several functional areas are required.

team-based structure

Horizontal or vertical teams define part or all of the organization

Lattice Structure

In organizations with a *lattice structure*, cross-functional and cross-level subteams are formed and dissolved as necessary to complete specific projects and tasks. This structure is common in consulting organizations.

W. L. Gore is a $3-billion, high-tech materials company headquartered in Newark, Delaware, that manufactures Gore-Tex fabric, Elixir guitar strings, and Glide dental floss, among many other things. Founder Bill Gore liked to say that at hierarchical companies, "communication really happens in the car pool" because that is the only place where employees freely talk without regard for the chain of command.[44] He also observed that during a crisis, companies create task forces that throw out the rules, take risks, and make big breakthroughs.[45] So Gore created a lattice structure with minimal hierarchy and few rules, organizing the company as if it were a bunch of small task forces. He insisted on direct, one-on-one communication where any associate (the Gore term for employees) can talk to any other. Gore does have a president and CEO, divisions, and business units, but there is no organizational chart, minimal hierarchy, and sponsors rather than bosses. There is no fixed or assigned authority. Goals are set by the same people who are accountable for making them happen, and tasks and functions are organized through a system of commitments. This allows employees to create roles for themselves that leverage their talents and interests rather than be assigned formal jobs.

The lattice structure of tomato processing company Morning Star is featured in this chapter's *Case Study*.

lattice structure

Cross-functional and cross-level subteams are formed and dissolved as necessary to complete specific projects and tasks

Network Organization

A *network organization* is a collection of autonomous units or firms that act as a single larger entity, using social mechanisms for coordination and control. Because network organizations contract out any function that can be done

network organization

A collection of autonomous units or firms that act as a single larger entity, using social mechanisms for coordination and control

CASE STUDY

The Morning Star's Lattice Structure

The Morning Star Company, a highly successful and growing $700 million California tomato-processing company, was founded on a philosophy of self-management. The company envisions "an organization of self-managing professionals who initiate communication and coordination of their activities with fellow colleagues, customers, suppliers, and fellow industry participants, absent directives from others."[46] The core of the company's management philosophy is freedom, which is seen as important to effective coordination. The company believes that freedom allows employees to be drawn to what they really like as opposed to having to do what they're told, increasing both enthusiasm and performance. Extensive applicant screening for fit with the company's philosophy and new hire training on self-management helps employees adapt to the autonomy and responsibility of working without a formal boss.

The company's lattice structure requires a high degree of self-management. Each year every employee writes a personal mission statement that identifies how he or she will contribute to Morning Star's overall objective of "producing tomato products and services which consistently achieve the quality and service expectations of our customers." Every employee also negotiates a Colleague Letter of Understanding (CLOU) with the associates most affected by his or her work. The letter creates an operating plan for each employee, spelling out the relevant performance metrics for as many thirty activities. Employees are also personally responsible for acquiring the training, resources, and cooperation necessary to fulfill their role.[47]

Like anywhere, disputes arise between employees that must be settled. If an employee believes that someone has not lived up to his or her CLOU commitments, the two meet to discuss the issue. If they cannot resolve the matter they choose a trusted internal mediator to hear their views. If the losing party objects to the proposed remedy, a panel of six colleagues assembles and either endorses the mediator's recommendation or proposes an alternative solution. If that is not accepted, the president brings both employees together and makes a binding decision. Reflecting employees' commitment to self-management, employee disputes rarely make it to the president.[48]

Questions:

1. How would working for Morning Star be different from working at a traditional, bureaucratic company? What would be the most positive and negative aspects of the experience?
2. Do you think the lattice structure is best for Morning Star? Can you identify another structure that might be more appropriate for the company's culture of empowerment and self-management?
3. Where do you think this type of lattice structure would be ineffective? What would make this type of structure inappropriate or difficult to implement?

better or more cheaply by outside firms (e.g., marketing and payroll), managers spend a lot of time coordinating and controlling the network of contractors and strategic alliances.

Clothing retailer H&M has a team of 100 in-house designers who work with buyers to develop its clothing, which is then outsourced to a network of 700 suppliers.[49] This allows H&M to be more flexible than many of its competitors and to keep its costs down.

H&M has a team of 100 in-house designers who work with buyers to develop its clothing, which is then outsourced to a network of 700 suppliers. This allows H&M to be more flexible than competitors, keeping costs down.

RICK DIAMOND/WIREIMAGE/GETTY IMAGES

Network organizations are best for functions that do not require frequent exchanges, do not suffer from supply uncertainty, and do not require customization. In this case, the costs of making and monitoring the transactions will not prevent the organization from hiring specialists to do the job. These specialist firms can often deliver a higher-quality product more cheaply because of the volume they do.

Because a network organization does not have a system of direct supervision or standardized rules and procedures, it must coordinate and control the participants in some other way. Some of the ways this is done are through joint payoffs and restricted access:

- *Joint payoffs:* Because networks are organized around specific products or projects, payments are arranged based on the final product, so that if the product does not make it, no firm makes a profit. This motivates everyone to do their best.

- *Restricted access:* By restricting their exchanges to just a few long-term partners, networked organizations are more dependent on each other. By increasing their chances for future business, long-term relationships decrease the incentive for one organization to take advantage of another because they will get kicked out of the network and lose the opportunity to have future work.

VIRTUAL ORGANIZATIONS

A *virtual organization* is one that contracts out almost all of its functions except for the company name and managing the coordination among the contractors. A virtual organization may not even have a permanent office. Virtual organizations often use virtual teams linked by technology, although employees may still meet face-to-face.

Virtual organizations tend to be very complex. The loss of control over the outsourced functions creates many challenges, including communication, ambiguity over organizational membership and career paths, and skills for managing at a distance. Nonetheless, the reduced costs and increased flexibility from being virtual create a competitive advantage for many firms.

Sigma is a German training and consulting company whose freelancing consultants and trainers build small or large teams as needed to work on projects. Sigma partners work from their home offices, some full-time for

virtual organization

An organization that contracts out almost all of its functions except for the company name and managing the coordination among the contractors

direct contact

Managers from different units informally work together to coordinate or to identify and solve shared problems

liaison role

A manager or team member is held formally accountable for communicating and coordinating with other groups

task force

A temporary committee formed to address a specific project or problem

cross-functional team

A permanent task force created to address specific problems or recurring needs

communities of practice

Groups of people whose shared expertise and interest in a joint enterprise informally binds them together

Sigma, and others temporarily if their competencies are needed on a project. Project managers find new partners through recommendations from current Sigma partners. An information technology system called SigSys enables communication.[50]

INTEGRATING EMPLOYEES

Segmenting employees into divisions, functional areas, or groups requires additional integrating mechanisms that facilitate coordination and communication among employees and groups. These mechanisms can be as simple as getting managers from different units to communicate and work together to coordinate or to identify and solve shared problems. When done informally, this is simply called ***direct contact***.

Alternatively, a manager or team member can be assigned a ***liaison role*** and held formally accountable for communicating and coordinating with other groups. When a specific project or problem needs to be addressed, organizations often create a temporary committee called a ***task force***. When integration needs are permanent and more complex, a ***cross-functional team*** is created. Cross-functional teams are like permanent task forces created to address specific problems or recurring needs.

COMMUNITIES OF PRACTICE

Communities of practice can also help to integrate employees and create the informal structure that nearly every business needs, regardless of its formal structure. ***Communities of practice*** are groups of people whose shared expertise and interest in a joint enterprise informally binds them together. Examples include consultants who specialize in designing training systems or environmental engineers willing to share their knowledge and insights with other environmental engineers. A community of practice may or may not meet regularly or even in person, and can be located in a single company or span companies. The people involved in a community of practice share their knowledge and experiences in open, creative ways that can create new solutions and approaches to problems.[51] In this way, the company intranet can cultivate a sense of community and employee loyalty.

Most companies have communities of practice, which often span across company boundaries. Field technicians share experiences and help each another troubleshoot problems, and researchers developing new products reach around the world to tap experts with specialized knowledge. Although these communities rarely show up on organizational charts and may not even be formally recognized by executive leadership, companies recognize their benefits and are increasingly promoting and enabling them.[52]

The Chevron Corporation has more than 100 "operational excellence" communities in place. One of those networks saved an estimated $30 million in damages by rapidly sharing information about the potential hazards of a gas-drilling technique that had caused problems in one location. Caterpillar Inc. has established more than 2,700 communities with more than 37,000 registered participants: employees, dealers, customers, and suppliers. The resulting quality and productivity improvements among dealers and suppliers have been enough to justify the investment seven times over.[53]

Managers cannot create effective communities of practice, only the conditions necessary for them to exist. A "command and control" management style is unlikely to foster successful communities of practice. Successful managers cultivate communities of practice by identifying and bringing the right people together, building trust, and providing an appropriate infrastructure.[54] Dictating goals and applying individual performance metrics can disintegrate communities of practice, and indiscriminately throwing money (or collaboration software) at them without a clear set of priorities can be equally wasteful.[55]

A relatively simple way to improve interconnectedness among community members is to develop a searchable database that identifies each community member's areas of expertise to help members quickly identify appropriate experts. Including some personal information in the database can help—knowing that the person you are contacting shares a hobby or alma mater can help break the ice.[56] The heart of a community of practice is the web of relationships among community members. Every e-mail, wiki posting, and phone call strengthens members' relationships and builds the community.

As a manager, how can you create the conditions that enable communities of practice to flourish? Here are some experts' tips:[57]

1. *Start with a clear area of business need*. Build communities that help the company work more effectively. For example, Hewlett Packard's Work Innovation Networks are a means of focusing effort on developing a creative approach to a current problem.[58]
2. *Start small*. Test ideas and try several formats to see what employees like and what works best. For example, any Hewlett Packard business can create a network by announcing itself as the host for a series of presentations, conferences, and seminars on a topic it is currently striving to understand. An invitation is broadcast to the rest of the company, and if the "market" responds, then the subject area takes on a life of its own in a community of practice.[59]
3. *Recruit management involvement*. If lower-level employees see their bosses actively participating in the community, they are more likely to participate as well.
4. *Use technology that supports the community's needs and that community members are able to use and are comfortable using*. Some training in using wikis, portals, and other technologies may be necessary. Some companies, including Ford Motor Company and Delta Airlines, have even provided home computers and Internet connections for employees for a very low price.
5. *Respect and build on informal employee initiatives already underway*. Employees may have already created a type of community of practice to help them do their jobs better—determine what is already in place and working, and build on it. Employees will already be somewhat familiar with the community's processes and practices, and more willing to use it.
6. *Celebrate contributions and build on small successes*. Building a community of practice takes time and requires employees to behave in new ways. Highlight on the company intranet or in the company newsletter ways the community has solved business problems and recognize employees who have meaningfully contributed.

A reason many companies invest in communities of practice is the ability of these communities to transfer knowledge among people. Organizations such as IBM, HP, and Unisys even prefer to call them "knowledge networks." In the knowledge economy, organizations need their employees to become "knowledge workers" who constantly draw on their expertise to respond to a rapidly changing market. Employees need to be able to participate in a flow of knowledge that consists of not only written and online information sources, but also the active exchange of ideas with others who have related experience and skills.[60] This also helps transfer knowledge from more senior to more junior employees, ensuring that key knowledge is not lost when some employees leave or retire.

SO WHAT

Communities of practice facilitate knowledge transfer across employees, facilitating employee transitions.

EFFECTS OF RESTRUCTURING ON PERFORMANCE

The turnover of a CEO is frequently followed by corporate restructuring.[61] Struggling organizations often look to restructuring as a way to improve their performance.[62] Although restructuring can certainly address some issues, it is not a panacea[63] and can lead to unintended consequences.[64]

The restructuring process is stressful and can decrease employee motivation if the changes are poorly communicated. High performers often leave if the change is chaotic or if their future with the firm is ambiguous. When the new structure requires fewer employees, the survivors of the resulting downsizing can suffer stress, decreased commitment, and higher turnover intentions.[65]

Restructuring efforts must focus on positioning the organization for the future.[66] Restructuring also must address the real cause of whatever the organization wants to change.[67] For example, if a performance problem is due to low employee motivation, reorganizing the structure is not likely to fix this core problem. Restructurings should take place as infrequently as possible to create stability, enhance performance, and minimize employee stress and confusion.

SO WHAT

Restructure organizations as infrequently as possible to create stability, enhance performance, and minimize employee stress and confusion.

SUMMARY AND APPLICATION

There is no one best way to organize a company. What is important is that there be a fit between the organization's structure and its environmental and strategic requirements. Structuring any organization is an ongoing process that adjusts the structure to match organizational needs. More centralized and bureaucratic organizational structures based on functional departments are well suited for getting routine work done efficiently. Matrix designs and teams improve coordination and relationships and promote effective decision making in the face of changing environments. Understanding a variety of organizational forms will help you to make an informed choice when you need to design an organization's structure.

TAKEAWAY POINTS

1. Organizational design is the process of selecting and managing aspects of organizational structure and culture to enable the organization to achieve its goals. Organizational structure is the formal system of task, power, and reporting relationships in an organization. Organizational charts are diagrams of the reporting relationships and chain of command in a company.

REAL WORLD RESPONSE

RESTRUCTURING AMERICAN AIRLINES

When American Airlines needed to redesign its organizational structure to better compete, it proceeded in a very strategic way. American wanted to reduce its total costs and put the customers' experience at the heart of American's operation. To do this it identified three objectives for its restructuring: (1) to have the right people in the right jobs, (2) improve cost efficiency, and (3) to "have a management structure that fosters accountability and high performance, adaptability and fast, effective decision-making."[68]

Beginning with the transition to Tom Horton as Chairman and CEO, American identified a restructuring goal in which all employee groups reduced costs by 20 percent. A layer of management was removed and the senior leadership team eliminated five officer positions, reducing American's most senior leadership positions by 20 percent. American's organization redesign purposefully began at the top, with each management level redesigning and staffing the next lower level.[69]

American has also taken steps to communicate frequently with employees and to recognize the difficulty the restructuring has imposed on them. Denise Lynn, American Airline's senior vice president of people said, "The need to reduce positions, and the impact this has on people, in this layer and throughout the process is difficult, without a doubt. Despite these changes, I'm pleased that we have taken advantage of the shifting structure to provide opportunities for our people where possible."[70]

American's restructuring is not yet complete, and the company's structure continues to evolve with each phase of the redesign. By staying focused on the company's strategy and business goals, the company hopes that it will be able to once again succeeded in the competitive airline industry.

2. Division of labor is the degree to which employees specialize or generalize. Span of control is the number of people reporting directly to an individual. Hierarchy is the degree to which some employees have formal authority over others. Centralization is the degree to which power and decision-making authority are concentrated at higher levels of the organization rather than distributed.

3. Delegation frees you to focus on more important tasks, develops others' skills, increases trust, and can lead to a higher-quality product.

4. An organization's structure is influenced by its business strategy, external environment, nature of the organization's talent, size, expectations of how employees should behave, production technology, and organizational change.

5. Prebureaucratic structures are most common in newer and smaller organizations. They are characterized by low standardization and total centralization, and most communication is one-on-one. Bureaucratic structures have more formal division of labor, greater hierarchy, and more standardization of work procedures.

6. Network organizations are best for functions that do not require frequent exchanges, do not suffer from supply uncertainty, and do not require customization. In this case, the costs of making and monitoring transactions will not prevent the organization from hiring specialists to do the job.

7. Mechanistic organizations are rigid, traditional bureaucracies with centralized power and hierarchical communications. Organic structures are more flexible, decentralized structures with less clear lines of authority, decentralized power, open communication channels, and a focus on adaptability in helping employees accomplish goals.

8. Communities of practice are groups of people whose shared expertise and interest in a joint enterprise informally binds them together. They help organizations share knowledge internally as well as across organizational boundaries.

DISCUSSION QUESTIONS

1. How do you think your career path might differ in a hierarchical versus flat organization?

2. Why do you think companies are moving toward flatter, more organic structures? Do you think this is appropriate?

3. What areas of an organization (e.g., what functions) do you think are the best to centralize? Which are the best to decentralize?

4. What keeps you from delegating more? How can you overcome these obstacles?

5. If you started your own company selling iPhone applications, what organizational structure would you create? Why?

6. If you wanted employees to work collaboratively and minimize conflict, what organizational structures would you consider adopting? Why? Which structures would you avoid? Why?

7. What type of person would be a good fit with Nordstrom's extremely organic and informal structure? Why?

8. What would you do during a corporate restructuring to ensure that your best employees did not leave?

EXERCISES

Am I an Effective Delegator?[71]

As you learned in this chapter, delegation is an important managerial skill in every organizational structure. This exercise gives you the chance to assess your delegation habits.

Source: Management review by T. J. Krein. Copyright 1982 by AMERICAN MANAGEMENT ASSOCIATION. Reproduced with permission of AMERICAN MANAGEMENT ASSOCIATION in the formats Textbook and Electronic book via Copyright Clearance Center.

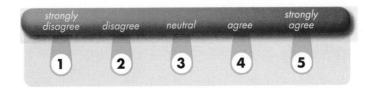

___ 1. I'd delegate more, but the jobs I delegate never seem to get done the way I want them to be done.

___ 2. I don't feel I have the time to delegate properly.

___ 3. I carefully check on subordinates' work without letting them know I'm doing it, so I can correct their mistakes if necessary before they cause too many problems.

___ 4. I delegate the whole job—giving the opportunity for the subordinate to complete it without any of my involvement. Then I review the end result.

___ 5. When I have given clear instructions and the job isn't done right, I get upset.

___ 6. I feel the staff lacks the commitment that I have. So any job I delegate won't get done as well as I'd do it.

___ 7. I'd delegate more, but I feel I can do the task better than the person I might delegate it to.

___ 8. I'd delegate more, but if the individual I delegate the task to does an incompetent job, I'll be severely criticized.

___ 9. If I were to delegate the task, my job wouldn't be nearly as much fun.

___ 10. When I delegate a job, I often find that the outcome is such that I end up doing the job over again myself.

___ 11. I have not really found that delegation saves any time.

___ 12. I delegate a task clearly and concisely, explaining exactly how it should be accomplished.

___ 13. I can't delegate as much as I'd like to because my subordinates lack the necessary experience.

___ 14. I feel that when I delegate I lose control.

___ 15. I would delegate more but I'm pretty much a perfectionist.

___ 16. I work longer hours than I should.

___ 17. I can give subordinates the routine tasks, but I feel I must keep non-routine tasks myself.

___ 18. My own boss expects me to keep very close to all details of my work.

Scoring: Add up your responses to the eighteen statements to calculate your delegating habits score.

Interpretation: If your score is *over 72,* you may be seriously failing to utilize the talents of your staff and should try to delegate more.

If your score is *between 36 and 71,* your delegating habits could probably be improved.

If your score is *below 35,* you are probably an effective delegator.

Review the statements to which you responded with a 4 or 5. This will give you some insights into the obstacles and excuses that might be keeping you from delegating more.

To improve your delegation skills, imagine that you must travel to an island and will not be able to contact anyone off the island for a week. Identify what you need to accomplish in the next week, and think about how you would delegate it to get it all done. Then start delegating some tasks and responsibilities and see if you are not surprised at the results!

Dow Corning's Cooperation Problem[72]

You learned in this chapter that restructuring does not always lead to improved performance. Working alone or in a small group, read the following description of Dow Corning's response to a cooperation problem, and then answer the questions below. Be prepared to share your answers with the class.

Dow Corning was having problems getting its country managers to cooperate with its U.S.-based product managers to introduce new products in their local markets. Corning's top management assumed that the problem was due to an inappropriate organizational structure, so Corning changed to a well-developed matrix structure. Unfortunately, the problem persisted. After a few years Corning realized that the problem was not actually due to its structure, but rather to its lack of a teamwork culture. Accordingly, the CEO introduced a teamwork culture, which successfully improved cooperation between the product and country managers.

Questions

1. Why do you think the matrix structure failed to solve Dow Corning's cooperation problem?
2. Which do you think is more important, a company's structure or its culture? Why?
3. What types of organizational structures do you think best facilitate teamwork? Why?

Designing Organizational Structure

Imagine that your chocolate company, Sweet Eats, has grown large enough to require a formal organizational structure. Assume that you have 250 employees organized around different mechanized manufacturing lines. One line makes chocolate lollipops, one makes chocolate bars, and one makes small bags of candy-covered chocolates. Draw an organizational chart to show how you would design a new organizational structure for this situation, and describe why you chose that organizational structure.

Now assume that your 250-employee chocolate company is designed around several handmade specialty products made in small batches by work teams. Orders tend to come from companies and individuals wanting to purchase custom, high-quality chocolates for corporate events and weddings. Draw an organizational chart for this situation and describe why you designed the company this way.

Johnson & Johnson's Unique Structure

Watch the video interview or read the transcript of the interview "Johnson & Johnson CEO William Weldon: Leadership in a Decentralized Company (17:06)" at http://knowledge.wharton.upenn.edu/article.cfm?articleid=2003, then answer the questions below.

Questions

1. How would you describe J&J's organizational structure?
2. How does J&J balance globalization with a local focus when needed?
3. How can a company like J&J promote consistent ethical behavior across all of its many autonomous operating companies?

VIDEO CASES

Now What?

Imagine being part of a group with the boss and another coworker discussing recently being beat to market by a competitor's new toy line. The boss asks the group what the company could do to prevent something similar from happening again. *What do you say or do?* Go to this chapter's "Now What?" video, watch the challenge video, and choose a response. Be sure to also view the outcomes of the two responses you didn't choose.

Discussion Questions

1. What organizational structures are illustrated in these videos? Explain.
2. How do these videos illustrate the influence of the external environment on organizational design?
3. What other ideas do you have to help Happy Time Toys faster develop and manufacture new toys?

Workplace | Evo: Designing Adaptive Organizations

When ski-enthusiast Bryce Phillips started selling ski and snowboard equipment on eBay, he managed everything—customer care, supply chain, technology, buying, and finance—all from his apartment. Nine years later, Phillips's company, Evo, runs a hugely successful e-commerce site, employs more than sixty people, manages its Seattle flagship store, and operates a 40,000 square foot distribution center. Evo has grown at least 70 percent every year and recently hit $10 million in sales. To effectively lead this expanding venture, Phillips continually looks for ways to delegate responsibilities to capable managers around him.

As a straightforward business, Evo is well served by its flat, functional structure. A recent companywide meeting showcased this organizational structure. Department heads introduced themselves and their staffs and explained the function of their departments so new employees and the whole company would have a better understanding of how all the pieces of the company fit together.

(Continued)

Beyond its formal structure, Evo works within a set of core values called "The Great 8," which provides another important operating framework. The Great 8 includes authenticity, balanced ambition, credibility, style, leadership, respect, communication, and evolución. On Evo's website, Phillips explained, "Even with all of the changes, many things have remained constant, and we are where we are because we have stayed true to the Great 8. We established the Great 8 to guide us through the decisions, big and small, that we make every day."

In 2004, when Evo employed only six people, flexibility was a way of life. Everyone wore multiple hats and did everything necessary to get the job done. As the number of employees on payroll approached sixty, it was time to make sure the people who dealt directly with customers possessed the authority and flexibility to deliver excellent service. This organizational soul-searching yielded a new customer care policy titled "Just Say YES!" As a result, customer service representatives now make their own decisions about how to make customers happy.

Today, Phillips is looking for ways to adapt again—this time to the troubled U.S. economy. Luckily, tackling monster moguls on the ski slopes has prepared him for almost anything.

Discussion Questions

1. Is Evo a centralized or decentralized company? Explain.
2. Are Evo's top managers likely to seek a taller, more mechanistic type of organization to accommodate growth and change? Why or why not?
3. Identify the factors that influence Evo's organizational structure.

DO WHAT?

CENGAGENOW

CENGAGENOW™ includes **teaching and learning resources** to supplement the text, and is designed specifically to **help students "think like managers"** by engaging and challenging them to think critically about managerial situations. **CengageNOW uses today's technology to improve the skills** of tomorrow's managers.

END NOTES

[1]Stewart, D.R. (2012). American's Managers Face 4th Round of Layoffs, Tulsa World, June 7. http://www.tulsaworld.com /business/article.aspx?subjectid=45&articleid=20120607_45_ E1_Afourt600974; Mutzabaugh, B. (2012). Full Text: American CEO's Letter to Employees Regarding Cuts, USA Today, February 1. http://travel.usatoday.com/flights/post/2012/02/american-letter/618147/1; AMR Restructuring News and Information,

American Airlines, 2012. http://www.aa.com/i18n/amrcorp/news-room/mn-restructuring-news.jsp.

[2]Ketchen, Jr., D. J., Combs, J. G., Russell C. R., Shook, C., Dean, M. A., Runge, J., Lohrke, F. T., Naumann, S. E., Haptonstahl, D. E., Baker, R., Beckstein, B. A., Handler, C., Honig, H., & Lamoureux, S. (1997). Organizational Configurations and Performance: A Meta-Analysis. *Academy of Management Journal, 40,* 223–240.

[3]Covin, J. G., & Slevin, D. P. (1989). Strategic Management of Small Firms in Hostile and Benign Environments. *Strategic Management Journal, 10,* 75–87; Jennings, D. F., & Seaman, S. L. (1990). Aggressiveness of Response to New Business Opportunities Following Deregulation: An Empirical Study of Established Financial Firms. *Journal of Business Venturing, 5,* 177–189.

[4]Morris, J. H., & Steers, R. M. (1980). Structural Influences on Organizational Commitment. *Journal of Vocational Behavior, 17,* 50–57.

[5]Pugh, D. S., Hickson, D. J., Hinings, C. R., & Turner, C. (1968). Dimensions of Organizational Structure. *Administrative Science Quarterly, 13,* 65–105.

[6]Katz, J. (2010). The Soul of Memphis. *Smithsonian,* 71.

[7]Blau, P. M., & Schoenherr, R. A. (1971). *The Structure of Organizations.* New York: Basic Books.

[8]Pugh, D. S., Hickson, D. J., Hinings, C. R., & Turner, C. (1969). Dimensions of Organizational Structure. *Administrative Science Quarterly, 13,* 65–105.

[9]Campion, M. A. (1989). Ability Requirement Implications of Job Design: An Interdisciplinary Perspective. *Personnel Psychology, 42,* 1–24.

[10]Revlon Implements Worldwide Organizational Restructuring. (2009, June 1). GCI. Available online: http://www.gcimagazine.com/business/marketers/announcements/46625697.html.

[11]Lashinsky, A., Burker, D., & Kaufman, S. (2006, April 17). The Hurd Way. *Fortune,* 92.

[12]Pugh, D. S., Hickson, D. J., Hinings, C. R., & Turner, C. (1969). Dimensions of Organizational Structure. *Administrative Science Quarterly, 13,* 65–105.

[13]Morris, J. H., & Steers, R. M. (1980). Structural Influences on Organizational Commitment. *Journal of Vocational Behavior, 17,* 50–57.

[14]Hartenian, L. S, Hadaway, F. J., & Badovick, G. J. (1994). Antecedents and Consequences of Role Perceptions: A Path Analytic Approach. *Journal of Applied Business Research, 10,* 40–52.

[15]Hage, J., & Aiken, M. (1969). Routine Technology, Social Structure, and Organizational Goals. *Administrative Science Quarterly, 14,* 366–376.

[16]Pugh, D. S., Hickson, D. J., Hinings, C. R., & Turner, C. (1968). Dimensions of Organizational Structure. *Administrative Science Quarterly, 13,* 65–105.

[17]Glew, D. J., O Leary-Kelly, A. M., Griffin, R. W., & Van Fleet, D. D. (1995). Participation in Organizations: A Preview of the Issues and Proposed Framework for Future Analysis. *Journal of Management, 21,* 395–421.

[18]Shadur, M. A., Kienzle, R., & Rodwel, J. J. (1999). The Relationship Between Organizational Climate and Employee Perceptions of Involvement. *Group & Organization Management, 24,* 479–503.

[19]Meyer, J., & Allen, N. (1991). A Three-Component Conceptualization of Organizational Commitment. *Human Resource Management Review, 1,* 69–89; Herscovitch, L., & Meyer, J. P. (2002). Commitment to Organizational Change: Extension of a Three Component Model. *Journal of Applied Psychology, 87,* 474–487.

[20]Gerstner, Jr., L. V. (2002). *Who Says Elephants Can't Dance? Inside IBM's Historic Turnaround* (p. 22). New York: HarperBusiness.

[21]Burns, T., & Stalker, G. M. (1961). *The Management of Innovation.* London: Tavistock; Lawrence, P. R., & Lorsch, J. W. (1967). *Organization and Environment.* Homewood, IL: Irwin.

[22]Rahman, M., & Zanzi, A. (1995). A Comparison of Organizational Structure, Job Stress, and Satisfaction in Audit and Management Advisory Services (MAS) in CPA Firms. *Journal of Managerial Issues, 7,* 290–305.

[23]Meyer, J. P., & Allen, N. J. (1997). *Commitment in the Work Place: Theory Research and Application.* London: Sage.

[24]Covin, J. G., & Slevin, D. P. (1989). Strategic Management of Small Firms in Hostile and Benign Environments. *Strategic Management Journal, 10,* 75–87.

[25]Spector, R. (2000). *Lessons from the Nordstrom Way: How Companies Are Emulating the #1 Customer Service Company.* New York: John Wiley.

[26]Burns, T., & Stalker, G. M. (1961). *The Management of Innovation.* London: Tavistock; Lawrence, P. R., & Lorsch, J. W. (1967). *Organization and Environment.* Homewood, IL: Irwin.

[27] Based on Burns, T., & Stalker, G. M. (1961). *The Management of Innovation.* London: Tavistock; Lawrence, P. R., & Lorsch, J. W. (1967). *Organization and environment.* Homewood, IL: Irwin.

[28]Chenhall, R.H., Kallunki, J.P., & Silvola, H. (2011). Exploring the Relationships Between Strategy, Innovation and Management Control Systems: The Roles of Social Networking, Organic Innovative Culture and Formal Controls, *Journal of Management Accounting Research, 23*(1), 99–128.

[29]Olson, E. M., Slater, S. F., & Hult, G. T. (2005). The Importance of Structure and Process to Strategy Implementation. *Business Horizons, 48,* 47–54.

[30]Gooding, R. Z., & Wagner, III, J. A. (1985, December). A Meta-Analytic Review of the Relationship Between Size and Performance: The Productivity and Efficiency of Organizations and Their Subunits. *Administrative Science Quarterly,* 462–481; Bluedorn, A. C. (1993, Summer). Pilgrim's Progress: Trends and Convergence in Research on Organizational Size and Environments. *Journal of Management,* 163–192.

[31]Harrison, F. L., & Lock, D. (2004). *Advanced Project Management: A Structured Approach* (4th ed.). Burlington, VT: Gower.

[32]Mathieu, J. E., & Zajac, D. M. (1990). A Review and Meta-Analysis of the Antecedents, Correlates, and Consequences of Organizational Commitment. *Psychological Bulletin 108,* 171–194.

[33]Samsung (2010). About Samsung Electronics. Available online: http://www.samsung.com/us/aboutsamsung/sustainability/sustainabilityreports/download/2009/2009%20About%20Samsung%20Electronics.pdf.

[34]Greene, T. (2009, March 26). Avaya's New CEO Sets Three Top Goals for Company. Network World. Available online: http://www.networkworld.com/news/2009/032609-avaya-new-ceo-discusses-restructuring.html.

[35]Hambrick, D., & Mason, P. (1984). Upper Echelons: The Organization as a Reflection of Its Top Managers. *Academy of Management Review,* 193–206; Lewin, A. Y., & Stephens, C. U. (1994). CEO Attitudes as Determinants of Organization Design: An Integrated Model. *Organization Studies, 15,* 183–212.

[36]Miller, D., & Droge, C. (1986). Psychological and Traditional Determinants of Structure. *Administrative Science Quarterly, 31,* 539–560.

[37]Deutschman, A. (2004, December). The Fabric of Creativity. *Fast Company, 89,* 54.

[38]H. H. Gerth and C. W. Mills. (1958). From *Max Weber: Essays in Sociology.* New York: Oxford University Press; Walton, E. (2005). The Persistence of Bureaucracy: A Meta-Analysis of Weber's Model of Bureaucratic Control. *Organization Studies, 26,* 569–600.

[39]Galbraith, J. (2009, August). How Do You Manage in a Downturn? *Talent Management Magazine,* 44–46.

[40]Kraft Foods Announces New Global Organizational Structure. (2004, August 1). *The Moodie Report.* Available online: http://www.moodiereport.com/document.php?c_id=1178&doc_id=2628.

[41]Kolodny, H. F. (1979). Evolution to a Matrix Organization. *Academy of Management Review, 4,* 543–544.

[42]Davidovitch, L., Parush, A., & Shtub, A. (2010). Simulator-Based Team Training to Share Resources in a Matrix Structure Organization, *IEEE Transactions on Engineering Management,* 57(2), 288-300.

[43]Fishman, C. (1996, April 30). Whole Foods Is All Teams. *Fast Company.* Available online: http://www.fastcompany.com/magazine/02/team1.html?page=0%2C0.

[44]Deutschman, A. (2004, December). The Fabric of Creativity. *Fast Company, 89,* 54.

[45]Deutschman, A. (2004, December). The Fabric of Creativity. *Fast Company, 89,* 54.

[46]The Morning Star Company (2012). Self-Management. Available online: http://www.morningstarco.com/index.cgi?Page=Self-Management. Accessed July 18, 2012.

[47] Flegal, S. (2012). 1 Company Thrives With No Managers, *The Telegraph,* January 18. Available online: http://www.nashuatelegraph.com/business/946895-192/1-company-thrives-with-no-managers.html.

[48] Hamel, G. (2011). First, Let's Fire All the Managers, *Harvard Business Review, 89*(12), 48–59.

[49]Capell, K. (2008, September 3). H&M Defies Retail Gloom. *BusinessWeek.* Available online: http://www.businessweek.com/globalbiz/content/sep2008/gb2008093_150758.htm.

[50]Jacobsen, K. (2004, Fall). *A Study of Virtual Organizations* (p. 36). Norwegian University of Science and Technology Department of Computer and Information Science. Available online: http://www.idi.ntnu.no/grupper/su/fordypningsprosjekt-2004/Jacobsen2004.pdf.

[51]Wenger, E. C., & Snyder, W. M. (2000, January–February). Communities of Practice: The Organizational Frontier. *Harvard Business Review,* 139–145.

[52]Laseter, T., & Cross, R. (2007, January 31). The Craft of Connection. Strategy + Business. Available online: http://www.strategy-business.com/press/enewsarticle/enews013107?pg=0.

[53]Laseter, T., & Cross, R. (2007, January 31). The Craft of Connection. Strategy + Business. Available online: http://www.strategy-business.com/press/enewsarticle/enews013107?pg=0.

[54]Wenger, E. C., & Snyder, W. M. (2000, January–February). Communities of Practice: The Organizational Frontier. *Harvard Business Review,* 139–145.

[55]Laseter, T., & Cross, R. (2007, January 31). The Craft of Connection. Strategy + Business. Available online: http://www.strategy-business.com/press/enewsarticle/enews013107?pg=0.

[56]Laseter, T., & Cross, R. (2007, January 31). The Craft of Connection. Strategy + Business. Available online: http://www.strategy-business.com/press/enewsarticle/enews013107?pg=0.

[57]Based on Stuckey, B., & Smith, J. D. (2004). Building Sustainable Communities of Practice. In *Knowledge Networks: Innovation Through Communities of Practice,* eds. P. M. Hildreth and C. Kimple (pp. 150–164). Hershey, PA: Idea Group; Vestal, W. C., & Lopez, K. (2004). Best Practices: Developing Communities That Provide Business Value. Building Sustainable Communities of Practice. In *Knowledge Networks: Innovation Through Communities of Practice,* eds. P. M. Hildreth and C. Kimple (pp. 142–149). Hershey, PA: Idea Group; Ambrozek, J., & Ambrozek, L. B. (2002, December). Building Business Value Through Communities of Practice. *Workforce Online.* Available online: http://www.workforce.com/section/10/feature/23/37/28/; Weigner, E. (2002). *Cultivating Communities of Practice.* Boston: Harvard Business School Press.

[58]Stewart, T. A. (1997). *Intellectual Capital: The New Wealth of Organizations.* New York: Doubleday.

[59]Stewart, T. A. (1997). *Intellectual Capital: The New Wealth of Organizations.* New York: Doubleday.

[60]Gongla, P., & Rizzuto, C. (2001). Evolving Communities of Practice: IBM Global Services Experience. *IBM Systems Journal, 40*(4), 842–862.

[61]Perry, T., & Shivdasani, A. (2005). Do Boards Affect Performance? Evidence from Corporate Restructuring. *Journal of Business, 78*(4), 1403–1432.

[62]Denis, D. J., & Kruse, T. A. (2000). Managerial Discipline and Corporate Restructuring Following Performance Declines. *Journal of Financial Economics, 55,* 391–424.

[63]Fraser, C. H., & Strickland, W. L. (2006, February). When Organization Isn't Enough. *McKinsey Quarterly.* Available online: http://www.mckinseyquarterly.com/When_organization_isnt_enough_1719.

[64]Bowman, E. H., & Singh, H. (1993). Corporate Restructuring: Reconfiguring the Firm. *Strategic Management Journal, 14,* 5–14.

[65]Probst, T. M. (2003). Exploring Employee Outcomes of Organizational Restructuring. *Group & Organization Management, 28,* 416–439.

[66]Marshall, R., & Yorks, L. (1994). Planning for a Restructured, Revitalized Organization. *MIT Sloan Management Review, 35*(4), 81–91.

[67]Carter, L., Ulrich, D., & Goldsmith, M. (2005). *Best Practices in Leadership Development and Organization Change: How the Best Companies Ensure Meaningful Change and Sustainable Leadership.* San Francisco, CA: John Wiley.

[68]Maxon, T. (2012). American Airlines CEO Promises Redesign of Airline's Management, Dallasnews.com, January 24. Available online: http://www.dallasnews.com/business/airline-industry/20120124-american-airlines-ceo-promises-redesign-of-airlines-management.ece.

[69]American Airlines Continues Its Organization Redesign to Build Its Team for the Future, PR Newswire, May 1, 2012. Available online: http://www.prnewswire.com/news-releases/american-airlines-continues-its-organization-redesign-to-build-its-team-for-the-future-149674795.html.

[70]Stewart, D.R. (2012). American's Managers Face 4th Round of Layoffs, Tulsa World, June 7. http://www.tulsaworld.com/business/article.aspx?subjectid=45&articleid=20120607_45_E1_Afourt600974; Mutzabaugh, B. (2012). Full Text: American CEO's Letter to Employees Regarding Cuts, USA Today, February 1. http://travel.usatoday.com/flights/post/2012/02/american-letter/618147/1; AMR Restructuring News and Information, American Airlines, 2012. http://www.aa.com/i18n/amrcorp/newsroom/mn-restructuring-news.jsp.

[71]Management review by T. J. Krein. Copyright 1982 by AMERICAN MANAGEMENT ASSOCIATION. Reproduced with permission of AMERICAN MANAGEMENT ASSOCIATION in the formats Textbook and Electronic book via Copyright Clearance Center.

[72]Ross, J. (1999). Dow Corning Corporation: Business Processes and Information Technology. *Journal of Information Technology, 14,* 253–266; Galbraith, J. R., & Nathanson, D. A. (1978). *Strategy Implementation: The Role of Structure and Process.* St. Paul, MN: West Publishing; Goggin, W. C. (1974, January–February). How the Multidimensional Structure Works at Dow Corning. *Harvard Business Review,* 56–57; Bartlett, C. A., & Nanda, A. (1990, November 16). Corning, Inc.: A Network of Alliances. Harvard Business School Case #391102. Available online at: http://hbr.org /product/corning-inc-a-network-of-alliances/an /391102-PDF-ENG.

CHAPTER **15**

Organizational Culture and Organizational Change

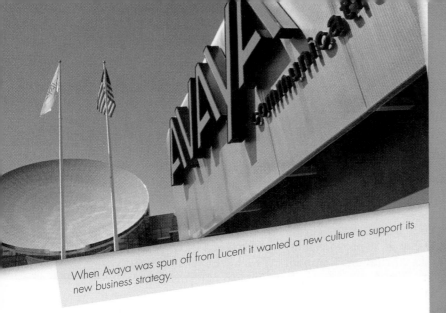

When Avaya was spun off from Lucent it wanted a new culture to support its new business strategy.

REAL WORLD CHALLENGE

CULTURE CHANGE AT AVAYA

Avaya is a global business communications company that was spun off from Lucent. Seven years later, the company was taken private by two private equity firms. This transition accelerated Avaya's strategy to become a business collaborator and provider of unified communications including web conferencing rather than just voice telephony. The change highlighted a need for a new culture that better supported its new business strategy.[1]

Avaya's bureaucratic culture reflected the strong influence of both AT&T and Lucent.[2] Avaya knew that this culture would not support its new business strategy. The company wanted to change Avaya's culture to better support creativity and collaboration. What advice would you give Avaya in making this organizational culture change? After reading this chapter, you should have some good ideas.

LEARNING OBJECTIVES

1. Explain why culture matters to organizations.

2. Describe how leaders create and maintain culture.

3. Explain why inclusive cultures are important to diversity and to organizational performance.

4. Describe why it is harder to acclimate remote employees to an organization's culture.

5. Describe the difference between incremental and transformative change.

6. List and explain the four stages of change.

7. Describe some of the most common barriers to change.

8. Describe after-action reviews and how they can be best used.

MICHAEL SMITH/GETTY IMAGES

Organizational culture is essential to organizational performance. Not only does it influence the decisions and behaviors of employees, but it also explains what is happening in an organization and why it is happening. Just as organizational structure can be thought of as an organization's skeleton, organizational culture can be thought of as its personality because it influences the way employees behave. Understanding and managing organizational culture is an important management role that can improve your own and your organization's performance.

Managing change is another key factor in organizational performance and even survival.[3] Change is prevalent in organizations as they adjust to changing internal and external environments. Two of the most common organizational changes involve changes to an organization's culture and changes to its structure. We will discuss both types of change in this chapter.

After reading this chapter, you should better understand both organizational culture and organizational change, and how to manage them.

WHAT IS ORGANIZATIONAL CULTURE AND WHERE DOES IT COME FROM?

organizational culture

A system of shared values, norms, and assumptions that guide members' attitudes and behaviors

When we say that an organization has a certain type of culture, what do we mean? *Organizational culture* is a system of shared values, norms, and assumptions that guides members' attitudes and behaviors[4] and influences how they perceive and react to their environment. These assumptions are usually taken for granted by organizational members, and are taught to new members as they are socialized into the group.

An organization's culture is reflected in how it gets work done and how employees interact with each other. It takes a long time for a culture to evolve, and a long time to change it. Trust is the foundation of culture, and is earned through repeated interactions over time. When a positive culture becomes strong enough, employee interactions become more efficient. Relationships improve, and employees cooperate to achieve common goals. When culture supports business strategy, the firm can become high performing. Common organizational culture themes include ethics, innovation, being casual or formal, and collaboration.[5]

As important as it is to create and maintain the right culture, doing so is not necessarily easy. As management experts Jack and Suzy Welch once stated, "It's Management 101 to say that the best competitive weapon a company can possess is a strong culture. But the devil is in the details of execution. And if you don't get it right, it's the devil to pay.[6]

artifacts

The physical manifestation of the culture including open offices, awards, ceremonies, and formal lists of values

Cultures are made up of formal and informal practices, artifacts, espoused values and norms, and assumptions. *Artifacts* are physical manifestations of the culture including the myths and stories told about the organization or its founder, awards, ceremonies and rituals, decorations, office space allocations, the dress code, how people address each other, published lists of organizational values, and so on.

When Lou Gerstner wanted to reinforce his culture change efforts at IBM, he abolished the firm's famous white shirt and tie dress code.[7] Steelmaker Nucor Corporation lists every single employee's name on the front cover of its annual report as a symbolic gesture to build and reinforce its team culture.[8]

espoused values and norms

The preferred values and norms explicitly stated by the organization

Espoused values and norms are those that are explicitly stated by the organization. For example, an organization might state that ethical behavior is a preferred value and norm, and it might hang signs in the office stating that ethical behavior is a driving principle of the company as an artifact of that cultural component. Nokia communicates its espoused values through videos, its intranet, and in its communications on company strategy.[9]

Enacted values and norms are those that employees exhibit based on their observations of what actually goes on in the organization. If a company's top managers engage in illegal or unethical behavior, these are the enacted values and norms of the firm no matter what its formally stated ethics values are. If the company has the espoused value that ethics are important, the difference between that espoused value and its enacted values creates a gap that can negatively affect employee attitudes and company performance.[10] Performance management, feedback, and compensation systems all help align espoused and enacted values and norms.

enacted values and norms
Values and norms that employees exhibit based on their observations of what actually goes on in the organization

Assumptions are those organizational values that have become so taken for granted over time that they become the core of the company's culture.[11] These basic assumptions are highly resistant to change, and guide organizational behavior. For example, outdoor clothing company Patagonia is noted for its social responsibility and environmental awareness.[12] Patagonia employees would be stunned to see their managers engage in environmentally irresponsible behavior.

assumptions
Those organizational values that have become so taken for granted over time that they become the core of the company's culture

Figure 15-1 illustrates these four levels of culture.[13]

Formal practices that influence culture include compensation strategies like profit sharing, benefits, training and development programs, and even the use of teleconferencing to enable some employees to work from home. Informal practices include "open-door management" to promote upward communication and the sharing of ideas, employees helping each other, and employees of different ranks eating lunch together to share ideas.

Does Culture Matter?

Does culture matter? Noted culture researcher Edgar Schein states, "Organizational culture is the key to organizational excellence . . . and the function of leadership is the creation and management of culture."[14] Research has shown that by actively managing culture, your organization and its employees will be more likely to deliver on strategic objectives over the long run. In particular, culture boosts organizational performance when it (1) is *strategically relevant*, (2) is *strong*, and (3) *emphasizes innovation and change* to adapt to a changing environment.[15] The effects of culture on a firm's effectiveness are even stronger when employees have positive attitudes.[16] A company's culture should reinforce its business strategy, and can give a firm a competitive advantage. If a business strategy and corporate culture are pulling in two different directions, the culture will win no matter how good the strategy is.[17]

BRENDAN HOFFMAN/ GETTY IMAGES NEWS/ GETTY IMAGES

Google's open office layout and amenities such as a cafeteria stocked with soda, candy, and free catered daily lunches encourage collaboration.

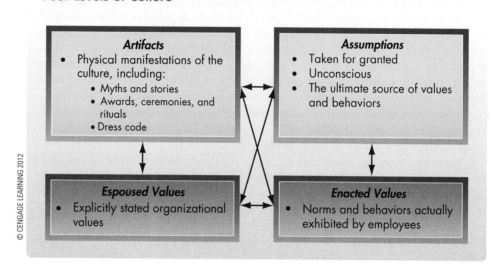

Figure 15-1

Four Levels of Culture

Artifacts	**Assumptions**
• Physical manifestations of the culture, including:	• Taken for granted
• Myths and stories	• Unconscious
• Awards, ceremonies, and rituals	• The ultimate source of values and behaviors
• Dress code	
Espoused Values	**Enacted Values**
• Explicitly stated organizational values	• Norms and behaviors actually exhibited by employees

© CENGAGE LEARNING 2012

SO WHAT

Actively managing an organization's culture improves the firm's competitive advantage and performance when the culture supports the business strategy, is strong, and enables innovation and change.

"Great companies create a culture where everyone believes we're all in this together and together we can accomplish anything." —Bill Emerson, CEO of Quicken Loans

Culture is a source of competitive advantage. Creating a culture that supports sharing and helping other employees can have positive performance results. Technology can make a sharing culture possible. For example, Xerox gave its 25,000 field-service engineers access to a knowledge-sharing system that they can consult during sales calls. The system led to a nearly 10 percent savings on parts and labor, worth $15 to $20 million per year. Dan Holtshouse, director of knowledge initiatives, is proud of "the 50,000 solution tips that have been entered into the knowledge base, all on a purely voluntary basis, in exchange for contributors being recognized. What we have learned is the importance of creating a work environment with a culture and incentives that are conducive to sharing, and to support that environment with improved work processes and strong technology."[18]

Organizational cultures can be strong or weak. Strong cultures clarify appropriate behavior, are widely shared, and are internally consistent. Strong cultures can enhance organizational performance in two ways. First, they improve performance by *energizing employees*—appealing to their higher ideals and values, and rallying them around a set of meaningful, unified goals. Because they are engaging, these cultures stimulate employee commitment and effort.[19] At Quicken Loans, CEO Bill Emerson believes that, "Great companies create a culture where everyone believes we're all in this together and together we can accomplish anything." To help strengthen the company's culture, he and Chairman and Founder Dan Gilbert spend an entire day of new employees' orientation discussing the company's culture and philosophies.[20]

Second, strong cultures improve performance by *coordinating employee behavior*. Shared values and norms focus employees' attention on company priorities and goals that then guide their behavior and decision making without impinging on employee autonomy like formal control systems do. This makes strong cultures particularly helpful for dealing with changing environments.[21]

Strong cultures are not always better than weak cultures, however—whether the culture is positive or negative also matters. A strong positive culture promotes employee commitment to the firm's value system and helps to align employee and company values. An example of employee behaviors in a strong positive culture would be employees' reaction to the arrival of the plant manager: "We're proud to have our plant manager come onto the production floor to observe our ethical, high-performance, high-quality work behaviors. We work this way whether the manager is here or not." In a strong negative culture, which means that employees have shared norms and values that are not consistent with what the organization wants or values, employee reactions to the plant manager's arrival would be: "Heads up! The plant manager is coming onto the production floor—look busy!"

Because strong cultures create stable and consistent employee values and behaviors, they are slow to change. If a company needs to change its culture to adapt to changing competition or a new business strategy, a strong culture can create difficulty in its ability to evolve. A company with a weaker culture (but not *too* weak) should be able to more quickly adapt to different circumstances. Culture is like the glue that holds things together in an organization—if it is too weak, it does not effectively guide employees. Research has found that long-term financial performance is highest for organizations with an adaptive culture receptive to change and innovation.[22]

When a culture is strong, it pushes employees to engage in behaviors that reinforce the firm's values and culture, whether good or bad. Strong ethical cultures are known to influence employees' ethical behavior and commitment through formal and informal organizational structures and systems.[23] An overall ethical environment that includes leadership, communication, reward systems, and a formal ethical behavior code of conduct decreases employees' unethical conduct.[24]

What ruined Enron? Accounting shenanigans is the easy answer. But underlying many of its problems was a culture that pushed for visible results and individual performance above all else. An emphasis on consistent earnings growth and individual initiative, combined with the absence of the usual corporate checks and balances, tipped the culture to one that reinforced unethical corner cutting.[25] During the recent housing crisis, rampant unethical corporate behavior led FBI Director Robert Mueller to call for a "culture of integrity" to combat the rampant mortgage fraud and other white-collar crime.[26]

A good example of how a company's culture influences employee behaviors is seen in the way Acadian Ambulance Service in New Orleans responded after hurricane Katrina hit in the fall of 2005. Employees from medics to mechanics, some of whom had lost their homes, quickly began delivering supplies, cooking, and keeping generators working. By the weekend, more than 5,000 patients and about 11,000 hospital staff and family members were evacuated. Ross Judice, M.D., Acadian Ambulance Service's medical director, said, "Acadian's culture has always been to 'Get the job done.' . . . Things happen because you have good people wanting to do good things who have the leadership and the motivation to do it. We saw a need and stepped up. That happened over and over again."[27]

Culture matters to organizations because it influences employees' discretionary behaviors, including what they do in situations when the rules and expectations are unclear or when there is no direct supervision. This is critical because organizations cannot create procedures or policies covering every possible situation. One of the most important sources of employee motivation is the firm's culture.

Understanding your corporate culture can create a personal competitive advantage by reducing the chances of your offending superiors or making a social blunder. Phrasing your ideas in ways consistent with actual company values and with the way top management views the world also increases your influence.

How Leaders Create and Maintain Culture

An organization's culture is influenced in part by its industry. Different industries develop different cultures. For example, nuclear power plants have a very different culture than do Internet or biotech firms. Organizational culture is also influenced by the national culture in which the organization is embedded. Russian, Chinese, and American companies tend to differ due to the national cultures in which they are embedded. Company founders and leaders also influence a firm's culture.

Most managers' training prepares them well to set the business strategy and ensure that the organization's capabilities are in line with this strategy. Shaping an organization's culture is harder to learn in school and takes personal involvement. A leader has to define the culture to support the business strategy, consistently behave in ways that demonstrate the culture, explain the culture to employees so they understand why it is critical, and then hold him- or herself and others accountable for maintaining it. It can be very time-consuming to create and maintain an organizational culture. Nevertheless, organizations like Nordstrom, Southwest Airlines, and Nike did not earn their success by letting their cultures happen accidentally.

An organization's founder and early management team shape a firm's culture, which is then reinforced by management's philosophy, values, vision, and goals. These cultural choices then influence the company's structure, compensation system, customer relations policies, human resources policies, and individual behavior and motivation, which reinforce the culture.

When beverage giant Molson Coors' new CEO Peter Swinburn took the reins after a series of ten acquisitions and joint ventures created a mishmash of workforces, he made it his top priority to forge a cohesive corporate culture.[28] As Swinburn says, "If you spend five years developing a brand, why shouldn't you spend five years developing a culture?"[29]

So how can leaders create, maintain, or change an organization's culture? Table 15-1 highlights some tactics several experts recommend.[30]

Employment and staffing service provider Randstad wanted its new hire training program to include information about the company's culture. What started as a one-week on-site course for new hires has grown into a sixteen-week program that combines e-learning, in-class training, on-the-job learning, and mentoring. During their first week at Randstad, new hires receive a virtual call in which executives welcome them to the company. Participants then take an e-learning course about the culture and the history of the organization and receive classroom training from their district managers on the culture and values of the company. Randstad believes that the training helps the business run more smoothly and gives employees a sense of having a career, not just a job.[34]

SO WHAT

Changing an organization's culture helps instill new employee attitudes, behaviors, and values.

PHOTO_ALTO/ISTOCKPHOTO.COM

Organizational culture is too important to leave to chance. Culture is communicated through formal training as well as daily routines, managerial role modeling, and company traditions.

Table 15-1

How Leaders Can Influence an Organization's Culture

- *Develop a clear sense of mission and values about what the company should be,* and communicate it to employees through what you pay attention to, measure, and control.

- *Select employees who can share, express, and reinforce the desired values* in order to help build the desired culture. Furniture retailer IKEA hires employees based on their attitudes, values, and fit with the company culture as much as for their qualifications. Steelmaker Nucor Corporation protects its culture by making cultural compatibility a key issue in acquiring other companies. In visiting companies it is interested in acquiring, Nucor pays careful attention to how plant managers and employees interact.[31]

- *Use daily routines and concrete actions and behaviors to demonstrate and exemplify appropriate values and beliefs.* For example, Walmart employees are constantly reminded of the company's cost-control culture. Reinforcing the company's thrift, a Walmart vice president responsible for billions of dollars' worth of business has his visitors sit in mismatched, cast-off lawn chairs likely left behind as free samples during a sales call.[32]

- *Consistently role-model behaviors that reinforce the culture.* Walmart CEO Lee Scott and Chief Financial Officer Tom Schoewe each earn millions of dollars a year, but on business trips, the two regularly share a modest hotel room. "Sharing rooms is a very symbolic part of what we do," Scott says. "It's also an equalizer. If I'm asking the district managers to share a room, but I won't share a room with Schoewe, then what am I saying? There are two different standards here? The customer is the most important thing for all of you, but for me I think I'll run a different standard."[33] Leaders set the culture, and employees learn what behaviors and attitudes are appropriate from their leaders' behaviors.

- *Make your human resource management procedures and criteria consistent.* Communicate your priorities in the way you reward employees. Linking raises and promotions to specific behaviors communicates leaders' priorities. When Lou Gerstner took the lead at IBM, he reinforced his performance focus with new performance appraisal and compensation systems.

- *Nurture traditions and rituals that express, define, and reinforce the culture.* Awards and recognition ceremonies, having the CEO address new employees during their orientations, and reciting stories of past company successes can all define and reinforce a firm's culture.

Changes in strategy, technology, and organizational structure all trigger a need for changes in employees' attitudes, behaviors, values, and skills. This can require changes in the organization's culture to reinforce these new employee behaviors and values. To assess important dimensions of their culture, companies like Coca-Cola use surveys and focus groups to regularly evaluate employees' perceptions of the company's support for diversity.[35]

Organizational culture has many layers. Outer layers of the culture, such as marketing strategies and customer service perceptions, can change fairly quickly. Inner layers, including fundamental values and ideologies, are much slower to change.

Organizations can also have different cultures in different areas. Different business units or subgroups of organizations can develop unique cultures supporting their unique business needs. This can actually mean that employees who belong to multiple subgroups simultaneously participate in several different organizational cultures.

SO WHAT

Effective employees understand their organization's conflict culture and how to appropriately resolve conflict.

conflict culture
Shared norms for managing conflict

active conflict management norms
Resolve conflict openly

passive conflict management norms
Avoid addressing conflict

agreeable conflict management norms
Resolve conflict in a cooperative manner

disagreeable conflict management norms
Resolve conflict competitively

CULTURES OF CONFLICT AND CULTURES OF INCLUSION

To better understand organizational culture, let's now discuss two specific types of culture: cultures of conflict and cultures of inclusion.

Cultures of Conflict

Conflict cultures are one example of a specific type of culture. Firms develop distinct *conflict cultures*, or shared norms for managing conflict, which reflect different degrees of active versus passive and agreeable versus disagreeable conflict management norms.[36] *Active conflict management norms* resolve conflict openly, whereas *passive conflict management norms* tend to avoid addressing conflict. *Agreeable conflict management norms* resolve conflict in a cooperative manner, whereas *disagreeable conflict management norms* resolve conflict competitively. This results in four types of conflict cultures: dominating, collaborative, avoidant, and passive-aggressive, as shown in Figure 15-2.[37]

Dominating Conflict Cultures. Dominating conflict cultures are active and disagreeable—open confrontations are accepted as well as heated arguments and threats.[38] The Digital Equipment Corporation had a dominating conflict culture as described by a former employee:

> People at Digital seemed to fight a lot with one another. Shouting matches were a frequent occurrence, and I came to conclude that Digital people didn't like one another. I was subsequently told by more senior members that it was okay to disagree with someone, because truth would ultimately prevail. . . . After one of these exchanges, one in which I almost came to blows with one of my peers, I was called in by my manager the next morning. Sensing that this time I had really exceeded the bounds of propriety, I thought about updating my resume. It was with great and pleasant surprise that I was told that my behavior the previous day had been admirable.[39]

Collaborative Conflict Cultures. Collaborative conflict cultures are active and agreeable. Employees actively manage and resolve conflicts cooperatively to find the best solution for all involved parties.[40] Southwest Airlines has a collaborative conflict culture, as described by a chief pilot:

Figure 15-2

Cultures for Managing Conflict

	Disagreeable	Agreeable
Active	Dominating	Collaborative
Passive	Passive-Aggressive	Avoidant

Source: Gelfand, M.J., Leslie, L.M., & Keller, K.M. (2008). On the etiology of conflict cultures, Research in Organizational Behavior, 28, 137–166.

Pilots and flight attendants—sometimes an interaction didn't go right between them. [If] they are upset, then we get them together and work it out, in a teamwork approach. If you have a problem, the best thing is to deal with it yourself. If you can't, then we take it to the next step—we call a meeting of all the parties.[41]

Avoidant Conflict Cultures. Avoidant conflict cultures are passive and agreeable. This type of culture strives to preserve order and control and/or to maintain harmony and interpersonal relationships.[42] Typical behaviors include accommodating or giving in to the other's point of view, changing the subject, or evading open discussion of the conflict issue.

Avoidant conflict norms often start at the top. At Wang Laboratories, a once-successful computer company that eventually went bankrupt, the founder and director developed and sustained a conflict avoidant culture by sending a strong message that he did not want to hear any conflicts or disagreements with his policies and practices. Although he acted in ways he believed would benefit the entire organization, which worked for a while, everyone prospered only as long as his instincts and actions were correct.[43]

Passive-Aggressive Conflict Cultures. Passive-aggressive conflict cultures are both passive and disagreeable. Rather than dealing openly with conflict, this culture develops norms to handle it via passive resistance such as refusing to participate in conflict-related discussions, giving the silent treatment, withholding information, or withdrawing from work and from interactions with coworkers.[44] Hospitals often have passive-aggressive conflict cultures due to the many layers of authority and strong bureaucracy.[45]

National and regional culture can influence which type of conflict culture develops in an organization. This chapter's *Global Issues* feature describes some of the cross-cultural influences on conflict cultures.

Cultures of Inclusion

Organizational culture is an important part of effective diversity management. An organization's values and culture interact with its demographic

GLOBAL ISSUES

CROSS-CULTURAL INFLUENCES ON CONFLICT CULTURES

Societal culture influences aspects of an organization's culture, including its conflict culture. Dominating conflict cultures may occur more often in national cultures emphasizing individualism, as in the United States. In the U.S. media and institutions, for example, conflict is often referred to adversarially as "a war" or something that should be "won."[46]

Collaborative conflict cultures may be more common in more egalitarian and collectivistic cultures and those that value cooperation over competition, such as The Netherlands.[47]

Conflict avoidant cultures may occur more often in cultures higher in uncertainty avoidance and collectivism, where people are motivated to submit to authorities and maintain group harmony, as is the case in many Asian cultures.[48]

Passive-aggressive conflict cultures may be more likely in societal cultures with higher power distance, or where less powerful members of society and organizations expect and accept unequal power distribution.[49] Passive-aggressive cultures may also be more prevalent in societies where there are abusive leaders.[50]

SO WHAT

A culture of inclusion helps leverage the potential benefits of diversity.

culture of inclusion

The extent to which majority members value efforts to increase minority representation, and whether the qualifications and abilities of minority members are questioned

composition to influence social interaction, conflict, productivity, and creativity.[51] Organizations that focus on collective interests better capitalize on the potential benefits of demographic diversity. Research has supported the idea that pro-diversity cultures are related to lower turnover among Blacks, Whites, and Hispanics.[52] Perceiving that the organization values diversity is also related to reduced absenteeism among Black employees.[53]

An organization's *culture of inclusion* reflects the extent to which majority members value efforts to increase minority representation, and whether the qualifications and abilities of minority members are questioned.[54] These perceptions may be affected by the firm's diversity actions as well as by the extent to which diversity is salient to a particular individual.[55]

When home finance company Fannie Mae wanted a corporate culture that values and retains employees, they asked employees, "From your own perspective, what could we do to improve the culture here?" They learned that Jewish, Muslim, and Hindu groups felt that the company always acknowledged Christmas, but never acknowledged Rosh Hashanah, Ramadan, or Diwali. The issue came up again when Fannie Mae was rushing to complete a financial restatement. Working twelve-hour days, six days a week cut into some people's religious observances. As a result, the company created a multicultural calendar noting religious celebrations throughout the year. When holidays approach, an article about the holiday's meaning and history written by an employee group is then posted on the company intranet; a note at the bottom directs managers on how to accommodate employees celebrating the holiday.[56]

This chapter's *Case Study* feature describes how Whirlpool built an inclusive culture.

This chapter's *Improve Your Skills* feature gives you some tips to better assess a company's culture.

CASE STUDY

Building a Culture for Inclusion at Whirlpool

Approximately 60 percent of the employees of Michigan-based Whirlpool Corporation, the world's largest manufacturer of home appliances, are located outside of North America. Even within North America, the company has a rich multicultural mix of employees.[57] Diversity and inclusion are central to Whirlpool Corporation's goal of placing its appliances in "every home, everywhere"—a vision that guides its employees around the world.[58] Whirlpool believes that acknowledging its diversity and practicing inclusiveness allows it to utilize all employees' unique strengths to increase Whirlpool's productivity, profit, and performance.

"At Whirlpool, we best serve the unique needs of our customers through diverse, inclusive and engaged employees who truly reflect our global customer base," says Jeff Fettig, chairman and CEO.[59] Because diverse employees help provide a keen understanding of its diverse global customers' needs, diversity and inclusion are encouraged throughout the organization. Whirlpool views diversity as about being different, and inclusion as the respectful involvement of all people and making use of everyone's talents. Whirlpool believes that differences create value, and they practice inclusion because it enables the company to best respond to the needs of its diverse customers.[60]

Senior leaders make inclusion a top priority. A diversity council oversees the efforts of the corporate diversity network, and a diversity network mentoring program addresses the needs of new hires. The company also hosted a diversity summit to discuss building a culture of inclusion.[61]

Whirlpool understands that its leaders must first show an understanding of and interest in diversity before it can become part of the company culture. To involve busy senior leadership and middle management in the company's diversity efforts, it creates short five- to ten-minute podcasts that report on the company's diversity initiatives, and gives iPod Shuffles to upper management so that they can listen to these programs while on the go. Executives can also print them out as short, two-page papers. A diversity and inclusion "lunch and learn" series, hosted by the employee-based diversity networks, offers a comfortable environment to generate discussion among peers. The engagement of Whirlpool's leaders has stimulated positive change throughout the organization.[62]

Whirlpool integrated diversity and inclusion into its business in three phases:[63]

1. *Awareness building*: Whirlpool began by building the business case for diversity in a changing consumer marketplace, and then delivered that message along with diversity training to the company's approximately 18,000 employees.
2. *Building competency and capacity*: Next, it developed tools to enable senior managers to effectively manage a global workforce and build employee engagement.
3. *Embedding best practices*: After training managers and employees, Whirlpool wove best practices into the fabric of the organization. It began by previewing the company's diversity strategy for new employees and continued through the development of an educational development curriculum that prepares senior managers to effectively manage a multicultural workforce.

Whirlpool's slogan even reflects its culture of diversity: "The only thing more diverse than our products . . . Are the people who create them."[64] Whirlpool was among Diversity Inc's Top 50 Companies for Diversity in 2011. In addition, Whirlpool has received a 100 percent rating in the Human Rights Campaign Corporate Equality Index.[65]

Questions:

1. Do you agree that Whirlpool can realize a competitive advantage through its diverse employees?
2. How else can technology be used to enhance Whirlpool's culture of inclusion?
3. Do you feel that Whirlpool's efforts to create a culture of inclusion are worthwhile? Explain your answer.

IMPROVE YOUR SKILLS

ASSESSING CULTURE

To be a successful and happy employee, it is important to match your values, preferences, and goals to the corporate culture. But how can you identify what a company's culture is before you become an employee? Here are some experts' suggestions:[66]

1. *Observe the physical surroundings.* Pay attention to how employees are dressed, how open the offices are, what type of furniture is used, and what is displayed on the walls. Signs warning of prohibited activities can also provide insights.
2. *Ask open-ended questions about the culture.* Ask several employees, "How would you describe your organization's culture?" and listen closely to their responses. Do they agree? Do they seem positive and enthusiastic?

3. *Check out the website.* How does the company choose to present itself? Do employee testimonials seem scripted or authentic?
4. *Listen to the language.* Do you hear a lot of talk about "customer service" and "ethics" or do you hear more emphasis on "making our numbers"?
5. *Note to whom you are introduced and how they act.* Are the people you meet formal or casual, serious or laidback? Do you feel you are being introduced to everyone in the unit or only to a few select employees?
6. *Get the views of outsiders, including vendors, customers, and former employees.* Do these sources of information consistently describe the company in terms such as "bureaucratic," "frustrating to deal with," "open and flexible," or "a positive and engaging place to work"?

EFFECTS OF TECHNOLOGY ON CULTURE

Creating and maintaining a desired culture can be facilitated by technology, but at the same time can be made more difficult by the consequences of using technology to work remotely. Let's explore these issues further.

Using Intranets to Build and Maintain Culture

SO WHAT

Effective managers use their company's intranet to establish and reinforce a desired culture.

By building and fostering a sense of community among employees, intranets can help reinforce an organization's culture. An organization's culture can vary across divisions and even across managers. Ask people who work in different parts of a large company to describe its culture and you are likely to get different answers. Because workgroups develop their own *subcultures*, intranets can be used to build a common cultural foundation that can help unify employees in different units and locations around common company values. This keeps people connected to the broader organization and also promotes consistency in how employees behave and make decisions.

The key issue for organizations is not about using the latest information technologies, but about leveraging the right technologies for creating and maintaining a culture of trust, openness, relationship building, and information sharing. An organization's intranet strongly reflects its culture, as highlighted in Table 15-2.

Table 15-2

How Intranets Can Reflect and Influence Organizational Culture

Each intranet design reflects a different type of organizational culture, and in turn reinforces the firm's culture by controlling the flow of information and establishing norms of behavior. Following are some of the ways intranets can both reflect and influence organizational culture:

1. *Their scope.* Intranets with a narrow scope can reinforce a culture of secrecy and information hoarding. Intranets that contain information on a variety of topics and links to other useful sites such as human resources, company and industry news, blogs, wikis, interviews with company leaders, and performance indicators reflect a culture of openness and teamwork.

2. *Their openness to employee feedback and contributions.* Intranets that contain "like it or not?" feedback tools and features that allow employees to contribute reflect a participative culture that values employee contributions. A more centralized, heavily edited and filtered site reflects a culture in which information flows less freely and employee contributions are less valued.

3. *The frequency with which they are updated.* Intranets that are rarely updated are not likely to influence the company's culture and can reflect a culture that does not value employee contributions, has poor internal communication, and has poor attention to detail. Lucent updates its intranet multiple times a day if appropriate. It also posts two weekly feature articles that reinforce the strategic vision and positioning of the company to entice employees to visit multiple times each week.

4. *The number of intranets.* This refers to whether there is just one company intranet, or several, each serving different groups of employees. For example, some organizations have one intranet for the sales force and another, completely different looking one, for the R&D group.

5. *The use of symbols, stories, and ceremonies.* Because these express a company's culture, intranets can convey such information via news of events affecting the organization, messages from CEOs, and announcements of employees' awards programs of importance to the organization.

Building and Maintaining Culture with Remote Employees

Being virtual challenges an organization's identity and culture, particularly when the company relies on free agents or alliances with other firms that have their own cultures. Because they spend little time face-to-face with coworkers, it is harder for virtual employees to become familiar with an organization's culture. It is also harder for the organization to reinforce its cultural values among remote employees. This has important implications for employee identification with the organization and for the management of employee behaviors.[67]

Because they are not able to see and experience the culture firsthand, acclimating teleworking employees to a corporate culture can be challenging. Business research firm Dun & Bradstreet's formal telework program requires employees to put in at least three months in an office before working remotely. This office time lets managers assess employees' strengths, weaknesses, and work habits in person. Employees also experience the company's unique corporate culture and work ethic firsthand. Working in the same place also allows team members to get to know one another before embarking on an e-mail and phone-based relationship.[68]

ORGANIZATIONAL CHANGE

As stated so well in the famous quote by François de la Rochefoucauld: "The only thing constant in life is change." Organizations must change in many ways to adapt to changing environments, labor markets, customer preferences, and other factors. Understanding the nature of organizational change and how to manage the inevitable barriers to change will make you more effective as a manager.

> "The only thing constant in life is change." —*François de la Rochefoucauld, Writer*

Organizational change can be described as incremental or transformative. *Incremental change* is linear, continuous change conducted to fix problems or change procedures. *Transformative change* is radical and tends to be both multidimensional and multilevel, involving discontinuous shifts in thinking or perceiving things. Incremental change is like rearranging the furniture in a room, while transformative change is like asking if this is even the building where we should be. Both types of change are important, but transformative change is obviously more difficult for both individuals and organizations.

incremental change
Linear, continuous change conducted to fix problems or change procedures

transformative change
Radical change that tends to be both multidimensional and multilevel, involving discontinuous shifts in thinking or perceiving things

Forces Creating a Need for Change

A variety of factors can create a need for organizational change. Some common external drivers of change include:

- Increased competition
- Globalization
- Changes in consumer demands
- Governmental regulations
- Deregulation
- Resource shortages

Some common internal drivers of change that occur within an organization include:

- Top management
- Technology changes

- Slack capacity
- Budget changes
- Talent shortages
- Growth

Recognizing a need for change in time to do something about it is the goal of forecasting and planning. Staying aware of current trends and possible change drivers will help you to anticipate what organizational changes will be needed.

Lewin's Model of Organizational Change

Kurt Lewin's force field analysis model of organizational change process[69] recognizes that there are always *driving forces* that push organizations toward a new state and *restraining forces* that act to maintain the status quo. Restraining forces create resistance to change that can block a change initiative. When driving and restraining forces are roughly equal, stability occurs because they are acting in opposite directions, as shown in Figure 15-3. Successful change occurs when either the driving forces are strengthened or the restraining forces are weakened.

Lewin's force field analysis model identifies a three-stage change process of unfreezing the current system, moving to a desired new system, and refreezing the new system. An additional diagnosis phase has since been added,[70] reflecting the need for planning and goal setting. This four-stage model is shown in Figure 15-4. The four stages are:

- *Phase 1: Diagnosis.* Before implementing any change, it is important to understand what requires change and what does not, and to set clear goals for the change initiative. The organization may already know this, or a more formal diagnostic effort may need to be made to analyze the need for change. Diagnosis involves identifying the problem; isolating its primary causes, which may not be obvious due to the complexity of most

Figure 15-3

Kurt Lewin's Force Field Analysis Model

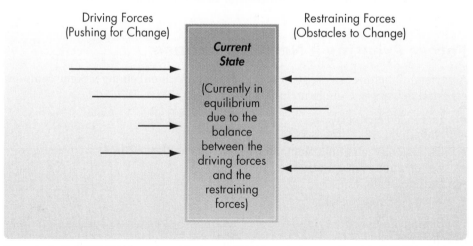

Source: Lewin, K. (1951). Field theory in social science; selected theoretical papers. Copyright © 1951 by the American Psychological Association. Reprinted by permission of APA.

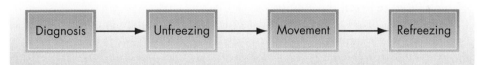

Figure 15-4

Four-Stage Model of the Change Process

Diagnosis → Unfreezing → Movement → Refreezing

Source: Northcraft, G.B., & Neale, M.A. (1994) *Organizational Behavior: A Management Challenge.* Hinsdale, IL: Dryden Press (2nd edition).

organizations; and developing an appropriate solution.[71] For example, low employee motivation may be due to many factors. Understanding the true cause is necessary to ensure that the chosen solution is likely to work in the intended way. There may be multiple or hidden causes, and many possible solutions. For example, should underperforming, unmotivated workers be given more pay, increased responsibilities, or better working conditions or should they be replaced with more motivated employees?

• *Phase 2: Unfreezing. Unfreezing* prepares people and organizations for change by creating a disequilibrium between driving and restraining forces that helps to dissolve the existing mindset and overcome defense mechanisms. Defining the organizational problem and recognizing the need for change help to overcome resistance to change. In addition, a change plan must be formulated, ways of evaluating change outcomes must be identified. The communication of the diagnosis and importance of the change must persuade the affected individuals and groups to accept and support the change.

unfreezing
Prepares people and organizations for change by creating a disequilibrium between driving and restraining change forces

• *Phase 3: Movement. Movement* involves the implementation of the change, and is usually a period of transition and confusion. Old ways are being dismantled, but the new ways are not clearly established yet. Even if the unfreezing stage is successful and employees support the change, implementation of the change may not be easy.[72] *Change agents*, employees or outside experts who assist with all phases of the change process, especially the resolution of conflicts, often facilitate this phase. If employees lose faith in the change agents, the change effort is likely to fail.[73]

movement
The implementation of the change

change agents
Employees or outside experts who assist with all phases of the change process, especially the resolution of conflicts

• *Phase 4: Refreezing. Refreezing* is the institutionalization of the changes into everyday life in the organization. In this stage, the firm's systems and structures support the desired behaviors. The effects of the change are also assessed against the goals of the change effort, and any unanticipated outcomes are identified.

refreezing
The institutionalization of the changes into everyday life

Kotter's Change Phases

After learning that as many as 70 percent of organizational change initiatives ultimately fail, Professor John Kotter identified eight reasons why many change processes do not succeed:[74]

1. Allowing too much complacency
2. Failing to build a substantial coalition
3. Not understanding the need for a clear vision
4. Failing to clearly communicate the vision
5. Permitting roadblocks against the vision
6. Not planning and securing short-term wins
7. Declaring victory too soon
8. Not anchoring changes in corporate culture

Kotter then developed a model of eight sequential change phases to prevent these mistakes:[75]

1. *Establish a sense of urgency*: Change is easier if people want it and are motivated to begin the change.
2. *Create a coalition*: Convince key people that the change is needed to build urgency and momentum.
3. *Develop a clear vision for the change*: Link ideas and solutions to an overall vision that people can easily understand and remember.
4. *Share the vision*: Keep the vision fresh in employees' minds and frequently demonstrate the change you are seeking.
5. *Empower people to remove obstacles*: This helps keep the change effort moving forward.
6. *Secure short-term wins*: Success is motivating—results can help to silence critics and negative thinkers.
7. *Build on the change*: After every success, analyze what went right and what can be improved; keep ideas fresh by bringing new change leaders into the coalition.
8. *Anchor the change in the corporate culture*: Because the corporate culture determines what gets done, the change will only stick if it becomes part of the core organizational culture.

Kotter emphasizes the importance of creating a sense of urgency, following the change phases in order, and recognizing that the entire system needs to support change if it is to last.

Appreciative Inquiry

appreciative inquiry

An organizational change philosophy and process building organizations around what works, rather than focusing on and trying to fix what doesn't work

The core idea of **appreciative inquiry** is building organizations around what works, rather than focusing on and trying to fix what doesn't work. This positively oriented organizational development philosophy or process engages individuals within the organization in its change efforts. Appreciative inquiry stems from the idea that an organization that focuses on its problems and difficulties will continue to find more of them whereas an organization that tries to identify and appreciate its strengths will discover more and more of what is good and can focus on creating more excellence.

Reactions to Change

Organizational change efforts result in a variety of employee reactions. Although quality, service, productivity, and risk taking often improve, employee outcomes such as stress, organizational commitment, employee morale, and workplace climate are often negative.[76] These unintended affective outcomes can undermine and even defeat an intended change. For many employees, a climate of constant change is a major cause of disengagement and withdrawal.[77]

Employees generally react to change in a predictable manner.[78] Employees are first in *denial* and refuse to believe that a change is necessary or that it will actually be implemented. This is followed by *resistance* as employees attempt to postpone the change implementation by withholding participation and trying to convince decision makers that the proposed change is inappropriate. Employees then engage in *exploration* and experiment with new behaviors as a test of their effectiveness in achieving the anticipated results. Finally, *commitment* takes place as the proposed change is embraced.

SO WHAT

Constant change can decrease employees' engagement.

Barriers to Change

Change is not easy for most people and organizations. Unless a change is perceived by all involved to be essential for personal or organizational survival, it tends to be resisted. This is why one of the best times for change is during an organizational crisis. Here we highlight some of the most common barriers to organizational change, summarized in Table 15-3.

Habits. All organizations, just like people, engage in habitual behaviors. Habits form regular, stable patterns of events that become routines and take time to change. Have you noticed that students tend to sit in the same seats during class, even when seats are not formally assigned? If you are feeling brave, sit in another person's regular seat during the next class or your next meeting and see what happens. Many people actually feel upset when "their" regular seat is occupied and they have to sit somewhere else. If people react to a change this small, imagine what people facing changes in work practices and expectations feel!

Power and Influence. Organizational change often involves both anticipated and unanticipated changes in the firm's power and influence structure. Some employees or employee groups may find their influence or power increased, and others may find theirs decreased as a result of a change. For example, the introduction of the Internet in many organizations shifted power toward employees skilled in the new technology and away from those unfamiliar with it. Because people do not generally want to lose power or influence, they are likely to resist any changes that threaten them in this manner.

Limited Resources. Resources—human, natural, intellectual, financial—are available to organizations in finite degrees. If employees need new skills to implement an organizational change but there is not enough money to invest in training, the change will be difficult to execute.

Misunderstandings. Misunderstandings due to communication problems or inadequate information can also create resistance to change. Not only does this increase uncertainty, but it also increases the chance that employees will not buy into the need for the change.

Table 15-3

Barriers to Change

Habits: Regular, stable patterns of events become routines and take time to change.

Power and influence: People are likely to resist changes that threaten to reduce their power or influence.

Limited resources: Insufficient resources (time, money, expertise, etc.) are a barrier to change.

Misunderstandings: Because misunderstandings increase uncertainty, they increase the chances that employees will not buy into the need for change.

Saving face: Sometimes people resist a change to "prove" that another option was better or to try to demonstrate that the person championing the change is incompetent.

Fear of the unknown: Many people are afraid of change because of the uncertainty over their future.

Tolerance for ambiguity: The personality trait that reflects the tendency to perceive ambiguous situations as desirable or as threatening helps to determine a person's ability to accept change.

Saving Face. Sometimes employees who preferred a different change strategy will resist a change to "prove" that the change is inappropriate or that the person championing the change is incompetent. For example, manufacturing employees resisting a change in work practices may intentionally reduce their productivity under the new system to try to prove that the old way of doing things was better.

Fear of the Unknown. Even if a proposed change has clear potential benefits, it is natural for those affected by the change to be concerned about the uncertainty of their future. Although a promotion might bring a desired raise or increase in status, for example, it may also trigger uncertainty over how to perform well with new supervisors, subordinates, and responsibilities. To the extent that the potential harm from a change is perceived to outweigh the potential benefit, fear of the unknown increases. Employees who understand that a change is needed may still be emotionally unable to make the transition and resist for reasons they may not consciously understand.

Tolerance for Ambiguity. The personality trait of tolerance for ambiguity has been shown to be positively related to the success of organizational change efforts.[79] *Tolerance for ambiguity* reflects a person's tendency to perceive ambiguous situations as desirable or threatening,[80] and reflects the extent to which a person is comfortable with situations that are uncertain or that cannot be adequately structured or categorized due to a lack of sufficient information. People with a lower tolerance for ambiguity tend to interpret and perceive ambiguous situations as threatening. People with a higher tolerance for ambiguity tolerate and cope with new experiences[81] and cope with change[82] better than people with a lower tolerance for ambiguity.[83] When top managers have a higher tolerance for ambiguity, organizational changes are more frequent.[84] This chapter's *Understand Yourself* feature gives you the opportunity to assess your own tolerance for ambiguity.

tolerance for ambiguity

A person's tendency to perceive ambiguous situations as desirable or threatening

UNDERSTAND YOURSELF
WHAT IS YOUR TOLERANCE FOR AMBIGUITY?

This feature gives you an opportunity to better understand your tolerance for ambiguity. Please respond to the following statements as honestly as possible using the following scale:

strongly disagree	somewhat disagree	neutral	somewhat agree	strongly agree
1	2	3	4	5

___ 1. I do not like to get started in group projects unless I feel assured that the project will be successful.

___ 2. In a decision-making situation where there is not enough information to process the problem, I feel very uncomfortable.

___ 3. I do not like to work on a problem unless there is a possibility of coming out with a clear-cut and unambiguous answer.

___ 4. I function poorly whenever there is a serious lack of communication in a job situation.

___ 5. In a situation in which other people evaluate me, I feel a great need for clear and explicit evaluations.

___ 6. If I am uncertain about the responsibility of a job, I get very anxious.

___ 7. A problem has very little attraction for me if I don't think it has a solution.

___ 8. It's satisfying to know pretty much what is going to happen on the job from day to day.

___ 9. The most interesting life is one that is lived under rapidly changing conditions.

___ 10. When planning a vacation, a person should have a schedule to follow if he or she is really going to enjoy it.

___ 11. Adventurous and exploratory people go farther in this world than do systematic and orderly people.

___ 12. Doing the same things in the same places for long periods of time makes for a happy life.

___ 13. I don't tolerate ambiguous situations well.

___ 14. I find it difficult to respond when faced with an unexpected event.

___ 15. I am good at managing unpredictable situations.

___ 16. I prefer familiar situations to new ones.

___ 17. I enjoy tackling problems that are complex enough to be ambiguous.

___ 18. I prefer a situation in which there is some ambiguity.

Scoring: For statements 1 through 8, 10, 12, 13, 14, and 16, subtract your score from 6 and replace your initial score with this new number (high scores should become low, and low scores should become high). Then add up your scores for all eighteen statements to calculate your tolerance for ambiguity score.

Interpretation: Possible scores range from 18 to 90. The higher your score, the greater your tolerance for ambiguity. Higher scores mean that you are more comfortable with change and are less likely to interfere with change efforts. Scores *above 72* reflect a particularly high tolerance for

ambiguity. If you have a lower score, you are less comfortable with uncertainty and with change. To increase your ambiguity tolerance, try to recognize why you are not more comfortable with ambiguity and work on developing the confidence that you can successfully handle ambiguous situations.

Source: Gupta, A.K. & Govindarajan, V. (1984). Business Unit Strategy, Managerial Characteristics, and Business Unit Effectiveness at Strategy Implementation. *Academy of Management Journal, 27*, 25–41; Lorsch, J.W. & Morse, J.J. (1974). *Organizations and Their Members: A Contingency Approach.* New York: Harper & Row; Norton, R.W. (1975). Measurement of Ambiguity Tolerance. *Journal of Personality Assessment, 39*, 607–619.

Overcoming Resistance to Change

Resistance to change can be thought of as any behavior that preserves the status quo in the face of pressure to change. Resistance to change can take many forms, including absenteeism, turnover, formal complaints, passive noncompliance, and even active noncompliance through strikes or walkouts. Organizational commitment helps to decrease resistance to change.[85] The success of change efforts is due not only to the nature of the change, but also to the process followed and actions taken during its implementation.[86] Many strategies exist for overcoming resistance to change, several of which are summarized in Table 15-4.

SO WHAT

Effective change initiatives require attending to both planning the change and overcoming resistance to the change during its implementation.

Table 15-4

Strategies for Overcoming Resistance to Change

- *Communication*: Communicating often and clearly reduces uncertainty and builds support.
- *Ensure that staffing and performance appraisals support the change*: This reinforces the permanence of the change.
- *Participation*: Letting employees participate in the diagnosis and planning phase of organizational change can increase their understanding of and support for the change.
- *Promote fairness perceptions*: Increased perceptions of the fairness of both change procedures and outcomes increase positive employee reactions to the change; treating people respectfully and fairly during the change process also decreases their resistance to it.
- *Negotiation*: Each side makes concessions to reach an acceptable change program and implementation plan.
- *Manipulation and coercion:* Using formal authority and power can result in compliance (although not necessarily genuine commitment).
- *Incentives*: Rewarding employees for supporting and facilitating a change can enhance their cooperation.
- *Pilot programs*: Implementing a smaller version of the change in one location or with one group and making improvements before rolling out the change project to the entire organization can increase employee buy-in after they see the successful results of the pilot effort.
- *Organization development*: A planned effort to increase an organization's long-term effectiveness will help to show the need for change and gain stronger employee support.

Communication. One of the most important things managers can do during an organizational change is to communicate often and communicate clearly, including through speeches and newsletters. Communication reduces subsequent employee efforts to derail the change effort, including sabotage.[87] The initial change announcement should build support and increase participation in the change effort while decreasing uncertainty during the unfreezing phase. During the movement phase, effective communication helps to maintain performance and morale during a period of instability and uncertainty, keeping employees focused on the anticipated benefits after the change is complete. During the freezing phase, communication helps to sustain momentum and focus employees on critical goals. Honest communication can help to decrease the stress associated with organizational change and improve employees' satisfaction, commitment, and intentions to remain with the firm.[88]

To convert the parties affected by a change into supporters of the change, the communication message should incorporate five components:[89]

1. Information about the need to change
2. Self-efficacy boosting elements, demonstrating that we have the capability to successfully change
3. Personal valence, showing that it is in our best interest to change
4. Information that those affected are behind the change
5. Information that the desired change is appropriate

Because Unilever believes that people at work tend to mirror the behavior of their managers, all of its change programs begin with senior managers, whose personal changes communicate the sincerity of a change to other organizational members.[90]

Ensure That Staffing and Performance Appraisals Support the Change. Aligning human resource policies and practices with the organization's new needs reinforces the permanence of the change. Evaluate employees on their adaptation to the new ways of doing things and to their performance in the new system, and be willing to separate employees who are unable or unwilling to change.

Participation. Letting employees participate in the diagnosis and planning phase of organizational change can increase their understanding of and support for the change.

Promote Fairness Perceptions. Perceptions of the fairness of both change procedures and outcomes are related to more positive employee reactions to the change.[91] Treating people respectfully and fairly during the change process also decreases their resistance to it.

Negotiation. When various organization members do not support a proposed change, negotiation can help. Each side usually makes concessions in reaching an acceptable change program and implementation plan. This is more common in unionized environments in which union support is critical to a successful change effort.

Manipulation and Coercion. Although not the preferred strategy, if the initiators of a change have more power than do those who oppose it, using formal authority and power can result in compliance. Changing organizational policies and transferring or terminating employees blocking the change may induce others to change. Note, however, that although this approach might generate compliance, it is not likely to create genuine commitment to the change, and it is likely to hurt employee motivation and trust.

Incentives. As Rosabeth Moss Kanter said, "People often resist change for reasons that make good sense to them, even if those reasons don't correspond to organizational goals. So it is crucial to recognize, reward, and celebrate accomplishments." Rewarding employees for supporting and facilitating a change can enhance their cooperation. Because financial incentives have been found to be effective in prompting people to improve their health habits and reduce health insurance premiums, hundreds of employers are using financial rewards, and sometimes penalties, to prompt employees to take demonstrable steps to improve their health habits.[92]

Pilot Programs. Before rolling out a change to the entire organization, organizations often run a smaller scale version of it, called a *pilot project*, in one division or business. This helps the firm learn from the smaller project and make improvements before rolling out the change project to the entire organization. Employee buy-in can be increased after seeing the successful results of the pilot program.

pilot project
A smaller version of an organizational change intended to test the proposed change and improve it before rolling it out to the entire organization

Organization Development. *Organization development* involves following a carefully planned and implemented process to support organizational change.[93] Organization development focuses on creating the structures, systems, and processes an organization needs to implement a change. By taking a long-term focus, organization development helps organizations overcome barriers to change.

organization development
A planned effort to increase an organization's long-term effectiveness

ORGANIZATIONAL LEARNING

As American capitalist icon and philanthropist Andrew Carnegie said, "The only irreplaceable capital an organization possesses is the knowledge and ability of its people. The productivity of that capital depends on how effectively people share their competence with those who can use it." As Ray Stata, President and CEO of Analog Devices, Inc., said, "The rate at which organizations learn may become the only sustainable source of competitive advantage."[94]

A *learning organization* is an organization that facilitates the learning of all its members and continually transforms itself.[95] In a learning organization, continual learning and change become part of the culture. Wikis, blogs, and searchable databases are sometimes used to collect employees' knowledge and make it available to others.

> "The rate at which organizations learn may become the only sustainable source of competitive advantage."
> —*Ray Stata, President and CEO of Analog Devices, Inc.*

learning organization
An organization that facilitates the learning of all its members and continually transforms itself

To facilitate organizational learning, it is important that learning happen during a project and continue after the project ends. As one expert says, "You need to have some coaching or debriefing afterward, to make sure that people learn what you want them to learn. You need to get them to think through the experience. If things worked, why did they work? If they were screwed up, why did things get screwed up?" Without reflection, tasks may be completed, but learning does not occur.[96]

One of the best ways to encourage continual learning is through an *after-action review*, or a professional discussion of an event that enables discovery of what happened, why it happened, and how to sustain strengths and improve on weaknesses.[97] After-action reviews are conducted for both successes and failures and occur after any identifiable event or milestone during a project or after the project is completed. The purpose is never to assign credit or blame, but to carefully identify the circumstances that led to successful and less successful outcomes to enable learning.

after-action review
A professional discussion of an event that enables discovery of what happened, why it happened, and how to sustain strengths and improve on weaknesses

SO WHAT

Effective leaders make time for learning from both successes and failures.

Learning from an after-action review is usually by the group and for the group, although individuals can also conduct such a review. The review is usually conducted fairly quickly using a simple process. In an open and honest meeting usually lasting twenty minutes or less, everyone who participated in the event or project discusses four simple questions:

1. What was supposed to happen?
2. What actually happened?
3. Why were there differences?
4. What did we learn?

Building trust and team integrity are additional outcomes of after-action reviews. To quote from a supervisor at Toledo Refinery in Ohio: "There are times when you think we don't have time to do this then you do it and think we don't have time *not* to do this."[98]

Another factor influencing an organization's ability to learn is its approach to failure. Many organizations punish failures through lower performance evaluations, lower bonuses, or even terminations. More learning-oriented firms recognize the learning opportunities presented by "intelligent failures," that is, the failures of events or projects that had a good chance of working, did not work out, but provide a good learning opportunity. At the computer chipmaker Intel, one manager threw a big dinner every month—not for the group that had been most successful, but for the "failure of the month," to honor the group that had made a valiant effort that just did not work out. That manager communicated to his people that failures were an inevitable accompaniment of risk taking that should be talked about openly, not hidden, papered over, or blamed on others.[99] High-quality relationships in which employees feel psychologically safe enables organizational members to engage in learning from failures.[100]

SUMMARY AND APPLICATION

Because organizational culture influences the norms, communication, socialization, and group dynamics within an organization, it ultimately influences employees' performance, satisfaction, and personal growth and development. Organizations can have cultures for different things, such as a customer service culture, an ethical culture, or an innovation culture promoting risk taking and experimentation.

✔ TAKEAWAY POINTS

1. By actively managing culture, your organization and its employees will be more likely to deliver on strategic objectives over the long run. Culture boosts organizational performance when it (1) is *strategically relevant*, (2) is *strong*, and (3) *emphasizes innovation and change*. A company's culture that reinforces its business strategy can give it a competitive advantage.

2. Leaders create and maintain culture by developing a clear sense of mission and values about what the company should be; selecting employees who can share, express, and reinforce the desired values; using daily routines and concrete actions and behaviors to demonstrate and exemplify appropriate values and beliefs; consistently role-modeling behaviors that reinforce the culture; making human resource management procedures and criteria consistent; and nurturing traditions and rituals that express, define, and reinforce the culture.

REAL WORLD RESPONSE

CULTURE CHANGE AT AVAYA

Avaya began its culture change initiative by identifying its desired culture and comparing it to its current culture. Marketing-style focus groups, interviews with departing employees, and conversations with the executive team helped the company identify what it needed to change and become.[101] Avaya learned that loyalty, integrity, and trust were a strong part of its culture, and that innovation was truly valued by employees. They also learned that employees were averse to taking risks, feeling that they needed to ask permission before making decisions, and that numerous restructurings and changes over the years created a mentality that employees needed to keep their heads down to survive. Avaya's change leaders realized that no one "owned" the culture and no one had taken the initiative to manage it during Avaya's formative years.[102]

Core values and beliefs were identified that Avaya needed to reinforce throughout the organization. "Success profiles" describing what employees at each organizational level would need to know and do to support the business strategy and desired culture were identified and communicated. Performance management, employee development, and pay-for-performance plans were put in place to support the desired employee behaviours.[103]

Avaya is now making big strides toward changing its culture[104] despite numerous challenges including a global recession.

3. Inclusive cultures value efforts to increase minority representation, and do not question the qualifications and abilities of minority members, which improves social interaction, conflict, productivity, and creativity.
4. Because remote employees spend little time face-to-face with coworkers, it is harder for them to become familiar with an organization's culture and it is harder for the organization to reinforce its cultural values.
5. Incremental change is linear, continuous, and conducted to fix problems or change procedures. Transformative change is larger, more radical change involving shifts in thinking or in how things are perceived.
6. The four stages of change are diagnosis, unfreezing, movement, and refreezing. *Diagnosis* involves identifying the problem and its primary causes, and developing a solution. *Unfreezing* prepares people and organizations for change by creating a disequilibrium between driving and restraining change forces. *Movement* is the implementation of the change solution identified in the diagnosis phase. *Refreezing* is the institutionalization of the changes into everyday organizational life.
7. The most common barriers to change include habit, changes in organizational power and influence, limited resources, misunderstandings, saving face, fear of the unknown, and ambiguity tolerance.

8. An after-action review is a professional discussion of an event that enables discovery of what happened, why it happened, and how to sustain strengths and improve on weaknesses. It is best done immediately following any identifiable event or milestone during a project or after a project is completed.

DISCUSSION QUESTIONS

1. Describe three different types of organizational cultures. When would each be most and least effective for a research and development company dependent on employee innovation?
2. Do you think that culture is important to organizational performance? Why or why not?
3. How do you learn about prospective employers' cultures? How important is a company's culture to you when you decide to apply or to accept a job offer?
4. Which of the four conflict management cultures would be the best fit for you? Why?
5. What can companies do to create and reinforce a culture of inclusion?
6. What do you think are the most difficult barriers to change? How can they be overcome?
7. Describe some factors or events that might stimulate organizational change. How would organizations need to change to respond to them?
8. How can learning-oriented companies encourage high performance while tolerating the inevitable failures that will result from experimentation and risk taking? What types of organizational policies and rewards would support these values?

EXERCISES

Learning from Change

Think about a major change you experienced over the past five years. While thinking about this experience, answer the following questions.

Questions

1. What was the greatest fear or difficulty you had to face?
2. How did you overcome this fear or difficulty? (What methods did you employ?)
3. What worked well? What would you do differently?
4. What have you learned? How could you apply these insights to manage change you are experiencing in your organization?

*We thank Professor Michael S. Duchon at Cleveland State University for suggesting this exercise.

Performance Improvement Through Culture Change

Imagine that you have just accepted a leadership position with Pirate Cove, an Internet retail company focused on a wide variety of pirate-themed products. The organization's financial performance has been worsening and its market share slipping, which is why the company hired you to come in and make some changes. You have been given the authority to do whatever you need to do to improve the company's performance.

After collecting a lot of information and speaking with a wide variety of employees, you have determined that the biggest cause of the company's underperformance is that its culture is too complex and consensus-oriented, which makes decision making too slow. The first thing you decide to do is to change the culture. What type of culture do you want to adopt? How will you change the culture? What will you do to reinforce the changes you suggest (e.g., through staffing, rewards, performance feedback, etc.)? You will have twenty minutes to work alone or in a small group. Be prepared to share your insights with the rest of the class.

VIDEO CASES

Now What?

Imagine attending a meeting with your boss and two coworkers to discuss declining sales for a previously popular product. A competitor introduced a similar but better product that has been taking your market share. The company knew about the competitor's product, but underestimated the threat. Happy Time Toys wants to make sure it recognizes potential threats faster in the future. *What do you say or do?* Go to this chapter's "Now What?" video, watch the challenge video, and choose a response. Be sure to also view the outcomes of the two responses you didn't choose.

Discussion Questions

1. How is resistance to change illustrated in these videos?
2. How is ethics illustrated in these videos?
3. Which other aspects of organizational behavior discussed in this chapter are illustrated in these videos? Explain your answer.

Workplace | The Environment and Corporate Culture at Recycline

Ever since green became the new black, U.S. companies have been scrambling to change their products, packaging, and energy consumption to stay in the game. Thanks to Eric Hudson's perceptive scanning of the

(Continued)

external environment in the mid-1990s, recycled products firm Recycline discovered an opportunity others missed.

Hudson broke into the natural product arena with an innovative toothbrush made from recycled materials—a bold decision in 1996. Hudson named his first product the Preserve Toothbrush, and Recycline was born. The toothbrush, with its nylon bristles and ergonomically curved handle made of 100 percent recycled material, was a hit with eco-conscious consumers. New converts flocked to it, and Hudson gradually added personal care and kitchenware items to his line of recycled products. Today, Preserve products can be found at top retail chains including Target, Whole Foods, and Wal-Mart.

For environmentally sensitive consumers, integrity is everything. Recycline believes that customers are getting wise to the "green-washing effect" in which businesses cultivate a superficial green image without the substance to back it up. A close look at Recycline's internal culture confirms that Hudson's company is authentically green. First, as Preserve's cultural leader, Hudson practices what he preaches; When he isn't pedaling twenty-two miles to and from work on his bicycle, he's cruising in a Volkswagen that has been converted to run on french-fry grease—an emerging symbol of the modern-day eco-hero. Additionally, everyone at Preserve tries to do right by the natural environment, whether it's composting, conserving energy, or using eco-friendly cleaning products.

But Recycline's organizational culture isn't just green—it's effective. Because of Recycline's small size, anyone interested in taking on a new initiative is encouraged to do so, regardless of position. The vice president of sales, John Turcott, believes that Preserve's size is critical for rapid response: "Our decision-making process is quicker. We pull together the resources we need to solve a problem, we get it done and move on to the next thing." Since everything at Preserve happens at high-speed, everyone has to be driven, creative, and adaptable.

Discussion Questions

1. What are some visible aspects of Recycline's culture that reflect the company's values and commitment to green issues?
2. What role do leaders play in shaping Recycline's organizational culture? Explain.
3. Could Recycline easily change its organizational culture if the green products market encounters a backlash? How would management know if a permanent change in culture has occurred?

DO WHAT

CENGAGENOW™

CENGAGENOW™ includes **teaching and learning resources** to supplement the text, and is designed specifically to **help students "think like managers"** by engaging and challenging them to think critically about managerial situations. **CengageNOW uses today's technology to improve the skills** of tomorrow's managers.

END NOTES

[1]Gaston, R. & Fitzgerald, S. (2010). Culture Change at Avaya. Denison Consulting. Available online: http://www.denisonconsulting .com/sites/default/files/documents/resources/culture_change_at _avaya_-_webinar_presenation__0.pdf.

[2] Denison (2011). Avaya: Culture Transformation through Alignment, *Denison, 6*(2), 1–4.

[3]The Nimble Giants: Hard-Learned Lessons in the Art of Change Are Paying Off at Last. (1994, March 28). *Business Week,* 64–69.

[4]O'Reilly, C., & Chatman, J. (1996). Cultures as Social Control: Corporations, Cults, and Commitment. In *Research in Organizational Behavior,* eds. L. Cummings and B. M. Staw (Vol. 18, pp. 157–200, p. 166). Greenwich, CT: JAI Press.

[5]Chatman, J. A., & Jehn, K. A. (1994). Assessing the Relationship Between Industry Characteristics and Organizational Culture: How Different Can You Be? *Academy of Management Journal, 37,* 522–553.

[6]Welch, J. & Welch, S. (2012). Goldman Sachs and a Culture-Killing Lesson Being Ignored, Fortune, April 30. Available online: http://management.fortune.cnn.com/2012/04/12 /goldman-sachs-culture-values/.

[7]Gerstner, II, L. V. (2002). *Who Says Elephants Can't Dance? Inside IBM's Historic Turnaround.* New York: HarperCollins.

[8]Byrnes, N. (2006, May 1). The Art of Motivation. *BusinessWeek,* 56–62.

[9]Embedding Our Values (2010). Nokia.com. Available online: http://www.nokia.com/corporate-responsibility/employees /employee-engagement/embedding-our-values.

[10]See, e.g., Clarke, S. (1999, March). Perceptions of Organizational Safety: Implications for the Development of Safety Culture. *Journal of Organizational Behavior,* 185–198.

[11]Schein, E. (1985). *Organizational Culture and Leadership.* San Francisco, CA: Jossey-Bass.

[12]Gardiner, L. (2010). From Synchilla to School Support. Markkula Center for Applied Ethics. Available online: http://www.scu .edu/ethics/publications/iie/v8n1/synchilla.html.

[13]Note: Three levels, combining espoused and enacted values, are referred to in Schein, E. (1992). *Organizational Culture and Leadership* (2nd ed.). San Francisco, CA: Jossey-Bass.

[14]Schein, E. (1992). *Organizational Culture and Leadership* (2nd ed.). San Francisco, CA: Jossey-Bass.

[15]Chatman, J. A., & Cha, S. E. (2003). Leading by Leveraging Culture. *California Management Review, 45,* 20–34.

[16]Gregory, B. T., Harris, S. G., Armenakis, A. A., & Shook, C. L. (2009). Organizational Culture and Effectiveness: A Study of Values, Attitudes, and Organizational Outcomes. *Journal of Business Research, 62,* 673–679.

[17]Neuhauser, P. C., Bender, R., & Stromberg, K. L. (2000). *Culture. com: Building Corporate Culture in the Connected Workplace.* New York: John Wiley.

[18]Ambrozek, J., & Ambrozek, L. B. (2002, December). Building Business Value Through "Communities of Practice." *Workforce Online.* Available online: http://www.workforce.com/section/10 /feature/23/37/28/.

[19]Walton, R. E. (1980). Establishing and Maintaining High Commitment Work Systems. In *The Organizational Life Cycle: Issues in the Creation, Transformation and Decline of Organizations,* eds. J. R. Kimberly and R. H. Miles, & Associates (pp. 208–290). San Francisco, CA: Jossey-Bass.

[20]Quicken Loans Named to *Fortune*'s "100 Best Companies to Work For" List for Third Consecutive Year. (2006). Quicken Loans. Available online: http://www.quickenloans.com/about /press_room/news_releases/fortune_best_company2006.html.

[21]Tushman, M. L., & O'Reilly, C. A. (1997). *Winning Through Innovation: A Practical Guide to Leading Organizational Change and Renewal.* Boston: Harvard Business School Press.

[22]Kotter, J. P., & Heskett, J. L. (1992). *Corporate Culture and Performance.* New York: Free Press.

[23]Treviño, L. K., Weaver, G. R., & Reynolds, S. J. (2006). Behavioral Ethics in Organizations: A Review. *Journal of Management, 32,* 951–990.

[24]Treviño, L. K. (1990). A Cultural Perspective on Changing and Developing Organizational Ethics. In *Research in Organizational Change and Development,* eds. R. Woodman and W. Passmore (Vol. 4, pp. 195–230). Greenwich, CT: JAI Press.

[25]Byrne, J. A., France, M., & Zellner, W. (2002, February 28). At Enron, the Environment Was Ripe for Abuse. *BusinessWeek.* Available online: http://www.businessweek.com/magazine /content/02_08/b3771092.htm.

[26]FBI: Beware of Mortgage Fraud. (2008). Money.CNN.com. Available online: http://money.cnn.com/2008/05/13/real_estate /mortgage_fraud/index.htm.

[27]Robyn, K. (2005, December). Acadian Ambulance Got It Done. *Emergency Medical Services.* Available online: http://www .emsmagazine.com/publication/article.jsp?pubId=1&id=2613.

[28]MacMillan, D. (2010, March 1). Survivor: CEO Edition, Bloomberg. *BusinessWeek,* 32–38.

[29]MacMillan, D. (2010, March 1). Survivor: CEO Edition, Bloomberg. *BusinessWeek,* 38.

[30]Brief, A. P., Schneider, B., & Guzzo, R. A. (1996). Creating a Climate and Culture for Sustainable Organizational Change. *Organizational Dynamics, 24*(4), 7–19; Schein, E. (1985). *Organizational Culture and Leadership* (pp. 224–237). San Francisco, CA: Jossey-Bass; Deal, T. E., & Peterson, K. D. (1998). *Shaping School Culture: The Heart of Leadership.* San Francisco, CA: Jossey-Bass.

[31]Byrnes, N. (2006, May 1). The Art of Motivation. *BusinessWeek,* 56–62.

[32]Fishman, C. (2006, January). The Man Who Said No to Wal-Mart. *Fast Company, 102,* 66.

[33]Faber, D. (2004). The Age of Wal-Mart: Inside America's Most Powerful Company. Digital Films. Available online: http://digital .films.com/play/UPAK6H#.

[34]Marquez, J. (2006, March 13). Randstad North America: Optimas Award Winner for Competitive Advantage. *Workforce Management,* 18.

[35]Lundquist, K. K. (2008). Coca-Cola Measures Progress on Diversity Journey. Talent Management, January, 21.

[36]Gelfand, M. J., Leslie, L. M., & Keller, K. M. (2008). On the Etiology of Conflict Cultures. *Research in Organizational Behavior, 28,* 137–166.

[37]Gelfand, M. J., Leslie, L. M., & Keller, K. M. (2008). On the Etiology of Conflict Cultures. *Research in Organizational Behavior, 28,* 137–166.

[38]Gelfand, M. J., Leslie, L. M., & Keller, K. M. (2008). On the Etiology of Conflict Cultures. *Research in Organizational Behavior, 28,* 137–166.

[39]DeLisi, P. S. (1998). A Modern-Day Tragedy. *Journal of Management Inquiry, 7,* 120.

[40]Gelfand, M. J., Leslie, L. M., & Keller, K. M. (2008). On the Etiology of Conflict Cultures. *Research in Organizational Behavior, 28,* 137–166.

[41]Gittell, J. H. (2003). *The Southwest Airlines Way: Using the Power of Relationships to Achieve High Performance.* New York: McGraw-Hill.

[42]Gelfand, M. J., Leslie, L. M., & Keller, K. M. (2008). On the Etiology of Conflict Cultures. *Research in Organizational Behavior, 28,* 137–166.

[43]Finkelstein, S. (2005). When Bad Things Happen to Good Companies: Strategy Failure and Flawed Executives. *Journal of Business Strategy, 26,* 19–28.

[44]Baron, R., & Neuman, J. (1996). Workplace Violence and Workplace Aggression: Evidence on Their Relative Frequency and Potential Causes. *Aggressive Behavior, 22,* 161–173; Geddes, D., & Baron, R. A. (1997). Workplace Aggression as a Consequence of Negative Performance Feedback. *Management Communication Quarterly, 10,* 433–454.

[45]Musiker, H. R., & Norton, R. G. (1983). The Medical System: A Complex Arena for the Exhibition of Passive-Aggressiveness. In *Passive-Aggressiveness: Theory and Practice,* eds. R. D. Parsons and R. J. Wicks (pp. 194–212). New York: Brunner/Mazel.

[46]Gelfand, M. J., Nishii, L. H., & Raver, J. L. (2006). On the Nature and Importance of Cultural Tightness-Looseness. *Journal of Applied Psychology, 91,* 1225–1244.

[47]Sigler, T., & Pearson, C. (2000). Creating and Empowering Culture: Examining the Relationship Between Organizational Culture and Perceptions of Empowerment. *Journal of Quality Management, 5,* 27–52; Leung, K., Bond, M. H., Carment, D. W., & Krishnan, L. (1990). Effects of Cultural Femininity on Preferences for Methods of Conflict Processing: A Cross Cultural Study. *Journal of Experimental Social Psychology, 26,* 373–388.

[48]Triandis, H. C., & Gelfand, M. J. (1998). Converging Measurement of Horizontal and Vertical Individualism and Collectivism. *Journal of Personality and Social Psychology, 74,* 118–128.

[49]Gelfand, M. J., Nishii, L. H., & Raver, J. L. (2006). On the Nature and Importance of Cultural Tightness-Looseness. *Journal of Applied Psychology, 91,* 1225–1244.

[50]Gelfand, M. J., Leslie, L. M., & Keller, K. M. (2008). On the Etiology of Conflict Cultures. *Research in Organizational Behavior, 28,* 137–166.

[51]Chatman, J. A., Polzer, J. T., Barsade, S. G., & Neale, M. A. (1998). Being Different Yet Feeling Similar: The Influence of Demographic Composition and Organizational Culture on Work Processes and Outcomes. *Administrative Science Quarterly, 43,* 749–780.

[52]McKay, P. F., Avery, D. R., Tonidandel, S., Morris, M. A., Hernandez, M., & Hebl, M. R. (2007). Racial Differences in Employee Retention: Are Diversity Climate Perceptions the Key? *Personnel Psychology, 60,* 35–62.

[53]Avery, D. R., McKay, P. F. Wilson, D. C., & Tonidandel, S. (2007). Unequal Attendance: The Relationships Between Race, Organizational Diversity Cues, and Absenteeism. *Personnel Psychology, 60,* 875–902.

[54]Kossek, E. E., & Zonia, S. C. (1993). Assessing Diversity Climate: A Field Study of Reactions to Employer Efforts to Promote Diversity. *Journal of Organizational Behavior, 14,* 61–81.

[55]Mor Barak, M. E., Cherin, D. A., & Berkman, S. (1998). Organizational and Personal Dimensions in Diversity Climate: Ethnic and Gender Differences in Employee Perceptions. *Journal of Applied Behavioral Science, 34,* 82–104.

[56]Toppling a Taboo: Businesses Go "Faith-Friendly." (2007, January 24). Knowledge @ Wharton. Available online: http://knowledge.wharton.upenn.edu/article.cfm?articleid=1644&

CFID=15563496 &CFTOKEN=55015521&jsessionid=a8307d84d98967424b15.

[57]Whirlpool (2012). Employees. Available online: http://www.whirlpoolcorp.com/responsibility/employees/default.aspx.

[58]Whirlpool (2012). About Whirlpool. Available online: http://www.whirlpoolcorp.com/about/overview.aspx.

[59]Diversity and Inclusion at Whirlpool. (2008, March). Diversityinc.com. Available online: http://www.diversityinc.com/pdf/specialsections/michigan-sect-march2008.pdf.

[60]Whirlpool (2012). Employees. Available online: http://www.whirlpoolcorp.com/responsibility/employees/default.aspx.

[61]Henneman, T. (2004, December). Diversity Training Addresses Sexual Orientation. Workforce Management Online. Available online: http://www.workforce.com/section/11/feature/23/90/44/239046.html.

[62]Diversity Best Practices. (2007, April). White Male Engagement: Inclusion Is Key. *CDO Insights 1,* 21–24.

[63]Diversity and Inclusion at Whirlpool. (2008). Diversityinc.com, March, 60.

[64]http://www.whirlpoolcorp.com.

[65]Whirlpool (2012). Awards and Recognition. Available online: http://www.whirlpoolcorp.com/about/awards_recognition.aspx.

[66]Based on Hunsaker, P. (2001). *Training in Management Skills* (p. 323). Upper Saddle River, NJ: Prentice Hall; Seidel, H. (2005). Assessing an Organization's Culture—Before You Join. Jobfind.com. Available online: http://www.keystonepartners.com/index.cfm/handlers?GID=14&ContentID=23; Paulson, C. (2009, September 14). How to Spot the Corporate Culture. Boston.com. Available online: http://www.boston.com/jobs/bighelp2009/september/articles/how_to_evaluate_corporate_culture/.

[67]Rousseau, D. M. (1998). Why Workers Still Identify with Organizations. *Journal of Organizational Behavior, 19,* 217–233; Pratt, M. G., & Foreman, P. O. (2000). Classifying Managerial Responses to Multiple Organizational Identities. *Academy of Management Review, 25,* 18–42.

[68]Mayor, T. (2001). Remote (Worker) Control. *CIO Magazine.* Available online: http://www.cio.com/article/30100/Management_Remote_Worker_Control.

[69]Lewin, K. (1951). *Field Theory in Social Science; Selected Theoretical Papers,* ed. D. Cartwright. New York: Harper & Row.

[70]Northcraft, G. B., & Neale, M. A. (1994). *Organizational Behavior: A Management Challenge* (2nd ed.). Hinsdale, IL: Dryden Press.

[71]Northcraft, G. B., & Neale, M. A. (1994). *Organizational Behavior: A Management Challenge* (2nd ed.). Hinsdale, IL: Dryden Press.

[72]Gold, B., & Miles, M. (1981). Whose School Is It Anyway? *Psychological Review, 84,* 191–215.

[73]Reichers, A. E., Wanous, J. P., & Austin, J. T. (2000). Cynicism About Organizational Change. *Group & Organization Management, 25,* 132–153.

[74]Kotter, J. (1996). *Leading Change.* Boston: Harvard Business Press.

[75]Kotter, J. (1996). *Leading Change.* Boston: Harvard Business Press.

[76]Gilmore, T., Shea, G., & Useem, M. (1997). Side Efects of Corporate Cultural Transformations. *Journal of Applied Behavioral Science, 33,* 174–189.

[77]McHugh, M. (1997). The Stress Facto: Another Item for the Change Management Agenda? *Journal of Organizational Change Management, 10,* 345–362.

[78]Jaffe, D., Scott, C., & Tobe, G. (1994). Rekindling Commitment: How to Revitalize Yourself, Your Work, and Your Organization. San Francisco, CA: Jossey-Bass; Isabella, L. (1990). Evolving Interpretations as a Change Unfolds: How Managers Construe Key Organizational Events. *Academy of Management Journal, 33,* 7–41.

[79]Judge, T. A., Thoresen, C. J., Pucik, V., & Welbourne, T. M. (1999). Managerial Coping with Organizational Change: A Dispositional Perspective. *Journal of Applied Psychology, 84,* 107–122.

[80]Budner, S. (1962). Intolerance of Ambiguity as a Personality Variable. *Journal of Personality, 30,* 29–50.

[81]Rydell, S. T. (1966). Tolerance of Ambiguity and Semantic Differential Ratings. *Psychological Reports, 19,* 1303–1312.

[82]Ashford, S. J. (1988). Individual Strategies for Coping with Stress During Organizational Transitions. *Journal of Applied Behavioral Science, 24,* 19–36; Rush, M. C., Schoel, W. A., & Barnard, S. M. (1995). Psychological Resiliency in the Public Sector: "Hardiness" and Pressure for Change. *Journal of Vocational Behavior, 46,* 17–39.

[83]Judge, T. A., Thoresen, C. J., Pucik, V., & Welbourne, T. M. (1999). Managerial Coping with Organizational Change: A Dispositional Perspective. *Journal of Applied Psychology, 84,* 107–122.

[84]Huber, G. P., & Glick, W. H. (1995). *Organizational Change and Redesign: Ideas and Insights for Improving Performance.* New York: Oxford University Press.

[85]Peccei, R., Giangreco, A., & Sebastiano, A. (2011). The Role of Organisational Commitment in the Analysis of Resistance to Change: Co-Predictor and Moderator Effects, *Personnel Review, 40*(2), 185–204.

[86]Hendry, C. (1996). Understanding and Creating Whole Organizational Change Through Learning Theory. *Human Relations, 49,* 621–641.

[87]Giesberg, J. (2006). The Role of Communication in Preventing Workplace Sabotage. *Journal of Applied Social Psychology, 31,* 2439–2461.

[88]Schweiger, D., & DeNisi, A. (1991). Communication with Employees Following a Merger: A Longitudinal Field Experiment. *Academy of Management Journal, 34,* 110–135.

[89]Armenakis, A., Harris, S., & Field, H. (1999). Paradigms in Organizational Change: Change Agent and Change Target Perspectives. In *Handbook of Organizational Behavior,* ed. R. Golembiewski. New York: Marcel Dekker.

[90]Health, Safety, and Well-Being. (2009). Unilever. Available online: http://www.unilever.com/sustainability/employees/well-being/.

[91]Ashkanasy, N. M., Zerbe, W. J., & Härtel, C. E. J. (2002). *Managing Emotions in the Workplace.* Armonk, NY: M. E. Sharpe.

[92]Barrett, J. (2008, April 7). Dieting for Dollars. *Newsweek.* Available online: http://www.newsweek.com/2008/04/06/dieting-for-dollars.html.

[93]Bennis, W. (1969). *Organization Development: Its Nature, Origin and Prospects.* Reading, MA: Addison-Wesley.

[94]Senge, P. (2006). *The Fifth Discipline: The Art and Practice of the Learning Organization* (p. 349). New York: Broadway Business.

[95]Pedler, M., Burgoyne, J., & Boydell, T. (1997). *The Learning Company: A Strategy for Sustainable Development* (2nd ed., p. 1). London: McGraw-Hill.

[96]Kiger, P. J. (2007, May). Task Force Training Develops New Leaders, Solves Real Business Issues, and Helps Cut Costs. *Workforce Management Online.* Available online: http://www.workforce.com/archive/feature/24/92/37/index.php?ht.

[97]Ellis, S., Ganzach, Y., Castle, E., & Sekely, G. (2010). The Effect of Filmed Versus Personal After-Event Reviews on Task Performance: The Mediating and Moderating Role of Self-Efficacy. *Journal of Applied Psychology, 95,* 122–131.

[98]Croft, L. (2001, August 9). Learning While Doing. *Inside Knowledge.* Available online: http://www.ikmagazine.com/xq/asp/sid.0/articleid.01E48E89-C11D-4050-B478-1DEAFEE53A1F/eTitle.Learning_while_doing_The_after_action_review_process/qx/display.htm.

[99]Simons, R. (2005). *Levers of Organization Design: How Managers Use Accountability Systems for Greater Performance and Commitment* (p. 184). Boston: Harvard Business School Press.

[100]Carmeli, A., & Gittell, J. H. (2008). High-Quality Relationships, Psychological Safety, and Learning from Failures in Work Organizations. *Journal of Organizational Behavior, 30,* 709–729.

[101] Denison (2011). Avaya: Culture Transformation through Alignment, *Denison,* 6(2), 14.

[102]Gaston, R. & Fitzgerald, S. (2010). Culture Change at Avaya. Denison Consulting. Available online: http://www.whirlpoolcorp.com/responsibility/employees/default.aspx.

[103]Denison (2011). Avaya: Culture Transformation through Alignment, *Denison,* 6(2), 1–4.

[104] Avaya (2012). Our Culture. Available online: http://www.avaya.com/usa/about-avaya/our-company/our-culture/our-culture.

CHAPTER 16

Managing Your Career

Because SAS Institute's believes that meeting employees' needs is good for the company as well as its people it invests in many programs to promote work-life balance.

LEARNING OBJECTIVES

1. Explain different definitions of career success.

2. Define career anchors and explain their role in career paths.

3. Describe the four different career patterns.

4. Explain what a personal brand is and why it is helpful.

5. Describe the three phases in the socialization process.

6. Describe social styles and explain how they are useful in relating to others.

7. Describe why work-life balance is important to employees and to their companies.

REAL WORLD CHALLENGE

WORK-LIFE BALANCE AT SAS INSTITUTE

The software company SAS Institute is headquartered in Cary, North Carolina, and employs more than 13,000 people.[1] The culture at SAS is based on trust between employees and the company. SAS believes that meeting employees' needs is good business sense.[2] The company wants to encourage work-life balance to decrease employees' stress, absenteeism, and illness.

Imagine that SAS asks for your help in improving employees' work-life balance in a way that helps employees both personally and at work. What advice would you give them? After reading this chapter, you should have some good ideas.

Managing your career is not something you do only when you are ready for a change—it is something you do on a day-to-day basis. As the Roman philosopher Seneca said in the first century, "luck is when preparation meets opportunity." Preparing yourself to capitalize on the opportunities you value the most will help you to maximize your career success. In this chapter we extend our discussion of organizational behavior to include topics relevant for your career success, and for managing others' careers.

We begin by encouraging you to discover what career success means to you, which is essential if you are to make informed choices to maximize your career outcomes. We then turn our attention to career planning, identifying the job you really want, and succeeding on the job. We conclude by discussing work-life balance and how to best achieve it.

HOW DO YOU DEFINE CAREER SUCCESS?

Does everyone who excels at their job feel that their career is a success? Do people without high pay and a fancy job title feel unsuccessful? There is no single definition of career success. Some people define their career success in terms of pride in a job well done,[3] the opportunity to continually learn new things or help others, or earning the respect of valued others.[4] Others define success in terms of their ability to spend quality time with family and friends and pursue outside interests.

How we define success is critical to feeling successful on a task or in our career. Imagine that you are running a marathon. Are you trying to win? Trying to run a personal best time? Trying to finish? Trying to have fun? Each of these is a reasonable goal, but they are impossible to achieve simultaneously. Your marathon success is determined by your personal goals. If you set out to have fun and finish and did so, then you are successful no matter how fast you ran. Similarly, it is important to identify your career and life priorities to ensure that you are pursuing what you value the most.

Given the many different ways to define career success,[5] it is important for you to understand your personal definition. But it is not enough to just imagine what success would look like—you must also translate that vision into specific goals. Goal setting is a cornerstone of personal growth and career success. For example, when improvement needs are translated into specific goals after performance appraisal interviews, they are much more likely to be met.[6]

How you view money can be a strong influence on how you define career success. Some people place great importance on money, and view it as a symbol of success. For others, money represents the freedom to do whatever they want to do. Still others view money as unimportant, or even shameful.[7] Understanding what money means to you will help you better understand how important it is for you to pursue a high-paying job. This chapter's *Understand Yourself* feature gives you the opportunity to better understand how you view money and how money motivates you.

What you do with your money now will affect how you live when you are older. Regardless of how you feel about money, it is important to recognize the importance of always having some monetary reserves as you move throughout your career. If you need a break to acquire new skills, look for a more challenging position, focus on your family, or get out of an abusive job situation, you will have the financial slack to do it. If you do not have financial resources put aside, you may find yourself trapped in an unsatisfying situation. Putting aside just 10 percent of your income will help you to acquire the financial resources that will give you greater choice and flexibility in the future. And if you can start saving at least 10 percent of your income with your first job, you will never get used to having and spending that 10 percent and will not miss having it in your pocket. If your employer offers to match your retirement contributions, be sure to contribute enough to secure the maximum employer contribution to maximize both your compensation and your retirement savings.

SO WHAT
Identifying what success means to you will help you pursue what you value the most.

UNDERSTAND YOURSELF

HOW DO YOU VIEW MONEY?

What does money mean to you? Money obviously impacts people's motivation and work-related behavior in organizations. But money means different things to different people. The better you understand how you view money, the better you will understand how strongly money motivates you at this point in your life (it may change over time).

This self-assessment gives you the opportunity to better understand your attitudes toward money. Place your response on the line to the left of each statement using the scale below and then follow the scoring instructions. Be honest—there are no right or wrong answers.

strongly disagree	disagree	neutral	agree	strongly agree
1	2	3	4	5

___ 1. I worry about being financially secure.
___ 2. I tend to get worried when making decisions involving money.
___ 3. I get nervous when I don't have much money.
___ 4. I keep a close watch on how much money I have.
___ 5. Money represents one's achievements.
___ 6. I sometimes boast about how much money I have or make.
___ 7. I sometimes buy things just to impress other people.
___ 8. Money makes people respect you in the community.
___ 9. Money gives you autonomy and freedom.
___ 10. Money in the bank is a sign of security.
___ 11. Money can give you the opportunity to be what you want to be.
___ 12. Money means power.

Scoring:
Money as Evil: Add up your responses to statements 1–4: _____
Money as Achievement: Add up your responses to statements 5–8: _____
Money as Freedom: Add up your responses to statements 9–12: _____

Interpretation: *Money as a Source of Worry*: If your score is *16 or lower*, money does not tend to cause you anxiety. Scores of *17 or above* reflect a stronger tendency for money to be a source of anxiety for you.

Money as Achievement: If your score is *12 or lower*, you do not view money as reflecting your achievements. Scores of *13 or above* reflect a stronger view that money does reflect your achievements. Research has found that high-income people tend to think that money reflects one's achievement and is less evil.[8] People who more highly value money as achievement also tend to experience a lower level of satisfaction with work, promotion, supervision, coworkers, and overall life satisfaction.[9]

Money as Freedom: If your score is *19 or lower*, you do not view money as being a source of freedom. Scores of *20 or above* reflect a stronger view that money is a source of freedom. Viewing money as freedom is related to intrinsic job satisfaction.[10]

Source: Adapted from Thomas Li-Ping Tang (1992), "The Meaning of Money Revisited", '*Journal of Organizational Behavior*', 13, 197–202.

As Vineet Nayar, CEO of IT and software development company HCL Technologies, says, "I believe that you can divide employees into two groups: those motivated by what they receive from their employer and those motivated by what they are allowed to do by their employer."[11] Understanding what motivates you can help you identify what career success looks like for you.

When thinking about how you define career success, it is helpful to think of the many outcomes you can receive from work, and the trade-offs you must make when you devote time to your career.[12] People define career success differently.[13] For example, how important is it for you to spend time with your family or friends? Some people are happy in careers requiring them to travel several days a week, while others prefer to spend every night with their families. How important is it for you to have a fancy job title or responsibility for others? Is your job title more important than the work you do? As one example, as many researchers get promoted in their companies they take on increasing managerial responsibilities supervising others' research and do less actual research themselves. This requires making a career choice between doing research, a love for which is why many people become researchers, and managing research, which means they do little research themselves.

Different cultures place different emphases on career success versus quality of life.[14] Societies focused on career success tend to be more materialistic, emphasizing the acquisition of money and things. In contrast, societies focused more on quality of life emphasize relationships, concern for others, and overall quality of life.[15] This chapter's *Global Issues* feature describes how cultures differ in their focus on career success versus quality of life.

Another career choice worth reflecting on is the degree of expertise you would like to develop in a particular area versus being a generalist. Also, how important is it to you to mentor others to higher levels in their own careers? Some people feel more successful in their careers when they help others improve their skills and knowledge and obtain personal success.

Identify your strengths, including education, work experience, people skills, language skills, computer skills, written and verbal communication skills, and learning abilities. Think about the things you most and least enjoy doing, and identify the career opportunities that allow you to live your most important core values. For the authors of this book, integrity, independence, creativity, and having a positive impact on the broader world are central to our sense of having successful careers. If we chose to work at a job that violated any of these values, we would not consider ourselves successful (and we probably would not be too happy, either).

It is important to remember that pursuing career success does not end. As you reach various career goals, you will set new ones. As your life changes, your personal goals and how you prioritize them will also change. Regularly revisit your career goals and strategy in light of what you currently value. The greater your awareness of what you really want, the greater the chances that you will make the decisions that allow you to get it.

SO WHAT

Because your life will change, regularly revisit your career goals and strategy to ensure that you are pursuing what you currently value the most.

CAREER PLANNING

Once you have thought about what having a successful career means to you, it is time to start planning to achieve it. In the beginning of your career, your major goal is choosing a career direction that meets your needs and interests. Edgar Schein developed one of the most popular models for diagnosing career interests, which he called *career anchors*. As Schein states, "Certain motivational, attitudinal, and

career anchor

Core interests that serve to anchor a career throughout a person's life

GLOBAL ISSUES

DIFFERING VALUES FOR QUALITY OF LIFE VERSUS CAREER SUCCESS

Cultures differ in their commitment to quality of life versus career success. Countries such as Japan, Venezuela, and the United States emphasize career success, whereas countries such as Sweden, Norway, and Denmark put greater emphasis on quality of life.[16] Although Sweden expects women to work outside the home, parents are given the choice of paternity or maternity leave to care for newborns, and the government provides care for older children in support of quality of life. In contrast, although the United States also encourages women to work, families are offered limited support for maternity leave and child care.

Differing values for career success and quality of life explain some of the conflicts felt when working with people from other cultures. Americans are sometimes resentful when Swedes end the work week at 5 P.M. on Friday or fly home at the end of the day to spend more time with their families, believing the Swedes are showing an inadequate commitment to work. Swedish businesspeople, on the other hand, often describe Americans as willing to work all evening and weekend just to finish a project. The Swedes' behavior simply reflects their strong commitment to a high quality of life, and the Americans are reflecting their equally strong commitment to the project and to their career success.[17]

value syndromes formed early in the lives of individuals apparently function to guide and constrain their entire careers."[18] When people stray too far from their core interests, these interests serve as an anchor that pulls them back to their original interests. Table 16-1 describes different types of career anchors along with the characteristics of people with these anchors and their typical career paths.

Table 16-1

Career Anchors

Career Anchor	Characteristics	Typical Career Paths
Managerial competence	• Likes analyzing and solving challenging business problems • Likes influencing people to work together • Enjoys exercising power	• Large, prestigious firms • Plant management and sales management • Executive-level positions
Service	• Enjoys work that manifests personal values • Having an impact, not money, is central • Expects management to share one's personal values	• Consultants • Nonprofit organizations • Socially responsible employers
Technical/functional competence	• Excited by the work itself • Willing to forego promotions • Dislikes corporate politics	• Functional department managers • Research positions • Specialized consulting • Project management
Security	• Motivated by job security and long-term career with one company • Dislikes travel and relocation • Tends to be conformist and compliant to the organization	• Government jobs • Large government-regulated industries • Small family-owned businesses
Challenge	• Values proving oneself • Seeks ever-greater challenges • Enjoys competing and winning	• Strategy consultants • Management consultants • Naval aviators
Independence	• Desires freedom from organizational constraints • Wants to set own pace • Avoids large firms and governmental agencies	• Writing and publishing • Academia • Small business proprietorships
Creativity/ entrepreneurship	• Enjoys starting own businesses • Restless; moves from project to project • Prefers small and up-and-coming firms to well-established ones	• General management consulting • Entrepreneurial ventures
Lifestyle	• Integrates needs of individual, family, and career • Desires flexibility (part-time work, sabbaticals, parental leaves, etc.) • Common with dual-career families	• Socially progressive companies • Consulting

Source: Adapted from the works of Schein, E.H. (1978). *Career Dynamics.* Reading, MA: Addison-Wesley; Schein, E.H. (1985). *Career Anchors: Discovering Your Real Values.* San Francisco, CA: Pfeiffer; Schein, E.H. (1987). *Individuals and Careers.* In J.W. Lorsch (ed)., *Handbook of Organizational Behavior.* Upper Saddle River, NJ: Prentice Hall, 155–171.

In cultures such as Egypt and Latin America that strongly believe in destiny, people tend to spend little time planning their careers. Although there are certainly some circumstances that influence our careers that are beyond our control, including economic downturns, there is usually a lot we can do to advance our careers.[19] People in other cultures including the United States put more emphasis on self-determination and tend to engage in more proactive career planning.

Choose Wisely

Over a thirty-year career, you can expect to spend at least 60,000 hours working. Given this huge investment of time and effort, it is important to ensure that it is work you enjoy doing! Put thought into the industry in which you will be working as well as into the kind of company in which you would like to work and the job you will be doing. If advancement is important to you, you may find greater opportunities in growing industries and companies. If you value doing a variety of tasks, working in a smaller company might be a better fit for you than a large organization. Declining industries and companies obviously offer less job security and fewer opportunities for advancement and salary growth.

> "Certain motivational, attitudinal, and value syndromes formed early in the lives of individuals apparently function to guide and constrain their entire careers." —*Edgar Schein, Management Expert*

Career Development

Career development is the process through which we come to understand ourselves as we relate to the world of work and our role in it.[20] Through the career development process, we form a work identity. As this identity becomes more realistic and stable over time, so do our work behaviors and career choices. We choose occupations that allow us to express our self-concepts and interests, and we are more satisfied with our careers when we are successful in doing so.

Some people quickly find a job and career path that works for them whereas others take longer to find work they can commit to. Our career behavior has been found to follow one of four patterns:[21]

1. *Stable pattern*: A person goes directly from school or training into work with which he or she stays.
2. *Conventional pattern*: A person tries several jobs until finding a stable one.
3. *Unstable pattern*: A person never becomes established in one area, instead going from trial jobs to a stable situation and then back to trial jobs.
4. *Multiple trial pattern*: A person tries a lot of different jobs for short periods of time, not staying in any field long enough to achieve stability.

GETTING THE JOB YOU REALLY WANT

Once you have identified your desired career path and set goals to obtain personal success, you need to get started. When choosing a job, be sure to consider not just your fit with the job requirements, but also your fit with the company culture and your likely career path if you take the job. It is also a good idea to try to determine, to the greatest extent possible, whether you

SO WHAT

We tend to have core interests that we pursue throughout our careers. Understanding your core interests will help to put you on a satisfying career path.

career development

The process through which we come to understand ourselves as we relate to the world of work and our role in it

SO WHAT

It is important to carefully choose the industry in which you will work, as well as your employer and job, to maximize the fit with your career goals.

will have the resources and support you will need to be successful and further develop your skills. Understanding the expectations and agendas of your future boss and other key players can help you evaluate your likely fit with a job opportunity.

Getting a job is based in part on your qualifications and talents, but is also influenced by your personal presentation during job interviews. The most qualified people in the world are not likely to get jobs if they are unable to communicate their abilities to the people making the hiring decisions. We next discuss how to more effectively communicate your talents and what you would bring to an organization.

When someone hears your name, what do they think of? The answer is your personal brand. A ***personal brand*** is a summary of our key talents and what differentiates us from others. It is a good idea to have a one-sentence personal brand that summarizes your talents and interests in a memorable way. A personal brand statement comes in handy whenever you meet someone at a party or elsewhere who asks about your profession. By concisely communicating what differentiates you and makes you a great hire, it increases the chances that the interviewer will understand your talents and remember you favorably. You can even include your personal brand statement on your résumé, business cards, e-mail signature, blog postings, and social network profiles (e.g., Facebook and LinkedIn).

A personal brand also helps to keep you focused on what you stand for and helps you to be consistent in your own behaviors.[22] This consistency can increase your credibility and build trust with others. By living your personal brand, your self-impression should be aligned with how others perceive you. Here are several examples of personal brand statements:

- I help you get found on the Internet—online reputation management coach[23]
- The Career Engineer—a career coach[24]
- The Wizard of Ahhs—a therapist[25]
- I'm the leading personal branding expert for gen-y—a personal advancement consultant[26]

Developing your personal brand requires both self-awareness and an understanding of how others perceive you. You might perceive yourself as task-oriented and efficient, but others might perceive you as bossy and domineering. Understanding how others perceive you and your strengths can help you to be more self-aware in how you relate to others and how you project your desired brand. Your personal brand should reflect reality, which is grounded in how others view you as well as your own awareness of your talents.

personal brand
A summary of our key talents and what differentiates us from others

You can include a personal brand statement on your resume, business cards, e-mail signature, blog postings, and social network profiles.

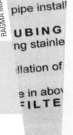

RAGMA IMAGES/SHUTTERSTOCK.COM

RESUME

CAREER SUMMARY

18 years in civil design and con structural designer in consulting commercial building and cement gas industry thru. Currently assi ongoing project Greenfield Area.

Familiar with ACI, AISC, ASCE, UE ISCP Standards

miliar with ASME, API AN
IA Stand

Table 16-2

What Is Your Personal Brand?

As you think about your personal brand, it can be helpful to answer the following questions:

1. What are you most proud of about yourself?
2. What are you best at doing?
3. What do you value the most (and therefore what do you represent)?
4. How are you unique?
5. What do you hope to accomplish over the next twenty-five years?
6. If you could be remembered for one thing, what would it be?
7. If you had to describe yourself with three adjectives, what would they be?

Source: Based on Super, D. (1957). The Psychology of Careers. New York: Harper.

SO WHAT

Developing a personal brand and elevator pitch will help you to be prepared to effectively communicate your strengths when the right opportunity comes along.

Table 16-2 gives you some suggestions for developing your personal brand.

It is also useful to practice a thirty-second to two-minute "elevator pitch" that reinforces your personal brand and describes why you are different from the many other people who do what you do. If someone is interested in learning more about you after your personal branding statement, you can elaborate through your elevator pitch. It is called an elevator pitch because you just might need to use it when you meet someone in an elevator (or any other brief encounter) who asks what you do and you need to be able to give a clear, memorable answer in less than two minutes. Your résumé, of course, should also highlight your talents, accomplishments, and what you would be able to do for the organization if it hires you.

The elevator pitch helps you to best answer interviewer questions like "Tell me about yourself" or "Why should we hire you?" You do not need to cover all your accomplishments and talents—if the other person is interested in what you say, that person can always ask to extend the conversation. When answering "Tell me about yourself" questions, it is a good idea to keep your answer clear and short, and go beyond what is on your résumé. Stay focused, and do not go into too much detail unless asked. Be prepared to answer follow-up questions to support any facts you provide. You do not need to provide information about any relevant protected characteristics (like your marital status or details about your family) if you do not want to. When you are using the pitch in a job interview, it is best to add information unique to the company you are interviewing with, elaborating on why you would be a great hire for them.

SUCCEEDING ON THE JOB

Career success is influenced by a range of factors such as education, intelligence, personality, motivation, family status, gender, career strategies (e.g., networking), and mentoring relationships.[27] Let's discuss the roles of socialization, mentoring, proactivity, social styles, social networks, continuous learning, and global perspective to job success.

Socialization

After accepting a job offer and starting the job, our attention turns to understanding our new surroundings, performing well, developing productive relationships with coworkers, and fitting into the organization.[28] On average, the time for new external hires to achieve full productivity ranges from eight weeks for clerical jobs to twenty weeks for professionals to more than twenty-six weeks for executives.[29] Companies and new hires can speed up this process and enhance newcomer satisfaction and commitment to the company.

We learn the knowledge, attitudes, and behaviors necessary to successfully participate as an organizational member through *socialization*. Socialization is an ongoing process that can last up to a year as we develop work relationships, adapt to organizational expectations, and find our place. Table 16-3 summarizes what employees learn and develop through the socialization process.[30]

The socialization process consists of three phases:[31]

1. *Anticipatory socialization*: occurs before a new hire begins work. New hires develop expectations about the job and organization through interactions with recruiters, managers, and other company representatives.
2. *Encounter*: happens as new employees begin working and learning about their job and company. Managers play an important role in helping new employees understand their roles and in reducing stress by developing a high-quality working relationship.
3. *Settling in*: happens as new employees become comfortable with their jobs and with their relationships with others in the organization. Interest in performance feedback and career opportunities increases during this stage.

Table 16-4 summarizes some of the different types of socialization tactics organizations use during the encounter stage of socialization.[32]

Research has found that collective, fixed, and supportive (investiture) tactics increase on-the-job embeddedness, or feelings of connectivity to the organization, which is negatively related to turnover.[33] When Corning, Inc., wanted to reduce voluntary turnover in the first three years of employment, it redesigned its socialization program to create a uniform understanding about the company and to build a positive attitude toward the company. The program contributed to a 69 percent reduction in newcomer turnover after two years.[34]

SO WHAT

Effective managers proactively socialize their new hires to speed up their time to productivity and enhance their commitment.

socialization
The process of learning the knowledge, attitudes, and behaviors necessary to successfully participate as an organizational member

SO WHAT

Effectively implementing OB concepts increases organizational performance.

Table 16-3

Socialization Content

History	Learning the organization's traditions, customs, and myths, and coworkers' personal and professional backgrounds
People	Establishing successful and satisfying work relationships with organizational members
Performance proficiency	Learning and mastering the knowledge, skills, and abilities to perform required work tasks
Politics	Obtaining information about formal and informal work relationships and power structures
Organizational goals and values	Understanding the rules or principles that maintain the organization's integrity
Language	Learning the profession's technical language including acronyms, slang, and firm-specific jargon

Source: Chao, G.T., O'Leary-Kelly, A.M., Wolf, S., Klein, H.J., & Gardner, P.D. (1994). Organizational socialization: Its content and consequences. *Journal of Applied Psychology, 79*, 5, 730–743. Reprinted by permission of APA.

Table 16-4

Socialization Tactics

Collective-individual	Newcomers experience common (collective) versus unique experiences in isolation from other new hires (individual)
Formal-informal	Specifically designed activities and materials are used while isolating newcomers from incumbents (formal) versus on-the-job learning with no exclusively prepared materials and immediate mixing with incumbents (informal)
Sequential-random	Communicating the sequence of discrete and progressive learning activities (sequential) versus unknown or ambiguous sequences (random)
Fixed-variable	Communicating specific time frames for completing each socialization step (fixed) versus no time frame and allowing each newcomer to be socialized at his or her own pace (variable)
Serial-disjunctive	Providing newcomers with access to experienced incumbents as role models and mentors (serial) versus no access to experienced models (disjunctive)
Investiture-divestiture	Providing newcomers with positive social support affirming their personal characteristics (investiture) versus providing more negative social feedback until newcomers adapt (divestiture)

Source: VanMaanen & Schein (1979). Van Maanen, J., & Schein, E. H. (1979). Toward a theory of organizational socialization. In B. M. Staw (Ed.), *Research in Organizational* Behaviour (vol. 1, pp. 209–264). Greenwich, CT: JAI Press.

proactive socialization

When a new hire takes initiative to better understand the work environment and work roles and adjusts his or her behaviors to improve socialization and career success

mentoring

A dynamic, reciprocal relationship in a work environment between an advanced career incumbent (mentor) and a protégé aimed at promoting the career development of both

When you begin a new job, you can proactively engage in tactics that expedite your adjustment and socialization. ***Proactive socialization*** occurs when a new hire takes initiative to better understand the work environment and work roles and adjusts his or her behaviors to improve socialization and career success.[35] Proactive socialization behaviors include seeking feedback and information about work-related topics, socializing with coworkers to get to know them better, and building good relationships with the boss and coworkers.[36] It is helpful to be proactive about your own socialization as you join organizations and accept new roles in them. As a manager, it is also helpful to encourage new hires to be proactive about their own socialization.[37]

Mentoring

Mentoring is "a dynamic, reciprocal relationship in a work environment between an advanced career incumbent (mentor) and a protégé aimed at promoting the career development of both."[38] Mentoring relationships are often intended to develop more junior employees, but mentoring relationships should benefit mentors as

CULTURA LIMITED / SUPERSTOCK

Mentoring is a reciprocal relationship in a work environment between an advanced career incumbent (mentor) and a protégé.

well as their protégés. Mentoring relationships are positively related to the mentors' job performance ratings and social status within the organization.[39]

Mentoring relationships can be established through formal mentoring programs in which a mentor is assigned to an employee. Coaching and social support can both positively influence managers' salary level and promotions,[40] and can serve as an effective training tool for smaller companies that cannot afford formal training programs. Abbott's formal mentoring program is web-based and matches protégés and mentors on qualities, competencies, and the experiences they both want.[41] Rockwell Collins uses a web-based matching tool to let all salaried employees be a mentor, mentee, or both. Senior leadership is also given directed matches for employees identified as having high leadership potential.[42]

Individual employees share in the responsibility for their career development, and should establish informal mentoring relationships as well. Protégés in informal mentorships have been found to benefit from more career-related support and higher salaries than protégés in formal mentorships.[43] Employee groups are a great way for employees to network and identify informal mentors. Abbott's employee group networking events help to foster mentoring relationships.[44] The company says, "Mentoring supports our inclusive culture in that it exposes participants to a diversity of thought, experience, education, culture, management, and personal styles."[45]

Setting goals and assessing mentoring performance are important to the success of a mentoring program.[46] IBM measures success by skill development, engagement, and retention.[47] American Express tracks employee engagement and new hire retention rates to evaluate its mentoring program.[48]

Table 16-5 identifies some best practices in mentoring.

Reverse mentoring, or the pairing of a junior and senior employee to develop the skills of the more senior employee, is also beneficial. General Electric used reverse mentoring when it assigned more junior and technology-savvy employees to teach more senior managers about technology and the Internet.[49]

Although mentors can make development suggestions, the primary responsibility for career progression lies with the employee. It is up to employees to identify career opportunities based on their interest and talents. These opportunities may be in areas of the company very different from where the person currently works. Creating a culture in which employees can move into other areas has helped Southwest Airlines recruit and retain the best people.[50]

SO WHAT

A quality mentoring relationship can facilitate your career advancement.

Table 16-5

Best Practices in Mentoring

1. Use both formal and informal mentoring.

2. Set goals and evaluate the results of the mentoring program.

3. The program should be led by someone passionate about and committed to mentoring.

4. The mentoring program should be given appropriate resources, including giving employees time for mentoring meetings.

5. Mentoring and supervising the mentors helps to model the relationship the mentors are expected to have with their own protégés.

Source: Based on VanMaanen & Schein (1979). Van Maanen, J., & Schein, E. H. (1979). Toward a theory of organizational socialization. In B. M. Staw (Ed.), *Research in Organizational Behavior* (vol. 1, pp. 209–264). Greenwich, CT: JAI Press.

Proactivity

Having a "proactive personality" is positively related to career satisfaction as well as higher pay.[51] People with more proactive personalities are more likely to influence their environment and to find and solve problems rather than being reactive and adapting to circumstances instead of changing them.[52] Being proactive is related to performance, particularly for people who are better able to self-manage themselves and their time.[53] Proactivity is related to greater networking ability and interpersonal influence.[54]

Managers often fail not because they lack intelligence or necessary technical knowledge, but because they lack the ability to turn their knowledge and skills into actions that matter to others.[55] Being proactive and focusing on delivering results can improve managerial performance. However, because extroverted leaders are less receptive to subordinates' proactivity, research has found that proactive groups perform best with less extraverted leaders.[56]

Social Styles

How we interact with other people greatly influences the quality of our relationships and the success we have in influencing others. Imagine that you are a supervisor intending to fairly and honestly evaluate a good subordinate's (Rita's) work, and motivate her to set even higher goals. You methodically review the facts of Rita's performance point by point, in detail. But your preference for being thorough and logical offends her. After she interprets your behavior as picky and micromanaging, Rita leaves the meeting less motivated to work hard. This misunderstanding can be explained by you and Rita having different social styles.

social style
A person's dominant pattern of interpersonal behaviors and communication styles

A *social style* is a person's dominant pattern of interpersonal behaviors and communication styles.[57] Although everyone has a dominant social style, the ability to flexibly adopt different styles to match the needs of different situations increases interpersonal effectiveness.[58] There are four social styles, shown in Figure 16-1, none of which is inherently better than any other. Each style is effective when it is implemented well and is appropriate to the situation.[59]

Much of our behavior is habitual and describable in the two dimensions of assertiveness and responsiveness shown in Figure 16-1. Assertiveness reflects how we are perceived as attempting to influence the thoughts and actions of other people. People range from being very deliberate, seldom interrupting, and tending to lean back (ask-directed assertiveness) to being quick to make decisions, making declarative statements, frequently interrupting, and tending to lean forward (tell-directed assertiveness).

Responsiveness reflects how we are perceived as expressing our feelings when relating to others. Responsiveness ranges from talking about facts, hiding personal feelings, and making minimal body gestures and facial expressions (task-directed responsiveness) to talking about relationships, using many gestures and facial expressions, and frequently exposing personal feelings (people-directed responsiveness). It is important to remember that people can fall in the middle of the two ranges rather than to one of the extremes.

Because observable behaviors are key to understanding a person's social style, one of the best ways of discovering your dominant social style is through feedback from other people. Many people, however, are able to recognize their dominant style from the descriptions in Figure 16-2. Once you understand your own social style, you need to identify the probable social style of the other person with whom you are interacting. With this knowledge, you can predict

Figure 16-1

Social Styles Based on Assertiveness and Responsiveness

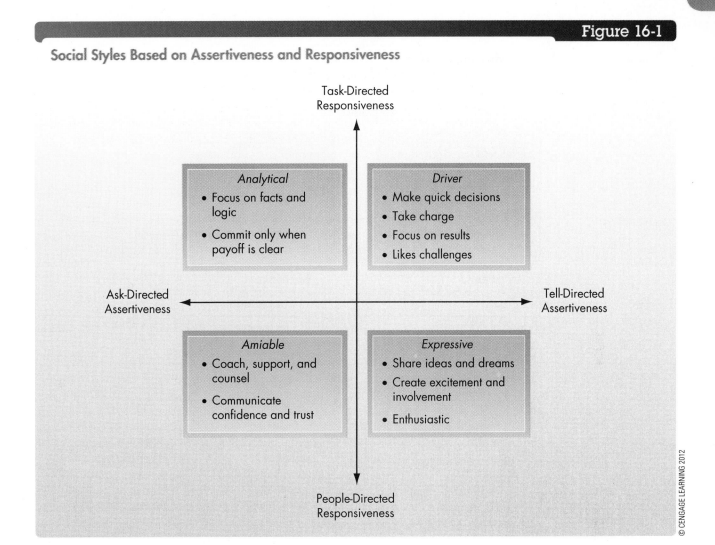

which aspects of your communication and behavior will be most and least comfortable for you and for the other person, and where your respective styles are likely to mesh and clash. This will help you to anticipate possible problems and miscommunications and prevent them from happening by adjusting your own social style.[60] Figure 16-2 gives you some tips for adjusting your social style to better appeal to another person.

Being aware of your social style and developing the skill to adapt it can help your career. Social styles influence performance evaluations[61] and how others evaluate our communication competence.[62] Managers with the less-responsive driver and analytical social styles may need to develop strategies to proactively compensate for their lower communication competency.[63]

SO WHAT

Understanding your preferred social style and developing the skill to flexibly adapt it to match the other person can enhance your effectiveness and help your career.

Social Networks

Social networks simply reflect the people you know to varying degrees in all aspects of your life. Networks can be personal, comprised of family and friends, or professional, comprised of people you know through your work. Internet networks reflect the people you know through online interactions in chat rooms and other online communities in which you participate. Networking is

social networks

The people you know to varying degrees in all aspects of your life

© CENGAGE LEARNING 2012

Figure 16-2

Relating to Other Social Styles

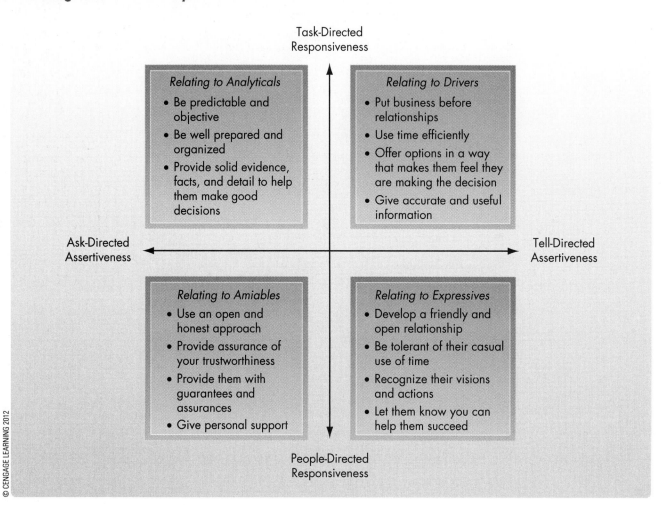

related to a higher salary and a faster salary growth rate as well as greater career satisfaction.[64]

Anyone you meet or know can potentially be considered part of your social network. Social ties with people you know well are considered to be strong, and those with people you know less well are considered to be weak. Both strong and weak ties can be useful. Table 16-6 summarizes and gives examples of some of the best sources for networking contacts. It is important to maintain connections with your network contacts through casual conversations, passing along information useful to them, or more formal meetings or letters.

Your network can help you get information you need to do your job better, and can also provide career assistance. When you are looking for a job, your network can help locate opportunities. When you let your contacts know that you are looking for a job, they can pass along information they know of and let their own contacts know that you are looking. This can greatly expand the number of opportunities of which you become aware. All types of networks can be useful to you when you need information or you are looking for job opportunities, particularly those involving specialized work, higher-level jobs, or jobs that are not widely advertised.

Table 16-6

Sources for Networking Contacts

Personal contacts: family, friends, current and former classmates, neighbors, club members, and church members

Professional contacts: colleagues, supervisors, suppliers, clients, and fellow professional association members

Internet contacts: anyone in your e-mail address book, and subscribers to chat rooms and other online communities in which you participate

Andrea Wong, CEO of Lifetime Networks, states, "You have this assumption that if you just put your head down and work, you will be rewarded for it. Relationships are critical, whether it's in your business or across adjacent businesses. They may not directly impact you immediately, but three years or five years later they come into play in some way, shape, or form."[65]

If someone in your network is an employee of an organization with an employee referral program that pays employees a bonus for successful referrals, they will be particularly motivated to help you get a job with their company. This is another reason that having a statement about your brand can help others understand the types of jobs that you would best fit with and that you are most interested in pursuing.

As Billie Williamson, Inclusiveness Officer for the Americas at Ernst & Young, said, "You absolutely must take time every day to build relationships with people all around you."[66] Research has shown that one of the consistent differentiators of high performers is their tendency to maintain ties outside their unit and outside the organization. In one organization, the employees with the most extensive personal digital networks were 7 percent more productive than those with smaller networks, suggesting that wikis and social networking tools may help improve productivity. However, in the same organization, employees with the most cohesive face-to-face networks were 30 percent more productive, suggesting that technology cannot always substitute for personal contact.[67]

> "You absolutely must take time every day to build relationships with people all around you." —*Billie Williamson, Inclusiveness Officer for the Americas at Ernst & Young*

Coaching, mentoring, and career development activities help employees diversify their networks and can have a powerful impact on individuals and on the organization as a whole.[68] A typical career trap is exemplified by a high-potential manager who had an insular personal network dominated by other functional professionals within her own company. Although technically savvy, the manager did not use communication technologies such as e-mail, instant messaging, and videoconferencing to reach outside her day-to-day network of colleagues. When her company helped her expand the diversity of her network, her effectiveness improved.[69]

SO WHAT

Developing relationships face-to-face and through social networking can enhance your effectiveness.

Continuous Learning

As IBM CEO Sam Palmisano said, "To be competitive, any individual—like any company, community or country—has to adapt continuously, learning new fields and new skills."[70] One of the most important things you can do for your career is to continually develop your skills and prepare yourself for future opportunities.

Individuals who continue to learn and improve themselves throughout their career can experience many benefits, including improved performance, increased value to their employers, greater career flexibility, and higher self-esteem.[71] For continuous learning to be successful, organizations must recognize the need for continuous learning, foster a continuous learning climate, and develop appropriate policies to support continuous learning. Similarly, individuals must participate in the continuous learning process.[72]

> "To be competitive, any individual—like any company, community or country—has to adapt continuously, learning new fields and new skills." —*Sam Palmisano, CEO of IBM*

Continuous learning is not just about taking courses or attending workshops. It is about developing knowledge and applying new skills to continuously improve your performance. In addition to employer-sponsored training and development, taking continuing education classes, belonging to professional associations, and utilizing online resources can help you to keep your skills fresh. Continuous learning can help you to develop both professional skills and leadership skills.

Global Perspective

SO WHAT

Continually improving your professional and leadership skills throughout your career will help to maximize your performance.

A global perspective is distinguished by a willingness to be open to and learn from the alternative systems and meanings of other people and cultures, and a capacity to identify complex interrelationships.[73] A person with a global perspective scans the world from a broader view, always seeking unexpected trends and opportunities. People with global perspectives are more likely to see the broader context and accept life as a balance of conflicting forces. They are not threatened by surprises or uncertainties, and value diversity.[74] They are also able to navigate through unfamiliar cultures with an open and external focus.[75] Given globalization trends and the multicultural nature of the U.S. workforce, managers increasingly need a global perspective and a supportive set of skills and knowledge to be most effective.[76] To meet this need, business schools are increasing their efforts to develop students' global managerial skills.[77]

This chapter's *Improve Your Skills* feature gives you the opportunity to assess your own global perspective and better understand how to enhance it.

WORK-LIFE BALANCE

SO WHAT

Reducing work-life conflict increases health, performance, ethical behavior, and attendance.

Companies including FedEx, General Mills, Accenture, Paychex, and SAS (featured in this chapter's *Real World Response*) offer at least some employees the opportunity to telecommute and work compressed workweeks. Cleaning product maker S.C. Johnson & Son's on-site concierge service mails employees' packages, sends flowers, picks up and delivers groceries, finds the best deals on car insurance, and even stands in line to wait for concert tickets.[79] Why do these companies do this?

Employees who experience low conflict and high facilitation between work and family roles are objectively healthier, less absent, and better-performing employees.[80] Research has found that viewing work as being more central to our lives neutralizes the negative relationship between work-family conflict and job satisfaction, organizational commitment, and retention.[81] Family-friendly work practices also have been shown to positively influence organizational performance.[82] Promoting work-life balance is often as good for the business as it is for employees.

Work-life policies such as flextime and telework do not always improve attraction, retention, and productivity.[83] Employees must believe that taking advantage of the policies and programs will not hurt them in any way. For example, in a law firm that offers paternity benefits for new fathers, employees

IMPROVE YOUR SKILLS

GLOBAL PERSPECTIVE

This self-assessment gives you the opportunity to better understand your global perspective. Place your response on the line to the left of each statement using the scale below, and then follow the scoring instructions and read the interpretation at the end.

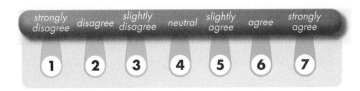

| strongly disagree | disagree | slightly disagree | neutral | slightly agree | agree | strongly agree |
| 1 | 2 | 3 | 4 | 5 | 6 | 7 |

Conceptualization

___ 1. I think it is necessary today to develop strategic alliances with organizations around the globe.
___ 2. Projects that involve international dealings are long-term.
___ 3. I believe that in the next ten years the world will be the same as it is today.
___ 4. In this interlinked world of ours, national boundaries are meaningless.
___ 5. We really live in a global village.
___ 6. In discussions, I always drive for a bigger, broader picture.
___ 7. I believe life is a balance of contradictory forces that are to be appreciated, pondered, and managed.
___ 8. I find it easy to rethink boundaries and to change direction and behavior.
___ 9. I feel comfortable with change, surprise, and ambiguity.
___ 10. I believe I can live a fulfilling life in another culture.

Contextualization

___ 11. I enjoy trying food from other countries.
___ 12. I enjoy working on world community projects.
___ 13. I mostly watch and/or read the local news.
___ 14. I am at my best when I travel to worlds that I do not understand.
___ 15. I get very curious when I meet somebody from another country.
___ 16. I enjoy reading foreign books or watching foreign movies.

___ 17. I have a lot of empathy for people who struggle to speak my own language.
___ 18. When something unexpected happens, it is easier to change the process than the structure.
___ 19. In trying to accomplish my objectives, I find that diversity and multicultural teams play a valuable role.
___ 20. I have close friends from other cultural backgrounds.

Scoring: The sum of your scores for statements 1 to 10 is your *Conceptualization* score: _____. Plot your score on the following continuum:

10 20 30 40 50 60 70

The sum of your scores for statements 11 to 20 is your *Contextualization* score: _____. Plot your score on the following continuum:

10 20 30 40 50 60 70

Interpretation: The higher your *Conceptualization* score, the better you are able to think globally. The higher your *Contextualization* score, the better you are able to act locally and adapt to the local environment. Global perspective is characterized by high levels of both conceptualization and contextualization. Training in international management, living in a foreign country, and working in a foreign country are all related to having higher global perspective.[78] Although both thinking globally and acting locally are important to managers, most managers are more adept at thinking globally than at acting locally because of the uniqueness of local cultures.

If you are interested in enhancing your global perspective, reflect on the statements above that you rated lower than others and identify ways of improving in those areas. Joining international organizations and seeking out multicultural experiences can enhance your global perspective.

Source: Adapted from Journal of International Management, 10, Arora, A., Jaju, A., Kefalas, A.G., & Perenich, T., An Exploratory Analysis of Global Managerial Mindsets: A Case of U.S. Textile and Apparel Industry, 393–411, Copyright © 2004, with permission from Elsevier.

will not take advantage of these benefits if they believe that doing so will prevent them from ever becoming a partner in the firm.

Organizations must address four issues in implementing work-life policies:[84]

1. *Supervisor support*: Do supervisors work with employees to utilize policies like telecommuting, or are important meetings scheduled when employees will be working from home?
2. *Universality*: Can everyone enjoy flextime, or are only those with certain job titles eligible?

3. *Negotiability*: Can all employees have a flexible schedule for caretaking, or are only the top performers granted this request?

4. *Quality of Communication*: Work-life policies are useless if few employees know about them, even if they are supported by the organization.

In balancing your own work and life responsibilities, it is important to understand what works best for you. Some people are able to integrate work and life responsibilities, whereas others prefer to create boundaries that separate their work from their lives. Actively managing and controlling how we use our time influences our satisfaction with our work-life balance.[85]

Some of the least expensive programs that effectively promote work-life balance include flextime, telecommuting, and compressed workweeks.[86] This chapter's *Case Study* feature explores how KPMG instituted a flexible work program to help it meet its business needs while meeting employee needs as well.

CASE STUDY

Flexibility at KPMG

Accounting firm KPMG's U.K. offices wanted to decrease payroll costs while maintaining the company's commitment to its employees. So KPMG gave its U.K.-based employees the choice of either volunteering for a four-day workweek at 90 percent of their salary (80 percent if fewer than 75 percent of employees signed up); a four- to twelve-week sabbatical at 30 percent of their base pay; either or both; or neither. Volunteering for the program, called Flexible Futures, triggered an eighteen-month change in the employee's employment contract giving KMPG the right to exercise the chosen option if and when it needed to. This allowed the company to reduce employee hours and pay on short notice and reduce the need for large-scale staff reductions if economic challenges arose.

To educate employees about their options, KPMG held conference calls, trained managers to answer potential questions, and posted a long list of questions and answers on a dedicated Flexible Futures page on its intranet. The website also included a calculator to enable employees to easily calculate what their take-home pay would be under any of the options. A link to KPMG's corporate responsibility website helped connect employees interested in sabbaticals with nonprofit organizations that needed accounting expertise.

Flexible Futures gives employees greater job security and control over their own destiny. This has allowed them to worry less about their jobs and focus more on their clients. More than 85 percent of KPMG employees signed up for at least one of the options. KPMG expects this to save the company up to 15 percent of payroll costs and to boost employee morale.

Questions:

1. How does this program help KPMG?
2. How does this program help KPMG's employees?
3. If you were employed by KPMG, would this program appeal to you? Why or why not?

Source: Campbell, R. & Payne, T. (2012). The Future is Flexible, KPMG, February. Available online: http://www .kpmg.com/global/en/issuesandinsights/articlespublications/frontiers-in-finance/publishingimages/february-2012 /march2010/16008.html; KPMG Asks Staff to Accept Temporary Flexible Contracts if the Need Arises (2009). People Management Magazine, January 29, 8; Hewlett, S.A. (2010). "KPMG's Flexible Futures, "Talent Management, January, 22; Huber, N. (2009)." Huge Demand for Flexible Working at KPMG," Accountancy Age, February 12. Available online: http://www.accountancyage.com/accountancyage/news/2236299/huge-demand-flexible-working-4476838.

Providing a work-life balance to employees can not only increase retention and job satisfaction, but may also create a more ethical workplace. One survey found that nine out of ten employed adults agreed that workers are more likely to behave ethically on the job when they have a good work-life balance.[87] In addition, 60 percent of respondents believed that job dissatisfaction is a significant reason why people make unethical decisions at work. As one expert says, "In the competitive environment to attract and retain talent, it is imperative that employers provide employees with the means to attain a healthy work-life balance. This is not only key to job satisfaction and retaining your most valued employees, but it is also critical in fostering an ethical workplace culture."[88]

SUMMARY AND APPLICATION

Your career path and ultimate career success is up to you. The better you are able to define what you want to accomplish, the better you will be able to prepare yourself to take advantage of opportunities to get there. Understanding your personal definition of career success will be critical to making the trade-offs you will face throughout your career.

Socialization, mentoring, and continuous learning will help you to succeed in your career. Being proactive, taking advantage of your social networks, and having a global perspective will also contribute to your effectiveness in our increasingly globalized world. Staying focused on what is important to you and striving for an appropriate work-life balance will help keep you on course throughout your journey.

We hope this book has helped you to acquire some of the skills and tools you will need to find and excel at a job you like. We want you to get a better job and a better career, and to be a better manager. We wish you every success in your life and career!

TAKEAWAY POINTS

1. Definitions of career success include making a lot of money, obtaining a high-status job title, taking pride in a job well done, learning new things, helping others, spending quality time with family and friends, and being able to pursue outside interests.
2. Career anchors are our core interests that anchor our careers throughout our lives. If we stray too far from our core interests, we tend to return to these anchors.
3. People who follow a stable pattern go directly from school or training into work with which they stay. People following a conventional pattern try several jobs until they find a stable one. A person following an unstable pattern never becomes established in one area, instead going from trial jobs to a stable situation and then back to trial jobs. Those who follow a multiple trial pattern try a lot of different jobs for short periods of time, not staying in any field long enough to achieve stability.
4. A personal brand is a summary of our key talents and what differentiates us from others. It helps us to concisely communicate what differentiates us, increasing the chances that those we meet will understand our talents and remember us favorably.
5. The first phase of socialization is anticipatory socialization, which occurs before a new hire begins work. In this stage new hires develop

REAL WORLD RESPONSE

WORK-LIFE BALANCE AT SAS INSTITUTE

SAS Institute's culture is based on trust between employees and the company. One of *Money* magazine's 100 Best Companies to Work For in all of the years the list has been compiled, SAS is known for encouraging employee work-life balance to decrease employee stress, absenteeism, and illness. To SAS, investing in these programs makes good business sense and increases employees' performance and loyalty. As CEO Goodnight says, "95 percent of my assets drive out the front gate every evening. It's my job to bring them back."[89] Because SAS recognizes that its employees have varied needs and are in different life stages, it offers a variety of services and policies to meet all employees' needs.

Employees at SAS headquarters in Cary, North Carolina, enjoy on-site amenities including free health care, subsidized child care, eldercare, a free 66,000-square-foot recreation and fitness center, and programs that promote employee wellness. As a result, SAS employees are unusually loyal. Annual turnover is about 4 percent in an industry in which 22 percent is the norm. This low turnover translates into high profits and long-term relationships with customers, knowledge retention, and low recruitment and training costs.[90]

When asked about the success of SAS's work-life initiatives, David Russo, SAS's Vice President for Human Resources, states, "It's not about programs and policies. It's about philosophy; it's about 'who you are' as a company."[91] As one SAS employee says, "There's an understanding about finding a healthy work-life balance that permeates SAS from top to bottom."[92]

expectations about the job and organization through interactions with recruiters, managers, and other company representatives. The second phase is the encounter phase, which happens as new employees begin working and learning about their job and company. The third phase is settling in. In this phase new employees become comfortable with their jobs and with their relationships with others, and their interest in performance feedback and career opportunities increases.

6. A social style is a person's dominant pattern of communication styles and interpersonal behaviors. People with different styles have different preferences for influencing others and communicating either facts or personal feelings. Because the communication preferences of different social styles can conflict, understanding your own social style and being able to flexibly adapt it to match the communication preferences of others can increase personal effectiveness.

7. Providing a work-life balance to employees can not only increase performance, retention, and job satisfaction, but may also create a more ethical workplace.

DISCUSSION QUESTIONS

1. How can managers help their subordinates manage their careers to best support the firm's business strategy?
2. How do you define career success?
3. Which do you think is more important, your career or your quality of life? Do you think that your answer will change over time? If so, what can you do now to meet your current goals and prepare yourself to best meet your different future goals?
4. How can companies help job candidates evaluate how happy they would be working for them?
5. What are your career anchors? What does this mean for the career you plan to pursue?
6. What is your personal brand? Why should a company hire you over the other candidates it is evaluating?
7. How can your school better socialize new students? Do you think that all students would prefer to be socialized in this way? Why or why not?
8. What is your social style? What behaviors do you need to be most aware of when interacting with others to increase your effectiveness?
9. Do you think companies should invest in programs promoting work-life balance or do you feel that this is not a good investment? Explain your answer.

EXERCISES

How Do You Define Success?

As you learned in this chapter, identifying your personal definition of success is critical in developing a career plan that will get you there.

Think about pay, health, job title, family, personal relationships, family goals, life and purpose, the desire to have a broader impact in both life and work, and outside interests and hobbies. Think about what you want to accomplish or do in the next five years, ten years, and by the end of your career.

Now write a list of what is important to you right now and what you think will be important in five years, ten years, and by the end of your career. Then think about what it will take in the context of your work to achieve these things. What can you do in the next year to get started? What are the skills, capabilities, and resources you will need? How will you manage your time? What trade-offs will you need to make?

Your definition of success may change over time. It is a good idea to revisit your definition as your life and goals change.

Career Management at Chipotle[93]

Chipotle Mexican Grill initially offered its workers few chances to advance in the company. They could only advance from hourly crew to assistant manager to manager, and advancing to manager only happened about 20 percent of the time. Many talented employees had to leave the company in order to advance their careers.

Recognizing its untapped talent, Chipotle created more levels for hourly workers to advance into, including kitchen manager, service manager, apprentice (formerly the assistant manager), general manager, and restaurateur (managing multilevel operations). After the changes, Chipotle now promotes 80 percent from within. As co-CEO Monty Moran says, "If you don't have a career path that is clear, good people won't want to stay with you. People want to know that their hard work is rewarded, and they can ascend through the ranks and become a bigger factor in the company's success."

Employees must start as hourly crew members in order to move into other positions. Chipotle's Culture and Language team supports Chipotle's goal of developing all of its restaurant managers from crew by bridging the cultural and linguistic gaps between Chipotle employees. The department empowers, educates, and trains employees to increase internal promotions, cultural sensitivity, and communication skills.

Chipotle hires people who are upbeat, ambitious, motivated, and hospitable. The key factor for advancement is a store manager identifying these attributes in an employee, and then providing challenges to broaden that employee's experience. Talented food servers typically advance to become kitchen managers where they learn more about the food, and then become service managers and handle customer-service issues. Service managers then train their replacements, which helps Chipotle discover who has the skills to be a manager and run a full-service restaurant.

Questions

1. How does career management help both Chipotle and its employees?
2. What role does diversity and inclusion play in Chipotle's career management practices?
3. How might Chipotle use mentoring and other concepts you learned about in this chapter to further support its career development efforts?

How Satisfied Are You with Your Job?

Point your favorite browser to http://wbs2.careervision.org/PerspectiveJobSatisfationSurvey.aspx and complete the Career Vision Job Satisfaction Survey. Print out your report and answer the following questions.

Questions

1. Do you agree with the ratings of where mismatches exist between your needs and expectations and the work you are doing?
2. What can you do to raise the ratings of your two lowest satisfier dimensions?
3. What obstacles might prevent you from improving the ratings of your two lowest satisfier dimensions? What can you do to overcome these obstacles?

Skills Profiler

Point your favorite browser to http://www.careerinfonet.org/skills/default.aspx?nodeid=20 and use the Skills Profiler tool to learn about some career options. Then answer the following questions.

Questions

1. What are your strongest skills?
2. What are some of the jobs identified by this tool that match your skills and interests which you might consider pursuing next in your career?
3. How can information from this type of tool help you make various career choices?

You can also visit http://www.careerinfonet.org/acinet/select_state.asp?next=carout1&level=&optstatus=&id=1&nodeid=210&soccode=&stfips=&jobfam= to learn about the employment trends for different occupations by state.

VIDEO CASES

Now What?

Imagine receiving a performance review from your boss that is less favorable than you expected. *What do you say or do?* Go to this chapter's "Now What?" video, watch the challenge video, and choose a response. Be sure to also view the outcomes of the two responses you didn't choose.

Discussion Questions

1. As a manager, how can you increase a subordinate's openness to your feedback?
2. Which aspects of organizational behavior discussed in this chapter are illustrated in these videos? Explain your answer.
3. How else might you handle this situation? Explain your answer.

Workplace | Numi Organic Tea: Danielle Oviedo

When Danielle Oviedo showed up for her first day as the manager of the Distribution Center at Numi Organic Tea in Oakland, California, her new direct reports were not happy about the change. They loved Oviedo's predecessor, who was more like a friend than a boss to them. But Numi's director of operations, Brian Durkee, was looking for someone with specific skills and experience when he hired Danielle, and popularity wasn't on the list. Durkee hired Danielle because of her effectiveness and success as a manager in previous positions. She also had experience leading much big teams in similar departments.

Prior to Danielle's arrival, lead times for Numi's customer orders were not competitive. Although Numi's loyal food service customers were happy with Numi products, some customers were considering taking their business elsewhere because deliveries were unpredictable. Upon her arrival at Numi, Danielle identified the problem: employees were performing tasks in isolation with little attention to anything else.

(Continued)

To solve the issue, Danielle trained the Distribution Center employees in every critical task and process, explaining how all the pieces fit together. Going forward, her staff would perform multiple tasks depending on what pressing deadlines loomed. Importantly, Danielle helped her team understand their jobs on a conceptual level so they could see how their work linked directly to Numi's larger goals. With newfound effectiveness aided by Danielle's planning and organizing, the team cut lead times for international orders by about 75 percent.

Numi's customer service manager, Cindy Graffort, is thrilled about Danielle's achievements and said none of these changes were possible before Danielle arrived. According to Cindy, the dramatic changes were a direct result of Danielle's ability to come up with innovative solutions to problems plaguing the Distribution Center.

When asked for specific insight into Danielle's managerial success, Cindy highlighted her impressive human skills. Unlike old-school managers who hide in their offices and manage employees from afar, Danielle is out on the floor working with teammates, ensuring they understand the process, and being supportive.

Discussion Questions

1. In what career stage is Danielle Oviedo?
2. In your view, what are Danielle Oviedo's career anchors?
3. Do you think Danielle Oviedo will attain senior leadership at Numi or elsewhere? Why or why not?

DO WHAT

CENGAGENOW™

CENGAGENOW™ includes **teaching and learning resources** to supplement the text, and is designed specifically to **help students "think like managers"** by engaging and challenging them to think critically about managerial situations. **CengageNOW** uses today's technology to improve **the skills** of tomorrow's managers.

END NOTES

[1]SAS (2012). *About SAS*. Available online: http://www.sas.com/company/about/index.html.

[2]Leung, R. (2003, April 20). Working the Good Life. *60 Minutes*. Available online: http://www.cbsnews.com/stories/2003/04/18/60minutes/main550102.shtml.

[3]Heslin, P. A. (2005). Experiencing Career Success. *Organizational Dynamics, 34*, 376–390.

[4]Heslin, P. A. (2003). Self- and Other-Referent Criteria of Career Success. *Journal of Career Assessment, 11*, 262–286.

[5]Heslin, P. A. (2005). Conceptualizing and Evaluating Career Success. *Journal of Organizational Behavior, 26*, 113–136.

[6]Kay, E., French, Jr., J. R. P., & Meyer, H. H. (1962). *A Study of the Performance Appraisal Interview. Management Development and Employee Relations Services*. New York: General Electric.

[7]Tang, T. L. P. (1992). The Meaning of Money Revisited. *Journal of Organizational Behavior, 13*, 197–202.

[8]Tang, T. L. P. (1992). The Meaning of Money Revisited. *Journal of Organizational Behavior, 13*, 197–202.

[9]Tang, T. L. P. (1992). The Meaning of Money Revisited. *Journal of Organizational Behavior, 13,* 197–202.

[10]Tang, T. L. P., & Gilbert, P. R. (1995). Attitudes Toward Money as Related to Intrinsic and Extrinsic Job Satisfaction, Stress and Work-Related Attitudes. *Personality and Individual Differences, 19,* 327–332.

[11] Hamel, G. (2010). HCL's CEO on its 'Management Makeover.' *The Wall Street Journal*, November 18. Available online at: http://blogs.wsj.com/management/2010/08/24/hcls-ceo-on-its-management-makeover/?KEYWORDS=HCL.

[12] Herrbach, O. & Mignonac, K. (2012). Perceived Gender Discrimination and Women's Subjective Career Success: The Moderating Role of Career Anchors, *Industrial Relations, 67*(1), 25–50.

[13]Enache, M., Sallan, J.M., Simo, P., & Fernandez, V. (2011). Career Attitudes and Subjective Career Success: Tackling Gender Differences, *Gender in Management: An International Journal, 26*(3), 234–250.

[14] Lazarova, M., Dany, F., & Mayrhofer, W. (2012) Careers Across National Contexts. In C. Brewster & Mayrhofer, W. (Eds) *Handbook of Comparative Human Resource Management*. Northampton, MA: Edward Elgar Publisher.

[15]Adler, N. J. (2008). *International Dimensions of Organizational Behavior* (5th ed.). Mason, OH: Thomson/South-Western.

[16]Hofstede, G. (2001). *Culture's Consequences: Comparing Values, Behaviors, Institutions, and Organizations Across Nations* (2nd ed.). Thousand Oaks, CA: Sage.

[17]Hampden-Turner, C. (1991). *Charting the Corporate Mind*. Oxford, England: Blackwell; Adler, N. J. (2008). *International Dimensions of Organizational Behavior* (5th ed.). Mason, OH: Thomson/South-Western.

[18]Schein, E. (1978). *Career Dynamics: Matching Individual and Organizational Needs* (p. 133). Reading, MA: Addison-Wesley.

[19]Laud, R. & Johnson, M. (2012). Upward Mobility: A Typology of Tactics and Strategies for Career Advancement, *Career Development International, 17*(3).

[20]Hansen, L. S. (2001). *Integrative Life Planning: Critical Tasks for Career Development and Changing Life Patterns*. San Francisco, CA: Jossey-Bass.

[21]Miller, D. C., & Form, W. H. (1951). *Industrial Sociology*. New York: Harper.

[22]Arrdua, W., & Dixson, K. (2007). *Career Distinction: Stand Out by Building Your Brand*. Hoboken, NJ: John Wiley.

[23]Feigenson, W. (2009, June 24). Forget the Elevator Pitch: You Have 6 Seconds for Your Personal Branding Statement. BrandYourself.com. Available online: http://feigenson.us/blog/?p=846.

[24]Siegel, R. (2009). Develop a Great Elevator Pitch. TheStreet Directory.com. Available online: http://www.streetdirectory.com/travel_guide/29391/sales/develop_a_great_elevator_pitch.html.

[25]Siegel, R. (2009). Develop a Great Elevator Pitch. TheStreetDirectory.com. Available online: http://www.streetdirectory.com/travel_guide/29391/sales/develop_a_great_elevator_pitch.html.

[26]Schawbel, D. (2012, September 12). Your Personal Brand Statement IS NOT a JOB TITLE (revision 1, 17:21 BST). *The CIPR Conversation*. Available online: http://conversation.cipr.co.uk/posts/dan.schawbel/your-personal-brand-statement-is-not-a-job-title/17953

[27]Heslin, P. A. (2005). Experiencing Career Success. *Organizational Dynamics, 34,* 376–390.

[28]Louis, M. R. (1980). Surprise and Sense Making: What Newcomers Experience in Entering Unfamiliar Organizational Settings. *Administrative Science Quarterly, 64,* 226–251.

[29]Williams, R. (2003). *Mellon Learning Curve Research Study*. New York: Mellon Corp.

[30]Chao, G. T., O'Leary-Kelly, A. M., Wolf, S., Klein, H. J., & Gardner, P. D. (1994). Organizational Socialization: Its Content and Consequences. *Journal of Applied Psychology, 79*(5), 730–743.

[31]Noe, R. A. (2005). *Employee Training and Development*. New York: McGraw-Hill/Irwin.

[32]Van Maanen, J., & Schein, E. H. (1979). Toward a Theory of Organizational Socialization. In *Research in Organizational Behaviour*, ed. B. M. Staw (Vol. 1, pp. 209–264). Greenwich, CT: JAI Press.

[33]Allen, D. G. (2006). Do Organizational Socialization Tactics Influence Newcomer Embeddedness and Turnover? *Journal of Management, 32,* 237–256.

[34]Cascio, W. F. (2003). *Managing Human Resources*. New York: McGraw-Hill/Irwin.

[35]Ashford, S. J., & Black, J. S. (1996). Proactivity During Organizational Entry: The Role of Desire for Control. *Journal of Applied Psychology, 81,* 199–214; Morrison, E. W. (1993). Newcomer Information Seeking: Exploring Types, Modes, Sources, and Outcomes. *Academy of Management Journal, 36,* 557–589; Ostroff, C., & Kozlowski, S. W. J. (1992). Organizational Socialization as a Learning Process: The Role of Information Acquisition. *Personnel Psychology, 45,* 849–874; Wanberg, C. R., & Kammeyer-Mueller, J. D. (2000). Predictors and Outcomes of Proactivity in the Socialization Process. *Journal of Applied Psychology, 85,* 373–385.

[36]Ashford, S. J., & Black, J. S. (1996). Proactivity During Organizational Entry: The Role of Desire for Control. *Journal of Applied Psychology, 81,* 199–214.

[37]Gruman, J. A., Saks, A. M., & Zweig, D. I. (2006). Organizational Socialization Tactics and Newcomer Proactive Behaviors: An Integrative Study. *Journal of Vocational Behavior, 69,* 90–104.

[38]Healy, C. C., & Welchert, A. J. (1990). Mentoring Relations: A Definition to Advance Research and Practice. *Educational Researcher, 19*(9), 17–21.

[39]Liu, D., Liu, J., Kwan, H. K., & Mao, Y. (2009). What Can I Gain as a Mentor? The Effect of Mentoring on the Job Performance and Social Status of Mentors in China. *Journal of Occupational and Organizational Psychology, 82,* 871–895.

[40]Scandura, T. A. (1992). Mentorship and Career Mobility: An Empirical Investigation. *Journal of Organizational Behavior, 13*(2), 169–174.

[41]Frankel, B. (2009, April 7). 5 Mentoring Best Practices. *Diversity Inc Error! Hyperlink reference not valid. Magazine*, 39–41.

[42]Frankel, B. (2009, April 7). 5 Mentoring Best Practices. *Diversity Inc. Magazine*, 39–41.

[43]Chao, G. T., Walz, P. M., & Gardner, P. D. (1992). Formal and Informal Mentorships: A Comparison on Mentoring Functions and Contrast with Nonmentored Counterparts. *Personnel Psychology, 45,* 619–636.

[44]Frankel, B. (2009, April 7). 5 Mentoring Best Practices. *Diversity Inc. Magazine* , 39–41.

[45]Frankel, B. (2009, April 7). 5 Mentoring Best Practices. *Diversity Inc. Magazine*, 39–41.

[46]United States Office of Personnel Management (2008, September). Best Practices: Mentoring. Available online: http://www.opm.gov/hrd/lead/BestPractices-Mentoring.pdf.

[47]Frankel, B. (2009, April 7). 5 Mentoring Best Practices. *Diversity Inc. Magazine*, 39–41.

[48]Frankel, B. (2009, April 7). 5 Mentoring Best Practices. *Diversity Inc. Magazine*, 39–41.

[49]Greengard, S. (2002). Moving Forward with Reverse Mentoring. *Workforce*, 81, 15.

[50]Gittel, J. H. (2005). The Southwest Airlines Way. New York: McGraw-Hill.

[51]Siebert, S. E., Crant, J. M., & Karimer, M. C. (1999). Proactive Personality and Career Success. *Journal of Applied Psychology, 84,* 416–427.

[52]Siebert, S. E., Crant, J. M., & Karimer, M. C. (1999). Proactive Personality and Career Success. *Journal of Applied Psychology, 84,* 416–427.

[53]Gerhardt, M., Ashenbaum, B., & Newman, W. R. (2009). Understanding the Impact of Proactive Personality on Job Performance. *Journal of Leadership and Organizational Studies, 16,* 61–72.

[54]Shi, J., Chen, Z., & Zhou, L. (2011). Testing Differential Mediation Effects of Sub-Dimensions of Political Skills in Linking Proactive Personality to Employee Performance, *Journal of Business and Psychology, 26*(3), 359–369.

[55]Caprioni, P. J. (2000). *The Practical Coach: Management Skills for Everyday Life.* Upper Saddle River, NJ: Prentice Hall.

[56]Grant, A.M., Gino, F., & Hofmann, D.A. (2011). Reversing the Extraverted Leadership Advantage: The Role of Employee Proactivity, *The Academy of Management Journal, 54*(3), 528–550.

[57]Bolton, R., & Bolton, D. G. (1984). *Social Style / Management Style* (p. 3). New York: American Management Associations.

[58]Merrill, D. W., & Reid, R. H. (1999). *Personal Styles and Effective Performance.* Boca Raton, FL: CRC Press.

[59]Bolton, R., & Bolton, D. G. (1984). *Social Style / Management Style.* New York: American Management Associations.

[60]Bolton, R., & Bolton, D. G. (1984). *Social Style / Management Style.* New York: American Management Associations.

[61]May, G. L. (2008). The Effect of Rater Training on Reducing Social Style Bias in Peer Evaluation. *Business Communication Quarterly, 71,* 297–313.

[62]Snavely, W. B., & Walters, E. V. (1983). Differences in Communication Competence Among Administrator Social Styles. *Journal of Applied Communication Research, 11,* 120–135.

[63]Snavely, W. B., & Walters, E. V. (1983). Differences in Communication Competence Among Administrator Social Styles. *Journal of Applied Communication Research, 11,* 120–135.

[64]Wolff, H. G., & Moser, K. (2009). Effects of Networking on Career Success: A Longitudinal Study. *Journal of Applied Psychology, 94,* 196–206.

[65]How Women Handle Success. (2009, November 2). *BusinessWeek,* 70–71.

[66]How Women Handle Success. (2009, November 2). *BusinessWeek,* 70–71.

[67]Pentland, A. (2008). *Honest Signals: How They Shape Our World.* Boston: The MIT Press.

[68]Laseter, T., & Cross, R. (2007, January 31). The Craft of Connection. Strategy + Business. Available online: http://www.strategy-business.com/press/enewsarticle/enews013107?pg=0.

[69]Laseter, T., & Cross, R. (2007, January 31). The Craft of Connection. Strategy + Business. Available online: http://www.strategy-business.com/press/enewsarticle/enews013107?pg=0.

[70]Schoeff, Jr., M. (2011, September 15). IBM Establishes Individual Learning Accounts for Employees. *Workforce Management Online.* Available online: http://www.workforce.com/article/20070726/NEWS01/307269993#.

[71]Eddy, E. R., Tannenbaum, S. I., Lorenzet, S. J., & Smith-Jentsch, K. A. (2005). The Influence of a Continuous Learning Environment on Peer Mentoring Behaviors. *Journal of Managerial Issues, 17,* 383–395.

[72]Eddy, E. R., Tannenbaum, S. I., Lorenzet, S. J., & Smith-Jentsch, K. A. (2005). The Influence of a Continuous Learning Environment on Peer Mentoring Behaviors. *Journal of Managerial Issues, 17,* 383–395.

[73]Kedia, B. L., & Mukherji, A. (1999). Global Managers: Developing a Mindset for Global Competitiveness. *Journal of World Business, 34,* 230–251.

[74]Rhinesmith, S. H. (1992). Global Mindsets for Global Managers. *Training & Development, 46,* 63–69.

[75]Levy, O., Beechler, S., Taylor, S., & Boyacigiller, N. (2007). What We Talk About When We Talk About "Global Mindset": Managerial Cognition in Multinational Corporations. *Journal of International Business Studies, 38,* 231–258.

[76]Wankel, C. (2007). *21st Century Management: A Reference Handbook* (Vol. 1). New York: Sage.

[77]Kedia, B.L. & Englis, P.D. (2011). Transforming Business Education to Produce Global Managers, *Business Horizons, 54*(4), 325–331.

[78]Arora, A., Jaju, A., Kefalas, A. G., & Perenich, T. (2004). An Exploratory Analysis of Global Managerial Mindsets: A Case of U.S. Textile and Apparel Industry. *Journal of International Management, 10,* 393–411.

[79]Unusual Perks: S.C. Johnson & Son. (2010, January 21). *Fortune.* Available online: http://money.cnn.com/galleries/2010/fortune/1001/gallery.bestcompanies_unusual_perks.fortune/14.html.

[80]van Steenbergen, E. F., Ellemers, N., & Mooijaart, A. (2007). How Work and Family Can Facilitate Each Other: Distinct Types of Work-Family Facilitation and Outcomes for Women and Men. *Journal of Occupational Health Psychology, 12,* 279–300.

[81]Carr, J., Boyar, S. L., & Gregory, B. T. (2008). The Moderating Effect of Work-Family Centrality on Work-Family Conflict, Organizational Attitudes, and Turnover Behavior. *Journal of Management, 34,* 244–262.

[82]Ngo, H. Y., Lau, C. M., & Foley, S. (2008). Strategic Human Resource Management, Firm Performance, and Employee Relations Climate in China. *Human Resource Management, 47,* 73–90.

[83]Sutton, K. L., & Noe, R. A. (2005). Family-Friendly Programs and Work-Life Integration: More Myth than Magic. In *Work and Life Integration: Organizational, Cultural, and Individual Perspectives,* eds. E. E. Kossek and S. J. Lambert (pp. 151–170). Mahwah, NJ: Erlbaum Associates.

[84]Ryan, A. M., & Kossek, E. E. (2008). Work-Life Policy Implementation: Breaking Down or Creating Barriers to Inclusiveness? *Human Resource Management, 47,* 295–310.

[85]Kossek, E. E., & Lautsch, B. A. (2008). *CEO of Me: Creating a Life That Works in the Flexible Job Age.* Philadelphia: Wharton School Publishing.

[86]Breaugh, J.A. & Farabee, A.M. (2012). Telecommuting and Flexible Work Hours: Alternative Work Arrangements that Can Improve the Quality of Work Life, *International Handbooks of Quality-of-Life, 4,* 251–274.

[87]Worthington, B. (2007, May 3). Work/Life Balance Influences Workplace Ethics. *Human Resource Executive Online.* Available online: http://www.hreonline.com/HRE/story.jsp?storyId=12614425.

[88]Worthington, B. (2007, May 3). Work/Life Balance Influences Workplace Ethics. *Human Resource Executive Online*. Available online: http://www.hreonline.com/HRE/story.jsp?storyId=12614425.

[89]Leung, R. (2003, April 20). Working the Good Life. *60 Minutes*. Available online: http://www.cbsnews.com/stories/2003/04/18/60minutes/main550102.shtml.

[90]SAS. (2010, February 8). *Money*. Available online: http://money.cnn.com/magazines/fortune/bestcompanies/2010/snapshots/1.html; SAS on FORTUNE Best Companies to Work For List in US, January 19, 2012. Available online: http://www.sas.com/news/preleases/2012fortuneranking.html.

[91]Litchfield, L., & Pitt-Catsouphes, M. (1999). A Perspective from SAS Institute, Boston College Center for Work & Family Research Highlights Series, p. 2.

[92]Ohri, A. (2009, July 1). Interview Alison Bolen, SAS.com. *Decision Stats*. Available online: http://decisionstats.com/2009/06/30/interview-alison-bolen-sas-com/.

[93]Chipotle Names 200th Restauranteur, Chipotle Mexican Grill, April 14, 2011. Available online: http://ir.chipotle.com/phoenix.zhtml?c=194775&p=irol-newsArticle&ID=1550462&hight=; Careers (2010). Chipotle.com. Available online: http://www.chipotle.com/en-US/company/careers.aspx; Job Description: Crew. (2010). Chipotle.com. Available online: http://www.chipotle.com/en-US/company/careers.aspx; People are People Too (2010). Chipotle.com.Available online at: http://www.chipotle.com/en-US/fwi/people/ people.aspx.

GLOSSARY

abuse of power Using any type of power to demean, exploit, or take advantage of another or influencing someone to do something the person later regrets

accommodating A cooperative conflict management style

achievement motivation Strong desires to accomplish something important, and take pleasure in succeeding at something important and demanding

active conflict management norms Resolve conflict openly

active listening Becoming actively involved in the process of listening to what others are saying and clarifying messages' meaning

adjourning When the team disbands

affective commitment Positive emotional attachment to the organization and strong identification with its values and goals

affectivity A general tendency of an individual to experience a particular mood or to react to things in a particular way or with certain emotions

after-action review A professional discussion of an event that enables discovery of what happened, why it happened, and how to sustain strengths and improve on weaknesses

agreeable conflict management norms Resolve conflict in a cooperative manner

alternative dispute resolution Involving a third party in a negotiation to overcome a stalemate between the parties

anchoring and adjustment Making assessments by starting with, or anchoring onto, a familiar starting value and then adjusting it based on other elements of the decision problem to arrive at a final decision

appreciative inquiry An organizational change philosophy and process building organizations around what works, rather than focusing on and trying to fix what doesn't work

arbitration A third party is involved and usually has the authority to impose a settlement on the parties

artifacts The physical manifestation of the culture including open offices, awards, ceremonies, and formal lists of values

assumptions Those organizational values that have become so taken for granted over time that they become the core of the company's culture

attitude Expresses our values, beliefs, and feelings toward something, and inclines us to act or react in a certain way toward it

attribution How people explain the causes of their own as well as other people's behaviors and achievements

autocratic leadership style Centralizing authority, making decisions alone, and expecting followers or subordinates simply to follow instructions

availability bias When we can readily remember past instances of an event, we tend to overestimate the likelihood that such an event will occur again

avoiding Ignoring the conflict or denying that it exists

behavioral intentions Reflect your motivation to do something with respect to the object of the attitude

beliefs Your judgments about the object of the attitude that result from your values, past experiences, and reasoning

Big Five A personality framework consisting of extroversion, emotional stability, agreeableness, conscientiousness, and openness to experience

body language A body movement such as a gesture or expression

bounded rationality Our rationality is limited by the amount of information, time, and resources available.

brainstorming A process for developing creative solutions

bureaucratic structure An organizational structure with formal division of labor, hierarchy, and standardization of work procedures

burnout Exhaustion of physical or emotional strength or motivation usually as a result of prolonged stress or frustration

career anchor Core interests that serve to anchor a career throughout a person's life

career development The process through which we come to understand ourselves as we relate to the world of work and our role in it

categorization Our tendency to put things into groups or categories

centralized organizations Concentrate power and decision making authority at higher levels of the organization

change agents Employees or outside experts who assist with all phases of the change process, especially the resolution of conflicts

channel The medium used to send the message

charismatic leaders Leaders idealized by followers who develop strong emotional attachments to them

code of conduct Specifies expected and prohibited actions in the workplace, and gives examples of appropriate behavior

code of ethics A decision-making guide that describes the highest values to which an organization aspires

coercive power A position power based on fear or a desire to avoid punishment

cognitive dissonance An incompatibility between behavior and an attitude or between two different attitudes

cohesiveness The degree to which members are attracted to the team and to its members, and how loyal team members are to the team and to each other

collaborating A conflict management style reflecting a desire to give both parties what they want

common good standard The ethical decision shows respect and compassion for all others, especially the most vulnerable

communication The transmission of information from one person to another to create a shared understanding and feeling

communities of practice Groups of people whose shared expertise and interest in a joint enterprise informally binds them together

competing Pursuing one's own interest at the expense of the other party

competitive advantage Anything that gives a firm an edge over rivals in attracting customers and defending itself against competition

complementary fit The degree to which an employee adds something that is missing in the organization or workgroup by being different from the others

compromising A conflict management style in which each side sacrifices something in order to end the conflict

conciliation A third party builds a positive relationship between the parties and directs them toward a satisfactory settlement

conflict A disagreement through which two or more parties perceive a threat to their interests, needs, or concerns

conflict culture Shared norms for managing conflict

conflicts of interest Conflict due to incompatible needs or competition over perceived or actual resource constraints

constructive conflict Adaptive, positive conflict (also called functional conflict)

consultative Seeking input from others but making the final decision alone

contingency theories of leadership Leadership theories that acknowledge that the appropriateness of any leadership style depends on the nature of the followers and the situation

continuance commitment Staying with an organization because of perceived high economic and/or social costs involved with leaving

continuous production Machines constantly make the product

contrast effect Evaluating a person's characteristics through comparisons with other people we have recently encountered who rank higher or lower on the same characteristics

core self-evaluations Fundamental premises people hold about themselves and their functioning in the world

corporate social responsibility Businesses living and working together for the common good and valuing human dignity

correlation Reflects the size and strength of the statistical relationship between two variables; ranges from −1 to +1

cost leadership strategy Striving to be the lowest-cost producer for a particular level of product quality

cross-functional team A team whose members come from different departments or functional areas; can be short- or long-term in duration

cross-team integrating teams A team member serves on a work team and a second team with the function of integrating multiple teams

cross-training Training employees in more than one job or in multiple skills to enable them to do different jobs

cultural competence The ability to interact effectively with people of different cultures

culture of inclusion The extent to which majority members value efforts to increase minority representation, and whether the qualifications and abilities of minority members are questioned

customer intimacy Delivering unique and customizable products or services to meet customers' needs and increase customer loyalty

decentralized decisions Employees, not managers, make decisions about their work, including staffing, production scheduling, and resource allocation

decentralized organizations The authority for making decisions affecting an organization is distributed

decoding Translating the message back into something that can be understood by the receiver

deep-level diversity Individual differences that cannot be seen directly, including goals, values, personalities, decisionmaking styles, knowledge, skills, abilities, and attitudes

defensive attributions Explanations for negative outcomes, such as tragic events, that help us to avoid feelings of vulnerability and mortality

Delphi method Experts' judgments gathered through successive iterations of a questionnaire result in a decision by consensus

democratic leadership style Sharing decision making with others and encouraging subordinates to be involved in setting goals

demographic characteristics Physical and observable characteristics of individuals, including gender, ethnicity, and age

demographic diversity Diversity in age, gender, race, and other demographic characteristics

dependent variable The variable predicted to be affected by something else

differentiation strategy Developing a product or service that has unique characteristics valued by customers

direct contact Managers from different units informally work together to coordinate or to identify and solve shared problems

disagreeable conflict management norms Resolve conflict competitively

disparity Differences in the concentration of valuable social assets or resources—dissimilarity in rank, pay, decision-making authority, or status, for example

display rules Shared expectations about which emotions ought to be expressed and which ought to be disguised

distributive fairness The perceived fairness of the outcome received

distributive negotiation Any gain to one party is offset by an equivalent loss to the other party

diversity The variety of observable and unobservable similarities and differences among people

division A collection of functions organized around a particular geographic area, product or service, or market

division of labor The degree to which employees specialize

dysfunctional conflict Destructive conflict focused on emotions and differences between the two parties

dysfunctional stress An overload of stress from a situation of either under- or overarousal that continues for too long

emotional contagion One person's expressed emotion causes others to express the same emotion

emotional intelligence An interpersonal capability that includes the ability to perceive and express emotions, to understand and use them, and to manage emotions in oneself and other people

emotional labor Displaying the appropriate emotion regardless of the emotion actually felt

emotions Transient physiological, behavioral, and psychological episodes experienced toward an object, person, or event that prepare us to respond to it

employee engagement A heightened emotional and intellectual connection that an employee has for his/her job, organization, manager, or coworkers that, in turn, influences him/her to apply additional discretionary effort to his/her work

empowerment Sharing power with employees and giving them the authority to make and implement at least some decisions

empowerment The degree to which an employee has the authority to make and implement at least some decisions

enacted values and norms Values and norms that employees exhibit based on their observations of what actually goes on in the organization

encoding Converting a thought, idea, or fact into a message composed of symbols, pictures, or words

equity norm People are rewarded based on their relative level of contributions

escalation of commitment Persisting with a failing course of action

espoused values and norms The preferred values and norms explicitly stated by the organization

ethical awareness The identification of an ethical issue

ethical leadership The demonstration of normatively appropriate conduct through personal actions and interpersonal relationships, and the promotion of such conduct to followers through two-way communication, reinforcement, and decision making

ethics Standards of behavior about how people ought to act in different situations

ethnocentrism The belief that one's own language, native country, and cultural rules and norms are superior to all others

expatriate Person temporarily or permanently living in a country other than that of legal residence.

expected utility All the objective and subjective outcomes associated with a decision

expert power A personal power based on an individual's knowledge or expertise

extrinsic work values Values related to the outcomes of the work

fairness standard The ethical decision treats all people equally, or at least fairly based on some defensible standard

faultlines Separation based on the existence and strength of subgroups due to the composition and alignments of different group member characteristics

fear of failure An anticipatory feeling of anxiety about attempting a challenging task, failing, and appearing incompetent

feedback A check on the success of the communication

feelings Reflect your evaluations and overall liking of the object of the attitude, and can be positive or negative

filtering Less than the full amount of information is received due to withholding, ignoring, or distorting information

forming First stage of team development in which members learn about each other and the team's goals, purpose, and life span

framing How a situation is described or framed influences the decision we make

functional stress Manageable levels of stress for reasonable periods of time that generate positive emotions including satisfaction, excitement, and enjoyment

functional structure An organizational structure that groups people with the same skills, or who use similar tools or work processes, together into departments

functional teams Members come from the same department or functional area

fundamental attribution error Our tendency to underestimate the impact of external factors and overestimate the impact of internal factors in explaining other people's behavior

general mental ability The capacity to rapidly and fluidly acquire, process, and apply information

general self-efficacy Your generalized belief that you will be successful at whatever challenges or tasks you might face

global mindset Set of individual attributes that enable you to influence individuals, groups, and organizations from diverse socio/ cultural/institutional systems

global teams Face-to-face or virtual teams whose members are from different countries

group polarization The tendency of people to make more extreme decisions in a group than when alone

groupthink A mode of thinking that people engage in when they are deeply involved in a cohesive in-group, when the members' strivings for unanimity override their motivation to realistically appraise alternative courses of action

growth strategy Company expansion organically or through acquisitions

halo effect Drawing a general impression about something or someone based on a single (typically good) characteristic

Hawthorne effect When people improve some aspect of their behavior or performance simply because they are being assessed

hierarchy The degree to which some employees have formal authority over others

high-context culture Situational and nonverbal cues are used to convey meaning

hindsight bias How our impression of how we acted or would have acted changes when we learn the outcome of an event

human relations movement Views organizations as cooperative systems and treats workers' orientations, values, and feelings as important parts of organizational dynamics and performance

hygiene factors Factors such as pay, status, and working conditions that produce an acceptable work environment and whose absence leads to dissatisfaction

hypotheses Written predictions specifying expected relationships between certain variables

implicit personality theories Assumptions about how personality traits are related

impression management The process of portraying a desired image or attitude to control the impression others form of us

inclusion The sense of being safe, valued, and engaged in a group

incremental change Linear, continuous change conducted to fix problems or change procedures

independent variable The variable that is predicted to affect something else

individualism Reflects the strength of the ties people tend to have with others in their community

individual-organization value conflict When an employee's values conflict with the values of the organization

influence tactics How people translate their power to affect the behavior of others

information conflict Conflict that occurs when people lack necessary information, are misinformed, interpret information differently, or disagree about which information is relevant

information overload The amount of information available exceeds a person's ability to process it

information processing   A change in the way groups integrate information and reconcile different perspectives

information processing capacity   The manner in which individuals process and organize information

informational diversity   Diversity in knowledge and experience

informational fairness   The extent to which employees receive adequate information and explanations about decisions affecting their working lives

informational power   Power derived from control over information

instrumental values   Our preferred means of achieving our terminal values or our preferred ways of behaving

instrumental voice   When the comments a person makes may influence the decision being made

integrative negotiation   A win-win negotiation in which the agreement involves no loss to either party

interactional fairness   Whether the amount of information about the decision and the process was adequate, and the perceived fairness of the interpersonal treatment and explanations received during the decision-making process

interpersonal fairness   The degree to which people are treated with politeness, dignity, and respect by authorities or third parties involved in executing procedures or determining outcomes

interpersonal value conflicts   When two different people hold conflicting values

intrapersonal value conflict   When highly ranked instrumental and terminal values conflict

intrinsic work values   Values related to the work itself

intuition   Knowing something instinctively based on expertise and experience solving similar problems

job characteristics   Attributes that describe the nature of the work

job characteristics model   Objective characteristics of the job itself, including skill variety, task identity, task significance, autonomy, and task feedback, lead to job satisfaction for people with a high growth need strength

job enlargement   Adding more tasks at the same level of responsibility and skill related to an employee's current position

job enrichment   An approach to job design that increases a job's complexity to give workers greater responsibility and opportunities to feel a sense of achievement

job rotation   Workers are moved through a variety of jobs to increase their interest and motivation

job satisfaction   Reflects our attitudes and feelings about our job

laissez-faire leadership style   Employees are given discretion to make decisions and perform their work any way they want

lattice structure   Cross-functional and crosslevel subteams are formed and dissolved as necessary to complete specific projects and tasks

law of individual differences   People have different abilities, needs, personalities, values, and self-concepts

leadership   Guiding and influencing others to work willingly toward the leader's objectives

leadership motive pattern   A high need for power (with high impulse control) and a low need for affiliation

leadership neutralizers   Factors that make leadership impossible

leadership substitutes   Factors that make leadership unnecessary

learning   A relatively permanent change in behavior that occurs because of experience

learning goal orientation   Characterized by a belief that abilities are changeable and a desire to increase task mastery or competence

learning organization   An organization that facilitates the learning of all its members and continually transforms itself

legitimate power   A position power based on a person's holding of the managerial position rather than anything the manager is or does as a person

Level 5 leadership   A combination of transactional and transformational leadership styles focused on long-term company performance

liaison role A manager or team member is held formally accountable for communicating with other groups and coordinating the teams' activities as needed

Lifelong learning A formal commitment to ensuring that employees have and develop the skills they need to be effective in their jobs today and in the future

"like me" bias A bias resulting from people's preference to associate with other people who they perceive to be like themselves

locus of control The degree to which a person generally perceives events to be under his or her control (internal locus) or under the control of others (external locus)

long-term orientation Reflects a focus on long-term planning, delivering on social obligations, and avoiding "losing face"

loss aversion Tendency to experience losses more strongly than gains

low-context cultures Cultures that rely on words to convey meaning

Machiavellianism An individual's general strategy for dealing with other people and the degree to which they feel they can manipulate others in interpersonal situations

management teams A higher-level team of managers manages lower-level cross-team integration

managers Organizational members who are responsible for the attainment of organizational goals by planning, organizing, leading, and controlling the efforts of others in the organization

masculinity How much a society values and exhibits traditional male and female roles and expects them to be distinct

mass production Producing large volumes of identical products

matrix structure Employees report to both a project or product team and to a functional manager

mechanistic organizations Rigid, traditional bureaucracies with centralized power and hierarchical communications

mediation An impartial third party (the mediator) facilitates a discussion using persuasion and logic, suggesting alternatives, and establishing each side's priorities

mental ability tests Assess general mental abilities including verbal and mathematical reasoning, logic, and perceptual abilities

mentoring A dynamic, reciprocal relationship in a work environment between an advanced career incumbent (mentor) and a protégé aimed at promoting the career development of both

message The encoded information

meta-analysis A statistical technique used to combine the results of many different research studies done in a variety of organizations and for a variety of jobs

misperception When a message is not decoded by the receiver in the way the sender intended

moods Short-term emotional states not directed toward anything in particular

motivation The intensity of a person's desire to begin or continue engaging in the pursuit of a goal

motivators Factors intrinsic to the job that can drive an employee to pursue excellence and whose presence increases satisfaction

movement The implementation of the change

Myers-Briggs Type Indicator A personality inventory based on Carl Jung's work on psychological types

need for power Wanting to control and influence others, or to be responsible for others

negative affect Comprises feelings of being upset, fearful, and distressed

negotiation A process in which two or more parties make offers, counteroffers, and concessions in order to reach an agreement

network organization A collection of autonomous units or firms that act as a single larger entity, using social mechanisms for coordination and control

noise Anything that blocks, distorts, or changes in any way the message the sender intended to communicate

nominal group technique A structured variation of a small-group discussion to reach consensus

noninstrumental voice   When a person's comments will have no bearing on the outcome

non-programmed decisions   Novel decisions that require unique solutions

nonverbal communications   Communications that are not spoken or written but that have meaning to others

normative commitment   Feeling obliged to stay with an organization for moral or ethical reasons

norming   The team becomes more cohesive and clarifies members' roles and responsibilities, team goals, and team performing

norms   Shared rules, standards, or guidelines for team member behavior and performance

ombudsman   Someone who investigates complaints and mediates fair settlements between aggrieved parties

operational decisions   Focus on the day-to-day running of the company

operational excellence   Maximizing the efficiency of the manufacturing or product development process to minimize costs

organic organizations   Flexible, decentralized structures with less clear lines of authority, decentralized power, open communication channels, and a focus on adaptability in helping employees accomplish goals

organization   Consists of people with formally assigned roles working together to achieve common goals

organization development   A planned effort to increase an organization's long-term effectiveness

organizational behavior   Explains and predicts how people and groups interpret events, react, and behave in organizations; describes the role of organizational systems, structures, and processes in shaping behavior

organizational chart   Diagram of the chain of command and reporting relationships in a company

organizational citizenship behaviors   Discretionary behaviors (e.g., helping others) that benefit the organization but that are not formally rewarded or required

organizational commitment   The degree to which an employee identifies with the organization and its goals and wants to stay with the organization

organizational communication   The exchange of information among two or more individuals or groups in an organization that creates a common basis of understanding and feeling

organizational culture   A system of shared values, norms, and assumptions that guide members' attitudes and behaviors

organizational design   The process of selecting and managing aspects of organizational structure and culture to enable the organization to achieve its goals

organizational fairness   Employees' perceptions of organizational events, policies, and practices as being fair or not fair

organizational networks   Patterns of task and personal relationships among employees

organizational politics   Social influence attempts directed at those who can provide rewards that will help promote or protect the self-interests of the actor

organizational structure   The formal system of task, power, and reporting relationships

overlapping team membership   One or more team members is also a formal member of another team

parochialism   Viewing the world solely through one's own eyes and perspective

participative   Giving employees a say in the decision

passive conflict management norms   Avoid addressing conflict

performance goal orientation   A belief that abilities are fixed and a desire to demonstrate high ability and to be positively evaluated by others

performing   The team is cohesive, productive, and makes progress toward its goals

personal brand   A summary of our key talents and what differentiates us from others

personal power   Based on the person's individual characteristics; stays with a person regardless of his or her job or organization

personality   The dynamic mental attributes and processes that determine individuals' emotional and behavioral adjustments to their environments

person-group fit   Match between an individual and his or her supervisor and workgroup

person-job fit   The fit between a person's abilities and the demands of the job and the fit between a person's desires and motivations and the attributes and rewards of a job

person-organization fit   Fit between an individual's values, beliefs, attitudes, and personality and the values, norms, and culture of the organization

person-vocation fit   The fit between a person's interests, abilities, values, and personality and a profession

persuasive power   Power due to the ability to use logic and facts to persuade

pilot project   A smaller version of an organizational change intended to test the proposed change and improve it before rolling it out to the entire organization

position power   Based on one's position in the organization influence tactics

positive affect   Reflects a combination of high energy and positive evaluation characterized in such emotions as elation

post-decisional justification   Remembering our decisions as better than they actually were

power   A person or group's potential to influence another person's or group's behavior

power distance   The degree of inequality that exists and that is accepted among people with and without power

prebureaucratic structure   Smaller organizations with low standardization, total centralization, and mostly one-on-one communication

proactive socialization   When a new hire takes initiative to better understand the work environment and work roles and adjusts his or her behaviors to improve socialization and career success

problem-solving teams   Teams created to solve problems and make improvements

procedural fairness   Perceptions of the fairness of the policies and procedures used to make decisions

process conflict   Conflict about how to accomplish a task, who is responsible for what, and how things should be delegated

process gain   The performance improvements that occur because people work together rather than independently

process loss   When a team of people working together performs worse than the individual members would have if they had worked alone

product innovation   Developing new products or services

programmed decisions   Routine decisions that address specific problems and result in relatively structured solutions

projection   Attributing our own characteristics to other people

psychographic characteristic   Any personality, value, attitude, interest, or lifestyle attribute

psychological contract   Employer and employee expectations of the employment relationship, including mutual obligations, values, expectations, and aspirations that operate over and above the formal contract of employment

rational decision-making process   Assumes that we make decisions systematically to maximize our expected utility

realistic job previews   Provide both positive and potentially negative information to job candidates

reciprocal mentoring   Matches senior employees with diverse junior employees to allow both people to learn more about a different group

referent power   A personal power based on a manager's charisma or attractiveness to others

refreezing   The institutionalization of the changes into everyday life

reinforcers   Anything that makes a behavior more likely to happen again

relational demography   A single group member's similarities to and differences from other group members.

relationship conflict   Conflict due to incompatibility or differences between individuals or groups

relationship conflict   Interpersonal conflict including personality clashes

representativeness bias   Occurs when we overestimate what we are familiar with, and underestimate things with which we are not familiar or that we do not remember as well

reverse mentoring Pairs a senior employee with a junior employee to transfer the skills of the junior employee to the senior employee

reward power A position power that involves the use of rewards to influence and motivate followers

rights standard The ethical decision is the one that best respects and protects the moral rights of all those affected by the decision

risky shift People who tend to make more risky decisions as individuals will make even riskier decisions in a group

roles The behaviors and tasks each team member is expected to perform because of their position

satisficing Making a satisfactory rather than optimal decision

schema Organized patterns of thoughts or behaviors to help us quickly interpret and process information

scientific management Based on the belief that productivity is maximized when organizations are rationalized with precise sets of instructions based on time-and-motion studies

scientific method Method of knowledge generation that relies on systematic studies that identify and replicate a result using a variety of methods, samples, and settings

selective perception Selectively interpreting what we see based on our interests, expectations, experience, and attitudes

self-concept A person's perceptions of him- or herself as a physical, spiritual, or moral being

self-directed teams Set their own goals and pursue them in ways defined by the team

self-efficacy A person's confidence in his or her ability to organize and execute the courses of action necessary to accomplish a specific task for different definitions for different definitions

self-esteem Our feelings of self-worth and our liking or disliking of ourselves

self-fulfilling prophecies When expectations create behaviors that cause the expectations to come true

self-monitoring Having a high concern with others' perceptions of us and adjusting our behavior to fit the situation

self-serving attributions Attributing our successes to ourselves and our failures to external factors

separation Differences in position or opinion among group members reflecting disagreement or opposition— dissimilarity in an attitude or value, for example, especially with regard to group goals or processes

social categorization theory Similarities and differences among people form the basis for sorting self and others into similar in-group members and dissimilar out-groups

social facilitation An increase in effort by a person working in a group

social integration When members feel they are a core part of the group

social loafing When people put less effort into a task when working with a team than they do when working alone

social network The set of relationships among people connected through friendship, family, work, or other ties

social perception The process through which we use available information to form impressions of others

social style A person's dominant pattern of interpersonal behaviors and communication styles

socialization The process of learning the knowledge, attitudes, and behaviors necessary to successfully participate as an organizational member

span of control The number of people reporting directly to an individual

specialization strategy Focusing on a narrow market segment or niche and pursuing either a differentiation or cost leadership strategy within that market segment

status quo bias Our tendency to not change what we are doing unless the incentive to change is compelling

stereotype A belief about an individual or a group based on the idea that everyone in that particular group will behave the same way

stereotype A dysfunctional schema that is essentially an oversimplified schema for a group of people

stereotype threat Awareness of subgroup differences on standardized tests creates frustration among minority test takers and ultimately lowers test scores

stereotyping Forming oversimplified beliefs about an individual or a group based on the idea that everyone in that particular group will behave the same way

storming A stage of conflict in which team members begin establishing goals, work processes, and individual roles

strategic decisions Address the long-term direction and focus of the organization

structural conflict Conflict resulting from structural or process features of the organization

supplementary fit The degree to which a person's characteristics are similar to those that already exist in the organization

surface-level diversity Observable differences in people, including race, age, ethnicity, physical abilities, physical characteristics, and gender

task conflict Conflict over task issues, such as goals, deadlines, or work processes

task force A temporary committee formed to address a specific project or problem

team contract Written agreement among team members establishing ground rules about the team's processes, roles, and accountabilities

team efficacy A team's shared belief that it can organize and execute the behaviors necessary to reach its goals

team-based structure Horizontal or vertical teams define part or all of the organization

teams An interdependent collection of at least two individuals who share a common goal and responsibility for specific outcomes

terminal values Long-term personal life goals

theory A collection of verbal and symbolic assertions that specify how and why variables are related, and the conditions under which they should and should not relate

theory of multiple intelligences There are a number of distinct forms of intelligence that each individual possesses in varying degrees

Theory X Belief that most people dislike work and will try to avoid it whenever possible

Theory Y Belief that people can enjoy responsibility and work, and are able to make good decisions and exercise self-direction

token Being in the numerical minority in a group based on some unique characteristic and being assumed to fully represent that minority group

tolerance for ambiguity A person's tendency to perceive ambiguous situations as either desirable or threatening

top-down decisions Directive decisions made solely by managers who then pass them down to lower-level employees for implementation

trait A person's tendency to behave in a certain way over time and in a variety of situations

transactional leadership Leadership based on a reciprocal exchange of something of value

transformational leadership Leadership that inspires followers to adopt the values and goals of the leader and put aside their own self-interests for the good of the organization

transformative change Radical change that tends to be both multidimensional and multilevel, involving discontinuous shifts in thinking or perceiving things

trust The expectation that another person will not take advantage of us regardless of our ability to monitor or control them

two-way communication Communication is from worker to chief executive, as well as vice versa

Type A personality Impatient, competitive, ambitious, and uptight; experiences a frustrated sense of wasting time when not actively engaged in productive activity

Type B personality Relaxed and easygoing; less overly competitive than Type A

uncertainty avoidance The degree of anxiety members feel in uncertain or unfamiliar situations

unfreezing Prepares people and organizations for change by creating a disequilibrium between driving and restraining change forces

unit production Producing in small batches or making one-of-a-kind custom products

upward influence   Influencing superiors

upward influence styles   Combinations of upward influence tactics that tend to be used together

utilitarian standard   The ethical decision is the one that strikes the best balance of good over harm

values conflict   Conflict arising from perceived or actual incompatibilities in belief systems

values   Ways of behaving or end-states desirable to a person or to a group

variety   Differences in a certain type or category, including group members' expertise, knowledge, or functional background

venture teams   Teams that operate semiautonomously to create and develop new products, processes, or businesses

verbal intonation   The emphasis given to spoken words and phrases

virtual organization   An organization that contracts out almost all of its functions except for the company name and managing the coordination among the contractors

virtual teams   Teams whose members are linked by technology

virtue standard   The ethical decision is consistent with certain ideal virtues, including honesty, courage, compassion, fairness, and generosity

workplace bullying   A repeated mistreatment of another employee through verbal abuse; conduct that is threatening, humiliating, or intimidating; or sabotage that interferes with the other person's work

NAME/COMPANY INDEX

SUBJECT INDEX